D0875734

108 530 7

American Prose and Criticism, 1820-1900

AMERICAN LITERATURE, ENGLISH LITERATURE, AND WORLD LITERATURES IN ENGLISH: AN INFORMATION GUIDE SERIES

Series Editor: Theodore Grieder, Curator, Division of Special Collections, Fales Library, New York University

Associate Editor: Duane DeVries, Associate Professor, Polytechnic Institute of New York, Brooklyn

---

The above series is part of the
GALE INFORMATION GUIDE LIBRARY

The Library consists of a number of separate series of guides covering major areas in the social sciences, humanities, and current affairs.

General Editor: Paul Wasserman, Professor and former Dean, School of Library and Information Services, University of Maryland

Managing Editor: Denise Allard Adzigian, Gale Research Company

Ref
PS
368
P37
1933

American Prose and Criticism, 1820-1900

A GUIDE TO INFORMATION SOURCES

*Volume 39 in the American Literature, English
Literature, and World Literatures in English
Information Guide Series*

Elinore Hughes Partridge

*Department of English
California State College
San Bernardino*

Gale Research Company
Book Tower, Detroit, Michigan 48226

DISCARDED

THE
UNIVERSITY OF WINNIPEG
PORTAGE & BALMORAL
WINNIPEG, MAN.   R3B 2E9
CANADA

Library of Congress Cataloging in Publication Data

Partridge, Elinore H. (Elinore Hughes)
   American prose and criticism, 1820-1900.

   (Volume 39 in the American literature, English
literature, and world literatures in English information
guide series)
   Includes index.
   1. American prose literature—19th century—
Bibliography. 2. Criticism—United States—Bibliography.
I. Title. II. Series: Gale information guide library.
American literature, English literature, and world
literatures in English ; v. 39.
Z1231.P8P37   1983   [PS368]   016.818'08   82-24241
ISBN 0-8103-1213-1

Copyright © 1983 by
Elinore H. Partridge

No part of this book may be reproduced in any form without permission in
writing from the publisher, except by a reviewer who wishes to quote brief
passages or entries in connection with a review written for inclusion in a
magazine or newspaper. Manufactured in the United States of America.

VITA

Elinore Hughes Partridge teaches in the department of English at California State College, San Bernardino. She received her B.A. in English from the University of Utah, 1958; M.A. in British and American literature from New York University, 1963; and Ph.D. in American literature from the University of California, Davis, 1970.

Her academic honors include Phi Beta Kappa, Phi Kappa Phi, Ford Foundation Early Admission Scholar, High Honors from the University of Utah and University of California, a Teaching Fellow from the University of Utah and University of California. Her areas of teaching interest and specialization are: American literature, English linguistics, and expository and technical writing.

Dr. Partridge is now writing A MAN FOR THE TIMES: THE OLPIN YEARS, a history of the University of Utah, 1946-1964, commissioned by the Utah Bicentennial Committee.

CONTENTS

Contents

Contents

ACKNOWLEDGMENTS

I have received assistance from the following libraries and their staffs: University of Wisconsin, Milwaukee; University of Utah; and campuses of the University of California at Berkeley, Los Angeles, and Santa Barbara.

I should like to express appreciation to Dr. Theodore Grieder, for his patience and painstaking editing, and to Denise Allard Adzigian and Pamela Dear of Gale Research Company. My thanks also to Elaine H. Partridge, for her help in collecting data and allowing the use of her excellent typewriter, to Helen Hughes for much material and moral support, to De Shea Rushing for assistance in checking the final manuscript, and to James Woodress, who suggested that I work on this project.

I should also like to thank Philip R. Hughes, Jonathan Hughes and Constance Hughes, who helped me maintain a sense of perspective, and Ernest Partridge, who lovingly and patiently endured.

INTRODUCTION

In his study, HISTORY AND THE CONTEMPORARY (Madison: Univ. of Wisconsin Press, 1964), Howard Mumford Jones criticized histories of American literature for being deficient in a number of areas:

> They seldom or never, for example, recognize the greatness of
> American biographical writing. . . . They scarcely know what to
> do with most nonfictional prose. . . . They do not know what to
> do with the powerful library of travel literature written by Ameri-
> cans. . . . But I think the greatest deficiency in these manuals
> is their failure to recognize the existence of that type of writer
> the French call the moralist. For him American literary criticism
> has small space (pp. 135-36).

What to do with the nonfiction prose of nineteenth-century America is, indeed, a large and often bewildering problem. Where should one draw the line, for example, between the literary essay and the philosophical treatise? Can one decide when scientific writing belongs to the category of the natural history essay, which has long been considered part of the body of American literature, and when it should be placed in the archives of obsolete science? What about the journals, memoirs, and diaries of the nineteenth century? Some of the best prose of Emerson and Thoreau, as well as that of many other writers, can be found in their journals and must be considered an important part of the body of their work. Travel writing contains some of the most vivid images and descriptions to be found in nineteenth-century literature, and, often, the most profound musings on the nature and character of human beings and circumstances. Should we ignore the literary qualities of this writing simply because it may also fit into such categories as history, science, or politics?

A familiarity with the writings of economists like Henry George and Thorstein Veblen is helpful in understanding some of the realistic and naturalistic fiction being produced at the end of the nineteenth and into the twentieth centuries. Some knowledge of the religious, philosophical, educational, and scientific writings is essential background for reading the transcendentalists and many of the essayists of the century. The outstanding historians of the century, including Motley, Parkman, and Bancroft, have been the subject of a number of recent studies which can only be called literary criticism. As the civil rights and feminist movements of the twentieth century have paralleled some of the events of the nineteenth century, works in the areas of abolition, woman's suffrage, and labor reform have been rediscovered, reprinted, and appreciated for their literary as well as their social and historical value. All of these somewhat amorphous writings, I would argue, can be fitted into the category of literature, sometimes that of great literature.

Biography was the form of expression for so many of the excellent writers of the century that this genre by itself could easily be the subject of an entire research guide. A survey of the great biographies of the nineteenth century is, therefore, a deserving subject but an enormous one. Because this is so, I have chosen, in this volume, to include only those biographies written by writers who have achieved distinction as essayists, historians, journalists, or writers of fiction and poetry. I have included, as well, the significant biographies about the major writers of the century. In the section on autobiographical writings, I have included a sampling of the literary memoir, such as those written by the publisher James T. Fields and his wife, of the "Famous Men I have Known . . ." type so popular in the nineteenth century.

Autobiography is another form which is abundant in the century, since keeping a diary or journal was often considered not just an exercise but a requirement for the literate person. Much travel writing, as well as the literature dealing with the Civil War, was really autobiography. Since the recording of the details of daily life and surroundings was considered important not only by the New England transcendentalists but also by the Western explorers and travelers, these nineteenth-century diaries often have a vivid immediacy not always achieved in fiction. In some cases, as, for example, in the writings of Caroline Kirkland, it is difficult to tell where factual narrative ends and realistic fiction begins.

Because much of the nonfiction prose writing of the nineteenth century was often initially published in periodicals, I have decided to include here only collections of periodical prose published as separate volumes. More work needs to be done on both the critical and the descriptive essays published in the journals and magazines of the 1800s. However, this study would necessarily be the subject of a separate volume or volumes. I have listed the important nineteenth-century periodicals, which contained many of the essays and much of the criticism, in section II.A.2 of this volume. In addition, guides to periodical literature are listed either in section I or in the "Secondary Sources" listings in section II.

In section I are listed general bibliographies and guides to American writings and some of the background studies particularly relevant to nonfiction prose and criticism. I have also included in this section studies that may focus upon a few individual writers (though more than one), but which provide valuable general information as well.

In section II are listed representative works (excluding the works listed under Individual Authors in section III) which gives a sample of the best of the various types of nonfiction prose being written in the century. Other works are also listed here because they have had significant impact upon American thought or were considered particularly innovative or influential in the nineteenth century. It will become apparent to anyone using this section that the categories sometimes overlap, for it is often difficult to fit a work into a single category--such as essay, criticism, history, or autobiography--when it clearly encompasses several categories.

Where a nineteenth-century work has been republished or reprinted in a modern edition, only the year of the original publication date is cited; the full imprint is given for the more available (and importantly for the librarian and scholar, the more easily acquired) modern edition; for example, LETTERS FROM THE WEST. 1828; reprinted with introd. John T. Flanagan, Gainesville, Fla.: Scholar's Facsimiles and Reprints, 1965. The same procedure is followed for earlier twentieth-century titles available in more recent editions and for the citations in section III.

Section III is a listing of individual authors, their major works of nonfiction prose, and a brief description of the most important full-length studies of their lives and works. I have included the nonfiction prose by several writers who are most often thought of primarily as poets (e.g., Bryant), or novelists (e.g., Henry James), or writers of poetry and fiction (e.g., Poe) simply because these men were also among the outstanding literary critics of the time, and to omit them would give a false picture of nineteenth-century criticism. For the most part, I have omitted serial studies of individual authors. Listings of such studies can readily be found in the PMLA BIBLIOGRAPHY, in the regular listings in AMERICAN LITERATURE, in AMERICAN LITERARY REALISM, and in other scholarly journals: Lewis Leary's two volumes of ARTICLES ON AMERICAN LITERATURE are also useful. Brief descriptions of the more important articles written since 1963 can be found in the annual AMERICAN LITERARY SCHOLAR-SHIP. All of these titles, and many more, are listed and annotated in section I.A. and B.

This guide carries its subject from Donald Yannella and John Roch, AMERICAN PROSE TO 1820 (Detroit: Gale Research Co., 1979), and is continued by Peter Brier and Anthony Arthur, AMERICAN PROSE AND CRITICISM, 1900-1950 (Detroit: Gale Research Co., 1981). Each of these three titles contains some material transitionally relevant to the preceding or succeeding volumes.

I. GENERAL GUIDES

A. BIBLIOGRAPHIES AND REFERENCE WORKS

Altick, Richard D., and Andrew Wright, eds. SELECTIVE BIBLIOGRAPHY FOR THE STUDY OF ENGLISH AND AMERICAN LITERATURE. 6th ed. New York: Macmillan, 1979.

> A partially annotated, selective bibliography, this is a useful guide for the undergraduate student. The listings include primarily major works by major authors; however, the reader is directed to other, more comprehensive bibliographies and reference guides.

Blanck, Jacob, ed. BIBLIOGRAPHY OF AMERICAN LITERATURE. 10 vols. projected. New Haven, Conn.: Yale Univ. Press, 1955-- .

> As of 1981, this study has been completed through volume 6 (the last entry is for Thomas William Parsons). Bibliographical descriptions of first editions of "certain American authors who, in their own time at least, were known and read" are given, together with some information about subsequent editions and a selected list of bibliographical, biographical, and critical works for each author.

Bruccoli, Matthew J., et al., eds. FIRST PRINTING OF AMERICAN AUTHORS: CONTRIBUTIONS TOWARD DESCRIPTIVE CHECKLISTS. 4 vols. Detroit: Gale Research Co., 1977-79.

> Four volumes of this checklist are proposed to aid scholars, librarians, researchers, book dealers, and collectors. Volume 4 contains the index for the set.

Burke, William J., and Will D. Howe, eds. AMERICAN AUTHORS AND BOOKS, 1640 TO THE PRESENT DAY. 3rd ed. Rev. by Irving Weiss and Anne Weiss. New York: Crown, 1972.

> This is a useful source of information on publication dates and places of works by both major and minor writers. It is particularly helpful in its listing of first printings in newspapers and magazines.

Callow, James T., and Robert J. Reilly, eds. GUIDE TO AMERICAN LITERA-
TURE FROM ITS BEGINNINGS THROUGH WALT WHITMAN. New York:
Barnes and Noble, 1976.

> This guide gives a good general overview of literary trends and
> major writers, and the sources listed provide a solid basis for re-
> search. The chapter on the transcendentalists, for example, de-
> fines transcendentalism, provides a background of sources and
> analogues, indicates its development in New England, and discusses
> the influence, life, and works of Emerson and Thoreau.

Clark, Harry Hayden, ed. AMERICAN LITERATURE: POE THROUGH GAR-
LAND. New York: Appleton-Century-Crofts, 1970.

> One of the Goldentree Bibliographies, this work deals with authors
> who were writing between 1830 and 1914, emphasizing their "con-
> tribution to the short story, literary theory and criticism, social or
> travel commentary, history, and letters." The listings include in-
> formation on bibliographical, biographical, and critical studies.
> Brief sections on more general secondary material are also included.

Cohen, Hennig, ed. ARTICLES IN AMERICAN STUDIES, 1954-1968: A CUMU-
LATION OF THE ANNUAL BIBLIOGRAPHIES FROM AMERICAN QUARTERLY.
2 vols. Ann Arbor, Mich.: Pierian Press, 1972. Index.

> The items collected include listings and studies of nineteenth-
> century nonfiction prose.

Davis, Richard Beale, ed. AMERICAN LITERATURE THROUGH BRYANT, 1585-
1830. New York: Appleton-Century-Crofts, 1969.

> A Goldentree Bibliography, this guide includes a section on "Liter-
> ary History and Criticism" which covers some of the nineteenth-
> century critics.

Day, Martin Steele, ed. A HANDBOOK ON AMERICAN LITERATURE: A
COMPREHENSIVE STUDY FROM COLONIAL TIMES TO THE PRESENT DAY.
New York: Crane, Russak and Co., 1976.

> The author views American literature in the context of world litera-
> ture, asking what unique contribution the United States has made
> through its significant writings. Two chapters, "Renaissance in
> New England" and "Prose and Nonfiction" (of the latter half of
> the nineteenth century), are useful general surveys of nonfiction
> prose.

Dobie, James Frank, ed. GUIDE TO LIFE AND LITERATURE OF THE SOUTH-
WEST. Dallas: Southern Methodist Univ. Press, 1952.

> The usefulness of this guide as a bibliographical tool is limited,
> but descriptions are given of the nineteenth-century natural history
> essay and the literature of travel and exploration. It also includes
> a listing of more comprehensive bibliographies.

Freidel, Frank, ed. HARVARD GUIDE TO AMERICAN HISTORY. 2 vols.
Rev. ed. Cambridge, Mass.: Harvard Univ. Press, 1974.

> This is the standard guide to American historical scholarship, in-
> cluding excellent primary and secondary material on nineteenth-
> century literary historians and noting works in political, economic,
> and social history which have become a part of the body of nine-
> teenth-century nonfiction prose.

Fullerton, Bradford M., ed. A SELECTIVE BIBLIOGRAPHY OF AMERICAN
LITERATURE, 1775-1900. New York: William Farquhar Payson, 1932.

> Fullerton's listing is useful primarily as a source of information on
> the works of several minor writers and as a consistently reliable
> source of publication dates.

Gohdes, Clarence, ed. BIBLIOGRAPHICAL GUIDE TO THE STUDY OF THE
LITERATURE OF THE U.S.A. 4th ed., rev. Durham, N.C.: Duke Univ.
Press, 1976.

> This is one of the most useful general guides to all aspects of
> American literature. The chapters related to nineteenth-century
> prose and criticism are "Transcendentalism in the U.S.," "Criticism,"
> "Essay, Humor, and other Minor Types," and "Philosophy and Psy-
> chology."

Hart, James D., ed. THE OXFORD COMPANION TO AMERICAN LITERATURE.
4th ed. New York: Oxford Univ. Press, 1965.

> A dictionary of American authors, works, and topics, this one in-
> cludes summaries of works of prose nonfiction and entries on social,
> scientific, political, and religious figures. It is a useful source of
> information on minor writers and works which may not be included
> in a literary history.

Havlice, Patricia P., ed. INDEX TO AMERICAN AUTHOR BIBLIOGRAPHIES.
Metuchen, N.J.: Scarecrow Press, 1971.

> American author bibliographies published in periodicals are listed,
> including many not to be found in standard indexes.

Herzberg, Max, Jr., ed. THE READER'S ENCYCLOPEDIA OF AMERICAN
LITERATURE. New York: Crowell, 1962.

> A comprehensive reference book, this volume is useful for checking
> obscure titles, little-known authors, brief descriptions of works and
> literary terms, and titles and publishing records of nineteenth-
> century periodicals.

Holman, C. Hugh, ed. A HANDBOOK TO LITERATURE. 4th ed. Indianapolis: Bobbs-Merrill, 1980.

Based on the original HANDBOOK by William Flint Thrall and Addison Hibbard, this gives definitions of literary terms, movements, schools, and institutions.

Johnson, Merle D., ed. AMERICAN FIRST EDITIONS. 4th ed. Rev. and enl. by Jacob Blanck, 1942. Waltham, Mass.: Mark Press, 1965.

Brief bibliographical descriptions are given, useful for book collectors and scholars and as a supplement to other bibliographies such as Blanck's BIBLIOGRAPHY OF AMERICAN LITERATURE, above.

Kaplan, Louis, ed. A BIBLIOGRAPHY OF AMERICAN AUTOBIOGRAPHIES. Madison: Univ. of Wisconsin Press, 1961.

One of the few listings of autobiographies, this briefly annotated compilation includes some 6,400 autobiographies written by Americans from colonial days through 1945.

Kelly, James, ed. THE AMERICAN CATALOGUE OF BOOKS, ORIGINAL AND REPRINTS PUBLISHED IN THE UNITED STATES FROM JAN., 1861, TO . . . 1871. 2 vols. 1866-71; New York: Peter Smith, 1938.

This catalog is useful for its listing of pamphlets, tracts, sermons, and addresses, particularly those generated during the Civil War.

Kennedy, Arthur G., and Donald B. Sands, eds. A CONCISE BIBLIOGRAPHY FOR STUDENTS OF ENGLISH. 5th ed. Rev. by William E. Colburn. Stanford, Calif.: Stanford Univ. Press, 1972.

Two sections of this handbook deal with nineteenth-century prose and criticism: chapter 6 lists studies of diaries, autobiographies, and essays, and chapter 12 lists criticism.

Kolb, Harold H., Jr., ed. A FIELD GUIDE TO THE STUDY OF AMERICAN LITERATURE. Charlottesville: Univ. Press of Virginia, 1976.

The author's annotations are clear and thorough, making this a valuable guide. The listings include a useful, although incomplete, section on literary history and criticism.

Kribbs, Jayne K., ed. AN ANNOTATED BIBLIOGRAPHY OF AMERICAN LITERARY PERIODICALS, 1741-1850. Boston: G.K. Hall, 1977. Index.

Periodicals that contain "a significant amount of literature or . . . are of distinctly literary interest" are listed here. Contributions described include biography, criticism, essays, and travel descriptions. Since much of the nonfiction prose of the century was originally published in periodicals, this is a valuable resource.

Leary, Lewis G., ed. ARTICLES ON AMERICAN LITERATURE, 1900-1950. Durham, N.C.: Duke Univ. Press, 1954.

> Most of the articles listed are on works of the major writers. A separate listing by topic and genre includes more general articles; some deal with criticism, the familiar essay, and the literature of travel.

_____, ed. ARTICLES ON AMERICAN LITERATURE, 1950-67. Durham, N.C.: Duke Univ. Press, 1970.

> This is an updated listing, similar to Leary's work above.

Leary, Lewis G., and John Auchard, eds. ARTICLES ON AMERICAN LITERATURE, 1968-1975. Durham, N.C.: Duke Univ. Press, 1979.

> Included in this new volume "are numerous additions and corrections to the two preceding volumes, especially in the sections listing genres or topical aspects of American literature."

_____. AMERICAN LITERATURE: A STUDY AND RESEARCH GUIDE. New York: St. Martin's, 1976.

> This useful guide provides a fairly comprehensive introduction to American literature. It includes a chapter on "Types and Schools of Criticism," which briefly discusses some of the nineteenth-century critics.

LITERARY WRITINGS IN AMERICA: A BIBLIOGRAPHY. 8 vols. Millwood, N.Y.: KTO Press, 1977.

> A compilation sponsored by the Federal WPA Historical Survey Program, this study lists the titles of major and minor American writers (1850-1940) that appeared in over six hundred journals and in more than six hundred volumes of literary history, criticism, and bibliography.

LITERATURE AND SOCIETY: A SELECTIVE BIBLIOGRAPHY. 3 vols. Coral Gables, Fla.: Univ. of Miami Press, 1950-67. Index.

> The books and articles in this listing are those that "reveal some literary expression of history, sociology, philosophy, religion, political science, folklore, aesthetics, psychology, publishing, and communications."

McNamee, Lawrence F., ed. DISSERTATIONS IN ENGLISH AND AMERICAN LITERATURE. New York: Bowker, 1968.

> This listing covers the years 1865-1964. Two supplements, one published in 1969 covering 1964-68, the second published in 1975 covering 1969-73, have appeared.

Marsh, John L., ed. A STUDENT'S BIBLIOGRAPHY OF AMERICAN LITERA-
TURE. Dubuque, Iowa: Kendall, Hunt, 1971.

> Concentrating on major literary genres and frequently anthologized
> figures, this is a useful introductory guide for undergraduate stu-
> dents of American literature. Sections on literary criticism, literary
> history, and history of ideas and society cover nineteenth-century
> essayists and critics.

Marshall, Thomas F., ed. AN ANALYTICAL INDEX TO AMERICAN LITERA-
TURE. Durham, N.C.: Duke Univ. Press, 1963.

> Volumes 1-30 (March 1929-January 1959) are covered.

Miller, Elizabeth W., ed. THE NEGRO IN AMERICA: A BIBLIOGRAPHY.
2nd ed. Rev. by Mary L. Fisher. Cambridge, Mass.: Harvard Univ. Press,
1970.

> The listings provide sources for cultural, historical, and sociologi-
> cal backgrounds. Chapters 5 and 6 include some nineteenth-
> century writers, and chapter 2 lists material on slavery and abolition
> with both secondary and primary material excerpted from and
> about nineteenth-century reform writings.

Mugridge, Donald H., and Blanche P. McCrum, eds. A GUIDE TO THE
STUDY OF THE UNITED STATES OF AMERICA: REPRESENTATIVE BOOKS RE-
FLECTING THE DEVELOPMENT OF AMERICAN LIFE AND THOUGHT. Wash-
ington, D.C.: Library of Congress, 1960.

> This guide gives a well-annotated listing of basic materials, includ-
> ing chapters on literary history and criticism, biography and auto-
> biography, and literature and language.

Nilon, Charles H., ed. BIBLIOGRAPHY OF BIBLIOGRAPHIES IN AMERICAN
LITERATURE. New York: Bowker, 1970.

> Nilon's work provides a useful starting point for research on partic-
> ular authors or subjects in American literature: it includes a com-
> prehensive listing of other bibliographies of American literature
> and lists specific bibliographies for authors, genres, and such an-
> cillary topics as biographies, humor, folklore, and literary history
> and criticism. The "Authors" section contains bibliographical
> material on many nineteenth-century writers who are not included
> in the bibliographies in LITERARY HISTORY OF THE UNITED
> STATES or in CAMBRIDGE HISTORY OF AMERICAN LITERATURE,
> listed below under Spiller and Trent respectively.

Pollard, Arthur, ed. WEBSTER'S NEW WORLD COMPANION TO ENGLISH
AND AMERICAN LITERATURE. New York: World Publishing, 1973.

> The brief biographical sketches and critical assessments offer a
> readable, reliable, and useful, though not comprehensive, guide
> to American authors.

Porter, Dorothy B., ed. THE NEGRO IN THE UNITED STATES: A SELECTED BIBLIOGRAPHY. Washington, D.C.: Government Printing Office, 1970.

"Designed to guide persons interested in acquiring books for public, private and university collections of Afro-Americana," this work includes listings of biographies and autobiographies, history and criticism, and essays by and about black writers and writings.

Rees, Robert A., and Earl N. Harbert, eds. FIFTEEN AMERICAN AUTHORS BEFORE 1900. Madison: Univ. of Wisconsin Press, 1971.

The bibliographical essays on the works by and critical studies of the writers covered are comprehensive and informative. Some of the individual essays are further described here in Section III.

Robbins, J. Albert, ed. AMERICAN LITERARY MANUSCRIPTS: A CHECKLIST OF HOLDINGS IN ACADEMIC, HISTORICAL, AND PUBLIC LIBRARIES, MUSEUMS, AND AUTHORS' HOMES IN THE UNITED STATES. 2nd ed. Athens: Univ. of Georgia Press, 1977.

The location of primary source materials provided in this checklist assists researchers in finding manuscripts.

Roorbach, Orville A., ed. BIBLIOTHECA AMERICANA: CATALOGUE OF AMERICAN PUBLICATIONS, INCLUDING REPRINTS AND ORIGINAL WORKS, FROM 1820-1852, INCLUSIVE: TOGETHER WITH A LIST OF PERIODICALS PUBLISHED IN THE UNITED STATES. 4 vols. New York: Peter Smith, 1939.

The 1939 compilation was reprinted from the 1852 edition, incorporating five additional supplements through 1861; it remains a useful source of publication data on early nineteenth-century works.

Rubin, Louis D., Jr., ed. A BIBLIOGRAPHICAL GUIDE TO THE STUDY OF SOUTHERN LITERATURE. Baton Rouge: Louisiana State Univ. Press, 1969. Appendix.

The guide contains lists of works on general topics (e.g., "Ante-Bellum Southern Writers," "The Civil War in Southern Literature," and "Humorists of the Old Southwest") and selective checklists on 135 Southern writers. An appendix by J.A. Leo Lemay lists 68 additional writers.

Sheehy, Eugene, ed. GUIDE TO REFERENCE BOOKS. 9th ed. Chicago: American Library Association, 1976. Supplement with assistance of Rita G. Keckeissen et al. Chicago: American Library Association, 1980.

Reference materials are listed in several areas, including the humanities, social sciences, and history. The annotations are informative, and cover many titles not usually included in bibliographical guides to literature, which may be useful in research on nonfiction prose. This is a basic, important research resource.

Spiller, Robert E., et al., eds. LITERARY HISTORY OF THE UNITED STATES: BIBLIOGRAPHY. 4th ed. Rev. New York: Macmillan, 1974.

> This is an indispensable source of primary and secondary materials on topics and writers.

Trent, William P., et al., eds. THE CAMBRIDGE HISTORY OF AMERICAN LITERATURE. 3 vols. New York: Macmillan, 1946.

> The bibliography included in THE CAMBRIDGE HISTORY OF AMERICAN LITERATURE is supplementary to Spiller's work, above, and is particularly valuable for its listings of nineteenth-century travel literature, oratory, and memoirs.

Truebner, Nicholas, ed. TRUEBNER'S BIBLIOGRAPHICAL GUIDE TO AMERI-CAN LITERATURE: A CLASSIFIED LIST OF BOOKS PUBLISHED IN THE UNITED STATES OF AMERICA DURING THE LAST FORTY YEARS, WITH BIBLIOGRAPHI-CAL INTRODUCTION, NOTES, AND ALPHABETICAL INDEX. 1859; Detroit: Gale Research Co., 1966.

> Truebner's guide is more reliable than Roorbach's (above) in deter-mining dates of travel accounts, of government documents, and of minor critical works. The place of publication and date, but not the publisher, are given in the listing.

Turner, Darwin T., ed. AFRO-AMERICAN WRITERS. New York: Appleton-Century-Crofts, 1970.

> A Goldentree Bibliography, this includes several nineteenth-century black writers of nonfiction prose and lists autobiographies, essay collections, and various background references.

Woodress, James, ed. DISSERTATIONS IN AMERICAN LITERATURE, 1891-1966. Durham, N.C.: Duke Univ. Press, 1968. Index.

> This is the most complete listing of dissertations in American litera-ture to 1966. A section covering dissertations on individual authors is followed by a variety of more general topics--e.g., criticism, humor and satire, transcendentalism, and travel. Author, title, institution, and the date of dissertation are listed.

_____, ed. EIGHT AMERICAN AUTHORS. Rev. ed. New York: Norton, 1971.

> Bibliographical essays on Poe, Emerson, Hawthorne, Thoreau, Whit-man, Melville, Clemens, and Henry James along with a listing and critical evaluation of bibliographies, editions, biographies, and criticism for each author. Individual essays are described in Sec-tion III.

B. PERIODICALS AND ANNUAL BIBLIOGRAPHIES

ABSTRACTS OF ENGLISH STUDIES. Urbana, Ill.: National Council of Teachers of English, 1958-- . 10 per year.

> Abstracts of articles screened from approximately 1,500 journals and monographs include those on American literature. Emerson and Thoreau are among the major writers listed, and abstracts of articles on nineteenth-century criticism occasionally appear.

AMERICAN LITERARY REALISM, 1870-1910. Arlington: Univ. of Texas, 1967-- . Quarterly.

> Intended "to serve as a primary research tool," the journal places special emphasis on the "lesser literary figures" of the latter half of the nineteenth century. The bibliographies of primary and secondary works and bibliographical essays on various writers included in the journal supplement and expand other standard bibliographies.

AMERICAN LITERARY SCHOLARSHIP: AN ANNUAL. Durham, N.C.: Duke Univ. Press, 1963-- .

> Chapters by the various contributors summarize and evaluate books and articles on major authors, themes, topics, and types of American literature. Of most relevance to nineteenth-century nonfiction prose and criticism are the chapters on "Emerson, Thoreau, and Transcendentalism," "Nineteenth-Century Literature," and "Themes, Topics, Criticism." Since 1979 James Woodress and J. Albert Robbins have been alternate editors.

AMERICAN LITERATURE. Durham, N.C.: Duke Univ. Press, 1929-- . 4 per year.

> A "journal of literary history, criticism, and bibliography," AMERICAN LITERATURE is published with the cooperation of the American literature section of the Modern Language Association. It includes articles and notes on topics in American literature, book reviews, and a listing of "Articles on American Literature Appearing in Current Periodicals."

AMERICAN QUARTERLY. Philadelphia: Univ. of Pennsylvania, 1949-- .

This periodical is published five times a year and includes articles of an interdisciplinary nature as well as an annual listing of "Articles in American Studies." It deals with "the characteristics, relationships and ramifications of various aspects of American civilization" and American nonfiction prose and criticism of the nineteenth century.

AMERICAN STUDIES. Lawrence: Univ. of Kansas, 1960-- . Biannual.

The articles in this interdisciplinary journal cover American literary, historical, and cultural studies and are often relevant to the study of nineteenth-century essayists and writers of nonfiction prose.

AMERICAN TRANSCENDENTAL QUARTERLY. Kingston: Univ. of Rhode Island, 1969-- .

This is "a journal of nineteenth-century New England writers and their culture." Formerly limited to publishing primarily bibliographies, checklists, and newspaper references to Emerson, Thoreau, Alcott, and other New England transcendentalists, it has recently included full-length studies, often devoted to one particular work.

ESQ: A JOURNAL OF THE AMERICAN RENAISSANCE. Pullman: Washington State Univ., 1955-- . Quarterly.

Formerly titled EMERSON SOCIETY QUARTERLY, the journal publishes critical studies, source and influence studies, biographical and bibliographical studies, and general discussions of literary history, theory, and the history of ideas in nineteenth-century American literature. Literary figures are examined with an emphasis on the New England romantic and transcendental traditions.

JOURNAL OF AMERICAN STUDIES. Cambridge, Engl.: Cambridge Univ. Press, 1967-- . Biannual.

This periodical includes works "by specialists of any nationality on American history, literature, politics, geography and related subjects."

MLA INTERNATIONAL BIBLIOGRAPHY OF BOOKS AND ARTICLES ON THE MODERN LANGUAGES AND LITERATURES. New York: Modern Language Association of America, 1921-- . Annual.

Two sections of the bibliography list books and articles published on nineteenth-century American literature. Since 1970 (bibliography for 1969), the listings for English, American, medieval and neo-Latin, and Celtic literatures have been published as a separate volume.

NEW ENGLAND QUARTERLY: A HISTORICAL REVIEW OF NEW ENGLAND LIFE AND LETTERS. Brunswick, Maine: Colonial Society of Massachusetts, 1928-- .

> The articles and book reviews relate to New England writers, including the literary historians and essayists, and the social, economic, religious, and intellectual movements that have influenced them.

RESOURCES FOR AMERICAN LITERARY STUDY. College Park: Univ. of Maryland, 1971-- . Biannual.

> This journal provides annotated checklists of critical and biographical scholarship, evaluations of bibliographical studies, notations of collections of research materials, and information on unpublished manuscripts. It also includes book reviews which are primarily of recently published bibliographies, reference guides, and checklists.

STUDIES IN THE AMERICAN RENAISSANCE. Boston: Twayne, 1977-- . Annual.

> This journal proposes to offer "original analyses of the lives and works of mid-19th-century American authors." Each volume includes biographical studies of authors, commentary on major editions of unpublished letters and journals as well as previously unpublished letters, calendars of manuscripts, accounts of publishing houses and literary publishing in general, and primary and secondary bibliographies.

THOREAU JOURNAL QUARTERLY. Orono: Univ. of Maine, 1969-- .

> Since 1973, the quarterly has published some good essays, book reviews, and editorials on material related to Thoreau.

THOREAU SOCIETY BULLETIN. Genesee, N.Y.: State Univ. College, 1941-- . 4 per year.

> The bulletin includes short essays, proceedings of meetings, and a brief bibliography devoted to studies of Thoreau.

WESTERN AMERICAN LITERATURE. Logan: Utah State Univ., 1967-- . Quarterly.

> This includes essays and reviews of books on writers and topics related to Western American literature.

THE YEAR'S WORK IN ENGLISH STUDIES. London: John Murray for the English Association, 1919-- . Annual.

> Beginning in 1954, bibliographies in American literature have been listed. Although not as thorough or complete as those in AMERICAN LITERARY SCHOLARSHIP, the bibliographical essays in YEAR'S WORK do provide useful supplementary material.

C. CULTURAL, HISTORICAL, AND LITERARY STUDIES

Aaron, Daniel. MEN OF GOOD HOPE: A STUDY OF AMERICAN PROGRES-SIVES. New York: Oxford Univ. Press, 1961.

> In discussing the political and social activities and philosophies of several nineteenth-century writers, including Emerson, Henry George, and Theodore Parker, the author argues that their influence depended on their ability to speak and write powerfully and persuasively. His analysis, an attempt "to rehabilitate the progressive tradition," shows that these "men of good hope" accomplished a great deal.

Anderson, Quentin. THE IMPERIAL SELF: AN ESSAY IN AMERICAN LITERARY AND CULTURAL HISTORY. New York: Knopf, 1971.

> This is an interesting, although sometimes obscure, discussion of the celebration of the self by Emerson, Whitman, and Henry James in contrast with the concern for social consciousness of Hawthorne, who felt that only in society do we "become human."

Banta, Martha. FAILURE AND SUCCESS IN AMERICA: A LITERARY DEBATE. Princeton: Princeton Univ. Press, 1978.

> The author's exploration of success and failure in terms of various attitudes and concepts covers the work of such writers as Emerson, Thoreau, Henry Adams, William James, and several of the literary historians, as well as other major writers of the nineteenth and twentieth centuries.

Bartlett, Irving H. THE AMERICAN MIND IN THE MID-NINETEENTH CEN-TURY. New York: Crowell, 1967.

> Designed for use in a basic American history course, this historical study is brief but solid. The bibliographical essay at the end is well annotated and informative.

Beer, Thomas. THE MAUVE DECADE: AMERICAN LIFE AT THE END OF THE NINETEENTH CENTURY. 1926. Intro. Frank Freidel. New York: Vintage, 1960.

> This is a popular history of the 1890s which outlines some of the attitudes and moral restraints that governed the standards of writers, critics, and reviewers.

Bercovitch, Sacvan. THE AMERICAN JEREMIAD. Madison: Univ. of Wisconsin Press, 1978.

> The author attempts to show how the American Puritan Jeremiad shaped attitudes into the nineteenth century and beyond. Unlike the European Jeremiad, which was a denunciation of the ways of the world, the American Jeremiad fused sacred and secular history and was concerned with both the city of God and the city of man. Bercovitch maintains that there existed a rhetoric of ambiguity capable of absorbing the discrepancies between fact and ideal. This study differs significantly from similar studies by Perry Miller and others and presents some interesting and persuasive arguments.

_____. THE PURITAN ORIGINS OF THE AMERICAN SELF. New Haven, Conn.: Yale Univ. Press, 1975.

> Bercovitch provides a difficult but valuable study of the characteristics of American Puritanism and "the rhetoric of American identity," extending the analysis to the nineteenth century and Emerson and focusing on the concept of self as it relates to a Puritan legacy.

Berthoff, Warner. THE FERMENT OF REALISM: AMERICAN LITERATURE 1884-1919. New York: Free Press, 1965.

> In a chapter on the "Literature of Argument," the author discusses the contributions of William Graham Sumner, William James, Thorstein Veblen, and Henry and Brooks Adams. He argues that these writers belong to the literary history of the period and presents some of their rhetorical strategies and critical premises. This chapter also includes a brief section on literary criticism.

Boas, George, ed. ROMANTICISM IN AMERICA. 1940; New York: Russell and Russell, 1961.

> The essays on historiography (by Eric Goldman) and on "romantic philosophy" (by George Boas) provide insight into the historical and ideological trends of American romanticism. The first essay fits George Bancroft into a larger context of historical trends. The second focuses on "the speculations of individuals outside universities," particularly of the New England transcendentalists and Poe.

Bode, Carl, ed. AMERICAN LIFE IN THE 1840S. New York: New York Univ. Press, 1967.

>Reprints of historical documents and photographs, some of which have not been previously reproduced, show the daily life of average Americans in the 1840s and provoke an unspoken comparison between the late 1840s and the late 1960s.

_____. MIDCENTURY AMERICA: LIFE IN THE 1850S. Carbondale: Southern Illinois Univ. Press, 1972.

>Similar in format to Bode's work cited above, this social history attempts to give a sense of the popular culture of the era, providing some insight into the serious and humorous essays and sketches in periodical literature of the time.

Boller, Paul F., Jr. FREEDOM AND FATE IN AMERICAN THOUGHT FROM EDWARDS TO DEWEY. Dallas: Southern Methodist Univ. Press, 1978.

>The author's examination of the attitudes of several writers sheds light upon an important aspect of American intellectual history. He aligns Tom Paine, Frederick Douglass, William James, and John Dewey on the side of freedom, and Jonathan Edwards, Emerson, and Mark Twain on the side of determinism and fatalism.

Branch, Edward Douglas. THE SENTIMENTAL YEARS, 1836-1860. 1934; New York: Hill and Wang, 1965.

>A discussion of the ideas and ideals of the members of the American middle class, this study focuses upon the "common" person rather than the intellectual leaders of the era and aids understanding the popular appeal of some of the descriptive essays and travel writings of the nineteenth century.

Bremner, Robert H., ed. ESSAYS ON HISTORY AND LITERATURE. Columbus: Ohio State Univ. Press, 1966. Bibliog.

>The essays by Edward Lurie on "American Scholarship" and Russell B. Nye on "History and Literature" are particularly useful. Lurie discusses Henry Adams, Peirce, and Agassiz, showing how their concept of events has affected subsequent histories. Nye contends that "to the historians and literary artists of a century ago, their function was in essence much the same--to interpret experience, for the purpose of guiding and elevating man."

Bridgman, Richard. THE COLLOQUIAL STYLE IN AMERICA. New York: Oxford Univ. Press, 1966.

>A chapter on nineteenth-century talk contains some valuable observations on the use of dialect by essayists and humorists; otherwise the study focuses upon the prose of fiction rather than that of nonfiction.

Brooks, Van Wyck. THE CONFIDENT YEARS, 1885-1915. New York: E.P. Dutton, 1952.

> This work and the four others by Brooks are volumes in "Makers and Finders. A History of the Writer in America, 1800-1915," a series of impressionistic accounts of writers and the times in which they wrote. All of the volumes include some discussion of literary criticism, but they provide more of a broad overview of the social and literary movements of the time than an intensive critical discussion of the literature.

_____. THE FLOWERING OF NEW ENGLAND, 1815-1865. New York: E.P. Dutton, 1936.

> This volume focuses on the New England transcendentalists and Nathaniel Hawthorne.

_____. NEW ENGLAND: INDIAN SUMMER, 1865-1915. New York: E.P. Dutton, 1940.

> A discussion of Francis Parkman and other literary historians is included in this volume.

_____. THE TIMES OF MELVILLE AND WHITMAN. New York: E.P. Dutton, 1947.

> A discussion of the critical controversies in New York gives a background for understanding the context of some of the essays and criticism published in periodicals of the era.

_____. THE WORLD OF WASHINGTON IRVING. New York: Doubleday, 1944.

Brownell, William Crary. AMERICAN PROSE MASTERS. 1909. Ed. Howard Mumford Jones. Cambridge, Mass.: Belknap Press, Harvard Univ. Press, 1963.

> Brownell's essays are intelligent, appreciative, and penetrating, and his comments on the need for art in the critical essay are valuable. His chapter on Emerson contains excellent commentary on Emerson's methods of gathering and expressing the ideas in his essays. Sections on the criticism and literary theory of Poe, Lowell, and Henry James relate the writer's criticism to his background, tastes, psychological characteristics, and cultural peculiarities.

Bruccoli, Matthew J., ed. THE CHIEF GLORY OF EVERY PEOPLE: ESSAYS ON CLASSIC AMERICAN WRITERS. Carbondale: Southern Illinois Univ. Press, 1973.

> This is a collection of twelve essays on authors represented in the first hundred editions produced by the Center for Editions of American Authors (CEAA, now Center for Scholarly Editions). The volume

includes three essays on nineteenth-century nonfiction prose writers: "The Relevance of John Dewey's Thought," by Sidney Hook; "Mr. Emerson--of Boston," by Eleanor M. Tilton; and "Henry Thoreau and the Reverend Poluphloisboios Thalassa," by Joel Parte.

Burke, John Gordon, ed. REGIONAL PERSPECTIVES: AN EXAMINATION OF AMERICA'S LITERARY HERITAGE. Chicago: American Library Association, 1973. Bibliog.

Essays on New England, the South, Midwest, frontier and Southwest, and "Archetype West" are by writers who live and work in those regions. The essays by Hayden Carruth on "The New England Tradition" and by Larry Goodwin on "The Frontier Myth and Southwestern Literature" provide interesting new perspectives on Emerson and Thoreau and on descriptive and travel literature.

Canby, Henry Seidel. THE AGE OF CONFIDENCE: LIFE IN THE 90'S. New York: Farrar and Rinehart, 1934.

The author, relying on his own experiences and observations, surveys institutions and ideas of the 1890s. His volume offers a pleasant way to gain some understanding of the decade.

Carpenter, Frederic Ives. AMERICAN LITERATURE AND THE DREAM. New York: Philosophical Library, 1955.

Carpenter argues that "American literature has differed from English literature because of the constant and omnipresent influence of the American dream upon it." The study focuses on nineteenth-century American literature and describes the American dream in terms of progress, freedom, and faith in the ideal democracy. It includes writers of philosophical, political, and personal essays, as well as writers of fiction and poetry. Viewing transcendentalists as philosophers who celebrated the dream, the author makes some worthwhile comments on the influences of and reactions to transcendentalism.

Carter, Everett. THE AMERICAN IDEA: THE LITERARY RESPONSE TO AMERICAN OPTIMISM. Chapel Hill: Univ. of North Carolina Press, 1977.

Carter looks chiefly at nineteenth-century American writers and examines them in terms of a shared idea which held "hopeful views of man's experience in the world and a sanguine regard for man's intrinsic value." While carefully qualifying the universal applicability of this thesis, the author argues that such writers as Emerson and Whitman supported the idea; Poe, Melville, and Dickinson tended to deny it; William James and Howells reshaped it; and Henry Adams never had it. This is a thoughtful, enlightening work of literary history and criticism.

Cawelti, John G. APOSTLES OF THE SELF-MADE MAN. Chicago: Univ. of Chicago Press, 1965.

> This study surveys how the concept of the ideal man is used as a model in periodical literature, including essays and criticism; in fiction; and in political rhetoric. The views of Emerson and Horatio Alger are discussed at some length.

Charvat, William. LITERARY PUBLISHING IN AMERICA. Philadelphia: Univ. of Pennsylvania Press, 1959.

> The author examines the struggle of American authors to sell their books, studying the formation of publishing centers in New York, Boston, and Philadelphia; how publishers affected and interpreted American taste; the relations between authors and publishers; and the position of the writer as influenced by publishing restrictions and popular tastes. The work includes observations about the development of critical standards and preferences among literary critics as it relates to the history of publishing in America.

_____. THE PROFESSION OF AUTHORSHIP IN AMERICA, 1800-1870: THE PAPERS OF WILLIAM CHARVAT. Ed. Matthew J. Bruccoli. Foreword by Howard Mumford Jones. Columbus: Ohio State Univ. Press, 1968.

> A collection of previously unpublished studies "salvaged from William Charvat's files," the essays are centered upon the author-publisher-reader relationship in literary history. The studies of specific authors do not include any major writers of nonfiction prose; however, Charvat's view of the publishing scene in the nineteenth century is useful background material.

Clark, Harry Hayden, ed. TRANSITIONS IN AMERICAN LITERARY HISTORY. Durham, N.C.: Duke Univ. Press, 1953.

> This collection of essays deals with "the problem of how and especially why American literature did change historically from one center of emphasis to another." Alexander Kern's essay, "The Rise of Transcendentalism," is an excellent survey of the sources, ideas, and influence of transcendentalism in America. Other essays on the nineteenth century are written by M.F. Heiser, G. Harrison Orians, Floyd Stovall, and Robert P. Falk.

Cohen, Hennig, ed. LANDMARKS OF AMERICAN WRITING. New York: Basic Books, 1969.

> The American writings discussed in the essays collected here include several works of nonfiction prose considered to have literary merit. Among the writers studied are Parkman, Frederick Douglass, Thoreau, John Wesley Powell, Thorstein Veblen, William James, and Henry Adams. Because these essays deal with "works that were written for other than primarily literary purposes," this is a useful collection for students interested in nonfiction prose.

Conrad, Susan Phinney. PERISH THE THOUGHT: INTELLECTUAL WOMEN IN ROMANTIC AMERICA, 1830-1860. New York: Oxford Univ. Press, 1976.

> A study of feminists, reformers, writers, and critics, this work surveys both the contributions of women and the responses of others to them, showing the difficulties in a culture slightly uneasy with and suspicious of both intellectuals and women. The study contains a perceptive section on Margaret Fuller's character and criticism and other useful commentary on women writers, reformers, and educators who are often neglected in typical literary and cultural histories.

Crawley, Thomas Edward, ed. FOUR MAKERS OF THE AMERICAN MIND: EMERSON, THOREAU, WHITMAN, AND MELVILLE. Durham, N.C.: Duke Univ. Press, 1976.

> Crawley's volume contains four fine essays, resulting from an exploration of "America's cultural heritage" at Hampden-Sydney College in 1974-75. The editor explains that "the purpose . . . was to arrive at a reasonably comprehensive view of what these key mid-nineteenth-century literary figures did consciously through their writings in giving voice to or projecting the American character as a shaping influence through which the values of the American experiment, as they saw them, might be clarified, strengthened, and ultimately realised." The essays are "The Four Faces of Emerson," by Robert E. Spiller; "Thoreau: His 'Lover's Quarrel with the World,'" by J. Lyndon Shanley; "Walt Whitman as American," by Floyd Stovall; and "Melville and the American Tragic Hero," by Leon Howard. Each piece is balanced, well informed, and appreciative.

Cunliffe, Marcus, ed. AMERICAN LITERATURE TO 1900. History of Literature in the English Language, vol. 8. London: Barrie and Jenkins, 1973. Bibliog.

> The editor's general introduction to this volume emphasizes some of the unique problems presented to American writers by the culture and the profession of authorship in America. Each chapter is written by a noted scholar. George Hochfield's discussion of New England transcendentalism is comprehensive, thorough, and does not generalize or oversimplify. Cunliffe's chapter, "New England --The Universal Yankee Nation," discusses the literary historians and the essays and criticism of Longfellow, Lowell, and Holmes.

Curti, Merle E. THE GROWTH OF AMERICAN THOUGHT. New York: Harper, 1951.

> The author discusses educational practices and institutions; influential political, literary, and religious figures; economic and political trends; and popular tastes. This study provides a thorough and well-documented cultural and social context for American writers and their forms of literary expression, including criticism, essays, and other kinds of significant, nonfiction prose writings.

_____. HUMAN NATURE IN AMERICAN THOUGHT: A HISTORY. Madison: Univ. of Wisconsin Press, 1980.

> This excellent intellectual history focuses upon the theories of human nature expressed in major works of American literature, history, political theory, and philosophy.

DeVoto, Bernard. THE YEAR OF DECISION, 1846. Boston: Little, Brown, 1943.

> DeVoto's thesis is that in 1846 America changed from an agrarian nation into an empire. He focuses on the pre-Civil-War far west, providing valuable historical background for a study of nineteenth-century accounts of travel and exploration, including those of Francis Parkman.

Falk, Robert, ed. LITERATURE AND IDEAS IN AMERICA: ESSAYS IN MEMORY OF HARRY HAYDEN CLARK. Athens: Ohio Univ. Press, 1975.

> Included in this volume are fine essays on the NORTH AMERICAN REVIEW by Neal Frank Doubleday; two on Emerson, one by Merton M. Sealts, Jr., and another by Gay Wilson Allen; and on Thoreau by Alexander C. Kern. The essays on Emerson and Thoreau explore aspects of their works (Emerson's oration on "Literary Ethics" and his interest in science; Thoreau's religious thought) which have been neglected.

Foerster, Norman, ed. THE REINTERPRETATION OF AMERICAN LITERATURE. 1928; New York: Russell and Russell, 1959.

> The essays collected here aim to provide "a new way" of looking at American literature in terms of European culture and the American environment. They deal with the literature in relation to the frontier spirit, the Puritan tradition, romanticism, and realism. The essay by Harry Hayden Clark, "Literary History and Literature," reviews some of the literary histories of the nineteenth century; Arthur M. Schlesinger's essay gives a useful discussion of nineteenth-century social backgrounds and periodical literature.

Foster, Edward Halsey. THE CIVILIZED WILDERNESS: BACKGROUNDS TO AMERICAN ROMANTIC LITERATURE, 1817-1860. New York: Free Press, 1975.

> In considering the effect of the reading public upon the literature of the nineteenth century, the author examines "the significance to Romantic American literature of popularly apprehended symbols, beliefs, and ideas." This is a useful survey of some of the descriptive travel literature, essays, and reform literature of the time; of the major writers, including Emerson and Thoreau; and of several minor writers, including Nathaniel Parker Willis.

Fussell, Edwin. FRONTIER: AMERICAN LITERATURE AND THE AMERICAN WEST. Princeton: Princeton Univ. Press, 1965.

> The central image of the West and the frontier as reality and myth were central, Fussell argues, to the works of several writers, including Thoreau, a writer he believes achieved an ideal balance between the West as metaphor and the West as substance. Fussell further states that "without the model of the pioneer, [Thoreau] would have lacked both vocation, in the overserious, Transcendental sense, and personal identity (he might never have eluded Emerson); without the frontier metaphor, he would have split down the middle and fallen open in two halves." This is an interesting study, and it points the way to discovering similar images in works of writers not included. However, the works treated are sometimes shaped to serve this particular emphasis, and the thesis is sometimes pushed too far.

Gardiner, Harold C., ed. AMERICAN CLASSICS RECONSIDERED: A CHRISTIAN APPRAISAL. New York: Scribner's, 1958.

> The essays in this volume represent the appraisal of nineteenth-century writers by a group of Catholic scholars. In addition to chapters on most of the major literary figures, there is a chapter on Orestes A. Brownson and one on literary historians (Prescott, Bancroft, Motley, and Parkman). In the latter chapter, Mason Wade documents the wide appeal their histories had and points out that all four were "affected by the anti-clericism of their intellectual world."

Girgus, Sam B. THE LAW OF THE HEART: INDIVIDUALISM AND THE MODERN SELF IN AMERICAN LITERATURE. Austin: Univ. of Texas Press, 1979.

> The author points out that the American insistence upon individualism has often led to alienation and lack of social responsibility. He discusses the works of Poe, Emerson, Brownson, Whitman, Howells, and William James.

Gohdes, Clarence, ed. ESSAYS ON AMERICAN LITERATURE IN HONOR OF JAY B. HUBBELL. Durham, N.C.: Duke Univ. Press, 1967.

> Two of the essays in this fine collection relate specifically to nineteenth-century nonfiction prose writers: Lewis Leary's piece on Lafcadio Hearn and Russel B. Nye's essay on Parkman.

Green, Martin, ed. REAPPRAISALS: SOME COMMONSENSE READINGS IN AMERICAN LITERATURE. New York: Norton, 1965.

> In an attempt to counter what he regards as the excesses and dangers of much recent criticism, the author examines several major American writers. He praises Emerson's discrimination and discernment as a critic and provides a valuable overview of trends in twentieth-century criticism of American literature.

Gross, Theodore L. THE HEROIC IDEAL IN AMERICAN LITERATURE. New York: Free Press, 1971.

> The author discusses the "Emersonian hero" and other ideals as they have affected both the literature and the criticism of the nineteenth and twentieth centuries. Works studied include criticism, biography, and autobiography, as well as fiction.

Gurian, Jay. WESTERN AMERICAN WRITING: TRADITION AND PROMISE. DeLand, Fla.: Everett, Edwards, 1975.

> This study examines journalism and descriptive writing as well as fiction, drama, and poetry. It provides a historical context for understanding exaggerations and romanticizing in Western descriptive and travel literature. It also demonstrates that much of the writing about the West is influenced more by literary traditions and cultural myths than by actual experience.

Hoffman, Michael J. THE SUBVERSIVE VISION: AMERICAN ROMANTICISM IN LITERATURE. Port Washington, N.Y.: Kennikat Press, 1972.

> The author emphasizes not what is unique about American Romanticism but rather how it relates to the "breakthrough in Western consciousness" characteristic of the Romantic movement, which was often subversive to existing institutions and dominant assumptions of the time. Each chapter focuses on major authors and closely analyzes a few works, including Emerson's NATURE and Thoreau's WALDEN and "Civil Disobedience," to show the struggle of the American Romantics for new insights.

Horton, Rod W., and Herbert W. Edwards. BACKGROUNDS OF AMERICAN LITERARY THOUGHT. 2nd ed. New York: Appleton-Century-Crofts, 1967.

> Intended to provide supplementary background material for courses in American literary history, this survey describes the intellectual, social, political, and economic currents underlying the literature. Five chapters are particularly relevant to the development of nineteenth-century prose and criticism: "Unitarianism and Transcendentalism," "Expansionism," "The Triumph of Industry," "Evolution and Pragmatism," and "Gentility and Revolt." The latter chapter, for example, shows how the economic problems of the 80s and 90s tempered the materialistic optimism of the previous decades leading to increased social criticism in the journalistic and literary essays of that era.

Howard, Leon. LITERATURE AND THE AMERICAN TRADITION. Garden City, N.Y.: Doubleday, 1960.

> This survey contains a useful chapter on transcendentalism which emphasizes the Harvard backgrounds of Emerson and Thoreau, discussing the books read there and ideas emphasized by that institution. The chapter includes a discussion of Lowell, in which he is praised

more for his criticism than for his poetry. Here, as elsewhere
in the book, the focus is more on the major writers and their
works than general movements and trends.

Hubbell, Jay B. THE SOUTH IN AMERICAN LITERATURE, 1607-1900. Durham,
N.C.: Duke Univ. Press, 1954.

This discussion of southern writing includes Civil War literature,
Southern humorists, criticism in southern periodicals, and anti-
and proslavery writings. The studies give historical, religious,
educational, and cultural backgrounds, as well as brief evaluations of important writers.

Irwin, John T. AMERICAN HIEROGLYPHICS: THE SYMBOL OF THE EGYP-
TIAN HIEROGLYPHICS IN THE AMERICAN RENAISSANCE. New Haven,
Conn.: Yale Univ. Press, 1981.

The author discusses the use of hieroglyphics as symbol and image
in the works of Emerson, Thoreau, Whitman, Hawthorne, Melville,
and Poe.

Jones, Howard Mumford. THE AGE OF ENERGY: VARIETIES OF AMERICAN
EXPERIENCE, 1865-1915. New York: Viking Press, 1971.

The "energy" in the title is not mechanical but that of personality,
prime movers, or words. This study, unified by the author's concept of the human energy which seems to him to have dominated
the age, provides a useful background covering developments which
affected reform literature, aesthetics and criticism, and writings
on science and natural history.

_____. AMERICA AND FRENCH CULTURE, 1759-1848. Chapel Hill: Univ.
of North Carolina Press, 1927.

In tracing the contacts and influences of the two cultures, the
author deals with the influence of French philosophers on transcendentalism, on criticism, and on the rise of realism.

_____. BELIEF AND DISBELIEF IN AMERICAN LITERATURE. Chicago: Univ.
of Chicago Press, 1967.

Jones places transcendentalism in the context of American religions
and, while considering Emerson a believer, points to some of the difficulties encountered in his philosophical system. Other sections of
the book provide a helpful understanding of religious trends and
reactions to them as seen in the works of other major writers.

_____. HISTORY AND THE CONTEMPORARY: ESSAYS IN NINETEENTH-
CENTURY LITERATURE. Madison: Univ. of Wisconsin Press, 1964.

Concerned about our "preoccupation with the present tense," the author attempts to show the contemporary value of historical consciousness. This study is useful for its wide view of American prose writers, from literary criticism to natural history, who explained, described, or commented upon the current scene.

_____. THE THEORY OF AMERICAN LITERATURE. Rev. and enl. ed. Ithaca, N.Y.: Cornell Univ. Press, 1965.

In this collection of essays on literary history, the chapter "A National Spirit in Letters" is particularly useful in tracing the expression of one concern of literary critics and essayists in the nineteenth-century; that is, the development of a significant and unique American literature.

Kaplan, Harold. DEMOCRATIC HUMANISM AND AMERICAN LITERATURE. Chicago: Univ. of Chicago Press, 1972.

The author investigates the interaction between democratic assumptions and literary performance in the works of Emerson, Thoreau, and others. He emphasizes the social and conservative aspects of the writers he discusses, focusing on their balance and judicial, critical temper rather than on their individualism or eccentric enthusiasms.

Knight, Grant C. THE CRITICAL PERIOD IN AMERICAN LITERATURE. 1951; Cos Cob, Conn.: John E. Edwards, 1968.

The years 1890-1900 constitute the "critical period" referred to in the title. The author focuses on the battle between the Romanticists and the realists which reached a crisis in the 1890s. The discussion cites literary criticism pertinent to the debate and notes some of the social issues which affected the literature.

Lewis, R.W.B. THE AMERICAN ADAM: INNOCENCE, TRAGEDY, AND TRADITION IN THE NINETEENTH CENTURY. Chicago: Univ. of Chicago Press, 1955.

This study has become a key statement of an American myth and its impact upon literature. The author shows, for example, how literary criticism was affected by the call for fresh, underivative accounts of the qualities and meaning of the new world. In a chapter, "The Function of History," Lewis discusses Prescott, Bancroft, and Parkman, demonstrating that even those whose task was to consecrate history developed new approaches and styles.

Lieber, Todd M. ENDLESS EXPERIMENTS: ESSAYS ON THE HEROIC EXPERIENCE IN AMERICAN ROMANTICISM. Columbus: Ohio State Univ. Press, 1973.

The author includes Emerson and Thoreau in his examination of the thesis that the "endless experiments" were directed toward mediating the dualism which was part of the Puritan inheritance.

McGiffert, Michael, ed. PURITANISM AND THE AMERICAN EXPERIENCE.
Reading, Mass.: Addison-Wesley, 1969.

> This is a collection of documents and interpretations designed to
> give "some account of our present understanding of Puritanism and
> its relevance to the American experience." The ideas presented
> contribute to an understanding of some of the influences looking
> on nineteenth-century essayists and literary critics.

Macy, John A. THE SPIRIT OF AMERICAN LITERATURE. Garden City, N.Y.:
Doubleday, Page, 1913.

> Although Macy's general assumptions about American literature have
> been challenged, his specific studies remain solid, judicial, and
> broad enough to provide a good introduction to the backgrounds of
> the major nineteenth-century writers.

_____, ed. AMERICAN WRITERS ON AMERICAN LITERATURE. New York:
H. Liveright, 1931.

> Several of the essays collected in this volume discuss the nonfiction
> prose and criticism of nineteenth-century American writers. Allan
> Nevins' essay on Prescott, Motley, and Parkman deals with the
> literary achievements as well as the historical perspectives of these
> writers.

Martin, Jay. HARVESTS OF CHANGE, AMERICAN LITERATURE, 1865-1914.
Englewood Cliffs, N.J.: Prentice-Hall, 1967.

> Martin's thesis is that the writers of the period, experiencing alien-
> ation and social instability, attempted to find the locus of the
> change, wishing to preserve old values and to accommodate change
> for humanistic uses. Among their basic concerns were the rise of
> wealth and the growth of science and technology. This study pro-
> vides an overview of the assumptions and ideas which affected
> writing after the Civil War. The writers discussed are primarily
> those who wrote fiction; however, there is commentary throughout
> on the philosophers, essayists, and reformers who were writing
> nonfiction prose.

Marx, Leo. THE MACHINE IN THE GARDEN: TECHNOLOGY AND THE
PASTORAL IDEAL. New York: Oxford Univ. Press, 1964.

> In analyzing the uses of the "pastoral ideal in the interpretation
> of American experience," the author discusses the views of Emer-
> son, Thoreau, and Henry Adams, among others. The study il-
> luminates significant images in nineteenth-century nonfiction prose
> as well as those in fiction and poetry. Emerson finds no incom-
> patibility between technology and nature: as a product of human
> ingenuity, machines can be beneficially used, while Thoreau sees
> the machine as a metaphor for intrusions on his inner landscape.
> To Henry Adams, the machine became an "elaborate, tragic, and
> all-inclusive thematic figure."

Matthiessen, F.O. AMERICAN RENAISSANCE: ART AND EXPRESSION IN THE AGE OF EMERSON AND WHITMAN. New York: Oxford Univ. Press, 1941.

> This is a significant study and an excellent exposition of the inter-action of form and meaning in works by Emerson, Thoreau, and others. The author relates Horatio Greenough's advocacy of the interconnection between form and function in art to the search by Emerson and Thoreau for the ideal organic writing form. By detailed illuminating discussion of the writers' styles, Matthiessen also sheds much light upon their ideas.

Miller, Perry. ERRAND INTO THE WILDERNESS. Cambridge, Mass.: Belknap Press, Harvard Univ. Press, 1956.

> Two essays in this volume are a particularly valuable analysis of nineteenth-century attitudes: "From Edwards to Emerson" and "Nature and the National Ego." In the first, Miller cautions against perceiving a direct intellectual line from Edwards to Emerson but does find a persistent attempt, from the Puritans through Edwards to Emerson, to confront nature directly, without intermediary. In the second, Emerson is seen as less important for his espousal of transcendentalism than for his ability to become the spokesman for "the inarticulate preoccupation of the entire community"--that is, nature, wilderness versus civilization.

_____. LIFE OF THE MIND IN AMERICA FROM THE REVOLUTION TO THE CIVIL WAR. New York: Harcourt, Brace and World, 1965.

> Although this study does not deal directly with transcendentalism, it is important reading for anyone who wishes to understand the period. Miller hoped to "distinguish the various strands of intellectual experience that went into the establishing of an American identity." The three sections of the work, the third of which was prepared from an outline after his death, are "The Evangelical Basis," "The Legal Mentality," and "Science--Theoretical and Applied."

_____. NATURE'S NATION. Cambridge, Mass.: Belknap Press, Harvard Univ. Press, 1967.

> Miller traces the movement of European culture into America from the seventeenth to the nineteenth century. Four of the essays focus on transcendentalism.

_____. THE RAVEN AND THE WHALE: THE WAR OF WORDS AND WITS IN THE ERA OF POE AND MELVILLE. New York: Harcourt, Brace, 1956.

> A study of the New York publishing world and its battles, this work provides an understanding of the background for some of the criticism appearing in the era's periodicals.

Minter, David L. THE INTERPRETED DESIGN AS A STRUCTURAL PRINCIPLE IN AMERICAN PROSE. New Haven, Conn.: Yale Univ. Press, 1969.

Two essays analyze the stylistic forms of Thoreau and Henry Adams in terms of the active, designing principle on the one hand, and the passive, interpretive principle on the other. The author concludes that by submitting his active experience at Walden to a poetic interpretation of that experience, Thoreau had "achieved more than he had in the beginning dared to dream." In the EDU-CATION, Henry Adams also achieved a triumph through the poetic interpretation of his experiences.

Moore, Merritt H., ed. MOVEMENTS OF THOUGHT IN THE NINETEENTH CENTURY. Chicago: Univ. of Chicago Press, 1936.

The discussions of Kant and the American "romantic philosophers" and of the effect of science on the American pragmatists provide useful background information.

Morgan, H. Wayne, ed. THE GILDED AGE: A REAPPRAISAL. Rev. ed. Syracuse, N.Y.: Syracuse Univ. Press, 1970.

This is a re-evaluation of the Gilded Age which contains essays on American culture, politics, business, and labor. Robert R. Roberts' "Gilt, Gingerbread and Realism: The Public and Its Taste" discusses patterns of evaluating the popular taste and provides a useful survey of the content of the periodicals of the age. Robert Falk's "The Search for Reality: Writers and Their Literature" includes a discussion of editorial practices and literary criticism. Paul F. Boller, Jr., discusses the impact of scientific thinking upon the time.

Morison, Samuel Eliot. THE OXFORD HISTORY OF THE AMERICAN PEOPLE. New York: Oxford Univ. Press, 1965.

One of the best general histories for the literary scholar, this traces movements, major figures, and significant events. Morison indicates both the reception of literary figures abroad and their influence at home, providing an extremely useful background for a study of such areas of nonfiction prose as travel literature and that of reform movements and of politics.

Mumford, Lewis. THE GOLDEN DAY: A STUDY IN AMERICAN EXPERIENCE AND CULTURE. New York: Boni and Liveright, 1926.

The "golden day" is the generation just prior to the Civil War. Mumford deals with the broad backgrounds influencing the "American mind" and with the national characteristics that affected the development of thought in America. He examines the institutions and ideas which influenced American literature, showing both its connections with the traditions and culture of the Old World and the unique qualities deriving from the New World.

Munson, Gorham B. STYLE AND FORM IN AMERICAN PROSE. Garden
City, N.Y.: Doubleday, 1929.

> The author's analysis of style is often abstract, general, and dated;
> still, in his discussion of rhetorical techniques he provides some
> valuable insights. One section, "Prose of Literary Criticism,"
> includes a description of and examples of Poe's style. Another
> section "Prose for Philosophy" discusses and gives examples of the
> work of Emerson, William James, and Santayana.

Myers, Gustavus. THE HISTORY OF AMERICAN IDEALISM. New York:
Boni and Liveright, 1925.

> This is a useful survey of the shaping events, institutions, and
> ideas in America up to the time of the robber barons of the late-
> nineteenth century. The author takes the view that both leaders
> and artists were representative and democratic, expressing what
> "the people themselves felt and thought." The study contributes
> to an understanding of the place of arts and literature in society
> and social protest.

Nye, Russel B. SOCIETY AND CULTURE IN AMERICA, 1830-1860. New
York: Harper and Row, 1974.

> This volume emphasizes the impact of Romanticism on American
> culture and the effect of material growth on social institutions.
> The chapter, "History and Literature in a Romantic Age," contains
> an informative discussion of the ideas and ideals which influenced
> the nineteenth-century literary historians.

Parrington, Vernon Louis. MAIN CURRENTS IN AMERICAN THOUGHT.
3 vols. New York: Harcourt, Brace and World, 1927-30.

> This remains a useful literary history despite some of the obvious
> biases of the author. His discussion of American writers and ideas
> considers the essays, political pieces, and other nonfiction prose
> that helped shape American thought.

Pattee, Fred Lewis. A HISTORY OF AMERICAN LITERATURE SINCE 1870.
1915; New York: Cooper Square, 1968.

> Pattee's judgments are interesting, and most were to be upheld by
> later evaluations. However, there are a few exceptions: he under-
> rates Thoreau and overrates Lafcadio Hearn. His study offers one
> of the few evaluations of essayists and natural history writers of
> the last quarter of the nineteenth century.

Paul, Sherman. REPOSSESSING AND RENEWING: ESSAYS IN THE GREEN
AMERICAN TRADITION. Baton Rouge: Louisiana State Univ. Press, 1976.

> This is a collection of essays, more personal than scholarly, which
> gives "an informal account of the Emersonian tradition and some of

the critics who have fostered it." The essays document Emerson's influence upon writers from John Jay Chapman and Paul Rosenfeld to William Carlos Williams and Gary Snyder. Those who are familiar with the author's work on Emerson and Thoreau will be interested in an autobiographical account of his attitudes toward them.

Perry, Bliss. THE PRAISE OF FOLLY AND OTHER PAPERS. Boston: Houghton Mifflin, 1923.

This is a collection of personal and eloquent biographical and critical essays. The essay on Dana, Burroughs, Emerson, Lowell, Woodrow Wilson, and literary criticism in American periodicals produces a vivid sense of the men and events discussed. The study of literary criticism is an interesting survey of changing attitudes about the nature and function of the genre.

Pizer, Donald. REALISM AND NATURALISM IN NINETEENTH-CENTURY AMERICAN LITERATURE. Carbondale: Southern Illinois Univ. Press, 1966.

The author discusses the effect of the theory of evolution upon late nineteenth-century critical theories, fiction, and poetry. His perceptive and informative analysis outlines the cultural backgrounds and social influences on the theories and criticism of Howells, Garland, and Norris.

Poirier, Richard. A WORLD ELSEWHERE: THE PLACE OF STYLE IN AMERI-CAN LITERATURE. New York: Oxford Univ. Press, 1966.

Poirier's study focuses on the style of major writers, from Cooper to Faulkner, demonstrating that the creative act of writing allows the writer to build his own realities. The comments on the prose styles of Emerson and Thoreau, particularly the analysis of Thoreau's use of puns and verbal irony, are illuminating.

Quinn, Arthur Hobson, et al. THE LITERATURE OF THE AMERICAN PEOPLE: AN HISTORICAL AND CRITICAL SURVEY. New York: Appleton-Century-Crofts, 1951.

The chapters "The Foundations of American Criticism," "Literature, Politics, and Slavery," and "The Literary Historians," by Arthur Hobson Quinn, and "Escape from the Commonplace" and "The Challenge of Social Problems and of Science," by Clarence Gohdes, deal with nonfiction prose and criticism, providing both a comprehensive view of literature and a solid judgment of its quality.

Richardson, Robert D., Jr. MYTH AND LITERATURE IN THE AMERICAN RENAISSANCE. Bloomington: Indiana Univ. Press, 1978.

In his examination of the use of myth by nineteenth-century writers, the author argues that "two polar traditions were operative, one

romantic and the other skeptical." His study provides some interesting insights and helps to explain some of the tension apparent in
Renaissance works.

Rosenthal, Bernard. CITY OF NATURE: JOURNEY TO NATURE IN THE AGE
OF AMERICAN ROMANTICISM. Newark: Univ. of Delaware Press, 1979.

This is a thoughtful study of the significance in American literature of the journey to the wilderness, the urban impulse, the concept of the "garden," and the growth of technology.

Spiller, Robert E. THE CYCLE OF AMERICAN LITERATURE: AN ESSAY IN
HISTORICAL CRITICISM. 1955; New York: Macmillan, 1967.

In a stimulating and highly readable literary history, the author
views major works of American literature in terms of recurring
cyclical patterns.

_____. THE OBLIQUE LIGHT: STUDIES IN AMERICAN LITERARY HISTORY
AND BIOGRAPHY. New York: Macmillan, 1968.

This study includes essays on Cooper as a social critic, and on
Channing, Emerson, and Henry Adams. Spiller concludes that
Cooper is more important for his social criticism than for his romantic novels. Channing's prose is oral--he "never left the pulpit"--but, Spiller argues, "there is no good reason why a good
sermon may not be as fit an object for the discussions of the literary critic as a good poem or essay." Emerson is seen as the
"spokesman" for his time and country, even though his philosophy
was not formal and his art not fully formed.

_____. THE THIRD DIMENSION: STUDIES IN LITERARY HISTORY. New
York: Macmillan, 1965.

This collection of essays, written over more than three decades on
the subject of American literary history, deals with such subjects
as nineteenth-century critical standards, science and literature,
and the province of literary history. In "Critical Standards in the
American Romantic Movement," the author emphasizes some of the
differences between Romanticism in America and in Europe, shed-
ding light on the culture and ideas shared by American critics and
essayists of the mid-nineteenth century.

Spiller, Robert E., et al., eds. LITERARY HISTORY OF THE UNITED STATES:
HISTORY. 4th ed. New York: Macmillan, 1974.

Containing essays by leading scholars on American literature and
major authors, this is, to date, one of the most useful and comprehensive volumes of U.S. literary history.

Stapleton, Laurence. THE ELECTED CIRCLE: STUDIES IN THE ART OF PROSE. Princeton: Princeton Univ. Press, 1973.

> Emerson and Thoreau are among the eight authors studied. The author says he is "concerned with the press of meaning upon structure, the varying ways in which the inner themes of . . . writers unfold, with their adaptations of existing kinds of discourse." He emphasizes the effect of the lecture upon Emerson's prose and praises Thoreau's ability to articulate concrete observations.

Stovall, Floyd. AMERICAN IDEALISM. Norman: Univ. of Oklahoma Press, 1943.

> The author uses "idealism" in both its philosophical and popular sense, and places a number of nineteenth-century writers, including essayists, philosophers, and critics within the framework of idealism. Stovall traces idealism as it reached a peak with Emerson and his contemporaries, and then declined in the late nineteenth century.

Sullivan, Wilson. NEW ENGLAND MEN OF LETTERS. New York: Macmillan, 1972.

> These biographical sketches of Emerson, Thoreau, Hawthorne, R. H. Dana, Jr., Melville, Parkman, Prescott, Longfellow, Lowell, and Holmes are sympathetic, stressing the writers' human qualities and contemporary relevance.

Tanner, Tony. THE REIGN OF WONDER: NAIVETY AND REALITY IN AMERICAN LITERATURE. Cambridge, Engl.: Cambridge Univ. Press, 1965.

> The author studies "the recurring use of wonder and the naive vision in American literature," examining writers from Emerson to the present. He discusses the transcendentalists, showing how they adapted ideas of Carlyle and other European Romantics to fit peculiarly American perspectives. This is an interesting study, tracing influences from the nineteenth century to such later writers as Stein, Anderson, Hemingway, Bellow, and Walker Percy.

Taylor, Walter F. THE STORY OF AMERICAN LETTERS. Chicago: Henry Regnery Co., 1956.

> An expanded and revised version of A HISTORY OF AMERICAN LETTERS (1936), this is a good general survey of literary movements and major writers. The author's discussion of the transcendentalists is well informed but biased, and the treatment of Emerson and Thoreau ignores the journals and notebooks of the two writers. The literary criticism of Lowell, Holmes, and several Southern writers is discussed, with their contributions and the contexts from which their criticism emerged.

Trent, William P., et al., eds. THE CAMBRIDGE HISTORY OF AMERICAN LITERATURE. 3 vols. New York: Macmillan, 1946.

> This work remains valuable for its well-ordered bibliographies and studies of minor writers. A SHORT HISTORY OF AMERICAN LITERATURE in one volume, based on the larger work, was published in 1922.

Vivas, Eliseo. CREATION AND DISCOVERY: ESSAYS IN CRITICISM AND AESTHETICS. New York: Noonday Press, 1955.

> This analysis includes chapters on Henry and William James, on John Dewey, and on theories of criticism and problems of aesthetics. A section containing William James's comments on his brother's art explores their differing visions and conceptions of intellect as well as their similarities in viewing experience, perception, and consciousness.

Warren, Austin. THE NEW ENGLAND CONSCIENCE. Ann Arbor: Univ. of Michigan Press, 1966.

> The study provides background for understanding the guiding impulses and activities of essayists and reformers of the nineteenth century by examining the development and characteristics of the "New England conscience" and its effect on several major figures. Thoreau is seen as somewhat rigid and offering less practical advice about living than did Emerson. William Lloyd Garrison seems closer in conscience to Quakerism than many other nineteenth-century reformers. Henry Adams' conscience is described as being intellectual rather than moral.

Wellek, Rene. CONFRONTATIONS: STUDIES IN THE INTELLECTUAL AND LITERARY RELATIONS BETWEEN GERMANY, ENGLAND, AND THE UNITED STATES DURING THE NINETEENTH CENTURY. Princeton: Princeton Univ. Press, 1965.

> The author emphasizes the common denominator of Romanticism which runs through the three literatures and presents an informative discussion of the relationship between American transcendentalism and Germany philosophy.

Welter, Barbara. DIMITY CONVICTIONS: THE AMERICAN WOMAN IN THE NINETEENTH CENTURY. Athens: Ohio Univ. Press, 1976.

> This historical survey explores attitudes toward and stereotypes of American women which are found in such sources as novels, letters, diaries, speeches, sermons, newspapers, and periodicals.

Welter, Rush. THE MIND OF AMERICA, 1820-1860. New York: Columbia Univ. Press, 1975.

> The author argues that the years covered in this study were crucial

in the development of American thought, placing emphasis upon shared attitudes expressed in public documents. There is a useful section on the idea of the West found in the writings of such historians as Bancroft, in political statements by legislators, and in newspapers. The study also demonstrates the influence of contemporary popular culture upon literary expression and the influence of literature upon popular opinion.

Westbrook, Perry D. FREE WILL AND DETERMINISM IN AMERICAN LITERATURE. Rutherford, N.J.: Fairleigh Dickinson Univ. Press, 1979.

The author's treatment of such themes as Calvinism, free will, moral responsibility, and the transition from Calvinistic determinism to naturalistic determinism is a useful review, but remains superficial in its survey of attitudes.

Wish, Harvey. SOCIETY AND THOUGHT IN AMERICA. 2nd ed. 2 vols. New York: McKay, 1962.

This survey carefully traces the development of American ideas and institutions including a discussion of the reception of prominent men of letters by critics and the public.

Woodress, James, ed., with the assistance of Townsend Ludington and Joseph Arpad. ESSAYS MOSTLY ON PERIODICAL PUBLISHING IN AMERICA: A COLLECTION IN HONOR OF CLARENCE GOHDES. Durham, N.C.: Duke Univ. Press, 1973.

Two essays in this volume are relevant to nineteenth-century non-fiction prose: one, written by Lewis Leary, describes the diary written by Elizabeth Clementine Dodge Stedman Kinney, mother of Edmund Clarence Stedman, while she was in Florence. Charles R. Anderson's essay on Thoreau's contributions to THE DIAL indicates that this little magazine "served as the real vehicle of his apprenticeship." Other essays contribute to an understanding of what was happening in American magazines in the nineteenth century.

Ziff, Larzer. THE AMERICAN 1890'S: LIFE AND TIMES OF A LOST GENERATION. 1966; Lincoln: Univ. of Nebraska Press, 1979.

The study includes useful information on the magazines and newspapers of the era, discussing influential literary opinions, tastes, and cultural attitudes. The author also traces the importance of the "big story" and the tradition of personal journalism, which led to muckraking stories as well as to particular types of humor in contemporary newspapers.

D. ANTHOLOGIES

Additional anthologies are listed in the various parts of Section II of this guide.

Alderman, Edwin A., et al., eds. LIBRARY OF SOUTHERN LITERATURE.
17 vols. Atlanta: Martin and Hoyt Co., 1909-22.

> This massive collection includes essays, criticism, and humorous
> sketches as well as fiction and poetry, by southern writers. The
> volumes are particularly useful as a source of short works, espe-
> cially humor, by minor authors, many of whom are difficult to
> find represented elsewhere. The evaluations written by the editors
> are perceptive and interesting as essays in their own right. This
> is an important resource.

Banks, Stanley, ed. AMERICAN ROMANTICISM: A SHAPE FOR FICTION.
New York: Capricorn, 1969.

> Intended to provide a background for understanding the fiction of
> the mid-nineteenth century, the primary material in this survey
> consists of letters, prefaces, reviews, essays, and some fiction
> excerpts. The critical essays and commentary include selections
> from Irving, Cooper, Poe, Simms, Hawthorne, and Melville. Re-
> actions to their work by some of their contemporaries in critical
> essays, reviews, and letters are also excerpted.

Benardete, Jane, ed. AMERICAN REALISM: A SHAPE FOR FICTION. New
York: Capricorn, 1972.

> This volume is similar in format to the one by Banks, above, in-
> cluding selections from the criticism of Whitman, Howells, Twain,
> Henry James, and Garland, focusing upon the social effect of
> literature and literary realism. Brief contemporary comments and
> evaluations of the writers' works are also included.

Blair, Walter, ed. NATIVE AMERICAN HUMOR 1800-1900. 1937; rev. ed.
San Francisco: Chandler, 1960.

> In addition to the samples of nineteenth-century humor, this col-

lection includes an informative discussion of such influences on American humor as the oral, narrative tradition. The revised edition includes an updated general bibliography and introduction. Blair's work is the basic resource for the subject.

Bronson, Walter C., ed. AMERICAN PROSE. 1916; Freeport, N.Y.: Books for Libraries, 1970.

This is a representative selection of fiction and nonfiction prose writings of major authors, covering the years 1607 to 1865. Included are speeches by Calhoun, Webster, and Lincoln with essays by Emerson, Holmes, and Lowell.

Brooks, Van Wyck, ed. A NEW ENGLAND READER. New York: Atheneum, 1962.

Brooks includes a number of works not usually found in anthologies, ranging from essays and criticism by N.P. Willis, Ticknor, Prescott, Motley, and Parkman to natural history essays by Frank Bolles and Edward Martin Taber.

Brown, Clarence Arthur, ed. THE ACHIEVEMENT OF AMERICAN CRITICISM: REPRESENTATIVE SELECTIONS FROM THREE HUNDRED YEARS OF AMERICAN CRITICISM. Foreword by Harry H. Clark. New York: Ronald Press, 1954.

This is one of the better collections of criticism by major authors from Richard Mather and the Puritans to Cleanth Brooks and the mid-twentieth century. Well over half the book is devoted to nineteenth-century essays. A foreword and an introduction (by the editor) provide excellent brief surveys of the historical development of American criticism.

Carpenter, George Rice, ed. AMERICAN PROSE. New York: Macmillan, 1911.

This collection is of interest because of the critical introductions and commentaries by such writers as Thomas Wentworth Higginson (on Charles Brockden Brown and Thoreau), Santayana (on Emerson and Whitman), Charles Eliot Norton (on James Russell Lowell), William Dean Howells (on George William Curtis), and Edward Everett Hale, Jr. (on Prescott and Motley).

Cohen, Hennig, and William B. Dillingham, eds. HUMOR OF THE OLD SOUTHWEST. Boston: Houghton Mifflin, 1964.

This offers an excellent survey of the field and includes a number of obscure but interesting writers.

ESSAYS FROM THE CRITIC. Boston: James R. Osgood, 1882.

Essays, reviews, eulogies, and literary criticism collected here from the periodical review are written by John Burroughs, Edmund C.

Stedman, Walt Whitman, R.H. Stoddard, F.B. Sanborn, and others on such writers as Longfellow, Thoreau, Whitman, Emerson, and Lanier.

Foerster, Norman, ed. AMERICAN CRITICAL ESSAYS, NINETEENTH AND TWENTIETH CENTURIES. New York: Oxford Univ. Press, 1930.

This volume represents an early recognition that there was something of value in American criticism. Several of the essays have been anthologized since Foerster's collection appeared, but, together with less well-known essays, still provide a useful spectrum of critical opinions and taste. Two essays not often found elsewhere, Lewis E. Gates's "Impressionism and Appreciation" and George Edward Woodberry's "Man and the Race," present two very different aspects of nineteenth-century American criticism-- that is, the romantic view and the historical view.

Fogle, Richard H., ed. THE ROMANTIC MOVEMENT IN AMERICAN WRITING. New York: Odyssey, 1966.

This anthology is more generous than most in its inclusion of nonfiction prose: criticism, reform writings, humor, and excerpts from the work of the literary historians.

Furness, Clifton J., ed. THE GENTEEL FEMALE: AN ANTHOLOGY. New York: Knopf, 1931.

The editor notes that "the greater part of American writing has been influenced by women more or less directly." The "representative" selections are strong on piety, melancholy, and "female frailty"; however, the chapter, "Woman's Rights and Wrongs," includes several excerpts from tracts on suffrage and emancipation which are both intelligent and eloquent.

Griswold, Rufus W., ed. THE PROSE WRITERS OF AMERICA: WITH A SURVEY OF THE INTELLECTUAL HISTORY, CONDITION, AND PROSPECTS OF THE COUNTRY. 1847. Rev. and enl. John H. Dillingham. Philadelphia: H.T. Coates, 1870.

This is interesting as a document in literary history and criticism because it was one of the first collections of its kind; its criticism affected the contemporary reputations of the authors involved, and the editor's biases make an interesting study in themselves.

Hart, John S., ed. THE FEMALE PROSE WRITERS OF AMERICA, WITH PORTRAITS, BIOGRAPHICAL NOTICES, AND SPECIMENS OF THEIR WRITINGS. Philadelphia: E.H. Butler and Co., 1852.

This is a more sophisticated and literary collection than THE GENTEEL FEMALE anthology edited by Furness, above. The essays represent some of the best writings of nineteenth-century women, including short works by Margaret Fuller, Susan Fenimore Cooper, Sarah J. Hale, and Caroline M. Kirkland.

Hochfield, George, ed. SELECTED WRITINGS OF THE AMERICAN TRANS-CENDENTALISTS. New York: New American Library, 1966.

> Although at present no longer in print, this is a useful paperback selection that includes many of the minor transcendentalists.

Leary, Lewis, ed. AMERICAN LITERARY ESSAYS. New York: Crowell, 1960.

> This is a good introduction to the American essay and includes a brief listing of additional essay collections. The editor's introduction includes a descriptive and historical definition of the essay and an account of American essayists.

Lynn, Kenneth S., ed. THE COMIC TRADITION IN AMERICA. Garden City, N.Y.: Doubleday, 1958.

> This work is a comprehensive survey of major humorists and the humor of major American writers, including those of the nineteenth century.

Matthews, Brander, ed. THE OXFORD BOOK OF AMERICAN ESSAYS. New York: Oxford Univ. Press, 1914.

> Matthews excludes purely literary criticism and set orations in his selection of representative essays, observing that America is some-what deficient in the lighter essay. This is one of the better col-lections of the nineteenth-century familiar essay; and, though the essays by the major writers are easily available in other collec-tions, this one also includes less accessible but interesting pieces by Charles Dudley Warner, Charles William Eliot, and Edward Sanford Martin.

Mayberry, George, ed. A LITTLE TREASURY OF AMERICAN PROSE: THE MAJOR WRITERS FROM COLONIAL TIMES TO THE PRESENT DAY. New York: Scribner's, 1949.

> Except for some excellent essays by Parkman, Prescott, William James, and John Dewey, this collection is unremarkable, since most of the other essays have been so often anthologized.

Miller, Hugh, ed. ESSAYS, HISTORICAL AND BIOGRAPHICAL, POLITICAL, SOCIAL, LITERARY AND SCIENTIFIC. Boston: Gould and Lincoln; New York: Sheldon and Company, 1866.

> This collection includes a wide range of essays, all having consider-able literary merit, which are rarely found elsewhere.

Miller, Perry, ed. AMERICAN THOUGHT: CIVIL WAR TO WORLD WAR I.
New York: Holt, Rinehart and Winston, 1954. Bibliog.

Miller has attempted to find statements of "controlling conceptions"
of American thought from the Civil War to World War I. The thir-
teen writers represented are Josiah Royce, Chauncey Wright, Henry
George, William Graham Sumner, Lester Ward, C.S. Peirce,
William James, Oliver Wendell Holmes, Jr., John Dewey, Brooks
Adams, Henry Adams, Thorstein Veblen, and Louis Brandeis.

_____. THE AMERICAN TRANSCENDENTALISTS: THEIR PROSE AND
POETRY. Garden City, N.Y.: Doubleday, 1957.

This paperback volume is an offshoot of Miller's more comprehensive
THE TRANSCENDENTALISTS, below. It gives a good general idea
of the range and temper of transcendentalism.

_____. THE TRANSCENDENTALISTS. Cambridge, Mass.: Harvard Univ.
Press, 1950.

This is an indispensable anthology for any study of the American
transcendentalists.

Payne, William Morton, ed. AMERICAN LITERARY CRITICISM. New York:
Longmans, Green, 1904.

This selection, with a useful introductory essay, presents an il-
lustrative sample of the genteel criticism of the nineteenth century.
The critics are Stedman, Whipple, Dana, Ripley, and Margaret
Fuller. Other critical essays are written by Emerson, Poe, Lowell,
Whitman, Lanier, and Howells.

Pizer, Donald, ed. AMERICAN THOUGHT AND WRITING: THE 1890'S.
Boston: Houghton Mifflin, 1972.

A valuable contribution to the study of late nineteenth-century
literary, social, and philosophical ideas, this anthology includes
selections from the works of philosophers, historians, journalists,
theologians, and political figures.

Rice, Allen Thorndike, ed. ESSAYS FROM THE NORTH AMERICAN REVIEW.
New York: D. Appleton, 1879.

This excellent collection includes essays by Prescott, Motley,
C.F. Adams, Longfellow, George William Curtis, Parkman (on
Cooper), Holmes (on "The Mechanism of Vital Actions"), and
Bancroft.

Ruland, Richard, ed. THE NATIVE MUSE: THEORIES OF AMERICAN LITERA-
TURE. Vol. I. New York: Dutton, 1972.

Views of American writers on American literature from Bradford to
Whitman are represented here.

Spiller, Robert E., ed. THE AMERICAN LITERARY REVOLUTION, 1783-1837. Garden City, N.Y.: Doubleday, 1967.

> Precursors to Emerson's "The American Scholar," the essays in this collection represent early attempts to find a national identity and a unique literature.

Spingarn, Joel E., ed. CRITICISM IN AMERICA: ITS FUNCTION AND STATUS. New York: Harcourt, Brace, 1924.

> Only two of the critics represented wrote in the nineteenth century: George E. Woodberry and W.C. Brownell. However, almost all of the essays deal with aspects of nineteenth-century criticism and its preoccupation with the search for a national literature or a "national genius" in the literature.

Stedman, Edmund Clarence, and Ellen M. Hutchinson, eds. A LIBRARY OF AMERICAN LITERATURE FROM THE EARLIEST SETTLEMENT TO THE PRESENT TIME. 11 vols. New York: C.L. Webster, 1888-90.

> The editors intended this collection for "popular use and enjoyment," placing before the reader "select and characteristic examples of the literature of this country" without critical comment. These volumes were important to the nineteenth century in that American writers were taken seriously, bringing them thus a measure of attention and respect. They remain useful as a source of the writings of a number of minor authors who have largely or entirely disappeared from later collections. This is an important resource.

Stegner, Wallace E., ed. SELECTED AMERICAN PROSE, 1841-1900: THE REALISTIC MOVEMENT. New York: Holt, Rinehart and Winston, 1958.

> Essays of the period collected in this anthology include selections from Clarence King's travels and criticism by Henry James, Howells, Garland, Edward Eggleston, and Twain.

Van Nostrand, Albert D., ed. LITERARY CRITICISM IN AMERICA. New York: Liberal Arts Press, 1957.

> This is a good representative selection of nineteenth-century criticism, with an emphasis on critics who focus on the art and architecture of literature more than on content or literary history. The critics include Bryant, Poe, Hawthorne, Howells, Emerson, and other nineteenth-century writers concerned with the theme of originality and the need for an independent American literature.

Wilson, Edmund, ed. THE SHOCK OF RECOGNITION: THE DEVELOPMENT OF LITERATURE IN THE UNITED STATES RECORDED BY THE MEN WHO MADE IT. Garden City, N.Y.: Doubleday, Doran, 1943.

> Wilson sets out to present, through essays, memoirs, journals, letters, and dialogues, "the developing self-consciousness of the

American genius" from the middle of the nineteenth to the second decade of the twentieth century. The essays, chiefly about their contemporaries, include writings by Lowell, Poe, Melville, Henry James, and Howells. There is a good selection of Poe's critical essays, and a report by Bayard Taylor, "Diversions of the Echo Club," first published in ATLANTIC, which parodies a number of nineteenth-century writers and has real critical value as a comment on contemporary literary style and thought.

Zabel, Morton D., ed. LITERARY OPINION IN AMERICA. 1937. Rev. ed. New York: Harper, 1951.

Original critical essays by James and Howells are included, as well as a discussion of the criticism of Poe, Emerson, James, and Howells.

II. PROSE WORKS

A. LITERARY THEORY AND CRITICISM

1. PRIMARY WORKS

Allston, Washington. LECTURES ON ART AND POEMS. 1850. Nathalia Wright. Gainesville, Fla.: Scholar's Facsimiles and Reprints, 1967.

> This volume collects Allston's most important prose literary compositions in which he combines both creative experience and a clearly defined philosophical position. Influenced by the German idealist philosophy and by Coleridge, Allston applied both neo-classical and romantic standards to art. In her introduction to the reprint, Wright observes that "in its conception of art as expression and communication . . . it anticipates developments in aesthetic theory in the present century."

Boyesen, Hjalmar Hjorth. A COMMENTARY ON THE WRITINGS OF HENRIK IBSEN. New York: Macmillan, 1894.

> Boyesen advocated an "idealized realism" similar to that of Howells and Garland. His critical standards were somewhat traditional and romantic, while, in letters and essays, he advocated social reforms and awareness of the conditions of the people and the times. Boyesen achieved neither the style nor the insight of Garland and Howells, but his critical ideas contributed to the rise of American realism. In his commentary on Ibsen, Boyesen championed his naturalism, and, although he did not agree with Ibsen's philosophical positions, he approved of his social criticism.

_____. ESSAYS ON GERMAN LITERATURE. New York: Scribner's, 1892.

> These essays, which originally appeared in ATLANTIC in 1875 and 1876, praise the growing realism in literature and condemn the romantic extremes of the previous generation's writers.

_____. ESSAYS ON SCANDINAVIAN LITERATURE. New York: Scribner's, 1895.

> This volume consists largely of previously published magazine arti-

cles on contemporary Scandinavian writers. Boyesen judged the
writers by their subject matter, praising them if they dealt with
controversial topics, social issues, or revolutionary ideas.

_____. GOETHE AND SCHILLER. New York: Scribner's, 1879.

Intended as a college text and widely used for that purpose, this
work consists more of exegesis and plot summary than of literary
criticism. Boyesen's efforts to explain German romanticism provoked reviewers to accuse him of being a partisan of the movement.

_____. LITERARY AND SOCIAL SILHOUETTES. New York: Harper and
Bros., 1894.

The essays in this volume, most of which were written in the late
1880s, include Boyesen's best writing. "The Ethics of Robert
Browning" is an excellent example of his literary criticism. The
other essays are a combination of social and literary criticism in
a form which is a cross between the topical article and discursive
essay. In these essays, Boyesen emphasized the importance of the
audience in determining the writer's subject matter. He particularly attacked the role of the American woman, the "iron Madon-
na," who forced novelists to avoid serious subjects.

Bristed, Charles Astor. PIECES OF A BROKEN-DOWN CRITIC. 4 vols. Baden-
Baden: Scotzniovsky, 1858-59.

Volume 1, reviews; volume 3, sketches and essays; and volume 4,
letters, show Bristed to be devoted to the classics and an advocate
of a scholarly discriminating taste. These volumes are difficult to
find in the original edition, but are available on microfilm: American Culture Series, 310:7, Ann Arbor, Michigan.

Clark, Willis Gaylord. LITERARY REMAINS. Ed. Lewis Gaylord Clark. 1844;
4th ed. New York: W.A. Townsend, 1859.

This volume includes criticism as well as essays contributed to the
KNICKERBOCKER magazine. The writing styles represented had
a great deal of popular appeal in the nineteenth century and remain good examples of the era's taste.

Cox, William. CRAYON SKETCHES. Ed. Theodore S. Fay. New York: Con-
nor and Cooke, 1833.

These essays originally appeared in the New York MIRROR from
1828 to 1848. Cox said that critics should act "rather as friendly
assistants than as dogmatical censors." His criticism resembles that
of Charles Lamb: it is optimistic, personal, informal, and sympathetic.

Crawford, Francis Marion. THE NOVEL--WHAT IT IS. 1893; Freeport, N.Y.: Books for Libraries Press, 1969.

> This is a superficial but interesting discussion of the novel by a popular writer. Crawford writes about popular tastes, the purposes of the novelist, a code of ethics for the novelist, and contemporary social problems which affect the reader and writer of novels. He defends his own use of "sentiment" as opposed to "sentimentality," and defines the novel as "an intellectual artistic luxury."

Curtis, George William. LITERARY AND SOCIAL ESSAYS. New York and London: Harper and Bros., 1894.

> A collection of essays from the NORTH AMERICAN REVIEW, PUT-NAM'S, HARPER'S, and HOMES OF AMERICAN AUTHORS, these are more personal essays than they are criticism. However, Curtis does maintain some detachment in discussing the writers' works, showing sound taste and candid but sympathetic judgment.

Duyckinck, Evert A., and George L. Duyckinck. CYCLOPAEDIA OF AMERI-CAN LITERATURE: EMBRACING PERSONAL AND CRITICAL NOTICES OF AUTHORS, AND SELECTIONS FROM THEIR WRITINGS, FROM THE EARLIEST PERIOD TO THE PRESENT DAY. 1855, Supplement 1866; Detroit: Gale Research Co., 1965.

> This remains a useful and readable work which, when it was published, surpassed Griswold's earlier anthology (p. 37) because of the authors' concern for fairness, comprehensiveness, and objectivity. In producing the CYCLOPAEDIA, the authors intended to show that there was a native tradition in American literature. A number of the statements about the writers included in this work were composed or revised by the writers themselves.

Eichelberger, Clayton L., ed. HARPER'S LOST REVIEWS: THE LITERARY NOTES BY LAURENCE HUTTON, JOHN KENDRICK BANGS, AND OTHERS. Millwood, N.Y.: Kraus-Thomson, 1976.

> This work collects critical reviews from HARPER'S from January 1886 to December 1899.

Ellet, Elizabeth Fries. CHARACTERS OF SCHILLER. Boston: Otis, Broaders and Co., 1839.

> Modeled on the work of Madame de Stael, this is regarded as one of the earliest specimens of American literary criticism.

Everett, Alexander Hill. CRITICAL AND MISCELLANEOUS ESSAYS. 2 vols. Boston: J. Monroe and Co., 1845-46.

> Many of these essays were originally published in the NORTH AMERICAN REVIEW, which Everett edited. The essays show a wide acquaintance with both European and Oriental literatures.

Everett's comments and estimates are wise, and concerned with morals without being overly rigid.

Gilman, Samuel. CONTRIBUTIONS TO LITERATURE. Boston: Crosby, Nichols and Co., 1856.

This is a collection of what the author considered the best of his publications, including criticism, essays, and poetry. His criticism is characterized by his wide reading in English and German theology, history, and literature.

Godwin, Parke. COMMEMORATIVE ADDRESSES. New York: Harper and Bros., 1894.

Although his style is dated, Godwin had a good sense of the movements which influenced the ideas and writers with whom he dealt. In addition to a brief biographical sketch about the author under discussion, these essays include a statement about the person's contributions to and reception by his contemporaries. Among the men praised here are George William Curtis, Edwin Booth, John James Audubon, and William Cullen Bryant.

_____. OUT OF THE PAST: CRITICAL AND LITERARY PAPERS. New York: G.P. Putnam's, 1870.

This collection of critical and literary papers includes essays on Bryant, Audubon, Shelley, Motley, Emerson, Dana, and others. Most of them were originally contributed to the DEMOCRATIC REVIEW. The criticism reflects Godwin's sympathy with reform movements; he praised Bryant for entering the political arena and Dana for his sympathetic brotherhood with an oppressed class.

Greenough, Horatio. FORM AND FUNCTION: REMARKS ON ART, DESIGN AND ARCHITECTURE. Ed. Harold A. Small; introd. A. Erle Loran. Berkeley and Los Angeles: Univ. of California Press, 1958.

The pieces in this volume express Greenough's influential theories and aesthetic principles.

_____. THE TRAVELS, OBSERVATIONS, AND EXPERIENCE OF A YANKEE STONECUTTER. 1852; Gainesville, Fla.: Scholar's Facsimiles and Reprints, 1958.

Originally published under the pseudonym "Horace Bender," this work contains eighteen chapters, about half of which deal with artistic subjects; the other half consists of opinions on a variety of social, moral, and political issues. The book is fragmented and uneven; however, it covers a wide range of interests and exemplifies the organic or functional theory as applied to literature.

Hudson, Henry Norman. LECTURES ON SHAKESPEARE. 2 vols. New York: Baker and Scribner, 1848.

> Hudson's critical comments show some original perceptions, as well as the influence of Schlegel and Coleridge, in his psychological analyses of the individual characters in Shakespeare's plays.

Jones, William Alfred. THE ANALYST: A COLLECTION OF MISCELLANEOUS PAPERS. New York: Wiley and Putnam, 1840.

> These short, concise review essays, together with the collections listed below, were published in a variety of journals, primarily the DEMOCRATIC REVIEW. Jones was widely known and well respected. Poe considered him one of the ablest critics of the day.

_____. CHARACTERS AND CRITICISMS. New York: I. Westervelt, 1857.

> These essays, as well as those in the other two volumes listed here, demonstrate Jones's contention that the critic should be a middleman between the poet and his audience, working with enthusiasm, candor, independence, accurate perception, clear judgment, and a lively sensibility.

_____. ESSAYS UPON AUTHORS AND BOOKS. New York: Stanford and Swords, 1849.

> See annotation above.

Knapp, Samuel L. ADVICE IN THE PURSUITS OF LITERATURE. New York: C.S. Francis, 1841.

> One of the first practical textbooks in literature, especially for English and American school children, this volume rewards study for its insight into factors influencing the judgment and ideas of many in the nineteenth century.

_____. LECTURES ON AMERICAN LITERATURE, WITH REMARKS ON SOME PASSAGES OF AMERICAN HISTORY. 1829; rpt. Gainesville, Fla.: Scholar's Facsimiles and Reprints, 1961.

> This first attempt to survey and evaluate American literature contains material on many other aspects of the country. Knapp encouraged American literary independence and emancipation from cultural prudishness. He wished "to establish the claims of the United States to the intellectual, literary, and scientific eminence, which . . . she deserves to have and ought to maintain." Knapp was interested in American legend, folklore, and "aborigine expression" as well as other literary forms. His works are worth looking at for their contemporary critical attempt to understand the workings of the American mind together with several ideas and images influencing American writers.

49

Legare, Hugh Swinton. THE WRITINGS OF HUGH LEGARE. 2 vols. Charleston, S.C.: Burges and James, 1845–46.

Legare, a linguist, legal scholar, and literary critic who focused upon the classics and was strongly oriented to classical literary theory, was cofounder of the SOUTHERN REVIEW. He had little respect for American creative literature but encouraged criticism as long as it was classically oriented. His influential critical opinions appeared in the NEW YORK REVIEW as well as in his own journal.

Marshall, Henry Rutgers. AESTHETIC PRINCIPLES. New York: Macmillan, 1895.

Marshall's common-sense approach to aesthetics influenced late nineteenth- and early twentieth-century theories of literature. In this work, the author argues that "the artist must alternate between the attitude of the producer and that of the observer, and he must be his own sternest critic."

_____. PAIN, PLEASURE AND AESTHETICS. London and New York: Macmillan, 1894.

In this volume, the author discusses the importance of the imagination in the areas of both science and art. He also gives a "psychological description" of the "mental state during the contemplation of artistic production" and the relationship between creator and observer.

Mathews, Cornelius. VARIOUS WRITINGS. New York: Harper, 1843.

This collection includes humorous essays, criticism, and miscellaneous pieces, most of which were derived from speeches given by the author championing the international copyright. Mathews' humor and commentary remain readable and interesting, but his criticism, justifiably criticized by Lowell, exhibits the awkward syntax and effusive adjectives of the "high" school of critics.

Matthews, Brander. AN INTRODUCTION TO THE STUDY OF AMERICAN LITERATURE. New York: American Book Co., 1896.

The essays on some of the major writers of the nineteenth century (Emerson, Hawthorne, Holmes, Lowell, Parkman, and others) are still worth reading for the author's own stylistic grace as well as his personal biographical observations and perceptive critical judgments. Matthews' comments in this history were objective and scholarly and thus differed from many of the eulogistic critical commentaries favored by his contemporaries.

Mitchell, Donald Grant [Ik Marvel]. AMERICAN LANDS AND LETTERS. 2 vols. New York: Scribner's, 1898–99.

Mitchell's humorous sketches and anecdotal comments make this survey more a delightful and discursive ramble than a work of criticism. It did influence European opinions about American literature, and it still includes valuable information about some minor writers who were far more prominent in the nineteenth century than at present.

Neal, John. AMERICAN WRITERS: A SERIES OF PAPERS CONTRIBUTED TO BLACKWOOD'S MAGAZINE, 1824-1825. Ed. with notes and bibliography by Fred Lewis Pattee. Durham, N.C.: Duke Univ. Press, 1937.

Neal wrote these observations as if he were an Englishman who knew something about American letters. Few Americans were fooled. Neal's style, in both his criticism and his fiction, influenced or anticipated many later writers--e.g., Ambrose Bierce, Frank Norris, Stephen Crane (in his direct, stark style), Henry James, and Edith Wharton (in his style of qualifying and requalifying in an attempt to represent intricacy of thought). Neal's comments on American writers tend to be impressionistic rather than scholarly, but they are always original and vital.

Peabody, Elizabeth. AESTHETIC PAPERS. 1849. Introd. Joseph Jones. New York: AMS Press, 1967.

This is the introductory volume of a publication that failed to survive the first number but which contained some outstanding articles, including the first publication of Thoreau's "Resistance to Civil Government," and essays by Emerson and Hawthorne. In his introduction Jones describes the contributors and outlines the goals of this and other Transcendentalist journals.

Perry, Thomas Sergeant. ENGLISH LITERATURE OF THE EIGHTEENTH CENTURY. New York: Harper and Brothers, 1883.

Oliver Wendell Holmes said that Perry was one of the best-read men he had ever known. Perry brought a scholarly awareness of European literature to bear in a search for tradition and values in literature. By doing so, he provided a more universal and cosmopolitan outlook than that given by critics focusing only upon a national literature.

_____. THE EVOLUTION OF A SNOB. Boston: Ticknor and Co., 1887.

This is a representative collection of critical articles commenting on writers and literary tastes.

_____. FROM OPITZ TO LESSING. Boston: J.R. Osgood and Co., 1885.

These studies of Russian, German, and French poets, novelists, critics and dramatists were influential in bringing several European authors to the attention of Americans.

Scott, Fred Newton, and Charles Mills Gayley. A GUIDE TO THE LITERA-
TURE OF AESTHETICS. Berkeley: Univ. of California Press, 1890.

> This guide is an essential starting point for an examination of the
> basis of American criticism in the nineteenth century, since it
> provides a listing of the works on literary criticism and aesthetic
> theory which were used as resources in college classes in the lat-
> ter part of the century. Some significant periodical contributions
> are noted.

Scudder, Horace E. ESSAYS IN CHARACTERIZATION AND CRITICISM. Boston: Houghton Mifflin, 1887.

> Scudder's criticism is scholarly, well disciplined, and much less
> impressionistic than that of many of his contemporaries. As editor
> of ATLANTIC (1890-98) and as an excellent biographer, Scudder
> expressed influential opinions. This collection on a variety of
> literary topics and authors gives a good idea of his critical and
> biographical abilities.

Stedman, Edmund Clarence. NATURE AND ELEMENTS OF POETRY. Boston:
Houghton Mifflin, 1892.

> These essays are based upon a series of lectures delivered in 1891
> at Johns Hopkins University. Stedman revered Coleridge and em-
> phasized the nature and function of the imagination and the neces-
> sity for a suitable theme in poetry. He was concerned with "the
> quality and attributes of poetry itself, of its sources and efficacy,
> and of enduring laws to which its true examples are conformed."
> His pronouncements were accepted in the 1880s and 1890s as those
> of a respected and admired literary arbiter. He remains a clear
> spokesman for a conservative poetic creed.

_____. POETS OF AMERICA. Boston: Houghton Mifflin, 1885.

> Stedman defends the inventiveness, vigor, and simplicity of Ameri-
> can poets, but criticizes some, including Emerson, for being di-
> verted by philosophy. In his judgments, Stedman was less con-
> cerned with technical skills or aesthetic effects than with substance,
> energy, and moral values. Despite some of the author's prejudices,
> this work remains one of the best contemporary studies of American
> poetry.

_____. VICTORIAN POETS. Boston: Houghton Mifflin, 1875.

> The first chapter of this study presents Stedman's critical standards
> and theory of poetry. He praised "simplicity and spontaneity, re-
> fined by art, exalted by imagination, and sustained by intellectual
> power." His comments on the Victorian poets combine judicial
> criticism with impressionistic appreciation. Stedman found Robert
> Browning a puzzle, Elizabeth Barrett Browning wanting in art but
> inspired, and Tennyson to be "the fullest representative of the
> Victorian age."

Timrod, Henry. THE ESSAYS OF HENRY TIMROD. Ed. E.W. Parks. Athens: Univ. of Georgia Press, 1942.

> Most of these essays originally appeared in RUSSELL'S MAGAZINE in 1857 and 1859. Timrod is concerned with aesthetic, ethical, and poetic problems. He was convinced that the greatest poetry must have ethical content. Although he did not deny the need for beauty, he did attempt to refute Poe's aesthetic principles. The editor of this volume provides a useful historical and critical analysis of Timrod's work.

Tuckerman, Henry Theodore. CHARACTERISTICS OF LITERATURE. Philadelphia: Lindsay and Blakiston, 1849.

> Difficult to read today, Tuckerman was highly regarded by his contemporaries. These twenty-one essays show a quiet, genteel taste. The intelligent, penetrating, and sympathetic essay on Hazlitt is outstanding.

_____. RAMBLES AND REVERIES. New York: J.P. Giffing, 1841.

> These critical essays exhibit Tuckerman's somewhat sentimental impressionism. He emphasizes the importance of empathy, sensitivity, and enthusiasm in criticism.

_____. THOUGHTS ON THE POET. New York: C.S. and J.H. Francis, 1846.

> These articles on Italian, English, and American poets show Tuckerman's inclination to favor the Romantics.

_____, ed. MEMORIAL OF HORATIO GREENOUGH. 1853; New York: B. Blom, 1968.

> This collection consists of a long memoir by Tuckerman, essays by Greenough, and tributes to Greenough by several of his contemporaries. The tributes give insight into critical tastes of the time, and the "essays and fragments" by Greenough contain some of his influential aesthetic theories.

Tyler, Moses Coit. A HISTORY OF AMERICAN LITERATURE, 1607-1765. 2 vols. 1878. One-vol. ed. with foreword by Howard Mumford Jones. 1949; Chicago: Univ. of Chicago Press, 1967.

> This first scholarly study of American literary history gives insight into nineteenth-century critical tastes, was influential in the nineteenth century, and remains a classic study today. It is an important resource.

_____. THE LITERARY HISTORY OF THE AMERICAN REVOLUTION, 1763-1783. 2 vols. 1897. Foreword by Howard Mumford Jones. New York: Frederick Ungar, 1966.

This remains a standard and authoritative history of early American literature. In his foreword, Howard Mumford Jones writes that "in the true sense Tyler's work is classical--the discussion of a great theme by a great writer." Tyler wished to document precisely what American colonists were thinking in their early struggle for independence.

Vedder, Henry Clay. AMERICAN WRITERS OF TO-DAY. New York: Silver Burdett Co., 1894.

Vedder discusses nineteen writers who, with the exceptions of Howells, Henry James, and Mark Twain, are forgotten today or regarded as minor writers. His critical comments indicate how these writers were regarded by their contemporaries.

Verplanck, Gulian Crommelin. THE ADVANTAGES AND DISADVANTAGES OF THE AMERICAN SCHOLAR. New York: Wiley and Long, 1836.

As were many essayists of the time, including Emerson, Verplanck was concerned with the possibility of scholarly activities in the New World. He argued that the stimulation of American society produced a mental activity which counterbalanced the nation's lack of opportunity for scholarly meditation and its pursuits.

_____. DISCOURSES AND ADDRESSES ON SUBJECTS OF AMERICAN HISTORY, ARTS, AND LITERATURE. New York: Wiley and Long, 1832.

In these essays, Verplanck talks of the relationship between artistic and manual labor, arguing that literary creators have "rights of property" just as manual laborers do. He enthusiastically reviewed and supported such writers as Bryant and was considered an important voice for nineteenth-century American nationalism.

Very, Jones. ESSAYS AND POEMS. 1839. Biographical sketch by James Freeman Clarke. Boston: Houghton Mifflin, 1886.

The three essays in this volume are "Epic Poetry," in which Very maintains that humankind has outgrown epic poetry in moving from outward physical action to emotional and mental conflict; "Shakespeare," in which he maintains that he alone understands the great dramatist; and "Hamlet," in which Very argues that Hamlet discloses the "basis of Shakespeare's own being."

Wallace, Horace Binney. LITERARY CRITICISM AND OTHER PAPERS. Philadelphia: Parry and McMillan, 1856.

This volume contains some of the critic's best writing. Wallace was responsible for introducing the philosophical ideas of Comte to many writers in the United States. The critical essays have philosophical detachment with both scientific and aesthetic perceptiveness.

Walsh, Robert. DIDACTICS: SOCIAL, LITERARY, AND POLITICAL. Philadelphia: Carey, Lea and Blanchard, 1836.

Walsh was influenced in his literary criticism by the German historical approach and by Scottish philosophy and aesthetics. He edited the AMERICAN QUARTERLY REVIEW and other journals. This volume consists of selections from his political commentary, social observations, and literary criticism.

Wendell, Barrett. LITERATURE, SOCIETY, AND POLITICS: SELECTED ESSAYS. Ed. Robert T. Self. St. Paul, Minn.: John Colet Press, 1977.

In his introduction to this collection, Robert T. Self writes of Wendell: he "represents the debilitation of a genteel mind divided between an idealistic appreciation of the classical and Puritan past and sensitivity for the new material energy, between moral idealism and crass materialism, between intellect and sentiment, between aesthetic taste and mass culture." A professor of English at Harvard, Wendell wrote these essays in the last decade of the nineteenth and first decade of the twentieth century. This collection includes excerpts from his study of Mather; comments from A HISTORY OF LITERATURE IN AMERICA (1911), which was written with Chester Noyes Greenough; criticism of Hawthorne and Poe; and his essay "The Relation of Literature to Life," on French literature and naturalism.

Whipple, Edwin Percy. AMERICAN LITERATURE AND OTHER PAPERS. 1887; Folcroft, Pa.: Folcroft Library Editions, 1973.

One of the leading critics of the time, Whipple surveys American literature in a lively way. He concludes this volume with essays on Emerson and Webster, showing considerable insight into their style and the reasons for their popular appeal.

_____. ESSAYS AND REVIEWS. 2 vols. Boston: Houghton Mifflin, 1850.

In several of these essays, most of which originally appeared in the NORTH AMERICAN REVIEW, Whipple discusses the function of the critic, sympathizing strongly with the original creative spirits who must endure analytical treatment. Whipple is generous with his praise, yet boldly exposes some of the biased criticism of his time. This collection includes two fine essays on Prescott, who, Whipple says, has a fine historical sense, seeing "with his heart as well as his head," writing in a vital lucid style.

_____. LECTURES ON SUBJECTS CONNECTED WITH LITERATURE AND LIFE. 1850. Enlarged as LITERATURE AND LIFE, 1871; Folcroft, Pa.: Folcroft Library Edition, 1973.

In these essays on various subjects ("Wit and Humor," "The Ludicrous Side of Life," "Genius," and "Intellectual Health and Disease"), Whipple's prose style is finely crafted. His focus is, how-

ever, on British writers, and his views tend to be pious and conservative.

_____. THE LITERATURE OF THE AGE OF ELIZABETH. 1869; Folcroft, Pa.:
Folcroft Library Editions, 1973.

These widely read essays were first printed in ATLANTIC in 1867
and 1868. Whipple praised the intensely human quality, the
breadth and preponderance of thought, and the high imagination
of the Elizabethan dramatists. He is not annoyingly prudish in
his judgment, but he does exalt the "spiritual delicacy" of the
female characters and the "heroic stoicism and loyalty" of the
male characters in the plays he treats.

_____. RECOLLECTIONS OF EMINENT MEN, WITH OTHER PAPERS. 1887;
Folcroft, Pa.: Folcroft Library Editions, 1973.

These essays on literary, political, scientific, and philanthropic
figures are critical more than biographical, in that they clearly
focus on the contributions and qualities of the writings of these
men. Whipple's "recollections" include comments on Emerson,
Motley, Agassiz, and Ticknor.

Woodberry, George Edward. LITERARY MEMOIRS OF THE NINETEENTH CEN-
TURY: LITERATURE AND LIFE. New York: Harcourt, Brace, 1921.

This is a collection of essays from the NATION and ATLANTIC,
many of which were written in the late 1890s. The writers discussed include Hawthorne, Longfellow, Motley, Bayard Taylor,
Holmes, and Lowell. Some essays are more biographical than
critical; others focus upon specific aspects of a writer's career.
Woodberry here praises the American writers with whom he deals,
although he was later to become increasingly pessimistic about
the state of literature in the United States.

_____. STUDIES IN LETTERS AND LIFE. Boston: Houghton Mifflin, 1891.

These essays, with the exception of one on Channing, are on
British writers. Woodberry combines brief biographical sketches
with comments on the general qualities of the writings. His style
is direct and clear; he tempers his critical statements with common sense observations. He clearly favors the Romantic and early
Victorian writers.

_____. TWO PHASES OF CRITICISM, HISTORICAL AND AESTHETIC. 1914;
Folcroft, Pa.: Folcroft Library Editions, 1969.

Published as a response to the upsurge of aesthetic criticism led
by Joel E. Spingarn, this volume contains Woodberry's ideas about
the importance of historical context in the study of literature. He
maintains that "art . . . cannot be understood as it was in its

original creation except by the full aid of historical criticism in all its forms and by a spiritual awareness of the author's message." The critic, Woodberry says, should be concerned with two questions: "What was in the mind of the artist?" and "Has he expressed it?"

See also the listing of anthologies of criticism, I.D., pp. 35-41.

2. NINETEENTH-CENTURY PERIODICALS

This listing and brief description of the major nineteenth-century periodicals may serve as a guide to those interested in further research into critical essays which have remained uncollected in separate volumes. POOLE'S INDEX TO PERIODICAL LITERATURE, 1802-81 (Rev. ed. 2 vols., 1891; New York: Peter Smith, 1963) and its SUPPLEMENTS, 1882-1907 (5 vols; Boston: Houghton Mifflin, 1887-1908) are the indexes to many of these periodicals. Also consult Eugene Sheehy (I.A., p. 9) GUIDE TO REFERENCE BOOKS, for the use of POOLE'S and aids to it (Sheehy's entries AE 164-68). Edward Chielens (p. 61) should also be consulted for general resources and particular studies of nineteenth-century periodicals. Frank Luther Mott (p.61) is the standard monumental work for the genre in this period.

THE AMERICAN QUARTERLY REVIEW. 1827-37.

Established by Robert Walsh, whose tastes were neoclassical, this journal published some fine scholarly criticism. George Bancroft contributed reviews of historical works; others, including the philologist Peter S. Duponceau, also produced excellent essays.

THE AMERICAN WHIG REVIEW. 1845-52.

An organ for Whig conservative principles, this review was established in opposition to THE DEMOCRATIC REVIEW. Early issues included George P. Marsh's papers and several essays in defense of the quality of American literature.

ARCTURUS. 1840-42.

Founded by Cornelius Mathews and Evert A. Duyckinck, the journal was aimed at encouraging the cultivation of good literature. William A. Jones's excellent literary criticism appeared frequently.

THE ATLANTIC MONTHLY. 1857-- .

The first few decades of this magazine's history are characterized by some excellent essays by three of its early editors: J.R. Lowell, W.D. Howells, and T.B. Aldrich. Early contributions were primarily from the major New England writers. This magazine is cited on these pages as ATLANTIC.

THE BOSTON QUARTERLY REVIEW. 1838-42.

As editor, Brownson was the most frequent early contributor to the journal, but there were also articles by Bancroft, Ripley, Alcott, Fuller, and Elizabeth Peabody. In 1843, this review merged with THE DEMOCRATIC REVIEW.

BROWNSON'S QUARTERLY REVIEW. 1844-64; 1873-75.

Brownson was both editor and author of this journal; his essays are concerned primarily with his attempts to reconcile himself with those Catholics who were then attacking his views.

THE CHRISTIAN EXAMINER. 1824-69.

The reviews concerned themselves with the moral qualities of the literature examined, but the moral standards were those of liberal optimistic Unitarianism. Contributors to the journal included Frederick Henry Hedge, who wrote several essays on Coleridge, the German writers and philosophers, and William Ellery Channing.

THE DEMOCRATIC REVIEW. 1837-59.

The views expressed in the review were liberal; essays and editorials frequently espoused the need for a distinctive national literature. Bryant and William A. Jones were among the contributors.

THE DIAL. 1840-44.

Edited by Margaret Fuller and Emerson, this was the mouthpiece of the New England transcendentalists. In 1860, Moncure Conway briefly edited another organ of transcendentalism with the same name; from 1880 to 1929 a literary monthly was also published under the same title.

THE HARBINGER. 1845-49.

Edited by George Ripley, John S. Dwight, and Parke Godwin, this journal was printed at Brook Farm. Not all of the contributors espoused the doctrines of transcendentalism, but these volumes are a useful source for a study of the Brook Farm experiment and some of the ideas of New England transcendentalism.

HARPER'S MAGAZINE. 1850-1980.

The magazine tended to be more cosmopolitan in outlook and choice of contributors than ATLANTIC was at first. The "Editor's Easy Chair," especially those columns written by Donald G. Mitchell and George William Curtis, has yielded some excellent prose.

THE INTERNATIONAL REVIEW. 1874-83.

> The review contained some good articles on literature and art, with special attention to book reviews. Contributors included Higginson, Holmes, and Henry James.

THE KNICKERBOCKER. 1833-65.

> The journal's role in literature and criticism was lively rather than profound. Its columns insisted upon a recognition of literature as equal to other arts; and it promoted a national literature but not in so insular a manner as some other contemporary journals.

LITERARY WORLD. 1847-53.

> Edited by Evert A. Duyckinck and Charles Fenno Hoffman, the WORLD published some forthright criticism by both Evert A. Duyckinck and George D. Duyckinck. Other contributors included James K. Paulding and Henry T. Tuckerman.

THE MASSACHUSETTS QUARTERLY REVIEW. 1847-50.

> The editors were Theodore Parker and a reluctant Emerson. Parker's contributions included some good literary criticism in his discussions of Prescott, Emerson, and Channing. Lowell contributed a review of Thoreau's WEEK ON THE CONCORD AND MERRIMACK RIVERS.

THE NATIONAL QUARTERLY REVIEW. 1860-80.

> Modeled on the English reviews, this journal contained much political and economic commentary, a good deal of it written by the editor, Edward I. Sears. The political writings are more noteworthy than is the literary criticism.

THE NEW ENGLAND MAGAZINE. 1831-35.

> Frank Luther Mott (see p. 61) considers this the most important general magazine published in New England before ATLANTIC. Its series of "Literary Portraits" by George Stillman Hillard is excellent.

THE NEW ENGLANDER. 1843-85.

> From 1885 to 1892, this was published as THE NEW ENGLANDER AND YALE REVIEW. It included theology, criticism of transcendentalism, and some excellent articles on history, science, and education.

NEW YORK MIRROR. 1823-43.

> The weekly contained a variety of articles, including many of N.P. Willis' travel essays and his comments on current literature and criticism.

THE NEW YORK QUARTERLY. 1852-55.

The general literary reviews were comprehensive, but the criticism was not outstanding.

NEW YORK REVIEW. 1837-42.

This was a quarterly organ of the Protestant Episcopal Diocese of New York, but its literary contributors were allowed much freedom. It secured some fine contributions on German literature and philosophy.

NEW YORK REVIEW AND ATHENEUM. 1825-26.

Edited by Robert C. Sands, this was an excellent critical journal.

THE NORTH AMERICAN REVIEW. 1815-- .

In the nineteenth century, the journal devoted itself to sponsoring native, nonderivative literature. Contributors included Bryant, Edward Everett, A.H. Everett, W.H. Prescott, Bancroft, and Andrews Norton.

THE PRINCETON REVIEW. 1825-84.

From 1886-1888 published as THE NEW PRINCETON REVIEW, the journal, after 1878, became less preoccupied with theology and was a worthy competitor to THE NORTH AMERICAN REVIEW.

PUTNAM'S. 1853-1910.

This publication was issued as PUTNAM'S MONTHLY MAGAZINE (1853-1857), PUTNAM'S MAGAZINE (1868-1870), and PUTNAM'S MONTHLY, with various subtitles (19C6-1910), and concentrated upon publishing original American writing, including some of the better criticism and essays of the time.

THE SOUTHERN LITERARY MESSENGER. 1834-64.

In addition to the contributions by Poe, the journal included articles by Mathew Carey, James K. Paulding, and William Gilmore Simms.

THE SOUTHERN QUARTERLY REVIEW. 1842-57.

The review published some good travel essays by William Gilmore Simms as well as criticism by D.K. Whitaker.

THE UNITED STATES LITERARY GAZETTE. 1824-26.

The numbers include four interesting prose sketches by Longfellow and some excellent reviews of current literature.

THE WESTERN MONTHLY MAGAZINE. 1830-39.

> From 1830-1832, the magazine was published as the ILLINOIS MONTHLY MAGAZINE. Its most notable contributions were Judge James Hall's Western sketches, and it was the most successful of the early Western Magazines.

THE WESTERN MONTHLY REVIEW. 1827-30.

> Edited by Timothy Flint, this journal predictably favored Western writers. The reviews are straightforward and well written.

THE WESTERN REVIEW AND MISCELLANEOUS MAGAZINE. 1819-21.

> The literary criticism is solid, and the contributions include some excellent articles on science by Constantine S. Rafinesque and on Indian antiquities by John D. Clifford.

3. REFERENCE GUIDES TO NINETEENTH-CENTURY PERIODICALS

Chielens, Edward E., ed. THE LITERARY JOURNAL IN AMERICA TO 1900. American Literature, English Literature, and World Literatures in English, vol. 3. Detroit: Gale Research Co., 1975.

> This survey includes an annotated listing of periodicals, a brief history of literary journals in America, and a listing of books and articles written about individual periodicals and periodical literature in general.

Gohdes, Clarence L. THE PERIODICALS OF AMERICAN TRANSCENDENTAL-ISM. 1931; New York: AMS Press, 1971.

> The author discusses what various periodicals published and how this material contributed to the transcendental climate, focusing upon content of the periodicals rather than publishing history.

Granger, Bruce. AMERICAN ESSAY SERIALS FROM FRANKLIN TO IRVING. Knoxville: Univ. of Tennessee Press, 1978.

> Although the time span of this study is 1722-1811, it provides an excellent background for understanding the development of the periodical essay later in the nineteenth century. The author analyzes twenty-three of what he defines as the most important literary serials, lists the dates and journals in which they appeared, and gives a bibliography of secondary sources.

Mott, Frank Luther. A HISTORY OF AMERICAN MAGAZINES. 5 vols. Cambridge, Mass.: Harvard Univ. Press, 1930-68.

> This study includes topics covered by the magazines, various types of magazines, and publishing histories. The section "Literary Types

and Judgments" discusses some of the obstacles to honest, substantial criticism and reviewing and evaluates and summarizes critical attitudes found in essays and reviews for a number of the magazines. This is the basic, standard reference for the subject. See also Jayne K. Kribbs, p. 6.

4. SECONDARY RESOURCES

Abel, Darrel, ed. CRITICAL THEORY IN THE AMERICAN RENAISSANCE. Hartford, Conn.: Transcendental Books, 1969.

> Published as the Spring 1969 number of EMERSON SOCIETY QUARTERLY, this work includes short essays which discuss important critical theories, standards, and tastes of a number of writers and artists, including Emerson, Poe, Fuller, Whitman, Lanier, and John Burroughs.

Baym, Max I. A HISTORY OF LITERARY AESTHETICS IN AMERICA. New York: Frederick Ungar, 1973.

> This is a valuable guide to American aestheticians and their theories. Baym defines literary aesthetics as being "primarily concerned with the criteria of beauty and pleasure in the creation and in the appreciation of literary works of art" and treats not only such explicit literary aestheticians as Poe and Lowell but a number of other authors concerned with an analysis of beauty in general--for example, Dewey, Santayana, and the sculptor Horatio Greenough. Chapters 2-8 deal specifically with nineteenth-century critical theories and aesthetics, survey foreign sources, and attempt to develop standard aesthetic principles.

Charvat, William. THE ORIGINS OF AMERICAN CRITICAL THOUGHT, 1810-1835. 1936; New York: Russell and Russell, 1968.

> This study provides a good understanding of the changing critical standards in the early nineteenth century and the gradual shift of emphasis from the moral and social values of a work to its aesthetic qualities. Charvat notes that the two major characteristics of the criticism of the period were its judicial tone (many of the critics had been trained for law) and its moral tone (many others were or had been ministers). The author also traces the influence of Scottish philosophy, aesthetics, and culture, discussing the influence of criticism appearing in periodicals.

DeMille, George E. LITERARY CRITICISM IN AMERICA. New York: Dial Press, 1931.

> The evaluation of ideas and assessment of influences in this study are well balanced and informative. Each chapter includes a list of primary critical writings and secondary works about the critics

as prose stylists. The survey of nineteenth-century criticism includes chapters on Lowell, Poe, Emerson, Margaret Fuller, Stedman, Howells, and THE NORTH AMERICAN REVIEW.

Eichelberger, Clayton L., ed. A GUIDE TO CRITICAL REVIEWS OF UNITED
STATES FICTION, 1870-1910. 2 vols. Metuchen, N.J.: Scarecrow Press,
1974.

This is "a guide to representative critical comment in thirty American, English, and Canadian periodicals." The second volume includes additional critical comment from another ten periodicals.
The work is a useful source of information for the student wishing
to examine the critical tastes of the period or of a particular periodical. There is also an index to reviews of minor works written
by minor authors. Such reviews are difficult to find in any other
guide.

Foerster, Norman. AMERICAN CRITICISM: A STUDY OF LITERARY THEORY
FROM POE TO THE PRESENT. 1928; New York: Russell and Russell, 1962.

In one of the best outlines of the critical theories of these four
writers, the author focuses upon the "literary creeds" expressed by
Poe, Emerson, Lowell, and Whitman in the nineteenth century.
Foerster finds that the answers to such questions as "What is the
relation of literature to morality?" "What is the relation of literature to reality?" and "What is the relation of American literature
to the national spirit?" had been most impressively given, prior
to the twentieth century, by these four.

Glasrud, Clarence A. HJALMAR HJORTH BOYESEN. Northfield, Minn.:
Norwegian-American Historical Assn., 1963.

This is one of the most thorough studies of an American critic who,
shared many of the ideas, though not the stature, of Garland and
Howells.

Hoover, M.M. PARK BENJAMIN: POET AND EDITOR. New York: Columbia Univ. Press, 1948.

This gives a fine account of the publishing of magazines and newspapers in the mid-nineteenth century and of the critical judgments
exercised by their editors, focusing on Benjamin as editor as well
as poet. The author notes that Poe praised Benjamin's literary
judgment and his prose style, but indicates that his critical opinions
were more influential through his editorial policies than by means of
his essays.

July, Robert William. THE ESSENTIAL NEW YORKER: GULIAN CROMMELIN
VERPLANCK. Durham, N.C.: Duke Univ. Press, 1951. Bibliog.

This excellent biography of the critic and essayist contains a great

deal of social and literary history. The bibliography is also valuable: it gives manuscript, newspaper, and periodical sources, and
lists the writings of Verplanck and general works related to the
era.

Lease, Benjamin. THAT WILD FELLOW JOHN NEAL AND THE AMERICAN
LITERARY REVOLUTION. Chicago: Univ. of Chicago Press, 1972.

A critical biography, this study traces the influence of Neal upon
other writers and discusses the general literary scene of the time.
The author notes the influence of Neal's critical ideas upon Poe
(who studied BLACKWOOD'S MAGAZINE, which published portions
of Neal's AMERICAN WRITERS series and his LATE AMERICAN
BOOKS) and discusses Neal's involvement in the quest for nationality in literature.

McKenzie, Gordon. CRITICAL RESPONSIVENESS: A STUDY OF THE PSYCHO-
LOGICAL CURRENT IN LATER EIGHTEENTH-CENTURY CRITICISM. Berkeley:
Univ. of California Press, 1949.

Although McKenzie focuses upon eighteenth-century criticism, he
provides a valuable background study for early nineteenth-century
criticism--for example, noting the widespread influence of Hugh
Blair's LECTURES ON RHETORIC AND BELLES LETTERS and of
other Scottish critics on American critical standards.

Minor, Benjamin Blake. THE SOUTHERN LITERARY MESSENGER: 1834-1864.
New York: Neale Publishing Co., 1905.

This history of the periodical includes an account of Poe, the second editor, and a list of other contributors: from the North, Paulding, Longfellow, Griswold, and R.H. Stoddard; from the South,
Timrod, Simms, and Lanier.

Moulton, Charles W., ed. THE LIBRARY OF LITERARY CRITICISM OF ENGLISH
AND AMERICAN AUTHORS. 8 vols. 1901-05. Rev. with Additions by
Martin Tucker. New York: Frederick Ungar, 1966.

American materials may be found in volumes 5 through 8. For
each of the authors included, a biographical sketch is followed by
brief contemporary evaluations and reviews describing each author's
work. The revised volumes include a listing of the standard editions
of each author's work and biographical and critical studies about
him published through 1964.

Newton, Annabel. WORDSWORTH IN EARLY AMERICAN CRITICISM. Chicago: Univ. of Chicago Press, 1928.

In tracing Wordsworth's influence in America, Newton discusses essays and criticism documenting a change in attitude toward Wordsworth's ideas. The study indicates that while American sentimen-

tality and desire for sensationalism resisted Wordsworth's influence, his moral and religious idealism and faith in democratic principles made him an American favorite.

Parks, Edd Winfield. ANTE-BELLUM SOUTHERN LITERARY CRITICISM. Athens: Univ. of Georgia Press, 1962.

The author traces the change in literary criticism from classicism and neoclassicism to romanticism. He provides a good study of the best Southern critics, including Simms, Chivers, and Timrod, but excluding Poe, and discusses their theoretical principles, their judgments of contemporaries, and their reputations.

Power, Julia. SHELLEY IN AMERICA IN THE NINETEENTH CENTURY. 1928; Lincoln: Univ. of Nebraska Press, 1946.

This work discusses the views of Shelley and his influence upon periodical literature, the transcendentalists, the mid-Atlantic writers, Poe, and Southern writers. The author argues that "Shelley criticism in America may be considered as representative of American literary criticism of the nineteenth century"; that is, she says, it is largely a matter of "personal prejudice." Reactions to Shelley in the first half of the century were largely favorable; his most severe critics opposed him on religious and moral grounds.

Pritchard, John Paul. CRITICISM IN AMERICA: AN ACCOUNT OF THE DEVELOPMENT OF CRITICAL TECHNIQUES FROM THE EARLY PERIOD OF THE REPUBLIC TO THE MIDDLE YEARS OF THE TWENTIETH CENTURY. 1956; Norman: Univ. of Oklahoma Press, 1967.

The author believes that American literature and critical theory "has consistently borrowed and adapted principles from other literatures until it has become original in the best sense of the word-- a new creation to fit novel situations." His study shows movements from conservative traditions through the following: Emersonian idealism; Poe's insistence that literary criticism be restricted solely to commentary on creative writing; the concern with a representative national literature; the campaign for realism, with impressionism, regionalism, and nationalism at the turn of the century.

_____. LITERARY WISE MEN OF GOTHAM: CRITICISM IN NEW YORK, 1815-1860. Baton Rouge: Louisiana State Univ. Press, 1963.

The study "attempts to describe significant theories and practices in New York literary circles," focusing upon the interpretive and critical articles in literary magazines published in New York. Thorough and well documented, this survey fills a gap in the history of nineteenth-century American literary criticism because most studies dealing with this period tend to emphasize the critics of New England and the South. Pritchard contends that the belief that letters and business must go hand in hand profoundly affected

New York's literary and critical thinking, that there were no dominant groups of writers (such as those from Harvard and Cambridge
in New England), and that the New York critics were free from
the presence of an inherited Puritanism, against which the New
England writers often felt bound to rebel. As a result, the "New
York litterateurs developed a characteristic inquiring attitude toward
new ideas" and were "more typically American" than New England
or Southern critics.

_____. RETURN TO THE FOUNTAINS: SOME CLASSICAL SOURCES OF
AMERICAN CRITICISM. Durham, N.C.: Duke Univ. Press, 1942.

The author traces the indebtedness to classical sources, primarily
Horace and Aristotle, in the criticism of American writers of the
nineteenth and early twentieth centuries. Among the writers
studied are Bryant, Poe, Emerson, Thoreau, Stedman, Howells,
Woodberry, and Brownell. Pritchard documents his point that
American critics were influenced by classical standards, and the
study provides a counter balance to those emphasizing the "Ameri-
canness" of American literary criticism.

Rollins, Hyder E. KEATS' REPUTATION IN AMERICA TO 1848. Cambridge,
Mass.: Harvard Univ. Press, 1946.

This short volume compiles opinions expressed in reviews, essays,
and critical prose in American periodicals, discusses the influence
of the British criticism of Keats, and traces the impact of Keats
on American poetry.

Scholnick, Robert J. EDMUND CLARENCE STEDMAN. Boston: Twayne, 1977.

This is a helpful short study of an author with a great deal of
prominence and influence in the nineteenth century.

Self, Robert T. BARRETT WENDELL. Boston: Twayne, 1975.

This study provides an understanding of the career of an important
critic and scholar.

Smith, Bernard. FORCES IN AMERICAN CRITICISM: A STUDY IN THE HIS-
TORY OF AMERICAN LITERARY THOUGHT. 1939; New York: Cooper Square,
1971.

This early survey outlines American literary theories and trends
from a Marxist point of view. Later studies tracing the development of American literary criticism are more thorough, but this
was, for a number of years, one of the few of its kind. As such
it was influential in shaping some of the opinions of nineteenth-
century criticism held by scholars of the mid-twentieth century.

Spencer, Benjamin Townley. THE QUEST FOR NATIONALITY: AN AMERICAN
LITERARY CAMPAIGN. Syracuse, N.Y.: Syracuse Univ. Press, 1957.

> The author of this study has examined particular critical pronounce-
> ments, essays, correspondence, speeches, and other sources from
> the colonial times through the nineteenth century for statements
> comprising a "history of the attempt of American authors, critics,
> and patriots to design and foster a national literature." Examina-
> tion of the naturalist theme in nineteenth-century criticism places
> familiar statements by major writers in a critical and historical
> context and also collects numerous lesser-known critical commen-
> taries appearing in periodical literature.

Spingarn, Joel Elias, ed. CRITICISM IN AMERICA: ITS FUNCTION AND
STATUS. New York: Harcourt, Brace, 1924.

> This collection contains essays published from 1910-23, many of
> which deal with principles of nineteenth-century criticism and
> which themselves were influenced by nineteenth-century critical
> standards and practices. Many of the essays expound the principle
> that the critic ought to deal with the ideas as well as the social
> and ethical values of a work rather than the techniques of the
> writer.

Stafford, John. THE LITERARY CRITICISM OF "YOUNG AMERICA": A STUDY
IN THE RELATIONSHIP OF POLITICS AND LITERATURE, 1837-1850. 1952;
New York: Russell and Russell, 1967.

> Stafford composed a standard survey of early American literary crit-
> icism showing how literary criticism was directly influenced by
> political situations, surveys the magazines and publishing practices
> of the time, discusses the chief literary critics and examines the
> critical theories and literary judgments.

Stedman, Laura, and G.M. Gould. LIFE AND LETTERS OF EDMUND CLAR-
ENCE STEDMAN. 2 vols. New York: Moffat, Yard and Co., 1910.

> This includes a useful bibliography, compiled by Alice Marsland,
> a biography, and a commentary on Stedman's previously uncollected
> writings.

Stein, Roger. JOHN RUSKIN AND AESTHETIC THOUGHT IN AMERICA,
1840-1900. Cambridge, Mass.: Harvard Univ. Press, 1967.

> This is an excellent analysis of Ruskin's impact on aesthetic and
> critical thought in America. The author uses the critical reaction
> to Ruskin as "a tool for the understanding of American taste and
> the state of American critical theory." He finds that American
> critics were drawn to Ruskin's "moral" approach in his early writ-
> ing but that his emphasis on technical matters in his later work
> eroded his authority in America.

Stovall, Floyd, ed. THE DEVELOPMENT OF AMERICAN LITERARY CRITICISM. Chapel Hill: Univ. of North Carolina Press, 1955.

> The essays collected in this volume grew out of papers read at the 1952 meeting of the American Literature Group of the Modern Language Association. The introduction by Floyd Stovall and the essays--by Harry H. Clark, "Changing Attitudes in Early American Literary Criticism: 1800-1840"; Richard H. Fogle, "Organic Form in American Criticism: 1840-1870"; and Robert P. Falk: "The Literary Criticism of the Genteel Decades: 1870-1900" trace American critical movement away from dependence upon European influences in the early part of the century to a gradual convergence with European thought toward the end of the century. Not attempting to present a thorough history, these essays do constitute an informative introduction to and outline for the development of literary criticism in America. A supplementary reading list of works published up to 1952 includes titles useful for an introduction to the field of American criticism.

Tucker, Martin, ed. THE CRITICAL TEMPER: A SURVEY OF MODERN CRITICISM ON ENGLISH AND AMERICAN LITERATURE FROM THE BEGINNINGS TO THE TWENTIETH CENTURY. 3 vols. New York: Frederick Ungar, 1969.

> This reference work uses the same format as Moulton (above). Vol. 3 gives critical estimates of thirty-six American authors.

Wellek, Rene. A HISTORY OF MODERN CRITICISM, 1750-1950. 1955; New Haven, Conn.: Yale Univ. Press, 1965.

> This study places American criticism in the context of the larger body of world literature and traces the interplay of influences on and by the authors discussed. A useful contrast between the theories of Poe and Emerson, as well as the critical ideas of Whitman, Lowell, and other nineteenth-century critics, is presented.

Wimsatt, William K., Jr., and Cleanth Brooks. LITERARY CRITICISM: A SHORT HISTORY. New York: Knopf, 1957.

> The section on nineteenth-century criticism includes a discussion of the ideas of Wordsworth and Coleridge, German literary theory and criticism, and the use of art as propaganda as factors affecting American criticism of the nineteenth century.

B. AUTOBIOGRAPHIES, MEMOIRS, AND DIARIES

1. PRIMARY WORKS

Note: Several diaries, journals, and memoirs are also included in section II.D., "Description and Travel," and in section II.F., "Historical and Political Writing."

Adams, Charles Francis. DIARY OF CHARLES FRANCIS ADAMS. Ed. Aida Di Pace Donald et al. 4 vols. Cambridge, Mass.: Belknap Press, Harvard Univ. Press, 1964-68.

> The editors describe the diary as containing "a cool, precise, and informed record of most important men and events in midnineteenth-century American history." The diary, containing a detailed account of Adams' daily activities, is clearly written, intelligent, and informative.

Adams, John Quincy. THE DIARY OF JOHN QUINCY ADAMS, 1794-1845. Ed. Allan Nevins. 1928. Ed. David Grayson Allen. 2 vols. Cambridge, Mass.: Belknap Press of Harvard Univ. Press, 1981.

> A selection from the twelve-volume MEMOIRS, below. This volume is a more accessible resource than the larger set for the student and those interested in the memoir as a literary form. Editor Nevins describes Adams as "self-centered," "pedantic," and "singularly humorless"; however, he also had "a keen eye for much that was picturesque in mankind and interesting in the events and changes of the day."

_____. MEMOIRS OF JOHN QUINCY ADAMS, COMPRISING PORTIONS OF HIS DIARY FROM 1795-1848. Ed. Charles Francis Adams. 12 vols. 1874-77; New York: AMS Press, 1970.

> See annotation above.

Breck, Samuel. RECOLLECTIONS OF SAMUEL BRECK WITH PASSAGES FROM HIS NOTE-BOOKS (1771-1862). Ed. Horace E. Scudder. Philadelphia: Porter and Coates, 1877.

This is an unusually interesting account of a man who was a state
senator, a proponent of emancipation, and a friend of John Quincy
Adams. This volume represents only a part of the thorough diaries
which Breck kept from 1800 to about 1860. The diaries are a valuable social and political record of Philadelphia for nearly sixty
years. Breck was compared by some contemporary critics to the
great diarist, Samuel Pepys.

Carey, Mathew. AUTOBIOGRAPHICAL SKETCHES. 1837; New York: Research Classics, 1942.

Issued first as a series of letters in THE NEW ENGLAND MAGA-
ZINE (July 1833–December 1834), SKETCHES was favorably reviewed by Poe, who considered it "one of the most instructive as well
as one of the most amusing of autobiographies." Carey's autobiography
includes many of the same themes as Franklin's, provides an interesting later contrast to it, and remains a delightful, readable work.

Cartwright, Peter. AUTOBIOGRAPHY OF PETER CARTWRIGHT, THE BACK-
WOODS PREACHER. Ed. W.P. Strickland. Cincinnati: Cranston and Curts,
1856.

Peter Cartwright was an itinerant preacher in Kentucky and Illinois
and an unsuccessful opponent to Lincoln in running for congress.
This volume and the one below give a lively account of the camp
meetings, sectarian disputes, and hard life of the frontier circuit
rider.

_____. FIFTY YEARS AS A PRESIDING ELDER. New York: Carlton and
Lanahan, 1871.

This volume and the one above are valuable in showing some of
the reasons for the strong appeal of frontier Methodism.

Clarke, James Freeman. AUTOBIOGRAPHY, DIARY AND CORRESPONDENCE.
Ed. Edward Everett Hale. 1891; New York: Negro Univ. Press, 1968.

The editor has tied together Clarke's brief autobiography with
material from his journal, diary, and correspondence. Clarke's
writing is full of details about scenery, people, and ideas as they
clearly reveal his own character and his influence as theologian,
abolitionist, and humanist. His comments upon contemporaries,
such as Holmes and Emerson, are also interesting and informative.

Cody, William F. THE LIFE OF WILLIAM F. CODY, KNOWN AS BUFFALO
BILL. . . . Hartford, Conn.: F.E. Bliss, 1879.

The 1879 autobiography is probably Cody's own often inaccurate
and exaggerated account. Later publications and biographies are
generally a rehash or distortion of source materials written second-
hand by other authors. For a complete bibliography of the various

versions, see Don Russell's THE LIVES AND LEGENDS OF BUFFALO
BILL (Norman: Univ. of Oklahoma Press, 1960).

Crockett, David. A NARRATIVE OF THE LIFE OF DAVID CROCKETT. 1834.
Ed. James A. Shackford and Stanley J. Folmsbee. Knoxville: Univ. of Tennessee Press, 1973.

> In an excellent introduction to the 1973 edition, the editors out-
> line the significance and the publishing history of the narrative
> detailing some of the spurious additions to the original. The editors
> find the NARRATIVE an important document in three major areas of
> American culture--as literature (one of the first of the "American
> success" stories), as an early extended example of American humor,
> and as a document in the history of American English. Another
> useful edition is that edited by Joseph J. Arpad (New Haven, Conn.:
> College and Univ. Press, 1974).

Emerson, Edward Waldo. THE EARLY YEARS OF THE SATURDAY CLUB, 1855-
1870. Boston: Houghton Mifflin, 1918.

> Edward W. Emerson was assisted by Bliss Perry, DeWolfe Howe, and
> others. The account includes many quotations from biographies,
> journals, diaries, and poems. It is a primary as well as secondary
> source of material about the eminent men (R.W. Emerson, Lowell,
> Motley, Agassiz, Prescott, Longfellow, Holmes, Hawthorne, and
> Henry James, Sr.) whose membership in this prestigious club played
> an important role in their life and work.

Fields, Annie Adams. AUTHORS AND FRIENDS. Boston: Houghton Mifflin,
1893.

> Although personal rather than profound, these recollections of such
> writers as Longfellow, Emerson, Holmes, Harriet Beecher Stowe,
> and Whittier, among others, are worth reading. Mrs. Fields, the
> wife of James T. Fields, reconstructs conversations including per-
> sonal details that give a dimension to all of the writers she dis-
> cusses. She focuses upon their attitudes toward writing--their own
> writing, and the work of others.

Fields, James T. YESTERDAY WITH AUTHORS. Boston: Houghton Mifflin,
1871.

> Publisher and successor to Lowell as editor of ATLANTIC, Fields
> deals at length here with only one American author, Hawthorne;
> but he reveals much about the publishing scene and other literary
> figures in clear sympathetic prose. This volume includes some re-
> vealing excerpts from letters to Fields which discuss various writers.
> See also FIELDS OF THE ATLANTIC MONTHLY: LETTERS TO AN
> EDITOR 1861-1870 (Ed. James C. Austin; San Marino, Calif.:
> Huntington Library, 1953).

Finley, James Bradley. AUTOBIOGRAPHY OF REVEREND JAMES B. FINLEY, OR PIONEER LIFE IN THE WEST. Cincinnati: Cranston and Curts, 1853.

> Along with Peter Cartwright, Finley was one of the more interesting and observant of the pioneer preachers. These descriptions of life and scenes in Kentucky and Ohio and the backwoods preacher's role in the settlement of the frontier are often centered upon conversions, spiritual experiences, and the sectarian hierarchy. The narrative is clear, direct, and often eloquent. Finley's experience with the Indians show an interesting mixture of missionary zeal and evident prejudice.

Frothingham, Octavius B. RECOLLECTIONS AND IMPRESSIONS, 1822-1890. New York: G.P. Putnam's, 1891.

> Frothingham was an intelligent observer of many of the major events and persons of nineteenth-century New England. His analysis of religious thought and institutions and his liberal conjectures about the religious future of the country are particularly interesting.

Goodrich, Samuel G. [Peter Parley]. RECOLLECTIONS OF A LIFETIME; OR, MEN AND THINGS I HAVE SEEN. 2 vols. 1856; Detroit: Gale Research Co., 1967.

> Written in the form of letters to a friend, this is considered the author's best work. In it, he writes of early Connecticut, the War of 1812, the "Hartford Wits," writing and publishing in England and America, and his life as a consul in France. Also included is a list of books written by Goodrich and a list of spurious Parley titles.

Grant, Ulysses S. PERSONAL MEMOIRS. 2 vols. 1885-1886. Ed. with notes and introd. E.B. Long. Cleveland: World Publishing Co., 1952.

> Grant published these reminiscences of the Civil War in the CENTURY to earn a bit of money. Despite claims to the contrary, most biographers agree that Grant himself wrote most of them. Aside from a few chapters on his early years, the focus is on Grant's military career, and the memoirs conclude with the end of the Civil War. Matthew Arnold praised the work as "the most remarkable work of its kind since the COMMENTARIES of Julius Caesar . . . a unique expression of the national character."

Greeley, Horace. RECOLLECTIONS OF A BUSY LIFE. . . . 1868; New York: Arno, 1970.

> This is a collection of essays originally published in the NEW YORK LEDGER, revised and rewritten for this volume. The essays are reflective as well as reminiscent, including a fine tribute to Margaret Fuller, a commentary on "Literature as a Vocation," and statements about his lifetime "convictions."

Hale, Edward Everett. A NEW ENGLAND BOYHOOD. Boston: Little, Brown, 1893.

> Hale's eloquent autobiography tells how he was influenced by his literary family and his later association with other writers and statesmen. He meant his account to be instructive; it is also interesting and readable.

Higginson, Thomas Wentworth. CHEERFUL YESTERDAYS. 1898; Cambridge, Mass.: Riverside Press, 1900.

> As the title indicates, this is a determinedly cheerful autobiography. Written while Higginson was ill, it touches only upon the happier parts of his life. In his review of the work, Henry James wrote, "Colonel Higginson has the interesting quality of having reflected almost everything that was in the New England air, of vibrating with it all round. . . ."

Howe, Mark A. De Wolfe. AMERICAN BOOKMEN: SKETCHES, CHIEFLY BIOGRAPHICAL, OF CERTAIN WRITERS OF THE NINETEENTH CENTURY. New York: Dodd, 1898.

> These sketches are evidence of Howe's fine biographical ability. His reminiscences of such writers as Bryant, Poe, Prescott, Emerson, Hawthorne, and Whitman contain many familiar anecdotes and humane judgments of the writer's works and characters. Howe focuses more upon the impact of the works than upon their quality.

_____. LATER YEARS OF THE SATURDAY CLUB. 1927; Freeport, N.Y.: Books for Libraries Press, 1968.

> This is a continuation of Edward W. Emerson's volume (see p. 71). Well over half the book deals with nineteenth-century writers, including Parkman, Howells, and William James. The essays include a biographical sketch, personal anecdotes, statements of appreciation, and evaluations of the authors by those who knew them.

_____. MEMORIES OF A HOSTESS: A CHRONICLE OF EMINENT FRIENDSHIPS DRAWN CHIEFLY FROM THE DIARIES OF MRS. JAMES T. FIELDS. Boston: Atlantic Monthly Press, 1922.

> Howe's volume is an interesting addition to Annie Adams Fields' own published reminiscences (see p. 71) because he allows the reader to visualize the publisher and his wife as well as their acquaintances. The anecdotes included are often trivial, but occasionally reveal insights into some of the more personal characteristics of a number of eminent nineteenth-century American writers.

Jefferson, Joseph. THE AUTOBIOGRAPHY OF JOSEPH JEFFERSON. 1890. Ed. Alan S. Downer. Cambridge, Mass.: Belknap Press, Harvard Univ. Press, 1964.

> Jefferson's acting career covered seventy-one years, and his por-

trayal of Rip Van Winkle became legendary. This autobiography, begun at the suggestion of William Dean Howells, includes vivid recollections and skillful descriptions. In his introduction, Downer sees Jefferson as a representative American and the autobiography as "a great document of theatrical and cultural history."

Jones, John Beauchamp. A REBEL WAR CLERK'S DIARY AT THE CONFEDERATE STATE CAPITAL. 1866. Ed. Earl S. Miers. Cranbury, N.J.: A.S. Barnes, 1961.

Jones has been compared with Pepys because he kept a minute and extensive diary which, although not so imaginative as Pepys' in style and content, provides an important record from the point of view of a conventional but perceptive minor Southern official.

Kemble, Fanny. THE JOURNAL OF FRANCES ANNE BUTLER. 1835; New York: B. Blom, 1970.

In this day-by-day account, the actress tells of her experiences on stage in London and America and gives candid, often naive, opinions about dramatists, actors, and associates, as well as florid descriptions of the landscapes through which she traveled. Her journal is valuable as a document of the early American stage and interesting as an account of the early years of an unusual woman. Henry James commented that her various journals "form together one of the most animated autobiographies in the language."

Kilgore, Manley W., and George F. Woodbury, eds. PERSONAL RECOLLECTIONS OF AMERICAN POETS BY EDWARD EVERETT HALE AND OTHERS. Boston: George H. Ellis, 1935.

This is a gathering of articles which first appeared in the ARENA in the 1890s. The recollections include interviews, anecdotes, eulogies, and comments upon the writers' influences upon their contemporaries. The volume is of interest chiefly because it provides several contemporary views of important nineteenth-century writers.

Leland, Charles Godfrey. MEMOIRS. 1893; Detroit: Gale Research Co., 1968.

The author, who wrote humor under the pseudonym of "Hans Breitman," tells us that he "wrote, as fully and honestly as I could, everything which I could remember which had made me what I am." Full of humor, vivid descriptions, delightful anecdotes, and a subtle desire to shock, this is a fine example of the autobiographical form.

Lucid, Robert F., ed. THE JOURNAL OF RICHARD HENRY DANA, JR. 3 vols. Cambridge, Mass.: Belknap Press, Harvard Univ. Press, 1968.

Written in precise clear prose, the record kept by Dana supplies primary historical data, resources for scholarly research in literary and cultural history, and some insight into the life and personality of the man.

Miller, Cincinnatus Hiner (or Heine) [Joaquin Miller]. OVERLAND IN A COVERED WAGON: AN AUTOBIOGRAPHY. 1930; New York: Arno, 1972.

Considered by most critics as Miller's best literary production, this was originally written as an introduction to the complete edition of Miller's poems. As literature, it is a colorful clearly detailed narrative of a journey from the Midwest to Oregon and California. As autobiography, it is unreliable.

Neal, John. WANDERING RECOLLECTIONS OF A SOMEWHAT BUSY LIFE: AN AUTOBIOGRAPHY. Boston: Roberts Brothers, 1869.

The writer gives an informal, rambling account of his life and provides opinions and anecdotes about such topics as temperance, woman's suffrage, abolition, and the EDINBURGH REVIEW. He emerges as very likable, though occasionally self-congratulatory. His descriptions are wordy and florid; his narrative is straightforward and lively.

Sanborn, Frank B. RECOLLECTIONS OF SEVENTY YEARS. 2 vols. Boston: R.G. Badger, 1909.

In volume 1, Sanborn writes of the political events surrounding the Civil War. In volume 2, he tells of his association with Thoreau, Alcott, Hawthorne, Margaret Fuller, and others, recalling personal characteristics and describing their families and friends.

Scott, Leonora Cranch. THE LIFE AND LETTERS OF CHRISTOPHER PEARSE CRANCH. Boston: Houghton Mifflin, 1917.

While Cranch was a minor literary figure, his close acquaintance with major authors and his awareness of their views makes this collection of pieces worthwhile. The author, Cranch's daughter, has patched together excerpts from her father's diaries, an autobiographical sketch, together with letters to and comments upon his colleagues.

Sherman, William T. MEMOIRS. 2 vols. 1875. One-vol. ed. with foreword by B.H. Liddell Hart. Bloomington: Indiana Univ. Press, 1957.

When they first appeared, Sherman's MEMOIRS were attacked as being distorted and self-serving; however, the criticism appears to have been politically motivated. The work is an interesting, readable, important personal record, as well as a contemporary interpretation of historical events.

Siringo, Charles A. A TEXAS COWBOY. . . . 1885. Introd. and biographical sketch by J. Frank Dobie. New York: Sloane, 1950.

> Widely distributed and read by other range men as well as curious easterners, this was an unglamorized, honest account of cowboy life. Of the work and the writer, Dobie writes, "Siringo was not only the first authentic cowboy to publish an autobiography; of all cowboys, both spurious and authentic, who have recollected in print he was the most prolific in autobiographic variations. No record of a cowboy life has supplanted his rollicky, reckless, realistic chronicle."

Stanton, Elizabeth Cady. EIGHTY YEARS AND MORE. . . . 1898. Ed. Theodore Stanton and Harriet Stanton Blatch. New York: Arno and the New York Times, 1969.

> This volume of reminiscences covering the years 1815 to 1897 shows Stanton's consciousness of the issues of abolition and women's rights at a very early age. More than half the volume is devoted to a description of the author's political and reform activities.

Stoddard, Richard Henry. RECOLLECTIONS PERSONAL AND LITERARY. Ed. Ripley Hitchcock. Introd. Edmund Clarence Stedman. New York: A.S. Barnes, 1903.

> Published after Stoddard's death, this volume contains comments on writers he knew, among them Poe, Bryant, Longfellow, and Stoddard's friend, Bayard Taylor. RECOLLECTIONS is honest about personal antipathies yet generous in critical judgments. The descriptions are concrete, and the tone is sympathetic and self-confident.

Sutter, John Augustus. DIARY. San Francisco: Grabhorn Press, 1932.

> The diary was originally published in four issues of the San Francisco ARGONAUT in 1878, although much of it was written in 1856 to help Sutter's legal advisers in a land-title struggle. The diary is not well written, but the events, which are clearly recalled, are absorbing.

Wallace, Lew[is]. LEW WALLACE: AN AUTOBIOGRAPHY. 2 vols. New York: Harper, 1906.

> Accounts of the Mexican War, the Civil War, and the Wirz trial are presented in a rambling but readable style.

Ward, Elizabeth Stuart Phelps. CHAPTERS FROM A LIFE. Boston: Houghton Mifflin, 1896.

> The author writes about problems of writing, her philosophy of literature ("art for truth's sake"), and other writers, including Whitter, Holmes, and Harriet Beecher Stowe. Although sometimes

critically off the mark, her comments on the work and character of other authors are generous and acute.

Willard, Frances E. GLIMPSES OF FIFTY YEARS: THE AUTOBIOGRAPHY OF AN AMERICAN WOMAN. 1889; New York: Source Book Press, 1970.

This record of the life of a hard-working, determined, zealous temperance worker describes a life dedicated to a cause. Despite its moral and theological tone, the work shows an independent, spirited, and intelligent woman.

Wise, John Sergeant. THE END OF THE ERA. Boston: Houghton Mifflin, 1899.

Although this is, in the writer's words, "the autobiography of an insignificant person," it is clearly and vividly written and gives important insights into Southern life and sentiments prior to and during the Civil War.

2. GUIDES

Blasing, Mutlu Konuk. THE ART OF LIFE: STUDIES IN AMERICAN AUTO-BIOGRAPHICAL LITERATURE. Austin: Univ. of Texas Press, 1977.

This examination of American autobiographical literature is concerned with "the structures and dynamics of writers' creating literature out of their historical selves." Among the specific studies of autobiographies are those on Thoreau's WALDEN and Henry Adams' EDUCATION.

Brigano, Russell C. BLACK AMERICANS IN AUTOBIOGRAPHY: AN AN-NOTATED BIBLIOGRAPHY OF AUTOBIOGRAPHIES AND AUTOBIOGRAPHICAL BOOKS WRITTEN SINCE THE CIVIL WAR. Durham, N.C.: Duke Univ. Press, 1974.

The annotations attempt to "provide basic information about the authors' public lives and . . . identify some of the geographical locations where those lives were led." The listings include libraries in which both rare volumes and information on reprints (since 1945) of works printed before the Civil War can be found. Diaries, travelogs, letters, essays, and reports, as well as more formal autobiographies, are also included.

Butterfield, Stephen. BLACK AUTOBIOGRAPHY IN AMERICA. Amherst: Univ. of Massachusetts Press, 1974.

In his study the author notes several themes emerging. Among them an uncertain sense of identity in the slave narrative based on the desire for freedom; and the fear of failure to escape, since failure meant punishment or death to the narrator. Butterfield also considers various influences upon the language of black Americans and the sense of mysticism which arises where a narrator confronts the wilderness.

Cooley, Thomas. EDUCATED LIVES: THE RISE OF MODERN AUTOBIOGRAPHY IN AMERICA. Columbus: Ohio State Univ. Press, 1976.

The author finds autobiographical writings by Twain and Howells, among others, to be analyzable in terms of the rhetoric of fiction. He also traces certain psychological patterns in American auto-biographies--for example, the sense of the "fallen self."

Couser, G. Thomas. AMERICAN AUTOBIOGRAPHY: THE PROPHETIC MODE. Amherst: Univ. of Massachusetts Press, 1979.

The author examines what he calls the "prophetic mode" of Ameri-can autobiography which has roots in Puritan literature and Old Testament prophecy. This type of autobiography represents a com-munal crisis requiring the autobiographer to comprehend that crisis and to inquire about what being an American means. The prophetic mode is represented in writings by Frederick Douglass, Thoreau, Whitman, and Henry Adams and must be read as religious literature.

Kaplan, Louis, et al. A BIBLIOGRAPHY OF AMERICAN AUTOBIOGRAPHIES. Madison: Univ. of Wisconsin Press, 1961.

The entries give editions, publication data, and library locations for the autobiographies listed. Only factual autobiographies are included; episodic accounts, reminiscences, and fictionalizations are excluded. Indexes provide cross listings under the occupation-al headings of autobiographies (e.g., "Engineers," "Dancers," or "Critics") and regions they wrote about.

Lillard, Richard Gordon. AMERICAN LIFE IN AUTOBIOGRAPHY: A DESCRIP-TIVE GUIDE. Stanford, Calif.: Stanford Univ. Press, 1956. Index.

The introduction gives a good survey and description of the genre. Titles are organized by the principal occupation of the autobiog-rapher. The annotations suggest content, style, and reader ap-peal. Since the titles included were printed or reprinted after 1900, the guide has limited use as a source listing for nineteenth-century writings.

Matthews, William. AMERICAN DIARIES: AN ANNOTATED BIBLIOGRAPHY OF AMERICAN DIARIES WRITTEN PRIOR TO THE YEAR 1861. 1945; Boston: J.S. Canner, 1959. Index.

The author provides a year-by-year listing, from 1629 to 1860, of published diaries written by Americans.

_____. AMERICAN DIARIES IN MANUSCRIPT, 1580-1954: A DESCRIPTIVE BIBLIOGRAPHY. Athens: Univ. of Georgia Press, 1974.

As supplement to the entry directly above, this work describes and lists the location of some six thousand manuscript diaries.

Shea, Daniel B., Jr. SPIRITUAL AUTOBIOGRAPHY IN EARLY AMERICA. Princeton: Princeton Univ. Press, 1968.

This is one of the few general studies of an important genre in the history of American literature. Although most of the writers discussed in this study are eighteenth-century figures, note is taken of Quaker and Puritan influences upon Thoreau, Whitman, Dickinson, and Henry Adams.

C. THE ESSAY AND SKETCH

1. PRIMARY WORKS

a. Descriptive and Reflective

Aldrich, Thomas Bailey. PONKAPOG PAPERS. Boston: Houghton Mifflin, 1903.

> Better known as a writer of poetry and fiction than as an essayist, Aldrich nevertheless produced some witty and readable descriptions and sketches. He followed Howells as editor of ATLANTIC from 1881 to 1890. This collection of essays, written after Aldrich had retired and was living in Ponkapog, Massachusetts, includes sketches for possible plots of short stories, descriptions of places from the Far East to the eastside slums of New York, and brief comments on such topics as civilization and slang. The longer pieces include profiles of well-known and unknown people plus literary estimates of poets, including Dickinson (he felt that Higginson had overrated her poetic performance). Aldrich's tone is light, humorous, and commonsensical.

Curtis, George William. FROM THE EASY CHAIR. New York: Harper, 1891.
See annotation below.

_____. FROM THE EASY CHAIR, THIRD SERIES. New York: Harper, 1894.
See annotation below.

_____. OTHER ESSAYS FROM THE EASY CHAIR. New York: Harper, 1893.

The three collections listed here consist of EASY CHAIR columns written while Curtis was editor of HARPER'S WEEKLY. His personal, discursive style shows his indebtedness to Addison, Lamb, and Irving. Curtis touches upon a great variety of topics: contemporary manners, reform movements, music, and literature. Although his social criticism is heavy handed at times, his literary criticism shows considerable flexibility.

_____. POTIPHAR PAPERS. New York: G.P. Putnam's, 1853.

These satirical sketches are a mixture of essay and fiction. In them, the author describes members of New York society in various favorite watering places. Curtis is witty and brilliant at times, but he also tends to become didactic and pontifical. He criticizes social artifices in the manner of Thackeray, but lacks Thackeray's subtlety and sense of the ridiculous.

Dana, Richard Henry, Sr. POEMS AND PROSE WRITINGS. 2 vols. 1833. Rev. ed., 1850; Upper Saddle River, N.J.: Literature House, Gregg Press, 1970.

The essays and reviews in these two volumes, some of which were published in the NORTH AMERICAN REVIEW and the journal which Dana edited, THE IDLE MAN, reveal his preoccupation with and romantic notions of the past. He maintained that Pope could not write poetry; Wordsworth and Coleridge were the masters. His essays deal with city life, domestic life, the past and the present, and some transcendental "Musings" on the ability of nature to link man with God. He includes sympathetic comments on Charles Brockden Brown's novels and generally high praise for Irving's SKETCH BOOK.

Higginson, Thomas Wentworth. ATLANTIC ESSAYS. Boston: J.R. Osgood, 1871.

Some of the best of the historical and critical essays which Higginson had written before 1870 are published here. The collection includes "Letter to a Young Contributor" which started his correspondence with Emily Dickinson. The other selections range from "The Greek Goddesses" to "Americanism in Literature." His essay, "On an Old Latin Text-Book," is in the reminiscent vein, as are many of his later works.

_____. BOOK AND HEART: ESSAYS ON LITERATURE AND LIFE. New York: Harper, 1897.

This volume includes essays written on a variety of topics for FORUM, NEW WORLD, CONTEMPORARY REVIEW, OUTLOOK, INDEPENDENT, PHILISTINE, and BOSTON TRANSCRIPT. They illustrate Higginson's fine critical sense, his sympathy, his humor, and his graceful style. The "Literature" section includes essays on Shelley, Lowell, Keats, and local-color fiction. The "Life" section discusses such topics as "Anglomania and Anglophobia," social classes, foreign visitors, and conversation.

_____. CARLYLE'S LAUGH AND OTHER SURPRISES. Boston: Houghton Mifflin, 1909.

This is the last of the collections of magazine pieces which Higginson published. It includes his ATLANTIC article on Dickinson in

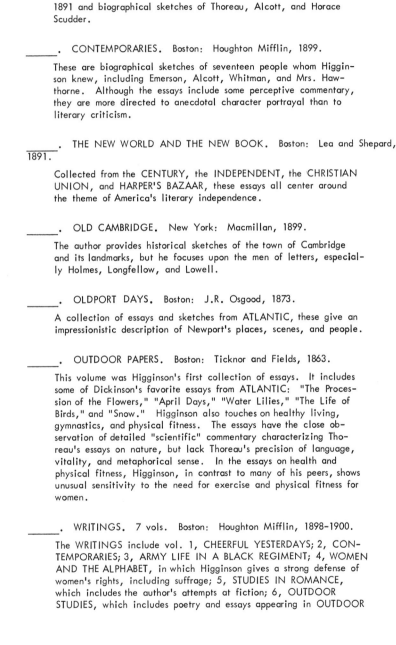

1891 and biographical sketches of Thoreau, Alcott, and Horace
Scudder.

_____. CONTEMPORARIES. Boston: Houghton Mifflin, 1899.

These are biographical sketches of seventeen people whom Higginson knew, including Emerson, Alcott, Whitman, and Mrs. Hawthorne. Although the essays include some perceptive commentary,
they are more directed to anecdotal character portrayal than to
literary criticism.

_____. THE NEW WORLD AND THE NEW BOOK. Boston: Lea and Shepard,
1891.

Collected from the CENTURY, the INDEPENDENT, the CHRISTIAN
UNION, and HARPER'S BAZAAR, these essays all center around
the theme of America's literary independence.

_____. OLD CAMBRIDGE. New York: Macmillan, 1899.

The author provides historical sketches of the town of Cambridge
and its landmarks, but he focuses upon the men of letters, especially Holmes, Longfellow, and Lowell.

_____. OLDPORT DAYS. Boston: J.R. Osgood, 1873.

A collection of essays and sketches from ATLANTIC, these give an
impressionistic description of Newport's places, scenes, and people.

_____. OUTDOOR PAPERS. Boston: Ticknor and Fields, 1863.

This volume was Higginson's first collection of essays. It includes
some of Dickinson's favorite essays from ATLANTIC: "The Proces-
sion of the Flowers," "April Days," "Water Lilies," "The Life of
Birds," and "Snow." Higginson also touches on healthy living,
gymnastics, and physical fitness. The essays have the close observation of detailed "scientific" commentary characterizing Thoreau's essays on nature, but lack Thoreau's precision of language,
vitality, and metaphorical sense. In the essays on health and
physical fitness, Higginson, in contrast to many of his peers, shows
unusual sensitivity to the need for exercise and physical fitness for
women.

_____. WRITINGS. 7 vols. Boston: Houghton Mifflin, 1898-1900.

The WRITINGS include vol. 1, CHEERFUL YESTERDAYS; 2, CON-
TEMPORARIES; 3, ARMY LIFE IN A BLACK REGIMENT; 4, WOMEN
AND THE ALPHABET, in which Higginson gives a strong defense of
women's rights, including suffrage; 5, STUDIES IN ROMANCE,
which includes the author's attempts at fiction; 6, OUTDOOR
STUDIES, which includes poetry and essays appearing in OUTDOOR

PAPERS; and 7, STUDIES IN HISTORY AND LETTERS, which reprints essays included for the most part in earlier publications.

Page, Thomas Nelson. THE OLD SOUTH. New York: Scribner's, 1892.

An outstanding regionalist and an apologist for the gentlemanly
cavalier tradition, Page, in this collection of essays and addresses,
attempts to correct myth and to provide a true history of the
South. In the first essay Page fervently defends southern culture
and civilization at length, praises its freedom from religious fana-
ticism, and champions its leaders. In other essays, he discusses
Southern men of letters, including Poe, and describes the life,
society, and town-and-country environs of the old South.

Repplier, Agnes. BOOKS AND MEN. Boston: Houghton Mifflin, 1888.

Despite the fact that Repplier was both a Roman Catholic and a
woman, her essays gained a wide audience among academics, in-
tellectuals, and sophisticates in the urban East. She was more
interested in manners and customs than in scenery, was more in
sympathy with Europe than America. Her essays show wide reading,
humor, and perceptiveness, but they also show a detachment from
social causes and reform movements. Repplier wrote into the first
three decades of the twentieth century; this volume and those
listed below include her best prose written before 1900. The
most noted of these were on the subject of useful and interesting
reading for children. Others touch on superstition and sentiment,
criticism and pessimism.

_____. ESSAYS IN IDLENESS. Boston: Houghton Mifflin, 1893.

The lead essay in this collection of eight papers is "Agrippina," a
delightful sketch of the author's favorite cat. The two best essays
are "Leisure," in which leisure and play are defended as means of
self-discovery, and "Wit and Humor," which offers a perceptive
and useful distinction between wit, "a cultivated art," and humor,
"a natural response."

_____. ESSAYS IN MINIATURE. Boston: Houghton Mifflin, 1892.

The sixteen essays here are generally not up to the standard of
Repplier's best work, but she has some interesting things to say
about Oscar Wilde and "Children in Fiction."

_____. IN THE DOZY HOURS AND OTHER PAPERS. Boston: Houghton Mif-
flin, 1894.

Considered by many critics to be Repplier's best volume of essays,
this recommends various kinds of reading--for example, the author's
favorite "bedside books," including the letters of Charles Lamb,
the novels of Jane Austen, and the poetry of Herrick. At her best,

Repplier's criticism of literature is penetrating, sympathetic, and witty, with flashes of insight but no coherent system.

_____. POINTS OF VIEW. Boston: Houghton Mifflin, 1891.

This volume includes eight papers from ATLANTIC and one from the CATHOLIC WORLD. They show wide reading, a sense of humor, and impatience with pretentiousness. Her topics include "A Plea for Humor" (the most powerful weapon against absurdity) and "Books that have Hindered Me" (especially school textbooks).

_____. VARIA. Boston: Houghton Mifflin, 1897.

The essays in this volume attack hypocrisy, self-righteousness, exaggeration, and cliches. "The Eternal Feminine," for example, denounces the practice of stereotyping. "Cakes and Ale" is a delightful analysis of drinking songs. "Old Wine and New" discourses on the use and misuse of history.

Saltus, Edgar. THE ANATOMY OF NEGATION. New York: Scribner and Welford, 1886.

Born into New York high society, Saltus used his essays and tales to discuss "manners, money, and morals," often comparing the scandals of New York society to the corruptions of imperial Rome. Most critics believe that his best work was written before 1900. Of the works listed here, only LOVE AND LORE fits into the category of "collected essays." ANATOMY and the remaining works listed below might be considered philosophy, history, or criticism. However, their discursive form and their ironic tone place them at least partially in the genres of description and reflection. In ANATOMY, Saltus traces evidences of antitheism from the ancient to the modern world by noting heretics and iconoclasts of all ages. He focuses on the theological doubts or disbeliefs of Montaigne, Spinoza, and Baudelaire, among others, but avoids the issue of his own agnosticism.

_____. IMPERIAL PURPLE. Chicago: Morrill, Higgins, 1892.

The best-known Saltus work, this provides a personalized and impressionistic history of the Caesars. He provokes a shudder at the horrors the empire produced. He also comments upon the contemporary power of the new Caesars--that is, the industrial titans of the 1890s.

_____. LOVE AND LORE. New York: Belford, 1890.

In these essays on fiction and love, Saltus praises what he calls "ornamental literature," uses the medieval courts of love to satirize contemporary courting and social codes, attempts to define love, and concludes with a definition of matrimony: "three months of

adoration, three months of introspection, and thirty years of tolera-
tion."

_____. THE PHILOSOPHY OF DISENCHANTMENT. Boston: Houghton Mif-
flin, 1885.

In this examination of the lives and doctrines of Schopenhauer,
Spinoza, and Edward von Hartmann, Saltus wanders through a
variety of religions and literatures, finding melancholy support for
the pessimistic view that "life is an affliction" and progress a
delusion.

Stoddard, Richard Henry. UNDER THE EVENING LAMP. New York: Scribner's, 1892.

Stoddard reviewed for the New York newspaper, the WORLD,
from 1860 to 1870 and served as literary editor for the New York
MAIL AND EXPRESS, 1880-1903. He also edited the writings of
Bryant and Poe and several journals and anthologies and wrote a
number of anecdotal biographies. His influence as an informal
critic and his position as a central figure in New York literary
circles were far more important contemporary forces than his own
writing, mostly poetry, which left little impression of consequence.
In LAMP, the studies of authors who were "worsted by misfortune"
are anecdotal rather than critical. Stoddard himself acknowledged
that he was more interested in the writers' lives than in their writings. Among the writers he considers are William Blake, Edward
Fitzgerald, and John Clare.

Warner, Charles Dudley. AS WE GO. New York: Harper, 1893.

This collection and the one immediately below consist primarily of
short pieces which Warner wrote for the "Editor's Drawer" of
HARPER'S MAGAZINE. These appeared from February 1887 to
June 1892. Many of them focus upon the American woman.
Warner speaks with some approval of their increasing emancipation.
His attitude displays a mixture of Victorian idealization and re-
formist interest in promoting equal rights. One fine essay deals
with the frenzied search for an American literature by those who
seem unaware that a fine literature has been developing all the
while by writers who are simply doing their best and are not particularly conscious of the need to be "American."

_____. AS WE WERE SAYING. New York: Harper, 1891.

Written for HARPER'S MAGAZINE from December 1887 to March
1891, these brief comments deal with society, politics, and human
nature. The writer is amused as well as a bit awed by the mech-
anisms of society as he discusses clothing, conversation, and the
roles of males and females. His tone is somewhat more serious as
he addresses and pessimistically remarks upon international affairs,

government, and business. Some of his pieces are dated, others remarkably fresh. His manner is mild, but he is always aware of human folly. These short pieces are not profound, but they do reflect the liberal, intelligent, gently critical views of a man who thinks and writes with clarity and precision.

_____. BACKLOG STUDIES. Boston: J.R. Osgood, 1893.

Most of the essays in this collection were originally contributed to SCRIBNER'S MONTHLY in 1871 and 1872. They are ruminations on a variety of topics, all prompted by or taking place beside the lighted fire in the fireplace, as the "back log" is moved to renew the flames. They range in subject matter from the pleasures and inspiration of the domestic fire, to the general repulsiveness of the male characters in sentimental novels by women, to the eccentricities of Charles Lamb.

_____. COMPLETE WRITINGS. 15 vols. Ed. Thomas Lounsbury. Hartford, Conn.: American Publishing Co., 1904.

Although this set does not contain all of Warner's writing, the titles listed in this present guide, as well as those described in other sections of this guide, are included. Best known for his collaboration with Mark Twain on THE GILDED AGE, Warner also edited the "American Men of Letters" series and the thirty-volume LIBRARY OF THE WORLD'S BEST LITERATURE. Warner offers no brilliant insights, but his keen observations and clarity of style make him still worth reading. He was a strong influence in bringing to the American essay a freshness, naturalness, and ease which marked the best prose of the late nineteenth century.

_____. FASHIONS IN LITERATURE. Introd. Hamilton Wright Mabie. New York: Dodd, Mead, 1902.

This posthumous collection derives its title from the first essay. Several of the essays were first delivered as addresses before various learned societies. In discussing "Fashions in Literature," Warner attempts to abstract qualities common to the masterpieces of literature: simplicity (that is, clarity of thought and language), knowledge of human nature, proportion, and perspective. In other essays, he discusses newspapers, American mobility, the prevailing discontent of the age, and education of the Negro. In his introduction, Mabie states that Warner "used the essay as Addison used it, not for sermonic effect but as a form of art which permitted a man to deal with serious things in a spirit of gayety and with that lightness of touch which conveys influence without employing force."

_____. MY SUMMER IN A GARDEN. Boston: Fields, Osgood, 1871.

This volume collects pieces which originally appeared in the HARTFORD COURANT in 1870. The newspaper sketches were a weekly log of Warner's struggles with weeds, bugs, and a neighbor's cow as he cultivated the garden of his newly purchased home near Hartford. The descriptions of his tribulations and pleasures are marvelously humorous. Warner regarded the garden more as a test of patience and character than as a means of producing vegetables and fruit. Warner's first book-length collection, this was extremely popular and went through several editions. Later editions add an essay, which manages to be touching without being sentimental, on Warner's cat, Calvin.

_____. THE PEOPLE FOR WHOM SHAKESPEARE WROTE. New York: Harper, 1897.

The first two chapters of this work appeared in the ATLANTIC in 1879. The last two were written subsequently and relate Elizabethan literature to its life and times. Warner concludes: "That the age was unable to separate [Shakespeare] from itself, and see his great stature, is probable; that it enjoyed him with a sympathy to which we are strangers there is no doubt."

_____. THE RELATION OF LITERATURE TO LIFE. New York: Harper, 1896.

The essays in this volume appeared in ATLANTIC, SCRIBNER'S, and the CENTURY, or were derived from some of Warner's speeches. Most are on such literary topics as the novel and contemporary fiction. Some move from literature to life and examine simplicity of style, the idea of equality, and the nature of culture.

Wasson, David Atwood. BEYOND CONCORD: SELECTED WRITINGS OF DAVID ATWOOD WASSON. Ed. with Intro. by Charles H. Foster. Bloomington: Indiana Univ. Press, 1965. Bibliog.

This volume includes the first extended biographical study of Wasson and a selection from his works. Wasson was highly praised by Alcott, Emerson, and William James, but his ideas are a contrast to those of other transcendentalists in their skepticism, in their recognition of evil, and in their insistence that individualism is tempered by culture and society. The pieces include essays and observations first appearing in ATLANTIC, the CHRISTIAN EX-AMINER, other periodicals, or letters, including one to Garrison and one to Carlyle. Foster writes, with some justification, that Wasson "advances . . . so far beyond Concord as to join hands with Irving Babbitt and T.S. Eliot." Wasson's style lacks the vigor of Thoreau and the felicitous phrasing of Emerson, but his perception and judgment are useful correctives to the transcendental enthusiasms.

_____. WASSON'S ESSAYS: RELIGIOUS, SOCIAL, POLITICAL. Collected by Octavius B. Frothingham. Boston: Lea and Shepard, 1889.

Most of the pieces collected by Frothingham were written late in

Wasson's life and represent an incomplete picture of his ideas and abilities. The volume includes an autobiographical sketch by Wasson and a brief memoir by Frothingham.

Whipple, Edwin Percy. CHARACTER AND CHARACTERISTIC MEN. Boston: Houghton Mifflin, 1894.

Whipple was a popular lecturer in the Lyceum Movement and an important figure in the literary life of Boston. His essays show the same keen wit and intelligent, though moralistic, judgment as his criticism. This volume collects statements published as essays in HARPER'S MAGAZINE or delivered as lectures on such topics as "Character," "The American Mind," and "Heroic Character" and such authors as Hawthorne and Thackeray.

_____. OUTLOOKS ON SOCIETY, LITERATURE, AND POLITICS. 1888; Folcroft, Pa.: Folcroft Library Editions, 1973.

These brief essays, mostly from the NORTH AMERICAN REVIEW, are on a variety of topics: politics, economics, personal habits, and literature. One essay, for example, "Mr. Hardhack on the Sensational in Literature and Life," directs clever wit against bad writing and contains some useful examples to show the difference between good prose and prose written to produce sentiment and sensation.

Willis, Nathaniel Parker. PROSE WRITINGS OF NATHANIEL PARKER WILLIS. Ed. Henry A. Beers. New York: Scribner's, 1885.

This collection selects the best of Willis' travel sketches, reminiscences, and descriptive notes, which mostly appeared as "letters" to the New York MIRROR. At the height of his fame, Willis was one of the most popular American essayists and could be considered the most characteristic New York man of letters between 1832 and the Civil War, noted for his descriptive journalism and the romantic, idealistic tone of writing. Probably the best of Willis' many volumes of essays is LETTERS FROM UNDER A BRIDGE (1840), which reprints several sketches published earlier as A L'ABRI; OR, THE TENT PITCHED (1839). This work has the pleasant chatty quality of the Willis' other travel notes and personal reminiscences, as well as vivid descriptions of the Glenmary Meadows area in New York state. The essays combine a delight in nature (with some nostalgia for the city) and criticism of various other contemporary writers, together with Willis' own, not very profound views of life.

b. Humorous Writings

Anderson, John Q., ed. WITH THE BARK ON: POPULAR HUMOR OF THE OLD SOUTH. Nashville, Tenn.: Vanderbilt Univ. Press, 1967.

This collects writings of minor humorists who wrote for newspapers and magazines from 1835 to 1860. Most of the pieces come from William T. Porter's journal, SPIRIT OF THE TIMES. The two sections, "The River" and "The Backcountry," provide some particularly valuable pieces heretofore uncollected for the serious student of American humor. The introduction and headnotes by the editor are useful and informative.

Baldwin, Joseph Glover. THE FLUSH TIMES OF ALABAMA AND MISSISSIPPI. 1853. Introd. William A. Owens. New York: Hill and Wang, 1957.

Baldwin was a young lawyer who took advantage of the "flush tide of litigation" created by the murdering, swindling, rioting, and larceny in north Alabama. These sketches in essay form lack the immediacy and oral tradition of the works of many other Southern humorists. However, Baldwin had excellent powers of observation, and regarded his creation of the sketches in FLUSH TIMES as a minor pastime. Baldwin later became a highly respected member of the California Supreme Court, but none of his other writings achieved the fame of this first work (see p. 107). His frontier character sketches and anecdotes were designed "to illustrate the periods, the characters, and the phases of society" of the movement to the Southwestern frontier; but Baldwin was not simply interested in recreating a time and place and a humorous tale. He also used irony and satire as a means of exposing the shams and vices of society in order to correct them. He created the rogue, Ovid Bolus, Esq., but he always makes clear his condemnation of Bolus' behavior.

Blair, Walter, ed. NATIVE AMERICAN HUMOR. 1937; San Francisco: Chandler, 1960.

Blair's introduction to this collection is an important analysis and survey of American humor. The bibliography of secondary sources is useful, although the 1960 edition is only slightly updated. The selections include the best or most representative works of some thirty-two authors and a few anonymous tall tales and sketches.

Browne, Charles Farrar. THE COMPLETE WORKS OF ARTEMUS WARD. 1875; New York: G.W. Carleton, 1903.

The best and most influential of the humorous lecturers before Mark Twain, Browne was also Twain's friend and mentor. Browne created Artemus Ward in a series of letters to the Cleveland PLAIN DEALER and adopted Ward as a persona in his popular lecture tours. Ward was a crackerbox philosopher, with a mixture of simplicity and showmanship, who satirized such popular butts as the fighters for "women's rites" and the "Mormins." The four volumes of writing which derived from his lectures are included in COMPLETE WORKS: ARTEMUS WARD: HIS BOOK (1863), ARTEMUS WARD: HIS TRAVELS (1865), ARTEMUS WARD IN LONDON (1867), and ARTEMUS WARD'S LECTURE (1869). In all of these, misspelling, nonstandard grammar, and other linguistic devices are skillfully used for their comic effect.

Derby, George Horatio. PHOENIXIANA; OR, SKETCHES AND BURLESQUES. New York: D. Appleton, 1855.

These are sketches published in the 1850s in California newspapers and magazines. Sometimes credited with being the father of a new school of Western humor, Derby followed a structural pattern which included protestations of truthfulness followed by impossible situations and grotesque exaggerations, as well as irreverence and ridiculous euphemisms. Among the objects of his satire are bureaucracies and perpetual office seekers.

Dunne, Finley Peter. MR. DOOLEY AND THE CHICAGO IRISH. Ed. Charles Fanning. New York: Arno, 1976.

These are pieces published in Chicago from 1893 to 1898, but not collected by Dunne in the books published during his lifetime. They express the Irish-American community's views which were often in conflict with those of other Chicagoans or Americans.

_____. MR. DOOLEY AT HIS BEST. Ed. Elmer Ellis with a Foreword by F.P. Adams. New York: Scribner's, 1938.

A Chicago Irish-American, Dunne created Mr. Dooley, a wise barkeep, and Hennessey, his straight-man, in order to comment upon Chicago politics and business and upon national affairs. Dunne collected the pieces, originally written for the Chicago SUNDAY POST, in several volumes, five of which appeared annually from 1898 to 1902. His best writings appeared in these five volumes, and the best of these reappear in this 1938 volume. Dunne's satire typically targets affectation, corruption, and imperialism, exposing their pretentions and deceptions at home and abroad. Both Theodore Roosevelt and McKinley avidly read and suffered from the clever barbs and burlesques of Dooley.

Field, Eugene. TRIBUNE PRIMER. Denver: Tribune Publishing Co., 1881.

Originally published in the Denver TRIBUNE, Field's humorous and satirical sketches won him a place in the list of "new humorous ists" of the last half of the nineteenth century. Their descriptions of practical jokes and their frank comedy make these sketches very different from Field's later sentimental verse and commentary.

Harris, George Washington. SUT LOVINGOOD'S YARNS. . . . 1867. Ed. with introd. Thomas M. Inge. New Haven, Conn.: College and Univ. Press, 1966.

Harris had little education and spent most of his life in Tennessee, but he read widely and had a broad range of experiences, including captaining a steamboat on the Tennessee River and farming in the foothills of the Great Smoky Mountains. He packs his narratives with action and tells his story directly and swiftly. His creation, Sut Lovingood, is a lusty, roughneck mountaineer of the Great Smokies whose ambition is to raise hell. The dialect and figures of speech are strikingly effective comic devices, although Harris' attempts to render the dialect phonetically are sometimes difficult to interpret. Sut is mischievous and even malevolent at times, but he also sees through pretenses and illusions. Many critics consider Harris to be one of the best of the Southwest humorists.

Holley, Marietta. MY OPINIONS AND BETSY BOBBET'S. Hartford, Conn.: American Publishing Co., 1873.

"Samantha" or "Josiah Allen's wife" was one of the most popular characters in American humor. Holley had a huge following with her character, Samantha, who used malapropisms and misspelled words, was shrewd but naive, and amused but also preached. In this book, Betsey Bobbet is a foil for Samantha's opinions on sentimentality (which she ridiculed), women's rights (which she supported), hypocrisy (which she exposed), and prejudice (which she attacked). Holley's other works generally followed this pattern of humor.

_____. SAMANTHA AT THE CENTENNIAL. Hartford, Conn.: American Publishing Co., 1878.

See annotation above.

_____. SAMANTHA AT SARATOGA. New York: F.M. Lupton, 1887.

See annotation above.

_____. SAMANTHA ON THE RACE PROBLEM. 1892; Upper Saddle River, N.J.: Literature House, Gregg Press, 1969.

See annotation above.

Hooper, Johnson Jones. ADVENTURES OF SIMON SUGGS, LATE OF THE TALLA POOSA VOLUNTEERS. 1845. Introd. Manly W. Wellman. Chapel Hill: Univ. of North Carolina Press, 1969.

Hooper was an Alabama lawyer and editor. Many of his Simon Suggs stories were first printed in his newspaper, THE EAST ALABAMIAN, and reprinted in William T. Porter's New York journal, THE SPIRIT OF THE TIMES. ADVENTURES is set forth as a burlesque campaign biography. Suggs is a shrewd and accomplished rogue and con-man; his motto is "It is good to be shifty in a new cuntry [sic]." Despite his dishonesty, Suggs amuses and appeals with his good humor and self-possession as he "lives as merrily and comfortably as possible at the expense of others" by taking advantage of the frailities of human nature.

_____. SIMON SUGGS' ADVENTURES AND TRAVELS . . . WITH WIDOW RUGBY'S HUSBAND, AND TWENTY-SIX OTHER HUMOROUS TALES OF ALA-BAMA. Philadelphia: T.B. Peterson, 1856.

This volume reprints most of Hooper's humorous writings.

Locke, David Ross. DIVERS VIEWS, OPINIONS, AND PROPHECIES OF YOURS TROOLY, PETROLEUM V. NASBY. Cincinnati: Carroll and Co., 1866.

Enjoyed by Lincoln, Grant, and Lowell, Petroleum V. Nasby was portrayed as a clever, vulgar scoundrel who thought up ways to avoid the draft, to attack Negroes, and to get himself a sinecure. Through Nasby's outrageous statements and behavior, Locke satirized traitors, cowards, and demagogues. Originating with Nasby letters in Locke's TOLEDO BLADE, the series ran for about twenty-six years.

_____. NASBY IN EXILE: OR, SIX MONTHS OF TRAVEL. Toledo: Locke Publishing Co., 1882.

Locke was an effective and successful propagandist, and the Nasby letters give a kind of psychological chronicle of the violence and follies of the quarter decade of the Civil War and the years following. This volume and the other four listed here collect some of the best of the letters.

_____. THE NASBY LETTERS. Toledo: Toledo Blade Co., 1893.

See annotation above.

_____. THE NASBY PAPERS. Indianapolis: C.O. Perrine, 1864.

See annotation above.

_____. THE STRUGGLES (SOCIAL, FINANCIAL AND POLITICAL) OF PE-TROLEUM V. NASBY. 1872. Abridged. Introd. Joseph Jones and Notes by Gunter Barth. Boston: Beacon Press, 1963.

Longstreet, Augustus Baldwin. GEORGIA SCENES, CHARACTERS, AND INCI-DENTS. 1835. 1969; Covington, Ga.: Cherokee Press, 1971.

Longstreet was a lawyer who became a minister, then a college president. The SCENES are humorous sketches of backwoods Georgia life and manners that had appeared in the STATES RIGHTS SENTINEL and other local Georgia papers. Published anonymously by the SENTINEL in 1835, the book was enthusiastically reviewed in the SOUTHERN LITERARY MESSENGER by Poe. Among the incidents Longstreet describes are a horse swap, an ear-and-nose-biting fight, a fox hunt, and a "gander pulling." Longstreet uses the sometimes coarse backwoods language, but distances himself by stepping aside and letting the storyteller speak for himself. With

GEORGIA SCENES, Longstreet established a pattern that was followed by later southern humorists, was a forerunner of regionalism and realism, and showed the humorous and narrative possibilities of southern frontier life.

Meine, Franklin J., ed. TALL TALES OF THE SOUTHWEST: AN ANTHOLOGY OF SOUTHERN AND SOUTHWESTERN HUMOR, 1830-1860. New York: Knopf, 1930.

In his fine introduction, Meine says that the early frontier humorists "have a two-fold importance for American literature: they were our first realists and they have exerted a far-reaching influence on later American humorists, notably Mark Twain." The humorous tales and sketches include excerpts from Longstreet, Thompson, Hooper, Harris, and others.

Newell, Robert Henry. THE ORPHEUS C. KERR PAPERS. 5 vols. New York: Carleton, 1862-71.

Considered by late nineteenth-century critics to be among the very best of the humorists, Newell, a New York journalist, burlesqued the campaigns of the U.S. army in the Civil War and political life in Washington, satirizing military types and bureaucrats. Newell has Kerr using impassioned purple prose, mixed metaphors, and anticlimactic sentences.

Nye, Edgar Wilson. THE BEST OF BILL NYE'S HUMOR. Ed. Louis Hasley. New Haven, Conn.: College and Univ. Press, 1972.

Unlike some of the earlier humorists, Nye did not set up a comic character but depicted himself alternately in the role of wise man and fool. His first book was BILL NYE AND BOOMERANG (1881) and his last to receive critical praise was the comic HISTORY OF THE UNITED STATES (1894). His works were widely enjoyed, and he was a popular lecturer. Nye generally avoided politics as a subject of satire. This is a good collection of parodies, essays, exaggerated anecdotes, and humorous letters, and is representative of Nye's use of anticlimax, incongruity, and mixed metaphors to achieve a comic effect.

Robb, John S. STREAKS OF SQUATTER LIFE, AND FAR-WEST SCENES. 1847. Ed. John Francis McDermott. Gainesville, Fla.: Scholar's Facsimiles and Reprints, 1962.

The volume collects tall tales and sketches of life and manners in the West, first published in the St. Louis Weekly REVEILLE, 1844-46. The REVEILLE was second only to Porter's SPIRIT OF THE TIMES in publishing humorous-realistic literature of the South and West in the middle of the nineteenth century. Robb was one of the most prolific contributors to the REVEILLE. Some of his pieces are social satire; others are sketches of character or local color, tall tales, and practical jokes.

Shaw, Henry Wheeler. JOSH BILLINGS: HIS WORKS, COMPLETE. 1888. Rev. ed. as THE COMPLETE WORKS OF JOSH BILLINGS. Chicago: M.A. Donohue, 1919.

> With JOSH BILLINGS, HIS SAYINGS (1865), Shaw won a national reputation for Josh, who was already widely popular because of the newspapers which had circulated his pieces. With his annual FARMER'S ALLMINAX (1869-1880), Shaw scored even greater success. Both the Billings stories and the almanacs are characterized by punning, occasionally banal, sometimes-wise aphorisms, and by vivid figures of speech. Billings expressed himself also in brief essays on such subjects as "Hoss Sense," "Love," "The Kondem Fool," and "Habits of Grate Men."

Shilaber, Benjamin Penhallow. LIFE AND SAYINGS OF MRS. PARTINGTON. 1854; Upper Saddle River, N.J.: Literature House, 1969.

> Mrs. Partington's sayings appeared in the Boston POST and the CARPET BAG before being collected in book form. Admired by Oliver Wendell Holmes and Henry Ward Beecher, Mrs. Partington was praised for her witty sayings, eccentric use of language (particularly malapropisms), and her mindless but benevolent gossip. Mrs. Partington may also have served as something of a prototype for Aunt Polly in Twain's TOM SAWYER.

Smith, Charles Henry. BILL ARP'S PEACE PAPERS. 1873; Upper Saddle River, N.J.: Literature House, 1969.

> Considered one of the best of the satirists writing during the Civil War, Smith, a Georgian, at first presented Bill Arp as a Northern sympathizer writing letters to Lincoln, whom he addressed as "Mr. Linkhorn," and offering ridiculous advice and supposed good wishes. Later, as Arp's character merged with that of his creator, he became more critical of Northern actions and pleaded the cause of his fellow Southerners. In addition to the usual humorous convention of errant grammar and phonetic spelling, Arp's pieces show keen observation, occasional bits of aphoristic wisdom, good regional sketches, and amusing anecdotes.

————. BILL ARP, SO-CALLED. New York: Metropolitan Record Office, 1866.

> This volume and the one above collect the best of the Arp letters and essays.

Smith, Seba. MY THIRTY YEARS OUT OF THE SENATE BY MAJOR JACK DOWNING. New York: Oaksmith, 1859.

> One of the first professional humorists, Smith created Jack Downing, the original Yankee oracle. In letters home, Jack, a small-town bumpkin, tells about his adventures in the big city and in politics. He learns fast and eventually becomes the confidant of

President Jackson. Beneath Downing's seemingly placid monologues is acute criticism of Jacksonian democracy. Smith reproduces Down East speech beautifully, and his various characters are clearly differentiated. The Downing papers continued for twenty years and were printed and imitated in newspapers throughout the country.

Taliaferro, Harden E. FISHER'S RIVER SCENES AND CHARACTERS. New York: Harper, 1859.

Taliaferro combined folk tales and social history in describing the inhabitants of the area near the Blue Ridge Mountains in the Carolinas. He has more sympathy with his characters than many of the Southern humorists, but he creates some memorable liars in Uncle Davy Lane, Oliver Stanley, and Larkin Snow.

Thompson, William Tappan. MAJOR JONES'S CHRONICLES OF PINEVILLE. Philadelphia: T.B. Peterson, 1845.

These are sketches of Georgia scenes, incidents, and characters which Thompson had written earlier and had decided to put together after his success with MAJOR JONES'S COURTSHIP, presenting, as he put it, a few "specimens of the genus 'Cracker'" the Georgia backwoodsman. These sketches include a circus scene, similar in many ways to the one described in HUCKLEBERRY FINN, in which a pretentious doctor is taken in by a supposedly drunken circus performer.

_____. MAJOR JONES'S COURTSHIP. Philadelphia: A. Hart, 1843.

Thompson was coeditor with Augustus Baldwin Longstreet of the Augusta, Georgia, SENTINEL and later became the editor of the SOUTHERN MISCELLANY. Jones's courtship is told in the form of letters which Jones has purportedly permitted Thompson to publish in the newspapers. The letters relate a connected series of episodes centered around the courtship, but they also reveal a great deal about contemporary middle-class southern plantation life. The humor is simple, unsophisticated, and easy-going.

_____. MAJOR JONES'S SKETCHES OF TRAVEL. Philadelphia: A. Carey and Hart, 1847.

These letters describe a tour from Georgia to Canada. The naive Major Jones is a southern counterpart of Seba Smith's Jack Downing (see Seba Smith, above), as he describes his travels to Washington, New York, Niagara Falls, and Quebec.

Thorpe, Thomas Bangs. THE HIVE OF THE BEE HUNTER. New York: D. Appleton, 1854.

This collection contains Thorpe's best and certainly his best-known piece, "The Big Bear of Arkansas." This tale was first printed in

William T. Porter's New York SPIRIT OF THE TIMES in 1841 and later reprinted in Porter's edition of a collection titled for Thorpe's piece. "The Big Bear" is a frame tale, which opens with a scene aboard a Mississippi riverboat. The passengers gather to hear a man tell the story about the bear who becomes almost mythical in his porportions and longevity. Parallels between this story and Faulkner's "The Bear" have been noted repeatedly.

_____. THE MYSTERIES OF THE BACKWOODS. Philadelphia: Carey and Hart, 1846.

In the sketches collected here, Thorpe focuses upon the realistic portrayal of a locality. He says that he wished to acquaint people with "the scenery of the Southwest, some idea of the country, of its surface, and vegetation." The "mysteries" of the title refer to the occupations of the people described. Contemporary reviews of the book often praised Thorpe's vivid descriptions and historical accuracy.

Whitcher, Frances Miriam. THE WIDOW BEDOTT PAPERS. 1855; Upper Saddle River, N.J.: Literature House, 1969.

First published posthumously, this volume consists of pieces collected from ARGUS, NEAL'S SATURDAY GAZETTE, and GODEY'S LADY'S BOOK. One of the first feminine American comic characters, the Yankee Widow wrote bad poetry and, in long digressive monologues, gossiped about her neighbors and described sewing circles, phrenology, and "courtin's." Her sketches greatly increased the circulation of the magazines in which they appeared and provide an insight into contemporary popular tastes. Whitcher deals very well with small-town concerns and characters.

Wilt, Napier, ed. SOME AMERICAN HUMORISTS. New York: T. Nelson, 1929. Bibliog.

This anthology includes selections from the writings of Seba Smith, William Tappan Thompson, Charles F. Browne, and David R. Locke, among others.

2. SECONDARY SOURCES

Bier, Jesse. THE RISE AND FALL OF AMERICAN HUMOR. New York: Holt, Rinehart and Winston, 1968.

This survey of American humor is best in its comments on modern humor; however, the author includes sections on nineteenth-century humorists before, during, and after the Civil War and examines humor in "selected major American writers," including Poe, Hawthorne, Cooper, Thoreau, Melville, Whitman, James, and Howells.

Blair, Walter. HORSE SENSE IN AMERICAN HUMOR, FROM BENJAMIN FRANKLIN TO OGDEN NASH. 1942; New York: Russell and Russell, 1962.

> This remains one of the most intelligent and appreciative studies of American humor and a basic work for the subject. Blair places the humorists in a solid context of traditions and times, traces influences, and gives illustrations of the humorists' work.

Blair, Water, and Hamlin Hill. AMERICA'S HUMOR, FROM POOR RICHARD TO DOONESBURY. New York: Oxford Univ. Press, 1978.

> This interesting and perceptive interpretation and survey of American humor adds depth to Blair's other fine studies. The authors present descriptive categories into which many humorists fit--for example, "the imposter," the man who pretends to be something he is not, and "the self-deprecator," the man who makes himself invulnerable by attacking himself.

Cary, Edward. GEORGE WILLIAM CURTIS. American Men of Letters Series. Boston: Houghton Mifflin, 1896.

> This is an early appreciative biography. Cary says that "Of the 'Easy Chair' especially it must be remembered that it was the chief product of Mr. Curtis' pen, was wrought in the pure literary spirit, and was, as much as the work of any prose-writer of his time, literature."

Fanning, Charles. FINLEY PETER DUNNE AND MR. DOOLEY: THE CHICAGO YEARS. Lexington: Univ. Press of Kentucky, 1978.

> Fanning focuses on the pieces Dunne did not collect for publication in book form during his lifetime. He argues that the columns Dunne wrote in Chicago between 1893 and 1898 give Dunne his chief claim to fame as a social historian: "These Dooley pieces constitute the most complete creative account we have of the late nineteenth-century urban Irish community."

Harrison, John M. THE MAN WHO MADE NASBY, DAVID ROSS LOCKE. Chapel Hill: Univ. of North Carolina Press, 1969.

> The author attempts to give a biography of Locke as a public figure, outlining his achievements in many areas, not just as a creator of Nasby. Harrison argues that Locke was more satirist than humorist, creating "some of the most devastatingly effective satire written by an American."

Inge, M. Thomas, ed. THE FRONTIER HUMORISTS: CRITICAL VIEWS. Hamden, Conn.: Archon, 1975.

> This critical collection includes essays by Walter Blair, John Donald Wade, Franklin J. Meine, and others on humor in general and on specific humorists, including Augustus B. Longstreet, William Tappan Thompson, and George Washington Harris. It also

contains "A Checklist of Criticism" on the humor of the old
Southwest by Charles E. Davis and Martha B. Hudson.

Levin, Harry, ed. VEINS OF HUMOR. Cambridge, Mass.: Harvard Univ.
Press, 1972.

> Only one essay in this critical collection focuses specifically on
> nineteenth-century humor: Joel Porte's "Transcendental Antics,"
> in which he argues persuasively that the comic impulse was a
> significant component of transcendentalism.

Milne, Gordon. GEORGE WILLIAM CURTIS AND THE GENTEEL TRADITION.
Bloomington: Indiana Univ. Press, 1956.

> In this excellent study, Milne uses Curtis to exemplify "the liter-
> ary achievement and the culture of the Genteel Tradition in the
> best light."

Rourke, Constance M. AMERICAN HUMOR: A STUDY OF THE NATIONAL
CHARACTER. 1931; Garden City, N.Y.: Doubleday, Anchor, 1953.

> In this classic study of the traditions of American humor, the author
> discusses main patterns in the development of various types of humor
> and focuses upon how they influenced some major writers, including
> Melville, Poe, Whitman, and Henry James. A good part of the
> study is devoted to demonstrating how humor emerges in fiction,
> drama, and poetry, as well as in the humorous sketch or tale.

Rubin, Louis D., Jr., ed. THE COMIC IMAGINATION IN AMERICAN LIT-
ERATURE. New Brunswick, N.J.: Rutgers Univ. Press, 1973.

> Several of the essays collected here deal with nineteenth-century
> humor, most notably those by James M. Cox, "Humor of the Old
> Southwest," Brom Weber, "The Misspellers," and C. Carroll Hollis,
> "Rural Humor of the Late Nineteenth Century."

Seitz, Don C. ARTEMUS WARD (CHARLES FARRAR BROWNE): A BIOGRAPHY
AND BIBLIOGRAPHY. 1919; New York: Beekman, 1974.

> This is a readable and objective biography, although many sources
> of information are not adequately documented. Seitz includes
> several of Ward's previously uncollected contributions to VANITY
> FAIR and the CARPET BAG.

Stewart, George R. JOHN PHOENIX, ESQ., THE VERITABLE SQUIBOB: A
LIFE OF CAPTAIN GEORGE H. DERBY, USA. New York: H. Holt, 1937.

> Stewart's biography of Derby is fascinating.

Tandy, Jennette R. CRACKERBOX PHILOSOPHERS IN AMERICAN HUMOR AND SATIRE. New York: Columbia Univ. Press, 1925.

> The author surveys the humorous caricature of the "homely American," the unlettered backwoods philosopher full of maxims and comic observations. She discusses the characters portrayed in the Biglow papers, in Southern humor, in the humor of the Civil War and reconstruction, and in the writings of such authors as Ward and Billings.

Thorp, Willard. AMERICAN HUMORISTS. Minneapolis: Univ. of Minnesota Press, 1964. Bibliog.

> This is a useful brief survey, particularly on the early Southern humorists. The selected bibliography is good on secondary resources to 1963, but the listing of primary sources is slight.

Tuttle, James. THOMAS WENTWORTH HIGGINSON. Boston: Twayne, 1978.

> This is a useful survey of Higginson's accomplishments as an editor, a man of letters, and a concerned citizen active in a number of reform movements.

D. TRAVEL AND DESCRIPTION

1. PRIMARY WORKS

a. Travel Abroad

Aldrich, Thomas Bailey. FROM PONKAPOG TO PESTH. Boston: Houghton Mifflin, 1883.

> In these essays, Aldrich presents himself as a provincial American, from Ponkapog, Massachusetts, awed by European sights and people, including those in Pesth (Budapest). He complains that the travel writer may be "aesthetic, or historic, or scientific, or analytic, or any kind of ic, except enthusiastic." His overall tone is, however, nostalgic, as he attempts to recreate and recapture the qualities of the Old World.

Bridge, Horatio. JOURNAL OF AN AFRICAN CRUISER. Ed. Nathaniel Hawthorne. 1845; Detroit: Negro History Press, 1969.

> In a format structured as a daily log, the writer, a U.S. Navy officer, describes the voyage to Africa and the visits to settlements along the coast. He is particularly interested in the settlements in Liberia; and, although he characterizes himself as being no abolitionist, he speaks with tolerance and avoids condescension in describing the customs and behavior of the Africans. Hawthorne is sometimes credited with writing the book, but evidence indicates that he simply edited his friend's notes.

Clarke, James Freeman. ELEVEN WEEKS IN EUROPE; AND WHAT MAY BE SEEN IN THAT TIME. Boston: Ticknor, Reed and Fields, 1852.

> Clarke describes cathedrals, castles, galleries, museums, monuments, towns, and scenery in his journey through England, France, Switzerland, Belgium, and the Rhineland. His work has the qualities of a guidebook, as he explains what travelers may expect in various places; of the personal essay, as he remembers amusing and touching anecdotes; and of the narrative and descriptive travel

sketch, as he describes the places and people he encounters. Clarke does not engage in elaborate, ornamental rhetoric. This was a much-read volume, and it remains one of the more readable of the many descriptions of European travel in the nineteenth century.

Curtis, George William. THE HOWADJI IN SYRIA. New York: Harper, 1852.

Both this book and the one below were based upon Curtis' travels through the Near East in 1849-1850. In this description of a journey from Cairo to Beirut, the narrative pace is casual, as the author stops for digressions, character sketches, moralizing, and descriptions. He produces an impressionistic picture, giving the reader a real sense of the places he talks about. He also encourages tolerance for strange places and customs.

_____. NILE NOTES OF A HOWADJI. New York: Harper, 1851.

This volume describes a journey on the Nile and scenes of Cairo. Curtis' sensual description of an Oriental dancer shocked the readers back home and caused him to prune and control similar passages in the later book. Both of these volumes contain trite and flowery diction, but the descriptions are generally lively and often humorous.

Davis, Richard Harding. ABOUT PARIS. New York: Harper, 1894.

One of the leading journalistic reporters of his time, and a managing editor of HARPER'S WEEKLY, Davis was idolized in the 1890s and early 1900s. He represented popular literary and political fashions in his reports and stories and had a wide audience. In this collection of observations of Paris scenes and people, Davis presents himself as a young American summer idler in Paris. He is interested in people, cafes, and show places of Paris, but he finds the French people callous, frivolous, and self-centered. He is also highly critical of the rudeness of American tourists. The writing is humorous and tasteful, but not particularly original or profound.

_____. RULERS OF THE MEDITERRANEAN. New York: Harper, 1894.

Davis was disappointed by many things in his journey to Gibraltar, Spain, Morocco, Tangier, Cairo, and Athens. Hoping to find exotic and lovely sights, he instead saw much that was ugly. He is particularly critical of the French and English conduct and influence in Egypt. However, he praises the blue of the Grecian skies and the sight of the Sphinx in the moonlight.

DeForest, John William. EUROPEAN ACQUAINTANCE; BEING SKETCHES OF PEOPLE IN EUROPE. New York: Harper, 1858.

> DeForest returned from the Near East (see ORIENTAL ACQUAIN-TANCE, below), stayed in America for a short time, and then re-turned abroad, this time to Europe, to seek the curative powers of various watering places. More interested in people than in places, he wittily describes the odd characters he met. There was little public demand for either of DeForest's travel books, but they are extraordinary in their humor and their good-natured satire of tourists and eccentric natives.

_____. ORIENTAL ACQUAINTANCE: OR, LETTERS FROM SYRIA. New York: Dix, Edwards, 1856.

> As a young man DeForest traveled abroad for his health, visiting Greece, Turkey, and the Holy Land, and spending about a year in Syria with his brother and sister-in-law, who were missionaries there. Like many Americans, DeForest finds a tremendous contrast between the past splendors and the decadent present of the Middle East. Although disgusted by the smells, dirt, and evidence of religious corruption and fanaticism, DeForest does broaden his horizons and learns to enjoy some Syrian customs. This volume was compiled from letters DeForest wrote home, to which he added material and smoothed the narrative. Some segments were published in PUTNAM'S. DeForest avoids the exoticism, society sketches, sentimentality, immature enthusiasms, and cliched descriptions of monuments and ruins which marred many other travel accounts. His wit is not in the class of Twain's in INNOCENTS ABROAD, but DeForest's books do bear comparison with Twain's work.

Fulton, Charles Carroll. EUROPE VIEWED THROUGH AMERICAN SPECTACLES. Philadelphia: J.B. Lippincott, 1874.

> This was a widely used guidebook which supplied 310 double-columned pages of facts and an appendix of useful "Hints to Euro-pean Tourists." It was originally published in the form of letters to the Baltimore AMERICAN in 1873.

Hale, Edward Everett. NINETY DAYS' WORTH OF EUROPE. Boston: Walker, Wise, 1860.

> Hale, a clergyman, one of the Overseers of Harvard, and chaplain of the Senate, was involved in many charitable causes and was responsible for the establishment of several philanthropic societies. He was also a prolific writer. In addition to autobiographical works, he contributed both fiction and essays to ATLANTIC, SCRIBNER'S, and to his own liberal Christian periodicals. This volume collects letters Hale sent to family members and to news-papers. Although he wrote with pleasure of the Alps, Rome, and the Louvre, he was more interested in institutions than in scenery. He visited the Working Man's College in London, praised the co-

operative organization of Protestant ministers in Paris, and explained the workings of the British Museum. Hale struggled against New England Puritanism to be open-minded about European art, and gradually developed an appreciation for the more unconventional examples he encountered.

_____. SEVEN SPANISH CITIES AND THE WAY TO THEM. Boston: Roberts Brothers, 1883.

This is probably the best of Hale's travel books. Here, he combines personal narrative, historical backgrounds, and advice about how to travel by train and stagecoach. The main topics are geography, transportation, religious ritual, museums, and archives at one point. He tells a delightful story about Perro Poco, the dog who became the center of interest when it was accidentally wounded by a matador at a bullfight. Hale also wrote more light-hearted, conventional, guidebook-type travel books with his sister, Susan, including A FAMILY FLIGHT THROUGH FRANCE, GERMANY, NORWAY AND SWITZERLAND (1881) and A FAMILY FLIGHT OVER EGYPT AND SYRIA (1882).

Hillard, George Stillman. SIX MONTHS IN ITALY. Boston: Ticknor, Reed and Fields, 1853.

A lawyer friend of Hawthorne, Hillard aided George Ripley on the CHRISTIAN REGISTER, edited the JURIST, and wrote several articles for the NORTH AMERICAN REVIEW. This is his most substantial work and tells much about his own character. It was one of the most widely quoted of the travel books of the time. Hillard's observations are informative and discriminating, and he urged American readers to learn from rather than condemn (as many did) the churchmen and rites of Catholicism.

Jarves, James Jackson. ITALIAN RAMBLES. New York: G.P. Putnam's, 1883.

Jarves served as U.S. vice-consul at Florence in 1880-82. He was an avid art collector and critic, urging Americans to renounce their prejudices, learn to see what was valuable in European culture, and create a climate in the new world favorable to artists. Jarves had a keen eye for significant details, and his other travel books (below) are valuable documentaries.

_____. ITALIAN SIGHTS AND PAPAL PRINCIPLES SEEN THROUGH AMERICAN SPECTACLES. New York: Harper, 1856.

Jarves reports on the usual tourist spots, but he sees far more than most travel writers. This volume includes a fine chapter on Pompeii.

_____. PARISIAN SIGHTS AND FRENCH PRINCIPLES SEEN THROUGH AMERICAN SPECTACLES. New York: Harper, 1852.

> A second series of observations about Paris was published in 1855 as PARISIAN SIGHTS. The two books present a vivid picture of Paris in the 1850s. Jarves uses the familiar tourist places as a starting point for an elaboration upon institutions, social classes, and culture.

Latrobe, John H.B. HINTS FOR SIX MONTHS IN EUROPE. Philadelphia: Lippincott, 1869.

> Son of architect and diarist Benjamin Henry Latrobe, John was a well-known lawyer, artist, and biographer. This is one of the better representatives of the popular guidebooks of the sixties which offered information and advice to tourists who wished to make the most profitable use of little time.

Norton, Charles Eliot. NOTES OF TRAVEL AND STUDY IN ITALY. Cambridge, Mass.: Riverside Press, 1860.

> In this volume, Norton attempted to formulate a moral and democratic explanation of art history. It is, therefore, as much a book of art criticism and social history as it is a travel account. Norton found the paintings of Florence to be a reflection of civic pride and the forceful clarity of those who painted from their hearts. With the worldliness of the Renaissance and the pomp of the papacy, art grew corrupt and false. In the Gothic cathedral, however, one may see a symbol and embodiment of sincerity in art, purity in religion, and an expression of popular will in society and government. His views on medieval art are inconsistent, but they foreshadow his later commentary and criticism on art in America.

Olmsted, Frederick Law. WALKS AND TALKS OF AN AMERICAN FARMER IN ENGLAND. New York: G.P. Putnam's, 1852.

> Pieced together from letters and a journal, this work interested Olmsted's contemporaries because of his account of English farming practices. It remains valuable for its acute social observation, which marked Olmsted's later works as well.

Silliman, Benjamin. A VISIT TO EUROPE IN 1851. 2 vols. New York: G.P. Putnam's, 1853.

> Silliman shows his scientific meticulousness and tendency to classify and generalize in his descriptions. He comments upon the natural history specimens at the Royal Institute, the roads and buildings of Europe, and compares the Europe of 1851 to that of forty-five years before, when he had previously visited it.

Smith, Francis Hopkinson. GONDOLA DAYS. Boston: Houghton Mifflin, 1897.

> Smith started to write when he began adding prose impressions to the drawings sketched during his travels. His descriptions of the sights, sounds, smells, and character types of Venice are pleasant, occasionally effusive.

_____. WELL-WORN ROADS OF SPAIN, HOLLAND, AND ITALY. Boston: Houghton Mifflin, 1887.

> As do many writers of travel books, Smith denies that his account is of any value as a guidebook. Instead, he insists he is merely writing about out-of-the-way places that have charmed and interested him. A sample of his leisurely pace and somewhat formal style can be seen in his prefatory note, saying that the sketches "were written some months after the discomforts and annoyances of travel had passed out of mind, when only the memory remained of many happy hours spent under cool archways, and along canals, and up curious, twisted streets, and into dark, old, smoked churches."

_____. A WHITE UMBRELLA IN MEXICO AND OTHER LANDS. Boston: Houghton Mifflin, 1889.

> The "white umbrella" is the parasol of the street artist; the "other lands" visited are Constantinople, Hungary, and Bulgaria.

Stoddard, Charles Warren. A CRUISE UNDER THE CRESCENT: FROM SUEZ TO SAN MARCO. Chicago: Rand, McNally, 1898.

> This account of travels through the Near East and Greece is less exciting than MASHALLAH! (below). As an observer, Stoddard is detached, almost indifferent, and the narrative shows signs of fatigue and boredom.

_____. MASHALLAH! A FLIGHT INTO EGYPT. New York: D. Appleton, 1881.

> This volume consists of twenty-one travel letters: five on France, the remaining on Egypt. Stoddard laments past glories and describes present decay, but his narrative is full of excitment and an occasional excellent flash of humor, sharper and wittier than Warner's (below), and sometimes matching of Clemens.

Warner, Charles Dudley. IN THE LEVANT. 2 vols. Boston: Houghton Mifflin, 1876.

> A sequel to MY WINTER ON THE NILE, this volume describes a tour through the Middle East, Cyprus, and Greece. Warner includes historical sketches, recounts incidents, describes people and scenes with an eye for incongruity, and records conversations with an ear for humor. He conveys the human qualities of the

various inhabitants of the regions through which he travels and the characteristic as well as the unique qualities of the places he visits.

_____. MY WINTER ON THE NILE. 1876. Rev. ed. Boston: Houghton Mifflin, 1880.

Titled MUMMIES AND MOSLEMS when it first appeared, this volume of travel sketches captures the activity and humor in the scenes and episodes which the author experienced. Like most of Warner's travel books, this one surpasses the usual guidebook. Warner is seldom profound, but he observes and describes with wit and originality.

_____. SAUNTERINGS. Boston: J.R. Osgood, 1872.

The first of Warner's travel books, this one includes sketches of scenes and incidents in Paris, London, Germany, Switzerland, and Italy. Some of the material originally appeared in the Hartford COURANT and the Boston magazine, OLD AND NEW. Warner writes that "almost everyone has been somewhere, and has written about it. The only compromise I can suggest is, that we shall go somewhere, and not learn anything about it." Warner is certainly never pedantic; he spikes descriptions with humor and a keen sense of the ridiculous. However, he also shows genuine appreciation for the sights and people he sees and is occasionally thoughtful about the meaning of what he experiences.

Williams, Samuel Wells. THE MIDDLE KINGDOM: A SURVEY OF THE . . . CHINESE EMPIRE AND ITS INHABITANTS. 2 vols. New York: Wiley and Putnam, 1848.

Williams went to China as a printer for the Board of Foreign Missions, mastered the Chinese language, and later accompanied Perry's expedition to Japan as an interpreter. This work remains one of the definitive studies of China. As the full title indicates, Wells studied the geography, government, literature, social life, arts, and history of China.

Wills, Nathaniel Parker. PENCILLINGS BY THE WAY: WRITTEN DURING SOME YEARS OF RESIDENCE AND TRAVEL IN EUROPE. 1835. 2nd ed. New York: Scribner's, 1852.

This volume collects letters which Willis wrote for the New York MIRROR. The sketches and descriptions compare favorably with the European notebooks of Hawthorne and Henry James. Willis is more interested in people in action and in landscapes than in museums or historic edifices. One reviewer criticized PENCILLINGS saying that it contained little "useful information." It was widely read, however, offending some, delighting many, and providing thousands of Americans who could not go to Europe with their impressions of what life there was like.

b. Travel in North America and the Pacific

Baldwin, Joseph Glover. THE FLUSH TIMES OF CALIFORNIA. Ed. Richard
E. Amacher and George W. Polhemus. Athens: Univ. of Georgia Press, 1966.

This is a well-edited volume that brings together the text of an
unpublished manuscript version of the author's adventures in California with fragments which were published in periodicals and
newspapers in the late 1850s and early 1860s. After publishing
the popular humorous sketches in THE FLUSH TIMES OF ALABAMA
AND MISSISSIPPI (see p. 89), Baldwin sailed for California and eventually was appointed to the California Supreme Court. His California sketches are delightful but do not represent so solid an achievement
as the earlier humorous sketches.

Ballou, Maturin M. THE NEW ELDORADO: A SUMMER JOURNEY TO ALASKA.
Boston: Houghton Mifflin, 1889.

Ballou, the first editor of the Boston DAILY GLOBE, traveled
widely and wrote descriptive letters which were published in periodicals of the time. His several travel books, including this one
which was one of his most popular accounts, were mostly compila-
tions of his published letters. For many years, this volume served
as a sort of tourists' guide to Alaska.

Bartlett, John Russell. PERSONAL NARRATIVE OF EXPLORATIONS AND IN-
CIDENTS IN TEXAS, NEW MEXICO, CALIFORNIA, SONORA, AND CHIHUA-
HUA. . . . 2 vols. 1854; Chicago: Rio Grande Press, 1965.

Bartlett was less of an explorer and leader than a scholar. After
having established something of a literary reputation, he received,
through political connections, the offer of the position of boundary commissioner (to establish the boundary between New Mexico
and Chihuahua). The expedition was not successful, but the account is a meticulous, scholarly, and clear, day-by-day narrative
of facts, observations, and incidents. It has been one of the most
widely used resources for scientists, historians, and travelers interested in the Southwest.

Beale, Edward F. WAGON ROAD FROM FORT DEFIANCE TO THE COLORA-
DO RIVER, 1857-58. Washington, D.C.: 35th Congress, Document 124,
1858.

Beale is credited with being the first to announce to Washington
the discovery of gold in California in 1848. He was a friend of
Bayard Taylor, the writer and critic, and was, at the time of his
appointment as leader of the road survey, superintendent of Indian
Affairs in California and Nevada. Partly because of his enthusiasm
for the idea of using camels to survey the Western desert, they were
procured and used by the group he led. His report is detailed and
interesting; however, he fails to give a precise account of the suc-

cess of the camel venture, although he occasionally praises the animal's survival capabilities.

Beckwourth, James P. THE LIFE AND ADVENTURES OF JAMES P. BECK-WOURTH, MOUNTAINEER, SCOUT, PIONEER, AND CHIEF OF THE CROW NATION OF INDIANS, WRITTEN FROM HIS OWN DICTATION BY T.D. BONNER. 1856; Foreword by Bernard DeVoto. 1931; Minneapolis, Minn.: Ross and Haines, 1965.

> Beckwourth joined General Ashley's Rock Mountain Fur Company expedition and spent the next fourteen years trapping and trading in the West; three years of this time he spent entirely with the Crow nation and was made a chief. He returned to St. Louis for a brief period, but then went West again. In the winter of 1853–54, Beckwourth found an excellent biographer in Bonner. Some of the bloody exploits rival those credited to Crockett and Boone and were doubtless exaggerated. In his foreword to the 1931 edition, DeVoto writes that "Jim was a mountain man and the obligation to lie gloriously was upon him."

Bishop, Isabella L. [Bird]. A LADY'S LIFE IN THE ROCKY MOUNTAINS. 1879. Introd. Daniel Boorstin. Norman: Univ. of Oklahoma Press, 1960.

> Mrs. Bishop, one of the most celebrated women travelers of the nineteenth century, traveled through the Rockies on her return route from the Hawaiian Islands to England. Compiled from the author's letters to her sister, these observations are humorous, perceptive, and well written.

Bowles, Samuel. OUR NEW WEST. RECORDS OF TRAVEL BETWEEN THE MISSISSIPPI RIVER AND THE PACIFIC OCEAN. . . . Hartford, Conn.: Hartford Publishing Co., 1869.

> Bowles, the editor of the Springfield, Massachusetts, REPUBLICAN describes the scenery of the West, including the Colorado Rockies and the Yosemite Valley, and urges that wild lands and scenic areas be set aside as public parks.

_____. THE SWITZERLAND OF AMERICA. A SUMMER VACATION IN THE PARKS AND MOUNTAINS OF COLORADO. Boston: Lea and Shepard, 1869.

> Bowles's accounts of the West are valuable because he was writing as a well-educated Easterner, highly appreciative of the scenic value of the West and able to influence those who were powerful in the East. In this work, Bowles praises the wonders of the Colorado Rockies.

Brackenridge, Henry Marie. RECOLLECTIONS OF PERSONS AND PLACES IN THE WEST. Philadelphia: James Kay, 1834.

> Son of the author of MODERN CHIVALRY, Brackenridge was sent

to a French settlement near St. Louis to learn the language. He
later returned there for a visit. These recollections are both entertaining and accurate, containing a fine account of frontier life.

Browne, J. Ross. J. ROSS BROWNE: HIS LETTERS, JOURNALS AND WRIT-
INGS. Ed. with Introd. and Commentary by Lina Fergusson Browne. Albuquerque: Univ. of New Mexico Press, 1969.

The material in this volume consists of excerpts from Browne's pri-
vate letters and journals. Browne took a whaling cruise to the
Indian Ocean, documented in his first book, ETCHINGS OF A
WHALING CRUISE (1846). He was later appointed a government
commissioner in California; his travels in the West led to ADVEN-
TURES IN THE APACHE COUNTRY (1859) and SKETCHES OF AD-
VENTURES IN CALIFORNIA AND WASHOE (1864). The etchings
and drawings included in his books became widely known and ad-
mired. Many of his travel essays were originally published in
HARPER'S, and these and his books influenced both Melville and
Twain. These excerpts provide an excellent background for his
travel writings.

Bunnell, Lafayette Houghton. DISCOVERY OF THE YOSEMITE, AND THE
INDIAN WAR OF 1851, WHICH LED TO THAT EVENT. Chicago: Fleming
H. Revell, 1880.

Bunnell was a young surgeon with the Thirty-sixth Regiment of
Wisconsin, which fought in the Indian War of 1851. He suggested
the name for the Yosemite Valley itself, and he was responsible for
naming many of the features in the area. Although this account
was written twenty-nine years after the event, Bunnell had been
sufficiently awed by the scenery to recapture the initial excitement
of the discovery.

Clappe, Louise Amelia Knapp Smith [Dame Shirley]. THE SHIRLEY LETTERS
FROM THE CALIFORNIA MINES, 1851-1852. Ed. with Introd. Carl I. Wheat.
New York: Knopf, 1965.

Some of the early "Shirley Letters" were originally published in the
Marysville, California, HERALD in 1851 and 1852. A later group
of letters, many of which were written to the author's sister, were
published serially in THE PIONEER magazine of San Francisco.
They were first issued in book form in 1822 as THE SHIRLEY LET-
TERS FROM CALIFORNIA MINES IN 1851-52. In his introduction
to the 1965 edition, Wheat writes that "These letters from the
Sierra diggings form a priceless contribution to our knowledge and
understanding of that long-vanished era." The letters, particularly
the later ones, are detailed and clearly written.

Colton, Walter. THREE YEARS IN CALIFORNIA. 1850; Stanford, Calif.:
Stanford Univ. Press, 1949.

Founder of the first newspaper in the state, THE CALIFORNIAN,

Colton was also a chief judge in Monterey, appointed to the position nine days after America had taken possession of the territory. He saw California grow from a population of 10,000 to over 200,000 and witnessed the Gold Rush. This is an important historical document as well as being a clearly written, compassionate, and humorous account.

Cox, Ross. THE COLUMBIA RIVER; OR, SCENES AND ADVENTURES DURING A RESIDENCE OF SIX YEARS ON THE WESTERN SIDE OF THE ROCKY MOUNTAINS. . . . Ed. with introd. Edgar I. Stewart and Jane R. Stewart. Norman: Univ. of Oklahoma Press, 1957.

Originally published in two volumes in 1832 as ADVENTURES ON THE COLUMBIA RIVER, this account by one of the members of Astor's Pacific Fur Company is not one of the best of the fur-trader journals; but it includes some interesting observations, especially of the Indians encountered. Although somewhat denigrated by Washington Irving as one of the "scribbling clerks" of Astor's company, Cox vividly describes both his adventures while he was lost for almost two weeks and the difficulties of constructing a new trading post in the wilderness.

Curtis, George William. LOTUS-EATING: A SUMMER BOOK. New York: Harper, 1852.

The author describes a tour of American summer resorts, including the Catskills, Niagara, Saratoga and Lake George in New York, Nahant in Massachusetts, and Newport, Rhode Island. He compares American scenery with that of Europe, although concluding that the European, with all of its romantic associations, is superior. He also finds flaws in the American people, commenting upon their general lack of culture and refinement. Some of his contemporaries found his judgments and descriptions patronizing; others saw them as being candid but fair.

Custer, Elizabeth. BOOTS AND SADDLE; OR, LIFE IN DAKOTA WITH GENERAL CUSTER. 1885. Introd. Jane R. Stewart. Norman: Univ. of Oklahoma Press, 1961.

Elizabeth Custer spent much of her life after her husband's death defending his reputation. This book is part of that defense; she ignores or glosses over anything critical of her husband and omits the rivalries and quarrels of the camp. However, the book does provide an interesting perspective on the hazards and humor of life in frontier army outposts.

Custer, George Armstrong. MY LIFE ON THE PLAINS; OR, PERSONAL EXPERIENCES WITH INDIANS. 1874. Introd. Edgar I. Stewart. Norman: Univ. of Oklahoma Press, 1962.

This is an autobiographical account of Custer's military service on the Plains. Much of the material first appeared serially in THE

GALAXY (which later merged with ATLANTIC). Although Custer does not directly mention the court martial which took place during these years, he probably wished to justify himself and defend other actions which were being criticized. Included in the 1962 edition is a pamphlet written by General Hazen, superintendent of the Southern Indian District, rebutting some of Custer's claims about the hostility of the Indians he encountered.

Dale, Harrison C., ed. THE ASHLEY-SMITH EXPLORATIONS AND THE DISCOVERY OF THE CENTRAL ROUTE TO THE PACIFIC, 1822-29, WITH THE ORIGINAL JOURNALS. Glendale, Calif.: Arthur H. Clark, 1941.

This volume is a compilation of the narratives and journals of William Henry Ashley, Jedediah Strong Smith, and Harrison G. Rogers. Fur traders Ashley and Smith helped to develop the overland route through the Platte Valley and over the South Pass to Oregon. Smith kept a detailed journal of their travels; Harrison Rogers was a clerk who kept a daybook of the expedition. These journals and reports give an excellent account of the mountain men and early fur trading.

Dana, Richard Henry, Jr. TWO YEARS BEFORE THE MAST. 1840; New York: Dutton, 1969.

Dana left Harvard because of poor eyesight and spent two years (1834-36) as a seaman. His sensitive and vivid account of his sea trip, which includes a description of the California coast, became immediately popular and remains a classic. Dana's descriptions of flogging led to movements protesting the severe treatment of seamen and to eventual reform. As a lawyer in later years, Dana handled a number of maritime cases. The book has appeared in a great number of editions since 1840.

Davis, Richard Harding. THE WEST FROM A CAR WINDOW. New York: Harper, 1892.

This was a highly popular account, illustrated by Frederick Remington, of a trip through Texas, Oklahoma, and Colorado. Although Davis attempted to record his impressions as accurately as possible, he was very much influenced by his previous reading and looked in vain for the wild men of the West described by Bret Harte. His humor and pretended naiveté do not quite mask his distaste for some aspects of the West. Although he enjoyed watching the cowboys and seeing mountains and canyons, he was glad to reach the relative civilization of Denver.

Delano, Alonzo. ACROSS THE PLAINS AND AMONG THE DIGGINGS. Ed. Rufus R. Wilson, with photographs by Louis Palenske. New York: Wilson-Erickson, Inc., 1936.

First published in 1854 as LIFE ON THE PLAINS AND AMONG

THE DIGGINGS, this is an account of an overland trip to California as part of the great migration there in 1849. Delano contributed reports on the mining district to the PACIFIC NEWS, and
many of his sketches were also published in the New York TIMES
and other eastern papers. This is an excellent chronicle of the
westward trek, a precursor to the humorous, absurd, occasionally
pathetic accounts of the West and westerners by Bret Harte and
Twain.

Doten, Alfred. THE JOURNALS OF ALFRED DOTEN, 1849-1903. 3 vols.
Ed. Walter Van Tilburg Clark. Reno: Univ. of Nevada Press, 1975.

This is a thorough and usually interesting account of the California
Gold Rush and subsequent events by a newspaperman who also
chronicled the Nevada silver boom. Doten's daily journals, from
1849-1903, amount to seventy-nine leather-bound volumes. Walter
Van Tilburg Clark died before the publication of the three volumes
he edited; however, in a prospectus to the edition, he said the
journals give in "graphic and often moving detail the tragic course
of a single representative life through the violent transformations
enforced by the predatory and essentially amoral life of the California Gold Rush and the Nevada Silver Rush."

Dwight, Theodore. SKETCHES OF SCENERY AND MANNERS IN THE UNITED
STATES. New York: A.T. Goodrich, 1829.

Brother of the better-known Timothy, and also a "Hartford Wit,"
Theodore Dwight here describes the Connecticut River, the White
Mountains, and traveling on the canals and recounts tales associated with the valleys. The travel narrative includes the advice
to travelers that they attempt to view the world as it is rather
than failing to enjoy the sights because of extravagant anticipations
or unfortunate comparisons.

Dwight, Timothy. TRAVELS IN NEW-ENGLAND AND NEW-YORK. 4 vols.
1821-22. Ed. Barbara Miller Soloman. Cambridge, Mass.: Belknap Press,
Harvard Univ. Press, 1969.

Dwight traveled around Vermont in 1798 and 1806 and regarded
the backwoodsmen as too idle, talkative, passionate, and shiftless
to acquire either property or acceptance in stable communities.
He felt that they merely wished to escape the restraints of law,
religion, morality, and government. Dwight notes, however,
that the farmers who moved in later were hardworking and virtuous.

Field, Stephen. PERSONAL REMINISCENCES OF EARLY DAYS IN CALIFOR-
NIA. 1893; New York: Da Capo, 1968.

Fields tells of his attempts as attorney, judge, and state supreme
court justice to interpret the law in midcentury California. His
descriptions are lively, and his style is clear. Little interest was

shown in the reports when they were originally published, but they provide an excellent source of material on the development of California from 1849 to around 1870.

Flint, Timothy. A CONDENSED GEOGRAPHY AND HISTORY OF THE WEST-ERN STATES, OR THE MISSISSIPPI VALLEY. 2 vols. 1828. Introd. Bernard Rosenthal. Gainesville, Fla.: Scholar's Facsimiles and Reprints, 1970.

Flint's writings were the source of information about the Mississippi Valley for a great many of his contemporaries. His statistics, charts, and catalogs are interspersed with anecdotes and descrip-tions. In his introduction Bernard Rosenthal writes that "If we wish to understand what the West meant for America in Flint's day, we are going to have to pay careful attention to the details of his GEOGRAPHY, and we are going to have to recognize his book as the authentic interpreter of America as it was."

_____. RECOLLECTIONS OF THE LAST TEN YEARS, PASSED IN OCCA-SIONAL RESIDENCES AND JOURNEYINGS IN THE VALLEY OF THE MISSIS-SIPPI. 1826. Reprinted as RECOLLECTIONS OF THE LAST TEN YEARS IN THE VALLEY OF THE MISSISSIPPI. Ed. with introd. George R. Brooks. Car-bondale: Southern Illinois Univ. Press, 1968.

Flint, who later was one of the editors of the KNICKERBOCKER MAGAZINE, went West in 1816 as a missionary. He wrote sever-al novels as well as nonfiction and became one of the leading men of letters of the westward movement. His RECOLLECTIONS intro-duced people to the physical beauty, agricultural potential, and commercial possibilities of the Ohio and Mississippi valleys; and his descriptions served as an inspiration for other writers, including James K. Paulding. This work remains a valuable record of the early West because of its author's shrewd and knowledgeable ob-servations of life and people along the rivers.

Foote, Mary Hallock. A VICTORIAN GENTLEWOMAN IN THE FAR WEST: THE REMINISCENCES OF MARY HALLOCK FOOTE. Ed. with introd. Rodman W. Paul. San Marino, Calif.: Huntington Library, 1972.

Mary Hallock Foote had studied art before she went West with her husband, a mining engineer, and she illustrated the novels, stories, and essays which she wrote about her experiences in a mining camp. This narrative has been prepared from a typescript which was probably intended for publication and from two manuscripts, one edited, the other unedited and intended for the author's family. Here Foote talks about her adventures and explains the role played in the development of the West by the group of well-educated en-gineers to which her husband belonged.

Fremont, Jessie Benton. A YEAR OF AMERICAN TRAVEL: NARRATIVE OF PERSONAL EXPERIENCE. 1878. Introd. Patrice Manahan. San Francisco: Book Club of California, 1960.

Daughter of Thomas Hart Benton and wife of John C. Fremont, Jessie Fremont skillfully edited her husband's official reports and wrote several descriptive accounts of her own, as well as the children's stories which she wrote to alleviate the family's financial distresses. In this narrative she avoids the Victorian embellishments which marred many other similar accounts and shows tolerance, sympathy, and courage in face of physical difficulties. This work, together with Louise Clappe's SHIRLEY LETTERS (see p. 109), represent the very best of the reminiscences of travel and settlement of the West written by women.

Fremont, John Charles. THE EXPEDITIONS OF JOHN CHARLES FREMONT. Ed. Donald Jackson and Mary Lee Spence. Urbana: Univ. of Illinois Press, 1970.

Fremont, a young second lieutenant of the Topographical Engineers in the U.S. Army, was chosen in 1842 to lead an expedition into the West. It surveyed the new Oregon Trail to the South Pass in Wyoming and prepared a report on the rivers and fertility of the country as well as a valuable map for emigrants. The following year, Fremont was sent to continue the exploration all the way to Oregon and California. He also led three other expeditions. His accounts, well-detailed and readable, offer both a scientific and an adventurous picture of the country and were widely read. This volume is an excellent compilation of material from the first two expeditions and includes letters, excerpts from journals and memoirs, reports, and a portfolio of maps.

Garrard, Lewis H. WAH-TO-YAH, AND THE TAOS TRAIL. . . . 1850. Introd. Carl I. Wheat. Palo Alto, Calif.: American West Publishing Co., 1968.

This is one of the more interesting and valuable accounts of the Santa Fe traders and belongs with those of Gregg and Ruxton (below) as the best of the descriptions of the early Southwest. In this autobiographical narrative, Garrard places great emphasis upon the freedom and self-sufficiency of the mountain men. As a young man of seventeen, he joined a caravan which traveled along the Santa Fe Trail to Bent's Fort and Taos. He participated enthusiastically in the life there and ably portrayed the character and speech of the trappers and traders.

Greeley, Horace. AN OVERLAND JOURNEY, FROM NEW YORK, TO SAN FRANCISCO, IN THE SUMMER OF 1859. 1860; New York: Knopf, 1964.

As founder and editor of the New York TRIBUNE, Greeley exerted a great influence on social and political ideas. This volume is made up of the letters which he wrote for the columns of the TRIBUNE on his trip across the Continent. Despite the rigors of the stagecoach journey, Greeley enjoyed the adventure. This is one of the best of the many books on Western travel written by eastern journalists.

Gregg, Josiah. COMMERCE OF THE PRAIRIES. . . . 1844. Ed. Max L. Moorhead. Norman: Univ. of Oklahoma Press, 1954.

> A Missourian, Gregg was engaged in the overland trade from Independence to Santa Fe from 1831 to 1840. He recorded a common belief that with cultivation and artificial forestation, the rainfall would increase and make the plains more fertile. Gregg recounts the history of the Santa Fe trade, describes the equipment and the adventures of the overland journey, and portrays Mexican life in Taos and Santa Fe. His book was popular when it first appeared. Gregg is still regarded as one of the best historians of the trail.

_____. DIARY AND LETTERS OF JOSIAH GREGG. 2 vols. Ed. Maurice G. Fulton. Norman: Univ. of Oklahoma Press, 1941-44.

> Compiled from diaries, letters, and reports written by Gregg from 1840 through 1850, this edition covers the years during which Gregg left Santa Fe, traveled through Texas and Arkansas, published COMMERCE, studied medicine, and went to Mexico as a volunteer expeditionary aide in the Mexican War.

Hall, Bayard Rush. THE NEW PURCHASE; OR, EARLY YEARS IN THE FAR WEST. New Albany, Ind.: J.R. Nunemacher, 1855.

> A humorous account of the author's adventures in Indiana, the descriptions of ludicrous events and often ridiculous characters and incidents invite comparison with Twain's ROUGHING IT. Hall also presents a valuable picture of the rude state of culture in one of Indiana's chief centers of higher education.

Hall, James. LETTERS FROM THE WEST. 1828. Introd. John T. Flanagan. Gainesville, Fla.: Scholar's Facsimiles and Reprints, 1967.

> Hall, a veteran of the War of 1812, a writer of verse, and a journalist of military life, decided to take a keelboat down the Ohio River. He remained in the Ohio Valley, living in Cincinnati as an editor, writer, and banker. LETTERS appeared originally in the Illinois GAZETTE in 1820, and some were printed in the PORT FOLIO. They tell of Hall's experiences on the river, of the scenery, the life ashore, and the country itself--its history, legends, and people. The commentary is light, sometimes flippant, and overtly patriotic. British reviews of the book were hostile because Hall was so critical of the supercilious view taken by most British travelers when they wrote about the American West.

_____. NOTES ON THE WESTERN STATES. Philadelphia: H. Hall, 1838.

> This is a compilation of papers dealing principally with Kentucky history. Most of the material here had already appeared in Hall's SKETCHES OF HISTORY, LIFE AND MANNERS IN THE WEST (1835) and in various periodicals.

Harris, Edward. UP THE MISSOURI WITH AUDUBON: THE JOURNAL OF EDWARD HARRIS. Ed. and annotated John F. McDermott. Norman: Univ. of Oklahoma Press, 1951.

> Made available for the first time in its entirety in this edition, the diary Harris kept of his trip with Audubon up the Missouri River to the Yellowstone is ably arranged and annotated by McDermott. Harris was an amateur ornithologist, a gentleman-farmer from New Jersey, and a patron and friend of scientific men. When Audubon needed money, Harris bought many of his drawings. Harris' careful, objective observations of the trip form a complement to the section of Audubon's JOURNALS which covers the same journey.

Hastings, Lansford W. THE EMIGRANTS' GUIDE TO OREGON AND CALIFORNIA. . . . 1845. Historical notes and bibliography by Charles H. Carey. 1932; New York: Da Capo, 1969.

> "This book," writes the editor of the 1932 reprint, "was an early specimen of a kind of descriptive literature, deliberately planned to promote settlement and to attract population for the West." It influenced many westward-bound settlers to change their objective from Oregon to California. Hastings advised several westward-bound groups, including the Donner party, to cut across the Great Salt Desert without adequately warning them of its dangers and difficulties.

Hoffman, Charles Fenno. A WINTER IN THE WEST. New York: Harper, 1835.

> Coeditor of the New York AMERICAN and for a short while editor of the KNICKERBOCKER MAGAZINE, Hoffman described a horseback trip through Michigan and Illinois in sketches written for the AMERICAN and published in 1835 in his first book. This is one of the earliest observations on frontier life by an Eastern author of any importance. Unlike the many British and American travelers who found the wilderness unattractive and the frontier settlements crude, Hoffman was charmed by the wilderness and found much to praise in some of the larger towns and settlements on the frontier.

Howe, Julia Ward. A TRIP TO CUBA. Boston: Ticknor and Fields, 1860.

> Howe's account of a trip to Cuba with her husband and Theodore Parker and his wife was first published in ATLANTIC. It includes humorous and occasionally perceptive sketches of the people and moralizing comments, which offended abolitionists at home, about the laziness of some of the Cuban natives.

Ingersoll, Ernest. THE CREST OF THE CONTINENT: A RECORD OF A SUMMER'S RAMBLE IN THE ROCKY MOUNTAINS AND BEYOND. Chicago: R.R. Donneley and Sons, 1885.

Ingersoll was a student of Agassiz, worked with him at the Smithsonian, joined the Hayden Survey as a naturalist, and became a correspondent for the New York TRIBUNE. He was also the natural history editor for FOREST AND STREAM. A result of three months' exploration in the Rockies, this was Ingersoll's most popular book, going through some forty printings from 1885 to 1901.

_____. KNOCKING 'ROUND THE ROCKIES. 1883; Santa Fe: New Mexico State Bureau of Mines and Mineral Resources, 1972.

Reworked from material published in various magazines, this volume collects the author's narratives of his experiences in the field work of the geological and geographical survey of the territories.

Jackson, Helen Hunt. BITS OF TRAVEL AT HOME. Boston: Roberts Brothers, 1878.

Although Jackson's travel reports are seldom read today, this account of her impressions of New England, California, and the Southwest was popular and gained a wide audience.

Kane, Elisha Kent. ARCTIC EXPLORATIONS IN THE YEARS 1853, '54, '55. 2 vols. Philadelphia: Childs and Peterson, 1857.

Kane was senior medical officer aboard the first search expedition sent out to discover the missing explorer, Sir John Franklin, and commanded the ship for the second expedition. The group found only sparse evidence of Franklin's passage, but they did discover Grinnell Land. The account is rich in scientific data and is very well written. Kane describes the natural features of the arctic landscapes with sensitive images, describing various fantastic forms of icebergs and glaciers and noting the shifting kaleidoscope of light and weather. His poetic prose as well as his drawings add to his excellent narrative.

King, Clarence, ed. REPORT OF THE GEOLOGICAL EXPLORATION OF THE FORTIETH PARALLEL. 7 vols. Washington, D.C.: Government Printing Office, 1870-80.

Contributions by John Wesley Powell, George M. Wheeler, and Ferdinand Hayden describe the exploration of the Cordilleran Range from eastern Colorado to California.

King, Edward. THE GREAT SOUTH. 2 vols. Ed. W. Magruder Drake and Robert Jones. Baton Rouge: Louisiana State Univ. Press, 1972.

This is a collection of articles which King wrote for SCRIBNER'S MONTHLY in 1873 and 1874 on the "material resources, and the present political condition, of the people of the States formerly under the dominion of Slavery." The author talked with people of all classes, including former slaves, and carefully investigated southern institutions. In his bibliography (p. 127), Clark calls this "the fullest and at the same time one of the most accurate and revealing of all the travel accounts written as a survey of the effects of reconstruction on the South."

Kirkland, Caroline M. FOREST LIFE. . . . 2 vols. Boston: J.H. Francis, 1842.

Kirkland spent five years in southern Michigan during the late 1830s and early 1840s. Her description of this experience in FOREST LIFE and the two volumes below was clear, lively, and humorous. Her books were widely read and reveal upper-class eastern attitudes toward the more primitive West. In this volume, her second, Kirkland tells of her attempts to identify more closely with the Michigan farmers and backwoodsmen. Written in the first person as a kind of travel diary, this work, as well as the others, also contains fictional sketches.

_____. A NEW HOME--WHO'LL FOLLOW? OR, GLIMPSES OF WESTERN LIFE. 1830. Ed. and introd. William S. Osborne. 1965. Introd. Douglas B. Hill, Jr. New York: Garrett, 1970.

This first volume of Kirkland's travel narratives takes the form of letters to friends in the East. She comments with humor and occasional indignation on Western indifference to class distinctions, but she appreciates the generosity of the pioneer farmers. This collection might be described as a journal of observations, a series of connected sketches and tales, or, even, a novel. Kirkland's realistic satire helped to dissipate the romantic view of the frontier, and her use of dialect gives a further sense of realism to her sketches. In his study, CAROLINE KIRKLAND (New York: Twayne, 1972), William S. Osborne argues that Kirkland has been neglected as a pioneer of American realism. Osborne includes a bibliography of Kirkland's essays and fiction.

_____. WESTERN CLEARINGS. . . . 1845; New York: Garrett, 1969.

In this, the last of her travel books, Kirkland most closely approaches narrative fiction, constructing plots incorporating the characters and incidents she describes. Most of the essays and tales in this collection had already been published in women's magazines. Kirkland demonstrated that the West offered interesting themes for fiction; however, she herself did not quite find the best form for dealing with those themes.

Larpenter, Charles. FORTY YEARS A FUR TRADER ON THE UPPER MISSOURI. Ed. with notes by Elliott Coues. New York: F.P. Harper, 1898.

Larpenter completed his autobiographical narrative in 1872; the editor received the manuscript some time later. Using Larpenter's somewhat disorganized memoir, as well as other journals which he had kept, the editor polished Larpenter's erratic spelling and grammar and his awkward syntax. Although some of the original flavor may have been lost by this editing, the work is vivid, interesting, and direct. It was one of the more popular accounts of Western fur trading and remains a valuable historical document.

Leonard, Zenas. ADVENTURES OF ZENAS LEONARD, FUR TRADER. Ed. John C. Ewers. Norman: Univ. of Oklahoma Press, 1959.

Leonard joined a fur trading company and spent four years in the Rocky Mountains and California, staying some of that time with the Crow Indians. His carefully kept journal was published in 1839 as NARRATIVE OF THE ADVENTURES OF ZENAS LEONARD and was responsible for acquainting the rest of the country with the life of a fur trader. It is a simple direct story of the isolation and dangers of the life of a trapper. Unlike some of the other narratives of the adventures of the fur trade, Leonard's does not attempt to present the writer as a hero or exaggerate his adventures. Ewers' edition combines Leonard's journal and his newspaper pieces.

Ludlow, Fitz Hugh. THE HEART OF THE CONTINENT: A RECORD OF TRAVEL ACROSS THE PLAINS AND IN OREGON. . . . New York: Hurd and Houghton, 1870.

A well-known editor, author, and critic, Ludlow traveled to the West in 1863. He met Mark Twain, among others, in California, and wrote a piece for a San Francisco journal praising the work of the then-unknown author. Ludlow was a keen observer and wrote well; his style is clear and relatively unadorned. Most of THE CONTINENT originally appeared as essays in ATLANTIC.

Manly, William L. DEATH VALLEY IN '49: AN IMPORTANT CHAPTER OF CALIFORNIA PIONEER HISTORY. . . . 1894. Ed. Milo M. Quaife. 1927; Los Angeles: Borden Publishing Co., 1949.

Manly wrote of the events of 1849 a generation after the event; but his descriptions are vivid and realistic, and his prose is immediate and convincing. The account published in 1894 was an extension and enlargement of several shorter pieces which had been previously published.

Perry, Commodore Matthew Calbraith. THE JAPAN EXPEDITION, 1852-1854: THE JOURNAL OF COMMODORE MATTHEW C. PERRY. Ed. Roger Pineau and introd. Samuel Eliot Morison. Washington, D.C.: Smithsonian Institution, 1968.

This edition of Perry's journal contains many original paintings, explicit descriptions of life in the Chinese treaty ports, other personal observations, Perry's occasional outbursts against Navy politics, and his correspondence, none of which were included in the official report (below).

_____. NARRATIVE OF THE EXPEDITION OF AN AMERICAN SQUADRON TO THE CHINA SEAS AND JAPAN. 3 vols. Comp. from the original notes and journals by Francis L. Hawks. 1856. Abridged and Edited by Sidney Walleck. London: Macdonald, 1952.

> This official report was based on Perry's own journals and the notes of several of his officers and crew members (among the latter was Bayard Taylor). Perry and Hawks worked together on the narrative, which describes the journey, the ports, and the signing of the 1854 treaty opening Japan to the influences of the West.

Pike, Albert. PROSE SKETCHES AND POEMS WRITTEN IN THE WESTERN COUNTRY. 1834. Ed. David J. Weber. Foreword by Tom L. Popejoy. Albuquerque, N.M.: Calvin Horn, 1968.

> Pike was an early visitor to the Rocky Mountains and the Southwest. In addition to poetry, this collection includes three fictional sketches and two travel narratives: "Narrative of a Journey in the Prairie" and "Narrative of a Second Journey in the Prairie," in which Pike tells of the adventures of trappers and voyageurs.

Powell, John Wesley. EXPLORATION OF THE COLORADO RIVER OF THE WEST AND ITS TRIBUTARIES. Washington, D.C.: Government Printing Office, 1875.

> Powell's revision of this account was later published as CANYONS OF THE COLORADO. It has been reprinted a number of times under various titles; an attractive recent edition, with photographs, is DOWN THE COLORADO (Milan, Italy: Promontory Press with E.P. Dutton, 1970). In his report, Powell combined two expeditions and failed to mention the men who accompanied him on his second trip. However, his EXPLORATION is a fine piece of writing which has not only historical importance but also significant literary value.

_____. REPORT ON THE LANDS OF THE ARID REGION OF THE UNITED STATES, WITH A MORE DETAILED ACCOUNT OF THE LANDS OF UTAH. 1878; Cambridge, Mass.: Belknap Press, Harvard Univ. Press, 1962.

> As director of the federal survey of the Rocky Mountain Region, Powell noted that the old methods of agricultural settlement would not work in the more arid lands of the Great Basin. He urged a change of policy in land use, pointing out that homestead units would have to be made larger to allow for grazing and the fact that land could be cultivated only with irrigation. The report was influential in establishing land-use laws in the West.

Preuss, Charles. EXPLORING WITH FREMONT: THE PRIVATE DIARIES OF CHARLES PREUSS. . . . Trans. and Ed. Erwin G. Gudde and Elizabeth K. Gudde. Norman: Univ. of Oklahoma Press, 1958.

> Preuss accompanied Fremont as official cartographer for the first,

second, and fourth expeditions. Preuss' maps were the first of the territory between the Mississippi and the Pacific Ocean based on modern principles of geodesy and cartography. His accounts supplement and sometimes correct Fremont's and give an interesting insight into the way in which people responded to one another in the rigors of the expeditionary camp.

Richardson, Albert D. BEYOND THE MISSISSIPPI: FROM THE GREAT RIVER TO THE GREAT OCEAN. LIFE AND ADVENTURE ON THE PRAIRIES, MOUNTAINS, AND PACIFIC COAST. . . . 1857-1867. Hartford, Conn.: American Publishing Co., 1867.

This volume was based upon Richardson's reports as correspondent for the New York TRIBUNE and was immensely successful. It describes the West before the completion of the Union Pacific Railroad in 1869. The book, issued by subscription only, was copiously illustrated with photographs and sketches.

Roosevelt, Theodore. THE WINNING OF THE WEST. 4 vols. New York: G.P. Putnam's, 1889-96.

This history of Western explorations, from 1763 through Lewis and Clark to Zebulon Montgomery Pike, promulgates Roosevelt's belief in the morality of Anglo-Saxon imperialistic expansion and in the heroism of the frontiersmen. He felt that the Indians should be removed as barbaric savages from fertile lands and that Americans should hold those lands by right of conquest and settlement. In expressing these ideas, Roosevelt was voicing the opinion of most of his countrymen.

Russell, Osborne. JOURNAL OF A TRAPPER; OR, NINE YEARS IN THE ROCKY MOUNTAINS, 1834-1843. 1914. Ed. with Biography by Aubrey L. Haines. Portland: Oregon Historical Society, 1955.

Russell's is one of the better accounts of the life of a fur trapper in the Rocky Mountains. As a young man, the author joined an overland expedition led by Nathaniel J. Wyeth to Oregon. He was left in charge of Fort Hall, and later joined Jim Bridger. Russell later studied law and eventually became a judge in the provisional government of Oregon. This journal is valuable because Russell made a point of being honest and correcting the inaccuracies and exaggerations of other accounts.

Ruxton, George Frederick Augustus. RUXTON OF THE ROCKIES; COLLECTED BY CLYDE AND MAE REED PORTER. Ed. LeRoy R. Hafen. Norman: Univ. of Oklahoma Press, 1950.

Ruxton spent several years travelling with traders and trappers. He was one of the more gifted writers to portray the life of mountain men, and his ADVENTURES IN MEXICO AND THE ROCKY MOUNTAINS (1847) was widely read. This volume compiles and connects various notes and letters, including Ruxton's account of his travels in the Rockies and Mexico.

Sanford, Mollie Dorsey. MOLLIE: THE JOURNAL OF MOLLIE DORSEY SAN-FORD IN NEBRASKA AND COLORADO TERRITORIES, 1856-1866. Introd. and notes by Donald F. Danker. Lincoln: Univ. of Nebraska Press, 1976.

Mollie Dorsey went to the newly opened Nebraska territory with her family in 1857 and later moved to Denver with her husband. Her journal records pioneer life on the Plains, the Colorado Gold Rush, and the effect of the Civil War on the Colorado frontier. It is simple and moving, a fine example of a pioneer memoir.

Schoolcraft, Henry R. NARRATIVE OF AN EXPEDITION THROUGH THE UP-PER MISSISSIPPI TO ITASCA LAKE. . . . New York: Harper, 1834.

Interested in geology and mineralogy as well as in the Indians whom he studied, lived with, and wrote about (see TRAVELS, be-low), Schoolcraft acted as official mineralogist for an expedition to search for the source of the Mississippi River. The second ex-pedition in 1832 was successful and is recorded here; the first, in 1820, resulted in the NARRATIVE JOURNAL OF TRAVELS, THROUGH THE NORTH-WESTERN REGIONS OF THE UNITED STATES (Ed. Mentor L. Williams. 1821. East Lansing: Michi-gan State College Press, 1953). Schoolcraft's reports are vivid; he considers the kinds of activities and people in the settlements through which he traveled as well as describing the physical and geographical details of the land.

_____. TRAVELS IN THE CENTRAL PORTIONS OF THE MISSISSIPPI VALLEY. New York: Collins and Hannay, 1825.

In 1821, Schoolcraft went from Detroit to Chicago by Lake Erie, the Maumee, the Wabash, and the Ohio, going overland only briefly to St. Louis and then traveling up the Mississippi and the Illinois. That journey, made almost entirely on these rivers, is well reported by the author.

Stanton, Robert Brewster. DOWN THE COLORADO. Ed. with Introd. Dwight L. Smith. Norman: Univ. of Oklahoma Press, 1965.

Stanton was appointed chief engineer for the Denver, Colorado Canyon, and Pacific Railroad survey to determine the feasibility of a railroad along the course of the Colorado River. He later put together the story of the 1889-90 expedition, wishing to correct erroneous impressions on and information about the river. He did a tremendous amount of research for the project and be-came one of the foremost authorities on the river. His manuscript would have become the standard treatise had it been published when he completed it. Smith's edition publishes the first eleven chap-ters of the second volume of the manuscript.

Stephens, John Lloyd. INCIDENTS OF TRAVEL IN YUCATAN. 2 vols. 1843. Ed. Victor Wolfgang von Hagen. Norman: Univ. of Oklahoma Press, 1962.

Described by Van Wyck Brooks (in THE WORLD OF WASHINGTON IRVING) as "the greatest of American travel writers," Stephens went to Mexico and Central America on a combined diplomatic and archeological expedition in 1839. His documentation of political events is excellent history, but his stimulation and development of interest in Central American archeology was even more important. His work is also significant in that it initiated a series of historical studies which were to be carried on by Prescott and Bancroft. A sense of adventure, humor, and vitality are evident in Stephens' style and give his work wide appeal. An earlier volume, INCIDENTS OF TRAVEL IN CENTRAL AMERICA, CHIAPAS, AND YUCATAN (1841), has been Edited with Introd. and Notes by Richard L. Predmore (New Brunswick, N.J.: Rutgers Univ. Press, 1949). Both the original books and the recent editions include engravings by Frank Catherwood.

Stoddard, Charles Warren. HAWAIIAN LIFE: BEING LAZY LETTERS FROM LOW LATITUDES. Chicago: F.T. Neely, 1894.

Stoddard, a San Francisco Bohemian and a friend of many distinguished writers including Bierce and Twain, was an indifferent poet who occasionally wrote magnificent prose. Although this work lacks unity, a characteristic typical of most of Stoddard's work, it contains some brilliant descriptions of scenery and is considered by some to be a minor classic. As well as colorful descriptive sketches of the locale, it includes history of the Hawaiian Islands. The best account of his works is Robert L. Gale's monograph, CHARLES WARREN STODDARD (Boise, Idaho: Boise State Univ. Press, 1977).

_____. IN THE FOOTPRINTS OF THE PADRES. San Francisco: A.M. Robertson, 1902.

Valuable because of its historical account of San Francisco, description of the qualities of the city and local-color touches, this work also reveals Stoddard's observant but slightly melancholy, passive, and detached point of view. Several pieces in this collection appeared first in the San Francisco CHRONICLE, the CENTURY, the OVERLAND MONTHLY, and other periodicals.

_____. THE ISLAND OF TRANQUIL DELIGHTS. Boston: H.B. Turner, 1904.

Essays mainly on Hawaii and Tahiti, this is the last of Stoddard's travel books containing some of his best and worst writings; while there are passages of truly fine prose, the tone, emotion, and mood are often inconsistent and jarring.

_____. SOUTH SEA IDYLS. Boston: J.R. Osgood, 1873.

This collection of autobiographical travel essays recounts adventures told by old seamen, speaks of friendships with "savage" islanders, describes sailing through coral reefs and hunting with young islanders, as well as relives the climbing up mountainsides and looking into volcanoes. Stoddard also discusses the conversion of natives to Christianity. Although he is a devout Christian, he criticizes those who deaden pagan souls. Some sections of the work compare well with Melville's ENCANTADAS, particularly the "Kahele" section. Stoddard's style is excellent, but he shows little real feeling for the scenery or the natives, and his philosophical speculations are hazy and inconsistent.

_____. A TRIP TO HAWAII. San Francisco: Oceanic Steamship Co., 1885.

This is a lovely guidebook by one who obviously knew the islands well. Much of it is duplication of material from the earlier SOUTH SEA IDYLS, above.

Stuart, Robert. ON THE OREGON TRAIL: ROBERT STUART'S JOURNEY OF DISCOVERY. Ed. Kenneth A. Spaulding. Norman: Univ. of Oklahoma Press, 1953. Appendix.

Stuart joined Astor's Pacific Fur Company and led the group that in 1813 discovered the South Pass, vital to westward migration and the establishment of the route which became the Oregon Trail. Parts of Washington Irving's ASTORIA were drawn directly from ON THE OREGON TRAIL, and it is interesting to compare the two works to see Irving's changes. Spaulding's edition is taken from the manuscript of the author's revision of his journal.

Thwaites, Reuben G., ed. EARLY WESTERN TRAVELS, 1748-1846: A SERIES OF ANNOTATED REPRINTS OF SOME OF THE BEST AND RAREST CONTEMPORARY VOLUMES OF TRAVEL . . . . 32 vols. Cleveland: A.H. Clark, 1904-07.

An active historian as well as an eminent librarian, Thwaites here collected reprints of early narratives of travel and description. For many years it was the only source of much early nineteenth-century travel literature. The volumes include useful introductions and notes to each of the works and the final two volumes supply an analytical index of material on frontier conditions. The set is an important resource.

Turner, Henry Smith. THE ORIGINAL JOURNALS OF HENRY SMITH TURNER WITH STEPHEN WATTS KEARNEY TO NEW MEXICO AND CALIFORNIA, 1846-1847. Ed. with Introd. Dwight L. Clarke. Norman: Univ. of Oklahoma Press, 1966.

Frank, intimate, varying between factual reporting and moody introspection, Turner's account of the march from New Mexico to

California is a valuable contribution to southwestern history and an interesting human document. His account of the return from Monterey to Fort Leavenworth is strictly factual and impersonal. The editor's introduction and biographical sketch are helpful.

Ward, Samuel. SAM WARD IN THE GOLD RUSH. Ed. Carvel Collins. Stanford, Calif.: Stanford Univ. Press, 1949.

This memoir was originally published serially in 1861 in Porter's SPIRIT OF THE TIMES under the pseudonym "Midas Jr." Sam Ward was the brother of Julia Ward Howe and a good friend to many contemporary writers. He joined the Gold Rush in 1849 and became involved in California civic affairs and business as well as in the mines. This work recounts his adventures in "the diggins" of 1851 and 1852. It is a highly literate narrative of the days in camp and the excitement of finding gold.

Warner, Charles Dudley. IN THE WILDERNESS. Boston: Houghton, Osgood, 1878.

This is a humorous sketch of a summer spent trout fishing, deer hunting, being lost, and getting chased by a bear in the Adirondacks. Warner is better at anecdote than description; he enjoys making an awkward situation appear ridiculous.

_____. ON HORSEBACK. A TOUR IN VIRGINIA, NORTH CAROLINA AND TENNESSEE, WITH NOTES OF TRAVEL IN MEXICO AND CALIFORNIA. Boston: Houghton Mifflin, 1883.

Warner here describes his trip through the southern Appalachian country, the scenery, and the people of the region. He also talks about his climb of Mt. Mitchell, the highest mountain in the East.

_____. OUR ITALY. New York: Harper, 1891.

First published as a series of articles in HARPER'S in 1890-91, these essays describe the fertile valleys of southern California, comparing them to the Mediterranean valleys of Italy. Warner sketches the history of the region, tells anecdotes and legends, and describes the landscape and beautiful climate without rhetorical flourishes. He also travels inland and describes the deserts and canyons, including the Grand Canyon.

Wilkes, Captain Charles. NARRATIVE OF THE UNITED STATES EXPLORING EXPEDITION, DURING THE YEARS 1838, 1839, 1841, 1842. 6 vols. Philadelphia: Lea and Blanchard, 1845.

Commissioned by the U.S. government to explore and survey the South Seas, Captain Wilkes, with six ships and a large company of scientists, visited Tahiti, Samoa, and Australia. The

company was the first to see the Antarctic continent and to explore the Antarctic coast. Explorations of the Oregon and California coasts and the Philippine Islands are also part of the narrative. The publishing history of these volumes is given in Daniel
C. Haskell's THE U.S. EXPLORING EXPEDITION, 1838-1842,
AND ITS PUBLICATION, 1844-1874 (New York: Greenwood Press,
1968).

Winthrop, Theodore. THE CANOE AND THE SADDLE, ADVENTURES AMONG
THE NORTH-WESTERN RIVERS AND FORESTS AND ISTHMANIA. 1863. Ed.
with introd. and notes by John H. Williams. Tacoma, Wash.: John H. Williams, 1913.

This narrative of exploration in Washington Territory in 1853 was
published after Winthrop was killed in battle in the Civil War.
It combines history, description, close observation, love of adventure, and intelligent commentary. The work was extremely popular, as were Winthrop's other writings.

Wislizenus, Frederick Adolph. A JOURNEY TO THE ROCKY MOUNTAINS IN
THE YEAR 1839. 1840. First English ed. 1912; Glorieta, N. Mex.: Rio
Grande Press, 1969.

A German immigrant, Wislizenus tells of a journey he took as a
means of gaining "mental and physical recreation." His account
is detailed, vivid, intelligent, and objective, although he indulges
in pedantic moralizing now and then.

2. BACKGROUNDS: ANTHOLOGIES AND SECONDARY SOURCES

Allen, Walter, ed. TRANSATLANTIC CROSSING: AMERICAN VISITORS TO
BRITAIN AND BRITISH VISITORS TO AMERICA IN THE NINETEENTH CENTURY.
New York: William Morrow, 1971.

This collection includes selections from the travel writings of N.P.
Willis, Cooper, Bryant, Bayard Taylor, Melville, Prescott, Park-
man, Emerson, Stowe, Hawthorne, Henry Adams, Elihu Burritt,
Joaquin Miller, J.R. Lowell, Holmes, William James, and Henry
James, as well as nineteen British writers on America. In his
introduction, Allen notes that the earlier American writers' atti-
tudes are characterized by criticism and a sense of inferiority.
Later writers are more openly appreciative of Great Britain.

Babcock, C. Merton, ed. THE AMERICAN FRONTIER: A SOCIAL AND
LITERARY RECORD. New York: Holt, Rinehart and Winston, 1965.

Illustrating "the special and literary record" of the American frontier, this volume includes nonfiction pieces from the writings of
J. Ross Browne, Timothy Flint, and Thoreau, as well as examples
and extracts from their fiction and poetry.

Bartlett, Richard A.   GREAT SURVEYS OF THE AMERICAN WEST.   Norman:
Univ. of Oklahoma Press, 1962.   Bibliog.

> This book, part of the American Exploration and Travel Series
> (many of the works listed in Section II.D.1. above, were also
> published as part of this series), provides a listing and discussion
> of the survey reports resulting from government expeditions.   Writers
> included are Ferdinand V. Hayden, Clarence King, John Wesley
> Powell, and George M. Sheeler--the latter being responsible for
> a topographical survey of a large area in the Southwest.   Although
> not complete, this is one of few such listings.

Buck, Solon J.   TRAVEL AND DESCRIPTION, 1765-1865.   Springfield: Illinois
State Historical Library, 1914.   Index.

> This is a useful key to the literature of travel in the Mississippi
> Valley before the Civil War, with a chronological list of travel
> narratives and a library census.

Clark, Thomas D.   FRONTIER AMERICA: THE STORY OF THE WESTWARD
MOVEMENT.   2nd ed.   New York: Scribner's, 1969.   Bibliography.

> With a chapter on "Frontier Arts and Sciences," this clear, co-
> herent survey of the westward movement is excellent background
> for those interested in the literature of the Western frontier.

_____.   TRAVELS IN THE NEW SOUTH: A BIBLIOGRAPHY.   2 vols.   Nor-
man: Univ. of Oklahoma Press, 1962.

> Designed for those interested in historical research, this work and
> the one directly below are excellent sources of information on the
> literature of travel and exploration in the South.   Each entry is
> described, summarized, and evaluated.   Volume 1 of TRAVELS IN
> THE NEW SOUTH is for the years 1865-1900.

_____.   TRAVELS IN THE OLD SOUTH: A BIBLIOGRAPHY.   3 vols.   Norman:
Univ. of Oklahoma Press, 1956-59.

> Volume 3 is for the years 1825-1860.   See Coulter, TRAVELS IN
> THE CONFEDERATE STATES, below, for travels in the South be-
> tween 1861-64.

Clough, Wilson O.   THE NECESSARY EARTH: NATURE AND SOLITUDE IN
AMERICAN LITERATURE.   Austin: Univ. of Texas Press, 1964.

> Clough insists that the practical, empirical qualities of frontier
> experience are more important than mythical patterns or arche-
> typal heroes.   Clough sees daily life routines as being at the
> heart of the American writer's reactions to nature and solitude.

Commager, Henry Steele, ed. BRITAIN THROUGH AMERICAN EYES. New York: McGraw-Hill, 1974.

> In his introduction, Commager speaks of a "special relationship" between America and Great Britain. He writes that "The majority of those who visited and wrote about [England] did so in order to satisfy themselves about the character of the Mother Country and about their own relationship with her." In his excellent survey, Commager explains some of the forces which conditioned American relations with the British and speculates upon the attitudes of the writers. The essays in the collection are arranged chronologically including observations by Edward Everett, Alcott, Henry James, Sr., Hawthorne, Motley, Booker T. Washington, Audubon, Burroughs, and Henry Adams.

Coulter, Ellis M. TRAVELS IN THE CONFEDERATE STATES: A BIBLIOGRAPHY. Norman: Univ. of Oklahoma Press, 1948.

> This bibliography covers travel in the South during the Civil War years (which Clark does not include in TRAVELS IN THE OLD SOUTH, above). Most of the works listed have to do with accounts of battles, campaigns, and reminiscences of the war.

Davidson, Levette Jay, and Prudence Bostwick, eds. THE LITERATURE OF THE ROCKY MOUNTAIN WEST, 1803-1903. Caldwell, Idaho: Caxton Printers, 1939. Bibliog.

> This is a good introductory selection of representative nineteenth-century writings about the Rocky Mountain West, and brief biographies of authors provide a useful background.

Dondore, Dorothy. THE PRAIRIE IN THE MAKING OF MIDDLE AMERICA. 1926; New York: Antiquarian Press, 1961.

> The author outlines the treatment of the Middle West by various writers—including explorers, travelers, reporters, poets, and novelists.

Etulain, Richard W. WESTERN AMERICAN LITERATURE: A BIBLIOGRAPHY OF INTERPRETIVE BOOKS AND ARTICLES. Vermillion, S.Dak.: Dakota Press, 1972. Bibliog.

> This is a comprehensive checklist of research on Western American literature. Most of the authors listed are twentieth-century writers, although some from the nineteenth century are included. The study is useful for the student of nineteenth-century literature, but the main focus is on later works.

Froncek, Thomas, ed. VOICES FROM THE WILDERNESS: THE FRONTIERS-MAN'S OWN STORY. New York: McGraw-Hill, 1974.

> This is a selection of recollections, notes, journals, narratives,

and reports by hunters, guides, traders, and travelers in the eighteenth and early nineteenth centuries. The pieces, many of them
by relatively unknown figures, are often fascinating documents of
the frontier experience.

Hazard, Lucy Lockwood. THE FRONTIER IN AMERICAN LITERATURE. 1927;
New York: Frederick Ungar, 1961.

The author states her purpose is "to trace in American literature
reflections of the pioneering spirit--the indirect but powerful influence of the frontier in shaping the conditions of American life
and the resultant American philosophies." Hazard concentrates
upon fiction writers, but includes nonfiction prose by Irving, Garland, Twain, and Whitman, as well as the writings of Henry George
and the transcendentalists.

Klose, Nelson. CONCISE STUDY GUIDE TO THE AMERICAN FRONTIER.
Lincoln: Univ. of Nebraska Press, 1964.

The guide "provides a topical treatment of the various main subjects of frontier history"--for example, "Problems and Features of
the Frontier," "Leading Types of Frontiers," "Mining," "Farming,"
and "Cattlemen." The author sketches the chronological history of
the exploration and settlement of various American frontiers, providing a useful listing of background readings.

Lee, Robert Edson. FROM WEST TO EAST. Urbana: Univ. of Illinois Press,
1966.

This study contains essays on Lewis and Clark, Timothy Flint and
James Hall, Washington Irving, and Francis Parkman. Lee analyzes
"the inability of Western writers to produce an imaginative record
worthy of the grandeur of the Western movement." He focuses
on "the men and women, Western or Eastern, who traveled into a
new country, who responded in some way to the particular quality
of the West, but who were unable, for a variety of reasons, to
transform the first-hand experience of history into a literature of
their own."

Lewis, Marvin, ed. THE MINING FRONTIER: CONTEMPORARY ACCOUNTS
FROM THE AMERICAN WEST IN THE NINETEENTH CENTURY. Norman: Univ.
of Oklahoma Press, 1967.

This is a collection of brief items, mostly newspaper articles, from
such sources as the ALTA CALIFORNIA, the San Francisco ARGO-
NAUT, the GOLDEN ERA, and the TERRITORIAL ENTERPRISE.
The editor writes that because the far Western frontier was the
scene of rapidly changing events, most of the writing on the frontier was "lost in columns of newspaper print. But the files of the
frontier press preserve a record . . . which mirrored the confident
and ebullient life of the times. The spell and traditions of frontier
mining . . . [are] represented in the pages of this book."

Long, Orie William. LITERARY PIONEERS: EARLY AMERICAN EXPLORERS OF EUROPEAN CULTURE. Cambridge, Mass.: Harvard Univ. Press, 1935.

> The author states that his purpose is "to record the many interesting relationships which . . . internationally minded men experienced in Europe, especially in Germany, and to show the part which they played afterwards in the advancement of American life." The "internationally minded men" include George Ticknor, Edward Everett, George Bancroft, Henry W. Longfellow, and John Motley. The survey also gives excerpts from journals and correspondence of these travelers.

McDermott, John Francis, ed. BEFORE MARK TWAIN: A SAMPLER OF OLD, OLD TIMES ON THE MISSISSIPPI. Carbondale: Southern Illinois Univ. Press, 1968.

> The editor wants "to illustrate what life on the Mississippi was like in the days before Mark Twain took it over as a literary property." This volume includes an excellent introduction, which surveys various accounts, and excerpts from the reports of Timothy Flint, Thomas Bangs Thorpe, Charles Lyell, and others.

Major, Mabel, Rebecca W. Smith, and T.M. Pearce. SOUTHWEST HERITAGE: A LITERARY HISTORY WITH BIBLIOGRAPHY. Albuquerque: Univ. of New Mexico Press, 1972. Bibliog., Index.

> This guide gives descriptions of some one thousand titles dealing with the literature of the southwestern frontier. Part 2, "Literature of Anglo-American Adventures and Settlers," includes chronicles, travel books, journals, and historical writings. Works are described in bibliographical essays that cover literary, cultural, and historical backgrounds.

Rader, Jesse L., ed. SOUTH OF FORTY, FROM THE MISSISSIPPI TO THE RIO GRANDE: A BIBLIOGRAPHY. Norman: Univ. of Oklahoma Press, 1947.

> Devoted to the diaries, journals, and narratives of explorers and travelers to the southern portion of the Louisiana Purchase, this bibliography is one of the few covering this particular geographical area. Secondary studies of southern travel literature are also included.

Rusk, Ralph L. THE LITERATURE OF THE MIDDLE WESTERN FRONTIER. 2 vols. 1925; New York: Frederick Ungar, 1962.

> This is a reliable and thorough survey of the literature of travel in the Middle West written before 1840. Rusk briefly reviews the history of the midwestern settlement, then describes and evaluates the literary accounts of the exploration and development of the area as well as the literature which influenced and was being produced by the settlers. Most of volume 2 consists of an extensive listing of works before 1841, published either by citizens of the Middle West or by travelers who describe the region.

Slotkin, Richard. REGENERATION THROUGH VIOLENCE: THE MYTHOLOGY OF THE AMERICAN FRONTIER, 1600-1860. Middletown, Conn.: Wesleyan Univ. Press, 1973.

> The author analyzes recurring images, themes, and values in frontier writings. He finds in the narrative of captivity and the tale of the frontier warrior the two forms which promulgated the frontier myth. His work is lengthy and sometimes ponderous, but it does present some interesting ideas about recurring themes which have subtley influenced American concepts.

Smith, Henry Nash. VIRGIN LAND: THE AMERICAN WEST AS SYMBOL AND MYTH. 1950; Cambridge, Mass.: Harvard Univ. Press, 1970.

> In this classic study, Smith examines the impact of the Western American frontier upon American thought and letters of the nineteenth century. Among the travel writers Smith mentions are Timothy Dwight, Fremont, William Gilpin, Greeley, and Powell.

Stegner, Wallace. THE GATHERING OF ZION: THE STORY OF THE MORMON TRAIL. New York: McGraw-Hill, 1964. Bibliog.

> Stegner's account of the settlement of Utah Territory utilizes many nineteenth-century journals, documents, and travel narratives.

Tuckerman, Henry Theodore. AMERICA AND HER COMMENTATORS, WITH A CRITICAL SKETCH OF TRAVEL IN THE UNITED STATES. New York: Scribner's, 1864.

> This early survey includes accounts by travelers and critics up to the mid-nineteenth century. It is especially valuable for early narratives and for Tuckerman's definition of good travel writing. The American travel writers discussed include Cooper, Bryant, Irving, and Hawthorne. Tuckerman stoutly defends American industriousness and democracy against all European criticism.

Turner, Frederick Jackson. THE FRONTIER IN AMERICAN HISTORY. 1920; New York: Holt, Rinehart and Winston, 1962.

> Although it was not published until 1920, Turner's paper, "The Significance of the Frontier in American History," was read in 1893 before the American Historical Society in Chicago. It was not the first essay on the subject, but it called the attention of scholars to the neglect of the frontier in the writing of American history. Turner briefly described the environmental influences which had transformed Old World ideas and institutions into American ideas and institutions. His discussion of the frontier's role provoked continuing discussion and inaugurated new study and reinterpretation of the West.

Venable, William Henry. BEGINNINGS OF LITERARY CULTURE IN THE OHIO VALLEY. 1891; New York: Peter Smith, 1949.

This is an unsystematic and rather miscellaneous collection of information, but it is a pioneer work, with sketches of Timothy Flint, James Hall, Daniel Drake, and other figures of the early Northwest in addition to notes on early Western magazines. It contains some interesting biographies on Western writers as well as a history of cultural institutions. It also includes items on Ohio Valley writers, lecturers, and orators, from published monographs, periodicals, and manuscript material.

Wagner, Henry R. HENRY R. WAGNER'S THE PLAINS AND THE ROCKIES: A BIBLIOGRAPHY OF ORIGINAL NARRATIVES OF TRAVEL AND ADVENTURE, 1800-1865. Rev. and enl. Charles L. Camp. 1937; Louisville, Ky.: Lost Cause Press, 1959.

This is a useful guide to travel literature and personal narrative, describing books and personal experience narratives written between the years 1800 and 1865 about the region lying between the Missouri River and the Sierra Nevada Cascades, from Mexico to the arctic (omitting Texas and Louisiana).

Walker, Franklin. SAN FRANCISCO'S LITERARY FRONTIER. 1939; Seattle: Univ. of Washington Press, 1969.

This survey of periodicals and personalities in California literature in the latter half of the nineteenth century includes material on Bierce, Harte, Clemens, Stoddard, Joaquin Miller, and others. Documentation of source materials from early California newspapers and magazines provides a useful reference for some first publications.

Webb, Walter Prescott. THE GREAT PLAINS. Boston: Ginn and Co., 1931.

This outstanding study of the growth of society in the plains, with a chapter devoted to its literature, gives an artistic account of the effect of the Great Plains upon its writers. Webb's thesis is that "the Great Plains environment . . . constitutes a geographic unit whose influences have been so powerful as to put a characteristic mark upon everything that survives within its borders." The section on literature focuses on fiction and poetry, but in a chapter on emotional and spiritual "mysteries" of the prairie, Webb deals with travel and description pieces.

Winther, Oscar O. A CLASSIFIED LIST OF THE PERIODICAL LITERATURE OF THE TRANS-MISSISSIPPI WEST, 1811-1957. Bloomington: Indiana Univ. Press, 1961.

Most of the material listed here, by topic (e.g., agriculture, fur trade, Indians, and utopian communities) or by state or area, consists of articles and essays written in the twentieth century about the history of the West and its explorers and settlers. The listing includes a few nineteenth-century pieces and is an extremely useful compilation of secondary sources.

E. WRITINGS IN EDUCATION, RELIGION, PHILOSOPHY, AND SCIENCE

1. PRIMARY WORKS

a. Education

Harris, William Torrey. PSYCHOLOGIC FOUNDATIONS OF EDUCATION.
New York: D. Appleton, 1898.

> After Harris moved from St. Louis, where he was a significant mem-
> ber of the "St. Louis School" of philosophers, he became involved
> for a time with Bronson Alcott and F.B. Sanborn in the Concord
> Summer School of Philosophy and Literature. He was later appointed
> U.S. commissioner of education. Here, he expounds a theory of
> education which represents a national, public education as the cul-
> minating embodiment of freedom. He wrote that "Education is the
> process of the adoption of the cosmical order in place of one's
> mere animal caprice. It is a renunciation of the freedom of the
> moment for the freedom of eternity."

Hopkins, Mark. THE LAW OF LOVE AND LOVE AS LAW: OR, MORAL
SCIENCE, THEORETICAL AND PRACTICAL. New York: Scribner's, 1869.

> Hopkins was one of the most influential teachers of moral philosophy
> of his time. Here, he reconstructs a series of lectures in which
> he argues that man's chief end is to love and enjoy God. It is
> more formal and stylistically less effective than the earlier lecture
> series, described below.

_____. LECTURES ON MORAL SCIENCE. Boston: Gould and Lincoln, 1862.

> This volume collects Hopkins' Lowell Institute Lectures, some of
> which were written as early as 1830. His arguments that human
> beings are capable of both rational choice and "holy love" of the
> Creator are eloquent, often-poetic treatises.

Mann, Horace. LECTURES ON EDUCATION. Boston: William B. Fowle and
N. Capen, 1845.

Horace Mann, an important figure in the mid-nineteenth-century humanitarianism, focuses upon reforms in education. As did the transcendentalists, Mann believed in the perfectibility of human life and institutions urging a common-school education for all children. Mann's idea that "The scientific or literary well-being of a community is to be estimated not so much by its possessing a few men of great knowledge as its having many men of competent knowledge" affected subsequent writers on education, whether they agreed or disagreed with Mann's premises.

_____. LIFE AND WORKS. 5 vols. Ed. Mary Tyler Peabody Mann. Boston: Walker, Fuller and Co., 1856–68.

Mann's second wife, Mary Tyler Peabody Mann, one of the Peabody sisters, prepared and edited most of Mann's important writings in these five volumes. Her biographical LIFE gives insight into Mann's character and motivations.

Parker, Francis W. TALKS ON PEDAGOGICS. New York: E.L. Kellogg, 1894.

Called by John Dewey the father of progressive education, Parker was influential in introducing the ideas of Pestalozzi, Froebel, and Herbart into the classrooms of the United States. His methods mark a transition from transcendentalism to a newer scientific pedagogy. This volume is one of the first American works on pedagogy to gain an international reputation.

Peabody, Elizabeth P. RECORD OF A SCHOOL. Boston: Russell, Shattuck and Co., 1835.

In 1834, Elizabeth Peabody and Amos Bronson Alcott opened a school based upon premises of transcendentalism. Their aim was to encourage a child to achieve "Self-Realization" through linking internal thoughts and outward objects. The RECORD is a mixture of Peabody's ideas and Alcott's practices as well as an exposition of the philosophy on which they based their methods. It also demonstrates their sometimes clumsy attempts to translate an abstract philosophy into practical pedagogy.

Spalding, John Lancaster. MEANS AND ENDS OF EDUCATION. Chicago: A.C. McClurg, 1895.

A leader in the Catholic church, Spalding wrote influential essays, gathered in the two publications listed here and below, arguing that Christian character, ideals, and values were needed to remedy the evils of American life. He deplored the exploitation of the immigrants and the avarice of the industrial titans.

_____. THOUGHTS AND THEORIES OF LIFE AND EDUCATION. Chicago: A.C. McClurg, 1897.

See annotation above.

b. Religious Movements

Abbott, Lyman. CHRISTIANITY AND SOCIAL PROBLEMS. 1896; New York: Johnson, 1970.

Abbott was a Congregational clergyman and editor of THE OUT-LOOK, a successor to Henry Ward Beecher's CHRISTIAN UNION; under Abbott's direction THE OUTLOOK became an organ for commenting upon a broad spectrum of social and political issues. CHRISTIANITY is a representative expression of Christian social thought in America. Abbott writes that church and ritual are in vain if they do not inspire justice, righteousness, and service. He hoped for an industrial democracy in which there would be a partnership between laborers and capitalists with profit-sharing and cooperatives. The system is not exactly socialistic, however, because Abbott feels that profits should be allocated according to each worker's contributions.

_____. THE EVOLUTION OF CHRISTIANITY. Boston: Houghton Mifflin, 1892.

Probably the most significant contribution which Lyman Abbott made to the "new theology" was his recognition and acceptance of the theory of evolution. Abbott was influenced by John Fiske, Henry Ward Beecher, Joseph Le Conte, and Henry Drummond--especially the latter's use of evolutionary theory to apply to both biological and spiritual development. This volume grew out of a course of lectures for the Lowell Institute in Boston. Abbott applies the evolutionary principal to the Bible, theology, the church, society, and the soul, arguing that as man's spiritual nature grew stronger, his animal nature was gradually eliminated.

_____. THE THEOLOGY OF AN EVOLUTIONIST. 1897; New York: Outlook, 1925.

Originating as a series of lectures in Plymouth Church, this book presents evolution as God's way of creation. Sin was a lapse into the animal nature from which man had risen. Man's hope was "in the power that shall lift him up and out of his lower self into his higher, truer, nobler self, until he shall be no longer the son of the animal, but in very truth a son of God."

Beecher, Lyman. AUTOBIOGRAPHY OF LYMAN BEECHER. 2 vols. 1864-65. Ed. Barbara Cross. Cambridge, Mass.: Belknap Press, Harvard Univ. Press, 1961.

Father of Catharine, Henry Ward and Harriet B. Stowe, Lyman

Beecher was a militant evangelist, a moral reformer (interested particularly in the temperance movement), and a revivalist who campaigned against Boston Unitarianism. His AUTOBIOGRAPHY gives an extraordinary picture of evangelical Protestantism in America and documents his own contribution of associating evangelicalism with moral reform and social benevolence.

_____. A PLEA FOR THE WEST. Cincinnati: Truman, 1835.

This is a classic statement of the significance of the West in the nation's growth. Beecher anticipated Frederick Jackson Turner's belief in the shaping force of the frontier; however, he also believed that the civilizing influence of New England was necessary to rescue the West from barbarism and license.

Bushnell, Horace. CHRISTIAN NURTURE. New York: Scribner's, 1861.

For Bushnell, rationalists, revivalists, and transcendentalists all overemphasized reason. He insisted that theology is not intellectual but intuitive, and he typified the transition from evangelicalism to pragmatism. He appealed to the rising middle class by preaching on the virtues of capitalism, on the religious nurture of children, and on the naturalness of progress. His ideas were central to the evolutionary optimism which nourished American liberal theology and was later popularized by Henry Ward Beecher.

_____. WORK AND PLAY; OR, LITERARY VARIETIES. New York: Scribner's, 1864.

Many of these essays deal with the same topics that Emerson used for his speeches and writings: loyalty, simplicity, and the pitfalls of materialism. The essays are serious, almost ponderous, in tone; while they are sometimes more formally coherent than Emerson's, they lack Emerson's brilliance and originality.

Clarke, James Freeman. TEN GREAT RELIGIONS. Boston: Houghton Mifflin, 1889.

An extremely popular work, this volume introduced the public to the subject of comparative religions and myths acknowledging the importance of the Oriental religions which influenced transcendentalism. Clarke was also an important medium of transfer for the German influence in America.

Frothingham, Octavius Brooks. BOSTON UNITARIANISM. New York: G.P. Putnam's, 1890.

Frothingham was converted from conservative Unitarian ministry to abolitionism and more radical views. This volume does represent, however, a clear expression of Unitarianism in the nineteenth century.

_____. THE RELIGION OF HUMANITY. New York: G.P. Putnam's, 1872.

As a promoter of a new humanistic, naturalistic concept of religious and ethical values, Frothingham argued that religion must be identified with ethics. This is the best expression of humanistic efforts to formulate a free and scientific religion for the American people. In it, Frothingham writes that "The new Liberal Church has a consistent scheme of thought; it goes to the mind for its ideas; it admits the claim of spontaneity; its method of obtaining truth is rational; the harmony it demands is harmony of principles-- the orderly sequence of laws."

_____. TRANSCENDENTALISM IN NEW ENGLAND. 1876. 1959; Gloucester, Mass.: Peter Smith, 1965.

This is an interesting history from a sympathetic observer and participant in the movement. Frothingham traces the philosophy, background, the place in history, the central message, and the practical accomplishments of transcendentalism and treats its major figures. His work was one of the first and remains one of the best accounts of transcendentalism in the United States.

Gladden, Washington. APPLIED CHRISTIANITY. Boston: Houghton Mifflin, 1886.

One of the earliest and most significant of the expounders of the Social Gospel, Gladden was a follower of Horace Bushnell who had been one of the country's most influential clergymen (see CHRISTIAN NURTURE, above). The four volumes listed here are the best and most representative of the thirty-six which Gladden published. Although he never became a Socialist, he did advocate public ownership of utilities, cooperative management of many industries, and was a major force in awakening the American social conscience.

_____. RULING IDEAS OF THE PRESENT AGE. Boston: Houghton Mifflin, 1895.

See annotation above.

_____. TOOLS AND THE MAN. Boston: Houghton Mifflin, 1893.

See annotation above.

_____. WORKING PEOPLE AND THEIR EMPLOYERS. 1876; New York: Arno, 1969.

See annotation above.

Hedge, Frederic Henry. REASON IN RELIGION. Boston: Walker, Fuller, 1865.

Hedge was a Unitarian minister who also taught ecclesiastical history and German literature at Harvard. He studied in Germany, knew German idealism well, and was the most reliable source for American transcendentalists who were interested in German thought. Although his visits to Concord and Boston were often the occasion for the meetings of the Transcendental Club, Hedge did not identify himself with the transcendentalists and defended the Christian church from their criticism. This work is a classic statement of transcendentalized Christianity.

_____. WAYS OF THE SPIRIT AND OTHER ESSAYS. Boston: Roberts Brothers, 1877.

Although Hedge was often at odds with the transcendentalists, the essays in this collection reveal many of the transcendentalist themes: the unity of nature and spirit, a positive view of successful reform, and avoidance of narrow dogmatism in religion.

Hitchcock, Edward. THE RELIGION OF GEOLOGY AND ITS CONNECTED SCIENCE. Boston: Phillips, Sampson, 1851.

A student of the geologist Benjamin Silliman and an eminent geologist himself, Hitchcock argued that the long geological history of the earth is a revelation of God's constancy, that the principles of science are a transcript of Divine character, and that the main use of science is its confirmation of religion. His advanced views were rarely accepted, but Hitchcock and Silliman both helped to harmonize the conflicting views of geology and Genesis.

Moody, Dwight Lyman. THE OVERCOMING LIFE AND OTHER SERMONS. New York: Fleming H. Revell, 1896.

Moody's fundamentalist evangelism was widely appealing. This collection of sermons gives a sample of the supernatural exhortations that were so attractive to vast numbers of people in the last two decades of the nineteenth century.

Norton, Andrews. THE EVIDENCE OF THE GENUINENESS OF THE GOSPELS. 3 vols. 1837-44; Boston: American Unitarian Association, 1880.

Andrews Norton, who was sometimes called the "Unitarian Pope," is significant primarily because of his conflict with the transcendentalists, particularly George Ripley. Norton argued that miracles (that is, external evidence) are the sole proof of the Divine origin of Christianity. Ripley argued that every person is capable of discerning truth through intuition (internal evidence) and examination of the moral doctrines which emerge from the Scriptures. Norton relied on learned authority; Ripley upon individual perceptions.

Reed, Sampson. OBSERVATIONS ON THE GROWTH OF THE MIND. 1826; 1838. Introd. Carl F. Strauch. Gainesville, Fla.: Scholar's Facsimiles and Reprints, 1970.

This forty-four page booklet is an important document in the history of American transcendentalism. Reed studied at the Harvard Divinity School, but, after reading and being profoundly affected by Swedenborg, disqualified himself from the Unitarian pulpit. In this pamphlet, Reed was expounding Swedenborg, although Swedenborg is not mentioned by name. Through Reed's interpretation of Swedenborg, the transcendentalists derived the basic content of their aesthetic theory. Reed explained the idea of correspondence, as of idea, object, word and thing, and the essentials of organic style, wherein the artist achieves form by freely expressing nature rather than by imposing artificial structures on it.

Sanborn, Franklin Benjamin. SIXTY YEARS OF CONCORD, 1855-1915: LIFE, PEOPLE, INSTITUTIONS AND TRANSCENDENTAL PHILOSOPHY IN MASSACHUSETTS--WITH MEMORIES OF EMERSON, THOREAU, ALCOTT, CHANNING AND OTHERS. Ed. with Notes and Index by Kenneth Walter Cameron. Hartford, Conn.: Transcendental Books, 1976.

This volume makes available a wide variety of primary materials written by Sanborn and organized by Cameron.

Schaff, Philip. AMERICA: A SKETCH OF ITS POLITICAL, SOCIAL, AND RELIGIOUS CHARACTER. 1855. Ed. Perry Miller. Cambridge, Mass.: Harvard Univ. Press, 1961.

Schaff, a historian and theologian educated in Germany, was one of the first important mediators of German critical thought in America. In the 1855 volume, consisting of two lectures given in Germany, to which the editor of the 1961 edition has added a third, Schaff attempts to explain and illuminate the problems of interpretation occurring in the exchange of ideas between Europe and America. He points out that religious diversity in the United States paradoxically led to a healthy unanimity rather than to chaotic dissent. In his "Editor's Introduction," Perry Miller calls this "one of the most searching analyses of the national character composed in [the nineteenth] century."

_____. CHURCH AND STATE IN THE UNITED STATES, OR THE AMERICAN IDEA OF RELIGIOUS LIBERTY AND ITS PRACTICAL EFFECTS. 1888; New York: Arno, 1972.

In this volume, Schaff argued that the Christian church should be responsive to historical change. Influenced at least indirectly by Hegel, Schelling, and others, Schaff maintained that Protestantism was not a revolt but an organic outgrowth from previous centuries. This work, and his seven-volume HISTORY OF THE CHRISTIAN CHURCH (1853), were milestones in American historical thinking and exegesis influencing contemporary theology, education, and literature.

Strong, Josiah. OUR COUNTRY. 1885. Introd. Jurgen Herbst. Cambridge, Mass.: Belknap Press, Harvard Univ. Press, 1963.

> Strong was a minister in the Congregationalist Home Missionary Society. In this volume, which went through several editions and influenced thousands of readers, Strong developed the idea of Anglo-Saxon superiority. Using Social Darwinism to give scientific sanction to his ideas, Strong argued that the United States mission was "to impress its institutions upon mankind." In the introduction to the 1963 edition, Jurgen Herbst writes that "The book . . . mirrors the thoughts and aspirations of this [Protestant] dominant segment of American society towards the close of the nineteenth century, and it is therefore a historical document of major importance." Strong also warned against the threat to old values of new waves of immigrants and the urbanization of America, celebrating the virtues of the agrarian past.

White, Andrew Dickson. A HISTORY OF THE WARFARE OF SCIENCE WITH THEOLOGY IN CHRISTENDOM. 2 vols. New York: D. Appleton, 1896.

> White was a cofounder and president of Cornell University. In this enlightened discussion, he airs his hopes for a unification of science and theology. The volume includes his famous Cooper Union speech, "The Battlefields of Science." This work was widely read and was highly influential, probably convincing many critics of the evolutionary theory that continued opposition to this theory and other scientific hypotheses would be both useless and harmful to organized Christianity.

See also anthologies of transcendental writings (pp. 25-41).

c. Philosophy and Psychology

Abbot, Francis Ellingwood. SCIENTIFIC THEISM. Boston: Little, Brown, 1885.

> In this major contribution to American philosophic realism, Abbot defends a realism based on independent analysis of objects and relationships. He also attempts to reconcile religion and evolutionary theories and was active with O.B. Frothingham in promoting a new humanistic concept of religious and ethical values.

Baldwin, James Mark. HANDBOOK OF PSYCHOLOGY. 2 vols. New York: H. Holt, 1889-90.

> Influenced by Darwin, Baldwin began as a psychologist propounding a complex evolutionary social psychology. His uniqueness lies in his emphasis on the play impulse and the primary aspect of the aesthetic consciousness. His most influential work was written after 1900; however, these earlier works affected the thinking of American and European aestheticians and psychologists.

_____. MENTAL DEVELOPMENT IN CHILD AND RACE: METHODS AND PROCESSES. New York: Macmillan, 1895.

See annotation above.

_____. SOCIAL AND ETHICAL INTERPRETATIONS IN MENTAL DEVELOP-MENT. New York: Macmillan, 1897.

See annotation above.

Blau, Joseph, ed. AMERICAN PHILOSOPHIC ADDRESSES, 1700-1900. New York: Columbia Univ. Press, 1946.

For this volume the editor chose addresses which had both outstanding literary merit and expressed a characteristic and representative philosophical position. Many of these addresses have been published elsewhere, but the collection gives context to the speeches of such nineteenth-century figures as Bancroft, Holmes, Emerson, W.E. Channing.

Fiske, John. OUTLINES OF COSMIC PHILOSOPHY. 2 vols. 1874; Boston: Houghton Mifflin, 1894.

Fiske was one of the most recognized American intellectual leaders of the late nineteenth century. His name is most closely associated with the interpretation of religion in evolutionary terms. For Fiske, evolution was not a godless process. It was, rather, a means by which man became increasingly like God. He wrote that "Below the surface din and clashing of the struggle for life we hear the undertone of the deep ethical purpose." His advocacy of Spencer brought him under suspicion at Harvard; however, with the advent of Charles W. Eliot there, Fiske was asked to give a series of lectures. This volume is based on lectures given at Harvard in 1869. Along with the next entry below, OUTLINES expresses Fiske's attempts to reconcile evolution with theistic concepts and to propose an ongoing evolutionary process. This work is reprinted as Volumes 13 through 16 of THE WRITINGS (below).

_____. THROUGH NATURE TO GOD. Boston: Houghton Mifflin, 1899.

See annotation above.

_____. THE WRITINGS OF JOHN FISKE. 24 vols. Cambridge, Mass.: Riverside Press, 1902.

See annotation above.

Harris, William Torrey. HEGEL'S DOCTRINE OF REFLECTION. New York: D. Appleton, 1881.

Probably the most academically respectable of the St. Louis group of philosophers, Harris cofounded the JOURNAL OF SPECULATIVE

PHILOSOPHY, which introduced Americans to Hegel, Fichte, Schelling, and other German philosophers. Harris approached a systematic study of Hegel, arguing that the finite particulars of sense perception are not ultimate reality as Hegel thought but depend on an environment. We must perceive relationships and mutual dependence of all objects within a dynamic whole. Harris believed that Hegel and Aristotle were saying similar things about ways of perceiving and knowing. He studied Greek which he thought revealed Hegel, and the understanding of Hegel essential for understanding psychology.

Ingersoll, Charles J. A DISCOURSE CONCERNING THE INFLUENCE OF AMERICA ON THE MIND. Philadelphia: A. Small, 1823.

This was an annual oration delivered before the American Philosophical Society in 1823. DISCOURSE is one of the more eloquent defenses which Americans were then offering to those who believed America was lacking in contributions to law, history, literature, and the arts. Ingersoll compared the cultural achievements of America with those of Europe, writing that "the average of intellect, and of intellectual power in the United States, surpasses that of any part of Europe," although "the range is not, in general, so great, either above or below the horizontal line." His concluding statement became a standard line of defense for the many who spoke on behalf of the American culture: "to prove to the world, that the best patronage of religion, science, literature, and the arts, of whatever the mind can achieve, is SELF GOVERNMENT."

James, Henry, Sr. CHRISTIANITY THE LOGIC OF CREATION. New York: D. Appleton, 1857.

Many of the ideas in this volume were originally contained in letters to John Garth Wilkinson, who introduced James to the ideas of Swedenborg. Although James acknowledged his indebtedness to Swedenborg, his own ideas were often quite original. He accepted the existence of the creator; what he sought was the meaning of creation. He distinguished between a false and showy self-hood--of which he accused the transcendentalists--and a true selfhood--which comes from God alone, including the acknowledgment of oneself as a kind of collective spiritual being that encompasses society.

_____. HENRY JAMES, SENIOR: A SELECTION OF HIS WRITINGS. Ed. Giles Gunn. Chicago: American Library Association, 1974.

This collection includes essays on Carlyle, Emerson, William James, and Henry James, Jr.

_____. LECTURES AND MISCELLANIES. New York: Redfield, 1850.

The six lectures and ten "Miscellanies" in this volume provide a

fairly comprehensive view of James's radical and sometimes complex
philosophy. In particular, they explain his peculiar antinomianism
which is given a secular form. He perceives political democracy
as an expression of faith in human nature. In the ideal society,
every man will freely abolish private differences and observe a
golden rule, so law, government, and other forms of compulsion
will disappear.

_____. THE LITERARY REMAINS OF THE LATE HENRY JAMES. Ed. with
Introd. William James. Boston: Houghton Mifflin, 1884.

In these pieces, Henry James, Sr., expounds his views of morality
and religion as merely means to an end. Both nature and society
are aspects of God. Nature represents unregenerate man; society,
man redeemed. Nature points toward man's moral and religious
consciousness; society points away from it. In his introduction
William James, while not agreeing with his father, acknowledged
the profundity of his ideas, writing that "The accord of moralism
and religion is superficial; their discord radical. Only the deepest
thinkers on both sides see that one must go."

_____. THE SOCIAL SIGNIFICANCE OF OUR INSTITUTIONS: AN ORATION
DELIVERED BY REQUEST OF THE CITIZENS OF NEWPORT, R.I., JULY 4,
1861. Boston: Ticknor and Fields, 1861.

Considered by most critics to be the most eloquent and dramatic
expression of James's philosophy of democracy, this represents the
United States as a nation in which the supreme task must be the
achievement of a collective democracy in which all men are sacred
as members of the spiritual union of mankind.

_____. SOCIETY THE REDEEMED FORM OF MAN, AND THE EARNEST OF
GOD'S OMNIPOTENCE IN HUMAN NATURE. Boston: Houghton, Osgood,
1879.

In this late work, James reiterates his conviction that in moving
out of the formative and into the redemptive phase of its process,
creation pivots on the consciousness of self--or morality--and the
conscience--or religion. Ultimately, however, morality and religion have no positive place in the redemptive process. They are
merely agents to wean men away from the false selfhood of the
formative process. In this work, also, James speaks of his own
"conversion" in terms that suggest the same experience of his two
sons.

Ladd, George Trumbull. THE ELEMENTS OF PHYSIOLOGICAL PSYCHOLOGY.
1887; New York: Scribner's, 1911.

A student of Noah Porter, who had been influenced by both the
German and the Scottish philosophers, Ladd was a leader in the
introduction of modern physiological psychology into America. He

attempted to link intellectual processes to observable physical events. He was, however, primarily interested in using these processes to make better Christian citizens; that is, to defend the church and the established moral and social order.

McCosh, James. HERBERT SPENCER'S PHILOSOPHY AS CULMINATED IN HIS ETHICS. New York: Scribner's, 1885.

In this volume and in THE RELIGIOUS ASPECT OF EVOLUTION (below), James McCosh used Darwinism to support his own Calvinistic belief in special providences. Natural selection was the same as Divine election: "Supernatural design produces natural selection." He criticized the uniformitarianism and mechanism of Spencer and other positivists.

_____. PSYCHOLOGY, THE COGNITIVE POWERS. New York: Scribner's, 1886.

This is one of the early influential texts expounding the "mental philosophy" which laid important groundwork for psychology.

_____. THE REALISTIC PHILOSOPHY. 2 vols. New York: Scribner's, 1887-90.

McCosh believed that the rational system of Scottish realism could help prevent the extremes of idealism and agnosticism. He called for a "genuine American philosophy," and argued that the most appropriate would be a brand of the Scottish common-sense school.

_____. THE RELIGIOUS ASPECT OF EVOLUTION. New York: G.P. Putnam's, 1888.

See annotation on HERBERT SPENCER'S PHILOSOPHY (above).

_____. THE SCOTTISH PHILOSOPHY, BIOGRAPHICAL, EXPOSITORY, CRITICAL, FROM HUTCHINSON TO HAMILTON. New York: R. Carter & Bros., 1875.

This is a clear, coherent introduction for Americans to the Scottish realistic philosophy.

Mahan, Asa. DOCTRINE OF THE WILL. Oberlin, Ohio: R.E. Gillet, 1845.

Mahan, who was president of Oberlin College, coupled an argument for freedom of will with a plea to analyze "the religious affections." This work, and others such as those by Noah Porter, approached philosophical problems with introspection, what they called a "mental philosophy," which helped to create the new "science" of psychology.

Marsh, James. COLERIDGE'S AMERICAN DISCIPLES: THE SELECTED CORRES-
PONDENCE OF JAMES MARSH. Ed. John J. Duffy. Amherst: Univ. of
Massachusetts Press, 1973. Index.

In his excellent introduction, the editor argues that Marsh's letters
"help to elucidate certain lines of continuity within American culture during the first third of the nineteenth century." He suggests
that they illuminate the tension between the Puritan mind and the
Romantic revolution.

_____. THE REMAINS OF THE REV. JAMES MARSH. Ed. Joseph Torrey.
Boston: Crocker and Brewster, 1843.

Marsh, a professor of classics at the University of Vermont, was
responsible for introducing Coleridge to the United States. His
American edition of Coleridge's AIDS TO REFLECTION contained
a long introduction and copious notes, which affected the curricu-
lum and the methods of instruction at the University of Vermont.
In these papers, Marsh expounded his interest in the philosophy of
life as a creative process, in a sense preaching the spiritual art
of reflection as an educated form of spirituality which gave a new
"inner" meaning to the old Puritan doctrine of redemption.

Morris, George Sylvester. PHILOSOPHY AND CHRISTIANITY. New York:
R. Carter, 1883.

Morris studied in Germany and taught at both Johns Hopkins and
Michigan. He attempted to put philosophy on a scientific basis,
arguing that the science of mind can be assimilated to the science
of other natural forms of energy. He is founder of the school of
"Dynamic Idealism." He also made accessible to English readers
the principal German philosophers, publishing a translation and interpretation of Kant's CRITIQUE OF PURE REASON (1886) and of Hegel
in HEGEL'S PHILOSOPHY OF THE STATE AND OF HISTORY (1887).

Peirce, Charles Sanders. COLLECTED PAPERS OF CHARLES SANDERS PEIRCE.
6 vols. Ed. Charles Hartshorne and Paul Weiss. Cambridge, Mass.: Harvard
Univ. Press, 1931-1935.

Although Peirce's papers were not collected during his lifetime,
he was a major influence upon late nineteenth- and twentieth-
century philosophy. His influence has increased since his death in
1914. Two highly influential papers were "The Fixation of Belief,"
and "How to Make our Ideas Clear," which were published in THE
POPULAR SCIENCE MONTHLY in 1877. In the first paper, Peirce
argues that man is forced into thinking by the discomfort of doubt.
Belief is to be defined as whatever will administer relief. In the
second, Peirce argues that only through action can concepts be
applied to existence, and only through such application can concepts
be given meaning. Concepts are thus not merely reflections of an
external reality: they are logical instruments for an active exploration of a world which can be known only through living. Elsewhere,

Peirce asserted several propositions which are fundamental to pragmatism, including the idea that experimental verification is based
on faith in an agreement among observers and that universals held
by the community of knowers constitute reality and truth.

Porter, Noah. THE HUMAN INTELLECT. New York: Scribner's, 1868.

Porter's many philosophy texts were comprehensive, clear, systematic, and preeminent for a whole generation. He combined German
idealism with "common sense" and scientific objectivity. The
volume above represents one of the best accounts of the "mental
philosophy" which was so important in America between 1830 and
1860. As a guide to the student, the text is printed in three
different type sizes. In the largest, Porter presents the views of
various British and German psychological theorists. In the inter-
mediate type, he gives a critical examination of these theories.
In the small type, he presents his original contributions.

Royce, Josiah. THE CONCEPTION OF GOD. New York: Macmillan, 1897.

Originally given as an address before the Philosophic Union of
California in 1895, this work approaches experiential proof of the
reality of the Absolute. One of the foremost of the Absolute
Idealists, Royce argues that we attempt to refer each experienced
fragment to some more organized whole of experience. To talk of
any real fact indicated by each fragmentary experience is to af-
firm the existence of an Absolute Reality and an Absolute Experience.

_____. THE PHILOSOPHY OF LOYALTY. New York: Macmillan, 1908.

In this volume, Royce argues that the individual must be devoted
to the concept of loyalty. Loyalty itself, regardless of the causes
of devotion, is a supreme good. One thus avoids the inevitable
conflict of loyalties and comes into a closer relation with the Absolute, whether that be God, Idea, or the Ideal Community.

_____. THE PROBLEM OF CHRISTIANITY. 2 vols. 1913; Chicago: Univ.
of Chicago Press, 1968.

Royce argues that if knowledge is social, then reality must be social. The world is a self-interpreting community of individuals;
however, the particular forms of space and time to which we are
limited should not be attributed to the structure of the whole. Although Christian churches as they exist do not represent a true community, "Great Community" does exist and is real because it is the
eternal moral basis of order.

_____. THE RELIGIOUS ASPECTS OF PHILOSOPHY. Boston: Houghton Mif-
flin, 1885.

Royce's first major work of philosophy, this is a dialectical explora-

tion of pessimism and skepticism searching for a universal principle
to serve as a guide for action in the morality of harmony. Pessimism, caused by moral conflict, exists to promote the good of moral
peace. Skepticism is not only a privilege but a duty. The study
of diversity produced by doubt, however, leads to the certainty of
inner unity. To admit the possibility of finite error implies absolute truth. If error is actual, then so must the Infinite Judge
be actual. Although Royce does not shift from the basic premises
of this volume, he does tighten the structure of his arguments by
studying mathematical logic. In later volumes, he also shifts from
the dualistic problem of knowledge (that is, idea and object, purpose and goal) to the problems of communications and interpretations (that is, language and the social use of symbols). He also
attempts to apply his dialectical arguments to ethics, science, and
politics.

_____. THE SPIRIT OF MODERN PHILOSOPHY. Boston: Houghton Mifflin,
1892.

In this volume, Royce shows himself to be an admirer of Darwin
but not of Spencer. He objected to the utilitarian aspects of the
latter's ideas. Royce attempts to link idealism and evolution by
showing that the nineteenth-century view of society's development
throughout history reveals an organic process which is part of a
whole; it links the present and the past, the natural with the human
world. Each of us is an inner self, but the "inner self is through
and through an appeal to a larger self." Every statement of natural science and of cultural organicism implies the existence of an
Absolute Self. Royce admits, however, the need for a synthesis
between the conclusions of evolution and the conclusions of metaphysics.

_____. STUDIES OF GOOD AND EVIL. New York: D. Appleton, 1898.

In this collection, Royce employs a dialectical system which re-
solves the seeming contradictions of good and evil into an encom-
passing affirmative synthesis. Evil exists to be hated but to be over-
come and condemned.

_____. THE WORLD AND THE INDIVIDUAL. 2 vols. New York: Macmil-
lan, 1900-1901.

This is a collection of Royce's Gifford Lectures, delivered in 1899
and 1900. Royce emphasizes the voluntary and active aspects of
absolute idealism. He makes room for individual purpose and
choice, just as he lays stress on the individual's appreciative capac-
ities and values. Royce's distinction for the cultural and literary
scholar lies in his giving an answer to some of the problems of the
individual in American society. He attempts to restore an individual's sense of purpose which has been threatened both by Darwinism and by the increasing complexities of industrialized society.

Santayana, George. THE SENSE OF BEAUTY: BEING THE OUTLINES OF AESTHETIC THEORY. 1896; New York: Random House, 1955.

The modern library edition of 1955 by Random House contains a useful foreword and introduction. Although this is Santayana's only significant publication before 1900, his response to nineteenth-century thought in both his critical works and his own ideas is important. In SENSE OF BEAUTY, Santayana presents his definition of beauty as the feeling of pleasure objectified. This objectification makes the feeling appear as an essential quality (beauty) of the thing being perceived. His poetic rhetoric, in this work and others, gives considerable literary value to his philosophical statements.

Schurman, Jacob Gould. KANTIAN ETHICS AND THE ETHICS OF EVOLU-TION. London: Hibbert Trustees, 1882.

Head of the Sage School of Philosophy at Cornell and later president of the university, Schurman also founded the PHILOSOPHICAL REVIEW in 1892. He developed the idea that critical idealism was especially significant for America since she is destined to be a mediator among nations. He also conceived philosophy's chief function to be to mediate between science and art. In this critical study of the ethics of Mill, Hamilton, Kant, and Spencer, he concludes that the ethics of evolution adds to hedonistic systems by emphasizing "the gradual development of moral notions, feelings, and beliefs." He also insisted upon distinguishing between science and speculation in the application of Darwinism to morals.

Snider, Denton Jacques. PSYCHOLOGY AND THE PSYCHOSIS. St. Louis: Sigma Publishing Co., 1896.

An associate of William T. Harris, and co-founder of the St. Louis Philosophical Society and the JOURNAL OF SPECULATIVE PHILOS-OPHY, Snider modified the Hegelian dialectic to a system which he called "Universal Psychology." His more significant work on the dialectic of American history was published after 1900.

Stallo, Johann Bernhard. THE CONCEPTS AND THEORIES OF MODERN PHYSICS. 1881; Cambridge, Mass.: Belknap Press, Harvard Univ. Press, 1960.

In this volume, Stallo repudiated much of his earlier study (below), expounding a more naturalistic system and a theory of physical relativism. "Thought," he wrote, "deals not with things as they are, or are supposed to be, in themselves, but with our mental representations of them."

_____. GENERAL PRINCIPLES OF THE PHILOSOPHY OF NATURE. Boston: W. Crosby and H.P. Nichols, 1848.

This was the first attempt to propogate in America the idealistic German NATURPHILOSOPHIE as a philosophy of science. It is an exposition of the Schelling, Hegel, and Oken philosophies of nature.

Wright, Chauncey. THE LETTERS OF CHAUNCEY WRIGHT. Collected by James Bradley Thayer. Cambridge, Mass.: J. Wilson, 1878.

Wright lived in Cambridge as a mathematician and a freelance journalist and was a member of "The Metaphysical Club" along with Charles S. Peirce and William James. The LETTERS, which include correspondence with Darwin, are an important source of his ideas. He faced Darwinism as purely scientific and made no attempt to reconcile it with theology. Wright pointed out that although he had focused upon scientific speculations, theological activities were also important.

_____. PHILOSOPHICAL DISCUSSIONS. Collected by Charles Eliot Norton. New York: H. Holt, 1877.

Of these collected papers, the most important is "Evolution of Self-Consciousness," which appeared in THE NORTH AMERICAN REVIEW in 1873. It is a study of the evolution of scientific thinking. Wright gives a naturalistic account with self-consciousness originating as a comprehensible extension of the biological powers of sensation and memory. He was one of the first in America to assert that the nonbeliever can be as much concerned with morality and civilization as the theist. Many of his ideas led to pragmatism.

_____. PHILOSOPHICAL WRITINGS: REPRESENTATIVE SELECTIONS. Ed. with Introd. Edward H. Madden. New York: Liberal Arts Press, 1958.

See annotation above.

d. Science, Natural History, and Nature Writing

Abbott, Charles Conrad. CLEAR SKIES AND CLOUDY. Philadelphia: Lippincott, 1899.

Abbott, a naturalist and archaeologist, contributed his nature essays to popular periodicals. This book and most of the volumes below are collections of these essays. Several of them have excellent illustrations. Abbott's style was influenced by Thoreau, whom Abbott admired, but it lacks Thoreau's concrete imagery and rhetorical skill.

_____. DAYS OUT OF DOORS. New York: D. Appleton, 1890.

_____. FREEDOM OF THE FIELDS. Philadelphia: Lippincott, 1898.

Many of the essays in this volume have titles reminiscent of Thoreau--for example, "Winter," "Company and Solitude," "Indian Summer."

_____. A NATURALIST'S RAMBLES ABOUT HOME. New York: D. Appleton, 1889.

_____. NOTES OF THE NIGHT, AND OTHER OUTDOOR SKETCHES. New York: Century, 1896.

This volume is particularly interesting because it contains an excellent and perceptive essay on Thoreau. Abbott counters the views of Thoreau eulogized by Emerson and Lowell, praising Thoreau for his rejection of the formalities of civilization, for his valuing ordinary labor, and for his forceful style. "Thoreau always said more than he meant," Abbott wrote, "knowing that, if he did not, his meaning would not reach home."

_____. OUTINGS AT ODD TIMES. New York: D. Appleton, 1890.

_____. PRIMITIVE INDUSTRY; OR, ILLUSTRATIONS OF THE HANDIWORK . . . OF THE NORTHERN ATLANTIC SEABORD OF AMERICA. Salem, Mass.: G.A. Bates, 1881.

This cultural description of the American Indians on the Atlantic seaboard is Abbott's most important contribution to American archaeology. Because of his interest in archaeology, Abbott worked on occasion with the Museum of Science and Art at the University of Pennsylvania.

_____. RECENT ARCHAEOLOGICAL EXPLORATIONS IN THE VALLEY OF THE DELAWARE. Boston: Ginn and Co., 1892.

_____. RECENT RAMBLES; OR, IN TOUCH WITH NATURE. Philadelphia: Lippincott, 1894.

_____. TRAVELS IN A TREE TOP. Philadelphia: Lippincott, 1894.

Agassiz, Louis. CONTRIBUTIONS TO THE NATURAL HISTORY OF THE UNITED STATES OF AMERICA. 4 vols. Boston: Little, Brown, 1857-62.

In his biographical study of Agassiz (p. 169), Edward Lurie notes that Agassiz's methodology helped lay the foundations for modern empirical science: "Possessed by universal compulsions, he taught men to appreciate specialized knowledge and impressed society with the need to support science and advance the professional status of its practitioners." Agassiz planned these volumes as an "American contribution to science" which would increase "the love of nature" among the people in this country. Although he had projected ten volumes, Agassiz died before his monumental work could be completed. It remains a landmark in zoology and biology.

_____. ESSAY ON CLASSIFICATION. 1857. Ed. with notes by Edward Lurie. Cambridge, Mass.: Harvard Univ. Press, 1962.

This work originally formed the major portion of CONTRIBUTIONS, volume 2. Agassiz constructs a system of classification based on the methods of the French naturalist, Baron Cuvier. In the process, Agassiz analyzes other taxonomies; therefore, the work presents an excellent survey of zoology at the time. He introduces laboratory methods to zoology, encouraging naturalists to explore internal functioning and animal behavior as well as external mannerisms. Although Agassiz's observations and descriptions are accurate and still useful, he opposed Darwin, insisting that the diversity of species resulted from creations by God after succeeding cataclysms and that the species, being the thoughts of God, were immutable.

_____. METHODS OF STUDY IN NATURAL HISTORY. Boston: Ticknor and Fields, 1863.

Probably the most popular of Agassiz's works, this volume consists of lectures delivered at the Lowell Institute in 1861-62 and first published as a series in the ATLANTIC MONTHLY in 1862. Agassiz sketched the history of natural science and praised those whose systems of classification affirmed the coherence and plan of the universe. He attacked Darwin's ideas, stated that "this theory is opposed to the processes of Nature," and gave arguments which were enthusiastically adopted by religious and political leaders opposed to the theory of evolution.

Bolles, Frank. LAND OF THE LINGERING SNOW: CHRONICLES OF A STROLLER IN NEW ENGLAND FROM JANUARY TO JUNE. Boston: Houghton Mifflin, 1891.

Bolles was a friend of James Russell Lowell, who suggested he publish these pieces. They are simple and appreciative, focusing attention on birds, trees, and other natural objects. The observations are not profound but, in their simplicity and directness, represent the era's better nature essays.

Brace, Charles Loring. THE RACES OF THE OLD WORLD: A MANUAL OF ETHNOLOGY. New York: Scribner's, 1863.

Brace was a pioneer in the development of social services in New York City. Distressed by the racism which he saw, Brace studied racial theories and prepared a synthesis of the best available works in the field. Published in the same year as the Emancipation Proclamation, this work countered the arguments of the radical Southerners for the inherent superiority of whites over blacks by presenting scientific evidence--including Darwin's theory of natural selection --against the separate origin of races. It was a significant study in ethnology and also as a resource for the abolitionists.

Cooper, Susan Fenimore. RURAL HOURS. 1850; 1887. Introd. David Jones. Syracuse, N.Y.: Syracuse Univ. Press, 1968.

First published anonymously as the work of "A Lady," this nature study by James Fenimore Cooper's daughter is appreciative, thoughtful, genteel, and sentimental. Less intense and pantheistic than many of the transcendentalists, Susan Cooper is similar as she observed and found the presence of God in nature. The work provides an excellent picture of life in the Cooperstown area during the mid-nineteenth century. Structured by the passage of the seasons, RURAL HOURS contains comments upon the ways in which human beings react to nature as well as descriptions of plants, animals, and changes in the landscape. The work was popular in England and the United States, demanding several editions and revisions.

Dana, James Dwight. MANUAL OF GEOLOGY. Philadelphia: T. Bliss, 1863.

Dana taught at Yale and was a responsible editor of the AMERICAN JOURNAL OF SCIENCE during a time when some American scientists, including Louis Agassiz and Asa Gray, were engaged in a controversy about geological studies in the United States. Dana was highly respected in both Europe and the United States and, since Dana's scientific interests were not restricted to geology, this work is a classic study in the field and an important document in the history of American scientific thought. Dana shared with Agassiz a theistic view of nature, arguing that God had a prearranged design for the evolution of the organic kingdom, and it was not until the final edition of the MANUAL (1895) that he accepted Darwinism without reservation.

Draper, John William. HISTORY OF THE CONFLICT BETWEEN RELIGION AND SCIENCE. New York: D. Appleton, 1874.

Draper was a research physicist and chemist. In this work, which was widely read and was condemned by many for its attack on religion and its faith in science and technology, Draper used the term "religion" to refer primarily to Catholic authoritarianism and suppression of thought. By "science" he meant the spirit of innovation and free inquiry, and was, therefore, a somewhat biased presentation. Draper wished to promote the idea of the "sovereign state" as opposed to the "sovereign church" as the way to encourage rather than inhibit scientific thought. Although Draper, like Asa Gray (below), was willing to call natural selection the means of asserting God's "intent," he justified the abandonment of religious literal interpretation of Genesis and the idea of supernatural intervention.

Dutton, Clarence Edward. THE PHYSICAL GEOLOGY OF THE GRAND CANYON DISTRICT. Washington, D.C.: Government Printing Office, 1887.

Dutton was assigned by the U.S. Geographical and Geological Survey to do field work in the West. Wallace Stegner described Dutton's monographs as "at least half nature writing, as far from stiff geology as they can be." Dutton's descriptions of the Grand Canyon are among the best that have been written; and Muir, Burroughs, and Charles Dudley Warner borrowed from him in their own descriptions.

_____. REPORT ON THE GEOLOGY OF THE HIGH PLATEAUS OF UTAH. Washington, D.C.: Government Printing Office, 1880.

This was a partial report of the geographical and geological survey of the Rocky Mountain region.

_____. THE TERTIARY HISTORY OF THE GRAND CANYON DISTRICT. Washington, D.C.: Government Printing Office, 1882.

Julius F. Stone, who reprints a good part of this report in his CANYON COUNTRY (New York: Putnam's, 1932), writes that "Government reports are not usually classed as literature, and for a very good reason." Dutton's reports, he says, are an exception: "Few government bulletins so splendidly combine such thorough mastery of subject matter with such a felicitous literary style." Dutton achieves this effect, in part, through his accurate observations combined with sensitive imagery. His accurate descriptions are almost conversational in style, but never condescending; and he invites the reader to share with him the processes of discovery, contemplation, and classification.

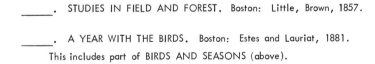

Flagg, Wilson. THE BIRDS AND SEASONS OF NEW ENGLAND. Boston: James R. Osgood, 1875.

Flagg was one of the first writers who sought to popularize natural history phenomena. Next to Burroughs, he was the most systematic and voluminous of the nature writers. He was not original; his style is ponderous and sometimes hackneyed; but he was a keen observer. He stoutly defended the natural as opposed to the artificial, and he spoke against human exploitation of nature or human attempts to "improve upon" nature. Flagg was admired by Higginson; this volume consists of essays originally published in ATLANTIC MONTHLY. Flagg was criticized by Thoreau, however, who found his style dull and sluggish.

_____. STUDIES IN FIELD AND FOREST. Boston: Little, Brown, 1857.

_____. A YEAR WITH THE BIRDS. Boston: Estes and Lauriat, 1881.

This includes part of BIRDS AND SEASONS (above).

_____. THE WOODS AND BY-WAYS OF NEW ENGLAND. Boston: James R. Osgood, 1872.

> This was reissued in 1881 as A YEAR AMONG THE TREES. It begins with a description of "the primitive forest"--the continent before the European colonists arrived. Flagg describes each species of tree in New England, gives illustrations and descriptions of the leaves, bark, and nuts or fruit, and indicates the relation of trees to the soil. He also describes seasonal variations in the forests and woods.

Gallatin, Albert. SYNOPSIS OF THE INDIAN WITHIN THE UNITED STATES EAST OF THE ROCKY MOUNTAINS AND IN THE BRITISH AND RUSSIAN POSSESSIONS IN NORTH AMERICA. New York: Bartlett and Welford, 1846.

> Gallatin was secretary of treasury under both Jefferson and Madison and minister to England under John Quincy Adams. His writings in economics made a significant contribution to American fiscal science and policy. After he retired from public life, he devoted himself to the pursuit of literature and science, and founded the American Ethnological Society in 1842. With this work, originally published in 1836 as a contribution to the TRANSACTIONS of the American Antiquarian Society, Gallatin has been credited with creating the science of American linguistics.

Gibbs, Josiah. ON THE EQUILIBRIUM OF HETEROGENEOUS SUBSTANCES. New Haven: Connecticut Academy of Arts and Sciences, 1876; 1878; also in THE SCIENTIFIC PAPERS OF J. WILLARD GIBBS, Vol. 1. London: Longmans, Green, 1906.

> Einstein termed Gibbs "the greatest mind in American history." This is Gibbs's most important contribution to physical science and a landmark in the history of American science. In it, Gibbs formulated the "phase rule" which determines the equilibrium between chemical substances present simultaneously in more than one phase (that is, liquid and gas, solid and liquid). The study is difficult for a nonscientist, but the author's summary, included with the study, is quite readable. The work influenced Henry Adams, who applied Gibbs's "phase rule" to human history.

Gibson, William Hamilton. HAPPY HUNTING GROUNDS, A TRIBUTE TO THE WOODS AND FIELDS. New York: Harper, 1887.

> Gibson, an accomplished artist, supplied his own drawings for his books. This volume and those listed below consist of essays contributed to HARPER'S, SCRIBNER'S, THE CENTURY, and other periodicals over a period of some twenty years. He achieved wide success as a popularizer of nature studies. He was not scientifically trained, but he was an acute observer; and his informal, intimate approach appealed to many readers. The interest and information given by his descriptions mitigate his sentimental overwriting; but his illustrations are better than his prose.

_____. HIGHWAYS AND BYWAYS, OR SAUNTERINGS IN NEW ENGLAND. New York: Harper, 1882.

_____. PASTORAL DAYS, OR MEMORIES OF A NEW ENGLAND YEAR. New York: Harper, 1882.

_____. SHARP EYES. New York: Harper, 1892.

_____. STROLLS BY STARLIGHT AND SUNSHINE. New York: Harper, 1891.

Godman, John D. RAMBLES OF A NATURALIST. Philadelphia: T.T. Ash, 1833.

> Godman wrote simply and clearly about various natural objects. He approached nature with scientific curiosity and wrote without sentimentality yet with a great deal of charm.

Gray, Asa. DARWINIANA: ESSAYS AND REVIEWS PERTAINING TO DARWIN. 1876. Ed. A. Hunter Dupree. Cambridge, Mass.: Belknap Press, Harvard Univ. Press, 1963.

> Considered by Darwin as one of the greatest botanists of his time, Gray became the outstanding scientific champion of Darwin's ideas and an opponent of Agassiz's non-Darwinian idealism. This work includes a review of ORIGIN OF SPECIES and several other articles by Gray which had appeared, many of them anonymously, in the ATLANTIC MONTHLY, the NATION, and other journals. The final chapter on teleology was written especially for this volume. Gray argued that natural selection was not inconsistent with natural theology, and did not exclude the doctrine of design.

_____. NATURAL SCIENCE AND RELIGION. New York: Scribner's, 1880.

> This work resulted from lectures given in New Haven to the Yale divinity students in which Gray identified himself clearly as being both an evolutionist and a theist. He surveyed scientific changes in the preceding thirty years and discussed his own views about species variation, evolution, and religion. The book both fortified the growing trend of the American Protestant clergy to find an accommodation with Darwinism and served as a starting point for the views of many liberal agnostics.

Higginson, Thomas Wentworth. OUTDOOR PAPERS. Boston: Ticknor and Fields, 1863.

> See II.C.1.a., above, for a listing and description of this and other titles by Higginson.

King, Thomas Starr. THE WHITE HILLS: THEIR LEGENDS, LANDSCAPE, AND POETRY. Boston: Estes and Lauriat, 1859.

> Unitarian minister of San Francisco, King admired William Ellery Channing, Emerson, and Thoreau. In this work, which is considered a classic of nature writing, King outlines the natural history of the White Mountains in New Hampshire and describes the scenery in vivid, concrete language. He urges people to take their time when they travel, writing "To learn to see is one of the chief objects of education and life." King's method of describing landscapes and scenery was copied by later nature writers. He also wrote some excellent descriptions of Yosemite Valley which were published in 1860-61 in the Boston EVENING TRANSCRIPT.

Lanman, Charles. LETTERS FROM THE ALLEGHENY MOUNTAINS. New York: G.P. Putnam's, 1849.

> Lanman's descriptive "summer books," largely collections of pieces which had appeared previously in magazines and journals, were popular and widely imitated. A writer, painter, and enthusiastic traveler, Lanman wrote about the wide variety of places which he visited in a style that was florid, romantic, and often trite. This collection of pieces originally published in the NATIONAL INTEL-LIGENCER is one of the better representatives of nature-travel books which were so successful in the 1840s and 1850s. Lanman describes the scenery, landmarks, and inhabitants of the mountains, including both the Cherokees and the mountain people, and re-counts amusing incidents and tales told by local people.

Marsh, George Perkins. MAN AND NATURE; OR, PHYSICAL GEOGRAPHY AS MODIFIED BY HUMAN ACTION. 1864. Revised as THE EARTH AS MODIFIED BY HUMAN ACTION, 1874; St. Clair Shores, Mich.: Scholarly Press, 1970.

> An early conservationist, Marsh argued for wilderness preservation on economic as well as aesthetic grounds. His purpose in writing was to point out the changes brought about by "human action in the physical conditions of the globe." He thought that "man has too long forgotten that the earth was given to him for usufruct alone, not for consumption, still less for profligate waste." He was aware that the frontier was important in the development of the national character which, he felt, was also affected by heredi-tary opinion, foreign relations, religious beliefs, climate and soil, modes of life, and institutional arrangements. This work is well written, interesting, and crucial in the history of American con-servationist thought.

Mitchell, Donald Grant. MY FARM AT EDGEWOOD. New York: Scribner's, 1864.

> This work consists of forty-four brief sketches describing Mitchell's farming theories and practices. The author combines knowledge of farm life with love of nature and literature, exposing the fallacies

of the pastoral ideal while remaining appreciative of the advantages of rural living. Mitchell does not mention Crevecoeur in his AMERICAN LANDS AND LETTERS (p. 50), but his sketches in this work are very similar to Crevecoeur's LETTERS FROM AN AMERICAN FARMER.

Morgan, Lewis Henry. ANCIENT SOCIETY; OR, RESEARCHES IN THE LINES OF HUMAN PROGRESS. 1877. Ed. Leslie A. White. Cambridge, Mass.: Belknap Press, Harvard Univ. Press, 1964.

Morgan, a pioneer anthropologist studying the American Indian, was a cultural evolutionist who argued that human institutions developed gradually and cumulatively with adaptation and survival as operating factors. Although the concept was greatly modified by later anthropologists, this work was, at the time of its publication, a revolutionary developmental study of primitive societies.

Schoolcraft, Henry Rowe. ALGIC RESEARCHES, COMPRISING INQUIRIES RESPECTING THE MENTAL CHARACTERISTICS OF THE NORTH AMERICAN INDIANS. 2 vols. 1839. Rev. as THE MYTH OF HIAWATHA. 1856; New York: Kraus, 1971.

In 1820, Schoolcraft accompanied General Lewis Cass as geologist in his expedition to the upper Mississippi and the Lake Superior copper region. In 1823, he was appointed government superintendent of Indian affairs for the Lake Superior country. He negotiated several treaties which ceded land to the Indians and married the granddaughter of an Indian chief. Schoolcraft published pioneering studies in both geology and ethnology. This account of Indian customs and folklore, occasionally romanticized by the author, opened a new source of materials for American literature. The relationship of Longfellow to Schoolcraft's collection has been the subject of several studies.

_____. HISTORICAL AND STATISTICAL INFORMATION RESPECTING THE HISTORY, CONDITION, AND PROSPECTS OF THE INDIAN TRIBES OF THE UNITED STATES. 6 parts. Philadelphia: J.B. Lippincott, 1851-57.

Issued under patronage of Congress and illustrated with 336 plates from original drawings, Schoolcraft wished to set down everything that could be learned about the Indians. It is a monumental study which, although unsystematic and containing some erroneous conclusions, provided the foundation for later researches.

Shaler, Nathaniel Southgate. NATURE AND MAN IN AMERICA. New York: Scribner's, 1891.

Shaler, a student of Agassiz, was professor of paleontology and geology at Harvard and director of the Atlantic Coast Division of the U.S. Geological Survey. He contributed essays to ATLANTIC, SCRIBNER'S, and was one of the first to note the geographical in-

fluences on American history. In this work--derived from a series
of Lowell Lectures and essays published in SCRIBNER'S--Shaler surveyed the geological and geographical history of North America
speculating on the relationship between climate and racial characteristics. He also argued that science need not destroy religious
faith, writing that "with each advance in our knowledge concerning
the conditions which have brought men to their present estate, we
come to a fuller sense as to the order and system that have made
men what they are."

Silliman, Benjamin. ELEMENTS OF CHEMISTRY. 2 vols. New Haven: H.
Howe, 1830-31.

Silliman was the outstanding contributor to the promotional organization of science in the United States. His lyceum lectures,
from which this volume and the one below were derived, were
extremely popular, stimulating an enthusiasm for science. In 1818,
he founded the AMERICAN JOURNAL OF SCIENCE which became
a vehicle for encouraging scientific investigation.

_____. OUTLINES OF THE COURSE OF GEOLOGICAL LECTURES, GIVEN
IN YALE COLLEGE. New Haven: H. Howe, 1829.

Silliman was a strong exponent of the reconciliation of geology
and scripture. He defended the literalness of the Biblical flood,
using geological "evidence" to support that belief. The controversy provoked by Silliman's theories about the deluge forced interested Americans to take sides, much as Darwinism created fac-
tions later in the century.

Torrey, Bradford. BIRDS IN THE BUSH. Boston: Houghton Mifflin, 1885.

Best known as the editor of Thoreau's journals, Bradford Torrey
worked in a shoe factory, briefly taught school, worked for the
American Board of Commissioners for Foreign Missions, and later
became an editor for YOUTH'S COMPANION. He was a New
Englander but traveled widely spending his last five years in California. Although Torrey was not a trained ornithologist and received no academic recognition, he was an accurate field observer contributing to the knowledge of habits and characteristics of
native American birds; he was probably the foremost authority on
hummingbirds during his lifetime. A skilled essayist, his writings
are much more than mere nature handbooks. He avoids sentimentality and excessive enthusiasm and, although not brilliantly original,
records definite experiences faithfully, simply, and with conversational intimacy. He provides his works with unity and coherence
by making his chapter headings guides to the sequences of months
or seasons.

_____. THE CLERK OF THE WOODS. Boston: Houghton Mifflin, 1893.

_____. A FLORIDA SKETCH BOOK. Boston: Houghton Mifflin, 1894.

_____. THE FOOT-PATH WAY. Boston: Houghton Mifflin, 1892.

_____. A RAMBLER'S LEASE. Boston: Houghton Mifflin, 1889.

_____. SPRING NOTES FROM TENNESSEE. Boston: Houghton Mifflin, 1896.

_____. A WORLD OF GREEN HILLS. Boston: Houghton Mifflin, 1898.

Webber, Charles Wilkins. THE HUNTER-NATURALIST. Philadelphia: Lippincott, Brambo, 1852.

> This and WILD SCENES AND SONGBIRDS, below, were the first two in a projected seven-volume study which Webber did not live to complete. Audubon's friend, Webber influenced Audubon's stylistic approach; Webber is forceful and enthusiastic, and he shows appreciation for both the vitality and the poetry of nature.

_____. WILD SCENES AND SONG BIRDS. Philadelphia: J.W. Bradley, 1852.

> This work and the one above have some fine illustrations by Webber's wife.

2. BACKGROUNDS: ANTHOLOGIES AND SECONDARY SOURCES

Addison, Daniel D. THE CLERGY IN AMERICAN LIFE AND LETTERS. New York: Macmillan, 1900.

> Addison studies the works of several American clergymen for their value "as an expression of religious life and national thought" and also for their contributions as literature. Among authors discussed are Horace Bushnell, Timothy Dwight, Theodore Parker, and Henry Ward Beecher.

Ahlstrom, Sydney E. A RELIGIOUS HISTORY OF THE AMERICAN PEOPLE. New Haven, Conn.: Yale Univ. Press, 1972. Bibliog.

> This is an enormous comprehensive survey of religious thought and religious leaders in America. The author traces both influences on and those exerted by religious figures and their writings, evaluating several important works.

Ayer, A.J. THE ORIGINS OF PRAGMATISM: STUDIES IN THE PHILOSOPHY OF CHARLES SANDERS PEIRCE AND WILLIAM JAMES. San Francisco: Freeman, Cooper, 1968.

A thorough explication of Peirce and James philosophies, this study clarifies the sometimes complex ideas of these two American philosophers.

Barbour, Brian M., ed. AMERICAN TRANSCENDENTALISM: AN ANTHOLOGY OF CRITICISM. Notre Dame, Ind.: Univ. of Notre Dame Press, 1973.

Barbour collects and reprints seventeen critical essays on the origins, characteristics, and effects of transcendentalism, including pieces by Perry Miller, H.C. Goddard, Yvor Winters, and Tony Tanner. The anthology provides an excellent critical introduction to transcendentalism; and in bringing together a number of important commentaries on the movement, it is a useful source for scholar and teacher.

Blau, Joseph L. MEN AND MOVEMENTS IN AMERICAN PHILOSOPHY. Englewood Cliffs, N.J.: Prentice-Hall, 1952.

This introductory historical survey of American philosophy traces the development of various philosophical "movements" such as pragmatism, idealism, transcendentalism and contrasts the philosophical ideas of Peirce, William James, and George Herbert Mead, within these movements. Blau neither generalizes nor oversimplifies, yet provides a thorough exposition of his topic.

Blinderman, Abraham. AMERICAN WRITERS ON EDUCATION BEFORE 1865. Boston: Twayne, 1975.

Blinderman surveys and summarizes the educational ideas of Emerson, Thoreau, Alcott, Fuller, Brownson, Ripley, and Peabody. Although occasionally overly simplistic, the account is one of the best available.

Boller, Paul F., Jr. AMERICAN TRANSCENDENTALISM, 1830-1860: AN INTELLECTUAL INQUIRY. New York: G.P. Putnam's, 1974.

The author examines transcendentalism as a religious movement, as a form of intuitional philosophy, as a way of viewing the natural order and the relation of spirit to matter, as a social reform movement, and as a gospel of cosmic optimism. He also compares the views of prominent transcendentalists. Although this intellectual overview is comprehensive, it is impressionistic; the sources are not carefully documented, and the author's conclusions are not always convincing.

Brown, Ira V. LYMAN ABBOTT, CHRISTIAN EVOLUTIONIST: A STUDY IN RELIGIOUS LIBERALISM. Cambridge, Mass.: Harvard Univ. Press, 1953. Bibliog.

Brown calls Lyman Abbott "the outstanding figure in the liberalizing movement" in American religion. Abbott, the author argues,

was an interpreter of his age. This study surveys the thought of
the time and is an interesting portrait of the liberal Christian.

Brown, Jerry W. THE RISE OF BIBLICAL CRITICISM IN AMERICA, 1800-1870:
THE NEW ENGLAND SCHOLARS. Middletown, Conn.: Wesleyan Univ. Press,
1969.

This study gives an excellent background of the religious controversy
which affected many of the nineteenth-century New England writers
before the end of the Civil War. Returning from Germany, such
New England thinkers as Edward Everett and George Bancroft sought
to transplant in America some of the critical techniques which
they had learned. The liberal thinkers "attempted to use the new
biblical studies as a destructive weapon against orthodox Calvinism."
In contrast, conservatives attempted to use biblical studies "within
the traditions of inherited Calvinism." In addition to Bancroft and
Everett, the discussion includes Andrews Norton, Theodore Parker,
Horace Bushnell, and William Ellery Channing. "Biblical studies,"
Brown writes, "occupied many of New England's best minds, and
theological battles between liberals and conservatives were waged
over questions of biblical interpretation and scholarship."

Brumm, Ursula. AMERICAN THOUGHT AND RELIGIOUS TYPOLOGY. New
Brunswick, N.J.: Rutgers Univ. Press, 1970.

Originally published in German in 1963, this study attempts "to
demonstrate how the theory and practice of symbolism in the
American classics developed out of Puritan forms of thought and
belief." Emerson is among the nineteenth-century writers considered. Like Perry Miller with whom she worked, Brumm compares and contrasts the ideas of Emerson and Edwards, finding that
"the same nature which the first Puritans found inimical and savage received by virtue of Emerson's heresy the consecration which
made it the ground of symbols and knowledge, and thus a vital
element in American literature."

Buell, Lawrence. LITERARY TRANSCENDENTALISM: STYLE AND VISION IN
THE AMERICAN RENAISSANCE. Ithaca, N.Y.: Cornell Univ. Press, 1973.

In this survey of "the literary art and criticism of the American
Transcendentalists," Buell focuses upon "the relationship between
style and vision in . . . nonfictional literature." He attempts
"through a combination of intellectual history, critical explication,
and genre study . . . to outline the nature and evolution of the
Transcendentalists' characteristic literary aims and approaches, and
the ways in which these express the authors' underlying principles
or vision." In his examination of the relationship between sub-
stance--aesthetic principles, self-examination, organic view--and
form--essay, sermon, autobiography, use of catalogue rhetoric--
Buell provides a novel perspective upon transcendentalism and a
perceptive analysis of language and structure in nonfiction prose.

162

Cameron, Kenneth Walter, ed. CONCORD HARVEST: PUBLICATIONS OF THE CONCORD SCHOOL OF PHILOSOPHY AND LITERATURE WITH NOTES ON ITS SUCCESSORS AND OTHER RESOURCES FOR RESEARCH IN EMERSON, THOREAU, ALCOTT AND THE LATER TRANSCENDENTALISTS. 2 vols. Hartford, Conn.: Transcendental Books, 1970.

> In this volume and those listed below, Cameron compiles a wide variety of resources ranging from previously unpublished manuscripts to newspaper accounts, public records, and library lists. He also outlines the history and publications of the Concord School, which was created on July 15, 1879 in the study in William Torrey Harris' home in Concord. On the school's first year's program were Bronson Alcott, Thomas W. Higginson, Emerson, and Franklin B. Sanborn. Sanborn's own history of Concord, brief biographies of those attending it, as well as pamphlets, tracts, flyers, and teaching materials produced by the school are also included.

_____. EMERSON, THOREAU, AND CONCORD IN EARLY NEWSPAPERS. Hartford, Conn.: Transcendental Books, 1958. Index.

> Here Cameron collects newspaper and magazine articles dealing with Emerson, Thoreau, or aspects of Concord life and events in which these men were or might have been involved. The amount of detailed material presented is almost overwhelming, but the reader can easily pinpoint items of interest.

_____. RESPONSE TO TRANSCENDENTAL CONCORD: THE LAST DECADES OF THE ERA OF EMERSON, THOREAU AND THE CONCORD SCHOOL AS RECORDED IN NEWSPAPERS. Hartford, Conn.: Transcendental Books, 1974.

> The reproductions of newspaper clippings for the years 1879-1887-- . reporting lectures, describing the speakers' performances, and outlining the discussions which followed--are sometimes highly interesting and useful sources; but they are difficult to read without a magnifying glass. Enlarged copies of the articles included are, however, available.

_____. TRANSCENDENTAL CLIMATE: NEW RESOURCES FOR THE STUDY OF EMERSON, THOREAU, AND THEIR CONTEMPORARIES. 3 vols. Hartford, Conn.: Transcendental Books, 1963.

> Among other source materials on transcendentalism gathered here are Emerson's treatise on Socrates, a manuscript diary of Franklin Sanborn, records of the Concord Lyceum, and Emerson's favorite songs.

_____. TRANSCENDENTAL EPILOGUE: PRIMARY MATERIALS FOR RESEARCH IN EMERSON, THOREAU, LITERARY NEW ENGLAND, THE INFLUENCE OF GERMAN THEOLOGY, AND HIGHER BIBLICAL CRITICISM. 3 vols. Hartford, Conn.: Transcendental Books, 1965.

> Materials on Emerson, Thoreau, Jones Very, Boston, New England,

the early lyceum, and Harvard University are included in these volumes, together with Franklin Sanborn's notebook and catalogues of personal libraries.

_____. TRANSCENDENTAL READING PATTERNS. Hartford, Conn.: Transcendental Books, 1970.

This volume lists the books taken from the Harvard and the Antheneum libraries by Theodore Parker, George Ripley, James Freeman Clarke, and others. It is interesting to note that shortly before Brook Farm was organized, Ripley borrowed a number of books on farming.

_____. TRANSCENDENTALISM AND AMERICAN RENAISSANCE BIBLIOGRAPHY. Hartford, Conn.: Transcendental Books, 1977.

Cameron here lists, with synopsis, the sixty-six collections of primary and secondary materials published in his previous works. Supplements have subsequently appeared in issues of the AMERICAN TRANSCENDENTAL QUARTERLY.

_____. THE TRANSCENDENTALISTS AND MINERVA: CULTURAL BACKGROUNDS OF THE AMERICAN RENAISSANCE WITH FRESH DISCOVERIES IN THE INTELLECTUAL CLIMATE OF EMERSON, ALCOTT AND THOREAU. 3 vols. Hartford, Conn.: Transcendental Books, 1958.

These volumes include a listing of Emerson's reading at Harvard, Boston, and Concord libraries, Thoreau's notes on books he read during his college years and shortly thereafter, indicating the influences upon the major transcendentalists.

Christy, Arthur. THE ORIENT IN AMERICAN TRANSCENDENTALISM: A STUDY OF EMERSON, THOREAU, AND ALCOTT. 1931; New York: Octagon Books, 1963. Appendix.

This study focuses on the Concord transcendentalists and "the literary and mystical results of Oriental influence in New England transcendentalism." The author argues that in a time of revolt from the dogma of the churches, men who "cared for the spirit" like Emerson, Thoreau and Alcott found "the catholicity of the Indian scriptures and the emphasis these books placed on inner resources" very attractive. The Oriental influence on these writers is probably overemphasized in this study, which still remains one of the best sources of information about that influence.

Clebsch, William A. FROM SACRED TO PROFANE AMERICA: THE ROLE OF RELIGION IN AMERICAN HISTORY. New York: Harper and Row, 1968.

The author organizes his discussion topically, considering religion as it affected areas of education, welfare, reform, morality, nationality, together with other aspects of American thought and action. While not directly a study of the literary figures, the work contributes to understanding the ideas of many of the nineteenth-century American nonfiction prose writers.

Conkin, Paul K. PURITANS AND PRAGMATISTS: EIGHT EMINENT AMERI-CAN THINKERS. New York: Dodd, Mead, 1968.

The eight thinkers are Edwards, Franklin, John Adams, Emerson, Peirce, William James, John Dewey, and Santayana. The author finds a common moral tenor in the thought of these men which found expression in various ways in the search for redemption and esthetic fulfillment.

Crowe, Charles. GEORGE RIPLEY: TRANSCENDENTALIST AND UTOPIAN SOCIALIST. Athens: Univ. of Georgia Press, 1967.

In this biography of Ripley, Crowe points out Ripley's intellectual ideals, his contributions to religious liberalism, and his commitment to social reform. The author feels that Ripley "went beyond Emersonian individualism to seek the social context which would provide maximum development of personality for all men." Crowe also argues that Ripley's ideal of social communion based on freedom and mutual consent led him to the Brook Farm experiment in communal living. The study gives Ripley a more significant place in the national reform activities of the 1840s than is assigned to him by most commentators.

Drachman, Julian Moses. STUDIES IN THE LITERATURE OF NATURAL SCIENCE. New York: Macmillan, 1930.

The author considers British and American literature of the nineteenth-century natural sciences, focusing upon the work's literary qualities. He makes a good case for approaching scientific writings as literature, arguing that many classics in the history of science also demonstrate expository art. The study is useful more as a model for treating the subject of scientific writings as literary analysis and evaluation than as a source of information about the writings themselves.

Dupree, A. Hunter. ASA GRAY, 1810-1888. Cambridge, Mass.: Belknap Press, Harvard Univ. Press, 1959.

The author's familiarity with botany, with the vast amount of material surrounding Darwin's evolutionary theories, among which are Gray's contributions, and with the main currents of thought in philosophy and religion make this not only a fine biography but an excellent survey of the history of science and culture in the nineteenth century.

Easton, Lloyd D. HEGEL'S FIRST AMERICAN FOLLOWERS: THE OHIO HEGELIANS: JOHN B. STALLO, PETER KAUFMANN, MONCURE CONWAY,

AND AUGUST WILLICH, WITH KEY WRITINGS. Athens: Ohio Univ. Press, 1966. Appendix.

> Organized a decade before the St. Louis group, the Ohio Hegelians were perceptive and influential. Stallo was responsible for introducing Hegel to many Americans, and Conway was an important influence upon both Emerson and Whitman. See pp. 149-50 for Stallo's work.

Ekirch, Arthur A. MAN AND NATURE IN AMERICA. New York: Columbia Univ. Press, 1963.

> The author, an historian, surveys national attitudes toward the relationship of man and nature from the early agrarian ideal, through Romantic and transcendental concepts, to modern industrialized economy. The work is polemical, urging the need for man to learn to live in harmony with nature and emphasizing the dangers of exploitation which could bring down "the whole human race in a collective mass suicide." The author considers the work and ideas of George Perkins Marsh, Emerson, Thoreau, and, more briefly, Henry Adams. The discussion of the backgrounds and influences of Marsh's work is valuable; the treatment of Emerson, Thoreau, and Adams less useful.

Fay, Jay W. AMERICAN PSYCHOLOGY BEFORE WILLIAM JAMES. New Brunswick, N.J.: Rutgers Univ. Press, 1939.

> This volume was one of the first to acknowledge that there were important psychological ideas in America prior to 1880. The author points out the importance of speculative philosophy to early psychological thought and surveys the influence of Scottish philosophy, with its emphasis upon the necessary role of consciousness in observation, and of the educators concerned with developing a "science of the mind." The work provides a good historical context for viewing the ideas of Dewey and William James.

Fleming, Donald. JOHN WILLIAM DRAPER AND THE RELIGION OF SCIENCE. Philadelphia: Univ. of Pennsylvania Press, 1950.

> The author sees Draper as an expositor who made accessible to the popular mind the controversies and scientific developments of the nineteenth century. "His work," Fleming writes, "is . . . an excellent case-history of the way in which innovations are knit up into continuity with tradition, and revolutions in thought made palatable."

Foerster, Norman. NATURE IN AMERICAN LITERATURE: STUDIES IN THE MODERN VIEW OF NATURE. New York: Macmillan, 1923.

> Foerster treats the attitudes toward nature of a number of nineteenth-century writers from Bryant to Burroughs; he includes Emerson, Thoreau, Lowell, and Muir and notes that most major American writers,

from the beginnings of the nineteenth century on, have displayed both curiosity about and devotion to nature. He also studies their interest in nature in relation to the classical and Christian traditions which preceded it.

Fox, Stephen. JOHN MUIR AND HIS LEGACY: THE AMERICAN CONSERVATION MOVEMENT. Boston: Little, Brown, 1981.

The author discusses Muir's philosophy of preserving nature for its moral or spiritual values and the conflict of Muir and his followers with conservationists such as Gifford Pinchot, who viewed nature as a resource for humanity.

Fuss, Peter L. THE MORAL PHILOSOPHY OF JOSIAH ROYCE. Cambridge, Mass.: Harvard Univ. Press, 1965.

The author focuses on Royce's ethical theory, arguing that if it is separated from his metaphysical absolutism, it is intelligible and coherent. This study clarifies Royce's social and moral philosophy and its applicability to actual social situations. It thus lucidly outlines those concepts of Royce which have had the most telling impact upon American thought.

Gaustad, Edwin S. A RELIGIOUS HISTORY OF AMERICA. New York: Harper and Row, 1966.

In this comprehensive history, the author documents the important role of religion in America's education, culture, and development. His chapters include excerpts from significant or representative speeches, journals, and other records by leaders in religious, social, and political movements, including utopianism, transcendentalism, and manifest destiny.

_____. RELIGIOUS ISSUES IN AMERICAN HISTORY. New York: Harper and Row, 1968.

The author argues that "religious conflict has been an integral part of the American scene." Here he collects essays by Emerson, Horace Bushnell, Lyman Beecher, William Ellery Channing, and Lyman Abbot in order to present what he calls "major cultural shifts" or "pivotal choices" in the history of religion in America which have interested and involved "the larger community."

Goddard, Harold Clarke. STUDIES IN NEW ENGLAND TRANSCENDENTALISM. 1908; New York: Hillary House, 1960.

Goddard was the first of many critics to note that New England transcendentalism was a blending of idealistic, Platonic metaphysics, European romanticism, and American puritanism. This early study remains one of the best.

Herbst, Jurgen. THE GERMAN HISTORICAL SCHOOL IN AMERICAN SCHOL-
ARSHIP: A STUDY IN THE TRANSFER OF CULTURE. Ithaca, N.Y.: Cornell
Univ. Press, 1965.

> The author investigates "the rise and decline of the German his-
> torical school of social science in the United States between the
> founding of the Johns Hopkins University in 1876 and the out-
> break of war in Europe in 1914." The study encompasses educa-
> tion, literature, philosophy, and historiography in its attempt to
> trace the influences of men who were trained in Germany and
> returned to the United States to teach in the universities and to
> determine just when and how the German concepts appear in
> American educational history.

Hicks, Philip M. THE DEVELOPMENT OF THE NATURAL HISTORY ESSAY
IN AMERICAN LITERATURE. Philadelphia: Univ. of Pennsylvania Press, 1924.

> Hicks focuses upon "the extent to which the facts of natural history
> have been made the basis of literary treatment in essay form."
> He briefly surveys the early literature, then focuses upon the nine-
> teenth and early twentieth centuries, giving major treatment to
> Burroughs, Emerson, and Thoreau. Other nineteenth-century writ-
> ers discussed are Audubon, Hawthorne, N.P. Willis, Alexander
> Wilson, Wilson Flagg, T.W. Higginson, Lowell, C.D. Warner,
> Donald G. Mitchell, and Gail Hamilton.

Howe, Daniel Walker. THE UNITARIAN CONSCIENCE: HARVARD MORAL
PHILOSOPHY, 1805-1861. Cambridge, Mass.: Harvard Univ. Press, 1970.

> The author includes Edward T. Channing, Andrews Norton, and
> William Ellery Channing in his study of twelve "Unitarian moral-
> ists" of the Harvard school, some of whom were professors at Har-
> vard and some who were ministers trained at Harvard. In their
> defenses of the Unitarian doctrine, these men marked a significant
> transition in American Christianity.

Hutchison, William R. THE TRANSCENDENTALIST MINISTERS: CHURCH RE-
FORM IN THE NEW ENGLAND RENAISSANCE. New Haven, Conn.: Yale
Univ. Press, 1959.

> The purpose of this work is "to find out what the members of the
> Concord group did and said as Christian ministers and also to re-
> assess the traditional account of the controversy in which they be-
> came involved." Hutchison concentrates on Theodore Parker,
> Andrews Norton, and the theological backgrounds of transcenden-
> talism, finding that the transcendentalists, while at odds with the
> early Unitarian conservatives, contributed a great deal to the more
> liberal form which Unitarianism later assumed.

Huth, Hans. NATURE AND THE AMERICAN: THREE CENTURIES OF CHANG-
ING ATTITUDES. 1957; Lincoln: Univ. of Nebraska Press, 1972. Bibliog.

In this study, Huth presents the development of attitudes, from the Puritans to the Roosevelt era, which led to the conservation movement in the United States. He argues that the nineteenth-century writer, painter, and scientist came to regard as a vocation the study and expression of nature. Excerpts from nineteenth-century essays and sketches indicate writers' attitudes, from the near-pantheism of the transcendentalists to the more utilitarian view of the urban gentleman. This comprehensive survey of views and expressions of nature touches upon many of the nineteenth-century nonfiction prose writers.

Koster, Donald. TRANSCENDENTALISM IN AMERICA. Boston: Twayne, 1975.

This is a short (97 p.) introductory survey which outlines the main events of transcendentalism--its leading ideas, literary qualities, reception, and influences--and discusses its major proponents. Although it covers the topic and presents various aspects of transcendentalism in a general way, the study is less than satisfactory for the serious scholar because the treatment of the subject is so brief and the sources cited not always reliable.

Kuklick, Bruce. THE RISE OF AMERICAN PHILOSOPHY: CAMBRIDGE, MASSACHUSETTS, 1860-1930. New Haven, Conn.: Yale Univ. Press, 1977.

Among those studied in this volume are William James, Peirce, Josiah Royce, and Santayana. This is an informative guide to the intellectual currents of the late nineteenth century.

Leighton, Walter L. FRENCH PHILOSOPHERS AND NEW-ENGLAND TRANS-CENDENTALISTS. 1908; Westport, Conn.: Greenwood Press, 1968.

Leighton discusses the influence of Cousin, Jouffroy, and Fourier on Ripley, Emerson, Fuller, and Alcott, maintaining that while the ideas of the French philosophers were not predominant, they were widely read and appreciated by the transcendentalists. He points out that the transcendentalists and the French philosophers did have similar precursors in the Vedas and in Plato, Pythagoras, Kant, and Hegel.

Lurie, Edward. LOUIS AGASSIZ: A LIFE IN SCIENCE. Chicago: Univ. of Chicago Press, 1960.

This biography outlines Agassiz's career, describes his accomplishments, and presents a comprehensive survey of the state of the biological sciences in the late nineteenth century. Agassiz's association with Emerson, William James, Asa Gray, and others is also discussed.

Madden, Edward H. CHAUNCEY WRIGHT AND THE FOUNDATIONS OF PRAGMATISM. Seattle: Univ. of Washington Press, 1963.

The author sees Wright as a pivotal figure in American philosophy and "the first in the series of technically proficient and original philosophers." Wright's philosophy and writings are clearly explained, and a useful selected bibliography of related writings and commentaries is included in this volume.

_____. CIVIL DISOBEDIENCE AND MORAL LAW IN NINETEENTH-CENTURY AMERICAN PHILOSOPHY. Seattle: Univ. of Washington Press, 1968.

In this study of some of the influential but relatively unknown academicians, such as Asa Mahan, Francis Wayland, Noah Porter, James Bradley Thayer, and George W. Curtis, Madden focuses upon "the conflict between intuitionistic and utilitarian interpretations of what constitutes moral law, and . . . the conflict between different attitudes toward reform in general and abolitionism in particular."

Meisel, Max. BIBLIOGRAPHY OF AMERICAN NATURAL HISTORY. 3 vols. Brooklyn, N.Y.: Premier Publishing Co., 1924-29.

This lists the relevant scientific titles published in America from 1765 to 1865, with some brief annotations.

Monroe, Will Seymour. HISTORY OF THE PESTALOZZIAN MOVEMENT IN THE UNITED STATES. Syracuse, N.Y.: C.W. Bardeen, 1907.

Introduced into the United States around 1853, Pestalozzi's ideas affected many nineteenth-century essayists as well as educators. Pestalozzi's commitment to moral education, to the idea of education as preparation for life, and to the schools as an instrument of society rather than an instrument of the church is reflected in the writings of Alcott, Emerson, Bancroft, Horace Mann, and John Dewey. This study provides an informative survey of the influence of the movement.

Moore, Edward C. AMERICAN PRAGMATISM: PEIRCE, JAMES AND DEWEY. New York: Columbia Univ. Press, 1961.

The author examines basic concepts in the three writers: Peirce's theory of reality, James's notion of truth, and Dewey's concept of the good. Although narrowly focused, the book clarifies the basic doctrines of pragmatism.

Morrison, Theodore. CHAUTAUQUA: A CENTER FOR EDUCATION, RELIGION AND THE ARTS IN AMERICA. Chicago: Univ. of Chicago Press, 1974.

This volume explores the hundred-year history of the institution which helped to form a part of American cultural history. It describes the original Chautauqua in southwestern New York state and tells how it became a summer center for a wide variety of activities. This is an attractive book, with many photographs, designed to interest and inform the general reader.

Mosier, Richard David. MAKING THE AMERICAN MIND: SOCIAL AND MORAL IDEAS IN THE McGUFFEY READERS. New York: Kings' Crown Press, 1947.

> The author's premise is that the readers both reflected and affected American culture. He argues that "a study of the main currents of thought in the McGuffey readers may legitimately hope to embrace some of the ideas which lie at the heart of American civilization." He concludes that the influential READERS were a manifestation of traditions underlying American culture from its beginnings, with political concepts derived from Locke, Webster, and others; theological concepts from Calvin and the middle-class Protestant ethic; and humanitarian concerns from a broad Judeo-Christian tradition.

Muelder, Walter G., et al., eds. THE DEVELOPMENT OF AMERICAN PHILOSOPHY: A BOOK OF READINGS. 2nd ed. Boston: Houghton Mifflin, 1960.

> The introductions to the selections in this anthology of American philosophical writings provide an excellent survey and background for understanding the ideas of the major American philosophers.

Mulder, William, and A. Russell Mortenson, eds. AMONG THE MORMONS: HISTORIC ACCOUNTS BY CONTEMPORARY OBSERVERS. 1958; Lincoln: Univ. of Nebraska Press, 1973.

> This volume collects comments upon the Mormons by early contemporaries and later observers who were friends, advocates, enemies, or simply curiosity seekers. The short pieces and excerpts are arranged chronologically and, with the connective notes by the editors, provide a view of the Latter Day Saints from the 1830s to the 1940s.

Nash, Roderick. WILDERNESS AND THE AMERICAN MIND. 1967. Rev. ed. New Haven, Conn.: Yale Univ. Press, 1973.

> Nash delineates and interprets "the changing American conception of wilderness." Beginning with a look at primitive fears of wilderness and Old World opinions, the author examines American attitudes from colonial days to (in the revised edition) the growing ecological consciousness of the early 1970s. Of the nineteenth century, Nash observes that Romanticism helped to promote a more favorable attitude, allowing Americans to regard wilderness as a unique characteristic of the New World and an asset rather than a liability. Among the nineteenth-century literary figures discussed are Bryant, Cooper, and Thoreau. The author also outlines the contributions of Audubon, Muir, and Parkman. This superb study provides a solid historical and cultural context for understanding the views of the wilderness which appear in nineteenth-century literature.

Osborne, Henry F. IMPRESSIONS OF GREAT NATURALISTS. New York: Scribner's, 1924.

> Osborne knew many of the nineteenth-century American and British natural scientists whom he discusses here in his rambling and, as the title indicates, impressionistic accounts. Of particular interest to the student of American literature is a chapter comparing Burroughs and Muir. Osborne also has a brief eulogistic chapter on Theodore Roosevelt as a naturalist.

Owings, Loren C., ed. ENVIRONMENTAL VALUES, 1860-1972: A GUIDE TO INFORMATION SOURCES. Man and the Environment Information Guide Series, vol. 4. Detroit: Gale Research Co., 1976. 324 p.

> The portions of this guide which are devoted to travel literature (chapter 2), American nature writing (chapter 7), and nature study (chapter 8) provide valuable listings, with excellent annotations, of primary and secondary material in these areas.

Persons, Stowe, ed. EVOLUTIONARY THOUGHT IN AMERICA. 1950; New York: George Braziller, 1956.

> Several of these pieces, originally delivered as lectures for the Princeton American Civilization Program, deal with nineteenth-century prose. The focus is upon the relationship of evolution to theories of nature, to American literature, and to moral theory. Three of the pieces--"Evolution in Its Relation to the Philosophy of Nature and the Philosophy of Culture," by F.S.C. Northrop; "The Influence of Evolutionary Theory upon American Psychological Thought," by Edwin G. Boring; and "Naturalism in American Literature," by Malcolm Cowley--provide particularly useful backgrounds and insights.

Pochmann, Henry A. GERMAN CULTURE IN AMERICA: PHILOSOPHICAL AND LITERARY INFLUENCES, 1600-1900. Madison: Univ. of Wisconsin Press, 1957.

> This is one of the best and most comprehensive studies of German thought in America, focusing upon the philosophical, political, religious, literary, and artistic ideas which have affected American culture. Of the influences in the nineteenth century which the author has considered are the effects of German thought upon American scholarship, including biblical and historical studies, upon New England Transcendentalism, upon the St. Louis Hegelians, and upon theology and philosophy in the major universities, as well as the German influence upon American poetry, fiction, and literary criticism.

_____. NEW ENGLAND TRANSCENDENTALISM AND ST. LOUIS HEGELIAN-ISM. Philadelphia: Carl Schurz Memorial Foundation, 1948.

> The author discusses the ideas and influences of Alcott and Emerson in comparing two phases of American idealism and notes that

while transcendentalism produced some fine literature, none of the work of the St. Louis movement had literary success. However, he argues, both movements revitalized that "strain of idealism that has been a vital part of American consciousness from earliest Puritan days."

Rayapati, J.P. Rao. EARLY AMERICAN INTEREST IN VEDANTA: PRE-EMERSONIAN INTEREST IN VEDIC LITERATURE AND VEDANTIC PHILOSOPHY. New York: Asia Publishing House, 1973.

By the term "Vedic literature," the author includes all English, Latin, French, and German translations of Sanskrit that were available up to 1840. He provides a checklist of the works which were available and reviews the literature discussed in periodicals. Giving emphasis to the influences upon Emerson, Thoreau, and Whitman, he concludes that these writers did not derive their ideas from their readings but rather found confirmation of them.

Sanborn, Franklin Benjamin. TRANSCENDENTAL AND LITERARY NEW ENGLAND: EMERSON, THOREAU, ALCOTT, BRYANT, WHITTIER, LOWELL, LONGFELLOW, AND OTHERS. Ed. Kenneth Walter Cameron. Hartford, Conn.: Transcendental Books, 1975.

This volume brings together the principal literary pieces and papers, seventy all together, written by Sanborn between 1854 and 1910. It includes reminiscences, criticism, reviews, and comments.

Santayana, George. CHARACTER AND OPINION IN THE UNITED STATES. New York: Scribner's, 1924.

These essays on William James and nineteenth-century academic backgrounds and philosophical leanings shed light on the neo-Hegelian movement as a whole and on Josiah Royce in particular.

_____. GEORGE SANTAYANA'S AMERICA: ESSAYS ON LITERATURE AND CULTURE. Ed. James Ballowe. Urbana: Univ. of Illinois Press, 1967.

The essays include some pieces which Santayana did for the HARVARD LAMPOON, some late nineteenth-century views of Boston, Yale, and Harvard, comments upon Emerson's optimism and his poetry, and "a dialogue" with Whitman. Santayana's perspective on nineteenth-century America is stimulating and his expression always eloquent.

_____. WINDS OF DOCTRINE. New York: Scribner's, 1913.

In the most widely known essay in this collection, "The Genteel Tradition in American Philosophy," originally an address delivered before the Philosophical Union of the University of California, Santayana discusses Emerson, transcendentalism, and William James. He finds the origins of the genteel tradition in both Calvinism and transcendentalism.

Schneider, Herbert W. A HISTORY OF AMERICAN PHILOSOPHY. 2nd ed. New York: Columbia Univ. Press, 1963.

> Of all histories of American philosophy, Schneider's is probably the most useful for the literary scholar. Schneider supplies excellent historical and cultural backgrounds as he discusses the ideas of American philosophers and their impact upon others.

Simon, Myron, and Thornton H. Parsons, eds. TRANSCENDENTALISM AND ITS LEGACY. Ann Arbor: Univ. of Michigan Press, 1966.

> These ten essays on Emerson, Dickinson, Thoreau, and others vary greatly in their usefulness and quality. The collection in general is valuable primarily for its examination of the relevance of transcendental thought to present problems. Two provocative essays are Kenneth Burke's study of Emerson's NATURE and Hebert W. Schneider's observations on "American Transcendentalism's Escape from Phenomenology."

Smallwood, William M., and Mabel Coon Smallwood. NATURAL HISTORY AND THE AMERICAN MIND. New York: Columbia Univ. Press, 1941.

> In this somewhat superficial study of the contributions of naturalists and scientists, the authors survey the years 1725 to around 1840, using the term "natural history" to refer to all of the concrete sciences, but focusing primarily upon the life sciences. The authors point out that many of the works of early American naturalists, such as Audubon, showed both literary and artistic skill. Their value lies in the accuracy of observation in both their verbal descriptions and their drawings rather than in their taxonomies or conclusions, which have often proved to be faulty. Although this study has limited value for the student of literature, it does provide historical context for the natural history writers.

Smith, James Ward, and A. Leland Jamison, eds. RELIGION IN AMERICAN LIFE. 4 vols. Princeton: Princeton Univ. Press, 1961.

> These volumes are an essential resource for anyone interested in studying religious writings and writers or in obtaining a comprehensive background of the development and effects of religion in America. Volumes 1 and 2 consist of essays by scholars such as Perry Miller, Stow Persons, and Richard P. Blackmur. Volumes 3 and 4, a critical bibliography compiled by Nelson R. Burr, provide a thorough survey of religious writings in America.

Smith, John Edwin. THE SPIRIT OF AMERICAN PHILOSOPHY. New York: Oxford Univ. Press, 1963.

> A study of the principal ideas of the five "classic American philosophers" (Peirce, William James, Royce, Dewey, and Whitehead), this work defines the uniquely "American" qualities of their thought as well as their attempt to make their ideas meaningful and applicable to the general populace.

Smithline, Arnold. NATURAL RELIGION IN AMERICAN LITERATURE. New Haven, Conn.: College and Univ. Press, 1966.

The study includes chapters on Theodore Parker, Emerson, and Whitman. "Natural religion" is the point of view which assumes that man is naturally moral and religiously self-sufficient. Theodore Parker is a transitional figure between deism and transcendentalism. Transcendentalism added an emotional and mystical quality to the basic belief of the deists. Whitman went beyond both, wedding natural religion to basic democratic concepts.

Stewart, Randall. AMERICAN LITERATURE AND CHRISTIAN DOCTRINE. Baton Rouge: Louisiana State Univ. Press, 1958.

Stewart examines "errors" (rationalism, romanticism--deification of man--and mechanistic naturalism) as opposed to the Christian view of man as a moral agent, as fallible, and as a tragic figure. While Emerson and Whitman erred in being too romantic, Hawthorne, Melville, and Henry James adopted a more Christian version of mankind.

Stoehr, Taylor. NAY-SAYING IN CONCORD: EMERSON, ALCOTT, AND THOREAU. Hamden, Conn.: Archon, 1979.

In contrast to those who see the transcendentalists as "Aye-sayers," Stoehr focuses upon their abstinence, self-discipline, and restraint. He examines and compares the positions of Emerson, Alcott, and Thoreau in relation to politics, communitarianism, and diet. The role of Charles Lane, an English journalist and transcendentalist who invested in Alcott's Fruitlands, is also discussed. Stoehr's perspective casts fresh light upon transcendentalist asceticism, and his perceptions are usually on the mark.

Sweet, William Warren. RELIGION ON THE AMERICAN FRONTIER. 2 vols. 1936; New York: Cooper Square, 1964.

This is a collection of source materials (minutes, documents, correspondence, autobiographical sketches) which traces the influence of the frontier preachers and missionaries upon the education and ideas of the early settlers and the Indians. Of interest to students of nineteenth-century prose are excerpts from the autobiographical writings of the frontier preachers.

_____. THE STORY OF RELIGION IN AMERICA. 1930. Rev. ed. New York: Harper, 1950.

This objective, thorough study remains one of the best surveys of the ideas, changes, leading figures, and influences of the major religions in America. The author also discusses the impact of social change (the changing frontier and abolition) on churches in America.

Thomas, John Wesley. JAMES FREEMAN CLARKE: APOSTLE OF GERMAN CULTURE TO AMERICA. Boston: John W. Luce, 1949.

> This study, originally a doctoral dissertation at Pennsylvania State College, discusses Clarke's studies in Germany and his role in making German philosophy and literature known and appreciated in America. The author uses primary documents in his study, including correspondence with Emerson, Fuller, Holmes, Longfellow, Theodore Parker, and others. He concludes that Clarke "exerted a great influence upon his age," making "a noteworthy contribution toward liberal Christianity, social improvement, and a proper appreciation of German literature in America."

Thomas, Russell Brown. THE SEARCH FOR A COMMON LEARNING: GENERAL EDUCATION, 1800-1960. New York: McGraw-Hill, 1962.

> The first section of this survey is useful in that it traces the influence of Charles W. Eliot as president of Harvard. More an administrator than a scholar, Eliot transformed Harvard from a small rather loosely organized institution into a great university. Eliot emphasized the need for a broad, general education, instituting the curricula that was experienced by those who attended Harvard after Eliot's inauguration in 1869.

Tracy, Henry Chester. AMERICAN NATURISTS. New York: Dutton, 1930.

> The author discusses American nature writing as a unique literary genre and considers the writings of Burroughs, Audubon, Thoreau, and Theodore Roosevelt, among others.

Vanderbilt, Kermit. CHARLES ELIOT NORTON: APOSTLE OF CULTURE IN A DEMOCRACY. Cambridge, Mass.: Belknap Press, Harvard Univ. Press, 1959.

> This biographical and critical study of an important figure of the latter part of the nineteenth century presents a view not only of Norton, who was an outstanding scholar, teacher, and social critic, but also of the transitional years between the pre-Civil War optimism of such writers as Emerson and Whitman and the more gloomy post-World War I writers such as T.S. Eliot, Paul Elmer More, and Irving Babbitt.

Vogel, Stanley M. GERMAN LITERARY INFLUENCES ON THE AMERICAN TRANSCENDENTALISTS. New Haven, Conn.: Yale Univ. Press, 1955. Appendix.

> The author first traces the history of German literary criticism outside the transcendental circle, then the German scholarship among the transcendentalists themselves. The author argues that while German thought was important to transcendentalism, particularly in the language it derived from Kant through Coleridge and Goethe, its value for them lay not in obtaining an exact doctrine but in the authorization it gave to their own ideas.

Walzl, John A.   GERMAN INFLUENCE IN AMERICAN EDUCATION AND CULTURE.   Philadelphia: Carl Schurz Memorial Foundation, 1936.

> In this brief but very informative study, the author maintains that German culture was one of the most significant factors affecting American education in the first half of the nineteenth century. He shows how German ideas both became part of the educational system and molded the thinking of many of the prominent scholars, writers, and teachers of the century.

Wells, Ronald V.   THREE CHRISTIAN TRANSCENDENTALISTS.   JAMES MARSH, CALEB SPRAGUE HENRY, AND FREDERIC HENRY HEDGE.   New York: Columbia Univ. Press, 1943.

> This study includes a discussion of the varieties of Christian transcendentalism and examines the "natural" and the "spiritual" views of the three men.

Whicher, George F., ed.   THE TRANSCENDENTALIST REVOLT AGAINST MATERIALISM.   Boston: D.C. Heath, 1949.

> This is a collection of essays by the transcendentalists themselves and by some twentieth-century scholars about the ideas and times of the transcendentalists, primarily about their concern with encouraging spiritual and intellectual qualities in an age of material prosperity and creature comforts.   The writers include Emerson, Thoreau, Theodore Parker, Louisa May Alcott, Arthur M. Schlesinger, Jr., and Henry Steele Commager.

White, Morton.   SCIENCE AND SENTIMENT IN AMERICA: PHILOSOPHICAL THOUGHT FROM JONATHAN EDWARDS TO JOHN DEWEY.   New York: Oxford Univ. Press, 1972.

> The author examines the major American philosophers in terms of their responses to "the challenge of modern science and scientific method."   The discussion of the impact of Darwin upon American philosophy is particularly useful to the student of nineteenth-century American writings.

Whittemore, Robert Clifton.   MAKERS OF THE AMERICAN MIND.   New York: Morrow, 1964.

> In this intellectual history, the author announces that his aim is to present "the essentials of the philosophy of those thinkers and doers whose influence upon our culture is, or has been, such as justify calling them 'the makers of the American mind.'"   Written for the general reader rather than the scholar, the work gives a good general overview of the writers discussed.   These writers include Emerson, Thoreau, Horace Mann, Theodore Parker, Lincoln, Fiske, Royce, Dewey, and others.

Wiener, Philip. EVOLUTION AND THE FOUNDERS OF PRAGMATISM. Cambridge, Mass.: Harvard Univ. Press, 1949.

The author "aims to shed light on the matrix of ideas about evolution from which diverse meanings of pragmatism emerged in the thinking of a brilliant group of philosophical liberals who met around Harvard in the 1860's and early 1870's." His historical survey illuminates the writings of such pragmatists as Chauncey Wright, Peirce, William James, and John Fiske.

F. THE LITERATURE OF HISTORY AND POLITICS

1. PRIMARY WORKS

a. Histories

Adams, Charles Kendall. CHRISTOPHER COLUMBUS, HIS LIFE AND WORKS. New York: Dodd, Mead, 1892.

> Adams' methodology influenced many later historians. This life is an excellent illustration of his sound, well-informed writing, and it is still a useful source in intelligent historical scholarship.

———. A MANUAL OF HISTORICAL LITERATURE. New York: Harper, 1882.

> A compilation of the kind rare in its day and invaluable to the nineteenth-century historians, this work indicates a growing awareness and appreciation of the accomplishments in American historical scholarship.

Adams, Hebert Baxter. THE LIFE AND WRITINGS OF JARED SPARKS. 2 vols. Boston: Houghton Mifflin, 1893.

> This thoughtful, accurate study restored Sparks to the status he deserved.

———. THE STUDY OF HISTORY IN AMERICAN COLLEGES AND UNIVERSITIES. Washington, D.C.: U.S. Bureau of Education, 1887.

> This influential work made the teaching and writing of history a specialized technique, derived from the German seminar method disseminated by Herbert Adams and others.

Bancroft, Hubert Howe, et al. HISTORY OF THE PACIFIC STATES OF NORTH AMERICA. 34 vols. San Francisco: A.L. Bancroft, 1882–90.

> H.H. Bancroft was the first to chronicle western U.S. history systematically and comprehensively and to collect materials

on the American West. The first five volumes of this collection were previously published as THE NATIVE RACES OF THE PACIFIC STATES . . . (1874-1876). Bancroft and others compiled this history from thousands of documents, and both his history and his ethnological studies of the native tribes remain valuable.

De Forest, John William. HISTORY OF THE INDIANS OF CONNECTICUT. Hartford, Conn.: J.W. Hammersley, 1851.

This is DeForest's first publication and the first work of any kind about the Connecticut tribes. It is painstaking, thorough, and accurate and was a reliable source of information for later ethnologists.

Gayarre, Charles Etienne Arthur. A HISTORY OF LOUISIANA. 4 vols. 1851-66; 3rd ed. New Orleans: A. Hawkins, 1885.

Considered by many to be the finest historian the South produced before the Civil War, Gayarre demonstrates, in these volumes, outstanding literary skill and imaginative scholarship. Written from original documents for the most part, the work is one of the best antebellum histories.

Hildreth, Richard. THE HISTORY OF THE UNITED STATES OF AMERICA. 6 vols. New York: Harper, 1849-52.

Regarded by many "scientific historians" as one of the most important histories of the nineteenth century, Hildreth's work is merely factual, consciously antiliterary, and dull. In the history, Hildreth attempts to construct "a science of man." His objective, matter-of-fact approach to historical writing is often cited as a direct contrast to the method of Bancroft.

McMaster, John Bach. HISTORY OF THE PEOPLE OF THE UNITED STATES, FROM THE REVOLUTION TO THE CIVIL WAR. 8 vols. New York: D. Appleton, 1883-1913.

Recognized as a unique contribution to American history, the work focuses on the social history of the people, concerning itself with dress, customs, morals, and institutions. Some historiographers regard McMaster as "the founder of the modern school of historians of the United States."

Mahan, Alfred Thayer. THE INFLUENCE OF SEA POWER UPON HISTORY, 1660-1783. 1890. 1957; Westport, Conn.: Greenwood Press, 1968.

An acute discussion of the effect of naval power and strategy on events leading to the development of nations, Mahan's work has been important and influential.

Meek, Alexander B. ROMANTIC PASSAGES IN SOUTHWESTERN HISTORY. Mobile, Ala.: S.H. Goetzel, 1857.

> A collection of orations and essays on the South, particularly Alabama, the work was a source for both Bancroft and Simms.

Page, Thomas Nelson. THE OLD SOUTH. New York: Scribner's, 1892.

> Consisting of social and historical essays together with Page's other writings on the South, this work is a fine example of cultural observation and regional awareness.

_____. SOCIAL LIFE IN OLD VIRGINIA. New York: Scribner's, 1897.

Palfrey, John Gorham. A COMPENDIOUS HISTORY OF NEW ENGLAND FROM THE DISCOVERY BY EUROPEANS TO THE FIRST GENERAL CONGRESS OF THE ANGLO-AMERICAN COLONIES. 5 vols. Boston: H.C. Shepard, 1858-90.

> Palfrey's work contains many useful details but it is weak in social and economic history. His loyalty to New England, pride in his New England ancestors, and desire to exalt the past are all evident in his work, arousing criticism by later historians.

Pitkin, Timothy. A POLITICAL AND CIVIL HISTORY OF THE UNITED STATES. 2 vols. 1828; New York: Da Capo, 1970.

> Pitkins' work was one of the best of its time, stressing political and civil rather than military events. His assessment of Franklin drew criticism for its severity from both Sparks and Bancroft.

Sabine, Lorenzo. BIOGRAPHICAL SKETCHES OF THE LOYALISTS OF THE AMERICAN REVOLUTION. 1864; Port Washington, N.Y.: Kennikat Press, 1966.

> Sabine's history had a great influence on later writers and was essential in revising the traditional views of the Tories before and during the revolution.

Schouler, James. HISTORY OF THE UNITED STATES UNDER THE CONSTITUTION. 7 vols. Washington, D.C.: W.H. and O.H. Morrison, 1880-1913.

> Written to fill the gap Schouler felt existed in historical writings, his history focuses on politics, is strictly chronological, and is structured according to presidential administrations. Schouler made full use of manuscript sources, was an early defender of Andrew Johnson's policies, and weighed his evidence carefully but he was also concerned with the need to "inculcate the lesson" of the Civil War, thereby revealing some of his Northern prejudices.

Sparks, Jared. LIFE OF GOUVERNEUR MORRIS, WITH SELECTIONS FROM HIS CORRESPONDENCE AND MISCELLANEOUS PAPERS. 3 vols. Boston: Gray and Bowen, 1832.

> Sparks was a pioneer in winning recognition for American history in American colleges; he is credited with being the first great editor of American history, and, despite their flaws, his works were a valuable resource for subsequent historians and biographers. He lacks the literary achievement of Bancroft or Prescott, but deserves a place in the vanguard of the literary historians. The two biographies listed here and below, together with his editions of the writings about Washington, Franklin, and the Revolution, remain among Sparks's important contributions.

_____. LIFE OF JOHN LEDYARD, THE AMERICAN TRAVELER: COMPRISING SELECTIONS FROM HIS JOURNALS AND CORRESPONDENCE. Cambridge, Mass.: Hilliard and Brown, 1828.

_____, ed. A COLLECTION OF THE FAMILIAR LETTERS AND MISCELLANEOUS PAPERS OF BENJAMIN FRANKLIN. Boston: C. Bowen, 1833.

_____. DIPLOMATIC CORRESPONDENCE OF THE AMERICAN REVOLUTION. 12 vols. Boston: N. Hale and Gray and Bowen, 1829-30.

_____. WORKS OF BENJAMIN FRANKLIN: WITH NOTES AND A LIFE OF THE AUTHOR. 10 vols. Boston: Hilliard, Gran, and Co., 1836-40.

_____. WRITINGS OF GEORGE WASHINGTON, BEING HIS CORRESPONDENCE, ADDRESSES, MESSAGES, AND OTHER PAPERS, OFFICIAL AND PRIVATE. 12 vols. Boston: J.B. Russell, 1834-37.

Tucker, George. THE HISTORY OF THE UNITED STATES FROM THEIR COLONIZATION TO THE END OF THE TWENTY-SIXTH CONGRESS IN 1841. 4 vols. Philadelphia: Lippincott, 1856-57.

> Written from a southern point of view, Tucker's history emphasizes sectional interests but is fairly dependable. He urged the use and preservation of original documents, but in writing his own history relied heavily upon Hildreth, Bancroft, and Sparks.

Winsor, Justin, ed. NARRATIVE AND CRITICAL HISTORY OF AMERICA. 8 vols. 1884-1889; New York: AMS Press, 1967. Notes, Bibliog.

> Thirty-nine scholars contributed to these eight volumes, but almost half were composed of Winsor's own writing. Its most important service was to bring together scattered pre-1850s material, for there is a preponderance of material on the period of discovery and exploration. The work, at the time of its publication, was a landmark of American historiography. Henry Adams and many other historians sought guidance from Winsor.

b. Political, Economic, and Sociological Studies

Adams, Brooks. LAW OF CIVILIZATION AND DECAY. 1896. Introd. Charles A. Beard. New York: Knopf, 1943.

In this study in social dynamics, Brooks proposed, before Henry did, the theory that civilization is the product of social energy, and that social energy obeys the physical law of mass, depending upon population densities. Many critics argue that in this volume Brooks made a better case for the application of Newton, Comte, Darwin, and Marx to the history of Western civilization than did Henry Adams. While not a major literary figure, Brooks was one of the clearest spokesmen for economic determinism.

Burgess, John W. POLITICAL SCIENCE AND COMPARATIVE CONSTITUTION-AL LAW. 2 vols. Boston: Ginn and Co., 1890-91.

Burgess was among the founding fathers of graduate education, a pioneer political scientist, and an early practitioner of "scientific" history. As a teacher, Burgess contributed to developing a genera-tion of historians, political scientists, lawyers, judges, and states-men. In this influential pioneering study in the field of interna-tional law, the author argues for a reconciliation over the issues of freedom and government.

Carey, Henry Charles. PRINCIPLES OF POLITICAL ECONOMY. 3 vols. Philadelphia: Carey, Lea and Blanchard, 1837-40.

Carey is often considered America's first professional economist. At first a free trader, Carey became a high-tariff advocate and an intense nationalist. He is of interest to literary historians because he was an occasional antagonist of William Cullen Bryant's on the question of protection for American manufacturers. His writings remain among the best economic treatises of the nineteenth century.

Carnegie, Andrew. THE GOSPEL OF WEALTH. 1889; Cambridge, Mass.: Belknap Press, Harvard Univ. Press, 1962.

Carnegie expounded principles of Spencerian economics, writing that "the concentration of business, industrial and commercial, in the hands of the few, and the law of competition between these, [is] not only beneficial, but essential to the progress of the race. . . . because it ensures the survival of the fittest in every depart-ment." However, he also felt that the man of wealth should live modestly and distribute his wealth for the community well-being. This work is a classic statement of the principles of Social Dar-winism mixed with private philanthropy that influenced the conduct of a number of nineteenth-century industrial titans.

George, Henry. THE COMPLETE WORKS OF HENRY GEORGE. 10 vols. Garden City, N.Y.: Doubleday, Page, 1906-11.

> The volumes include what were perhaps Henry George's three most influential works: OUR LAND AND LAND POLICY (1871), PROTECTION OR FREE TRADE (1886), and PROGRESS AND POVERTY (1879). Volumes 9 and 10 include THE LIFE OF HENRY GEORGE by Henry George, Jr. This is the first and is considered by critics to be one of the best of the biographies. It includes quotations from unpublished sources, family reminiscences, and personal conversations. Henry George, Jr., also edited the Memorial Edition, published as THE WRITINGS OF HENRY GEORGE (10 vols; New York: Doubleday and McClure, 1898-1901). A bibliography of the writings of Henry George was published by the New York Public Library under the title of HENRY GEORGE AND THE SINGLE TAX (1926).

_____. PROGRESS AND POVERTY: AN INQUIRY INTO THE CAUSE OF INDUSTRIAL DEPRESSIONS AND OF INCREASE OF WANT WITH INCREASE OF WEALTH: THE REMEDY. 1879. Ed. R.G. George. 1925; New York: Robert F. Schalkenbach Foundation, 1965. Bibliog.

> Henry George's writings are among the best of the nineteenth-century economists. By reason of style and influence, his prose deserves a place in studies of the literature of the period. Central to progress is the idea that every person has the right to enjoy the fruits of his own labor on the land. George proposed that a tax on the "unearned increment" of the land enjoyed by landholders be returned to any community whose members had contributed to the increased value of the land.

_____. SIGNIFICANT PARAGRAPHS FROM HENRY GEORGE'S PROGRESS AND POVERTY. Ed. Harry G. Brown. Introd. John Dewey. Garden City, N.Y.: Doubleday, 1928.

> This is an accessible edition of Henry George's most important work; the introduction by John Dewey provides an interesting commentary on George's influence.

Holmes, Oliver Wendell, Jr. THE COMMON LAW. 1881. Ed. Mark A. De Wolfe Howe. Cambridge, Mass.: Belknap Press, Harvard Univ. Press, 1963.

> In this work, published fairly early in his career, Holmes studies the evolutionary and pragmatic influences upon the law, stating that "the life of the law has not been logic: it has been [the] experience . . . of a nation's development through many centuries and . . . in order to know what it is, we must know what it has been, and what it tends to become." THE COMMON LAW was an influential achievement as scholarship, literature, and the legal philosophy which came to dominate American jurisprudence.

Lloyd, Henry Demarest. A STRIKE OF MILLIONAIRES AGAINST MINERS. 1890; New York: Johnson, 1971.

> Lloyd's writings on economic issues were excellent. This appeal for industrial justice showed a strong sympathy for labor problems.

———. WEALTH AGAINST COMMONWEALTH. 1894; Westport, Conn.: Greenwood Press, 1976.

> The author points out, in clear, appealing prose, how few control the natural wealth of the nation. This is a forerunner of the work done later by the muckrakers and remains a classic in the literature of journalistic exposure.

Veblen, Thorstein. THEORY OF THE LEISURE CLASS. 1899. Introd. John Kenneth Galbraith. Boston: Houghton Mifflin, 1973.

> Veblen's language is as important as his ideas in making this a classic study. In his introduction to the 1973 edition, Galbraith writes that while Veblen enjoyed uttering the outrageous at times, "no man of his time, or since, looked with such a cool and penetrating eye not so much at pecuniary gain as at the way its pursuit makes men and women behave." This work and Henry George's PROGRESS AND POVERTY, above, are probably the two most important books of the nineteenth century by American economists.

Ward, Frank Lester. DYNAMIC SOCIOLOGY. 2 vols. 1883; New York: D. Appleton, 1926.

> Ward ranks with Spencer and Comte in the founding of modern sociology. This is a pioneering work, and one of the first in English to employ the term "sociology." Although the style is ponderous, the study is thorough and meticulous. Ward quite rightly criticized many of Comte's simplistic nations and was largely responsible for making sociology a respectable academic discipline.

Wells, David A. PRACTICAL ECONOMICS: A COLLECTION OF ESSAYS RESPECTING CERTAIN OF THE RECENT ECONOMIC EXPERIENCES OF THE UNITED STATES. New York: G.P. Putnam's, 1885.

> This is a collection of articles which originally appeared in ATLANTIC and other periodicals. Wells was an unusually clear and facile writer on economic issues. He advocated laissez-faire policies, foresaw some of the problems of "technological unemployment," and sought to bring some system into taxation. This collection is a good example of his popularized interpretations of economic principles.

Willard, Josiah Flynt. TRAMPING WITH TRAMPS. 1893; College Park, Md.: McGrath Publishing, 1969.

> This is a unique study in that the author lived as one among

the "vagabonds" whom he wrote about. He sought to determine
the basis and characteristics of their often criminal behavior. This
is a significant pioneering sociological study; it is also a highly
articulate and fascinating narrative.

c. Writings and Rhetoric by Orators and Statesmen

Benton, Thomas Hart. ABRIDGMENT OF THE DEBATES OF CONGRESS FROM
1789 TO 1856. . . . 16 vols. New York: D. Appleton, 1857–61.

> Benton's speeches were admired for their clarity and wit; yet, as
> recorded they lack coherence and conciseness. His greatest in-
> fluence as a public speaker was in his advocacy of western ex-
> pansion and development and promoting a solid union.

_____. THIRTY YEARS' VIEW: A HISTORY OF THE WORKING OF THE
AMERICAN GOVERNMENT FOR THIRTY YEARS, FROM 1820–1850. 2 vols.
New York: D. Appleton, 1854–56.

> The volumes consist of material from congressional debates, some
> of the papers of Jackson, speeches of Benton, and his views "of
> men and affairs." These views are well written, judicious, infor-
> mative, worthwhile as both literature and history, and valuable
> as a contemporary source of information about the men and their
> speeches on current topics.

Beveridge, Albert J. MEANING OF THE TIMES. Indianapolis: Bobbs–Merrill,
1908.

> This is a collection of Beveridge's principal speeches. He was a
> political speaker in every national and congressional campaign
> from 1884–1924, except 1918. Together with Theodore Roosevelt
> and William J. Bryan, he was considered the best of a "new
> breed" of orators.

Black, Jeremiah S. ESSAYS AND SPEECHES OF JEREMIAH S. BLACK. Ed.
C.F. Black. New York: D. Appleton, 1885.

> Black, U.S. attorney general (1857–60) and secretary of state
> (1860–61), defended the constitutional Bill of Rights and the
> people's rights against corporate interests. This is the official
> collection of his speeches. He was considered by many of his
> contemporaries as "the most magnificent orator at the American
> bar" and a brilliant controversial writer.

Blaine, James G. POLITICAL DISCUSSIONS, LEGISLATIVE, DIPLOMATIC,
AND POPULAR. Norwich, Conn.: Henry Bill, 1887.

> This representative selection of Blaine's speeches as the Republican
> nominee for president in 1884 show him to be a careful, methodical,
> and sometimes brilliant public speaker.

Brooks, Phillips. ESSAYS AND ADDRESSES. New York: E.P. Dutton, 1894.

Speaking from the pulpit, Brooks felt his tasks were to reaffirm man's confidence in his spiritual nature and to harmonize old doctrine with modern scientific knowledge. This collection contains most of his best addresses.

Bryan, William Jennings. THE FIRST BATTLE: A STORY OF THE CAMPAIGN OF 1896. Chicago: B.B. Conkey, 1896.

This account of the leading events and issues of the campaign includes a collection of Bryan's speeches and a biographical sketch written by his wife.

_____. THE SPEECHES OF WILLIAM JENNINGS BRYAN. 2 vols. New York: Funk and Wagnals, 1913.

As the bulwark of the Democratic party, Bryan rose to be the foremost political and platform orator of America. This collection includes "The Cross of Gold," "On the Tariff," "On the Income Tax," and other significant speeches.

Calhoun, John C. THE PAPERS OF JOHN C. CALHOUN. 7 vols. Ed. Robert L. Meriwether (Vol. 1) and Edwin Hemphill (Vols. 2-7). Columbia: Univ. of South Carolina Press, 1959-73.

Calhoun eloquently defended slavery and argued for states' rights, first through nullification, later through the threat of secession. He also violently opposed the protective tariffs of 1824 and 1828. These papers and the WORKS below are valuable not only for their historical significance but also because of their considerable literary merit.

_____. THE WORKS OF JOHN C. CALHOUN. 6 vols. Ed. Richard K. Cralle. 1851-56. New York: Russell and Russell, 1968.

Channing, Edward T. LECTURES READ TO THE SENIORS IN HARVARD COLLEGE BY EDWARD T. CHANNING. 1856. Ed. Dorothy I. Anderson and Waldo W. Braden. Foreword by David Potter. Carbondale: Southern Illinois Univ. Press, 1968.

Channing's lectures reflect the prevailing oratorical and rhetorical principles of the day and exerted considerable influence on Emerson and Thoreau.

Choate, Rufus. ADDRESSES AND ORATIONS. Boston: Little, Brown, 1878.

Choate's oratorical fame rests upon his eloquence in court; he has the reputation of being the outstanding jury-orator of the nineteenth century. Speeches that remain of interest in this collection are "On Occupying Oregon" (1844), "On the Annexation of Texas" (1844), and "On Preservation of the Union" (1850).

_____. WORKS. . . . 2 vols. With a Memoir of his life by S.G. Brown. Boston: Little, Brown, 1862.

The volumes include a number of important political documents.

Clay, Henry. LIFE AND SPEECHES. 2 vols. Ed. D. Mallory. New York: Greeley and McElrath, 1843.

For a period of about forty years, 1812-50, Clay was in the front ranks of American statesmen, maintaining his position almost solely by his oratorical powers. This collection of speeches and the papers and works listed below help to establish his record as rhetoretician.

_____. THE PAPERS OF HENRY CLAY. 10 vols. Ed. James F. Hopkins. Lexington: Univ. of Kentucky Press, 1959-73.

_____. WORKS. 10 vols. Ed. C. Colton. New York: G.P. Putnam's, 1857-1904. Bibliog.

Contains a history of tariff legislation.

Curtis, George William. THE ORATIONS AND ADDRESSES OF GEORGE WIL-LIAM CURTIS. 3 vols. Ed. Charles Eliot Norton. New York: Harper, 1894.

Expressing many of the same views as the essays written when Curtis was an editor of HARPER'S MAGAZINE, these speeches are samples of his popular lyceum lectures on literary, moral, and political subjects.

Douglas, Stephen A. THE LETTERS OF STEPHEN A. DOUGLAS. Ed. Robert W. Johannsen. Urbana: Univ. of Illinois Press, 1961.

The dominating figure in Congress in the decade before the Civil War, Douglas is remembered primarily for his support of the Kansas-Nebraska bill, his opposition to Lincoln, and his speeches to the northern Democrats just before the war. The letters provide a sample of his rhetorical abilities and his outside interests.

Evarts, William Maxwell. THE ARGUMENTS AND SPEECHES OF WILLIAM MAXWELL EVARTS. 3 vols. Ed. Sherman Evarts. New York: Macmillan, 1919.

Evarts was a justice of the Supreme Court noted for his eloquence and intelligence. This collection includes legal arguments as well as political and commemorative speeches.

Everett, Edward. ORATIONS AND SPEECHES ON VARIOUS OCCASIONS. 4 vols. 1850-68; 7th ed. Boston: Little, Brown, 1865-72.

President of Harvard and an influential spokesman for his generation

and perhaps of his century, Everett believed that the American
system was theoretically and operationally perfect: any failure
was due to the folly of statesmen. Everett also argued for the
"duty" to educate--as distinct from the "right" to education--and
for a closer union of theoretical and practical sciences. This collection indicates the range and power of Everett's appeal.

Grady, Henry Woodfin. THE COMPLETE ORATIONS AND SPEECHES OF
HENRY W. GRADY. Ed. Edwin DuBois Surter. Austin, Tex.: South-West
Publishing, 1910.

Grady was a brilliant post-Civil War orator who saw his task as
convincing the South to expand its industry and reconciling North
and South by acting as mediator.

_____. THE NEW SOUTH AND OTHER ADDRESSES. New York: R. Bonner
and Sons, 1890.

In these speeches, Grady describes conditions in postwar southern
states; he also considers economic problems and the Negro question.

Ingersoll, Robert Green. THE WORKS OF ROBERT G. INGERSOLL. 12 vols.
New York: C.P. Farrell, 1896.

Ingersoll was a spokesman for the Republicans following the Civil
War and a celebrated agnostic who supported Darwinism and science.
He had a popular following because he was an extremely successful
lecturer, some viewing him as a notorious infidel, others as a liber-
ator from superstition.

Phillips, Wendell. SPEECHES, LECTURES, AND LETTERS. 2 vols. 1863-91.
New York: Negro Univ. Press, 1968.

As a platform orator on the lyceum circuit and later as one of the
prominent orators in the country, Phillips argued for abolition and,
after the Civil War, for reconstruction and reform. His other subjects ranged from economics and commerce to feminism and education. His last speech, a Phi Beta Kappa address at Harvard in
1881, "The Scholar in a Republic," is one of his most eloquent.

Schurz, Carl. SPEECHES, CORRESPONDENCE, AND POLITICAL PAPERS.
6 vols. New York: G.P. Putnam's Sons, 1913.

Schurz campaigned for Lincoln, wrote a report on conditions in the
South in 1865--which Johnson suppressed because it recommended
extending the franchise to the blacks--and decried growing post-
Civil War materialism. These papers demonstrate Schurz's liberal
sensitivity to oppression.

Sumner, Charles. ORATIONS AND SPEECHES. 2 vols. Boston: Ticknor,
Reed and Fields, 1850.

_____. COMPLETE WORKS. 20 vols. 1870–93; New York: Negro Univ. Press, 1969.

> Sumner's fame as an orator is based upon his eloquent opposition to the Mexican War, to war in general as a means of settling disputes, and to slavery. Among his best speeches are "The Crime Against Kansas" (1856), "Fame and Glory" (1847), and "The True Grandeur of Nations" (1845). As examples of refined rhetorical skill, his speeches earn themselves a place in both literature and history.

d. Utopianism

Alcott, Louisa May. TRANSCENDENTAL WILD OATS AND EXCERPTS FROM THE FRUITLANDS DIARY. Cambridge, Mass.: Harvard Common Press, 1981.

> Bronson Alcott's daughter here describes, with skepticism and humor, the Fruitlands experience.

Brisbane, Albert. SOCIAL DESTINY OF MAN: OR, ASSOCIATION AND REORGANIZATION OF INDUSTRY . . . . 1840; New York: A.M. Kelley, 1969.

> As one of the earliest American accounts of Fourierism, Brisbane's was instrumental in the establishment of a number of Fourieristic phalanxes. He advocated social and industrial reform through communal living, cooperative enterprise, and "discovering God's plan for the human race." He also supported equality for women, realizing that most of them spent their lives in demeaning repetitious labor. Some of Brisbane's characteristics may have inspired Hawthorne's character, Hollingsworth, in THE BLITHEDALE ROMANCE.

Codman, John T. BROOK FARM: HISTORIC AND PERSONAL MEMOIRS. Boston: Arena Publishing Co., 1894.

> Codman was a young participant in the Brook Farm community who remained, as can be seen in this account, enthusiastic about the principles espoused by the group and optimistic about the ability of such cooperative enterprises to reform society. The author was present during the later "industrial" period rather than the early "transcendental" period, but he conscientiously documents the years with which he was not personally familiar. His account of life at Brook Farm is idealistic and euphoric.

Godwin, Parke. A POPULAR VIEW OF THE DOCTRINE OF CHARLES FOURIER. 1844; Philadelphia: Porcupine Press, 1972.

> Godwin's study of Fourierism is shorter, less thorough, and less original than Brisbane's. He attempts, however, to convey the appeal and worth of the doctrine in a methodical rational way.

Gronlund, Laurence. THE CO-OPERATIVE COMMONWEALTH: AN EXPOSITION OF MODERN SOCIALISM. 1884. Ed. Stowe Persons. Cambridge, Mass.: Harvard Univ. Press, 1965.

Gronlund lectured widely on the cause of socialism. His book reflects the transitional stage between communitarian utopianism and advocacy of class struggle. In his introduction, Stowe Persons writes that "As a political movement Marxism was to be of negligible importance in the United States, but as a style of thinking, the somewhat diluted version represented by Gronlund was to have a far-reaching and pervasive influence." William Dean Howells probably derived his ideas of Marx at least partly from Gronlund, and some of these are reflected in Howells' utopian novels. Gronlund also influenced Eugene Debs and, perhaps, Edward Bellamy.

Haraszti, Zoltan. THE IDYLL OF BROOK FARM: AS REVEALED BY UNPUBLISHED LETTERS IN THE BOSTON PUBLIC LIBRARY. Boston: Trustees of the Public Library, 1937.

This collection provides valuable source material in the letters gathered here from the Brook Farm papers held by the Boston Public Library.

Nordhoff, Charles. THE COMMUNISTIC SOCIETIES OF THE UNITED STATES . . . . 1875. Prefatory essay by Frank H. Littell. New York: Schocken, 1965.

One of the more comprehensive studies of nineteenth-century communitarian views, Nordhoff's work includes studies of the Amana, Shaker, and Oneida societies, some of which survived for a number of years, and some to the present day, in order "to see if their experience offers any useful hints toward the solution of the labor question." He presents a sympathetic but objective account which is important because it is based upon his personal observations of the societies.

Orvis, Marianne Dwight. LETTERS FROM BROOK FARM, 1844-47. Ed. Amy L. Reed. Poughkeepsie, N.Y.: Vassar College, 1928.

Dwight was a member of the Brook Farm community. Her letters record the details of daily living and the discussions of ideas which occupied the residents. From beginning to end, the letters record the rising then declining hopes of those who wished the experiment to succeed. Dwight's lively prose style indicates she was intelligent, completely committed to the community, and a keen observer.

e. Suffrage and Other Reform Movements

Altgeld, John Peter. THE MIND AND SPIRIT OF JOHN PETER ALTGELD. Ed. Henry M. Christman. Introd. Vachel Lindsay. Urbana: Univ. of Illinois, 1960.

As a judge, Altgeld pardoned the "Chicago Anarchists" in 1893; as governor of Illinois, he often acted from conscientious principles not always in accord with political popularity. This is a collection of his selected writings and speeches.

_____. OUR PENAL MACHINERY AND ITS VICTIMS. Chicago: A.C. McClurg, 1884.

> In this work Altgeld criticized the entire system of law enforcement and prosecution: "It seems, first, to make criminals out of many that are not naturally so; and, second, to render it difficult for those convicted ever to be anything else than criminals; and, third, to fail to repress those that do not want to be anything but criminals." He aslo pointed out that the American judicial systems were weighted against the poor. His proposed reforms in both the judicial and the penal systems have been largely ignored by the legal system and bureaucracy but influenced other reformers and some lawyers, including Darrow.

Anthony, Susan B., et al. HISTORY OF WOMAN SUFFRAGE. 6 vols. 1881-87; New York: Arno, 1969.

> The volumes include reminiscences by Anthony, Stanton and others; reports of meetings; a brief history of reform movements, tracing the shifting emphasis from abolition and temperance to suffrage and women's rights; brief essays on women's positions in church and state; a report on the impact of the Civil War; and, finally, a discussion of the worldwide impact of the movement. The reports are made more interesting through the lively anecdotes and descriptions which are liberally scattered throughout.

Beecher, Catharine Esther. AN ESSAY ON THE EDUCATION OF FEMALE TEACHERS. New York: Van Nostrand and Dwight, 1835.

> Daughter of Lyman and sister of Henry Ward and Harriet, Catharine became an educator, opening the School for Females in Hartford, Connecticut. In this volume and the two listed below, she argues for educating women in the "domestic virtues" and against the kinds of oppression that prevent women from developing vocationally and intellectually. She called upon American women to exert their influence to "save the world" by honoring their "peculiar womanly duties as nurses, teachers, and mothers." She felt, however, that women's influence should be in the home and classroom not on the platform or at the polls. She extolled the virtues of home and family and provided a healthy argument for increased exercise for women, more sensible clothing, and greater activity in general.

_____. THE EVILS SUFFERED BY AMERICAN WOMEN AND . . . CHILDREN. New York: Harper and Brothers, 1846.

_____. THE TRUE REMEDY FOR THE WRONGS OF WOMAN. . . . Boston: Phillips, Sampson and Co., 1851.

Blake, Lillie Devereaux. WOMAN'S PLACE TODAY. New York: J.W. Lovell, 1883.

This book created a sensation in the contemporary press and did much to awaken women into active workers for suffrage.

Buhle, Mari Jo, and Paul Buhle, eds. THE CONCISE HISTORY OF WOMAN SUFFRAGE: SELECTIONS FROM THE CLASSIC WORK OF STANTON, ANTHONY, GAGE, AND HARPER. Urbana: Univ. of Illinois Press, 1978.

This volume includes eighty-two selections from the six-volume HISTORY OF WOMAN SUFFRAGE (above). The editors provide introductory essays to the selections.

Burritt, Elihu. LECTURES AND SPEECHES. London: Sampson Low and Son and Marston, 1869.

Largely self-taught, Burritt learned to read numerous languages and lectured on self-culture. He then devoted himself to temperance, abolition, and world peace. He organized the League of Universal Brotherhood and was instrumental in forming the International Land and Labor Agency, which helped to find work for emigrants. He blamed North and South equally for slavery and proposed several schemes to avoid the Civil War. After the war, he worked for education and equality for blacks. This is the only published volume of his ideas, although excerpts from letters and journals are included in Curti's study (Section II.F.2, p. 216). As seen in these speeches, the clarity of his arguments in behalf of unpopular social causes is remarkable. He deserves a prominent place in the history of nineteenth-century humanitarianism.

Cross, Barbara M., ed. THE EDUCATED WOMAN IN AMERICA: SELECTED WRITINGS OF CATHARINE BEECHER, MARGARET FULLER, AND M. CAREY THOMAS. New York: Teachers College Press, Columbia Univ., 1965.

All three women are represented with generous selections of their writings on educational reform.

Dix, Dorothea Lynde. MEMORIAL TO THE LEGISLATURE OF MASSACHUSETTS. Boston: Munroe and Francis, 1843.

In this appeal, Dix urges a study and reform of prisons, almshouses, and insane asylums. Her awareness of the debilitating effect of institutions, particularly those for the insane, is sensitive and intelligent.

Dodge, Mary Abigail. WOMAN'S WRONGS. 1868; New York: Arno, 1972.

The author was a liberal thinker and an abolitionist, but she opposed woman suffrage. As a popular writer, she used her influence to speak out against the distortions she felt had been perpetrated by the women's rights movement. At the same time, she argued that "neither heaven nor physiology" condemned women to household drudgery and that there was nothing exalted about mere "natural maternity." Giving life was not enough, she said; one

should also be "able to make provision to turn life to the best account,--to give life, careless whether it will be bale or boon to
the recipient,--is the sin of sins."

Eisler, Benita, ed. THE LOWELL OFFERING: WRITINGS BY NEW ENGLAND
MILL WOMEN (1840-45). Philadelphia: Lippincott, 1977.

The LOWELL OFFERING was a newsletter designed to reflect an
"ideal system": that of the mill workers in Lowell, Massachusetts.
This collection includes the letters, essays, and poems by the women mill workers, drawn to Lowell by the promise of self-improvement and by the salary of about 3 dollars a week. Although conditions in the Lowell mills were better than those in many other
New England factories and there were opportunities for the workers
to attend lectures and discussion groups, the hours were long and
the environment unhealthy. As conditions in the mill worsened,
editorials and articles reflected this. This anthology gives a clear
account of the attractions for farm girls and the conditions under
which they were expected to work.

Finley, James Bradley. MEMORIALS OF PRISON LIFE. 1850; New York:
Arno, 1974.

Finley was a chaplain to the penitentiary of Ohio, and in this account describes the miseries and degradations of prison life, gives
anecdotes about the prisoners, and tells of religious leader's visits
to the prison. He saw most criminals as sinful, deserving both
punishment and separation from the rest of society; however, he
also saw them as human beings capable of rehabilitation. He asserts
that he has no intent to preach or reform, yet he does urge the
development of prison libraries. Memorials resulted in a reexamina-
tion of several aspects of criminal justice in America.

Foner, Philip S., ed. THE FACTORY GIRLS: A COLLECTION OF WRITINGS
ON LIFE AND STRUGGLES IN THE NEW ENGLAND FACTORIES OF THE 1840S
BY THE FACTORY GIRLS THEMSELVES, AND THE STORY, IN THEIR OWN
WORDS, OF THE FIRST TRADE UNIONS OF WOMEN WORKERS IN THE UNITED
STATES. Urbana: Univ. of Illinois Press, 1977.

In contrast to the milder LOWELL OFFERING, this collection
samples the writing of several militant female workers. The "girls"
were aware that they had much to be grateful for and believed in
progress, but they were also aware that they were being exploited.
The documents represent the thoughts and feelings of these women
and their battle for shorter working days and better working conditions.

Grimke, Sarah Moore. LETTERS ON THE EQUALITY OF THE SEXES AND THE
CONDITION OF WOMAN. 1838; New York: Source Book Press, 1970.

Although better known as abolitionists, both Grimke sisters were
also active in the women's rights movement. This volume is a col-

lection of letters to Mary S. Parker, president of the Boston Anti-Slavery Society. Grimke gives scriptural as well as secular evidence for her argument for equality of the sexes. She notes, however, that equality would impose greater responsibility upon many women.

Hale, Sarah Josepha. WOMAN'S RECORD. 1854; New York: Source Book Press, 1970.

Sarah Hale was an editor of GODEY'S LADY'S BOOK; she was active in the woman's rights movement and encouraged female writers. In this survey, she attempted to illustrate, by means of over fifteen hundred biographical sketches and selections from the writings of women, the history of woman and her influence on society and literature.

Howe, Julia Ward. JULIA WARD HOWE AND THE WOMAN SUFFRAGE MOVEMENT: A SELECTION FROM HER SPEECHES AND ESSAYS. Ed. Florence Howe Hull. 1913; New York: Arno, 1969.

_____, ed. SEX AND EDUCATION. 1874; New York: Arno, 1972.

Howe assembled this collection of essays and reviews as a reply to Dr. E. Clarke's SEX IN EDUCATION, which argued against higher education for women because of their "delicate and complex" reproductive apparatus. Women should avoid diverting energy needed by their reproductive systems to "the region of brain activity," Dr. Clarke argued. Howe recruited a number of contributors to this collection, including many who were a living refutation of Clarke's assertions. Thomas Wentworth Higginson's review of Clarke's book, included here, is a scholarly attack upon its unscientific premises and unwarranted inferences.

Jackson, Helen Maria Hunt. A CENTURY OF DISHONOR. 1881; Minneapolis: Ross and Haines, 1964.

Helen Hunt Jackson is remembered today primarily for two literary reasons. One is that she recognized the greatness of Emily Dickinson's poetry. Late in life, after having largely ignored the causes of abolition and suffrage, Jackson became interested in the plight of the Poncas Indians in Nebraska. She carefully researched the treatment of the native Americans in the United States and documented, in this volume, the hypocrisy and cruelty of white Americans. She presented a clear case for the needed widespread reform within the Department of Interior. RAMONA (1884), her famous novel, grew in part out of her research and her resentment of the cruelties and injustices she had documented.

Riis, Jacob August. THE CHILDREN OF THE POOR. 1892; New York: Arno, 1971.

Written as a "supplement" to HOW THE OTHER HALF LIVES, below, this volume focuses on the children of the tenements: what happens to them and what might be done to help them.

_____. HOW THE OTHER HALF LIVES. 1890; New York: Hill and Wang, 1964.

As a reporter on the New York SUN, Riis saw the tenement environment as fostering crime. In these "studies among the tenements of New York," he provides a valuable social record of such urban conditions at the turn of the century as well as proposals to improve them.

Smith, Elizabeth Oakes. WOMAN AND HER NEEDS. New York: Fowler and Wells, 1851.

This is a collection of articles published in the New York TRIBUNE and lectures given on the lyceum circuit by an influential advocate of woman's suffrage. Elizabeth Smith, the wife of the humorist Seba Smith, also pleads for the recognition of the capabilities of women in arenas other than the home.

Sumner, William Graham. ESSAYS OF WILLIAM GRAHAM SUMNER. Ed. Albert G. Keller and Maurice R. Davie. New Haven, Conn.: Yale Univ. Press, 1934.

An economist and professor of political and social science at Yale, Sumner was a reformer in the sense that he urged defeat of "unjust" institutions and laws opposing "the process of natural selection and survival" of those who worked hardest and produced most.

_____. WHAT SOCIAL CLASSES OWE TO EACH OTHER. New York: Harper and Brothers, 1883.

In this volume, Sumner argues that rather than recognizing privileged classes and sets of duties and obligations to redistribute wealth, society should create new opportunities for production, allowing those who are less well off the opportunity to improve their financial status.

Willard, Frances E. WOMAN AND TEMPERANCE: OR, THE WORK AND WORKERS OF THE WOMAN'S CHRISTIAN TEMPERANCE UNION. 1883; New York: Arno, 1972.

The author, who founded the Women's Christian Temperance Union, worked for woman's suffrage and also for the labor movement, here gives a brief history of WCTU, biographical sketches of the workers, excerpts from letters and speeches, and "case studies" which provides an occasional fascinating narrative. Willard's reform platform was a broad one: "No sectarianism in religion, no sectionalism in politics, no sex in citizenship." In this volume, she hoped to portray temperance as improving both society and government.

Woodhull, Victoria Claflin. ORIGIN, TENDENCIES, AND PRINCIPLES OF GOVERNMENT. New York: Woodhull, Claflin and Co., 1871.

> This work created something of a sensation when it was published. It includes papers on human equality and pleas for women suffrage, the right to abortion, and a single standard of morality and free love. Woodhull's opposition to prostitution was consistent with these views.

Wright, Carroll D. THE WORKING GIRLS OF BOSTON. 1889. Ed. Leon Stein and Philip Taft. New York: Arno, 1969.

> Wright was the director of the Massachusetts Bureau of Statistics and was instrumental in the establishment of the Bureau of Labor. He urged that management organizations and labor unions handle conflicts and injustices. This study includes data on wage rates, living costs, and industrial conflicts caused by the problems of housing, illiteracy, and poverty. It presents an objective and informed picture of the female's working conditions in the mills.

f. Slavery and Abolition

Beecher, Catharine Esther. AN ESSAY ON SLAVERY AND ABOLITION WITH REFERENCE TO THE DUTY OF AMERICAN FEMALES. Boston: Perkins and Marvin, 1837.

> Catharine Beecher was a moderate abolitionist; however, she criticized female participation in public discussions and condemned abolitionist interference with southern slaves who were well treated. This short book is addressed to Angelina Grimke, see below.

Birney, James G. LETTER ON THE POLITICAL OBLIGATIONS OF ABOLITIONISTS. 1839; New York: Arno, 1969.

> An early antislavery leader in the South, Birney freed his slaves and organized the Kentucky Society for the Gradual Relief of the State from Slavery. He opposed William Lloyd Garrison, but consented to be a presidential candidate for the Liberty party in 1840 and 1844 as a political abolitionist. He accused the Southern churches of supporting slavery, but he noted that churches elsewhere were active in the antislavery movement.

_____. LETTERS OF JAMES GILLESPIE BIRNEY, 1831-57. 2 vols. Ed. Dwight L. Dumond. 1939; Gloucester, Mass.: Peter Smith, 1966.

> Birney's letters give insight into the personal as well as the public concern of an important nineteenth-century abolitionist.

Bontemps, Arna, ed. GREAT SLAVE NARRATIVES. Boston: Beacon Press, 1969.

> Bontemps provides an introduction and notes for the three slave narratives reprinted here: "The Life of Olaudah Equiano; or Gustavus

Vassa, the African" (1789); "The Fugitive Blacksmith; or Events in
the History of James W.C. Pennington" (1849); and "Running a
Thousand Miles for Freedom; or The Escape of William and Ellen
Craft" (1860). The editor views the slave narratives as an "influential contribution to American cultural history of the nineteenth
century." The narratives were popular, and hundreds were published with the approach of the Civil War. Pennington's narrative shows him to be well educated and articulate; the Crafts's story
is vivid and well detailed.

Brown, William Wells. THE BLACK MAN: HIS ANTECEDENTS, HIS GENIUS,
AND HIS ACHIEVEMENTS. 1863. New York: Johnson, 1968.

This is a collection of brief biographical sketches of nearly sixty
individuals who, as the author puts it, "by their own genius, capacity, and intellectual development, have surmounted the many obstacles which slavery and prejudice have thrown in their way, and
raised themselves to positions of honor and influence." Many of
these black leaders and writers had not been recognized formally
in print before. Brown aimed at refuting the contention that the
black is intellectually inferior to the white. To do so, he structured his biographies to include anecdotes and evaluations by a
subject's contemporaries. His prose demonstrates a control of
material and a gift for interesting narrative.

_____. MY SOUTHERN HOME: OR, THE SOUTH AND ITS PEOPLE. 1880;
Upper Saddle River, N.J.: Gregg Press, 1968.

This volume includes sketches, narratives, descriptions, and observations based upon the author's experiences as a southern slave and,
later, as a visitor returning to the South. The narratives are well
told and always interesting. The incidents described seem occasionally melodramatic, but the author does not dwell upon the injustices
which create the sense of melodrama. Brown captures the speech
and dialect of the people he writes about without being condescending.

_____. NARRATIVE OF WILLIAM W. BROWN: A FUGITIVE SLAVE. Boston:
Anti-Slavery Office, 1847.

In the narrative, Brown tells how he escaped from slavery, acquired
an education, and became a leading spokesman for black's claim to
freedom. Brown studied medicine and was also interested in temperance, woman's suffrage, and prison reform. He was an intelligent,
fluent, and forceful spokesman for these causes.

_____. THE NEGRO IN THE AMERICAN REBELLION: HIS HEROISM AND
HIS FIDELITY. 1867; New York: Johnson, 1968.

The author describes the Negro's role in the Revolutionary War,
the War of 1812, and the Civil War, obtaining information about

the latter through newspaper correspondents and personal contact with volunteer black regiments. Accounts of battles are interspersed with humorous anecdotes and stories of injustices, prejudice, and mistreatment of the free blacks in the war.

_____. THE RISING SON: OR, THE ANTECEDENTS AND ADVANCEMENT OF THE COLORED RACE. 1874; Miami, Fla.: Mnemosyne Publishing, 1969.

Brown attempts a history of the African race from Ethiopia to post-Civil War America. In his preface, the author states: "After availing himself of all the reliable information obtainable, the author is compelled to acknowledge the scantiness of materials for a history of the African race. He has throughout endeavored to give a faithful account of the people and their customs, without concealing their faults." Although Brown did not approach his subject entirely scientifically, for many years he was acknowledged as the outstanding authority on black history.

Cable, George Washington. THE NEGRO QUESTION. 1890. Ed. Arlin Turner. New York: Norton, 1958.

The 1958 publication edited by Arlin Turner includes both THE NEGRO QUESTION and THE SILENT SOUTH, as well as six previously unpublished essays. Considered by many critics to be among Cable's most valuable writings and "classics in their field," these volumes collect a series of articles and addresses on the condition of the former Confederate states. Cable points out that the present condition of many southern blacks was little better than it had been prior to the Civil War. He presents an eloquent argument for Negro civil rights, although he argues against intermarriage and other social mixing of the races.

_____. THE SILENT SOUTH. 1885. Ed. Arlin Turner as part of THE NEGRO QUESTION. New York: Norton, 1958.

One of Cable's main points in this volume is that many Southerners who have remained silent agree with his arguments for black civil rights and with his objections to the mistreatment of southern blacks. He calls upon these people to raise their voices and be heard.

Child, Lydia Maria. AN APPEAL IN FAVOR OF THAT CLASS OF AMERICANS CALLED AFRICANS. 1833. Pref. by James M. McPherson. New York: Arno, 1968.

The APPEAL is a mixture of emotionalism, common sense, unscientific anthropology, and practical economics. McPherson calls it "a key document in the history of the antislavery movement." Lydia Maria Child was a popular writer of domestic novels and of nonfictional domestic advice. When APPEAL was published, it alienated many of her Boston friends, and sales of her other books declined. However, her tract had an important role in converting many to the cause of abolition; in it the author traces the history of slavery and points out the injustice of the position of American slaves.

_____. LETTERS OF LYDIA M. CHILD. 1882; New York: AMS Press, 1971.

The correspondence includes letters to Whittier on abolition and letters admonishing capital punishment, two causes in which Child was active. Whittier, moved by her pleas, wrote the introduction to LETTERS.

Douglass, Frederick. THE LIFE AND WRITINGS OF FREDERICK DOUGLASS. 5 vols. Ed. Philip S. Foner. New York: International Publishers, 1950-64.

These volumes collect Douglass' writings and speeches other than the AUTOBIOGRAPHY. They present a solid argument for Douglass as an important contributor to nineteenth-century oratory and literature.

_____. NARRATIVE OF THE LIFE OF FREDERICK DOUGLASS: AN AMERICAN SLAVE. 1845. Ed. Benjamin Quarles. Cambridge, Mass.: Belknap Press, Harvard Univ. Press, 1960.

Douglass' NARRATIVE was one of the most widely read and by far the most effective of the slave narratives as a weapon in the abolitionist crusade. The prose is simple, forceful, and vivid, showing the intelligence and articulateness of the author. Douglass twice expanded his autobiography. In MY BONDAGE AND MY FREEDOM (1855; ed. with an Introd. Philip S. Foner, New York: Dover, 1969), Douglass was able to say things about the treatment of the black slaves which he had not dared put in the first NARRATIVE. THE LIFE AND TIMES OF FREDERICK DOUGLASS (1881), which was later revised and enlarged (1892), includes an account of Douglass' Civil War and Reconstruction activities.

DuBois, William E. Burghardt. THE PHILADELPHIA NEGRO. 1899; New York: B. Blom, 1967.

One of the first systematic sociological studies of American blacks, this places much of the burden of blame for their condition on the blacks themselves. The author is conservative, calling upon blacks to be patient, persevering, and temperate.

_____. THE SUPPRESSION OF THE AFRICAN SLAVE-TRADE TO THE UNITED STATES OF AMERICA. 1896; New York: Social Science Press, 1954.

DuBois' Harvard dissertation, published as the first volume in the Harvard Historical Series, this is an examination of the attempt by the United States to stop the importation of Africans. It is readable, authoritative, and clearly demonstrates that most of the anti-importation laws were not enforced.

Dumond, Dwight L., and G.H. Barnes, eds. LETTERS OF THEODORE WELD, ANGELINA GRIMKE WELD, AND SARAH GRIMKE. 1934; Gloucester, Mass.: Peter Smith, 1965.

> The discovery and publication of these letters led many historians to revise their view from that of the antislavery movement's being centered primarily around Garrison in New England to a greater emphasis upon the role in abolitionism of evangelical religious movements further west.

Elliott, E.N., ed. COTTON IS KING, AND PRO-SLAVERY ARGUMENTS: COMPRISING THE WRITINGS OF HAMMOND, HARPER, CHRISTY, STRING-FELLOW, HODGE, BLEDSOE, AND CARTWRIGHT. 1860; New York: Negro Univ. Press, 1969.

> Collected in order to avoid North-South conflicts and "to convince the abolitionists of the utter failure of their plans," these argu-ments presented by the primary spokesmen for slavery are economic, religious, social, and ethnological. The editor defines slavery as "the duty and obligation of the slave to labor for the mutual bene-fit of both master and slave, under a warrant to the slave of pro-tection, and a comfortable subsistance, under all circumstances."

Fitzhugh, George. CANNIBALS ALL! OR, SLAVES WITHOUT MASTERS. 1857; Cambridge, Mass.: Belknap Press, Harvard Univ. Press, 1960.

> The most influential proslavery propagandist of the decade before the war, Fitzhugh argued that the protective-dependent relationship of master and slave was much more benevolent than the competi-tiveness of free enterprise. He wrote that "all good and respect-able people are 'cannibals all' who do not labor, or who are suc-cessfully trying to live without labor, on the unrequited labor of other people." Employers in a free society get their labor at cheaper rates, Fitzhugh maintained, because they don't support their laborers when business slumps or when the laborers become too old or sick to work.

_____. SOCIOLOGY FOR THE SOUTH: OR, THE FAILURE OF FREE SO-CIETY. 1854; New York: B. Franklin, 1965.

> Fitzhugh was in the forefront of "Reactionary Enlightenment," a movement providing contrast to and objectivity toward the Ameri-can liberal formula. He argued that slavery was the only avenue of escape from the evils of a "Free Society" (i.e., laissez-faire capitalism) because it identified the interests of the strong with those of the weak.

Fletcher, John. STUDIES ON SLAVERY. Natchez, Miss.: Jackson Warner, 1852.

> In an influential reply to W.E. Channing and others, Fletcher argued that slavery was a "moral contract," service in exchange

for security. He also cited the biblical curse of Cain and the "wanted conformity to the laws of God" by the Negroes in Africa as justification for slavery. Fletcher opposed Channing's idea of conscience and the innate moral nature of man by stating that morality and conscience are learned qualities, developed through education and conformity to some law. He also argued that labor must always be dependent on capital; the slave, being capital, is always assured of work and sustenance.

Foner, Philip S., ed. THE VOICE OF BLACK AMERICA: MAJOR SPEECHES BY NEGROES IN THE UNITED STATES, 1791-1971. New York: Simon and Schuster, 1972.

> Many of the speeches given in the nineteenth century regarding emancipation are highly interesting and are good examples of the oratorical and literary accomplishments of the black Americans who gave them. The editor observes that "Despite the literature in the field, scores of important speeches by black Americans have never been reprinted and published in book form. Many of these appear in the present collection for the first time." Each speech is preceded by a biographical introduction and includes explanatory notes.

Garrison, William Lloyd. THE LETTERS OF WILLIAM LLOYD GARRISON. 6 vols. projected. Ed. Walter M. Merrill and Louis Ruchames. Cambridge, Mass.: Belknap Press, Harvard Univ. Press, 1971-- .

> These letters serve as a primary source for those interested in evaluating Garrison's role as an abolitionist. They are candid, well written, and intelligent, providing insight into Garrison's character and his ability to communicate his ideas and into the issues of the time.

_____ . SELECTIONS FROM THE WRITINGS AND SPEECHES OF WILLIAM LLOYD GARRISON. 1852; New York: Negro Univ. Press, 1968.

> This provides a representative sampling of the expression of one of the foremost abolitionists.

_____ . THOUGHTS ON AFRICAN COLONIZATION. 1832; New York: Arno, 1968.

> Garrison's cogent and eloquent document had a profound effect on white abolitionists and marked a turning point in the movement. While he had for a time argued in favor of returning American blacks to Africa, Garrison became convinced that such a move would only keep whites from facing their responsibilities to all citizens, including the blacks.

Grimké, Angelina Emily. APPEAL TO THE CHRISTIAN WOMEN OF THE SOUTH. 1836; New York: Arno, 1969.

> Grimké's appeal is powerfully and intelligently written, and it is

an important document of the involvement of women in the cause
of abolition. Grimké speaks as a woman from the South to southern
women, giving scriptural support for her views and calling upon
them to recognize the cruelties, inhumanity, and ultimately cor-
rupting qualities of slavery.

_____. LETTERS TO CATHARINE E. BEECHER. 1838; New York: Arno,
1969.

A reply to the short book which Catharine Beecher had addressed
to her (see above), these letters present both Grimké's abolitionist
and feminist position. Grimké argues that human rights should not
be affected by either race or sex and that sensitive women should
defend the rights of every human being.

Henson, Josiah. THE LIFE OF JOSIAH HENSON. 1849. Reading, Mass.:
Addison-Wesley, 1969.

Henson came to be identified with Harriet Beecher Stowe's Uncle
Tom. It is not clear whether or not Stowe had read Henson's
autobiography, which had been written with the help of Samuel A.
Eliot, before she wrote UNCLE TOM'S CABIN; however, many of
the episodes recounted by Henson paralleled her narrative, and
subsequent editions of his autobiography were altered to conform
to Stowe's story. The reprint is based on an edition published in
Ontario in 1881, edited by John Lobb. Many other editions have
also been reprinted--for example, the 1849 edition was reprinted
in Dresden, Ontario (Observer Press, 1965); the 1858 edition,
with an introduction by Harriet Beecher Stowe, was reprinted in
Williamstown, Massachusetts (Corner House, 1973).

Hildreth, Richard. DESPOTISM IN AMERICA. 1840; New York: Negro Univ.
Press, 1968.

An "inquiry into the nature, results, and legal basis of the slave-
holding system in the United States," written by a much-respected
historian and political philosopher, this presents a history of slavery
and a discussion of its practice from the point of view of one who
regarded it as a "malevolent disease" in the South.

Lester, Julius, ed. TO BE A SLAVE. New York: Dial Press, 1968.

This collection of nineteenth-century slave narratives includes both
accounts recorded and rewritten by abolitionists of the pre-Civil
War era and interviews taken down in a Federal Writers Project
in the 1930s. The narratives preserve the speech patterns and
language of the ex-slaves who were interviewed. The editor adds
a commentary on the social and historical conditions of the times.
The accounts are brief, informative, and often eloquent.

Pillsbury, Parker. ACTS OF THE ANTI-SLAVERY APOSTLES. 1883; New York: Negro Univ. Press, 1969.

> These letters, narratives, arguments, and descriptions deal with the ideas and effects achieved by those who lectured against slavery, primarily in New England. A few pro-slavery arguments are also presented. Garrison and others whom the author knew personally are sketched by means of brief biographies and anecdotes.

Ross, F.A. SLAVERY ORDAINED OF GOD. 1857; New York: Negro Univ. Press, 1969.

> One of the more influential proslavery treatises, this attempted to demonstrate "that slavery is part of the government ordained in certain conditions of fallen mankind . . . for the good of the slave, the good of the master, the good of the whole American family, until another and better destiny may be unfolded." Using both scriptural and social support for his argument, the author contends that the southern slave is "better off than his brethren in Africa."

Starobin, Robert S., ed. BLACKS IN BONDAGE: LETTERS OF AMERICAN SLAVES. New York: New Viewpoints, 1974.

> These slave letters, written or dictated by the slaves themselves while they were still in bondage, provide an excellent primary resource for both literary and cultural historians interested in the slaves' point of view, style, and general literacy.

Truth, Sojourner. THE NARRATIVE OF SOJOURNER TRUTH: A BONDSWO-MAN OF OLDEN TIMES. 1850. Enlarged as THE NARRATIVE OF SOJOURN-ER TRUTH, WITH A HISTORY OF HER LABORS AND CORRESPONDENCE DRAWN FROM HER BOOK OF LIFE BY FRANCES W. TITUS. 1878; New York: Arno, 1968.

> First recorded by Frances W. Titus, a white friend, the narrative influenced both the abolitionist and the women's rights movements. Many of the events and episodes were written in Sojourner Truth's own words; others were written from the point of view of Frances Titus. Truth's was one of the few accounts of a woman's experience as a slave or of the experience of a slave in the North.

Weld, Theodore Dwight. AMERICAN SLAVERY AS IT IS. 1839; New York: Arno, 1968.

> An indictment of slavery using evidence gathered from materials in southern newspapers from 1837 to 1839, this is considered by many historians to be one of the most important books in antislavery literature. Wendell Phillips called it the best possible "storehouse of arguments."

_____. THE BIBLE AGAINST SLAVERY. New York: American Anti-Slavery Society, 1838.

> This pamphlet was the unquestioned authority for abolitionists for years. Tens of thousands of copies were printed; all ministers and theological students who applied for a copy received one free.

Woodson, Carter G., ed. THE MIND OF THE NEGRO AS REFLECTED IN LETTERS WRITTEN DURING THE CRISIS, 1800-1860. 1926; New York: Russell and Russell, 1969.

> Letters which had previously been published in the JOURNAL OF NEGRO HISTORY are faithfully reproduced as they were found in the sources. They provide a fine resource for cultural history, social history, and insight into the views of blacks prior to the Civil War.

g. The Civil War

Alcott, Louisa May. HOSPITAL SKETCHES. 1863. Ed. Bessie Z. Jones. Cambridge, Mass.: Belknap Press, Harvard Univ. Press, 1960.

> Based on the author's brief tour of duty as a volunteer nurse in the Civil War, the book won a wide audience when it was first published. The descriptions and anecdotes are humorous as well as sympathetic and largely avoid the sentimentality of some other contemporary accounts of the wounded and dying.

Alexander, Edward Porter. MILITARY MEMOIRS OF A CONFEDERATE. New York: Scribner's, 1907.

> This interesting well-written analysis utilizes official reports of both the Union and the Confederate armies to criticize each campaign "as one would criticize a game of chess, only to point out the good and bad plays on each side, and the moves which have influenced the result." The author emphasizes the southern struggle for self-government, although he does admit that the Union victory led to the economic betterment of the South.

Andrews, J. Cutler, ed. THE SOUTH REPORTS THE CIVIL WAR. Princeton: Princeton Univ. Press, 1970.

> This is a collection of excerpts of Civil War reports from southern journalists, many of which are vivid and eloquent.

Beecher, Edward. NARRATIVE OF RIOTS AT ALTON. 1838; New York: E.P. Dutton, 1965.

> Beecher describes the murder of Elizah P. Lovejoy, abolitionist editor and minister, who was killed while defending his press, the Alton OBSERVER. The author was a perceptive interpreter of

events, and the NARRATIVE is considered by many historians to be a major document, crucial to an understanding of America in 1837. Beecher was a "conservative abolitionist," his own views about the evils of slavery tempered by an awareness of biblical precedents for slavery.

Bellard, Alfred. GONE FOR A SOLDIER: THE CIVIL WAR MEMOIRS OF PRIVATE ALFRED BELLARD. Ed. David Herbert Donald. Boston: Little, Brown, 1975.

During the Civil War, Bellard's father placed in a notebook the diaries, letters, and drawings sent by the eighteen-year-old Alfred while he was an infantryman in the Army of the Potomac. After the war, Alfred Bellard drafted a more coherent and extended account, adding many concrete details. The notebooks dropped out of sight until 1962 and were brought to Donald a few years later for editing. The value of the account lies in its authenticity and its unpretentious clear prose.

Billings, John Davis. HARDTACK AND COFFEE: THE UNWRITTEN STORY OF ARMY LIFE. 1887; Williamstown, Mass.: Corner House, 1973.

Billings was a member of the Army of the Potomac. In this lively, well-detailed, third-person account, he tells about army rations, punishments, sleeping quarters, together with more general information about hospitals, inventions of the war, building roads and bridges, and the development of the signal corps.

Cate, Wirt, ed. TWO SOLDIERS: THE CAMPAIGN DIARIES OF THOMAS J. KEY, C.S.A., AND ROBERT J. CAMPBELL, U.S.A. Chapel Hill: Univ. of North Carolina Press, 1938.

Begun in 1864 by Campbell, who was in the Union army, the diary was "captured" by Key, who was a newspaperman and a soldier in the Confederate Army. Key continued the day-by-day recording of life in the army and contemporary events, this time from the Southern view. Campbell was a fairly young man and a casual observer of what went on. Key was older and more bitter about the war; he was a better writer than Campbell and had considerable journalistic and literary skill.

Chesnut, Mary. MARY CHESNUT'S CIVIL WAR. Ed. C. Van Woodward. New Haven, Conn.: Yale Univ. Press, 1981

Originally published as A DIARY FROM DIXIE, this memoir, now presented in a definitive edition restoring the language and several passages from the original diary, presents one of the best Confederate accounts of the war years. Chesnut, the wife of a southern senator, was intelligent and widely read. She was also in touch with others in the Confederacy who were public-spirited and well educated. She sensed not only the importance of the war but also its literary possibilities. Edmund Wilson called the diary "an extraordinary document--in its informal department, a masterpiece."

Davis, Jefferson. RISE AND FALL OF THE CONFEDERATE GOVERNMENT. 2 vols. 1881. Abridged with a Foreword by Earl Schenk Miers. New York: Collier Books, 1961.

> Prepared by Davis himself, this history is his attempt to justify himself, hoping thereby to justify the South. As a justification of secession and the resulting war, the work is a worthy contribution; as history, it is partisan and sometimes unreliable. Davis spends much time on personal quarrels and misunderstandings without revealing a great deal about his own thoughts and concerns and showing little of the sympathy seen in Grant's memoirs or the breadth of vision of Lincoln's writings.

Dawson, Sarah Morgan. A CONFEDERATE GIRL'S DIARY. 1913; Louisville, Ky: Lost Cause Press, 1957.

> Sarah Morgan was twenty when the war broke out; her diary begins on March 9, 1862. She describes in great detail the devastation brought to the family's Baton Rouge house, presumably by Union officers. Although she was loyal to the Confederacy, she was horrified by the war. The diary contains joyful as well as painful experiences and is an articulate and sensitive account by one who has mixed feelings about the causes of both North and South.

De Forest, John William. A VOLUNTEER'S ADVENTURES: A UNION CAPTAIN'S RECORD OF THE CIVIL WAR. Ed. with Notes by James H. Crousshore and David Morris Potter. New Haven, Conn.: Yale Univ. Press, 1946; Hamden, Conn.: Archon, 1968.

> This is a collection of letters, selections from a journal, and magazine articles contributed to HARPER'S while De Forest was serving as a captain in the Louisiana and Shenandoah campaigns. Both the letters and the articles are direct and forcefully written. De Forest spared his wife few of the details of the brutality and hardship of war as he describes events in his letters, and he gives an objective account of his own thoughts and feelings in battle.

Duganne, Augustine J.H. CAMPS AND PRISONS: TWENTY MONTHS IN THE DEPARTMENT OF THE GULF. New York: J.F. Robens, 1865.

> Better known as a satirist and poet, Duganne was captured in Louisiana and spent much of the war in prisons in Texas. In a style reminiscent of Melville, the author talks of contemplated escapes, the conditions of the prisons and camps, and of his companions. He emerges as a courageous, articulate, and highly sensitive narrator.

Eggleston, George Cary. A REBEL'S RECOLLECTIONS. 1874; Bloomington: Indiana Univ. Press, 1959.

> Written by Edward Eggleston's younger brother at the suggestion of William Dean Howells, the reminiscences first appeared in ATLANTIC in 1874. Because they presented a human and humorous view of a rebel soldier, they helped to ease the bitterness between North and South. The account is cheerful, amusing, high-spirited, often exaggerated, and very readable. Although Eggleston loved Virginia and joined the southern army, he retained some loyalty to the North and wished to preserve the Union.

Forten, Charlotte. THE JOURNAL OF CHARLOTTE L. FORTEN. Introd. and notes by Ray Allen Billington. 1953; New York: Collier, 1967.

> Born in Philadelphia, the granddaughter of James Forten, a Philadelphia Negro whose grandfather had fought in the Revolutionary War, Forten was well-educated, beginning her diary when she was a young girl. She was sent to Massachusetts because she was refused admission to white schools in Philadelphia, and she records the discrimination she experienced in both of these places. She was later sent by a relief organization to teach the liberated blacks of the islands south of Charleston. After the war, Charlotte married Francis Grimke, the mulatto son of the slaveholding brother of Angelina and Sarah Grimke, the abolitionists. Her journal, particularly of the war years, is an articulate and interesting account by a free, well-educated black woman.

Giddings, Joshua Reed. THE HISTORY OF THE REBELLION. New York: Follet, Foster and Co., 1870.

> An abolitionist's account, much of this is devoted to events leading up to the war. The author emphasizes the role of the antislavery spokesmen and dwells upon incidents of southern brutality toward the slaves. Decisions by legislators and arguments in the legislature are documented in great detail.

Helper, Hinton Rowan. THE IMPENDING CRISIS OF THE SOUTH. 1857; Cambridge, Mass.: Belknap Press, Harvard Univ. Press, 1968.

> Either condemned or ignored by Southerners, this work was widely circulated by northern reformers. It finally became the most disturbing and influential work contributing to abolition since UNCLE TOM'S CABIN. Helper, the son of an illiterate farmer from North Carolina, combined statistics with argument and rhetoric to attack slavery and to point out its economic unfeasibility.

Higginson, Thomas Wentworth. ARMY LIFE IN A BLACK REGIMENT. Boston: Fields, Osgood and Co., 1870.

> Higginson was chosen to lead the First South Carolina Volunteers, the first black regiment fighting for the Union cause in the Civil

War. Much of this account comes from his war diary. His emotions, impressions, and descriptions are presented in a clear, precise, and unpretentious style. Although he is sometimes insensitive to the suffering of the Southerners and is smug about the moral righteousness of the northern position, he observes his soldiers without preconceptions and prejudices.

Holmes, Sarah Katherine Stone. BROKENBURN: THE JOURNAL OF KATE STONE, 1861-1868. Ed. John Q. Anderson. Baton Rouge: Louisiana State Univ. Press, 1955.

Forced to flee when Grant's army approached Vicksburg, Kate Stone and her mother, residents of a cotton plantation, had the typical Southern dislike of Yankees and disloyal former slaves. Although the journal itself contains no comments on the institution of slavery, Kate Stone later wrote, in an introduction to the journal, "Always I felt the moral guilt of it." She regretted the aftermath of the war but not the freeing of the slaves.

Knox, Thomas Wallace. CAMP-FIRE AND COTTON FIELD. 1865; New York: Da Capo, 1969.

Knox was a correspondent who covered the war. This lengthy document integrates various events with significant details to produce a vivid account of the conditions in the South during the Civil War. It is clearly written and generously laced with anecdotes.

Lee, Robert E. RECOLLECTIONS AND LETTERS OF GENERAL ROBERT E. LEE. 1904; Garden City, N.Y.: Garden City Publishers, 1924.

The memoirs and letters of Lee are restrained and dignified, and they indicate why he was held in so much respect by both North and South.

_____. THE WARTIME PAPERS OF R.E. LEE. Ed. Clifford Dowdey and Louis H. Manarin. Boston: Little, Brown, 1961.

This contains the most important letters, dispatches, orders, and reports together with a connective narrative by Clifford Dowdey. They document the difficulty under which Lee functioned both because of his tenuous command of forces in the Confederacy other than his own army and because of his troubles in obtaining supplies.

May, Samuel J. SOME RECOLLECTIONS OF OUR ANTISLAVERY CONFLICT. 1869; New York: Arno, 1968.

A Unitarian clergyman, May was an active abolitionist and was interested in the women's rights movement. May was an active participant in the events he describes, and he presents incidents, anecdotes, and thumbnail sketches of prominent reform figures.

His descriptions are vivid and convey a genuine sense of the times and the people involved.

Morrison, James L., Jr., ed. THE MEMOIRS OF HENRY HETH. Westport, Conn.: Greenwood Press, 1974.

Begun in 1897, these memoirs give a clear record, with a surprising number of details, of Heth's involvement in the Civil War. He was a Virginia West Pointer who became a Confederate general. He reveals his own personality and gives intimate glimpses of Winfield Scott, Grant, Lee, and others. Heth's first battle as a major-general was Gettysburg, and he bore the burden of his defeat there for the rest of his life. Heth sometimes skims over details that are painful, but he also maintains objectivity and humor about himself.

Mosby, John Singleton. THE MEMOIRS OF COLONEL JOHN S. MOSBY. 1917. Ed. Charles Wells Russell. Bloomington: Indiana Univ. Press, 1959.

Legendary for his exploits as a Confederate guerrila leader, Mosby was also a good storyteller, had a sense of humor, and was widely read. Both the memoirs and the earlier reminiscences (below) are liberally sprinkled with classical references, have a fine sense of narrative, and a certain detachment. His own exploits during the war are fascinating portrayals. S. Melville's narrative poem, "The Scout Toward Aldie," was based upon tales of Mosby's activities.

_____. MOSBY'S WAR REMINISCENCES AND STUART'S CAVALRY CAMPAIGN. Boston: G.A. Jones, 1887.

Nicolay, John George. THE OUTBREAK OF THE REBELLION. New York: Scribner's, 1881.

Utilizing the just-published Official War Records, the author describes events from secession to Bull Run--clearly, objectively, and intelligently.

Olmsted, Frederick L. THE COTTON KINGDOM. 2 vols. 1861. Ed. Arthur M. Schlesinger. New York: Knopf, 1953.

Better known as a landscape architect, Olmsted was also a journalist and was sent by the New York TIMES in 1852 to report on conditions in the South. This account and the one below--consisting of descriptions of people, remarkably faithful recordings of conversations, and other observations--lead to the conclusion that the South is doomed, slavery economically unsound, and the idea of southern culture a myth. The reports made a considerable impression in the North, and even in the South their conclusions were acknowledged to have some justification.

_____. A JOURNEY IN THE SEABOARD SLAVE STATES. 2 vols. 1856; New York: G.P. Putnam's, 1904.

_____. THE SLAVE STATES BEFORE THE CIVIL WAR. Ed. Harvey Wish.
New York: Capricorn, 1959.

> Wish collects and condenses sections of Olmsted's A JOURNEY IN
> THE SEABOARD SLAVE STATES, A JOURNEY THROUGH TEXAS,
> A JOURNEY IN THE BACK COUNTRY, and THE COTTON KING-
> DOM.

Shepherd, Jesse [Francis Grierson]. THE VALLEY OF SHADOWS. 1909. Ed.
Bernard DeVoto and an Introd. Theodore Spencer. New York: Harper and
Row, 1966.

> This memoir of the middle West just before the Civil War deserves
> more recognition than it has received. Written by an expatriate,
> mystic, and musician, who later turned to writing, this is probably
> the best prose Grierson wrote. Edmund Wilson says of this book
> that "No other book so gives us the sense of the imminence of the
> national crisis for which people dimly felt they were being pre-
> pared without having been given the power to control it." DeVoto
> also praises the work as a classic.

Smedes, Susan Dabney. MEMORIALS OF A SOUTHERN PLANTER. 1887. Ed.
with Introd. and Notes by Fletcher M. Green. New York: Knopf, 1965.

> In simple, effective prose, the author tells the story of her father,
> a planter of Mississippi, and a way of life abolished by the war.
> She never questioned the institution of slavery and wished to leave
> a record of the kindness and humaneness of the slaveowners she
> knew.

Stephens, Alexander H. A CONSTITUTIONAL VIEW OF THE LATE WAR BE-
TWEEN THE STATES: ITS CAUSES, CHARACTER, CONDUCT AND RESULTS
PRESENTED IN A SERIES OF COLLOQUIES AT LIBERTY HALL. 2 vols. Chi-
cago: Zeigler, McCurdy and Co., 1867-70.

> Stephens argues his case in a series of dialogues that take place
> between Stephens and three imaginary Unionists. It is long,
> heavily documented, and includes passages from speeches and pro-
> ceedings recorded in the CONGRESSIONAL RECORD.

_____. RECOLLECTIONS OF ALEXANDER H. STEPHENS. New York: Double-
day, Page, 1910.

> Vice-president of the Confederacy, Stephens was imprisoned at
> Fort Warren in 1865, was held incommunicado for several weeks,
> and thought he might be executed. While he was in prison, he
> kept a diary, published as the RECOLLECTIONS, in which he
> recorded his stoical despair, his fight with bedbugs and friend-
> ship with mice, and, most importantly, the justification of his
> policy on states' rights and in connection with the war. This
> policy is elaborated in A CONSTITUTIONAL VIEW.

Strong, George Templeton. DIARY OF THE CIVIL WAR, 1860–65. Ed. Allan Nevins. New York: Macmillan, 1962.

> Strong, a conservative New York lawyer, kept a diary between the years 1835 and 1875. Although Strong opposed slavery, he resisted abolitionism and deplored disunion. This diary, a literary achievement as well as a historical source, comments with humor, thoughtfulness, despair, and exultation upon the war and the events surrounding it.

Taylor, Richard. DESTRUCTION AND RECONSTRUCTION: PERSONAL EXPERIENCES OF THE LATE WAR. Ed. Charles P. Roland. Waltham, Mass.: Blaisdell, 1968.

> Son of Zachary Taylor, Richard bought a large plantation in Louisiana after his father's death. He was not particularly in favor of slavery but was a conscientious and stern officer of the Confederacy. His account contains some interesting portraits, including one of Stonewall Jackson.

Trowbridge, John T. THE SOUTH: A TOUR OF ITS BATTLEFIELDS AND RUINED CITIES, A JOURNEY THROUGH THE DESOLATED STATES, AND TALKS WITH THE PEOPLE. Abridged and Edited by Gordon Carroll as THE DESOLATE SOUTH, 1865-1866; published as A PICTURE OF THE BATTLEFIELDS AND OF THE DEVASTATED CONFEDERACY. New York: Duell, Sloan and Pearce, 1956.

> A friend and biographer of Whitman and Emerson, Trowbridge traveled to the South just after the fighting had stopped. He reports the same semifeudal system and injustices that had existed previously and argues that God had a hand in the devastation of the South.

Watson, William. LIFE IN THE CONFEDERATE ARMY. London: Chapman and Hall, 1887.

> Watson was a Scotsman who lived in the South during the Civil War and participated in the volunteer army. His account is straightforward and objective as he observes the causes of the war and its effects on the South.

Wilkeson, Frank. RECOLLECTIONS OF A PRIVATE SOLDIER IN THE ARMY OF THE POTOMAC. New York: G.P. Putnam's, 1887.

> The author gives an enlisted man's view of the daily conditions of camp and battlefield. His account is full of details and humor as well as serious criticism of the way the war was conducted. He felt that two great military mistakes in the North were the call for volunteers rather than the institution of a draft and the assumption that West Pointers were uncritically accepted as the most fit to command the armies.

2. BACKGROUNDS: ANTHOLOGIES AND SECONDARY SOURCES

Aaron, Daniel. THE UNWRITTEN WAR: AMERICAN WRITERS AND THE CIVIL WAR. New York: Knopf, 1973.

> The author argues that although "the War more than casually touched and engaged a number of writers, . . . it produced no major work which probed its causes and meaning." The major writers of non-fiction prose discussed are William Gilmore Simms, Oliver Wendell Holmes, Jr., Lowell, Emerson, and Henry Adams. A minor writer, George Templeton Strong, is also considered at some length.

Adler, Mortimer J., and Charles Van Doren, eds. THE NEGRO IN AMERICAN HISTORY. 3 vols. Chicago: Encyclopaedia Britannica Educational Corp., 1969.

> This collects essays, speeches, songs, poems, excerpts from fiction, documents, and other material, some of which, for example, Emerson's essay on "The Fugitive Slave Law," have become part of the general body of nineteenth-century nonfiction prose.

Aptheker, Herbert, ed. ONE CONTINUAL CRY: DAVID WALKER'S APPEAL TO THE COLORED CITIZENS OF THE WORLD, 1829-1830. New York: Humanities Press, 1965.

> A black Bostonian, Walker was reviled in the South and even condemned in the North as too impassioned and inflammatory in his statements. His APPEAL, first published in 1829, was one of the earliest and boldest statements in behalf of freedom in the early years of the antislavery movement. It had a strong impact on its own and succeeding generations and is today regarded by most historians as a great piece of antislavery literature. This edition provides backgrounds as well as the text of the 1830 edition of the APPEAL.

Barnes, Harry Elmer. A HISTORY OF HISTORICAL WRITING. Norman: Univ. of Oklahoma Press, 1937.

> One of the few comprehensive surveys of historical writing, this work provides a crucial context for an understanding of the writing of such nineteenth-century historians as Sparks, Bancroft, Motley, and Fiske. Barnes discusses their place and importance as historians and their methods of historiography.

Bassett, J.S. THE MIDDLE GROUP OF AMERICAN HISTORIANS. New York: Macmillan, 1917.

> Along with an introductory chapter on the earlier historians, this study provides a descriptive account of the careers of the most eminent historians of the nineteenth century: Sparks, Bancroft, Prescott, Motley, and Peter Force, the archivist. The contributions of each to the profession are clearly and intelligently assessed.

Beisner, Robert L. TWELVE AGAINST EMPIRE: THE ANTI-IMPERIALISTS, 1898-1900. New York: McGraw-Hill, 1968.

This study of historians, essayists, academics, and others, who for no obvious partisan reasons opposed the expansionist developments in the U.S. at the close of the nineteenth century, provides an insight into the motivations behind many literary productions of the period. Beisner believes that the same sentiments which earlier prompted abolitionist writings also prompted anti-imperialist expressions in such writers as Carl Schurz, Thomas B. Aldrich, Thomas W. Higginson, Charles Francis Adams, and William James.

Bestor, Arthur E., Jr. BACKWOODS UTOPIAS: THE SECTARIAN AND OWEN-ITE PHASES OF COMMUNITARIAN SOCIALISM IN AMERICA, 1663-1829. Philadelphia: Univ. of Pennsylvania Press, 1950.

In studying early communal utopian schemes, the author provides an excellent background and context for understanding the rise of the utopian community in the nineteenth century.

Bliss, William D., ed. ENCYCLOPEDIA OF SOCIAL REFORM. 1897; Rev. ed. New York: Funk and Wagnalls, 1908.

The volume lists persons who were involved in reform movements, describes the movements and activities, and provides "the economic, industrial, and sociological facts and statistics of all countries and all social subjects." Among the contributors and consultants for the volume were Jane Addams, William J. Bryan, William Lloyd Garrison, and Booker T. Washington.

Brigance, William N. JEREMIAH SULLIVAN BLACK: A DEFENDER OF THE CONSTITUTION AND THE TEN COMMANDMENTS. Philadelphia: Univ. of Pennsylvania Press, 1934. Bibliog.

Considered by many of his contemporaries "the most magnificent orator at the American bar" and a brilliant and controversial writer, Black was a prolific writer, but most of his pieces remain uncollected. This work lists all manuscripts, documents, and articles written by Black.

_____, ed. A HISTORY AND CRITICISM OF AMERICAN PUBLIC ADDRESS. 2 vols. 1943; 1960. Ed. Marie Kathryn Hochmuth. London: Longmans, Green, 1955.

The case for oratory as a legitimate literary genre is well made by both Brigance and Hochmuth. Hochmuth presents an excellent description of the genre. Chapters on the orators, mostly from the nineteenth century, have been written by collaborating specialists who consider the ideas, permanence, aesthetic qualities, and influence of the speakers. The study includes a number of authors (Emerson), religious leaders (Parker and Beecher), leaders in reform (Wendell Phillips), and education (Charles W. Eliot), as well as the statesmen and politicians.

Burton, Katherine. PARADISE PLANTERS: THE STORY OF BROOK FARM. London: Longmans, Green, 1939.

> The author regards the Brook Farm experiment as "one of the most important of America's social attempts." She uses letters, documents, and recollections to describe the personalities and ideas of those involved. The account is lively and interesting, but it is marked by the author's bias in favor of the experiment.

Cameron, Kenneth Walter. THE MASSACHUSETTS LYCEUM DURING THE AMERICAN RENAISSANCE: MATERIALS FOR THE STUDY OF THE ORAL TRADITION IN AMERICAN LETTERS: EMERSON, THOREAU, HAWTHORNE AND OTHER NEW-ENGLAND LECTURERS. Hartford, Conn.: Transcendental Books, 1969.

> Reprinting and/or editing histories and records of the Salem and Concord Lyceums, the Lowell Institute, and other organizations, Cameron gives new information on Thoreau's lecturing, identifies the subjects spoken about in several of Emerson's unpublished speeches, and outlines the pattern of lyceum education in Massachusetts.

Commager, Henry Steele. THE SEARCH FOR A USABLE PAST AND OTHER ESSAYS IN HISTORIOGRAPHY. New York: Knopf, 1967.

> A collection of readable and invariably interesting essays, these studies purportedly focus upon how historical writers have both interpreted and used the past. In fact, the essays focus more upon specific figures, publications, and movements--for example, Theodore Parker, THE DIAL, Joseph Storey, and nineteenth-century reform movements. Of Parker, the author writes that his contributions suffer from two limitations: "On their practical side they were so largely in the spirit of the times that they have been incorporated into the body of American thought"; on their philosophical side, he sees them as crippled by dualism. The effect of THE DIAL was minimal because it was ahead of its times.

Cunliffe, Marcus, and Robin W. Winks, eds. PASTMASTERS: SOME ESSAYS ON AMERICAN HISTORIANS. New York: Harper and Row, 1969.

> Three essays in this collection deal with nineteenth-century historians. William R. Taylor states that Francis Parkman adhered to a conception of history as story. J.C. Levenson believes that Henry Adams used the vehicle of historicism to "set his own experience in order." Howard R. Lamar cites Frederick Jackson Turner's intuitive sensitivity as a mark of genius, even if he was not "a great historian in the orthodox sense."

Curti, Merle E. THE AMERICAN PEACE CRUSADE, 1815-1861. Durham, N.C.: Duke Univ. Press, 1929.

> The author studies the American peace movement as part of a larger, international crusade.

_____. THE LEARNED BLACKSMITH: THE LETTERS AND JOURNALS OF ELIHU BURRITT. New York: Wilson-Erickson, 1937.

> Curti ties together his account of Burritt's life with Burritt's own description of his educational and reform efforts in his letters and journal. Burritt was largely self-educated, a leader in peace movements, and in these excerpts manifests the idealism and optimism of the nineteenth century. See also Section II.F.1, p. 193.

Curtis, Edith Roelker. A SEASON IN UTOPIA: THE STORY OF BROOK FARM. New York: Thomas Nelson and Sons, 1961.

> This readable account, emphasizing the relationships and interreactions of the participants rather than their ideas, provides an interesting narrative of the community.

Dillon, Merton Lynn. BENJAMIN LUNDY AND THE STRUGGLE FOR NEGRO FREEDOM. Urbana: Univ. of Illinois Press, 1966.

> This social history and biography is an important contribution to understanding the beginnings and the development of abolition. The author describes Lundy, a Quaker leather worker, as being not only "a pioneer abolitionist," but also, through his role in influencing attitudes brought about by the Texas revolution, "a major participant in the later phase of the antislavery movement."

Dorfman, Joseph. THE ECONOMIC MIND IN AMERICAN CIVILIZATION, 1606-1933. 5 vols. New York: Viking, 1946-59.

> In volumes 2 and 3 of this comprehensive study of economic theory and political philosophy, the author provides a rich background for the views of a number of nineteenth-century nonfiction prose writers, including Orestes Brownson, Rufus Griswold, George Tucker, and Henry George.

Duberman, Martin, ed. THE ANTISLAVERY VANGUARD: NEW ESSAYS ON THE ABOLITIONISTS. Princeton: Princeton Univ. Press, 1965.

> A collection of essays by some of the best scholars in the field on such topics as the Negro abolitionists, antislavery and utopia, abolitionism in the South, and the northern response to slavery, this volume was aimed at encouraging a reevaluation of abolitionism.

Dumond, Dwight L. A BIBLIOGRAPHY OF ANTISLAVERY IN AMERICA. Ann Arbor: Univ. of Michigan Press, 1961.

> The volume lists the literature "written and circulated by those active in the antislavery movement" and includes pamphlets, speeches, and various publications of abolitionist organizations, giving the complete title, publisher, place, and date of publication for each entry.

Farrison, William Edward. WILLIAM WELLS BROWN: AUTHOR AND REFORM-
ER. Chicago: Univ. of Chicago Press, 1969.

> Brown was a well-known historian, a leading abolitionist, a writer,
> a physician, and a fugitive slave. Farrison argues that Brown's
> "work as an author and reformer has merited for him an important
> place in the literary and social history of America." This study
> gives attention to a neglected nineteenth-century figure and places
> him in a well-delineated social and cultural context.

Fellman, Michael. THE UNBOUNDED FRAME: FREEDOM AND COMMUNITY
IN NINETEENTH CENTURY AMERICAN UTOPIANISM. Westport, Conn.:
Greenwood Press, 1973.

> This study examines the history of utopianism "as an intrinsic part
> of American reform," by focusing upon the ideas of several key
> figures including Margaret Fuller, George W. Curtis, Edward Bel-
> lamy, and William Dean Howells.

Floan, Howard R. THE SOUTH IN NORTHERN EYES, 1831-1861. 1958;
New York: Haskell, 1972.

> The author attempts to show how attitudes and events led to a
> "psychological conditioning for civil war." He presents material
> from representative New England and New York periodicals, noting
> that many conceptions were based upon hearsay, conjecture, stereo-
> types, and secondhand reports rather than any real knowledge.
> Most of the major men of letters from the North, such as Lowell,
> Holmes, Emerson, and Thoreau, were able to see beyond immediate
> stereotypes and were pessimistic about the coming conflict.

Freemarck, Vincent, and Bernard Rosenthal, eds. RACE AND THE AMERICAN
ROMANTICS. New York: Schocken, 1971.

> The editor discusses and reprints the views of major nineteenth-
> century authors on race and slavery. The collection includes two
> reviews by Poe, brief essays and excerpts by Whitman, excerpts
> from Melville's fiction, Hawthorne's LIFE OF FRANKLIN PIERCE,
> and Cooper's political comments, as well as statements from the
> writings of Emerson, Thoreau, Whittier, Bryant, and Lowell. Poe,
> reflecting the predominant southern view, defended slavery. Whit-
> man, a segregationist, opposed slavery largely on economic grounds.
> Melville was very much aware of the contradictions and paradoxes
> of slavery in a democracy. Hawthorne condemned extreme aboli-
> tionism and praised Pierce for defending southern rights. Cooper's
> argument was more political than moral--that free states should
> defer to slave states. Emerson opposed slavery but could not fully
> commit himself to public activity. Thoreau moved from private
> growth to public commitment in opposing slavery. Whittier's litera-
> ture was nourished by his abolitionism. Bryant editorially opposed
> slavery but would not campaign for the liberation of those already
> in bondage. Lowell, the most sophisticated analyst of the problem,

was ready to call himself an abolitionist, but he opposed the fan-
aticism in the cause.

Frothingham, Paul R. EDWARD EVERETT: ORATOR AND STATESMAN. 1925;
Port Washington, N.Y.: Kennikat, 1971.

This biography not only draws attention to the oratorical abilities
of Everett but also outlines the role of the orator in nineteenth-
century political events and gives a rhetorical analysis of some of
Everett's speeches.

Geiger, George R. THE PHILOSOPHY OF HENRY GEORGE. Introd. John
Dewey. New York: Macmillan, 1933.

This study contains the fullest discussion of George's ideas.

Hall, Wade H. REFLECTIONS OF THE CIVIL WAR IN SOUTHERN HUMOR.
Gainesville: Univ. of Florida Press, 1962.

The author argues that "the Southerner's sense of humor helped him
to fight a war he believed honorable and to accept the bitter defeat which ended it." In this survey of southern humor, he examines war memoirs, novels, plays, short stories, poetry, and songs
written between the beginning of the Civil War and the beginning
of World War I. Many of the resources used are out-of-print monographs and books; the writers discussed include Charles H. Smith,
George Washington Cable, George Cary Eggleston, Thomas Nelson
Page, and George Washington Harris.

Henderson, Harry B., III. VERSIONS OF THE PAST: THE HISTORICAL IMA-
GINATION IN AMERICAN FICTION. New York: Oxford Univ. Press, 1974.

In examining how American fiction has employed history, the author
opens with an analysis of the major nineteenth-century historians--
Bancroft, Prescott, Motley, and Parkman--in order to construct two
different frames of reference which he believes controlled the
historical imagination of these men. The "holistic" frame of reference, or, as the author terms it "frame of acceptance," typical
of Prescott and Parkman, took a relativistic view of time and
historical change. The "progressive" view, that of Bancroft and
Motley, held that history consisted of measurable change on an
absolute scale.

Herreshoff, David. AMERICAN DISCIPLES OF MARX: FROM THE AGE OF
JACKSON TO THE PROGRESSIVE ERA. Detroit: Wayne State Univ. Press,
1967.

The author finds a great deal of American socialism in the writings
of Brownson, Emerson, Thoreau, and others associated with transcendentalism. In its survey of both literary and nonliterary authors,
the study provides a valuable background for understanding currents
of thought in nineteenth-century transcendentalism.

Hersh, Blanche. THE SLAVERY OF SEX: FEMINIST ABOLITIONISTS IN NINE-TEENTH-CENTURY AMERICA. Urbana: Univ. of Illinois Press, 1978.

> The author examines the link between abolitionism and feminism, surveying the beginnings of organized activity for women's rights and the early women's movement, giving portraits of Stone, Stanton, and Anthony and noting shared characteristics in the lives of fifty-one key leaders in the movement from abolitionism to antebellum suffrage reform.

Holland, DeWitte, ed. AMERICA IN CONTROVERSY: HISTORY OF AMERICAN PUBLIC ADDRESS. Dubuque, Iowa: William C. Brown Co., 1973.

> Designed as a text for courses in the history of American public address, this includes chapters written by different scholars on the rhetoric centered around major issues in American history (slavery, labor agitation), providing a general background for the study of orators rather than focusing upon their individual contributions.

Jameson, J. Franklin. THE HISTORY OF HISTORICAL WRITING IN AMERICA. 1891; New York: Antiquarian Press, 1961.

> These four lectures were read at Johns Hopkins and Brown Universities and originally published in NEW ENGLAND MAGAZINE. The latter two, on nineteenth-century historians, provide an interesting contemporary evaluation of Bancroft, Sparks, Hildreth, Prescott, Motley, and Parkman.

Jenkins, William Sumner. PRO-SLAVERY THOUGHT IN THE OLD SOUTH. Chapel Hill: Univ. of North Carolina Press, 1935.

> The author discusses the ancient and medieval sources for the arguments in the slavery controversy and the way in which those arguments were developed as the proslavery defendants became more and more belligerent toward the abolitionists. He concludes that the southern mind was absorbed in making a defense of slavery—so much so that mental energy was so "used up in the perfection of an irrefutable justification of slaves that the finer features of Southern life were neglected and consequently imperilled."

Kraus, Michael. THE HISTORY OF AMERICAN HISTORY. New York: Farrar and Rinehart, 1937.

> This study of those "who have contributed most to the writing of American history in a comprehensive manner" remains one of the best surveys of historiography and of such nineteenth-century historians as Sparks, Bancroft, Palfrey, Hildreth, Tucker, Gayarre, Benton, Irving, and Parkman, as well as some lesser-known writers.

Lader, Lawrence. THE BOLD BRAHMINS: NEW ENGLAND'S WAR AGAINST SLAVERY, 1831-1863. New York: E.P. Dutton, 1961.

> The author discusses Garrison, the Grimke sisters, Theodore Parker,

Harriet B. Stowe, William G. Sumner, Thomas W. Higginson, John Brown, Emerson, and other abolitionists, giving a chronological account of the development and direction of the antislavery crusade, primarily in and around Boston.

Levin, David. HISTORY AS ROMANTIC ART: BANCROFT, PRESCOTT, MOTLEY AND PARKMAN. Stanford, Calif.: Stanford Univ. Press, 1959.

The author examines the histories written by Bancroft, Prescott, Motley, and Parkman, delineating the literary conventions that function in their work and examining the relationship between the historian's assumptions and his literary technique. He also considers American versions of romantic thought which appear in the histories, concluding that all four "regarded romantic conventions not as meaningless stereotypes, but as effective ways of communicating a message that all their literate contemporaries would understand."

Lewis, Edward R. A HISTORY OF AMERICAN POLITICAL THOUGHT FROM THE CIVIL WAR TO THE WORLD WAR. New York: Macmillan, 1937.

This is a solid study, providing a significant understanding of the political writers of the last half of the nineteenth century. The political theories of Lincoln, William J. Bryan, Theodore Roosevelt, Henry George, and Woodrow Wilson are discussed as well as some of their ideas which continue to influence political ideology.

Lockwood, George B. THE NEW HARMONY MOVEMENT. 1905; New York: A.M. Kelley, 1970.

One of the best early studies of Robert Owens' community, this is particularly interesting for its detailed account of the educational system.

Loewenberg, Bert James. AMERICAN HISTORY IN AMERICAN THOUGHT. New York: Simon and Schuster, 1972.

The author's purpose is less to record what American historians have said about the past than to explore why they have written as they have and how their writing of history has shaped the views of their leaders. He discusses the contributions, and social and philosophical views of Sparks, Bancroft, Parkman, Hildreth, Prescott, Motley, and Henry Adams, among others.

Loggins, Vernon. THE NEGRO AUTHOR: HIS DEVELOPMENT IN AMERICA TO 1900. 1931; Port Washington, N.Y.: Kennikat, 1964.

This is an excellent early survey which discusses biographers, sociologists, historians, poets, and abolitionists. At the time of publication of Loggins' work, most of the figures had been ignored by other surveys of American literature. He includes a useful bibliography of works by black American writers.

Loubere, Leo. UTOPIAN SOCIALISM: ITS HISTORY SINCE 1800. Cambridge, Mass.: Schenkman, 1974.

> The author discusses theories and ideals behind what he sees as socialistic utopian ventures and places American utopianism in the larger context of the whole of Western culture. He attempts "to discover the contrapuntal relations between economic and social evolution on the one hand and ideology and action on the other."

Lynd, Staughton. INTELLECTUAL ORIGINS OF AMERICAN RADICALISM. New York: Pantheon, 1968.

> Lynd believes that the radical content of the Declaration of Independence is a heritage from British dissent. Nineteenth-century reformers, especially the abolitionists, revitalized this radicalism.

McCurdy, Francis Lea. STUMP, BAR AND PULPIT: SPEECHMAKING ON THE MISSOURI FRONTIER. Columbia: Univ. of Missouri Press, 1969.

> The author examines the topics and terminology of surviving speeches, providing information about what appealed to audiences, devices used by speakers, and reflections of the popular mind in the subjects. He finds that the rhetoric reflects frontier ideals: the virtue of the yeoman, belief in the power of the people (excepting, in many cases, blacks and Indians), optimism, and ambivalence about the past.

Madison, Charles A. CRITICS AND CRUSADERS: A CENTURY OF AMERICAN PROTEST. New York: H. Holt, 1948.

> The study examines the abolitionists; the utopians; the anarchists, among whom the author includes Thoreau; and the dissident economists, including Henry George.

Marshall, Helen E. DOROTHEA DIX, FORGOTTEN SAMARITAN. Chapel Hill: Univ. of North Carolina Press, 1937.

> This is an appreciative scholarly biography which includes material on the history of the ways in which societies dealt with the insane and documents the activities of the woman who did so much to reform institutional treatment of the mentally disturbed.

Merideth, Robert. THE POLITICS OF THE UNIVERSE: EDWARD BEECHER, ABOLITION, AND ORTHODOXY. Nashville, Tenn.: Vanderbilt Univ. Press, 1968.

> Edward Beecher was the third child of Lyman and brother of Catharine, Harriet, and Henry Ward. The author finds Edward "a paradigm of the inner life of his generation" in that through him "we may see the dilemmas of a generation as felt ideas" and discover how "the special dilemmas of his generation were temporarily resolved by politicizing theology." Edward was more spiritual and less optimistic than his better-known brother, Henry Ward.

Meyers, Marvin. THE JACKSONIAN PERSUASION: POLITICS AND BELIEF. Stanford, Calif.: Stanford Univ. Press, 1957. Bibliog.

> The author discusses the attitudes toward economy and politics of those who shared a general Jacksonian view. This study is of particular interest for its analysis of Cooper's social criticism, finding in both the fiction and nonfiction of Cooper "a direct commentary on Jacksonian manners and morals." There is mention also of attitudes expressed in the nonfiction prose of Howells, Henry Adams, and others.

Myerson, Joel. BROOK FARM: AN ANNOTATED BIBLIOGRAPHY AND RE-SOURCES GUIDE. New York: Garland, 1978.

> Because of the large amount of available material related to Brook Farm, this is an extremely useful and informative resource guide.

Nevins, Allan, et al., eds. CIVIL WAR BOOKS: A CRITICAL BIBLIOGRAPHY. 2 vols. Baton Rouge: Louisiana State Univ. Press, 1967-69. Index.

> Designed to serve scholars and general readers, these volumes are restricted to the prose literature (excluding poetry, fiction, and drama) bearing solely on the war years. Each volume is divided into several sections having to do with various aspects of Civil War writings (campaigns, soldier life, biographies, memoirs).

Noble, David W. HISTORIANS AGAINST HISTORY. Minneapolis: Univ. of Minnesota Press, 1965.

> The author examines the work of six historians, including Bancroft and Frederick Jackson Turner of the nineteenth century, in light of their interpretation of the Puritan covenant: that covenant with God "which delivered them and their children from the vicissitudes of history as long as they did not fail in their responsibility to keep their society pure and simple." Bancroft viewed the role of historian as that of a "secular theologian." Turner was concerned with the effect of European-imported industrialization on the frontier.

Oakley, Mary Ann B. ELIZABETH CADY STANTON. Old Westbury, N.Y.: Feminist Press, 1972.

> The biography focuses on the first women's rights convention at Seneca Falls in 1848 and the friendship between Stanton and Susan B. Anthony.

Perkins, Alice J.G., and Theresa Wolfson. FRANCES WRIGHT: FREE EN-QUIRER. 1939; Philadelphia: Porcupine Press, 1972.

> This is a well-documented account of a woman who was involved in abolition, labor reform, the crusade for sexual freedom, and women's rights.

Pessen, Edward, ed. THE MANY-FACETED JACKSONIAN ERA: NEW INTER-
PRETATIONS. Westport, Conn.: Greenwood Press, 1977.

> These essays by contemporary historians present a stimulating dis-
> cussion of the social, economic, and political developments of the
> era and provide an interesting perspective on many of the ideas
> central to the nonfiction prose of the time.

Roemer, Kenneth M. THE OBSOLETE NECESSITY: AMERICA IN UTOPIAN
WRITINGS, 1888-1900. Kent, Ohio: Kent State Univ. Press, 1976.

> The author examines 160 American fictional and nonfictional uto-
> pian works, making their ideas more accessible and evaluating
> their relevance to American culture.

Rourke, Constance M. TRUMPETS OF JUBILEE. New York: Harcourt, Brace,
1927.

> An anecdotal account of the lyceum and popular orators of the
> mid-nineteenth century, Rourke's study includes Lyman Beecher,
> Harriet Beecher Stowe, Henry Ward Beecher, Horace Greeley,
> and P.T. Barnum.

Ruchames, Louis, ed. THE ABOLITIONISTS: A COLLECTION OF THEIR
WRITINGS. New York: G.P. Putnam's, 1963.

> The editor provides extensive introductory notes and comments to
> these selections, most of which were written in the 1830s and early
> 1840s, including excerpts from the writings of Garrison, Whittier,
> Theodore and Angelina Grimke Weld, James Birney, and Wendell
> Phillips.

Sams, Henry W., ed. AUTOBIOGRAPHY OF BROOK FARM. Englewood
Cliffs, N.J.: Prentice-Hall, 1958.

> Designed as a casebook for college students, this collects excerpts
> from articles, letters, and journals which pertain to the history of
> Brook Farm.

Saveth, Edward N. AMERICAN HISTORIANS AND EUROPEAN IMMIGRANTS,
1875-1925. New York: Columbia Univ. Press, 1948.

> This study, primarily "concerned with the attitudes of the various
> American historians toward immigrants and immigration," discusses
> several nineteenth-century historians, including Francis Parkman
> and Henry Adams. The author contends that late-nineteenth-century
> historians wavered between the view that historians should search
> only for facts and the view that they should formulate general
> historical truths or laws. One of the prevalant theories was that
> American institutions were Teutonic in origin, unfamiliar or alien
> to many immigrants.

Shaw, Warren C. HISTORY OF AMERICAN ORATORY. Indianapolis: Bobbs-Merrill, 1928. Bibliog.

> The author argues that "the appeals made by orators . . . are part of the vast body of permanent American literature." He treats the major nineteenth-century orators, providing historical backgrounds and contexts, biographies, and texts of speeches.

Sklar, Kathryn Kish. CATHARINE BEECHER: A STUDY IN AMERICAN DOMESTICITY. New Haven, Conn.: Yale Univ. Press, 1973.

> In this excellent biography, the author presents her subject as a woman who was devoted to "both nationalizing and personalizing the American domestic environment." For example, she attempted to express both freedom of choice and homogeneous values in the domestic layout of the home. Catharine Beecher (see pp. 192 and 197) was opposed to the women's rights movement but sought to teach women how to wield social and cultural influence through the home and family.

Smith, Hilrie Shelton. IN HIS IMAGE, BUT . . . : RACISM IN SOUTHERN RELIGION, 1780-1910. Durham, N.C.: Duke Univ. Press, 1972.

> In the eighteenth century, church leaders viewed Negro bondage as compatible with Christianity. Quakers, though many were slaveholders, pioneered the antislavery movement. In the nineteenth century, Southern ministers argued the Biblical precedents for the master-slave relationship. Those believing that blacks might some day be prepared for emancipation placed that date far in the future. During the war, clergymen argued that Southerners were favored by God because they had "never corrupted the gospel of Christ" by substituting "higher law" for "divine revelation" (the latter supporting slavery). In the final chapter, George Washington Cable's campaign for Negro rights, both in and out of the religious community, is presented briefly against the background of racial views in the churches of his time.

Smith, Timothy Lawrence. REVIVALISM AND SOCIAL REFORM IN MID-NINETEENTH CENTURY AMERICA. New York: Abingdon Press, 1957.

> The author focuses upon the importance of revivalism in urban areas, rather than on the frontier, and its role in shaping the views of ordinary people, rather than those of the most prominent social and cultural figures.

Snyder, Charles M., ed. THE LADY AND THE PRESIDENT: THE LETTERS OF DOROTHEA DIX AND MILLARD FILLMORE. Lexington: Univ. of Kentucky Press, 1975.

> The editor's commentary provides a useful background for these letters, which are of interest because of their literary value, their rhetorical arguments which Dix used to convince Fillmore of the

need for reforming prisons and mental institutions, and their value as documents in the nation's social history.

Sproat, John G. "THE BEST MEN": LIBERAL REFORMERS IN THE GILDED AGE. New York: Oxford Univ. Press, 1968.

In this discussion of reform movements from the reconstruction era to the 1890s, the author includes the activities and attitudes of several men of letters, among them Henry Adams, Howells, Twain, Thomas W. Higginson, and Charles E. Norton. The NORTH AMERICAN REVIEW, under the editorships of Norton and Lowell, and HARPER'S WEEKLY, with George Curtis as editor, were organs of what the author calls "restrained Radicals."

Stepto, Robert B. FROM BEHIND THE VEIL: A STUDY OF AFRO-AMERICAN NARRATIVE. Urbana: Univ. of Illinois Press, 1979.

The author's discussion of the similarities between the antebellum slave narratives and later black autobiography includes excellent discussions of Booker T. Washington's UP FROM SLAVERY and Frederick Douglass' NARRATIVE.

Swift, Lindsay. BROOK FARM: ITS MEMBERS, SCHOLARS, AND VISITORS. 1900; Introd. Joseph Schiffman. Secaucus, N.J.: Citadel, 1973.

A student of Henry Adams at Harvard, Swift uses this account of Brook Farm and the school, the members, and the visitors associated with it to celebrate a lost cause of "noble illusions" in an age of materialism.

Thompson, Lawrence S. THE SOUTHERN BLACK, SLAVE AND FREE: A BIBLIOGRAPHY OF ANTI- AND PRO-SLAVERY BOOKS AND PAMPHLETS AND OF SOCIAL AND ECONOMIC CONDITIONS IN THE SOUTHERN STATES FROM THE BEGINNINGS TO 1950. Troy, N.Y.: Whitston, 1970.

This is a list of books and pamphlets which have been issued in microcard editions by the Lost Cause Press, Louisville, Kentucky, relative to American slavery and the American South. It includes some 4,500 works, listed by author or title.

Turner, Lorenzo D. ANTI-SLAVERY SENTIMENT IN AMERICAN LITERATURE PRIOR TO 1865. 1929; Port Washington, N.Y.: Kennikat, 1966. Bibliog.

The author outlines antislavery arguments in writings from 1641 to the Civil War. Arguments based upon moral, religious, and sentimental grounds were most frequent, although some were based upon social, economic, and political necessity.

Vitzthum, Richard C. THE AMERICAN COMPROMISE: THEME AND METHOD IN THE HISTORIES OF BANCROFT, PARKMAN, AND ADAMS. Norman: Univ. of Oklahoma Press, 1974.

Discussing the writing of history "as one of the major forms of literary art," this volume is a perceptive work of literary criticism with an unusual approach to historiography. The author argues that Bancroft, Parkman, and Adams all saw America's history "as basically a conflict between separatist, decentralizing, anarchic forces on the one hand and unifying forces of central authority and sovereignty on the other."

Walker, Peter F. MORAL CHOICES: MEMORY, DESIRE, AND IMAGINA-TION IN NINETEENTH-CENTURY AMERICAN ABOLITION. Baton Rouge: Louisiana State Univ. Press, 1978.

The author focuses upon the abolitionist activities and the contri-butions of Moncure D. Conway, Jane Swisshelm, Frederick Doug-lass, Henry C. Wright, Salmon P. Chase, and Thomas M. Cooley, who were all involved in the final phase of the antislavery move-ment. By doing an "autobiographical" study of these abolitionists through their own writings, speeches, and autobiographies, Walker attempts to discover what led each of them to work for abolition.

Weeks, Edward. THE LOWELLS AND THEIR INSTITUTE. Boston: Little, Brown, 1966.

Founded in 1839 by John Lowell, Jr., the Lowell Institute invited many speakers (including Lyell, Agassiz, Judge Holmes, and William James) and avoided others (Emerson and Darwin). In addition to describing the various speakers, the author assesses the intellectual climate in Boston.

Wilson, Edmund. PATRIOTIC GORE: STUDIES IN THE LITERATURE OF THE AMERICAN CIVIL WAR. New York: Oxford Univ. Press, 1962.

This is the best general study of the nonfiction prose literature of the Civil War. In his introduction, Wilson points out that although belles lettres did not flourish during the war, the war did produce "a remarkable literature which mostly consists of speeches and pam-phlets, private letters and diaries, personal memoirs and journalis-tic reports." In this survey, the bulk of attention is given to these forms of writing. Many interesting manuscripts, particularly diaries, have been unearthed and published since Wilson's study was done; but he calls attention to a number of unknown and excellent writers about the Civil War and places the better-known writers (Stowe, Lincoln, Grant, and Sherman) in a literary and cultural context.

Wilson, William Edward. THE ANGEL AND THE SERPENT: THE STORY OF NEW HARMONY. Bloomington: Indiana Univ. Press, 1964.

In one of the most readable and well-researched discussions of nineteenth-century reform communities, Wilson discusses the found-ing of New Harmony and its religious and philosophical backgrounds.

Wish, Harvey. THE AMERICAN HISTORIAN: A SOCIAL-INTELLECTUAL HIS-
TORY OF THE WRITING OF THE AMERICAN PAST. New York: Oxford Univ.
Press, 1960.

The author discusses American historians, primarily those concerned
with American history itself, "with a primary view to determining
their social conditioning." He finds the influence of social ideas
particularly evident in pre-twentieth-century historians, including
Bancroft (influenced by both German idealism and Jacksonian democracy) and Parkman (affected by elitism and anticlericalism). Jared
Sparks, Richard Hildreth, and Henry Adams are also discussed.

III. INDIVIDUAL AUTHORS

INTRODUCTION

The authors chosen for listing in this section, with the exceptions of George Ticknor and Booker T. Washington, are listed in the BIBLIOGRAPHY to the LITERARY HISTORY OF THE UNITED STATES. Many of these writers are known principally for their fiction or poetry but have, nevertheless, made significant contributions to American nonfiction prose or criticism. The brief introductory paragraphs place each author within the context of this present guide. Under the section headed Principal Works are listed those works published during the author's lifetime. Such authors as Poe, Lincoln, and Webster, whose major contributions appeared in separate publications or collections only after their deaths, are treated accordingly.

As in the first two sections, I have included few periodical contributions. Excellent guides to periodical literature are available: the PMLA Bibliography; listings in AMERICAN LITERATURE, AMERICAN LITERARY REALISM, ESQ: A JOURNAL OF THE AMERICAN RENAISSANCE, and the AMERICAN TRANS-CENDENTAL QUARTERLY; and the bibliographical essays in AMERICAN LITER-ARY SCHOLARSHIP; Leary's ARTICLES ON AMERICAN LITERATURE also provides a comprehensive listing. In addition to these general listings, bibliographies for many of the authors have appeared in the BULLETIN OF BIBLIOG-RAPHY or have been collected in separate volumes by such publishers as G.K. Hall, Twayne, and Scarecrow. The listing of reprints and later editions has been selective; major posthumous editions, even if they are no longer in print, have been included as have some of the better, later editions, selections, and reprints. The listing of biographical and critical studies has also been selective, particularly when most of the criticism has been directed toward the poetry or fiction rather than the nonfiction prose or criticism of a particular writer. Under Related General Studies are included general works listed in sections I and II of this volume and works dealing primarily with other writers which have been listed in III, below, under that writer. These general studies provide information relevant to the artistic and historical milieus of authors for whom they are cited.

Because of the ongoing activities of academic and commercial publishers in re-issuing editions of standard primary and secondary sources or in publishing new scholarly editions of such sources in hardcover or paperback format, anyone working in American literature should keep in mind the most recent reference guides to books currently in print. These guides are explained in Eugene Shee-hy's GUIDE TO REFERENCE BOOKS (9th ed., Chicago: American Library Association, 1976); see particularly entries AA471-74, p. 42.

HENRY (BROOKS) ADAMS (1838-1918)

Much of the recent criticism of Adams' work has focused upon the literary qualities of his nonfiction prose. In his later historical studies, biographies, and
autobiography, Adams moved away from factual historical documentation toward
a consideration of the paradoxes and problems of human experience and a style
that relied increasingly upon the images and allusiveness of creative literature.

PRINCIPAL WORKS

LIFE OF ALBERT GALLATIN. 1879.
DEMOCRACY: AN AMERICAN NOVEL. 1880.
JOHN RANDOLPH. 1882.
ESTHER: A NOVEL. 1884.
HISTORY OF THE UNITED STATES DURING THE ADMINISTRATIONS OF JEF-
     FERSON AND MADISON. 9 vols. 1889-91.
HISTORICAL ESSAYS. 1891.
MEMOIRS OF MARAU TAAROA, LAST QUEEN OF TAHITI. Privately printed
     1893. Rev. ed. MEMOIRS OF ARII TAIMAIE. 1901.
MONT-SAINT-MICHEL AND CHARTRES. Privately printed 1904. Publ. 1913.
THE EDUCATION OF HENRY ADAMS. Privately printed 1907. Publ. 1918.
THE LIFE OF GEORGE CABOT LODGE. 1911.
Ed. ESSAYS IN ANGLO-SAXON LAW. 1876.
Ed. DOCUMENTS RELATING TO NEW ENGLAND FEDERALISM, 1800-1815.
     1877.
Ed. THE WRITINGS OF ALBERT GALLATIN. 3 vols. 1879.
Ed. LETTERS OF JOHN HAY AND EXTRACTS FROM DIARY. 3 vols. 1908.
Ed. with Charles Francis Adams, Jr. CHAPTERS OF ERIE AND OTHER ESSAYS.
     1871.

LETTERS

A CYCLE OF ADAMS LETTERS, 1861-1866. 2 vols. Ed. Worthington C. Ford.
Boston: Houghton Mifflin, 1920.

HENRY ADAMS AND HIS FRIENDS: A COLLECTION OF HIS UNPUBLISHED LETTERS. Ed. Harold Dean Cater. 1947; New York: Octagon, 1970.

LETTERS OF HENRY ADAMS, 1858-1891. Ed. Worthington C. Ford. Boston: Houghton Mifflin, 1930.

LETTERS OF HENRY ADAMS, 1892-1918. Ed. Worthington C. Ford. Boston: Houghton Mifflin, 1938.

LETTERS TO A NIECE AND PRAYER TO THE VIRGIN OF CHARTRES, WITH A NIECE'S MEMORIES. Ed. Mabel La Farge. Boston: Houghton Mifflin, 1920.

THE SELECTED LETTERS OF HENRY ADAMS. Ed. Newton Arvin. New York: Farrar, Straus and Young, 1951.

A complete edition of Adams's letters, edited by Ernest Samuels, Charles Van-dersee, and J.C. Levenson, is forthcoming from Harvard Univ. Press.

LATER EDITIONS, SELECTIONS, AND REPRINTS

CHAPTERS OF ERIE AND OTHER ESSAYS. New York: A.M. Kelley, 1967.

THE DEGRADATION OF THE DEMOCRATIC DOGMA. Ed. with introd. Brooks Adams. New York: Harper, 1919.

DOCUMENTS RELATING TO NEW ENGLAND FEDERALISM, 1800-1815. New York: B. Franklin, 1960.

THE EDUCATION OF HENRY ADAMS. Ed. with introd. and notes by Ernest Samuels. Boston: Houghton Mifflin, 1974.

> This is the authoritative edition, incorporating Adams' revisions and including excellent biographical notes and comments.

THE FORMATIVE YEARS: A HISTORY OF THE UNITED STATES DURING THE ADMINISTRATIONS OF JEFFERSON AND MADISON. 2 vols. Condensed and ed. by Herbert Agar. Boston: Houghton Mifflin, 1947.

"THE GREAT SECESSION WINTER" AND OTHER ESSAYS. Ed. George Hoch-field. 1958; Cranbury, N.J.: A.S. Barnes, 1962.

> The title essay was originally published in 1910 in the PROCEED-INGS OF THE MASSACHUSETTS HISTORICAL SOCIETY.

A HENRY ADAMS READER. Comp. Elizabeth Stevenson. Garden City, N.Y.: Doubleday, 1958.

HISTORY OF THE UNITED STATES DURING THE ADMINISTRATIONS OF JEF-
FERSON AND MADISON. 9 vols. New York: Antiquarian Press, 1962;
Abridged and ed. in one volume by Ernest Samuels with introd. Henry S. Com-
mager, 1967; Chicago: Univ. of Chicago Press, 1979.

> The six-chapter opening to HISTORY OF THE UNITED STATES is
> available in paperback as THE UNITED STATES IN 1800 (Ithaca,
> N.Y.: Cornell Univ. Press, 1955).

JOHN RANDOLPH. Introd. Milton Cantor. 1961; Gloucester, Mass.: Peter
Smith, 1969.

LIFE OF ALBERT GALLATIN. New York: Peter Smith, 1943.

MONT-SAINT-MICHEL AND CHARTRES. Boston: Houghton Mifflin, 1963.

TRAVELS IN TAHITI, BY HENRY ADAMS . . . MEMOIRS OF MARAU TAAROA,
LAST QUEEN OF TAHITI. Ed. with introd. and notes by Robert Spiller. 1947;
New York: Scholar's Facsimiles and Reprints, 1976.

BIBLIOGRAPHY

A descriptive listing of Adams' works is in Blanck's BIBLIOGRAPHY OF AMERI-
CAN LITERATURE, 1:1-11 and in the BIBLIOGRAPHY to the LITERARY HISTORY
OF THE UNITED STATES, pp. 373, 865, 1137.

Harbert, Earl N. "Henry Adams." In FIFTEEN AMERICAN AUTHORS BEFORE
1900. Ed. Robert A. Rees and Earl N. Harbert. Madison: Univ. of Wisconsin
Press, 1971, pp. 3-36.

> This is an excellent bibliographical essay and evaluation of work
> about Adams.

_____. HENRY ADAMS: A REFERENCE GUIDE. Boston: G.K. Hall,
1978.

> This useful guide includes a year-by-year listing of writings about
> Adams, 1879-1975, with informative annotations.

Vandersee, Charles. "Henry Adams (1838-1918)." AMERICAN LITERARY
REALISM, 2 (Summer 1969), 89-120, and 8 (Winter 1975), 13-34.

> These bibliographical listings are particularly useful for their sur-
> vey of shorter criticism of Adams, 1957-74.

Ernest Samuels' volumes of biography contain a chronology of Adams' writings.
Selected bibliographies, including secondary sources, may also be found in the
studies by Baym, Hochfield, Hume, Lyon, and Jordy. All of these titles are
listed below.

Henry (Brooks) Adams

BIOGRAPHY AND CRITICISM

Adams, James Truslow. THE ADAMS FAMILY. Boston: Little, Brown, 1931.

This biographical study provides background for understanding Adams' heritage. Henry Adams is included in the chapter, "The Fourth Generation."

_____. HENRY ADAMS. 1933; St. Clair Shores, Mich.: Scholarly Press, 1970.

For many years the best biography, this has now been supplanted by Samuels' scholarly volumes, below.

Auchincloss, Louis. HENRY ADAMS. Minneapolis: Univ. of Minnesota Press, 1971.

Auchincloss is not always sympathetic to Adams, finding the novels mere "footnotes for Adams enthusiasts" and his biographies a failure. However, Auchincloss explains Adams's ideas clearly, finding the synthesis of Adams' philosophy in the "Prayer to the Virgin of Chartres," and demonstrates that Adams offers much of interest to the general reader. Auchincloss' study is reprinted in Ralph Ross's MAKERS OF AMERICAN THOUGHT (p. 239).

Baym, Max I. THE FRENCH EDUCATION OF HENRY ADAMS. 1951; New York: Columbia Univ. Press, 1969.

Baym considers Adams' use of the French literary heritage and demonstrates that Adams' thought and techniques derive much from French sources.

Beringause, Arthur. BROOKS ADAMS: A BIOGRAPHY. New York: Knopf, 1955.

This study adds to an understanding of the influence of their father upon both Henry and Brooks and the relationship of the brothers. It includes a description of and generous excerpts from Henry's critique of Brooks's unpublished biography of John Quincy Adams.

Bishop, Ferman. HENRY ADAMS. Boston: Twayne, 1979.

Bishop closely examines the major works and several of the essays, noting particularly Adams' use of satire. The study provides backgrounds, summarizes major ideas, evaluates the work, and is a useful introduction to Adams.

Blackmur, R.P. HENRY ADAMS. Ed. Veronica A. Makowsy. New York: Harcourt Brace Jovanovich, 1980.

This collection of pieces on Henry Adams, written before Blackmur's death in 1965 and edited by a Princeton graduate student, are, taken together, a coherent and perceptive body of criticism by a critic who identified with and understood his subject.

Conder, John J. A FORMULA OF HIS OWN: HENRY ADAMS'S LITERARY EXPERIMENT. Chicago: Univ. of Chicago Press, 1970.

> Conder concentrates on the literary forms and techniques of CHARTRES and the EDUCATION in an attempt to explain Adams' major literary strategies. He finds Adams using recurrent methods of treatment in different contexts and creating "a unified structure as well as a dynamic kind of tension between an apparently free narrator and a world of more powerful forces."

Donovan, Timothy P. HENRY ADAMS AND BROOKS ADAMS: THE EDUCATION OF TWO AMERICAN HISTORIANS. Norman: Univ. of Oklahoma Press, 1961.

> Donovan identifies and describes various "traditions" in family thinking, arguing that Henry Adams sought "to justify the determinism of the nineteenth century."

Dusinberre, William. HENRY ADAMS: THE MYTH OF FAILURE. Charlottesville: Univ. Press of Virginia, 1979.

> Dusinberre considers the nine-volume HISTORY to be Adams' most impressive work and discusses it with close attention to Adams's style and technique. He argues that the HISTORY should be set against the writings of Macaulay and Gibbon rather than against those of Adams' fellow Americans, Parkman and Prescott.

Guttmann, Allen. THE CONSERVATIVE TRADITION IN AMERICA. New York: Oxford Univ. Press, 1967.

> Guttmann finds in literature conservative attitudes missing in politics. Writers like Henry Adams are distinguished by their sense of the past. The sense of past traditions, Guttmann feels, has served as a much-needed corrective to liberal thought. Henry Adams is "a pessimistic Liberal who understood the ideologies of the century too well to accept any of them."

Harbert, Earl N., ed. THE FORCE SO MUCH CLOSER HOME: HENRY ADAMS AND THE ADAMS FAMILY. New York: New York Univ. Press, 1977.

> In his analysis of Adams' major works, Harbert argues that Adams owes his self-understanding, much of his motivation, and many of his ideas to his family's literary traditions, principles, and active interests. Adams' self-doubt occurs when he is led into new areas of thought. This study of his work, particularly the EDUCATION, is perceptive and stimulating.

_____, ed. CRITICAL ESSAYS ON HENRY ADAMS. Boston: G.K. Hall, 1981.

> This collection includes essays by Ernest Samuels, R.P. Blackmur, and Henry Steele Commager.

Hochfield, George. HENRY ADAMS: AN INTRODUCTION AND INTERPRE-TATION. New York: Barnes and Noble, 1962.

> In his attempt "to demonstrate the continuity of Adams's mind in his books, and to define the order of relation among them," Hochfield finds the search for an ideal and a failure of that ideal to be the dominating pattern of the works. He proposes that the sense of failure is due to the frustration of the literary artist in Adams.

Hume, Robert A. RUNAWAY STAR: AN APPRECIATION OF HENRY ADAMS. Ithaca, N.Y.: Cornell Univ. Press, 1951.

> Intended for the general reader rather than the scholar, this study is nevertheless a reliable and useful account of Adams' career and an appreciative examination of the literary qualities of his works.

Jaher, Frederic Cople. DOUBTERS AND DISSENTERS: CATACLYSMIC THOUGHT IN AMERICA, 1885-1918. London: Free Press of Glencoe, 1964.

> The author discusses the views of Henry and Brooks Adams in some detail, seeing Henry as a rebel who sought refuge in an aesthetic and aristocratic "fastidiousness."

Jordy, William H. HENRY ADAMS: SCIENTIFIC HISTORIAN. 1952; New Haven, Conn.: Yale Univ. Press, 1963. Bibliog.

> Jordy examines the historical essays and places them within a scientific, biographical, and literary framework. The 1963 paperback edition contains a new preface.

Levenson, J.C. THE MIND AND ART OF HENRY ADAMS. 1957; Stanford, Calif.: Stanford Univ. Press, 1968.

> In this thorough, comprehensive study, Levenson traces the chronology of Adams' literary development, examines the major works, places them in a larger context of Adams' thought, and notes that Adams seems to dwell increasingly on the negative.

Lyon, Melvin. SYMBOL AND IDEA IN HENRY ADAMS. Lincoln: Univ. of Nebraska Press, 1970.

> The author focuses on Adams' use of symbols, finding that the illusion-reality theme is most clearly expressed through these symbols. Lyon's critical notes cover most of the scholarship on Adams to about 1968.

Mane, Robert. HENRY ADAMS ON THE ROAD TO CHARTRES. Cambridge, Mass.: Harvard Univ. Press, 1971.

> Reviewing the methods which Adams used to prepare to write, Mane argues that CHARTRES is a work of art and not history and that Adams is ultimately an imaginative writer rather than a scholarly historian.

Murray, James G. HENRY ADAMS. New York: Twayne, 1974.

> Murray focuses upon Adams' personal philosophy, tracing it from nineteenth-century transcendentalism to twentieth-century existentialism. Murray concludes that Adams' "indecisions do not invalidate his thought. Rather they are a distinctive feature of it."

Ross, Ralph, ed. MAKERS OF AMERICAN THOUGHT: AN INTRODUCTION TO SEVEN AMERICAN WRITERS. Minneapolis: Univ. of Minnesota Press, 1974.

> Ross attempts, in his introduction, to fit Adams into the intellectual history of his period. The brief study of Adams by Louis Auchincloss (p. 236) is included in this collection.

Rowe, John Carlos. HENRY ADAMS AND HENRY JAMES: THE EMERGENCE OF A MODERN CONSCIOUSNESS. Ithaca, N.Y.: Cornell Univ. Press, 1976.

> This study shows the approaches of James and Adams to history, society, language, and art and shows the relationships of their development of new ideas and their struggle with questions which came to dominate twentieth-century thought.

Samuels, Ernest. THE YOUNG HENRY ADAMS [1855 TO 1877]. Cambridge, Mass.: Belknap Press, Harvard Univ. Press, 1948.

> Scholarly, thorough, and objective, this and the two volumes below form the standard, definitive biography.

_____. HENRY ADAMS: THE MIDDLE YEARS [1878 TO 1891]. Cambridge, Mass.: Belknap Press, Harvard Univ. Press, 1958.

_____. HENRY ADAMS: THE MAJOR PHASE [1892 AND AFTER]. Cambridge, Mass.: Belknap Press, Harvard Univ. Press, 1964.

Sayre, Robert F. THE EXAMINED SELF. Princeton: Princeton Univ. Press, 1964.

> In this study of the autobiographies of Franklin, Adams, and Henry James, Sayre points out that the latter two writers were very much influenced by Franklin and that all three autobiographies contain perceptive and profound comments upon contemporary culture and institutions.

Scheyer, Ernst. THE CIRCLE OF HENRY ADAMS: ART AND ARTIST. Detroit: Wayne State Univ. Press, 1970.

> The author, an art historian, notes that the painter, John La Farge, the architect, Henry H. Richardson, and the sculptor, Saint-Gaudens, shared not only a friendship with Adams but also the attempt to achieve a synthesis between idealism and realism, aristocracy and democracy. Scheyer also discusses the development of Adams' artistic taste and his judgments on the visual arts.

Stevenson, Elizabeth. HENRY ADAMS: A BIOGRAPHY. 1956; New York: Octagon, 1977.

> Focusing upon the relationship between Henry Adams, the writer, and Henry Adams, the subject of the EDUCATION, the author concludes that Adams' "gift and his flaw was pride."

Wagner, Vern. THE SUSPENSION OF HENRY ADAMS: A STUDY OF MANNER AND MATTER. Detroit: Wayne State Univ. Press, 1969.

> The author analyzes Adams' literary techniques as a means of discovering the meaning of Adams' works through his style. Wagner argues that Adams uses juncture and ironic humor to create an "inconclusive, irresolute, uncertain, doubtful" silence.

Wasser, Henry. THE SCIENTIFIC THOUGHT OF HENRY ADAMS. Thessaloniki, Greece: Univ. of Salonika Press, 1956.

> Neither as original nor as provocative as the similar study by Jordy, Wasser nevertheless focuses more explicitly upon the science in Adams' work and thought. The author notes that the accuracy of many of Adams' speculations, including those on entropy, have not been proven wrong by subsequent scientific pronouncements.

RELATED GENERAL STUDIES

Banta, Martha. FAILURE AND SUCCESS IN AMERICA: A LITERARY DEBATE. (p. 14)
Berthoff, Warner. THE FERMENT OF REALISM. (p. 15)
Bremner, Robert H., ed. ESSAYS ON HISTORY AND LITERATURE. (p. 16)
Cohen, Hennig, ed. LANDMARKS OF AMERICAN WRITING. (p. 19)
Cunliffe, Marcus, and Robin W. Winks, eds. PASTMASTERS. (p. 215)
Loewenberg, Bert. AMERICAN HISTORY IN AMERICAN THOUGHT. (p. 220)
Meyers, Marvin. THE JACKSONIAN PERSUASION: POLITICS AND BELIEF. (p. 222)
Minter, David L. THE INTERPRETED DESIGN AS A STRUCTURAL PRINCIPLE OF AMERICAN PROSE. (p. 28)
Saveth, Edward N. AMERICAN HISTORIANS AND EUROPEAN IMMIGRANTS, 1875-1925. (p. 223)
Vitzthum, Richard C. THE AMERICAN COMPROMISE. (p. 225)
Wish, Harvey. THE AMERICAN HISTORIAN. (p. 227)

AMOS BRONSON ALCOTT (1799-1888)

Alcott's central role in New England transcendentalism has often been slighted or ignored because his writings lack the impact which his ideas and conversations apparently had upon his now more famous contemporaries. As an admiring and occasionally inspirational friend, he had an important effect upon Hawthorne, Emerson, and Thoreau, among others. At the Temple School in Boston, with the help of Sophia and Elizabeth Peabody and sometimes Margaret Fuller, Alcott put into practice some of his transcendental notions, primarily the belief that the power of intuition is freshest in young children. Alcott's own generation laughed at his "Orphic Sayings," yet some of them have real power and insight. Like Thoreau, Alcott spent a brief time in the Concord jail for refusing to pay taxes to support slavery and the Mexican War. He believed in woman's suffrage and urged women to devise their own best methods for reform. There are contradictions and paradoxes in his thought and career which no critic or biographer has satisfactorily explored, but excerpts from his journals and his letters attest to his steadfast loyalty to his ideals and to his friends.

PRINCIPAL WORKS

OBSERVATIONS ON THE PRINCIPLES AND METHODS OF INFANT INSTRUC-
TION. 1830.
THE DOCTRINE AND DISCIPLINE OF HUMAN CULTURE. 1836.
CONVERSATIONS WITH CHILDREN ON THE GOSPELS. 2 vols. 1836-37.
TABLETS. 1868.
CONCORD DAYS. 1872.
TABLE-TALK. 1877.
NEW CONNECTICUT. 1881. (Autobiographical poem)
RALPH WALDO EMERSON: AN ESTIMATE OF HIS CHARACTER AND GENIUS:
IN PROSE AND VERSE. 1882.
SONNETS AND CANZONETS. 1882.

LETTERS AND JOURNALS

THE JOURNALS OF BRONSON ALCOTT. Ed. Odell Shepard. 1938; New York: Kennikat, 1966.

Shepard publishes here less than one-twentieth of the total mass of the fifty volumes of Alcott's journals. The selection emphasizes Alcott's role as a generous, understanding friend and neglects to some extent the sources for and influences of his thought and doctrines. Shepard's critical introduction, however, is an excellent short piece on Alcott's life and influence.

THE LETTERS OF A. BRONSON ALCOTT. Ed. Richard L. Herrnstadt. Ames: Univ. of Iowa Press, 1969.

This collects over one thousand letters, chiefly from the Alcott-Pratt collection at Harvard. The letters cover gaps in the journals and the later years of Alcott's life, which his biographers have only briefly touched upon. Although the letters to his family are interesting and revealing, it is disappointing to find so few letters to such contemporaries as Emerson, Thoreau, and Hawthorne.

Myerson, Joel, ed. "Bronson Alcott's 'Journal for 1836.'" In STUDIES IN THE AMERICAN RENAISSANCE. Ed. Joel Myerson. Boston: Twayne, 1978.

Myerson reproduces the entire journal for a year which, as he tells us in his brief introduction, "marked the beginning of New England Transcendentalism as a unified force."

LATER EDITIONS, SELECTIONS, AND REPRINTS

ESSAYS ON EDUCATION, 1830-1862. Ed. with introd. Walter Harding. Gainesville, Fla.: Scholar's Facsimiles and Reprints, 1960.

NEW CONNECTICUT. Philadelphia: A. Saifer, 1970.

ORPHIC SAYINGS. . . . Rpt. from the DIAL. Introd. William P. Randel. Mt. Vernon, N.Y.: Golden Eagle Press, 1939.

RALPH WALDO EMERSON. . . . New York: Haskell, 1968.

SONNETS AND CANZONETS. New York: AMS Press, 1969.

TABLETS. Philadelphia: A. Saifer, 1970.

Significant selections from Alcott's journals, letters, and other papers are occasionally printed or reprinted in ESQ: A JOURNAL OF THE AMERICAN RENAISSANCE, in the NEW ENGLAND QUARTERLY, in the AMERICAN TRANSCENDENTAL QUARTERLY, and in Cameron's collections (see below and section II.E.2. above). "Bronson Alcott's 'Scripture for 1840,'" which Joel Myerson originally printed in ESQ 20 (4th quarter, 1974), is available as a monograph.

BIBLIOGRAPHY

A descriptive listing of Alcott's writings is in Blanck's BIBLIOGRAPHY OF
AMERICAN LITERATURE 1:20-26. Alcott is listed in the BIBLIOGRAPHY to
the LITERARY HISTORY OF THE UNITED STATES, pp. 381, 869, 1142. Shirley W. Dinwiddie and Richard Herrnstadt compiled a bibliography of primary
and secondary sources in the BULLETIN OF BIBLIOGRAPHY, 21, nos. 3 and
4 (1954).

BIOGRAPHY AND CRITICISM

Bedell, Madelon. THE ALCOTTS: A BIOGRAPHY OF A FAMILY. Vol. 1 of
2 vols. New York: Clarkson N. Potter, 1980.

> The family background, character, and relationship of Bronson Al-
> cott and his wife, Abigail, are traced here in great detail. Al-
> though aimed at a general audience, the study is well researched
> and places the Alcotts in the context of nineteenth-century thought
> and other well-known figures. Some of Alcott's previously unpub-
> lished poetry is included in the volume.

Haefner, George E. A CRITICAL ESTIMATE OF THE EDUCATIONAL THEORIES
AND PRACTICES OF A. BRONSON ALCOTT. New York: Columbia Univ.
Press, 1937.

> Based entirely upon published writings by and about Alcott's edu-
> cational theories and practices, Haefner's account credits Alcott
> with being innovative and more practical than he is usually thought
> to be.

Hoeltje, Hubert H. SHELTERING TREE: A STORY OF THE FRIENDSHIP OF
RALPH WALDO EMERSON AND AMOS BRONSON ALCOTT. 1943; New York:
Kennikat, 1965.

> An impressionistic rather than a critical account of the relationship
> of Emerson and Alcott based upon the letters and journals of the
> two men.

McCuskey, Dorothy. BRONSON ALCOTT, TEACHER. New York: Macmillan,
1940

> McCuskey, unlike Haefner, bases her analysis of Alcott as an edu-
> cator upon extensive use of Alcott's unpublished journals and papers.
> She notes that Alcott's ideas helped to pave the way for the pro-
> gressive education of the twentieth century. The author also in-
> cludes a useful bibliography of Alcott's writings on education and
> of sources which comment upon Alcott as an educator and the state
> of education in the mid-nineteenth century.

Morrow, Honore W. THE FATHER OF LITTLE WOMEN. Boston: Little, Brown, 1927.

An account of Alcott as an educator, this sentimental, unreliable work often confuses fact and fiction.

Sanborn, Frank B. BRONSON ALCOTT AT ALCOTT HOUSE, ENGLAND, AND FRUITLANDS, NEW ENGLAND, 1842-1844. 1908. Rpt. in MEMORABILIA OF HAWTHORNE, ALCOTT AND CONCORD. Ed. Hartford, Conn.: Transcendental Books, 1970.

This reminiscence covers years for which there are no extant journals, but Sanborn's accounts of Alcott's reception in England and his attempt to organize the rural community at Fruitlands are not always reliable.

Sanborn, Frank B., and William T. Harris. A. BRONSON ALCOTT: HIS LIFE AND PHILOSOPHY. 2 vols. Boston: Roberts Brothers, 1893.

Sanborn gives details of Alcott's life; but he relies upon hearsay and recollection, and his statements are not always accurate. Harris outlines Alcott's philosophy and claims for him "an eminent place among philosophers." The study includes numerous excerpts from Alcott's lectures and journals.

Sears, Clara E. BRONSON ALCOTT'S FRUITLANDS. Boston: Houghton Mifflin, 1915.

Clara Sears became the owner of Fruitlands and made a museum of the place. This is an informative collection of documents about an agricultural experiment which failed. It includes Louisa May Alcott's "Transcendental Wild Oats," a humorous account of the would-be farmers.

Shepard, Odell. PEDLAR'S PROGRESS: THE LIFE OF BRONSON ALCOTT. Boston: Little, Brown, 1937.

Based upon a careful reading of Alcott's journals and other sources, this presents a well-balanced portrait of Alcott the idealist, teacher, and friend; and it remains the standard biography. Shepard took the title from a section of Alcott's autobiographical poem in which he describes his peddling experiences in the South. Shepard proposed "to find out how a Connecticut Yankee who began his active life as a pedlar of trinkets became an acknowledged leader in the most purely idealist movement of thought that America has ever known." Shepard concludes that Alcott, who failed in so many enterprises, was finally successful in the nonmaterial achievements which mattered most to him.

Willis, Frederick L.H. ALCOTT MEMOIRS. Boston: R.G. Badger, 1915.

Compiled from firsthand accounts, this is a useful, brief source.

RELATED GENERAL STUDIES

Alcott, Louisa May. TRANSCENDENTAL WILD OATS. (p. 190)
Blinderman, Abraham. AMERICAN WRITERS ON EDUCATION BEFORE 1865.
(p. 161)
Cameron, Kenneth. CONCORD HARVEST. (p. 163)
_____. TRANSCENDENTAL CLIMATE. (p. 163)
_____. THE TRANSCENDENTALISTS AND MINERVA. (p. 164)
Christy, Arthur. THE ORIENT IN AMERICAN TRANSCENDENTALISM. (p. 164)
Frothingham, Octavius B. TRANSCENDENTALISM IN NEW ENGLAND.
(p. 138)
Goddard, Harold C. STUDIES IN NEW ENGLAND TRANSCENDENTALISM.
(p. 167)
Higginson, T.W. CONTEMPORARIES. (p. 82)
Monroe, Will S. THE HISTORY OF THE PESTALOZZIAN MOVEMENT IN
THE UNITED STATES. (p. 170)
Peabody, Elizabeth. RECORD OF A SCHOOL. (p. 135)
Pochmann, Henry A. NEW ENGLAND TRANSCENDENTALISM AND ST.
LOUIS HEGELIANISM. (p. 172)
Sanborn, Franklin B. RECOLLECTIONS OF SEVENTY YEARS. (p. 75)
_____. TRANSCENDENTAL AND LITERARY NEW ENGLAND. (p. 173)
Stoehr, Taylor, NAY-SAYING IN CONCORD. (p. 175)

JOHN JAMES AUDUBON (1785-1851)

Audubon was a keen observer of people and places as well as of birds and mammals, and his prose sketches are a valuable record of frontier America. He wrote the ORNITHOLOGICAL BIOGRAPHY to accompany the drawings in THE BIRDS OF AMERICA, supplying descriptive "bird biographies" which closely followed his illustrations. In addition, he wrote what he called "Episodes" or "Delineations of American Scenery and Character," which were narrative and descriptive sketches of people and places in the wilderness and on the frontier. Audubon's journals, although bowdlerized, polished, and corrected by family members and other editors, also contain some excellent description and narrative. His style is marred by exaggerated poetical rhetoric, but he managed to give the same sense of life and motion to his subjects with his prose as he did with his brush.

PRINCIPAL WORKS

THE BIRDS OF AMERICA FROM ORIGINAL DRAWINGS. 4 vols. 1827-38.
ORNITHOLOGICAL BIOGRAPHY; OR, AN ACCOUNT OF THE HABITS OF
    THE BIRDS OF THE UNITED STATES OF AMERICA. 5 vols. 1831-39.
A SYNOPSIS OF THE BIRDS OF AMERICA. 1839.
THE BIRDS OF AMERICA FROM DRAWINGS MADE IN THE UNITED STATES
    AND THEIR TERRITORIES. 7 vols. 1840-44.
THE VIVIPAROUS QUADRUPEDS OF NORTH AMERICA. 3 vols. 1845-48.
THE QUADRUPEDS OF NORTH AMERICA. 3 vols. 1849-54.

LETTERS AND JOURNALS

AUDUBON AND HIS JOURNALS. 2 vols. Ed. Maria R. Audubon with Zoological Notes by Elliott Coues. 1897; Gloucester, Mass.: Peter Smith, 1962.

> Despite the fact that a recent discovery of a manuscript journal
> proves this compilation to be bowdlerized and heavily edited, it
> is a valuable record.

AUDUBON IN THE WEST. Ed. John Francis McDermott. Norman: Univ. of Oklahoma Press, 1965.

> This is the first publication of twenty letters written during Audubon's search for specimens for his VIVIPAROUS QUADRUPEDS.

AUDUBON'S WESTERN JOURNALS. 2 vols. 1906; Introd. and notes Frank Heywood Hodder. Glorieta, N.Mex.: Rio Grande Press, 1969.

THE 1826 JOURNAL OF JOHN JAMES AUDUBON. Ed. Alice Ford. Norman: Univ. of Oklahoma Press, 1967.

> This is in fact an unedited version of one of Audubon's important journals.

JOURNAL OF JOHN JAMES AUDUBON MADE DURING HIS TRIP TO NEW ORLEANS IN 1820-21. 2 vols. Ed. Howard Corning. Boston: Club of Odd Volumes, 1929.

LETTERS OF JOHN JAMES AUDUBON, 1826-1840. Ed. Howard Corning. 1930; New York: Kraus, 1969.

LATER EDITIONS, SELECTIONS, AND REPRINTS

AUDUBON BY HIMSELF: A PROFILE. Selected, arranged, and edited by Alice Ford. Garden City, N.Y.: Natural History Press, 1969.

AUDUBON'S AMERICA: THE NARRATIVES AND EXPERIENCES OF JOHN JAMES AUDUBON. Ed. Donald C. Peattie. Boston: Houghton Mifflin, 1940.

> These selections from Audubon's writings and the accompanying facsimiles of his prints and paintings provide an excellent introduction to Audubon.

AUDUBON'S ANIMALS: THE QUADRUPEDS OF NORTH AMERICA. Compiled and ed. Alice Ford. New York: Studio Publications, in association with Crowell, 1951.

> The volume contains selections from both the VIVIPAROUS QUADRUPEDS and THE QUADRUPEDS OF NORTH AMERICA.

AUDUBON'S WILDLIFE. Ed. Edwin Way Teale. New York: Viking, 1964.

THE BIRD BIOGRAPHIES OF JOHN JAMES AUDUBON. Ed. Alice Ford. New York: Macmillan, 1957.

> This is the abridged text from the ORNITHOLOGICAL BIOGRAPHY.

DELINEATIONS OF AMERICAN SCENERY AND CHARACTERS. Introd. Francis H. Herrick. 1926; New York: Arno, 1970. Bibliog.

> These selected essays from the ORNITHOLOGICAL BIOGRAPHY clearly demonstrate Audubon's narrative skill. Herrick's introduction is a fine critical essay.

THE IMPERIAL COLLECTION OF AUDUBON ANIMALS. Ed. Victor H. Cahalane. Maplewood, N.J.: Hammond, 1967.

> The volume reprints much of THE QUADRUPEDS with the addition of new material by Victor H. Cahalane.

In addition to the reprints listed above, THE BIRDS OF AMERICA has been reprinted several times. A SYNOPSIS OF THE BIRDS OF AMERICA has been frequently reprinted by Macmillan. Illustrations from THE BIRDS OF AMERICA and THE QUADRUPEDS have been included in THE ART OF AUDUBON (New York: Harper and Row for Times Books, 1979).

BIBLIOGRAPHY

A complete descriptive bibliography of Audubon's works and a listing of books, pamphlets, monographs, and articles about Audubon to 1916 is in volume 2 of Herrick's AUDUBON THE NATURALIST, pp. 401-56. In her biography, JOHN JAMES AUDUBON, Alice Ford lists manuscript sources, articles, biographies, and memoirs, pp. 451-69. Audubon is listed in the BIBLIOGRAPHY to the LITERARY HISTORY OF THE UNITED STATES, pp. 390, 872, 1145.

BIOGRAPHY AND CRITICISM

Articles on Audubon and his works appear frequently in AUDUBON MAGAZINE (formerly BIRD LORE), 1899-- .

Adams, Alexander B. JOHN JAMES AUDUBON: A BIOGRAPHY. New York: G.P. Putnam's, 1966.

> This biography, aimed at a popular audience, is superficial but fairly accurate.

Arthur, Stanley C. AUDUBON: AN INTIMATE LIFE OF THE AMERICAN WOODSMAN. New Orleans: Harmanson, 1937.

> The study includes a complete bibliography of Audubon's works and focuses upon Audubon's Western experiences.

Audubon, Lucy G. THE LIFE OF JOHN JAMES AUDUBON, THE NATURALIST. New York: G.P. Putnam's, 1869.

> This revised version of Buchanan's LIFE, below, amateurishly elimi-

nates "objectionable" passages and in general simply reprints excerpts from both Audubon's own writings and Buchanan's biography.

Buchanan, Robert. LIFE AND ADVENTURES OF AUDUBON THE NATURALIST.
New York: E.P. Dutton, 1868.

This life was compiled largely from Audubon's writings and from
notes kept by Mrs. Audubon, who publicly renounced the publication.

Burroughs, John. JOHN JAMES AUDUBON. Boston: Small, Maynard, 1902.

Audubon awakened in Burroughs a lifelong delight in ornithology,
and this is a highly appreciative sketch. Some of Burroughs' critical comments are perceptive; however, he was working with few
primary sources, and, as biography, the book is not entirely reliable.

Ford, Alice Elizabeth. JOHN JAMES AUDUBON. Norman: Univ. of Oklahoma Press, 1964.

This generally replaces the work of Francis H. Herrick, below,
taking advantage of journals, letters, and other material not available to him.

Herrick, Francis H. AUDUBON THE NATURALIST: A HISTORY OF HIS LIFE
AND TIME. 2 vols. New York: D. Appleton, 1917.

Until the publication of Ford's work, this was the standard biography. It remains a good one, showing careful use of sources and
a sure style, along with a warmth for the subject that Ford's biography sometimes lacks.

Kolodny, Annette. THE LAY OF THE LAND: METAPHOR AS EXPERIENCE
AND HISTORY IN AMERICAN LIFE AND LETTERS. Chapel Hill: Univ. of
North Carolina Press, 1976.

Although Kolodny discusses a number of American writers, including Cooper, in this study of writers' responses to the land, the
work is included here rather than elsewhere because her comments
on Audubon offer some of the most provocative insights on his work
to date.

Muschamp, Edward A. AUDACIOUS AUDUBON: THE STORY OF A GREAT
PIONEER, ARTIST, NATURALIST AND MAN. New York: Brentano's, 1929.

Despite occasional inaccuracies, this is a vivid and readable account.

Peattie, Donald C. SINGING IN THE WILDERNESS: A SALUTE TO JOHN
JAMES AUDUBON. New York: G.P. Putnam's, 1935.

This evaluation of Audubon as a scientific observer is intended for a young audience, but it is beautifully written, informative, and a pleasure to read. Peattie defends Audubon's scientific accuracy, showing that most of his detractors have since been proven wrong.

Proby, Kathryn Hall. AUDUBON IN FLORIDA. WITH SELECTIONS FROM THE WRITINGS OF JOHN JAMES AUDUBON. Coral Gables, Fla.: Univ. of Miami Press, 1974.

Much of this work consists of Audubon's own writing about Florida, particularly from the ORNITHOLOGICAL BIOGRAPHY. The author provides a brief biography and backgrounds for the excerpts as well as observations that compare Audubon's Florida with Florida in the 1960s and 1970s.

Rourke, Constance. AUDUBON. New York: Harcourt, Brace, 1936.

Rourke focuses upon Audubon's frontier experiences, maintaining that "Audubon's writings, imperfect as he knew them to be, are essential to a knowledge of frontier life along the Ohio and in Louisiana during a significant period."

St. John, Mrs. Horace. AUDUBON: THE NATURALIST OF THE NEW WORLD. New York: C.S. Francis, 1856.

This is noteworthy as the first published life of Audubon, but it has been superseded by subsequent biographies and proven inaccurate by the careful researches of Herrick and Ford.

Welker, Robert Henry. BIRDS AND MEN: AMERICAN BIRDS IN SCIENCE, ART, LITERATURE, AND CONSERVATION, 1800-1900. Cambridge, Mass.: Belknap Press, Harvard Univ. Press, 1955.

Welker discusses the birds in America as a subject for dispassionate study, as creatures of beauty and inspiration, and as objects of unusual speculations by Audubon and other American writers and naturalists.

RELATED GENERAL STUDIES

Harris, Edward. UP THE MISSOURI WITH AUDUBON: THE JOURNAL OF EDWARD HARRIS. (p. 116).

GEORGE BANCROFT (1800-1891)

Bancroft believed that history followed a moral law or divine plan and that it was the duty of the historian to arrange events in their proper relation to these forces. The subjects treated in Bancroft's histories are predominantly political, military, and religious. He tended to stress New England over other sections of the country and to be emotionally nationalistic, believing fervently in the liberating qualities of democracy. As a historian, Bancroft made mistakes, but he was a pioneer in researching and synthesizing a massive collection of material. He was sometimes inclined to read into history what he wanted to see there, yet he was also impartial in judging the actions and motives of men in history. His style was florid and flamboyant, but he had a sense of drama which gave life and readability to his historical narratives. As a master of coherent narrative prose, Bancroft deserves a place in American literature.

PRINCIPAL WORKS

POEMS. 1823.
A HISTORY OF THE UNITED STATES FROM THE DISCOVERY OF THE AMERI-
CAN CONTINENT. 10 vols. 1834-75. Author's last review. 6 vols.
1883-85.
LITERARY AND HISTORICAL MISCELLANIES. 1855.
JOSEPH REED: AN HISTORICAL ESSAY. 1867.
HISTORY OF THE FORMATION OF THE CONSTITUTION OF THE UNITED
STATES OF AMERICA. 2 vols. 1882.
A PLEA FOR THE CONSTITUTION OF THE UNITED STATES. 1886.
MARTIN VAN BUREN TO THE END OF HIS PUBLIC CAREER. 1889.
HISTORY OF THE BATTLE OF LAKE ERIE AND MISCELLANEOUS PAPERS. 1891.

LETTERS AND JOURNALS

A number of letters are included in Mark A. De Wolfe Howe's LIFE AND LET-
TERS. Additional letters have been collected in "The Correspondence of George Bancroft and Jared Sparks, 1823-1832," SMITH COLLEGE STUDIES IN HISTORY 2, no. 2 (1917).

LATER EDITIONS, SELECTIONS, AND REPRINTS

THE HISTORY OF THE UNITED STATES OF AMERICA. Ed. and abr. in one vol. from the centenary edition by Russel B. Nye. Chicago: Univ. of Chicago Press, 1966.

BIBLIOGRAPHY

A listing of Bancroft's writing is in Blanck's BIBLIOGRAPHY OF AMERICAN LITERATURE, 1, 118-38. Selected bibliographies can be found in Canary's study and in the 1944 and 1964 editions of Nye's biography, below. Bancroft is listed in the BIBLIOGRAPHY to the LITERARY HISTORY OF THE UNITED STATES, pp. 394, 873, 1146.

BIOGRAPHY AND CRITICISM

Canary, Robert H. GEORGE BANCROFT. New York: Twayne, 1974.

This study focuses primarily upon THE HISTORY OF THE UNITED STATES; but it also provides useful biographical information and historical, philosophical, and political backgrounds for understanding Bancroft's place in American history and literature. The author concludes that Bancroft's works were significant literary achievements and that they "remain important for historians, for he helped to establish the framework within which we see our early history." The author also maintains that narrative form and manner are no different in history than they are in other literary genres.

Howe, Mark A. De Wolfe. LIFE AND LETTERS OF GEORGE BANCROFT. 2 vols. 1908; New York: Da Capo, 1970.

This remains an essential source for Bancroft scholars. It presents a sympathetic and well-informed account of Bancroft's life and generous excerpts from his correspondence.

Nye, Russel B. GEORGE BANCROFT. New York: Washington Square Press, 1964. Bibliog.

This new edition rearranges and condenses material from the 1944 biography (below).

_____. GEORGE BANCROFT: BRAHMIN REBEL. 1944; New York: Octagon, 1972.

In this standard modern biography, Nye points out that Bancroft made history as a diplomat and an intellectual force as well as wrote it and was, perhaps above all others, representative of the nineteenth-century renaissance. Nye also notes that Bancroft's works show considerable literary art and a sincere attempt to see in the past the pattern for the future.

RELATED GENERAL STUDIES

Barnes, Harry E. A HISTORY OF HISTORICAL WRITING. (p. 213)
Bassett, J.S. THE MIDDLE GROUP OF AMERICAN HISTORIANS. (p. 213)
Bremner, Robert H., ed. ESSAYS ON HISTORY AND LITERATURE. (p. 16)
Gardiner, Harold C., ed. AMERICAN CLASSICS RECONSIDERED. (p. 22)
Henderson, Harry B. VERSIONS OF THE PAST. (p. 218)
Jameson, J. Franklin. THE HISTORY OF HISTORICAL WRITING IN AMERICA.
    (p. 219)
Kraus, Michael. THE HISTORY OF AMERICAN HISTORY. (p. 219)
Levin, David. HISTORY AS ROMANTIC ART. (p. 220)
Lewis, R.W.B. THE AMERICAN ADAM. (p. 25)
Loewenberg, Bert J. AMERICAN HISTORY IN AMERICAN THOUGHT. (p. 220)
Noble, David. HISTORIANS AGAINST HISTORY. (p. 222)
Vitzthum, Richard C. THE AMERICAN COMPROMISE. (p. 225)
Welter, Rush. THE MIND OF AMERICA, 1820-1860. (p. 33)
Wish, Harvey. THE AMERICAN HISTORIAN. (p. 227)

HENRY WARD BEECHER (1813-87)

Having rejected the Calvinism of his father, Beecher turned to a concern for social conditions and an open optimism that made him one of the most popular ministers and speakers of his time. As an orator, Beecher's skills were remarkable; his defense of the northern cause in speeches against slavery, collected in AMERICAN REBELLION, are models of persuasive rhetoric. As editor of the INDEPENDENT and later of the CHRISTIAN UNION, Beecher wrote some powerful editorials linking Christian theology and the increasingly industrialized society of the Reconstruction era. Although Sinclair Lewis categorized Beecher as "a powerful writer of trash," the essays in the STAR PAPERS and EYES AND EARS, with their concrete examples, vivid images, and practical tone, still make good reading. As embodiments of an age of practical Christianity, combining materialism, idealism, and social reform, Beecher's writings remain valuable historical documents.

PRINCIPAL WORKS

SEVEN LECTURES TO YOUNG MEN. 1844.
STAR PAPERS, EXPERIENCES OF ART AND NATURE. 1855.
DEFENCE OF KANSAS. 1856.
LIFE THOUGHTS, GATHERED FROM EXTEMPORANEOUS DISCOURSES. 1858.
NEW STAR PAPERS; OR, VIEWS AND EXPERIENCES OF RELIGIOUS SUBJECTS. 1859.
PLAIN AND PLEASANT TALK ABOUT FRUITS, FLOWERS, AND FARMING. 1859.
EYES AND EARS. 1862.
FREEDOM AND WAR. 1863.
AMERICAN REBELLION: REPORT OF THE SPEECHES OF THE REVEREND HENRY WARD BEECHER, DELIVERED AT PUBLIC MEETINGS IN MANCHESTER, GLASGOW, EDINBURGH, LIVERPOOL, AND LONDON. . . . 1864.
NORWOOD; OR, VILLAGE LIFE IN NEW ENGLAND. 1867. (Fictionalized sketches)
SERMONS. 2 vols. 1869.
THE LIFE OF JESUS, THE CHRIST. 1871.
LECTURE ROOM TALKS. 1872.
YALE LECTURES ON PREACHING. 3 vols. 1872-74.

EVOLUTION AND RELIGION. 1885.
PATRIOTIC ADDRESSES IN AMERICA AND ENGLAND. 1887.

LETTERS AND JOURNALS

AUTOBIOGRAPHICAL REMINISCENCES. Ed. Truman J. Ellinwood. New York: Frederick A. Stokes. 1898.

Although there is no collection of Beecher's letters, the volume above and several of the biographical studies listed below include letters.

LATER EDITIONS, SELECTIONS, AND REPRINTS

AMERICAN REBELLION. Freeport, N.Y.: Books for Libraries, 1971.

FREEDOM AND WAR. Freeport, N.Y.: Books for Libraries, 1971.

LECTURES AND ORATIONS. Ed. Newell D. Hillis. 1913; New York: AMS Press, 1970.

STAR PAPERS. Freeport, N.Y.: Books for Libraries, 1972.

YALE LECTURES ON PREACHING. St. Clair Shores, Mich.: Scholarly Press, 1976.

BIBLIOGRAPHY

There is no standard bibliography of Beecher's writings; but Lyman Abbott's biography includes a list of writings by Henry Ward Beecher compiled by W.E. Davenport, and Lionel G. Crocker's 1934 study gives a selected listing of the speeches and writings. Beecher is listed in the BIBLIOGRAPHY to the LITERARY HISTORY OF THE UNITED STATES, pp. 400, 875.

BIOGRAPHY AND CRITICISM

Abbott, Lyman. HENRY WARD BEECHER. Boston: Houghton Mifflin, 1903.

This is a sympathetic but discriminating account of Beecher's life.

Beecher, William C., and Samuel Scoville. A BIOGRAPHY OF REVEREND HENRY WARD BEECHER. New York: C.L. Webster, 1888.

This official biography was written with the assistance of Beecher's

widow. It is eulogistic and not always reliable but includes useful information about Beecher's activities.

Caskey, Marie. CHARIOT OF FIRE: RELIGION AND THE BEECHER FAMILY.
New Haven, Conn.: Yale Univ. Press, 1978.

The author shows the sharp disagreements about religion among the
members of the Beecher family and notes that even Lyman, the
father, had already modified Calvinism to some extent, although
his children rebelled even further against his version.

Clark, Clifford E., Jr. HENRY WARD BEECHER: SPOKESMAN FOR A MID-
DLE-CLASS AMERICA. Urbana: Univ. of Illinois Press, 1978.

This biography provides insight into the relationship between religion
and culture in the mid-nineteenth century. Clark argues that
"Beecher was able to reinforce central tenets of the Victorian middle-class outlook--the belief in fixed moral laws, the emphasis on
individual self-reliance, the faith in education and high culture,
and the stress on economic security and social control."

Crocker, Lionel G. HENRY WARD BEECHER'S ART OF PREACHING. Chicago:
Univ. of Chicago Press, 1934.

A thorough analysis of Beecher's oratorical and rhetorical techniques
are provided by this study and the two following.

_____. HENRY WARD BEECHER'S SPEAKING ART. New York: Fleming H.
Revell, 1937.

_____. THE RHETORICAL THEORY OF HENRY WARD BEECHER. Chicago:
Univ. of Chicago Press, 1933.

Elsmere, Jane Shafer. HENRY WARD BEECHER: THE INDIANA YEARS, 1837-
1847. Indianapolis: Indiana Historical Society, 1973.

This well-researched study surveys the years in which Beecher was
married, suffered various personal tragedies, and became a prominent reformer and revivalist.

French, Earl A., and Diana Royce, eds. PORTRAITS OF A NINETEENTH
CENTURY FAMILY: A SYMPOSIUM ON THE BEECHER FAMILY. Hartford,
Conn.: Stowe-Day Foundation, 1976.

A collection of papers presented at a symposium honoring Lyman
Beecher's two hundredth birthday anniversary, this includes Joseph
S. Van Why's study of Henry Ward in "Crusaders of the Pen and
Podium."

Hibbin, Paxton. HENRY WARD BEECHER: AN AMERICAN PORTRAIT. 1927. Foreword by Sinclair Lewis. 1942; New York: Beekman, 1974.

> Hibbin is highly critical of Beecher, seeing his life as a mirror of a materialistic, greedy age. Hibbin also presents support for the charge of adultery aimed at Beecher.

McLoughlin, William Gerald. THE MEANING OF HENRY WARD BEECHER: AN ESSAY ON THE SHIFTING VALUES OF MID-VICTORIAN AMERICA, 1840–1870. New York: Knopf, 1970.

> More generous to Beecher than most biographers, the author here discusses how and why Beecher achieved the popularity and following which he did. The study attempts to explain how in 1840 to 1870 "Beecher's theological and intellectual evolution corresponded to (or were correlated with) the major social, economic, political, and religious shifts in American society in those years."

Rugoff, Milton. THE BEECHERS: AN AMERICAN FAMILY IN THE NINE-TEENTH CENTURY. New York: Harper and Row, 1982.

> This is a fine biography of the family as a whole, with sensitive treatments of both Harriet Beecher Stowe and Henry Ward Beecher.

Stowe, Lyman Beecher. SAINTS, SINNERS AND BEECHERS. Indianapolis: Bobbs-Merrill, 1934.

> This largely anecdotal account of Beecher family activities also discusses how they affected the times in which they lived. Stowe argues that "the children [seven sons and four daughters] of Lyman Beecher helped to build the intellectual bridge between the theologians of the past . . . and the spiritual leaders of the present."

RELATED GENERAL STUDIES

ORESTES AUGUSTUS BROWNSON (1803-76)

Almost entirely self-taught, Brownson responded early to the influences, particularly those of Cousin, which led to the transcendental movement in New England. He founded the vital and controversial BOSTON QUARTERLY REVIEW in 1838, writing much of it himself. In its pages, he argued that American literature is not merely a branch of English literature but in fact has more in common with Continental literature. Brownson also used the pages of his REVIEW to denounce the Whigs, support the Democratic party, and champion the laborer. Influenced by the French philosopher Pierre Leroux and his own changing perceptions, Brownson turned to Catholicism and, in 1844, established BROWNSON'S QUARTERLY, which supported Calhoun's candidacy and criticized transcendentalism. The REVIEW was often partisan, but its critical treatments of secular books remain valuable for the student of American literature and thought. Despite his apparent vacillations, Brownson was often prophetic about both the economic and the political consequences of particular actions. He observed the American scene with intelligence, commenting upon the important questions of the day in clear forceful prose.

PRINCIPAL WORKS

ADDRESS ON INTEMPERANCE. 1833.
NEW VIEWS OF CHRISTIANITY, SOCIETY, AND THE CHURCH. 1836.
THE MEDIATORIAL LIFE OF JESUS. 1842.
ESSAYS AND REVIEWS, CHIEFLY ON THEOLOGY, POLITICS, AND SOCIAL-
ISM. 1852.
THE SPIRIT-RAPPER: AN AUTOBIOGRAPHY. 1854. (Novel)
THE CONVERT; OR, LEAVES FROM MY EXPERIENCE. 1857. (Autobiography)
THE AMERICAN REPUBLIC: ITS CONSTITUTION, TENDENCIES, AND DESTINY.
1865.
CONVERSATIONS ON LIBERALISM AND THE CHURCH. 1870.

LETTERS AND JOURNALS

THE BROWNSON-HECKER CORRESPONDENCE. Ed. Joseph F. Gower and
Richard M. Leliaert. Notre Dame, Ind.: Univ. of Notre Dame Press, 1979.

Like Brownson, Isaac T. Hecker was a transcendentalist who converted to Catholicism.

Daniel Barnes of Ohio State University has announced a forthcoming volume of letters. Several important letters are reprinted in the three-volume biography by Brownson's son and in Ryan's centennial biography, below. Brownson's papers in the University of Notre Dame Archives are available on microfilm.

LATER EDITIONS, SELECTIONS, AND REPRINTS

THE AMERICAN REPUBLIC: ITS CONSTITUTION, TENDENCIES, AND DESTINY. Ed. Americo D. Lapati. New Haven, Conn.: College and University Press, 1974.

This paperback reissue contains an informative introduction.

THE BROWNSON READER. Ed. Alvan S. Ryan. New York: P.J. Kennedy, 1955.

ESSAYS AND REVIEWS. New York: Arno, 1972.

THE LABORING CLASSES. Delmar, N.Y.: Scholar's Facsimiles and Reprints, 1978.

LITERARY, SCIENTIFIC, AND POLITICAL VIEWS OF ORESTES A. BROWNSON. Ed. Henry F. Brownson. New York: Benziger, 1893.

ORESTES BROWNSON: SELECTED ESSAYS. Ed. Russell Kirk. Chicago: Henry Regnery, 1955.

WATCHWORDS FROM DR. BROWNSON. Ed. D.J. Scannell O'Neill. Techny, Ill.: Society of the Divine Word, 1910.

THE WORKS OF ORESTES A. BROWNSON. 20 vols. Collected and arranged by Henry F. Brownson. 1882-1907; New York: AMS Press, 1966.

These volumes collect virtually all of Brownson's essays after 1844 and a selection of those written before, although the bulk of these earlier essays, most of which appeared in the BOSTON QUARTERLY REVIEW, remain uncollected.

BIBLIOGRAPHY

There is no standard bibliography for Brownson, but a fairly complete listing can be found in the studies by Lapati, Maynard, and Ryan, below. These also include selected bibliographies of secondary sources. THE GUIDE TO CATHOLIC LITERATURE, 1888-1940, pp. 142-43, lists some secondary sources. Brownson is listed in the BIBLIOGRAPHY to the LITERARY HISTORY OF THE UNITED STATES, pp. 421, 880, 1154.

BIOGRAPHY AND CRITICISM

Brownson, Henry F. ORESTES A. BROWNSON'S EARLY LIFE, MIDDLE LIFE, AND LATER LIFE. 3 vols. Detroit: H.F. Brownson, 1898-1900.

> Written by Brownson's son, this poorly organized study does contain essential material for the study of Brownson, particularly several important letters.

Corrigan, Sister M. Felicia. SOME SOCIAL PRINCIPLES OF ORESTES A. BROWNSON. Washington, D.C.: Catholic Univ. of America, 1939.

> Originally a doctoral dissertation, this work examines the application of Brownson's social principles to religion, politics, education, and the family.

Farrell, Bertin. ORESTES BROWNSON'S APPROACH TO THE PROBLEM OF GOD. Washington, D.C.: Catholic Univ. of America, 1950.

Gilhooley, Leonard. CONTRADICTION AND DILEMMA: ORESTES BROWNSON AND THE AMERICAN IDEA. Bronx, N.Y.: Fordham Univ. Press, 1972.

> In his issue-by-issue description of the articles in Brownson's periodicals, the author of this study "hopes to make available for the current reader Brownson's views of the American Idea as he thought them through during the main part of his career." Some critical comments and backgrounds are presented in notes and in the introduction and afterword; otherwise, Brownson's ideas are presented largely without evaluation or commentary. Although he tries too hard to find consistency in Brownson's thought, Gilhooley's study is sympathetic, carefully documented, and thoroughly explains the ideas represented in Brownson's periodicals.

Lapati, Americo D. ORESTES A. BROWNSON. New York: Twayne, 1965.

> Despite difficulties in its prose style, this study contains solid information about Brownson's ideas, works, and influence.

Malone, George K. THE TRUE CHURCH: A STUDY IN THE APOLOGETICS OF ORESTES A. BROWNSON. Mundelein, Ill.: St. Mary of the Lake Seminary, 1957.

> The author focuses almost entirely on Brownson's arguments for the truth of Catholicism.

Marshall, Hugh, S.T. ORESTES BROWNSON AND THE AMERICAN REPUBLIC: AN HISTORICAL PERSPECTIVE. Washington, D.C.: Catholic Univ. of America, 1971.

> The author attempts to explain the shifts in Brownson's political thinking.

Maynard, Theodore. ORESTES BROWNSON: YANKEE, RADICAL, CATHOLIC. 1943; New York: Hafner, 1971.

> This sympathetic, fair, and generally well-documented biography emphasizes the years after Brownson's conversion to Catholicism. Maynard argues that Brownson never entirely got rid of his Protestantism and cites as evidence his Calvinist learnings and his lack of confidence in human nature.

Michel, Virgil G. THE CRITICAL PRINCIPLES OF ORESTES A. BROWNSON. Washington, D.C.: Catholic Univ. of America, 1918.

> Although the author's assumption that Brownson's aesthetic ideas were consistent over a period of thirty years seems unfounded, this is an interesting study of Brownson's critical and aesthetic premises and judgments. An excellent criticism of Michel's conclusions can be found in Charles Carroll Hollis' "The Literary Criticism of Orestes Brownson" (Dissertation, Univ. of Michigan, 1954).

Raemers, Sidney A. AMERICA'S FOREMOST PHILOSOPHER. Washington, D.C.: Catholic Univ. of America, 1931.

> As the title indicates, this is a highly laudatory study of Brownson's epistemology. The assertion in the title is not adequately supported by the evidence given.

Roemer, Lawrence. BROWNSON ON DEMOCRACY AND THE TREND TOWARD SOCIALISM. New York: Philosophical Library, 1953.

> The author emphasizes the arguments Brownson used to support his beliefs and notes the development of trends toward socialism and communism in the nineteenth century.

Ryan, Thomas R.C.; PP.S. ORESTES A. BROWNSON: A DEFINITIVE BIOGRAPHY. Huntington, Ind.: Our Sunday Visitor, 1976.

> This centennial biography integrates new material, particularly letters, shedding light on Brownson's life. It focuses upon Brownson's years and activities as a Catholic; and the author juxtaposes the careers of Brownson and John Henry Newman, finding a number of similarities in their lives and experiences. Given the biases of the biographer, however, one questions the use of the word "definitive" in the title of this large volume.

Schlesinger, Arthur M., Jr. ORESTES A. BROWNSON: A PILGRIM'S PROG-
RESS. 1939; rpt. as A PILGRIM'S PROGRESS: ORESTES A. BROWNSON,
Boston: Little, Brown, 1966.

> This expansion of a senior honor essay at Harvard, which the author
> wrote under the direction of Perry Miller, gives insight into the
> circumstances which affected Brownson's radically changing convic-
> tions and arguments. Schlesinger's observations are carefully docu-
> mented, and his evaluations of Brownson seem well-founded and
> objective.

Sveino, Per. ORESTES A. BROWNSON'S ROAD TO CATHOLICISM. New
York: Humanities Press, 1971.

> The author analyzes Brownson's conversion; attempts to rationalize
> it in terms of Brownson's philosophical leanings, psychological
> needs, and responses to tendencies in the Christianity of Europe
> and the United States; and measures it against Brownson's own
> autobiographical narrative in THE CONVERT. Sveino argues that
> Brownson's search for synthesis and unity was a lifelong pursuit of
> a father. The analysis is a useful supplement to what we know of
> the development of Brownson's thought.

Whalen, Doran [Sister Rose Gertrude Whalen, C.S.C.]. GRANITE FOR GOD'S
HOUSE: THE LIFE OF ORESTES AUGUSTUS BROWNSON. New York: Sheed
and Ward, 1941.

> This popular biography gives a sympathetic portrait of the man;
> but it is speculative, carelessly documented, often inaccurate,
> and obviously partisan.

RELATED GENERAL STUDIES

Burton, Katherine. PARADISE PLANTERS: THE STORY OF BROOK FARM.
(p. 215)
Curtis, Edith R. A SEASON IN UTOPIA. (p. 216)
Dorfman, Joseph, THE ECONOMIC MIND IN AMERICAN CIVILIZATION,
1606-1933. (p. 216)
Gardiner, Harold C., ed. AMERICAN CLASSICS RECONSIDERED. (p. 22)
Gohdes, Clarence. THE PERIODICALS OF AMERICAN TRANSCENDENTALISM.
(p. 61)
Guttmann, Allen. THE CONSERVATIVE TRADITION IN AMERICA. (III.,
under Henry Adams, p. 237)
Herreshoff, David. AMERICAN DISCIPLES OF MARX. (p. 218)
Mott, Frank L. A HISTORY OF AMERICAN MAGAZINES. (p. 61)
Sams, Henry W., ed. AUTOBIOGRAPHY OF BROOK FARM. (p. 223)
Swift, Lindsay. BROOK FARM: ITS MEMBERS, SCHOLARS, AND VISITORS.
(p. 225)

WILLIAM CULLEN BRYANT (1794-1878)

As editor of the New York EVENING POST, Bryant helped to shape opinion in America. He was an advocate of abolition, free speech, and labor rights as well as literary nationalism. Although his travel writing contains solid journalistic description, in his prose Bryant tends to be ponderous and impersonal. As a writer, he achieved his greatest successes with his poetry but was viewed by his contemporaries as primarily an editor and a journalist. He is second only to Poe in his importance as an early critic, embodying the change in literary taste from neoclassical to Romantic. His four LECTURES ON POETRY (first published in Godwin's edition of the PROSE WRITINGS and reprinted in Mc-Dowell's WILLIAM CULLEN BRYANT, below) are significant statements in the early development of American criticism.

PRINCIPAL PROSE WORKS

AN ADDRESS TO THE PEOPLE OF THE UNITED STATES IN BEHALF OF THE AMERICAN COPYRIGHT CLUB. 1843.

A FUNERAL ORATION OCCASIONED BY THE DEATH OF THOMAS COLE. 1848.

LETTERS OF A TRAVELLER; OR, NOTES OF THINGS SEEN IN EUROPE AND AMERICA. 2 vols. 1850.

REMINISCENCES OF THE EVENING POST. 1851.

A DISCOURSE ON THE LIFE AND GENIUS OF JAMES FENIMORE COOPER. 1852.

LETTERS OF A TRAVELLER, SECOND SERIES. 1859.

A DISCOURSE ON THE LIFE, CHARACTER AND GENIUS OF WASHINGTON IRVING. 1860.

LETTERS FROM THE EAST. 1869.

GULIAN CROMMELIN VERPLANCK: A DISCOURSE ON HIS LIFE, CHARACTER, AND WRITINGS. 1870.

ORATIONS AND ADDRESSES. 1873.

With S.H. Gay. A POPULAR HISTORY OF THE UNITED STATES. 4 vols. 1876-81.

LETTERS

THE LETTERS OF WILLIAM CULLEN BRYANT. 6 vols. projected. Ed. William Cullen Bryant II, and Thomas G. Voss. New York: Fordham Univ. Press, 1975-- .

> This edition of Bryant's letters has long been needed and will supplant Godwin's collection of letters in the biographical volumes of his edition of THE LIFE AND WORKS. Vol. 1 was published in 1975; vol. 2 in 1977; vol. 3 in 1981.

WILLIAM CULLEN BRYANT AND ISAAC HENDERSON: NEW EVIDENCE ON A STRANGE PARTNERSHIP. Ed. Theodore Hornberger. New York: Haskell House, 1973.

> This prints twenty-one letters, with an introduction and notes.

LATER EDITIONS, SELECTIONS, AND REPRINTS

PROSE WRITINGS. 2 vols. Ed. Parke Godwin. 1884; New York: Russell and Russell, 1964.

> Published as volumes 1 and 2 of Godwin's six-volume edition of THE LIFE AND WORKS OF WILLIAM CULLEN BRYANT (New York: D. Appleton, 1883-84), this work includes much of Bryant's criticism.

WASHINGTON IRVING: HIS LIFE, CHARACTER AND GENIUS. Norwood, Pa.: Norwood Editions, 1976.

> This is a reprint of Bryant's 1860 study of Irving.

WILLIAM CULLEN BRYANT: REPRESENTATIVE SELECTIONS. Ed. with Introd. and Notes by Tremaine McDowell. New York: American Book Co., 1935. Bibliog.

> Besides the excellent notes and introduction, this includes poetry, reviews, editorials, and correspondence as well as several critical essays on Bryant's work.

WILLIAM CULLEN BRYANT: SELECTIONS FROM HIS POETRY AND PROSE. Ed. Samuel Sillen. New York: International Publications, 1945.

BIBLIOGRAPHY

A listing of Bryant's works is in Blanck's BIBLIOGRAPHY OF AMERICAN LITERATURE 1:331-84. Bryant is listed in the BIBLIOGRAPHY to the LITERARY HISTORY OF THE UNITED STATES, pp. 422, 880, 1155.

Phair, Judith Turner. A BIBLIOGRAPHY OF WILLIAM CULLEN BRYANT AND HIS CRITICS, 1808-1972. Troy, N.Y.: Whitston, 1975.

> The guide lists, with brief annotations, secondary sources for Bryant: books and articles, book reviews, foreign references, and graduate research.

Rock, James E. "William Cullen Bryant." In FIFTEEN AMERICAN AUTHORS BEFORE 1900. Ed. Robert A. Rees and Earl N. Harbert. Madison: Univ. of Wisconsin Press, 1971, pp. 37-62.

> This bibliographical essay also evaluates Bryant criticism, with attention to studies of Bryant himself as critic and journalist.

Spivey, Herman E. "Manuscript Resources for the Study of William Cullen Bryant." PAPERS OF THE BIBLIOGRAPHICAL SOCIETY OF AMERICA, 44 (3rd quarter 1950), 254-68.

Sturges, Henry C. CHRONOLOGIES OF THE LIFE AND WRITINGS OF WILLIAM CULLEN BRYANT WITH A BIBLIOGRAPHY OF HIS WORKS IN PROSE AND VERSE. 1903; New York: B. Franklin, 1968.

> A useful source, Sturges must be used with some caution because the listing is incomplete and occasionally inaccurate.

Voss, Thomas G. WILLIAM CULLEN BRYANT: AN ANNOTATED CHECKLIST OF THE EXHIBIT IN THE MULLEN LIBRARY OF THE CATHOLIC UNIVERSITY OF AMERICA. Washington, D.C.: Catholic Univ. of America, 1967.

BIOGRAPHY AND CRITICISM

The critical works listed below include only those which give some discussion of Bryant's nonfiction prose and criticism.

Bigelow, John. WILLIAM CULLEN BRYANT. Boston: Houghton Mifflin, 1890.

> One of the more valuable biographies, by a friend and associate on the EVENING POST, this gives a good account of Bryant's public life and his work as an editor.

Bradley, William A. WILLIAM CULLEN BRYANT. New York: Macmillan, 1905.

> This contains no new biographical material. The criticism is perceptive, although Bradley overemphasizes Bryant's Puritanism.

Brown, Charles H. WILLIAM CULLEN BRYANT. New York: Scribner's, 1971.

> Relying upon extensive use of manuscript materials, this is the first biography to give a comprehensive view of the wide range

of Bryant's activities and influence. Meticulous, well-researched, and factual, the study focuses upon the life and times of Bryant rather than his mind and art. By presenting the editorial views in the New York EVENING POST and placing them in the context of the times, Brown reviews much of the social and cultural history of mid-century New York.

Curtis, George W. THE LIFE, CHARACTER, AND WRITINGS OF WILLIAM CULLEN BRYANT. New York: Scribner's, 1879.

This is primarily a memorial tribute, with little biographical or critical material, but it is useful as an indication of how Bryant was regarded by many of his contemporaries.

Godwin, Parke. A BIOGRAPHY OF WILLIAM CULLEN BRYANT WITH EX-TRACTS FROM HIS PRIVATE CORRESPONDENCE. 2 vols. 1883; New York: Russell and Russell, 1967.

Part of Godwin's six-volume edition of Bryant's LIFE AND WORKS, this includes autobiographical passages written by Bryant in 1874 and 1875. As Bryant's son-in-law, Godwin had access to hundreds of letters as well as diaries and journals, and his account is a valuable source of primary material. However, his biography betrays some personal biases and is most informative on the middle and later years of Bryant's life.

Johnson, Curtiss S. POLITICS AND A BELLY-FULL: THE JOURNALISTIC CAREER OF WILLIAM CULLEN BRYANT, CIVIL WAR EDITOR OF THE NEW YORK EVENING POST. New York: Vantage Press, 1962.

This is a short survey with a summary assessment of Bryant's years as an editor.

McClean, Albert F., Jr. WILLIAM CULLEN BRYANT. New York: Twayne, 1964.

After a brief biographical sketch, the author provides one of the most complete critical discussions of Bryant's poetry to date. The author also touches upon Bryant's critical theories, his achievements in nonfiction prose, and his prose style. McClean notes that Bryant's prose "voice" is that of "the literate, cosmopolitan gentleman who may observe, note, and express a few pertinent sentiments without fully engaging himself in the flow of life."

McDowell, Tremaine. "Introduction." In WILLIAM CULLEN BRYANT: REPRE-SENTATIVE SELECTIONS. New York: American Book Co., 1935.

McDowell's critical introduction is one of the best evaluations of Bryant's contributions to American literature.

Nevins, Allan. THE <u>EVENING POST</u>: A CENTURY OF JOURNALISM. New
York: Boni and Liveright, 1922.

> This provides an excellent examination of Bryant's editorial career,
> noting that Bryant's influence in the area of politics and economics
> was very important and that he was the first to bring "culture" to
> the American newspaper.

Wilson, James Grant. BRYANT AND HIS FRIENDS: SOME REMINISCENCES
OF THE KNICKERBOCKER WRITERS. New York: Fords, Howard and Hulbert,
1886.

> Wilson presents Bryant's relationships with Irving, Verplanck, and
> Halleck, quotes from correspondence, and includes personal anec-
> dotes.

RELATED GENERAL STUDIES

Brooks, Van Wyck. THE WORLD OF WASHINGTON IRVING. (p. 17)
Charvat, William. LITERARY PUBLISHING IN AMERICA. (p. 19)
_____. THE ORIGINS OF AMERICAN CRITICAL THOUGHT, 1810-1835.
    (p. 62)
Clark, Harry Hayden, ed. TRANSITIONS IN AMERICAN LITERARY HISTORY.
    (p. 19)
July, Robert W. THE ESSENTIAL NEW YORKER: GULIAN CROMMELIN
    VERPLANCK. (p. 63)
Miller, Perry. THE RAVEN AND THE WHALE. (p. 27)
Pritchard, John. CRITICISM IN AMERICA. (p. 65)
_____. LITERARY WISE MEN OF GOTHAM. (p. 66)
_____. RETURN TO THE FOUNTAINS. (p. 66)
Spencer, Benjamin T. THE QUEST FOR NATIONALITY: AN AMERICAN
    LITERARY CAMPAIGN. (p. 67)
Stafford, John. LITERARY CRITICISM OF YOUNG AMERICA. (p. 67)
Stovall, Floyd. THE DEVELOPMENT OF AMERICAN LITERARY CRITICISM.
    (p. 68)
_____. AMERICAN IDEALISM. (p. 32)

JOHN BURROUGHS (1837-1921)

Burroughs and Muir were very much responsible for developing the "nature essay" in American literature. In his prose, Burroughs was influenced by the
eighteenth-century British essayists, by Montaigne, and by such earlier American
nature writers as Audubon and Flagg, as well as by Emerson. Unlike many of
the transcendentalists, Burroughs did not view the relation of man and nature
metaphysically, but directly and practically. He was a careful observer and
for a time insisted that he was a scientist and not primarily a philosopher or
author. Ultimately, however, his treatment of nature was reflective rather than
scientific. In INDOOR STUDIES, he writes, "Until science is mixed with emotion, and appeals to the heart and imagination, it is like dead inorganic matter,
and when it is so mixed and so transformed it is literature." In LITERARY VAL-
UES he states that "vitality, sincerity, and genuineness" as well as "limpidness,
sweetness, and freshness" should characterize the nature writer's style. Burroughs' own style was spontaneous; the effect was leisurely but direct. His
criticism was impressionistic yet sincere; he is particularly good on Thoreau,
whose style and profundity he appreciated, and Whitman, a man whom he admired without reservation.

PRINCIPAL WORKS

NOTES ON WALT WHITMAN AS POET AND PERSON. 1867.
WAKE-ROBIN. 1871.
WINTER SUNSHINE. 1876.
BIRDS AND POETS. 1877.
LOCUSTS AND WILD HONEY. 1879.
PEPACTON. 1881.
FRESH FIELDS. 1885.
SIGNS AND SEASONS. 1886.
INDOOR STUDIES. 1889.
RIVERBY. 1894.
WHITMAN: A STUDY. 1896.
THE LIGHT OF DAY. 1900.
SQUIRRELS AND OTHER FUR-BEARERS. 1900. (Simplified version of previously
    published essays).
JOHN JAMES AUDUBON. 1902.

LITERARY VALUES AND OTHER PAPERS. 1902.
FAR AND NEAR. 1904.
WAYS OF NATURE. 1905.
BIRD AND BOUGH. 1906. (Poems)
CAMPING WITH PRESIDENT ROOSEVELT. 1906. (Published as CAMPING
  AND TRAMPING WITH ROOSEVELT, 1907)
LEAF AND TENDRIL. 1908.
TIME AND CHANGE. 1912.
THE SUMMIT OF THE YEARS. 1913.
THE BREATH OF LIFE. 1915.
UNDER THE APPLE-TREES. 1916.
FIELD AND STUDY. 1919.
ACCEPTING THE UNIVERSE. 1920. (This volume and those below were pre-
  pared by Burroughs but published posthumously by Clara Barrus.)
UNDER THE MAPLES. 1921.
THE LAST HARVEST. 1922.
MY BOYHOOD, WITH A CONCLUSION BY HIS SON, JULIAN BURROUGHS.
  1922.
MY DOG FRIENDS. Ed. Clara Barrus. 1928.
THE WRITINGS OF JOHN BURROUGHS. Riverby Edition. 23 vols. 1904-23.

LETTERS AND JOURNALS

THE HEART OF BURROUGHS'S JOURNALS. Ed. Clara Barrus. 1928; Port
Washington, N.Y.: Kennikat, 1967.

> These excerpts from Burroughs' notebooks and journals are valuable
> as the only published examples of that large body of writing. Al-
> though she was untrained as a scholar or critic, the editor's bio-
> graphical details and general comments throughout the volume are
> useful.

JOHN BURROUGHS AND LUDELLA PECK. New York: Harold Vinal, 1925.

> Ludella Peck was a professor at Smith College and a good friend
> of Burroughs. This is a collection of correspondence.

LATER EDITIONS, SELECTIONS, AND REPRINTS

CAMPING AND TRAMPING WITH ROOSEVELT. New York: Arno, 1970.

INDOOR STUDIES. Philadelphia: R. West, 1973.

JOHN BURROUGHS AT TROUTBECK: BEING EXTRACTS FROM HIS WRITINGS
PUBLISHED AND UNPUBLISHED. Ed. J.E. Spingarn. Introd. Vachel Lindsay.
Amenia, N.Y.: Troutbeck Press, 1926.

JOHN BURROUGHS TALKS: HIS REMINISCENCES AND COMMENTS AS RE-
PORTED BY CLIFTON JOHNSON. Ed. Clifton Johnson. Boston: Houghton
Mifflin, 1922.

JOHN BURROUGHS'S AMERICA: SELECTIONS FROM THE WRITINGS OF THE
HUDSON RIVER NATURALIST. Ed. with Introd. Fairda A. Wiley. Foreword
by Julian Burroughs. 1951; New York: Anchor, 1961.

LITERARY VALUES. Philadelphia: R. West, 1973.

WHITMAN: A STUDY. Philadelphia: R. West, 1973.

WITH JOHN BURROUGHS IN FIELD AND WOOD. Ed. and illus. by Elizabeth
Burroughs Kelley. South Brunswick, N.J.: A.S. Barnes, 1969.

THE WRITINGS OF JOHN BURROUGHS. Rpt. of the Riverby Edition. 23 vols.
New York: Russell and Russell, 1968.

BIBLIOGRAPHY

A listing of Burroughs' writings is in Blanck's BIBLIOGRAPHY OF AMERICAN
LITERATURE 1:433-48. Perry Westbrook surveys Burroughs' critical essays on
Emerson, Thoreau, and Whitman (over fifty of them) in ESQ 55 (1969): 47-55.
A selected listing of primary and secondary sources is in Westbrook's 1974 study,
below.

Burroughs is listed in the BIBLIOGRAPHY to the LITERARY HISTORY OF THE
UNITED STATES, pp. 427, 881, 1156.

BIOGRAPHY AND CRITICISM

Barrus, Clara. JOHN BURROUGHS, BOY AND MAN. 1921; New York:
Russell and Russell, 1968.

> This popular biography was originally intended for young people,
> but it is of interest to adults as well. It contains a number of
> Burroughs' letters.

_____. THE LIFE AND LETTERS OF JOHN BURROUGHS. 2 vols. Boston:
Houghton Mifflin, 1925.

> Dr. Clara Barrus was a psychiatrist who admired Burroughs and be-
> came, during the last years of his life, a friend, physician, typist,
> and editor. She was his literary executor and intended this LIFE
> as his official biography. It includes excerpts from Burroughs'
> diaries, journals, and correspondence. Although this is the most

comprehensive biography so far and a good source, it contains much trivial material.

_____. OUR FRIEND JOHN BURROUGHS. 1914; Philadelphia: R. West, 1973.

This adulatory biography includes autobiographical sketches written by Burroughs in letters to Barrus.

_____. THE RETREAT OF A POET NATURALIST. Boston: The Poet Lore Co., 1905.

This sketch describes "Slabsides," Burroughs' cabin retreat, and his life there.

_____. WHITMAN AND BURROUGHS, COMRADES. Boston: Houghton Mifflin, 1931.

This volume contains a number of letters, manuscripts, and other useful source material as well as a description of the relationship between Whitman and Burroughs.

DeLoach, Robert J.H. RAMBLES WITH JOHN BURROUGHS. Boston: R.G. Badger, 1912.

An appreciative reminiscence, this describes the author's acquaintance with Burroughs and briefly assesses Burroughs as a writer.

Frisbee, Lucy. JOHN BURROUGHS: BOY OF FIELD AND STREAM. Indianapolis: Bobbs-Merrill, 1964.

Intended for a young audience, this presents Burroughs as a kind of folk hero.

Haring, H.A., ed. THE SLABSIDES BOOK OF JOHN BURROUGHS. Boston: Houghton Mifflin, 1931.

This is a collection of reminiscences of John Burroughs as seen at his country retreat by a number of his friends.

Kelley, Elizabeth Burroughs. JOHN BURROUGHS: NATURALIST, THE STORY OF HIS WORK AND FAMILY. New York: Exposition Press, 1959.

Written by Burroughs' granddaughter, this is primarily a family history and does not deal with Burroughs' work. It is based upon a number of papers not available to Barrus and adds new material and insights.

Kennedy, William Sloane. THE REAL JOHN BURROUGHS, PERSONAL RECOLLECTION AND FRIENDLY ESTIMATE. New York: Funk and Wagnalls, 1924.

This study includes an estimate of Burroughs as a writer and a na-

turalist. Some of the biographical material has been questioned
by Kelley, above, and the descriptions of Burroughs and his achievements are colored by sentimentality.

Osborne, Clifford H. THE RELIGION OF JOHN BURROUGHS. Boston:
Houghton Mifflin, 1930.

An excellent summary of Burroughs' religious and philosophical views,
this is a useful study.

Sharp, Dallas Lore. THE SEER OF SLABSIDES. Boston: Houghton Mifflin,
1921.

This is a collection of pieces which Sharp wrote about Burroughs,
including an essay originally published in the ATLANTIC in 1910
praising Burroughs' work and ranking him among the greatest of
nature writers.

Westbrook, Perry D. JOHN BURROUGHS. New York: Twayne, 1974.

Burroughs' contributions in the areas of literary criticism, nature,
travel writings, philosophy, science, and theology are examined
in this study. The author focuses particularly upon Burroughs'
criticism and philosophy in this useful summary of his life and career.

RELATED GENERAL STUDIES

Abel, Darrel, ed. CRITICAL THEORY IN THE AMERICAN RENAISSANCE.
(p. 62)
Foerster, Norman. NATURE IN AMERICAN LITERATURE. (p. 166)
Hicks, Philip M. THE DEVELOPMENT OF THE NATURAL HISTORY ESSAY IN
AMERICAN LITERATURE. (p. 168)
Tracy, Henry C. AMERICAN NATURISTS. (p. 176)
Welker, Robert H. BIRDS AND MEN. (p. 250) under Audubon)

WILLIAM ELLERY CHANNING (1780-1842)

Channing was considered one of the most influential religious thinkers of his time, was ranked with Irving and Cooper as a writer, and was eminent both in the United States and in Europe. He was one of the first to realize the significance for religion of the changing spirit of the age and was a bridge between those holding the views of early Unitarianism and the proponents of New England Transcendentalism, his goal being the perfection of society through individual self-improvement. While his style is abstract and neither as brilliant as Emerson's nor as powerful as Thoreau's, it is clear and direct. His published essays and sermons show his remarkable ability to synthesize conflicting ideals and their possible resultant actions. In his aiming at a more humanitarian Christian theology, his emphasis upon human possibility, and his pleas for an American intellectual independence, Channing was a precursor to the scholars, transcendentalists, and writers who came to dominate nineteenth-century culture.

PRINCIPAL WORKS

A SERMON DELIVERED AT THE ORDINATION OF THE REV. JOHN CODMAN. . . . 1808.
A SERMON ON WAR. 1816.
A SERMON DELIVERED AT THE ORDINATION OF THE REV. JARED SPARKS. . . . 1819.
RELIGION, A SOCIAL PRINCIPLE. 1820.
A DISCOURSE ON THE EVIDENCES OF REVEALED RELIGION. 1821.
SERMONS AND TRACTS, INCLUDING THE ANALYSIS OF THE CHARACTER OF NAPOLEON AND REMARKS ON THE LIFE AND WRITINGS OF JOHN MILTON. 1828.
DISCOURSES, REVIEWS, AND MISCELLANIES. 1830.
THE IMPORTANCE AND MEANS OF A NATIONAL LITERATURE. 1830.
DISCOURSES. 1832.
SLAVERY. 1835.
AN ADDRESS ON TEMPERANCE. 1837.
ESSAYS, LITERARY AND POLITICAL. 1837. (Includes "Remarks on a National Literature")
A LETTER TO THE ABOLITIONISTS. 1837.
A LETTER TO THE HONORABLE HENRY CLAY, ON THE ANNEXATION OF TEXAS TO THE UNITED STATES. 1837.

CHARACTER OF NAPOLEON AND OTHER ESSAYS, LITERARY AND PHILO-
SOPHICAL. 2 vols. 1837.
SELF-CULTURE. 1838.
LECTURE ON WAR. 1839.
REMARKS ON THE SLAVERY QUESTION. 1839.
EMANCIPATION. 1840.
LECTURES ON THE ELEVATION OF THE LABOURING PORTION OF THE COM-
MUNITY. 1840.
THE DUTY OF THE FREE STATE; OR, REMARKS SUGGESTED BY THE CASE OF
THE CREOLE. 1842.

LETTERS AND JOURNALS

CHANNING'S NOTE-BOOKS: PASSAGES FROM THE UNPUBLISHED MANU-
SCRIPTS OF WILLIAM ELLERY CHANNING. Ed. Grace Ellery Channing.
1887; St. Clair Shores, Mich.: Scholarly Press, 1977.

CORRESPONDENCE OF WILLIAM ELLERY CHANNING AND LUCY AIKIN,
FROM 1826 TO 1842. Ed. Anna L. LeBreton. 1874; St. Clair Shores, Mich.:
Scholarly Press, 1977.

William H. Channing's MEMOIR contains excerpts from diaries and correspondence, some of them heavily edited. Elizabeth Peabody's REMINISCENCES includes valuable information about some of Channing's correspondence.

LATER EDITIONS, SELECTIONS, AND REPRINTS

CHANNING DAY BY DAY. . . . Ed. Jose Chapiro. Boston: Beacon, 1948.

CHARACTER AND WRITINGS OF JOHN MILTON. Philadelphia: R. West,
1978.

DISCOURSES ON WAR. Introd. Edwin D. Mead. 1903; with Introd. Ralph
E. Weber. New York: Garland, 1972.

EMANCIPATION. New York: Arno, 1969.

REMARKS ON THE CHARACTER AND WRITINGS OF JOHN MILTON. New
York: AMS Press, 1975.

SELF-CULTURE. New York: Arno, 1969.

SLAVERY. New York: Arno, 1969.

SLAVERY AND EMANCIPATION. New York: Negro Univ. Press, 1968.

THE WORKS OF WILLIAM E. CHANNING, D.D. 6 vols. 1841-43; New York: B. Franklin, 1970.

BIBLIOGRAPHY

There is no standard bibliography of Channing's writings. Arthur W. Brown's WILLIAM ELLERY CHANNING and the studies by David Edgell and Jack Mendelsohn, below, include useful selected bibliographies. Channing is listed in the BIBLIOGRAPHY to the LITERARY HISTORY OF THE UNITED STATES, pp. 438, 886, 1161.

BIOGRAPHY AND CRITICISM

Brooks, Charles T. WILLIAM ELLERY CHANNING: A CENTENNIAL MEMORY. Boston: Roberts Brothers, 1880.

> Like most accounts by those who knew Channing, this centenary biography tends to canonize the man.

Brown, Arthur W. ALWAYS YOUNG FOR LIBERTY: A BIOGRAPHY OF WILLIAM ELLERY CHANNING. Syracuse, N.Y.: Syracuse Univ. Press, 1956.

> This biographical study is well informed, emphasizing the personal as well as the public aspects of Channing's life.

_____. WILLIAM ELLERY CHANNING. New York: Twayne, 1961.

> This is a good introduction to Channing's life, importance, and reputation. Brown concludes his study by saying that "No one stood above [Channing] in the power to arouse enthusiasm and to compel belief in the exciting doctrine of human improvement."

Chadwick, John W. WILLIAM ELLERY CHANNING: MINISTER OF RELIGION. Boston: Houghton Mifflin, 1903.

> This is the best early biography, considering Channing's influence in the areas of religion, abolition, and social reform.

Channing, William Henry. MEMOIR OF WILLIAM ELLERY CHANNING, WITH EXTRACTS FROM HIS CORRESPONDENCE AND MANUSCRIPTS. 3 vols. Boston: Crosby and Nichols, 1848.

> The official biography, this contains valuable source material and was for many years the best account of Channing's life. However, its lack of an index makes it difficult to use.

_____. THE LIFE OF WILLIAM ELLERY CHANNING. 1880; Hicksville, N.Y.: Regina Press, 1975.

This centenary memorial edition condenses the earlier MEMOIR and includes some new material.

Edgell, David P. WILLIAM ELLERY CHANNING: AN INTELLECTUAL POR-TRAIT. Boston: Beacon, 1955.

Although this study is somewhat limited in scope, the author presents an objective and perceptive evaluation of Channing's role in American culture. He notes Channing's capacity to bear ambiguity, to see profoundly, and to commit himself passionately to social causes. Channing's greatness, the author concludes, was that he "helped to solidify and give contemporary expression to American liberalism, social as well as religious."

Holt, Anne. WILLIAM ELLERY CHANNING: HIS RELIGIOUS AND SOCIAL THOUGHT. London: Lindsay Press, 1942.

A short volume prepared to mark the centenary of Channing's death, this emphasizes the human qualities of Channing, countering the "plaster saint" image of the earlier memoirs.

Mendelsohn, Jack. CHANNING, THE RELUCTANT RADICAL: A BIOGRAPHY. Boston: Little, Brown, 1971.

The author focuses upon Channing's self-identification as a minister of religion, a prophet, and a reformer of the moral life. He points out that Channing has been regularly resurrected, each time fulfilling the particular needs of the age. In terms of our own needs, he sees Channing as perceiving the necessity to start "with the human situation" and work from there to fulfill the greatest possibilities of human growth and social improvement.

Parker, Theodore. AN HUMBLE TRIBUTE TO THE MEMORY OF WILLIAM EL-LERY CHANNING, D.D. Boston: Little, Brown, 1842.

In this tribute, Parker gives a good contemporary account of Channing's liberalism.

Peabody, Elizabeth. REMINISCENCES OF REVEREND WILLIAM ELLERY CHAN-NING, D.D. Boston: Roberts Brothers, 1880.

Peabody's account is anecdotal and affectionate, but she gives a clear account of Channing's profound effect upon his congregation and associates. The work is valuable as a source of primary material, but the facts and dates are not always reliable.

Rice, Madeleine Hook. FEDERAL STREET PASTOR: THE LIFE OF WILLIAM ELLERY CHANNING. New York: Bookman, 1961.

This biographical study focuses upon the important social influences

which Channing had as a minister for almost forty years of the
Federal Street Church in Boston.

RELATED GENERAL STUDIES

Ahlstrom, Sydney E. A RELIGIOUS HISTORY OF THE AMERICAN PEOPLE.
    (p. 160)
Curti, Merle. THE AMERICAN PEACE CRUSADE. (p. 215)
Gaustad, Edwin S. RELIGIOUS ISSUES IN AMERICAN HISTORY. (p. 167)
Howe, Daniel W. THE UNITARIAN CONSCIENCE. (p. 168)
Smith, James W., and Leland Jamison, eds. RELIGION IN AMERICAN LIFE.
    (p. 174)

SAMUEL LANGHORNE CLEMENS
[MARK TWAIN] (1835-1910)

Although Twain did not hesitate to change the facts to suit his artistic purposes, some of his works may be tentatively placed in the category of nonfiction prose and criticism and therefore deserve to be dealt with here. The artistry of these works was not immediately recognized. His most popular travel books, INNO-CENTS ABROAD and ROUGHING IT, were enjoyed for their humor without being taken seriously as literature, and LIFE ON THE MISSISSIPPI was appreciated primarily for its historical and regional interest. Only later were these and similar works given credit for the satire, the social and critical perceptiveness, the literary techniques, and the observations about the nature of experience and humanity which made effective the descriptive details, the images, and the humor. These "nonfiction" travel writings are essential in assessing Twain not only as a deeply sensitive representative of American experience and literature but also as a representative of an American abroad, offering to other Americans penetrating insights about the places which he visited. His study of Christian Science analyzes both the merits and faults of the movement, showing psychological sensitivity as well as awareness of broad social issues. His contributions to the field of literary criticism were often obscured by his more obvious achievement as a humorist, but Howells called Twain "a really great literary critic." Kraus's study noted below, MARK TWAIN AS CRITIC, demonstrates that Twain was a "close reader" whose judgments were based upon systematic principles and that his criticism should be seriously recognized.

PRINCIPAL PROSE WORKS

THE INNOCENTS ABROAD; OR, THE NEW PILGRIM'S PROGRESS. 1869.
ROUGHING IT. 1872.
SKETCHES, NEW AND OLD. 1875.
A TRAMP ABROAD. 1880.
LIFE ON THE MISSISSIPPI. 1883.
HOW TO TELL A STORY AND OTHER ESSAYS. 1897.
FOLLOWING THE EQUATOR. 1897.
MY DEBUT AS A LITERARY PERSON WITH OTHER ESSAYS AND STORIES.
     1903.
WHAT IS MAN? 1906.
CHRISTIAN SCIENCE. 1907.
IS SHAKESPEARE DEAD? 1909.

LETTERS AND JOURNALS

THE AUTOBIOGRAPHY OF MARK TWAIN. Ed. Charles Neider. New York: Harper, 1959; New York: Washington Square Press, 1961.

> Using mostly previously unpublished material, this largely, but not entirely, supersedes the Paine edition, below.

THE LOVE LETTERS OF MARK TWAIN. Ed. Dixon Wecter. 1949; Westport, Conn.: Greenwood Press, 1976.

MARK TWAIN-HOWELLS LETTERS . . . 1872-1910. 2 vols. Ed. Henry Nash Smith and William M. Gibson. Cambridge, Mass.: Belknap Press, Harvard Univ. Press, 1960.

> A one-volume edition, THE SELECTED MARK TWAIN-HOWELLS LETTERS, was published by Belknap Press, Harvard University in 1967.

MARK TWAIN AND GEORGE WASHINGTON CABLE. Ed. Arlin Turner. East Lansing: Michigan State Univ. Press, 1960.

> Most of the letters are written by Cable, but this is a useful collection for understanding the relationship between the two.

MARK TWAIN'S AUTOBIOGRAPHY. 2 vols. Ed. Albert B. Paine. 1924; New York: Haskell, 1970.

MARK TWAIN'S CORRESPONDENCE WITH HENRY HUTTLESTON ROGERS: 1893-1909. Ed. Lewis Leary. Berkeley: Univ. of California Press, 1969.

> This is a volume in the MARK TWAIN PAPERS (see below). The correspondence tells a great deal about Twain's business problems in the years covered.

MARK TWAIN'S LETTERS. 2 vols. Ed. Albert B. Paine. 1917; New York: AMS Press, 1975.

MARK TWAIN'S LETTERS TO HIS PUBLISHER, 1867-1894. Ed. Hamlin Hill. Berkeley: Univ. of California Press, 1967.

MARK TWAIN'S LETTERS TO MARY. Ed. Lewis Leary. New York: Columbia Univ. Press, 1961.

> Mary was the wife of Henry Huttleston Rogers. This volume contains some useful biographical details.

MARK TWAIN'S LETTERS TO THE ROGERS FAMILY. Ed. with Notes and Introd. Earl J. Dias. New Bedford, Mass.: Reynolds-DeWalt, 1970.

> This includes forty letters from Twain and his wife.

MARK TWAIN'S NOTEBOOK. Ed. Albert B. Paine. 1935; Philadelphia: R. West, 1973.

MARK TWAIN'S NOTEBOOKS AND JOURNALS. Ed. Frederick Anderson et al. Vol. 1 (1855-1873); vol. 2 (1877-1883); vol. 3 (1883-1891). Berkeley and Los Angeles: Univ. of California Press, 1976-- .

> These are volumes in the CEAA (Center for Editions of American Authors, now Center for Scholarly Editions) - approved edition and provide definitive texts which must meet rigorous bibliographical standards.

TWINS OF GENIUS. Ed. Guy A. Cardwell. East Lansing: Michigan State College Press, 1953.

> This includes eighteen letters from Mark Twain and describes the tour of public readings by Twain and George Washington Cable.

LATER EDITIONS, SELECTIONS, AND REPRINTS

CLEMENS OF THE CALL: MARK TWAIN IN SAN FRANCISCO. Ed. Edgar M. Branch. Berkeley: Univ. of California Press, 1969.

> This covers Twain's contributions to the San Francisco CALL from June to October 1864. The material is arranged topically.

THE COMPLETE ESSAYS. Ed. Charles Neider. Garden City, N.Y.: Doubleday, 1963.

> This is a useful collection, although it is not as all-inclusive as the title indicates.

THE COMPLETE TRAVEL BOOKS OF MARK TWAIN: THE EARLY WORKS--THE INNOCENTS ABROAD AND ROUGHING IT. Ed. Charles Neider. Garden City, N.Y.: Doubleday, 1966.

> Neider's introduction gives good historical background, but is weak in its critical appraisal of the two works.

THE COMPLETE TRAVEL BOOKS OF MARK TWAIN: THE LATER WORKS--A TRAMP ABROAD, LIFE ON THE MISSISSIPPI, FOLLOWING THE EQUATOR. Ed. Charles Neider. Garden City, N.Y.: Doubleday, 1967.

CONTRIBUTIONS TO THE GALAXY, 1868-1871. Ed. Bruce R. McElderry, Jr. 1961; Gainesville, Fla.: Scholar's Facsimiles and Reprints, 1977.

> This includes a useful bibliographical listing of some of Twain's journalistic work.

EUROPE AND ELSEWHERE. Introd. Albert Bigelow Paine. New York: Harper, 1923.

"THE GREAT LANDSLIDE CASE," BY MARK TWAIN: THREE VERSIONS. Ed. with comment by Frederick Anderson and Edgar M. Branch. Berkeley: Univ. of California Press for the Friends of the Bancroft Library, 1972.

> The editors analyze Twain's revisions of the lawsuit described in ROUGHING IT and provide historical annotation.

THE IOWA-CALIFORNIA EDITION OF THE WORKS OF MARK TWAIN. Ed. John C. Gerber et al. 24 vols. projected. Berkeley and Los Angeles: Univ. of California Press, 1969-- .

> This CEAA-approved edition will provide definitive texts. Nonfiction works in this edition are cited separately here by title.

LETTERS FROM THE EARTH. Ed. Bernard DeVoto. New York: Harper and Row, 1962.

> Henry Nash Smith has added a short preface to this material, which is otherwise essentially the same as the edition which DeVoto prepared in 1939.

LIFE AS I FIND IT: ESSAYS, SKETCHES, TALES, AND OTHER MATERIAL. Ed. Charles Neider. 1961; New York: Harper and Row, 1977.

LIFE ON THE MISSISSIPPI. Ed. Wiltis Wager. Introd. Edward Wagenknecht. New York: Heritage, 1944.

> This is a complete edition based on manuscripts.

LIFE ON THE MISSISSIPPI. Introd. Dixon Wecter. New York: Harper, 1950.

> The introduction to this edition is important.

MARK TWAIN: REPRESENTATIVE SELECTIONS. Ed. Fred L. Pattee. New York: American Book Co., 1935.

MARK TWAIN AND HAWAII. Ed. Walter T. Frear. Chicago: Lakeside Press, 1947. Appendix.

> A collection of Twain's writings with extensive commentary, this is a thorough treatment of his visit to Hawaii and its influence.

MARK TWAIN AND THE THREE R'S: RACE, REVOLUTION AND RELATED MATTERS. Ed. Maxwell Geismar. Indianapolis: Bobbs-Merrill, 1973.

> This is "an anthology of Twain's radical social commentary" from 1869 to his death.

MARK TWAIN IN ERUPTION: HITHERTO UNPUBLISHED PAGES ABOUT MEN AND EVENTS. Ed. Bernard DeVoto. New York: Harper, 1940.

> This publishes memoirs which Paine did not use in his edition of the autobiography.

MARK TWAIN OF THE ENTERPRISE. Ed. Henry Nash Smith and Frederick Anderson. Berkeley: Univ. of California Press, 1957.

> This well-edited text provides newspaper correspondence, personal letters, and other papers.

MARK TWAIN ON THE ART OF WRITING. Ed. Martin B. Fried. Buffalo, N.Y.: Salisbury Club, 1961.

> This includes material from the Buffalo EXPRESS, 1869-70.

MARK TWAIN ON THE DAMNED HUMAN RACE. Ed. Janet Smith. New York: Hill and Wang, 1962.

> This includes excerpts from writings on politics, race, war, and other topics.

MARK TWAIN PAPERS. Ed. Frederick Anderson et al. 14 vols. projected. Berkeley: Univ. of California Press, 1967-- .

> Published in conjunction with the IOWA-CALIFORNIA EDITION, above, this consists primarily of previously unpublished work.

MARK TWAIN SPEAKING. Ed. Paul Fatout. Iowa City: Univ. of Iowa Press, 1976.

> The editor has prepared texts for 195 lectures and speeches, includes useful explanatory notes, and gives a chronological listing of Twain's appearances before an audience.

MARK TWAIN SPEAKS FOR HIMSELF. Ed. Paul Fatout. West Lafayette, Ind.: Purdue Univ. Press, 1978.

> This collection of newspaper sketches, interviews, and informal statements shows the contradictions in Twain's character.

MARK TWAIN'S LETTERS FROM HAWAII. Ed. A. Grove Day. 1966; Honolulu: Univ. Press of Hawaii, 1975.

> Twenty-five letters from the Sacramento UNION are reprinted here.

MARK TWAIN'S LETTERS FROM THE SANDWICH ISLANDS. Ed. G. Ezra Dane. 1938; New York: Haskell, 1972.

MARK TWAIN'S SAN FRANCISCO. Ed. Bernard Taper. 1963; Westport, Conn.: Greenwood Press, 1977.

> The introductory essay and notes to these eighty-three pieces written for Nevada and California newspapers between 1863 and 1866 provide useful backgrounds.

MARK TWAIN'S SPEECHES. Introd. Albert B. Paine. New York: Harper, 1923.

MARK TWAIN'S TRAVELS WITH MR. BROWN. . . . Ed. Franklin Walker and G. Ezra Dane. 1940; New York: Russell and Russell, 1971.

> This includes sketches written for the ALTA CALIFORNIA in 1866 and 1867 before the sailing of the QUAKER CITY.

THE PATTERN FOR MARK TWAIN'S ROUGHING IT: LETTERS FROM NEVADA BY SAMUEL AND ORION CLEMENS, 1861-1862. Ed. Franklin R. Rogers. Berkeley and Los Angeles: Univ. of California Press, 1961.

> This correspondence, published in Iowa and Missouri newspapers, gives valuable backgrounds for ROUGHING IT.

A PEN WARMED-UP IN HELL: MARK TWAIN IN PROTEST. Ed. Frederick Anderson. New York: Harper and Row, 1972.

> This collects political and social satire.

THE PORTABLE MARK TWAIN. Ed. Bernard DeVoto. New York: Viking, 1946.

ROUGHING IT. Introd. and notes Franklin R. Rogers. Textual Ed. Paul Baender. Berkeley: Univ. of California Press for the Iowa Center for Textual Studies, 1972.

A TRAMP ABROAD. Introd. Edward Wagenknecht. New York: Heritage, 1966.

A TRAMP ABROAD BY MARK TWAIN. Abridged and edited with Introd. Charles Neider. New York: Harper and Row, 1977.

TRAVELING WITH INNOCENTS ABROAD: MARK TWAIN'S ORIGINAL REPORTS FROM EUROPE AND THE HOLY LAND. Ed. Daniel Morley McKeithan. Norman: Univ. of Oklahoma Press, 1958.

> Fifty-eight letters for various newspapers are presented in this well-edited collection, showing backgrounds for and some of the changes in INNOCENTS ABROAD.

THE TRAVELS OF MARK TWAIN. Ed. Charles Neider. Garden City, N.Y.: Doubleday, 1961.

> These are selections from all of the travel writings arranged according to the place described.

WHAT IS MAN? AND OTHER PHILOSOPHICAL WRITINGS. Ed. with Introd. Paul Baender. Berkeley and Los Angeles: Univ. of California Press, 1973.

THE WRITINGS OF MARK TWAIN. Ed. Albert B. Paine. 37 vols. New York: Harper, 1922-25.

BIBLIOGRAPHY

Clark, Harry Hayden. "Mark Twain." In EIGHT AMERICAN AUTHORS. Rev. Ed. James Woodress. New York: Norton, 1971, pp. 273-320.

Gale, Robert L. PLOTS AND CHARACTERS IN THE WORKS OF MARK TWAIN. 2 vols. Foreword by Frederick Anderson. Hamden, Conn.: Archon, 1973.

> Volume 1 summarizes book and notebook material, autobiographical writings, and collected letters.

Johnson, Merle. A BIBLIOGRAPHY OF THE WORKS OF MARK TWAIN. Rev. ed. New York: Harper, 1935.

Long, E. Hudson. MARK TWAIN HANDBOOK. New York: Hendricks House, 1957.

> This guide surveys biography and criticism and gives a brief summary of the life and works.

Tenney, Thomas A. MARK TWAIN: A REFERENCE GUIDE. Boston: G.K. Hall, 1977.

> This thorough and intelligently annotated guide attempts to collect all listings of books, reviews, and articles concerning Mark Twain through 1974. The listing is corrected, enlarged, and updated yearly in AMERICAN LITERARY REALISM.

The MARK TWAIN JOURNAL (formerly the MARK TWAIN QUARTERLY) and THE TWAINIAN include bibliographical items. An extensive listing of Twain's works is in Blanck's BIBLIOGRAPHY OF AMERICAN LITERATURE 2:173-254. An excellent listing is in the survey below by Asselineau. The International Mark Twain Society has occasionally published items to be added to the bibliography. Twain is listed in the BIBLIOGRAPHY to the LITERARY HISTORY OF THE UNITED STATES, pp. 442, 888, 1163.

BIOGRAPHY AND CRITICISM

The listing below does not include critical works which deal primarily with the fiction.

Anderson, Frederick, and Kenneth M. Sanderson, eds. MARK TWAIN: THE CRITICAL HERITAGE. London: Routledge and Kegan Paul, 1971.

> This includes contemporaneous evaluations, largely from reviews, of the major publications. Two Twain letters are also included.

Andrews, Kenneth. NOOK FARM: MARK TWAIN'S HARTFORD CIRCLE. 1950; Seattle: Univ. of Washington Press, 1960.

> A carefully documented account, this deals with the influence of the Hartford community and nearby friends upon Mark Twain.

Asselineau, Roger. THE LITERARY REPUTATION OF MARK TWAIN. Paris: Marcel Didier, 1954. Bibliog.

> The study provides a valuable survey of criticism, 1910-50.

Baetzhold, Howard G. MARK TWAIN AND JOHN BULL: THE BRITISH CON- NECTION. Bloomington: Indiana Univ. Press, 1970.

> The author discusses Twain's visit to England, his lectures there, and the influence of Britain on his thought and writings.

Baldanza, Frank. MARK TWAIN: AN INTRODUCTION AND INTERPRETATION. New York: Barnes and Noble, 1961.

> A good survey of Twain's life and works, this treats the travel and autobiographical material as well as the fiction.

Bellamy, Gladys Carmen. MARK TWAIN AS A LITERARY ARTIST. Norman: Univ. of Oklahoma Press, 1950.

> The author deals at some length with the travel books in this analy- sis of Twain's craftsmanship.

Benson, Ivan. MARK TWAIN'S WESTERN YEARS. . . . 1938; New York: Russell and Russell, 1966.

> This includes a partial bibliography of Twain's journalistic writing, 1861-66, and a sampling of writings which he did for California and Nevada newspapers.

Branch, Edgar M. THE LITERARY APPRENTICESHIP OF MARK TWAIN. Urbana: Univ. of Illinois Press. 1950; New York: Russell and Russell, 1966.

> This includes "Selections from Mark Twain's Apprenticeship Writings, 1852-67" and is concerned primarily with Twain's career to 1867.

Brooks, Van Wyck. THE ORDEAL OF MARK TWAIN. 1920; 1933; New York: AMS Press, 1976.

> A controversial but highly influential study, this considers Twain a victim of his environment and the genteel influence of his wife and W.D. Howells. It led to DeVoto's response, below.

Budd, Louis J. MARK TWAIN: SOCIAL PHILOSOPHER. Bloomington: Indiana Univ. Press, 1962.

> The author discusses the development of and changes in Mark Twain's political and social thinking and allies him with nineteenth-century liberalism and commitment to the doctrine of progress.

Canby, Henry S. TURN WEST, TURN EAST: MARK TWAIN AND HENRY JAMES. Boston: Houghton Mifflin, 1951.

> Canby examines the response of James and Twain to their age and circumstances and finds Twain actively participating in the mainstream of American literary production, James turning away from it.

Clemens, Will M. MARK TWAIN: HIS LIFE AND WORK. Chicago: F.T. Neely, 1892.

> This memoir contains some useful primary material not in Paine's biography.

DeVoto, Bernard. MARK TWAIN'S AMERICA. 1932; Boston: Houghton Mifflin, 1967.

> In this study, which is partially a response to Brooks' study, above, DeVoto emphasizes the importance of the frontier and frontier humor in Twain's writings.

Ensor, Allison. MARK TWAIN AND THE BIBLE. Lexington: Univ. of Kentucky Press, 1969.

> The author shows that Twain knew the Bible well, used it, and was much influenced by it.

Fatout, Paul. MARK TWAIN IN VIRGINIA CITY. 1964; New York: Kennikat, 1973.

> The author concentrates on the period from September 1862 to May 1864, and cites contemporary newspaper accounts as well as other previously unpublished material about Twain.

_____. MARK TWAIN ON THE LECTURE CIRCUIT. 1959; Gloucester, Mass.: Peter Smith, 1966.

Citing newspaper reviews, the author traces Twain's career as a
speaker, pointing to his talent as orator as well as writer.

Ferguson, DeLancey. MARK TWAIN: MAN AND LEGEND. 1943; New York:
Russell and Russell, 1966.

A good general study, this reflects all the scholarship then available.

Foner, Philip S. MARK TWAIN: SOCIAL CRITIC. 1958; New York: International Publishers, 1972.

Carefully documented and using numerous quotations from Twain,
this is a Marxist interpretation of his views.

Ganzel, Dewey. MARK TWAIN ABROAD: THE CRUISE OF THE "QUAKER
CITY." Chicago: Univ. of Chicago Press, 1968.

This gives a detailed account of Mark Twain's trip to Europe and
the Holy Land in 1867.

Geismar, Maxwell. MARK TWAIN: AN AMERICAN PROPHET. Boston:
Houghton Mifflin, 1970.

Geismar quotes at length from Twain's writings and accuses Twain
scholars of repressing "a whole area of Twain's social criticism of
the United States . . . because it is so bold, so brilliant, satirical, and prophetic."

Gibson, William M. THE ART OF MARK TWAIN. New York: Oxford Univ.
Press, 1976.

The author examines Twain's style and technique in various genres,
concluding that he "was more a man of letters in the traditional
sense than anyone has yet argued" and that he was best in his
shorter pieces.

Hill, Hamlin. MARK TWAIN: GOD'S FOOL. New York: Harper and Row,
1973.

This gives an account of the last ten years of Twain's life, using
much unpublished material.

Kaplan, Justin. MR. CLEMENS AND MARK TWAIN, A BIOGRAPHY. 1966;
New York: Simon and Schuster, 1970.

An objective, informative, and readable biography, this deals primarily with the years after 1866.

Krause, Sidney J. MARK TWAIN AS CRITIC. Baltimore, Md.: Johns Hopkins Univ. Press, 1967.

> The author contends that Twain adopted various poses as a critic, but that he was also a sensitive reader and a serious student of his literary craft.

Lorch, Fred W. THE TROUBLE BEGINS AT EIGHT: MARK TWAIN'S LECTURE TOURS. Ames: Iowa State Univ. Press, 1968.

> The author traces Twain's career as a lecturer and discusses his manner, techniques, and reception.

Lynn, Kenneth S. MARK TWAIN AND SOUTHWESTERN HUMOR. 1960; Westport, Conn.: Greenwood Press, 1972.

> The study treats Twain as a conscious literary artist who uses humor deliberately and effectively.

Macnaughton, William R. MARK TWAIN'S LAST YEARS AS A WRITER. Columbia: Univ. of Missouri Press, 1979.

> A critical appraisal of the writings from 1897-1910, this study focuses on the completed works rather than the fragments or manuscripts. The author argues that Twain's output in those years was not of inferior quality and tempers the view that the last years were filled with despair.

Neider, Charles. MARK TWAIN. New York: Horizon, 1967.

> This is a collection of essays by Neider, most of which were originally published as introductions to volumes of Twain's work.

Paine, Albert Bigelow. MARK TWAIN: A BIOGRAPHY. 3 vols. New York: Harper, 1912.

> Paine's authorized biography has been criticized for omissions and other problems, but it remains a valuable source.

Pettit, Arthur G. MARK TWAIN AND THE SOUTH. Lexington: Univ. of Kentucky, 1974.

> This monograph discusses Twain's ambivalent attitude toward the South and toward racial problems and how these attitudes affected his writing.

Scott, Arthur L. MARK TWAIN AT LARGE. Chicago: Henry Regnery, 1969.

> Scott discusses Twain's travels and travel books, concluding that he became a kind of "ambassador at large" for America.

Smith, Henry Nash. MARK TWAIN: THE DEVELOPMENT OF A WRITER. Cambridge, Mass.: Belknap Press, Harvard Univ. Press, 1962.

> Smith considers Twain's handling of style and structure in nine

principal works—including INNOCENTS ABROAD, LIFE ON THE MISSISSIPPI, and ROUGHING IT—and deals also with Twain's ethical ideas and "how his writing reveals a conflict between the dominant culture of his day and an emergent attitude associated with the vernacular language of the native American humorist."

Spengemann, William C. MARK TWAIN AND THE BACKWOODS ANGEL: THE MATTER OF INNOCENCE IN THE WORKS OF SAMUEL L. CLEMENS. Kent, Ohio: Kent State Univ. Press, 1966.

The study examines Twain's "myth of American innocence" in several works, including the travel and autobiographical writings.

Strong, Leah A. JOSEPH HOPKINS TWICHELL: MARK TWAIN'S FRIEND AND PASTOR. Athens: Univ. of Georgia Press, 1966.

Twichell traveled with Twain in Bermuda and Europe and remained a good friend from 1867 to Twain's death in 1910. The book deals with the friendship and with Twichell's influence on Twain and his writings.

Wagenknecht, Edward. MARK TWAIN: THE MAN AND HIS WORK. 1935; 1961; rev. with additional bibliography, Norman: Univ. of Oklahoma Press, 1967.

In this sympathetic study, Wagenknecht relies on available evidence in both his original study and his revisions. He concludes that Twain was both a realist and an idealist but was undisciplined.

Wecter, Dixon. SAM CLEMENS OF HANNIBAL. Ed. Elizabeth Wecter. 1952; New York: AMS Press, 1977.

Emphasizing the influence of Twain's Hannibal experiences, this is a thorough, scholarly study.

Welland, Dennis. MARK TWAIN IN ENGLAND. Atlantic Highland, N.J.: Humanities Press, 1978.

Using the archives of Twain's English publisher, Chatto and Windus, the author discusses Twain's relationship with his publisher and the English printings of his books.

RELATED GENERAL STUDIES

Blair, Walter. NATIVE AMERICAN HUMOR. (pp. 35 and 89)
Blair, Walter, and Hamlin Hill. AMERICA'S HUMOR. . . . (p. 97)
Boller, Paul F., Jr. FREEDOM AND FATE IN AMERICAN THOUGHT. (p. 16)
Bridgman, Richard. THE COLLOQUIAL STYLE IN AMERICA. (p. 16)
Brooks, Van Wyck. THE TIMES OF MELVILLE AND WHITMAN. (p. 17)
Carter, Everett. THE AMERICAN IDEA. (p. 18)

Cooley, Thomas. EDUCATED LIVES. (p. 78)

Garland, Hamlin. ROADSIDE MEETINGS (p. 328, under Garland)

Hazard, Lucy L. THE FRONTIER IN AMERICAN LITERATURE. (p. 129)

Howells, Mildred. LIFE IN LETTERS OF WILLIAM DEAN HOWELLS. (p. 351, under Howells)

Howells, William D. MY MARK TWAIN. (pp. 351 and 352, under Howells)

Lee, Richard E. FROM WEST TO EAST. (p. 129)

Lewis, Marvin, ed. THE MINING FRONTIER. (p. 129)

Macy, John. AMERICAN WRITERS ON AMERICAN LITERATURE. (p. 26)

Martin, Jay. HARVESTS OF CHANGE. (p. 26)

Mumford, Lewis. THE GOLDEN DAY. (p. 28)

Poirier, Richard. A WORLD ELSEWHERE. (p. 30)

Roemer, Kenneth M. THE OBSOLETE NECESSITY: AMERICA IN UTOPIAN WRITINGS. (p. 223)

Rourke, Constance. NATIVE AMERICAN HUMOR. (p. 35)

Walker, Franklin. IRREVERENT PILGRIMS. (p. 413, under Melville)

_____. SAN FRANCISCO'S LITERARY FRONTIER. (p. 132)

Warner, Charles D. BACKLOG STUDIES. (p. 86)

Ziff, Larzer. THE AMERICAN 1890'S. (p. 34)

JAMES FENIMORE COOPER (1789-1851)

Cooper's historical, critical, and descriptive prose works are well informed and carefully written. Robert Spiller has in fact observed that in his nonfiction Cooper's prose is freed from many of its worst defects. Cooper was a sensitive observer of contrasts in society, behavior, attitudes, and government between the United States and Europe; his volumes on Europe are distinguished contributions to our literature of travel. However, he offended both Europeans and Americans in his comparative judgments, Europeans seeing him as a champion of democracy and American life, Americans as a defender of aristocracy. His honesty as a naval historian caused further criticism from his countrymen. In his pieces on democracy, Cooper argued that an aristocracy of worth was not inconsistent with guaranteed equality of opportunity, but affirmed his belief in liberty and nationalism and encouraged American intellectual independence. Although Cooper was not a formal literary critic or theorist, and his opinions tended to be both violent and impressionistic, his prefaces show his appreciation for native material and for the power of the narrative form. With the passage of time, Cooper's social criticism has earned him respect for its penetrating analysis of some of the problems and dangers of democracy.

PRINCIPAL PROSE WORKS

NOTIONS OF THE AMERICANS. 1828. (Semifictional letters)
A LETTER TO GENERAL LAFAYETTE. 1831.
A LETTER TO HIS COUNTRYMEN. 1834.
SKETCHES OF SWITZERLAND. 1836.
SKETCHES OF SWITZERLAND, PART SECOND. 1836.
GLEANINGS IN EUROPE [France]. 1837.
GLEANINGS IN EUROPE: ENGLAND. 1837.
GLEANINGS IN EUROPE: ITALY. 1838.
THE AMERICAN DEMOCRAT. 1838.
THE CHRONICLES OF COOPERSTOWN. 1838.
HISTORY OF THE NAVY OF THE UNITED STATES. 2 vols. 1839.
LIVES OF DISTINGUISHED AMERICAN NAVAL OFFICERS. 1846.

LETTERS AND JOURNALS

CORRESPONDENCE OF JAMES FENIMORE COOPER. Ed. James Fenimore Cooper. 1922; New York: Haskell, 1971.

> Edited by Cooper's grandson, this volume contains some letters not reprinted in LETTERS AND JOURNALS, but most of the letters are to rather than from Cooper.

THE LETTERS AND JOURNALS OF JAMES FENIMORE COOPER. 6 vols. Ed. James Franklin Beard. Cambridge, Mass.: Belknap Press, Harvard Univ. Press, 1960-68.

LATER EDITIONS, SELECTIONS, AND REPRINTS

THE AMERICAN DEMOCRAT. Introd. H.L. Mencken. 1931. Reissued with introd. Robert E. Spiller, 1956; introd. George Dekker and Larry Johnston. Gretna, La.: Pelican, 1970.

EARLY CRITICAL ESSAYS BY JAMES FENIMORE COOPER. 1955. Introd. and Headnote by James F. Beard. Gainesville, Fla.: Scholar's Facsimiles and Reprints, 1977.

> This collection consists of book reviews written for THE LITERARY AND SCIENTIFIC REPOSITORY AND CRITICAL REVIEW between 1820 and 1822.

GLEANINGS IN EUROPE: FRANCE. Ed. Robert E. Spiller. 1928; Philadelphia: R. West, 1979.

GLEANINGS IN EUROPE: ENGLAND. Ed. Robert E. Spiller. New York: Oxford Univ. Press, 1930.

GLEANINGS IN EUROPE: SWITZERLAND. Ed. Kenneth Staggs and James P. Elliott. Albany, N.Y.: State Univ. of New York Press, 1979.

> This is one of the volumes of definitive texts being prepared under the auspices of CEAA (Center for Editions of American Authors, now CSE), to be published by the State University of New York Press with the joint scholarship of the American Antiquarian Society and Clark University.

HISTORY OF THE NAVY OF THE UNITED STATES. Upper Saddle River, N.J.: Gregg Press, 1970.

JAMES FENIMORE COOPER: REPRESENTATIVE SELECTIONS. Ed. Robert E. Spiller. 1936; Westport, Conn.: Greenwood Press, 1977.

This selection restricts itself to the critical prose, including excerpts from the prefaces, from the travel writings, and from the social criticism. Spiller's introduction is an excellent discussion and evaluation of Cooper's nonfiction prose and social criticism.

LIVES OF DISTINGUISHED AMERICAN NAVAL OFFICERS. New York: Somerset, 1964.

NEW YORK. Introd. Dixon Ryan Fox. New York: S.A. Jacobs for William Farquhar Payson, 1930.

This reprints a collection first published in 1864.

NOTIONS OF THE AMERICANS. Introd. Robert E. Spiller. New York: Frederick Ungar, 1963.

BIBLIOGRAPHY

Beard, James Franklin. "James Fenimore Cooper." In FIFTEEN AMERICAN AUTHORS BEFORE 1900. Ed. Robert A. Rees and Earl N. Harbert. Madison: Univ. of Wisconsin Press, 1971, pp. 63-96.

This is a comprehensive bibliographical essay and summary of Cooper criticism to 1970.

Spiller, Robert E., and Philip C. Blackburn. A DESCRIPTIVE BIBLIOGRAPHY OF THE WRITINGS OF JAMES FENIMORE COOPER. 1934; New York: B. Franklin, 1968.

This describes first and early editions of Cooper's works and includes an appendix containing correspondence between Cooper and various publishers.

A full listing of Cooper's works is in Blanck's BIBLIOGRAPHY OF AMERICAN LITERATURE 2:276-310. Volume 6 of THE LETTERS AND JOURNALS, above, lists Cooper's writings; Spiller's JAMES FENIMORE COOPER: REPRESENTATIVE SELECTIONS, above, lists books and articles about Cooper up to 1930 and gives a calendar of published letters. Cooper is listed in the BIBLIOGRAPHY to the LITERARY HISTORY OF THE UNITED STATES, pp. 450, 891, 1168.

BIOGRAPHY AND CRITICISM

The selection below includes works which deal with Cooper's nonfiction or primarily with his social and political ideas. Works which focus on the fiction are not included.

Barba, Preston A. COOPER IN GERMANY. Bloomington: Univ. of Indiana Press, 1914.

This brief study examines Cooper's travels in Germany, his influence on German literature, and the relationship of German criticism to Cooper's literary theories and practices.

Boynton, Henry W. JAMES FENIMORE COOPER. 1931; New York: Haskell, 1968.

A good short biography, this is based largely upon Cooper's letters to Admiral Shubrick.

Cunningham, Mary E., ed. JAMES FENIMORE COOPER: A REAPPRAISAL. Introd. Howard M. Jones. New York: State Historical Association, 1954.

This collection of Cooper centenary papers discusses various aspects of his life and career.

Dekker, George, comp. FENIMORE COOPER: THE CRITICAL HERITAGE. Ed. George Dekker and John P. McWilliams. London: Routledge and Kegan Paul, 1973.

A collection of nineteenth-century critical discussions and reviews, this reflects Cooper's reception by American and European contemporaries from 1822 to 1898. The editors also provide an essay surveying the criticism.

Grossman, James. JAMES FENIMORE COOPER. New York: W. Sloane, 1949.

Grossman's is one of the better biographies and provides perceptive evaluations of the works.

Lounsbury, Thomas R. JAMES FENIMORE COOPER. Boston: Houghton Mifflin, 1882.

This scholarly study, which is still a valuable resource, was the standard biography for many years.

McWilliams, John P. POLITICAL JUSTICE IN A REPUBLIC: JAMES FENIMORE COOPER'S AMERICA. Berkeley: Univ. of California Press, 1972.

The author discusses Cooper's "self-assumed role as fictional spokesman for the American republic" and analyzes selected fiction and nonfiction to outline the political values in Cooper's writing.

MEMORIAL OF JAMES FENIMORE COOPER. New York: G.P. Putnam's, 1852.

These collected tributes to Cooper include Bryant's "Discourse on the Life, Genius, and Writings of James Fenimore Cooper."

Outland, Ethel R. THE "EFFINGHAM LIBELS" ON COOPER. Madison: Univ. of Wisconsin Press, 1929.

Although the author's conclusions are questionable, this study includes valuable documentation of Cooper's quarrels with the press.

Ringe, Donald A. JAMES FENIMORE COOPER. New York: Twayne, 1962.

Ringe's study concerns itself mostly with the fiction, but also provides good perspective on the social and political views of Cooper.

Ross, John F. SOCIAL CRITICISM OF FENIMORE COOPER. Berkeley: Univ. of California Press, 1933.

Ross's monograph is based on the critical prose and focuses upon the relationship between Cooper's work and the concurrent development of America.

Shulenberger, Arvid. COOPER'S THEORY OF FICTION. 1955; Folcroft, Pa.: Folcroft Press, 1970.

Based upon the prefaces to Cooper's work, the overview is somewhat misleading because of the discrepancies between Cooper's theory and practice.

Spiller, Robert E. FENIMORE COOPER: CRITIC OF HIS TIMES. New York: Minton, Balch, and Co., 1931.

Spiller focuses upon Cooper's social and political criticism, his European travels, and his relationship with publishers. See also his introduction to JAMES FENIMORE COOPER: REPRESENTATIVE SELECTIONS, above.

_____. JAMES FENIMORE COOPER. Minneapolis: Univ. of Minnesota Press, 1965.

This is a brief but masterful summary of Cooper's life, career, and achievements.

Walker, Warren S. JAMES FENIMORE COOPER: AN INTRODUCTION AND INTERPRETATION. New York: Barnes and Noble, 1962.

This brief but useful introductory summary gives some consideration to the nonfiction prose.

Waples, Dorothy. THE WHIG MYTH OF JAMES FENIMORE COOPER. New Haven, Conn.: Yale Univ. Press, 1938.

The author attempts to show that Cooper was a victim of politically opposed Whig editors.

RELATED GENERAL STUDIES

Brooks, Van Wyck. THE WORLD OF WASHINGTON IRVING. (p. 17)
Brownell, William C. AMERICAN PROSE MASTERS. (p. 17)
Callow, James T. KINDRED SPIRITS. (p. 362, under Irving)
Charvat, William. THE PROFESSION OF AUTHORSHIP IN AMERICA. (p. 19)
Gardiner, Harold C. AMERICAN CLASSICS RECONSIDERED. (p. 22).
Jones, Howard M. HISTORY AND THE CONTEMPORARY. (p. 24).
Macy, John. AMERICAN WRITERS ON AMERICAN LITERATURE. (p. 26)
Meyers, Marvin. THE JACKSONIAN PERSUASION. (p. 222)
Simms, William G. VIEWS AND REVIEWS IN AMERICAN LITERATURE. (pp.
    446 and 447, under Simms)
Wilson, James G. BRYANT AND HIS FRIENDS. (p. 267, under Bryant)

EDWARD EGGLESTON (1837-1902)

While Eggleston is known primarily as a writer of realistic local color fiction, he also made substantial contributions to American nonfiction prose. The prefaces to his tales helped to establish a philosophy of composition for realistic fiction. He wrote numerous articles and editorials for journals, including some fine descriptive essays and some pieces which document his role in establishing international copyright protection. THE BEGINNERS OF A NATION and THE TRANSIT OF CIVILIZATION are not only solid traditional histories but also pioneering works in the genre of social history, a relatively new form at the time.

PRINCIPAL NONFICTION PROSE WORKS

A HISTORY OF THE UNITED STATES AND ITS PEOPLE. 1888. (Designed for
    school use)
THE BEGINNERS OF A NATION. A HISTORY OF THE SOURCE AND RISE
    OF THE EARLIEST ENGLISH SETTLEMENTS IN AMERICA WITH SPECIAL
    REFERENCE TO THE LIFE AND CHARACTER OF THE PEOPLE. 1896.
SETTLEMENTS IN AMERICA WITH SPECIAL REFERENCE TO THE LIFE AND
    CHARACTER OF THE PEOPLE. 1896.
THE TRANSIT OF CIVILIZATION FROM ENGLAND TO AMERICA IN THE
    SEVENTEENTH CENTURY. 1901.
With Lille Eggleston Seelye:
TECUMSEH AND THE INDIAN PROPHET. 1878.
POCAHONTAS. 1879.
BRANT AND RED JACKET. 1879.
MONTEZUMA AND THE CONQUEST OF MEXICO. 1880.

LETTERS

A large collection of letters, including virtually all letters written by Eggleston to members of his family, is in the Collection of Regional History at Cornell University. Most of the letters held by libraries in the United States are listed in AMERICAN LITERARY MANUSCRIPTS, Ed. J. Albert Robbins (Athens: Univ. of Georgia Press, 1977).

LATER EDITIONS, SELECTIONS, AND REPRINTS

THE BEGINNERS OF A NATION. 1896. Introd. Arthur M. Schlesinger. 1959;
New York: Johnson, 1970.

> Schlesinger's introduction to the 1959 edition and his introduction
> to the volume below are the best available discussions of Eggles-
> ton's contributions as an historian.

TRANSIT OF CIVILIZATION. Introd. Arthur M. Schlesinger. Gloucester,
Mass.: Peter Smith, 1972.

BIBLIOGRAPHY

A listing of Eggleston's works is in Blanck's BIBLIOGRAPHY OF AMERICAN
LITERATURE 3:1-15. Randel's two studies, below, contain selected bibliogra-
phies, including an extensive listing of Eggleston's periodical contributions.
Eggleston is listed in the BIBLIOGRAPHY to the LITERARY HISTORY OF THE
UNITED STATES, pp. 485, 905, 1188.

BIOGRAPHY AND CRITICISM

Eggleston, George Cary. THE FIRST OF THE HOOSIERS. Philadelphia: D.
Biddle, 1903.

> These reminiscences by Edward's brother, himself a writer, provide
> an intimate portrait.

Randel, William Peirce. EDWARD EGGLESTON. New York: Twayne, 1963.

> This is a good critical introduction to Eggleston's works, and, ex-
> cept for Schlesinger's introductions to the histories, is one of the
> few in-depth studies of Eggleston's nonfiction.

_____. EDWARD EGGLESTON: AUTHOR OF THE HOOSIER SCHOOL-MASTER.
New York: King's Crown Press, 1946.

> A well-documented biography, this is the best to date.

RELATED GENERAL STUDIES

Dondore, Dorothy. THE PRAIRIE AND THE MAKING OF MIDDLE AMERICA.
(p. 128)
Garland, Hamlin. ROADSIDE MEETINGS. (p. 328, under Garland)
_____. MY FRIENDLY CONTEMPORARIES. (p. 328, under Garland)
Kraus, Michael. A HISTORY OF AMERICAN HISTORY. (p. 219)

RALPH WALDO EMERSON (1803-82)

Emerson has a secure place in American literary history as a liberal spokesman
for nineteenth-century America and as a focal figure in American letters. His
standing as a great thinker and writer is less certain. Contemporary accounts
testify to the personal force of Emerson's character, which exerted tremendous
influence upon others. By the 1903 centenary of his birth, Emerson was regarded as a classic American writer. Despite the general decline of Emerson's
reputation, beginning in the 1930s and continuing into the 1960s, his works
were regularly reprinted in new editions, collections, and anthologies; he continued to stimulate other writers, to interest scholars, and to be appreciated by
a few kindred minds.

Critical opinion has been markedly divided. Emerson has been seen by some to
be a shallow optimist, a sloppy thinker, and either too emotional or too intellectual. Others have argued that he was highly disciplined, a great thinker,
and a revitalizer of desperate souls. Some have seen his prose style as vague,
amorphous, and platitudinous; others have felt it pertinent, vital, and pithy.
He has been considered by a few to be an outmoded, stuffy Victorian.

In 1971, however, a symposium on "Emerson's Relevance Today" (see Carlson
and Dameron below) produced arguments that Emerson was relevant for his liberalism, his existential concerns, and his psychological insights. The CEAA (Center for Editions of American Authors, now Center for Scholarly Edition)--ap-
proved edition of THE JOURNALS AND MISCELLANEOUS NOTEBOOKS,
with its exceedingly detailed and precise textual apparatus, has helped to
stimulate a growing interest in Emerson's craftsmanship: his style, language,
imagery, and use of dialectic strategies. Biographical and critical studies,
beginning with Whicher's FREEDOM AND FATE (1953), have also indicated
an awareness of Emerson's complexity, the depth of thought and discipline sup-
porting his optimism, and the sense of culture and tradition which lay behind
his liberalism. These recent studies reveal Emerson to be both more human and
more profound than most of the earlier studies had acknowledged.

PRINCIPAL WORKS

LETTER . . . TO THE SECOND CHURCH AND SOCIETY. 1832.

A HISTORICAL DISCOURSE DELIVERED BEFORE THE CITIZENS OF CONCORD,
    12TH SEPTEMBER, 1835. 1835.
NATURE. 1836.
THE AMERICAN SCHOLAR. 1837.
AN ADDRESS DELIVERED BEFORE THE SENIOR CLASS IN DIVINITY COLLEGE,
    CAMBRIDGE. . . . 1838.
AN ORATION DELIVERED BEFORE THE LITERARY SOCIETIES OF DARTMOUTH
    COLLEGE. 1838
THE METHOD OF NATURE. 1841.
ESSAYS. 1841.
MAN THE REFORMER. 1842.
THE YOUNG AMERICAN. 1844.
NATURE: AN ESSAY, AND LECTURES OF THE TIMES. 1844.
AN ADDRESS DELIVERED IN . . . CONCORD. . . . 1844
ORATIONS, LECTURES AND ADDRESSES. 1844.
ESSAYS: SECOND SERIES. 1844.
POEMS. 1847.
REPRESENTATIVE MEN: SEVEN LECTURES. 1850.
ENGLISH TRAITS. 1856.
THE CONDUCT OF LIFE. 1860.
THE COMPLETE WORKS OF EMERSON. 2 vols. 1866.
MAY-DAY AND OTHER PIECES. 1867.
THE PROSE WORKS OF EMERSON. 2 vols. 1869. (Vol. 3 was added in
    1878)
SOCIETY AND SOLITUDE. 1870.
LETTERS AND SOCIAL AIMS. 1876.
SELECTED POEMS. 1876.
FORTUNE OF THE REPUBLIC. 1878.
THE PREACHER. 1880.

LETTERS AND JOURNALS

A CORRESPONDENCE BETWEEN JOHN STERLING AND RALPH WALDO EMER-
SON. Ed. Edward W. Emerson. 1897; Port Washington, N.Y.: Kennikat,
1975.

CORRESPONDENCE BETWEEN RALPH WALDO EMERSON AND HERMAN GRIMM.
Ed. F. William Holls. 1903; Port Washington, N.Y.: Kennikat, 1971.

THE CORRESPONDENCE OF THOMAS CARLYLE AND RALPH WALDO EMER-
SON. 2 vols. Ed. Charles Eliot Norton. 1883. Rev. ed. 1888; Ed. Joseph
Slater in one vol. as THE CORRESPONDENCE OF EMERSON AND CARLYLE.
New York: Columbia Univ. Press, 1964. Index, bibliog.

    Slater's edition restores passages omitted by Norton.

EMERSON-CLOUGH LETTERS. Ed. H.F. Lowry and R.L. Rusk. 1934; Folcroft, Pa.: Folcroft, 1977.

THE HEART OF EMERSON'S JOURNALS. Ed. Bliss Perry. Boston: Houghton Mifflin, 1926.

THE JOURNALS AND MISCELLANEOUS NOTEBOOKS OF RALPH WALDO EMERSON. Ed. William H. Gilman et al. 16 vols. projected. Cambridge, Mass.: Belknap Press, Harvard University Press, 1960-- .

Volume 14, edited by Susan Sutton Smith and Harrison Hayford and covering the notebooks for the years 1854-61, was published in 1978. With the deaths of Gilman and Ferguson, Ralph H. Orth assumed the duties of chief editor. This is the definitive edition of the journals and notebooks and includes an elaborate textual apparatus and variant readings.

THE JOURNALS OF RALPH WALDO EMERSON. 10 vols. Ed. Edward W. Emerson and W.E. Forbes. Cambridge, Mass.: Riverside Press, 1909-14.

This is still a useful edition for the lay reader, although the definitive text has been established by the volumes edited by Gilman et al., above.

JOURNALS OF RALPH WALDO EMERSON. Ed. Robert N. Linscott. New York: Random House, 1960.

This Modern Library abridgement contains a good selection from the journal as they were edited by Edward W. Emerson and Waldo Emerson Forbes, above.

LETTERS FROM RALPH WALDO EMERSON TO A FRIEND, 1838-1853. Ed. Charles E. Norton. 1899; Port Washington, N.Y.: Kennikat, 1971.

These letters document Emerson's friendship with Samuel Gray Ward.

THE LETTERS OF RALPH WALDO EMERSON. 6 vols. Ed. Ralph L. Rusk. New York: Columbia Univ. Press, 1939.

This is the most useful and complete collection of the letters.

RALPH WALDO EMERSON TO ELIZABETH HOAR. Ysleta, Tex.: Edwin B. Hill, 1942.

RECORDS OF A LIFELONG FRIENDSHIP, 1807-1882. Ed. Howard H. Furness. Boston: Houghton Mifflin, 1910.

This collection of correspondence documents the friendship between Emerson and William Henry Furness.

Selections from the letters and journals are included in several of the collections listed below.

LATER EDITIONS, SELECTIONS, AND REPRINTS

"THE AMERICAN SCHOLAR" TODAY: EMERSON'S ESSAY AND SOME CRITI-
CAL VIEWS. Ed. David C. Mead. New York: Dodd, Mead, 1970.

> Intended as a casebook for students, this includes, in addition to
> the essay, four critical articles, questions for discussion, and topics
> for themes.

THE COLLECTED WORKS OF RALPH WALDO EMERSON. 10 to 12 vols. projected. Ed. Alfred R. Ferguson et al. Cambridge, Mass.: Belknap Press,
Harvard Univ. Press, 1971-- .

> Vol. 1, NATURE, ADDRESSES, AND LECTURES, was published in
> 1971, Vol. 2, ESSAYS: FIRST SERIES, edited by Joseph Slater in
> 1979. This is the definitive CEAA[CSE] edition.

THE COMPLETE WORKS OF RALPH WALDO EMERSON. Centenary Edition.
10 vols. Ed. Edward W. Emerson. 1903-04; New York: AMS Press, 1968.

> This has been the standard edition, but it will be superseded by
> the CEAA-approved volumes in THE COLLECTED WORKS, above.

THE EARLY LECTURES OF RALPH WALDO EMERSON. 3 vols. Ed. Robert E.
Spiller et al. Cambridge, Mass.: Belknap Press, Harvard Univ. Press, 1959-72.

EMERSON: THE BASIC WRITINGS OF AMERICA'S SAGE. Ed. Eduard C.
Lindeman. New York: New American Library, 1947.

EMERSON: A MODERN ANTHOLOGY. Ed. Alfred Kazin and Daniel Aaron.
Boston: Houghton Mifflin, 1959.

EMERSON ON EDUCATION: SELECTIONS. Ed. with Introd. Howard Mumford
Jones. New York: Teachers' College Press, 1966.

EMERSON'S LITERARY CRITICISM. Ed. Eric W. Carlson. Lincoln: Univ.
of Nebraska Press, 1979.

> This collection presents more than sixty selections on various critical
> topics arranged thematically with headnotes which provide back-
> grounds and cross-references to other writings. The introduction is
> a good discussion of Emerson's critical perspectives. This work is
> illustrative of current emphasis on the importance of Emerson's
> thought.

EMERSON'S NATURE: ORIGIN GROWTH, MEANING. Ed. Merton M.
Sealts, Jr. and Alfred R. Ferguson. 1969. Enlarged ed. Carbondale: Southern Illinois Univ. Press, 1979.

> This reprints the 1836 text with notes, as well as selected, pre-

viously published critical essays on NATURE written by a number of scholars ranging from Emerson's contemporaries to modern critics.

ENGLISH TRAITS. Ed. Howard Mumford Jones. Cambridge, Mass.: Belknap Press, Harvard Univ. Press, 1966.

ESSAYS BY RALPH WALDO EMERSON. Introd. Irwin Edman. New York: Crowell, 1951.

This edition presents the first and second series in one volume.

FIVE ESSAYS ON MAN AND NATURE. Ed. Robert E. Spiller. Northbrook, Ill.: AHM, 1954.

LECTURES AND BIOGRAPHICAL SKETCHES. Boston: Houghton Mifflin, 1884.

NATURAL HISTORY OF THE INTELLECT AND OTHER PAPERS. Boston: Houghton Mifflin, 1893.

THE PORTABLE EMERSON. Ed. Mark Van Doren. 1946; New York: Penguin, 1977.

RALPH WALDO EMERSON: ESSAYS AND JOURNALS. Ed. Lewis Mumford. Garden City, N.Y.: International Collectors Library, 1968.

RALPH WALDO EMERSON: REPRESENTATIVE SELECTIONS. Ed. Frederick I. Carpenter. New York: American Book Co., 1934.

RALPH WALDO EMERSON: SELECTED PROSE AND POETRY. 2nd ed. Ed. and introd. Reginald L. Cook. New York: Holt, Rinehart and Winston, 1950.

SELECTED ESSAYS, LECTURES AND POEMS OF RALPH WALDO EMERSON. Ed. Robert E. Spiller. New York: Washington Square Press, 1965.

THE SELECTED WRITINGS OF RALPH WALDO EMERSON. Ed. and introd. Brooks Atkinson. New York: Random House, Modern Library, 1940.

SELECTED WRITINGS OF RALPH WALDO EMERSON. Ed. with Foreword by William H. Gilman. New York: New American Library, 1965.

Gilman's comments and editing of this paperback volume are excellent.

SELECTIONS FROM RALPH WALDO EMERSON: AN ORGANIC ANTHOLOGY. Ed. Stephen E. Whicher. Boston: Houghton Mifflin, 1957.

These selections are good, but Whicher arranges them to reinforce his ideas about Emerson's changing views.

THE SENSES AND THE SOUL, AND MORAL SENTIMENT IN RELIGION: TWO ESSAYS. . . . London: Foulger, 1884.

TANTALUS . . . WITH A MEMORIAL NOTE BY F.B. SANBORN. Canton, Pa.: Kirgate Press, 1903.

TWO UNPUBLISHED ESSAYS. . . . Introd. Edward Everett Hale. Boston: Lamson Wolffe, 1896.

THE UNCOLLECTED LECTURES BY RALPH WALDO EMERSON. Ed. Clarence F. Gohdes. 1932; Folcroft, Pa.: Folcroft, 1973.

Much of the text is based upon newspaper accounts of the lectures.

THE UNCOLLECTED WRITINGS: ESSAYS, ADDRESSES, POEMS, REVIEWS AND LETTERS BY RALPH WALDO EMERSON. Ed. Charles C. Bigelow. 1912; Port Washington, N.Y.: Kennikat, 1971.

YOUNG EMERSON SPEAKS: UNPUBLISHED DISCOURSES ON MANY SUBJECTS. Ed. Arthur C. McGiffert. 1938; Port Washington, N.Y.: Kennikat, 1971.

This contains twenty-five of Emerson's sermons as well as an illuminating introduction and useful notes.

BIBLIOGRAPHY

Boswell, Jeanetta. RALPH WALDO EMERSON AND THE CRITICS: A CHECK-LIST OF CRITICISM, 1900–1977. Metuchen, N.J.: Scarecrow, 1979.

This is a fairly complete, unannotated checklist, but it contains a few errors of publication data. The ebb and flow of interest in Emerson can be traced here.

Bryer, Jackson R., and Robert A. Rees. A CHECKLIST OF EMERSON CRITICISM, 1951–1961. Hartford, Conn.: Transcendental Books, 1964.

This is a good listing with useful annotations.

Cameron, Kenneth Walter. AN EMERSON INDEX. Hartford, Conn.: Transcendental Books, 1958.

Words, examples, motifs, and other subjects are indexed from selected notebooks.

_____. INDEX-CONCORDANCE TO EMERSON'S SERMONS WITH HOMI-
LETICAL PAPERS. 2 vols. Hartford, Conn.: Transcendental Books, 1963.

> This is a concordance of 150 sermons, essays, notes, and outlines.

Carpenter, Frederick Ives. EMERSON HANDBOOK. 1953; New York: Hendricks House, 1967.

> This surveys biographies, criticism, sources, reputation and influence
> in works about Emerson to 1953. It is also an excellent summary
> of Emerson's writings and ideas.

Charvat, William. EMERSON'S AMERICAN LECTURE ENGAGEMENTS: A
CHRONOLOGICAL LIST. New York: New York Public Library, 1961.

Cooke, George Willis. A BIBLIOGRAPHY OF RALPH WALDO EMERSON.
1908; New York: B. Franklin, 1966.

Ferguson, Alfred R. CHECKLIST OF RALPH WALDO EMERSON. Columbus,
Ohio: Charles E. Merrill, 1970.

Harding, Walter. EMERSON'S LIBRARY. Charlottesville, Va.: Bibliographical
Society of the University of Virginia, 1967.

Sowder, William J. EMERSON'S REVIEWERS AND COMMENTATORS: NINE-
TEENTH-CENTURY PERIODICAL CRITICISM. Hartford, Conn.: Transcendental
Books, 1968.

Stovall, Floyd. "Ralph Waldo Emerson." In EIGHT AMERICAN AUTHORS.
Rev. ed. Ed. James Woodress. New York: Norton, 1971, pp. 37-84.

Checklists of criticism appear periodically in ESQ and in THE AMERICAN
TRANSCENDENTAL QUARTERLY. An extensive listing of Emerson's works is
in Blanck's BIBLIOGRAPHY OF AMERICAN LITERATURE 3:16-70. Cameron's
TRANSCENDENTALISM AND AMERICAN RENAISSANCE BIBLIOGRAPHY (Hartford, Conn.: Transcendental Books, 1977) gives a listing, with synopsis, of
the collections of primary materials previously issued from Hartford. Emerson
is listed in the BIBLIOGRAPHY to the LITERARY HISTORY OF THE UNITED
STATES, pp. 492, 909, 1192.

BIOGRAPHY AND CRITICISM

Albee, John. REMEMBRANCES OF EMERSON. 1901; Folcroft, Pa.: Folcroft,
1974.

> Albee, one of the younger men who was greatly influenced by
> Emerson, gives a good firsthand reminiscence.

Ralph Waldo Emerson

Anderson, John Q. THE LIBERATING GODS: EMERSON ON POETS AND POETRY. Coral Gables, Fla.: Univ. of Miami Press, 1971.

> This brief study selects passages from Emerson to show his poetic principles or his critical commentary on poets and poetry. Included are a summary of and comment on Emerson's theories and criticism.

Baritz, Loren. CITY ON A HILL: A HISTORY OF IDEAS AND MYTHS IN AMERICA. New York: Wiley, 1964.

> The author emphasizes Emerson's idealism, his isolation from society, and his criticism of social and materialistic concerns. He sees Emerson's role as one of stimulating individual pride and optimism and national hope for the future. By insisting upon Emerson's idealism, the author ignores much of importance in Emerson's life and work; however, he places Emerson within a wide social and intellectual context, providing some useful insights about the impact of his thought.

Berry, Edmund G. EMERSON'S PLUTARCH. Cambridge, Mass.: Harvard Univ. Press, 1961.

> The author demonstrates that Emerson was well acquainted with and much influenced by Plutarch, formulating a blend of Platonism and stoicism much like Plutarch's and using themes and passages from Plutarch in his writings.

Bishop, Jonathan. EMERSON ON THE SOUL. Cambridge, Mass.: Harvard Univ. Press, 1964.

> In this original and sensitive study of Emerson's style, the author discusses how Emerson's concept of the soul is reflected in his tone, metaphor, rhythm, and imagery. Bishop argues that Emerson's changing concept of "the soul" is reflected in his language.

Bode, Carl, ed. RALPH WALDO EMERSON: A PROFILE. New York: Hill and Wang, 1968.

> This title reprints eleven essays by Holmes, Rusk, Hubbell, Aaron, and others which touch on Emerson's life and works.

Brooks, Van Wyck. EMERSON AND OTHERS. 1927; New York: Octagon, 1973.

> In an anecdotal account, Brooks deals with episodes of Emerson's life in Concord.

_____. THE LIFE OF EMERSON. New York: Dutton, 1932.

> This impressionistic sketch, presented in the language of Emerson's journals, provides some psychological insights but little penetrating criticism.

Bruel, Andre. EMERSON ET THOREAU. Paris: Société d'edition Les Belles Lettres, 1929.

> This study shows the similarities, the friendship, and the growing coolness between the two men.

Cabot, James E. A MEMOIR OF RALPH WALDO EMERSON. 2 vols. 1887; New York: AMS Press, 1969.

> Written by Emerson's literary executor and authorized biographer, this is the best early biography and remains a useful source and an important contemporary account.

Cameron, Kenneth Walter. A COMMENTARY ON EMERSON'S EARLY LEC-TURES (1833-1836). Hartford, Conn.: Transcendental Books, 1961.

> Although sometimes badly organized and, because of the printing process, difficult to read, Cameron's collections of contemporary reviews, commentaries, articles, sources, influences, and check-lists are invaluable resources for students and scholars. For a summary of the contents of this volume and those listed below, see his TRANSCENDENTALISM AND AMERICAN RENAISSANCE BIBLIOGRAPHY, above.

_____. EMERSON AMONG HIS CONTEMPORARIES. Hartford, Conn.: Transcendental Books, 1967.

> This collects reviews of Emerson's books and other comments by his contemporaries from the 1840s to the end of the nineteenth century.

_____. EMERSON THE ESSAYIST. Hartford, Conn.: Transcendental Books, 1945.

> This reprints and discusses articles and excerpts from contemporary literature which influenced Emerson. See also EMERSON'S WORK-SHOP, below.

_____. EMERSON AND THOREAU AS READERS. Hartford, Conn.: Trans-cendental Books, 1958.

> This is a useful selection of listings and notes from Cameron's THE TRANSCENDENTALISTS AND MINERVA.

_____. EMERSON'S WORKSHOP. 2 vols. Hartford, Conn.: Transcendental Books, 1964.

> Supplementary to EMERSON THE ESSAYIST, this work collects more of Emerson's sources.

_____. RALPH WALDO EMERSON'S READINGS. 1941; revised and corrected, 1962; Philadelphia: R. West, 1973.

Carlson, Eric W., and J. Lasley Dameron, eds. EMERSON'S RELEVANCE TODAY: A SYMPOSIUM. Hartford, Conn.: Transcendental Books, 1971.

> This collection of essays on the topic gives evidence of Emerson's modern relevance in a number of areas--political, psychological, and literary. SYMPOSIUM is an important sign on the academic road to current interest in Emerson.

Carpenter, Frederic I. EMERSON AND ASIA. 1930; New York: Haskel, 1969.

> Carpenter emphasizes the influence of Oriental philosophy, especially Hinduism, upon Emerson and discusses several of his poems and the essay "Illusions."

_____. EMERSON HANDBOOK. 1953; New York: Hendricks House, 1967.

> In addition to covering bibliographical items, this study presents an excellent summary and evaluation of Emerson's sources, ideas, influence, and reputation.

Célieres, Andre. THE PROSE STYLE OF EMERSON. 1936; Darby, Pa.: Arden, 1978.

> In his analysis of Emerson's style, Célieres sees Emerson's success to be a product of his ability to express more aptly than anyone else the important thoughts prevalent in his time and to instill those thoughts with force and vigor.

Chapman, John Jay. EMERSON AND OTHER ESSAYS. New York: Scribner's, 1898.

> In his important essay on Emerson, Chapman noted the psychological effects of Emerson's literary method--that is, his technique of presenting conflicting statements to be resolved by the listener or reader.

Cheyfitz, Eric. THE TRANS-PARENT: SEXUAL POLITICS IN THE LANGUAGE OF EMERSON. Baltimore, Md.: Johns Hopkins Press, 1981.

> The author examines the conflict between the masculine and feminine in Emerson's life and works.

Conway, Moncure D. EMERSON AT HOME AND ABROAD. 1882; New York: Haskel, 1968.

> A friend and disciple of Emerson, Conway presents anecdotes and conversations which provide biographical insights.

Cooke, George Willis. RALPH WALDO EMERSON: HIS LIFE, WRITINGS, AND PHILOSOPHY. 1881; Folcroft, Pa.: Folcroft, 1974.

An important contemporary estimate, this attempts to present Emerson's philosophy as well as providing useful biographical information.

Cowan, Michael H. CITY OF THE WEST: EMERSON, AMERICA, AND THE URBAN METAPHOR. New Haven, Conn.: Yale Univ. Press, 1967.

In his close reading of several essays, the author focuses upon Emerson's fusion of a number of American literary themes, including the idea of progress, technological change, and the reconciliation of man and nature. Cowan concludes that Emerson was basically optimistic about urban civilization and technological progress, seeing "the machine" as part of a future "organic city."

Crothers, Samuel McCord. RALPH WALDO EMERSON: HOW TO KNOW HIM. 1921; Port Washington, N.Y.: Kennikat, 1975.

This introductory study of Emerson is still useful for the beginning student.

Dana, William F. THE OPTIMISM OF RALPH WALDO EMERSON. 1886; Folcroft, Pa.: Folcroft, 1976.

This early study helped to establish an image of Emerson which influenced later critics and commentators.

Dugard, Marie. RALPH WALDO EMERSON, SA VIE ET SON OEUVRE. Rev. ed. 1907; Paris: Armand Colin, 1913.

This is one of the best early critical biographies by a European. Despite her enthusiasm for Emerson, Dugard had little sympathy with transcendentalism and is perceptive in criticizing some of Emerson's ideas.

Duncan, Jeffrey L. THE POWER AND FORM OF EMERSON'S THOUGHT. Charlottesville: Univ. Press of Virginia, 1973.

In an explication of Emerson's philosophical ideas, Duncan emphasizes the importance of polarity in Emerson's literary method and philosophy.

Emerson, Edward Waldo. EMERSON IN CONCORD: A MEMOIR WRITTEN FOR THE "SOCIAL CIRCLE" IN CONCORD, MASS. 1888; Detroit: Gale Research Co., 1970.

An account of Emerson's private life by his son, this is a valuable sourcebook.

Emerson, Ellen Tucker. THE LIFE OF LIDIAN JACKSON EMERSON. Ed. Delores Bird Carpenter. Boston: Twayne, 1981.

This biography, written by Emerson's daughter, not only presents a portrait of a strong and influential woman but also provides an insight into nineteenth-century domestic life and attitudes. The editor's introduction includes material from unpublished letters by Ellen Emerson and several photographs of sketches by Ellen from the original manuscript.

Firkins, Oscar W. RALPH WALDO EMERSON. 1915; New York: Russell and Russell, 1965.

A valuable assessment of Emerson's ideas, this biographical and critical study is based upon a close and sympathetic reading of Emerson's writings. Firkins argues that Emerson was not "logical" in presenting his ideas because his organic method of presenting them was closer to actual experience.

Foster, C.H. EMERSON'S THEORY OF POETRY. Iowa City: Univ. of Iowa Press, 1939.

This study of Emerson's aesthetics makes use of extensive quotations and the impressionistic method of Van Wyck Brooks.

Francis, Elamanamadathil V. EMERSON AND HINDU SCRIPTURES. Cochin, India: Academic Publications, 1972.

This work adds to the information about the influence of the Hindu scriptures on Emerson.

Garnett, Richard. LIFE OF EMERSON. 1888; New York: Haskell, 1974.

Written for the British Great Writers Series, Garnett's LIFE is based primarily on Cabot's memoir, above; but it has some interesting original criticism.

Gay, Robert M. EMERSON: A STUDY OF THE POET AS SEER. Garden City, N.Y.: Doubleday, Doran, 1928.

In this thoughtful study, the author argues that Emerson's purpose was not to inculcate ideas but to stimulate the creative imagination.

Gonnaud, Maurice. INDIVIDU ET SOCIETE DANS L'OEUVRE DE RALPH WALDO EMERSON: ESSAI DE BIOGRAPHIE SPIRITUELLE. Paris: Didier, 1964.

One of the best European studies, this focuses upon Emerson's concern with the problem of vocation, his career as a lecturer, and his attitudes toward social and political problems prior to, during, and after the Civil War. Gonnaud argues that Emerson was led to an acceptance of the need for the individual to sacrifice some freedom to fulfill his duties as a member of society.

Goren, Leyla. ELEMENTS OF BRAHMANISM IN THE TRANSCENDENTALISM OF EMERSON. 1959; Hartford, Conn.: Transcendental Books, 1964.

Goren's study traces Emerson's Orientalism in a number of works and points out the affinity between Emerson's contemplative nature and his interest in Indian thought.

Gray, Henry David. EMERSON: A STATEMENT OF NEW ENGLAND TRANS-CENDENTALISM AS EXPRESSED IN THE PHILOSOPHY OF ITS CHIEF EXPON-ENT. 1917; 1958; Folcroft, Pa.: Folcroft, 1976.

One of the best early works on transcendentalism and Emerson's philosophical position, this argues that Emerson wished to remain open to new ideas and approached philosophy with a religious and poetical attitude.

Gregg, Edith W., ed. ONE FIRST LOVE: THE LETTERS OF ELLEN LOUISA TUCKER TO RALPH WALDO EMERSON. Cambridge, Mass.: Harvard Univ. Press, 1962.

Edited by Emerson's great-granddaughter, these letters add to the biographical information. None of Emerson's letters to Ellen sur-vive.

Hale, Edward Everett. RALPH WALDO EMERSON. 1899; 1904; Norwood, Pa.: Norwood, 1976.

This is a well-written, appreciative early account.

Harris, Kenneth Marc. CARLYLE AND EMERSON: THEIR LONG DEBATE. Cambridge, Mass.: Harvard Univ. Press, 1978.

The author examines the writings as well as the correspondence of Carlyle and Emerson and assesses the two men in relation to each other. He does a critical comparison of some parallel works, for example Carlyle's ON HEROES AND HERO WORSHIP and Emerson's REPRESENTATIVE MEN, and finds that the two writers are more often "in dialogue" than in unison.

Harrison, John Smith. THE TEACHERS OF EMERSON. 1910; New York: Haskell, 1966.

This study sees Platonism as the dominant influence upon Emerson's philosophy.

Haskins, David Greene. RALPH WALDO EMERSON: HIS MATERNAL ANCES-TORS WITH SOME REMINISCENCES OF HIM. 1887; Port Washington, N.Y.: Kennikat, 1971.

These firsthand reminiscences about Emerson's mother and father and the childhood of Emerson are useful sources.

Hopkins, Vivian C. SPIRES OF FORM: A STUDY OF EMERSON'S AESTHETIC THEORY. Cambridge, Mass.: Harvard Univ. Press, 1951.

In this fine study, Hopkins illuminates Emerson's theory and practice by analyzing his works in terms of the creative process, the completed organic work of art, and the reception of the work by the audience.

Ireland, Alexander. RALPH WALDO EMERSON: HIS LIFE, GENIUS, AND WRITINGS. 1882; Port Washington, N.Y.: Kennikat, 1972.

Ireland's work is a useful primary source which includes his own recollections of Emerson's visits to England.

Irie, Yukio. EMERSON AND QUAKERISM. Tokyo: Kenkyusha, 1968.

This study traces the influences of New England Quakerism on Emerson's thought.

Jones, Howard M. EMERSON ONCE MORE: THE WARE LECTURE. Boston: Beacon, 1953.

Jones's appreciation of Emerson points out his relevance to the world of the 1950s.

Jordan, Leah E. THE FUNDAMENTALS OF EMERSON'S LITERARY CRITICISM. 1945; Folcroft, Pa.: Folcroft, 1973.

This is an early attempt to formalize Emerson's critical principles.

Konvitz, Milton R., ed. THE RECOGNITION OF RALPH WALDO EMERSON: SELECTED CRITICISM SINCE 1837. Ann Arbor: Univ. of Michigan Press, 1972.

In this collection are important estimates of Emerson's contributions and influence by Theodore Parker, Matthew Arnold, and D.H. Lawrence.

Konvitz, Milton R., and Stephen Whicher, eds. EMERSON: A COLLECTION OF CRITICAL ESSAYS. 1962; Westport, Conn.: Greenwood Press, 1978.

Collected here are previously printed essays by critics including Henry Nash Smith, Perry Miller, Newton Arvin, Daniel Aaron, and Sherman Paul.

Leary, Lewis. RALPH WALDO EMERSON: AN INTERPRETIVE ESSAY. Boston: Twayne, 1980.

This is a useful general survey of Emerson's writings, thought, and influence intended for the general reader rather than the scholar.

Levin, David, ed. EMERSON-PROPHECY, METAMORPHOSIS, AND INFLUENCE: SELECTED PAPERS FROM THE ENGLISH INSTITUTE. New York: Columbia Univ. Press, 1975.

The papers are concerned with Emerson's artistic development, his place in American literary history, and his influence on today's society.

McQuiston, Raymar. THE RELATION OF RALPH WALDO EMERSON TO PUBLIC AFFAIRS. Lawrence: Univ. of Kansas Press, 1923; Folcroft, Pa.: Folcroft, 1973.

The study focuses upon Emerson's political, economic, and social ideas and his attitudes toward slavery and the Civil War.

Mead, Edwin Doak. EMERSON AND THEODORE PARKER. Boston: American Unitarian Assn., 1910.

Mead's two works cited here give a good account of Emerson's influence on his contemporaries, particularly Parker, and on American ideas.

_____. THE INFLUENCE OF EMERSON. Boston: American Unitarian Assn., 1903.

Metzger, Charles R. EMERSON AND GREENOUGH, TRANSCENDENTAL PIONEERS OF AN AMERICAN ESTHETIC. 1954; Westport, Conn.: Greenwood Press, 1971.

Metzger compares the expressions of the two men on their organic theory of art, suggesting that both were attempting to reach through nature toward God.

Michaud, Regis. EMERSON, THE ENRAPTURED YANKEE. Trans. from French by George Boas. 1930; New York: AMS Press, 1976.

A popular rather than a scholarly biography, this emphasizes the mystical side of Emerson's thought.

Miles, Josephine. RALPH WALDO EMERSON. Minneapolis: Univ. of Minnesota Press, 1961.

In an excellent short account of Emerson's ideas and works, Miles is particularly useful in her discussion of Emerson's poetic principles and practice.

Neufeldt, Leonard N., ed. RALPH WALDO EMERSON: NEW APPRAISALS, A SYMPOSIUM. Hartford, Conn.: Transcendental Books, 1973.

These collected papers evaluate Emerson's literary techniques and ideas. Like Levin's collection, above, this edition is another illustration of current emphasis on Emerson's importance.

Nicoloff, Philip L. EMERSON ON RACE AND HISTORY: AN EXAMINATION OF "ENGLISH TRAITS." New York: Columbia Univ. Press, 1961.

> In discussing Emerson's cyclical theory of history and his analysis of race, this study also presents a broad analysis of Emerson's thought.

Paul, Sherman. EMERSON'S ANGLE OF VISION: MAN AND NATURE IN AMERICAN EXPERIENCE. Cambridge, Mass.: Harvard Univ. Press, 1952.

> The author uses Emerson's metaphors and diction to show how important to him was the sense of sight and the "circle" of vision made possible by a particular perspective; also studied is Emerson's application of the principle of "correspondence" to "man's spiritual experience, his communion with nature, his self expression in language and method, his self-fulfillment individually and in society."

Perry, R. Bliss. EMERSON TODAY. 1931; Hamden, Conn.: Shoe String, 1969.

> This remains a superb brief introduction to Emerson. Perry sketches the life, outlines Emerson's ideas, and summarizes critical discussions of Emerson.

Pommer, Henry F. EMERSON'S FIRST MARRIAGE. Carbondale: Southern Illinois Univ. Press, 1967.

> Pommer's biographical approach reveals a warmth in Emerson which is not usually seen.

Porte, Joel. EMERSON AND THOREAU: TRANSCENDENTALISTS IN CONFLICT. Middletown, Conn.: Wesleyan Univ. Press, 1966.

> Thoreau is seen by the author as a much better human being than Emerson. Porte accuses Emerson of hypocrisy in his attitude toward Thoreau and points out major differences in their outlook and ideas.

_____. REPRESENTATIVE MAN: RALPH WALDO EMERSON IN HIS TIME. New York: Oxford Univ. Press, 1979.

> More sympathetic to Emerson than the previous account, this study traces Emerson's development as a person and as a writer. Porte regards Emerson's choice of the essay form as a means of expression to be appropriate, because the essay is a "tentative and fragmentary record of the mind in search of its meaning." His analysis of what he calls "the Emerson Idiom" provides perspective upon both Emerson and several modern writers.

Porter, David. EMERSON AND LITERARY CHANGE. Cambridge, Mass.: Harvard Univ. Press, 1978.

Porter suggests that much of Emerson's poetry fails because Emerson was too much concerned with theory. On the other hand, the persona which he adopts in his prose (Man-Thinking or Man-Becoming) and his open structure are significant contributions to American literature.

Rayapati, J.P. Rao. EARLY AMERICAN INTEREST IN VEDANTA: PRE-EMERSONIAN INTEREST IN VEDIC LITERATURE AND VEDANTIC LITERATURE. New York: Asia House, 1973.

In his thorough study Rayapati provides essential backgrounds for understanding the Oriental influence in nineteenth-century New England.

Reaver, Joseph R. EMERSON AS MYTHMAKER. Gainesville: Univ. of Florida Press, 1954.

Reaver comments on the relationship between Emerson's writings, particularly his poetry, and his world view, showing recurring images and allusions with which Emerson constructs his own reality.

Rountree, Thomas J., ed. CRITICS ON EMERSON. Coral Gables, Fla.: Univ. of Miami Press, 1973.

This collection of previously published essays has a useful introduction and bibliography.

Rusk, Ralph L. THE LIFE OF RALPH WALDO EMERSON. New York: Scribner's, 1949.

Rusk remains indispensable as the most thorough and reliable biography of Emerson.

Sanborn, Franklin B. THE GENIUS AND CHARACTER OF EMERSON. 1885; Port Washington, N.Y.: Kennikat, 1970.

This collects reminiscences of Emerson by friends in the Concord School of Philosophy.

_____. THE PERSONALITY OF EMERSON. 1903; Folcroft, Pa.: Folcroft, 1977.

An important recollection by a younger man who was influenced by Emerson, this includes letters and records of conversations.

_____. RALPH WALDO EMERSON. Ed. Mark A. De Wolfe Howe. Boston: Small, Maynard, 1901.

In a brief minor biography, Sanborn here repeats much of the material in his two volumes above.

Scheick, William J. THE SLENDER HUMAN WORD: EMERSON'S ARTISTRY IN PROSE. Knoxville: Univ. of Tennessee Press, 1978.

> Starting from Emerson's own theory of language, the author argues that the development of Emerson's "hieroglyphs" through images shows more artistry than most critics have given him credit for. Although the author's interpretations and attempts to relate various images seem at times to be overreaching, his reading of several of the important essays is perceptive and stimulating.

Scudder, Townsend. THE LONELY WAYFARING MAN: EMERSON AND SOME ENGLISHMEN. London: Oxford Univ. Press, 1936.

> This work is an interesting discussion of Emerson's friendship with Carlyle, Clough, and others.

Snider, Denton J. THE LIFE OF EMERSON. 1921; Folcroft, Pa.: Folcroft, 1977.

> A member of the St. Louis School of Hegelianism attempts to relate the events in Emerson's life to his intellectual development.

Sowder, William J. EMERSON'S IMPACT ON THE BRITISH ISLES AND CANADA. Charlottesville: Univ. Press of Virginia, 1966.

> A comprehensive survey of reviews in British and Canadian periodicals, 1840-70, Sowder's study demonstrates the great amount of invective as well as praise directed at Emerson.

Staebler, Warren. RALPH WALDO EMERSON. New York: Twayne, 1973.

> A rather superficial study, this work in the Great American Thinkers Series attempts "an introduction to the character and thought" of Emerson.

Stein, William B., ed. TWO BRAHMIN SOURCES OF EMERSON AND THOREAU. Gainesville, Fla.: Scholar's Facsimiles and Reprints, 1968.

> Stein reprints translations of THE VEDS (1832) and THE SIX DARSHANAS (1822) which were available to Emerson and Thoreau.

Strauch, Carl F., ed. CHARACTERISTICS OF EMERSON: TRANSCENDENTAL POET: A SYMPOSIUM. Hartford, Conn.: Transcendental Books, 1975.

> These collected papers represent new insights into Emerson's poetry and an increasing appreciation for his poetic techniques.

Sutcliffe, Emerson G. EMERSON'S THEORIES OF LITERARY EXPRESSION. 1923; New York: Phaeton, 1972.

> The author attempts to establish some connection between Emerson's ideas and his performance, supporting generalizations about Emerson's theories by excerpting quotations from his writings.

Thayer, James B. A WESTERN JOURNEY WITH MR. EMERSON. 1884; Port Washington, N.Y.: Kennikat, 1971.

Thayer served as historian for the trip which he, Emerson, and eight others took in 1871 to San Francisco and back to Boston. One interesting account is about Emerson's meeting with John Muir in Yosemite Valley.

Thomas, Amelia Forbes, ed. LETTERS AND JOURNALS OF WALDO EMERSON FORBES. Philadelphia: Dorrance, 1977.

This includes some interesting material relating to Ralph Waldo Emerson from the journals of his grandson.

Thurin, Erik I. THE UNIVERSAL AUTOBIOGRAPHY OF RALPH WALDO EMERSON. Lund, Sweden: C.W.K. Gleerup, 1974.

A psychological-archetypal approach to Emerson, this study presents Emerson's bipolar vision as a dichotomy of the male principle versus the female principle. Thurin offers some original and provocative, if somewhat disorganized, insights.

Wagenknecht, Edward. RALPH WALDO EMERSON: PORTRAIT OF A BALANCED SOUL. New York: Oxford Univ. Press, 1974.

A scholarly thoughtful study, this presents Emerson as thinker, writer, and man, and shows a sympathetic appreciation for his attitudes, ideas, and influence.

Waggoner, Hyatt. EMERSON AS POET. Princeton: Princeton Univ. Press, 1975.

The author summarizes Emerson's poetic reputation and attempts to point out qualities in the poetry which give it the greatness which most perceptive readers seem to recognize intuitively.

Whicher, Stephen E. FREEDOM AND FATE: AN INNER LIFE OF RALPH WALDO EMERSON. 1953; 2d ed. Philadelphia: Univ. of Pennsylvania Press, 1969.

In this crucial study of the development of Emerson's thought, Whicher focuses on the years 1833–47 and finds a great deal more skepticism, as well as wisdom, than previous critics and biographers have recognized.

Woodberry, George Edward. RALPH WALDO EMERSON. 1907; New York: Haskell, 1968.

A readable and well-balanced biography, this contains some good early criticism as well.

Woodbury, Charles J. TALKS WITH EMERSON. 1890; New York: Horizon Press, 1970.

> These are interesting reminiscences by a student of Emerson. The 1970 reprint provides a useful introduction by Henry Le Roy Finch.

Wynkoop, W.M. THREE CHILDREN OF THE UNIVERSE: EMERSON'S VIEW OF SHAKESPEARE, BACON AND MILTON. The Hague: Mouton, 1966.

> The author attempts to show how the three writers represent, for Emerson, the "Knower," the "Doer," and the "Sayer." Shakespeare is identified with the "classic mode," Bacon with the "romantic," and Milton as a synthesis transcending both. The author also provides a good discussion of Emerson's theories of knowledge and art.

Yoder, R.A. EMERSON AND THE ORPHIC POET IN AMERICA. Berkeley and Los Angeles: Univ. of California Press, 1978.

> Although the author focuses on Emerson's poetry and maintains that Emerson the poet is quite distinct from Emerson the essayist, the study does provide some evidence for Emerson's declining faith.

Young, Charles L. EMERSON'S MONTAIGNE. New York: Macmillan, 1941.

> In his discussion of Montaigne's influence on Emerson and Emerson's essay on Montaigne in REPRESENTATIVE MEN, Young argues that Emerson cared more for Montaigne as a moralist than as a skeptic.

RELATED GENERAL STUDIES

Aaron, Daniel. MEN OF GOOD HOPE. (p. 14)
Abel, Darrel, ed. CRITICAL THEORY IN THE AMERICAN RENAISSANCE. (p. 62)
Anderson, Quentin. THE IMPERIAL SELF. (p. 14)
Banta, Martha. FAILURE AND SUCCESS IN AMERICA. (p. 14)
Baym, Max I. A HISTORY OF LITERARY AESTHETICS IN AMERICA. (p. 62)
Bercovitch, Sacvan. THE PURITAN ORIGINS OF THE AMERICAN SELF. (p. 15)
Blau, Joseph L. MEN AND MOVEMENTS IN AMERICAN PHILOSOPHY. (p. 161)
Blinderman, Abraham. AMERICAN WRITERS ON EDUCATION BEFORE 1865. (p. 161)
Boas, George, ed. ROMANTICISM IN AMERICA. (p. 15)
Boller, Paul F. AMERICAN TRANSCENDENTALISM, 1830-1860. (p. 161)
Brigance, William N. A HISTORY AND CRITICISM OF AMERICAN PUBLIC ADDRESS. (p. 214)
Brooks, Van Wyck. THE FLOWERING OF NEW ENGLAND. (p. 17)
Brownell, William C. AMERICAN PROSE MASTERS. (p. 17)
Brumm, Ursula. AMERICAN THOUGHT AND RELIGIOUS TYPOLOGY. (p. 162)
Buell, Lawrence. LITERARY TRANSCENDENTALISM. (p. 162)

Poirier, Richard. A WORLD ELSEWHERE. (p. 30)
Pritchard, John P. CRITICISM IN AMERICA. (p. 65)
_____. RETURN TO THE FOUNTAINS. (p. 66)
Richardson, Robert D., Jr. MYTH AND LITERATURE IN THE AMERICAN RE-
     NAISSANCE. (p. 30)
Sanborn, F.B. RECOLLECTIONS OF SEVENTY YEARS. (p. 75)
_____. TRANSCENDENTAL AND LITERARY NEW ENGLAND. (p. 173)
Santayana, George. WINDS OF DOCTRINE. (p. 173)
Schneider, Herbert W. A HISTORY OF AMERICAN PHILOSOPHY. (p. 174)
Simon, Myron, and Thornton H. Parsons, eds. TRANSCENDENTALISM AND ITS
     LEGACY. (p. 174)
Smith, Henry N. VIRGIN LAND. (p. 131)
Spencer, Benjamin T. THE QUEST FOR NATIONALITY. (p. 67)
Stafford, John. THE LITERARY CRITICISM OF YOUNG AMERICA. (p. 67)
Stapleton, Laurence. THE ELECTED CIRCLE. (p. 31)
Stoehr, Taylor. NAY-SAYING IN CONCORD. (p. 175)
Stovall, Floyd. AMERICAN IDEALISM. (p. 32)
Tanner, Tony. THE REIGN OF WONDER. (p. 32)
Vogel, Stanley. GERMAN LITERARY INFLUENCES ON THE AMERICAN TRANS-
     CENDENTALISTS. (p. 176)
Warren, Austin. THE NEW ENGLAND CONSCIENCE. (p. 33)
Wellek, Rene. A HISTORY OF MODERN CRITICISM. (p. 68)
Whipple, Edwin P. RECOLLECTIONS OF EMINENT MEN. (p. 56)

Although they are no longer principal biographical sources, the studies of Emerson by Alcott and Holmes and Fuller's comments on Emerson, especially in WO-
MAN IN THE NINETEENTH CENTURY, should be noted.

[SARAH] MARGARET FULLER [OSSOLI] (1810-50)

During her lifetime, Margaret Fuller was regarded as a far more brilliant speak-er than writer, both in her informal discourse and in her more formal "Conver-sations." Early biographies emphasized the romantic aspects of her life, while more recent biographies have stressed her role as a pioneer journalist and feminist. Although she was not a major writer, she deserves a significant place in American literature for her work. Excerpts from her journals reveal more sharply than any other record the emotional drives behind transcendentalism. She was an early, original critic, disavowing the role of moralist, but assum-ing that of critic of all aspects of life. She not only edited the DIAL but also filled many of its pages when lack of contributions forced her to do so. As a translator and critic, she was the interpreter of European culture for many Americans. Recent critical studies of her works have added to her stature.

PRINCIPAL WORKS

SUMMER ON THE LAKES IN 1843. 1844.
WOMAN IN THE NINETEENTH CENTURY. 1845.
PAPERS ON LITERATURE AND ART. 2 vols. 1846.

LETTERS AND JOURNALS

LOVE-LETTERS OF MARGARET FULLER, 1845-1846. Introd. Julia Ward Howe. 1903; New York: AMS Press, 1970.

> This edition of the letters to James Nathan also includes short reminiscences by Emerson, Horace Greeley, and Charles T. Congdon.

The MEMOIRS and the anthologies edited by Perry Miller and Mason Wade, below, include letters and excerpts from notebooks. A complete collection of Fuller's letters, edited by Robert N. Hudspeth, Pennsylvania State Univ., is forthcoming.

LATER EDITIONS, SELECTIONS, AND REPRINTS

ART, LITERATURE, AND THE DRAMA. Ed. Arthur B. Fuller. Boston: Brown, Taggard and Chase, 1860.

> This includes a translation of Goethe's TASSO and much of PAPERS ON LITERATURE AND ART.

AT HOME AND ABROAD. Ed. Arthur B. Fuller. 1856; New York: Kennikat, 1971.

THE EDUCATED WOMAN IN AMERICA: SELECTED WRITINGS OF CATHARINE BEECHER, MARGARET FULLER, AND M. CAREY THOMAS. Ed. Barbara M. Cross. New York: Teachers' College Press, 1965.

> The introduction and notes by the editor provide a useful commentary and comparison.

LIFE WITHOUT AND LIFE WITHIN. Ed. Arthur B. Fuller. 1860; Boston: Gregg Press, 1974.

MARGARET AND HER FRIENDS, OR, TEN CONVERSATIONS WITH MARGARET FULLER. Reported by Caroline W. Healey [Dall]. 1895; New York: Arno, 1972.

MARGARET FULLER, AMERICAN ROMANTIC: A SELECTION FROM HER WRITINGS AND CORRESPONDENCE. Ed. Perry Miller. 1963; Gloucester, Mass.: Peter Smith, 1974.

MARGARET FULLER: ESSAYS ON AMERICAN LIFE AND LETTERS. Ed. Joel Myerson. New Haven, Conn.: College and Univ. Press, 1978.

MEMOIRS OF MARGARET FULLER OSSOLI. 2 vols. Ed. Ralph Waldo Emerson et al. 1852; New York: B. Franklin, 1972.

> The excerpts here from the journals and letters and from the European correspondence are valuable primary sources. However, as numerous later critics have pointed out, the nature of the selections and the eulogies by the editors and others tend to distort the nature of the woman and her work.

PAPERS ON LITERATURE AND ART. New York: AMS Press, 1972.

SUMMER ON THE LAKES. Atlantic Highlands, N.J.: Humanities Press, 1979.

THE WOMAN AND THE MYTH: MARGARET FULLER'S LIFE AND WRITINGS. Ed. with commentary by Bell Gale Chevigny. Old Westbury, N.Y.: Feminist Press, 1976.

In addition to selections of Fuller's writings, this volume includes comments by Fuller's contemporaries and biographical-critical essays for each of the chapters, tracing the evolution of Fuller's thought from idealism to social radicalism.

WOMAN IN THE NINETEENTH CENTURY. Introd. Madeleine B. Stern. Columbia: Univ. of South Carolina Press, 1980.

This is the first authoritative text of the 1845 edition of Fuller's study.

THE WRITINGS OF MARGARET FULLER. Ed. Mason Wade. 1941; Clifton, N.J.: A.M. Kelley, 1973.

This collection includes SUMMER ON THE LAKES, WOMAN IN THE NINETEENTH CENTURY, thirteen critical essays, letters, and passages from the MEMOIRS.

BIBLIOGRAPHY

Myerson, Joel. MARGARET FULLER: AN ANNOTATED SECONDARY BIBLIOGRAPHY. New York: B. Franklin, 1977.

This lists 1,245 items published from 1834 to 1975 and not only provides excellent commentary on secondary resources but also surveys Fuller's reputation for over a century.

_____. MARGARET FULLER: A DESCRIPTIVE BIBLIOGRAPHY. Pittsburgh: Univ. of Pittsburgh Press, 1978.

This is a full listing of Fuller's works, including writings in collections and writings which appeared in magazines and newspapers during her lifetime.

Although supplanted by Myerson's two listings of primary and secondary sources, Blanck's sections on Fuller in the BIBLIOGRAPHY OF AMERICAN LITERATURE 3:262-69, is still useful. A "Calendar of the Letters of Margaret Fuller" was published by Robert N. Hudspeth in STUDIES IN THE AMERICAN RENAISSANCE (1977). Fuller is listed in the BIBLIOGRAPHY to the LITERARY HISTORY OF THE UNITED STATES, pp. 522, 922, 1209.

BIOGRAPHY AND CRITICISM

Allen, Margaret Vanderhaar. THE ACHIEVEMENT OF MARGARET FULLER. University Park: Pennsylvania State Univ. Press, 1979.

In her discussion of Fuller's achievement as a writer, a critic, a feminist, a reformer, and a humanist, the author stresses that the interest in the superficial facts of Fuller's life has displaced and distorted her lasting accomplishments. After considering those who influenced Fuller, most notably Emerson and Goethe, the author focuses upon Fuller's social and political activities and evaluates her writings. She concludes that Fuller deserves a place in American literary history equal to that of Emerson and Thoreau.

Anthony, Katharine. MARGARET FULLER: A PSYCHOLOGICAL BIOGRAPHY. 1920; Philadelphia: R. West, 1977.

The study gives a Freudian account of Fuller's life and activities, thus subjecting her to a great many preconceptions which tend to distort the historical facts.

Bell, Margaret. MARGARET FULLER: A BIOGRAPHY. Introd. Eleanor Roosevelt. New York: C. Boni, 1930.

This is a semifictional, somewhat unsatisfactory biography.

Blanchard, Paula. MARGARET FULLER: FROM TRANSCENDENTALISM TO REVOLUTION. New York: Delacorte Press, Seymour Lawrence, 1978.

In this biography, intended more for a general audience than the specialist, the author concludes that Margaret Fuller was not a first-rate writer but that "in carving a niche for herself on the enormous wall of resistance that faced her, she left a foothold for others." The study is well-informed and sympathetic but objective, despite the author's announced feminist perspective.

Braun, Frederick A. MARGARET FULLER AND GOETHE. New York: H. Holt, 1910.

The author demonstrates the importance of Goethe's thought in Fuller's criticism and views and recognizes her importance in interpreting his ideas for her American audience. He also argues that Fuller was more practical than speculative in her approach to self-development.

Brown, Arthur W. MARGARET FULLER. New York: Twayne, 1964.

Brown's brief study is one of the first to give Fuller the credit she deserves for her accomplishments as a literary critic and a journalist. The author also notes her importance in introducing European literature to America at the same time she was promoting a native American culture and literature.

Chipperfield, Faith. IN QUEST OF LOVE: THE LIFE AND DEATH OF MARGARET FULLER. New York: Coward-McCann, 1957.

This romanticized biography is very readable but not always reliable.

Clarke, James Freeman. THE LETTERS OF JAMES FREEMAN CLARKE TO MARGARET FULLER. Ed. John Wesley Thomas. Hamburg: Cram, de Gruyter, 1957.

> These letters written by Clarke to Fuller cover the years 1829–48 and provide information about Fuller's activities and ideas during those years.

Deiss, Joseph. THE ROMAN YEARS OF MARGARET FULLER: A BIOGRAPHY. New York: Crowell, 1969.

> In a good partial biography, the author uses Fuller's travel letters to the TRIBUNE, together with other materials, to fill a gap in earlier biographies.

Durning, Russell. MARGARET FULLER, CITIZEN OF THE WORLD: AN INTER-MEDIARY BETWEEN EUROPEAN AND AMERICAN LITERATURE. Heidelberg: Carl Winter, 1969.

> This is a solid, reliable source of information about the influences on Margaret Fuller and her effect as a critic and commentator. The topics covered include Fuller's teaching and conversations, her analysis of continental literature, and her theory and practice of translation.

Higginson, Thomas W. MARGARET FULLER OSSOLI. 1884; New York: Haskell, 1968.

> Higginson's gentlemanly account partially corrects the distorted image presented in the MEMOIRS, above, and includes several selections from journals and letters.

Howe, Julia Ward. MARGARET FULLER, MARCHESA OSSOLI. Boston: Roberts Brothers, 1883.

> Useful as a source of primary material, this sympathetic study is an attempt to portray Fuller's personality rather than to present an objective account of her life.

McMaster, Helen N. MARGARET FULLER AS A LITERARY CRITIC. 1928; Folcroft, Pa.: Folcroft Press, 1969.

> In a well-balanced view of Fuller's theories and practices, McMaster indicates Fuller's importance as a critic of literature and her defects as a critic of music and the visual arts.

Myerson, Joel, ed. CRITICAL ESSAYS ON MARGARET FULLER. Boston: G.K. Hall, 1980.

> These essays include comments by such contemporaries as Bronson Alcott and Henry James as well as twentieth-century criticism by Oscar Cargill, V.L. Parrington, Madeleine Stern, and others.

Stern, Madeleine B. THE LIFE OF MARGARET FULLER. 1942; New York: Haskell, 1968.

> Detailed and well researched, this biography occasionally fiction-
> alizes events to make them "more alive."

Urbanski, Marie Mitchell Olesen. MARGARET FULLER'S WOMAN IN THE NINETEENTH CENTURY: A LITERARY STUDY OF FORM AND CONTENT, OF SOURCES AND INFLUENCE. Westport, Conn.: Greenwood Press, 1980.

Wade, Mason. MARGARET FULLER, WHETSTONE OF GENIUS. 1940; Clifton, N.J.: A.M. Kelley, 1973.

> This is a good biography, although the lack of footnotes obscures
> sources. Wade also betrays a bias in his distaste for Fuller's "mas-
> culine" side.

Wellisz, Leopold. THE FRIENDSHIP OF MARGARET FULLER D'OSSOLI AND ADAM MICKIEWICZ. New York: Polish Book Import, 1947.

> This useful primary source includes letters from the poet and pro-
> fessor of Slavic languages who became one of Fuller's best friends
> in Europe.

Wilson, Ellen. MARGARET FULLER, BLUESTOCKING, ROMANTIC, REVOLU-TIONARY. New York: Harcourt, Farrar, Straus and Giroux, 1977.

> Although Wilson's straightforward, objective biography gives little
> interpretation of Fuller's life and achievements and no evaluation
> of her works, it is honest, well researched, and reliable.

RELATED STUDIES AND SOURCES

Abel, Darrel, ed. CRITICAL THEORY IN THE AMERICAN RENAISSANCE.
    (p. 62)
Alcott, A. Bronson. CONCORD DAYS. (p. 241, under Alcott)
Buell, Lawrence. LITERARY TRANSCENDENTALISM: STYLE AND VISION IN
    THE AMERICAN RENAISSANCE. (p. 162)
Clarke, James F. AUTOBIOGRAPHY, DIARY AND CORRESPONDENCE.
    (p. 70)
Curtis, Edith R. A SEASON IN UTOPIA: THE STORY OF BROOK FARM.
    (p. 216)
DeMille, George E. LITERARY CRITICISM IN AMERICA. (p. 62)
Emerson, Ralph Waldo. THE CORRESPONDENCE OF EMERSON AND CAR-
    LYLE. (p. 300, under Emerson)
_____. JOURNALS AND MISCELLANEOUS NOTEBOOKS. (p. 301, under
    Emerson)
_____. THE LETTERS OF RALPH WALDO EMERSON. (p. 301, under Emerson)

Fellman, Michael. THE UNBOUNDED FRAME. (p. 217)

Goddard, Harold C. STUDIES IN NEW ENGLAND TRANSCENDENTALISM. (p. 167)

Gohdes, Clarence. THE PERIODICALS OF AMERICAN TRANSCENDENTALISM. (p. 61)

Greeley, Horace. RECOLLECTIONS OF A BUSY LIFE. (p. 72)

James, Henry. WILLIAM WETMORE STORY AND HIS FRIENDS. (pp. 365 and 369, under H. James)

Pritchard, John P. CRITICISM IN AMERICA. (p. 65)

Pochmann, Henry A. GERMAN CULTURE IN AMERICA. (p. 172)

Shepard, Odell, ed. THE JOURNALS OF BRONSON ALCOTT. (pp. 241-42, under Alcott)

HAMLIN GARLAND (1860-1940)

Hamlin Garland's place in American literature is assured by his vivid and sensitive treatment, in his fiction and autobiographical volumes, of the poverty and difficulty of farm life on the prairie. In addition, both his fiction and nonfiction reflect the most important social and aesthetic issues of his time. His CRUMBLING IDOLS defined for a new generation of writers a new kind of fiction. In this volume of essays, Garland expounded his theory of "veritism," which was a kind of impressionistic realism, neither systematic nor profound but opening fiction to the possibilities of finding truth in immediate experience, intensely felt and faithfully recorded. His late biographical reminiscences are not major works, but they constitute a rich record of the people and the times. Garland urged writers to "write of those things which you know most, and for which you care most. By doing so you will be true to yourself, true to your locality, and true to your time." In his best fiction and autobiography, Garland achieved something of that truth.

PRINCIPAL NONFICTION PROSE WORKS

CRUMBLING IDOLS: TWELVE ESSAYS ON ART. 1894.
ULYSSES S. GRANT: HIS LIFE AND CHARACTER. 1898.
BOY LIFE ON THE PRAIRIE. 1899. (Fictionalized autobiography)
A SON OF THE MIDDLE BORDER. 1917.
A DAUGHTER OF THE MIDDLE BORDER. 1921.
A PIONEER MOTHER. 1922.
TRAIL-MAKERS OF THE MIDDLE BORDER. 1926.
THE WESTWARD MARCH OF AMERICAN SETTLEMENT. 1927.
BACK-TRAILERS FROM THE MIDDLE BORDER. 1928.
ROADSIDE MEETINGS. 1930.
COMPANIONS ON THE TRAIL. 1931.
MY FRIENDLY CONTEMPORARIES. 1932.
AFTERNOON NEIGHBORS. 1934.
FORTY YEARS OF PSYCHIC RESEARCH. 1936.

JOURNALS

HAMLIN GARLAND'S DIARIES. Ed. Donald Pizer. San Marino, Calif.:
Huntington Library, 1968.

LATER EDITIONS, SELECTIONS, AND REPRINTS

BOY LIFE ON THE PRAIRIE. Ed. with Introd. Bruce R. McElderry, Jr. Lincoln: Univ. of Nebraska Press, 1961.

CRUMBLING IDOLS. Introd. Robert Spiller. Ed. and introd. Jane Johnson.
1952; Cambridge, Mass.: Harvard Univ. Press, 1960.

A DAUGHTER OF THE MIDDLE BORDER. New York: Peter Smith, 1960.

A SON OF THE MIDDLE BORDER. Lincoln: Univ. of Nebraska Press, 1979.

BIBLIOGRAPHY

Bryer, Jackson R., and Eugene Harding with Robert A. Rees. HAMLIN GARLAND AND THE CRITICS: AN ANNOTATED BIBLIOGRAPHY. Troy, N.Y.:
Whitston, 1973.

> This includes annotated listings of reviews of books by Garland,
> periodical articles about Garland, and books and parts of books
> about Garland.

Silet, Charles L.P. HENRY BLAKE FULLER AND HAMLIN GARLAND: A
REFERENCE GUIDE. Boston: G.K. Hall, 1977.

> This contains a listing of works about Garland, 1891-1975.

A catalog of Garland papers bequested to the Univ. of Southern California is
included in Arvidson, below. Garland is listed in the BIBLIOGRAPHY to the
LITERARY HISTORY OF THE UNITED STATES, pp. 526, 923, 1210.

BIOGRAPHY AND CRITICISM

Arvidson, Lloyd, ed. CENTENNIAL TRIBUTES AND A CHECKLIST OF THE
HAMLIN GARLAND PAPERS IN THE UNIVERSITY OF SOUTHERN CALIFORNIA
LIBRARY. Los Angeles: Univ. of Southern California, 1962.

> TRIBUTES includes about two dozen brief essays reviewing Garland's
> career and works.

Holloway, Jean. HAMLIN GARLAND: A BIOGRAPHY. Austin: Univ. of Texas Press, 1956.

> The author gives a thorough chronology and a background of the genesis and composition of Garland's works, along with the critical reactions of his contemporaries, in an attempt to discover the "enigma of a talented writer who squandered his talent."

McCullough, Joseph B. HAMLIN GARLAND. Boston: Twayne, 1978.

> This study gives an excellent introduction to and brief analysis of Garland's works. The author notes that Garland's "desire to write more acceptable material in order to gain respectability seriously damaged his art" and that he was unable "to integrate his social and literary theories with the materials he gathered from personal experience and observation." However, McCullough judges that Garland did achieve a few works of lasting interest and value.

Mane, Robert. HAMLIN GARLAND: L'HOMME ET L'OEUVRE (1860-1940). Paris: Didier, 1968.

> Mane's comprehensive analysis of Garland's life and works includes a listing of writings by and about Hamlin Garland.

Pizer, Donald. HAMLIN GARLAND'S EARLY WORKS AND CAREER. Berkeley: Univ. of California Press, 1960.

> The study covers the years 1884-95, emphasizing Hamlin Garland as a social reformer, Populist, local colorist, arts reformer, and impressionist.

RELATED GENERAL STUDIES

Brooks, Van Wyck. THE CONFIDENT YEARS. (p. 17)
_____. HOWELLS: HIS LIFE AND WORLD. (p. 354, under Howells)
Carter, Everett. HOWELLS AND THE AGE OF REALISM. (p. 355, under Howells)
Clough, Wilson O. THE NECESSARY EARTH. (p. 127)
Dondore, Dorothy. THE PRAIRIE AND THE MAKING OF MIDDLE AMERICA. (p. 128)
Foerster, Norman. AMERICAN CRITICISM. (p. 63)
Hazard, Lucy L. THE FRONTIER IN AMERICAN LITERATURE. (p. 129)
Martin, Jay. HARVESTS OF CHANGE. (p. 26)
Pattee, Fred L. A HISTORY OF AMERICAN LITERATURE SINCE 1870. (p. 29)
Pritchard, John P. CRITICISM IN AMERICA. (p. 65)
Smith, Bernard. FORCES IN AMERICAN CRITICISM. (p. 66)
Smith, Henry N. VIRGIN LAND. (p. 131)
Ziff, Larzer. THE AMERICAN 1890'S. (p. 34)

NATHANIEL HAWTHORNE (1804-64)

Hawthorne's NOTEBOOKS, excellent texts of which are being established in the Centenary edition of his works, and, to a lesser extent, his prefaces, his essays and English sketches in OUR OLD HOME, and his biographical stories for children are important resources for understanding the novelist. However minor they may appear in the total body of Hawthorne's writings, these genres also deserve recognition as contributions to American nonfiction prose and criticism.

PRINCIPAL PROSE WORKS

BIOGRAPHICAL STORIES FOR CHILDREN. 1842.
LIFE OF FRANKLIN PIERCE. 1852.
OUR OLD HOME. 1863.

LETTERS AND JOURNALS

THE AMERICAN NOTEBOOKS. Ed. Claude M. Simpson. Columbus: Ohio State Univ. Press, 1972.

> Volume 7 of the centenary edition, this supersedes Stewart's edition, below. Simpson includes the five notebooks of the 1941 edition plus three more. The historical commentary and textual notes are excellent, giving a background of the publication of the notebooks and a clear account of the material they contain.

THE AMERICAN NOTEBOOKS BY NATHANIEL HAWTHORNE. Ed. Randall Stewart. New Haven, Conn.: Yale Univ. Press, 1932.

THE ENGLISH NOTEBOOKS. Ed. Randall Stewart. 1941; New York: Russell and Russell, 1962.

THE FRENCH AND ITALIAN NOTEBOOKS. Ed. William Charvat et al. Columbus: Ohio State Univ. Press, 1980.

Volume 14 of the centenary edition, this includes textual apparatus and historical notes.

HAWTHORNE AND HIS PUBLISHER. Ed. Caroline Ticknor. 1913; Port Washington, N.Y.: Kennikat, 1969.

HAWTHORNE'S FIRST DIARY, WITH AN ACCOUNT OF ITS DISCOVERY. Ed. Samuel T. Pickard. 1897; Philadelphia: R. West, 1973.

HAWTHORNE'S LOST NOTEBOOK 1835-1841. Transcript and Pref. by Barbara S. Mouffe. University Park: Pennsylvania State Univ. Press, 1978.

The entries in this earliest of Hawthorne's notebooks extend from May 28, 1835, to June 29, 1841. Although unedited in this publication, the notebook reveals a great deal about Hawthorne's state of mind and preoccupations at the time.

THE HEART OF HAWTHORNE'S JOURNALS. Ed. Newton Arvin. Boston: Houghton Mifflin, 1929.

LETTERS OF NATHANIEL HAWTHORNE TO WILLIAM D. TICKNOR, 1851-1864. 2 vols. 1910; Foreword by C.E. Frazer Clark, Jr. Washington, D.C.: Microcard Editions, 1972.

LOVE LETTERS OF NATHANIEL HAWTHORNE, 1839-41, 1841-63. 2 vols. Pref. by Roswell Fields. 1907; Foreword by C.E. Frazer Clark, Jr. Washington, D.C.: Microcard Editions, 1972.

In his preface to this offset reprinting, Clark corrects errors in the dating of some of the letters and prints a few passages omitted from the printed texts.

PASSAGES FROM THE AMERICAN NOTE-BOOKS. 2 vols. Ed. Sophia Hawthorne. Boston: Ticknor and Fields, 1868.

In the notes to the centenary edition of the AMERICAN NOTE-BOOKS, above, Claude M. Simpson gives an account of Sophia Hawthorne's editing of this version of the NOTEBOOKS.

PASSAGES FROM THE ENGLISH NOTE-BOOKS. 2 vols. Ed. Sophia Hawthorne. Boston: Fields, Osgood, 1870.

PASSAGES FROM THE FRENCH AND ITALIAN NOTE-BOOKS. 2 vols. Ed. Una Hawthorne. Boston: J.R. Osgood, 1872.

PASSAGES FROM THE NOTE-BOOKS OF THE LATE NATHANIEL HAWTHORNE. Introd. Moncure D. Conway. London: John Camden Hotten, 1869.

LATER EDITIONS, SELECTIONS, AND REPRINTS

THE CENTENARY EDITION OF THE WORKS OF NATHANIEL HAWTHORNE.
Ed. William Charvat et al. Columbus: Ohio State Univ. Press, 1962-- .

> This edition will provide the definitive texts for Hawthorne's works.
> Nonfiction prose works in this edition published to date are listed
> by title, below.

THE COMPLETE WORKS OF NATHANIEL HAWTHORNE. 12 vols. Ed. by
G.P. Lathrop. Boston: Houghton Mifflin, 1883.

HAWTHORNE AS EDITOR. SELECTIONS FROM HIS WRITINGS IN THE
AMERICAN MAGAZINE FOR USEFUL AND ENTERTAINING KNOWLEDGE.
Baton Rouge: Louisiana State Univ. Press, 1941.

HAWTHORNE IN ENGLAND. Ed. Cushing Shout. Ithaca, N.Y.: Cornell
Univ. Press, 1965.

> This includes selections from OUR OLD HOME and from the EN-
> GLISH NOTEBOOKS.

THE LIFE OF FRANKLIN PIERCE. Foreword by Richard C. Robey. New York:
Garrett, 1970.

NATHANIEL HAWTHORNE: REPRESENTATIVE SELECTIONS. Ed. Austin Warren. 1934; St. Clair Shores, Mich.: Scholarly Press, 1971.

OUR OLD HOME: A SERIES OF ENGLISH SKETCHES. Ed. William Charvat
et al., with introd. Claude M. Simpson and Textual Introd. Fredson Bowers.
Columbus: Ohio State Univ. Press, 1970.

> This is volume 5 in the centenary edition.

THE PORTABLE HAWTHORNE. Rev. ed. Malcolm Cowley. New York: Viking, 1969.

TRUE STORIES FROM HISTORY AND BIOGRAPHY. Historical Introd. Roy Harvey Pearce; Textual Introd. Fredson Bowers. Columbus: Ohio State Univ. Press,
1972.

> Pearce's introduction to this volume, volume 6 of the Centenary
> Edition discusses Hawthorne as a writer of stories and biographies
> for children.

BIBLIOGRAPHY

Babiiha, Thaddeo K. THE JAMES-HAWTHORNE RELATIONS: BIBLIOGRAPHI-
CAL ESSAYS. Boston: G.K. Hall, 1980.

> These essays provide a definitive account of the relationship; much
> material by James on Hawthorne is included.

Blair, Walter. "Nathaniel Hawthorne." In EIGHT AMERICAN AUTHORS.
Rev. Ed. James Woodress. New York: Norton, 1971, pp. 85-128.

> This excellent bibliographical essay describes texts and editions
> and evaluates biography and criticism to 1970.

Browne, Nina E. A BIBLIOGRAPHY OF NATHANIEL HAWTHORNE. 1905;
New York: B. Franklin, 1967.

> This listing includes collected and separate works by Hawthorne
> and early biography and criticism.

Cathcart, Wallace H. BIBLIOGRAPHY OF THE WORKS OF NATHANIEL HAW-
THORNE. 1905; Ann Arbor: Univ. of Michigan Microfilms, 1971.

Clark, C.E. Frazer, Jr. CHECKLIST OF NATHANIEL HAWTHORNE. Columbus, Ohio: Charles E. Merrill, 1970.

_____. A DESCRIPTIVE BIBLIOGRAPHY OF THE WRITINGS OF NATHANIEL
HAWTHORNE. Pittsburgh: Univ. of Pittsburgh Press, 1978.

> This lists separate publications, collected works, and contributions
> to books, pamphlets, magazines, and newspapers.

_____. HAWTHORNE AT AUCTION. Detroit: Gale Research Co., 1972.

> This reprints sales catalogs of important auctions of Hawthorne
> material, 1894-1971.

FIRST EDITIONS OF THE WORKS OF NATHANIEL HAWTHORNE TOGETHER
WITH SOME MANUSCRIPTS, LETTERS, AND PORTRAITS. New York: Grolier
Club, 1904.

Gross, Theodore L., and Stanley Wertheim. HAWTHORNE, MELVILLE, STE-
PHEN CRANE: A CRITICAL BIBLIOGRAPHY. New York: Free Press, 1971.

> The annotations to the listings are excellent and consistently more
> reliable and informative than those by Ricks et al., below.

Jones, Buford. A CHECKLIST OF HAWTHORNE CRITICISM, 1951-1966. Hartford, Conn.: Transcendental Books, 1967.

Ricks, Beatrice, Joseph D. Adams, and Jack O. Hazlerig. NATHANIEL HAW-
THORNE: A REFERENCE BIBLIOGRAPHY. Boston: G.K. Hall, 1972.

> This is a comprehensive listing, but it contains errors in annotation
> and indexing.

Hawthorne's works are listed in Blanck's BIBLIOGRAPHY OF AMERICAN LITERA-
TURE 3:1-36. The NATHANIEL HAWTHORNE JOURNAL publishes updated
checklists and new primary materials. Hawthorne is listed in the BIBLIOGRAPHY
to the LITERARY HISTORY OF THE UNITED STATES, pp. 544, 927, 1215.

BIOGRAPHY AND CRITICISM

The works listed below include the standard biographies and critical works dealing with Hawthorne's aesthetic and literary ideas and those relating Hawthorne
specifically to his nineteenth-century milieu. Works dealing chiefly with the
fiction have been excluded.

Arvin, Newton. HAWTHORNE. 1929; New York: Russell and Russell, 1961.

> Arvin's study is good biography, although it contains some errors.
> He uses Hawthorne's works to explicate his life, relating Haw-
> thorne's preoccupation with guilt to his supposed reclusiveness.

Bell, Millicent. HAWTHORNE'S VIEW OF THE ARTIST. Albany, N.Y.:
State Univ. of New York Press, 1962.

> The study surveys Hawthorne's critical theories in relation to roman-
> ticism and presents Hawthorne as an alienated artist.

Bridge, Horatio. PERSONAL RECOLLECTIONS OF NATHANIEL HAWTHORNE.
1893; Philadelphia: R. West, 1973.

> Bridge's JOURNAL OF AN AFRICAN CRUISER (1834) was exten-
> sively edited by Hawthorne from Bridge's notes on the voyage.
> These reminiscences also include some significant letters from Haw-
> thorne to the author.

Cameron, Kenneth W., ed. HAWTHORNE AMONG HIS CONTEMPORARIES.
Hartford, Conn.: Transcendental Books, 1968.

> This is a somewhat confused compilation of critical discussions and
> anecdotes about Hawthorne.

Cantwell, Robert. NATHANIEL HAWTHORNE: THE AMERICAN YEARS. New
York: Rinehart, 1948.

> Cantwell presents Hawthorne as a well-adjusted New Englander, em-
> phasizing the social world in which Hawthorne moved and describ-
> ing the places where he lived and worked.

Cohen, B. Bernard. THE MERRILL GUIDE TO NATHANIEL HAWTHORNE. Columbus, Ohio: Charles E. Merrill, 1970.

> This provides a useful introductory overview of Hawthorne's career and works.

_____, ed. THE RECOGNITION OF NATHANIEL HAWTHORNE: SELECTED CRITICISM SINCE 1828. Ann Arbor: Univ. of Michigan Press, 1969.

> This is valuable for providing a summary of the growth of Hawthorne's reputation.

Conway, Moncure D. LIFE OF NATHANIEL HAWTHORNE. 1890; New York: Haskell, 1969.

> A good early biography, this provides useful source material.

Crowley, Joseph D., ed. HAWTHORNE: THE CRITICAL HERITAGE. New York: Barnes and Noble, 1970.

> Crowley collects reviews of Hawthorne's works written by his contemporaries and includes prefaces and letters which reflect Hawthorne's views of his critics.

Elder, Marjorie J. NATHANIEL HAWTHORNE: TRANSCENDENTAL SYMBOLIST. Athens: Ohio Univ. Press, 1969.

> An imaginative and well-documented study, this discusses the transcendental influences on Hawthorne's theories.

Faust, Bertha. HAWTHORNE'S CONTEMPORANEOUS REPUTATION: A STUDY OF LITERARY OPINION IN AMERICA AND ENGLAND, 1828-1864. Philadelphia: Univ. of Pennsylvania Press, 1939.

> Faust surveys and gives extracts of contemporary reviews and opinions. The material is arranged in chronological order, giving some idea of the growth of Hawthorne's reputation. The author concludes that at the time of his death, "no one in America at least, questioned his classic status."

Hall, Lawrence Sargent. HAWTHORNE, CRITIC OF SOCIETY. 1944; Gloucester, Mass.: Peter Smith, 1966.

> The study presents a useful discussion of Hawthorne's relationship to his society and his attitudes toward it. The author argues that Hawthorne's social consciousness was an important but subtle factor in his thoughts and perceptions.

Hawthorne, Julian. HAWTHORNE AND HIS CIRCLE. 1903; Hamden, Conn.: Archon, 1968.

> These recollections, and those below, by Hawthorne's son provide useful primary material and backgrounds.

_____. NATHANIEL HAWTHORNE AND HIS WIFE. 2 vols. 1884; Philadelphia: R. West, 1973.

Hoeltje, Hubert H. INWARD SKY: THE MIND AND HEART OF NATHANIEL HAWTHORNE. Durham, N.C.: Duke Univ. Press, 1962.

The author attempts to present Hawthorne's thought and daily life and to see him in the context of his nineteenth-century world, basing the analysis of what kind of man Hawthorne was upon a close study of his works. This is a careful study, although Hawthorne's affinity to Emerson may seem overemphasized.

Jacobson, Richard J. HAWTHORNE'S CONCEPTION OF THE CREATIVE PROCESS. Cambridge, Mass.: Harvard Univ. Press, 1965.

The author places Hawthorne in the mainstream of romantic thought, relating his ideas to those of other romantic theorists. The study is carefully researched but tends to portray Hawthorne as too much of an abstract theorist.

James, Henry. HAWTHORNE. 1879; New York: Cornell Univ. Press, 1956.

James's critical approach to Hawthorne has been an influential study, revealing much about James as well as his attitudes toward Hawthorne. The factual material is based largely on Lathrop, below.

Lathrop, George Parsons. A STUDY OF HAWTHORNE. Boston: J.R. Osgood, 1876; New York: AMS Press, [1972].

Written by Hawthorne's son-in-law, this contains portions of Hawthorne's journal and provides insights into Hawthorne's ideas as well as details of his life. Lathrop's factual material served as the basic source for James's biography.

Lathrop, Rose. MEMOIRS OF HAWTHORNE. 1897; New York: AMS Press, [1972].

Written by Hawthorne's daughter, this remains a good primary source.

Martin, Terence. NATHANIEL HAWTHORNE. New York: Twayne, 1965.

Martin's brief but intelligent and well-rounded study of Hawthorne's career and works is a useful survey and introduction.

Normand, Jean. NATHANIEL HAWTHORNE: AN APPROACH TO AN ANALYSIS OF ARTISTIC CREATION. Trans. Derek Coltman. Cleveland, Ohio: Case Western Reserve Univ., 1970.

Normand's stylistic analysis of Hawthorne's work is excellent, although his conclusions about Hawthorne's ideas and psychological makeup rests upon some faulty assumptions.

_____, ed. HAWTHORNE CENTENARY ESSAYS. Columbus: Ohio State Univ. Press, 1964.

These essays by outstanding scholars and writers provide an important views of Hawthorne's reputation and influence one hundred years after his death.

Stewart, Randall. NATHANIEL HAWTHORNE, A BIOGRAPHY. 1948; Hamden, Conn.: Shoe String, 1970.

This sensible study reevaluates Hawthorne's personality and presents him as more of a social being than had many previous biographers, although it oversimplifies aspects of Hawthorne's character and art.

Turner, Arlin. NATHANIEL HAWTHORNE: AN INTRODUCTION AND INTERPRETATION. New York: Barnes and Noble, 1961.

Effectively using material from Hawthorne's notebooks, the author discusses Hawthorne's social attitudes and aesthetic theories and the processes and influences which shaped them.

Woodberry, George E. NATHANIEL HAWTHORNE. 1902; Detroit, Mich.: Gale Research Co., 1967.

This influential early biography helped perpetuate the image of Hawthorne as a solitary being.

RELATED GENERAL STUDIES

Brownell, William. AMERICAN PROSE MASTERS. (p. 17)
Curtis, George. FROM THE EASY CHAIR. (p. 80)
Fields, James T. YESTERDAYS WITH AUTHORS. (p. 71)
Henderson, Harry. VERSIONS OF THE PAST. (p. 218)
Lewis, R.W.B. THE AMERICAN ADAM. (p. 25)
Long, Robert E. THE GREAT SUCCESSION. (p. 373, under H. James)
Marx, Leo. THE MACHINE IN THE GARDEN. (p. 26)
Matthiessen, F.O. AMERICAN RENAISSANCE. (p. 27)
Pochmann, Henry. GERMAN CULTURE IN AMERICA. (p.172)
Poirier, Richard. A WORLD ELSEWHERE. (p. 30)
Stoddard, Richard H. RECOLLECTIONS. (p. 76)
Whipple, E.P. CHARACTER AND CHARACTERISTIC MEN. (p. 88)

[PATRICIO] LAFCADIO [TESSIMA CARLOS]
HEARN (1850-1904)

Hearn's writings almost defy classification; for he freely mixed essays, sketches, legends, prose poems, speculations, and fantasies in his volumes. The listing below of "Prose Works" is, thus, necessarily arbitrary. It does not include "romances," such as CHITA or YOUMA, or the collections consisting primarily of folk tales, such as KWAIDAN. Hearn's greatest contributions to American literature were probably his reworking of the tales and legends from various cultures. However, his travel sketches and descriptions, though unique in form, are still interesting explorations for readers; his criticism, collected by others after his death, reveals him to have been a sensitive interpreter of literature.

PRINCIPAL PROSE WORKS

TWO YEARS IN THE FRENCH WEST INDIES. 1890.
GLIMPSES OF UNFAMILIAR JAPAN. 2 vols. 1894.
OUT OF THE EAST. 1895.
KOKORO: HINTS AND ECHOES OF JAPANESE INNER LIFE. 1896.
GLEANINGS IN BUDDHA-FIELDS. 1897.
EXOTICS AND RETROSPECTIVES. 1898.
IN GHOSTLY JAPAN. 1899.
SHADOWINGS. 1900.
A JAPANESE MISCELLANY. 1901.
KOTTO. 1902.
JAPAN: AN ATTEMPT AT INTERPRETATION. 1904.

LETTERS AND JOURNALS

DIARIES AND LETTERS. Ed. Ryuji Tanabe. Tokyo: Hokuseido Press, 1921.

THE JAPANESE LETTERS OF LAFCADIO HEARN. Ed. Elizabeth Bisland. 1910; Wilmington, Del.: Scholarly Resources, 1973.

LETTERS FROM THE RAVEN: BEING THE CORRESPONDENCE OF LAFCADIO HEARN WITH HENRY WATKIN. Ed. Milton Bronner. New York: Brentano's, 1907.

SOME NEW LETTERS AND WRITINGS OF LAFCADIO HEARN. Ed. Sanki Ichi-kawa. Tokyo: Kenkyusha, 1925.

A number of letters are included in Bisland's LIFE AND LETTERS and a selection is included in LETTERS/LAFCADIO HEARN, below.

LATER EDITIONS, SELECTIONS, AND REPRINTS

In addition to the volumes cited below, much of Hearn's canon has been re-printed by Arno, AMS Press, Folcroft, Books for Libraries, or Scholarly Press. Such publishing activity demonstrates current interest in Hearn's work.

AN AMERICAN MISCELLANY. 2 vols. Ed. Albert Mordell. New York: Dodd, Mead, 1924.

APPRECIATIONS OF POETRY. Ed. John Erskine. 1916; New York: Arno, 1973.

> Hearn's lectures were recorded by his students and were later edited by John Erskine, Ryuji Tanabe, and others; they were published in seventeen volumes, including this and several of those listed below.

ARTICLES ON LITERATURE AND OTHER WRITINGS FROM THE CINCINNATI ENQUIRER. New York: AMS Press, 1975.

BOOKS AND HABITS. Ed. John Erskine. 1921; Folcroft, Pa.: Folcroft, 1974.

THE BUDDHIST WRITINGS OF LAFCADIO HEARN. Introd. Kenneth Rexroth. Santa Barbara, Calif.: Ross-Erikson, 1977.

BUYING CHRISTMAS TOYS AND OTHER ESSAYS. Ed. Ichiro Nishizaki. Tokyo: Hokuseido Press, 1939.

CHILDREN OF THE LEVEE. Ed. O.W. Frost; Introd. John Ball. Lexington: Univ. of Kentucky Press, 1957.

CREOLE SKETCHES. Ed. Charles W. Hutson. Boston: Houghton Mifflin, 1926.

EDITORIALS. Ed. Charles W. Hutson. 1926; New York: Beekman, 1974.

> This collects articles which Hearn wrote for New Orleans news-papers, 1878-87.

ENGLISH ROMANTIC POETS. Folcroft, Pa.: Folcroft, 1973.

ESSAYS IN EUROPEAN AND ORIENTAL LITERATURE. Ed. Albert Mordell. 1923; Darby, Pa.: Arden, 1977.

ESSAYS ON AMERICAN LITERATURE. Ed. Sanki Ichikawa. Tokyo: Hokuseido Press, 1929.

A HISTORY OF ENGLISH LITERATURE. 2 vols. Tokyo: Hokuseido Press, 1927.

INTERPRETATIONS OF LITERATURE. Ed. John Erskine. 2 vols. 1915; Port Washington, N.Y.: Kennikat, 1965.

LAFCADIO HEARN: EDITORIALS FROM THE KOBE CHRONICLE. Tokyo: Hokuseido Press, 1960.

LAFCADIO HEARN'S AMERICAN ARTICLES. Ed. Ichiro Nishizaki. Tokyo: Hokuseido Press, 1939.

LAFCADIO HEARN'S LECTURES ON TENNYSON. Ed. Sigestsugu Kishi. Tokyo: Hokuseido Press, 1941.

LEAVES FROM THE DIARY OF AN IMPRESSIONIST. Introd. Ferris Greenslet. Boston: Houghton Mifflin, 1911.

LECTURES ON PROSODY. Tokyo: Hokuseido Press, 1929.

LECTURES ON SHAKESPEARE. Ed. Iwao Inagaki. Tokyo: Hokuseido Press, 1931.

LIFE AND LITERATURE. Ed. John Erskine. New York: Dodd, Mead, 1917.

LITERARY ESSAYS. Ed. Ichiro Nishizaki. Tokyo: Hokuseido Press, 1939.

THE NEW RADIANCE AND OTHER SCIENTIFIC SKETCHES. Ed. Ichiro Nishizaki. Tokyo: Hokuseido Press, 1939.

OCCIDENTAL GLEANINGS. 2 vols. Ed. Albert Mordell. New York: Dodd, Mead, 1925.

ON LITERATURE. Ed. T. Ochiai. Tokyo: Hokuseido Press, 1922.

ON POETS. Ed. Ryuji Tanabe et al. Tokyo: Hokuseido Press, 1934.

ORIENTAL ARTICLES. Ed. Ichiro Nishizaki. Tokyo: Hokuseido Press, 1939.

PRE-RAPHAELITE AND OTHER POETS. Ed. John Erskine. New York: Dodd, Mead, 1922.

THE SELECTED WRITINGS OF LAFCADIO HEARN. Ed. Henry Goodman; Introd. Malcolm Cowley. New York: Citadel, 1949.

> Cowley's important introduction gives a sympathetic and well-informed portrait of the writer and the man.

SKETCHES OF NEW ORLEANS. Franklin, N.H.: Hillside Press, 1964.

SOME STRANGE ENGLISH LITERARY FIGURES. . . . 1916; Freeport, N.Y.: Books for Libraries, 1965.

TALKS TO WRITERS. Ed. John Erskine. New York: Dodd Mead, 1920.

TWO YEARS IN THE FRENCH WEST INDIES. Upper Saddle River, N.J.: Literature House, 1970.

VICTORIAN PHILOSOPHY. Ed. Ryuji Tanabe. Tokyo: Hokuseido Press, 1930.

THE WRITINGS OF LAFCADIO HEARN. 16 vols. Boston: Houghton Mifflin, 1922.

BIBLIOGRAPHY

DESCRIPTIVE CATALOGUE OF THE HEARNIANA IN THE HEARN LIBRARY OF THE TOYAMA UNIVERSITY. Toyama, Japan: Toyama Univ., 1959.

LETTERS/LAFCADIO HEARN. New York: AMS Press, 1975.

> This gives a descriptive listing and selection of the letters at Tenri University, Japan.

MANUSCRIPTS/LAFCADIO HEARN. Tokyo: Tenri Central Library, Yushodo, 1974.

Perkins, P.D., and Ione Perkins. LAFCADIO HEARN: A BIBLIOGRAPHY OF HIS WRITINGS. 1934; New York: Burt Franklin, 1968.

An extensive listing of Hearn's writings is in Blanck's BIBLIOGRAPHY OF AMERICAN LITERATURE 4:75-106. Selected bibliographies, including secondary sources, are in the studies by Gould, Kunst, and Yu, below. Hearn is listed in the BIBLIOGRAPHY to the LITERARY HISTORY OF THE UNITED STATES, pp. 556, 931, 1220.

BIOGRAPHY AND CRITICISM

Bisland, Elizabeth. THE LIFE AND LETTERS OF LAFCADIO HEARN. 2 vols. Boston: Houghton Mifflin, 1906.

> A friend of the writer, Bisland provides basic biographical information. The two volumes are included in THE WRITINGS OF LAFCADIO HEARN, above.

Frost, Orcutt W. YOUNG HEARN. Tokyo: Hokuseido Press, 1958.

> This is a carefully researched account of the years before Hearn went to Japan.

Gould, George M. CONCERNING LAFCADIO HEARN. Philadelphia: George W. Jacobs, 1908.

> Gould's evaluation of Hearn's work is rigid and unsympathetic; at the time it greatly damaged Hearn's reputation in the United States.

Huneker, James. IVORY, APES AND PEACOCKS. New York: Scribner's, 1915.

> Huneker was Hearn's contemporary and a fellow journalist.

Kennard, Nina H. LAFCADIO HEARN. 1912; Port Washington, N.Y.: Kennikat, 1967.

> This provides basic biographical information and includes a few letters from Hearn to his half-sister.

Kirkwood, Kenneth P. UNFAMILIAR LAFCADIO HEARN. Tokyo: Hokuseido Press, 1936.

> The author spends a considerable portion of his study examining some of Hearn's eccentricities, such as his fascination with insects.

Koizumi, Kazuo. FATHER AND I. Boston: Houghton Mifflin, 1935.

> These warm reminiscences by Hearn's oldest son provide some vivid glimpses of the author as a family man.

Kunst, Arthur E. LAFCADIO HEARN. New York: Twayne, 1969.

> In his brief study Kunst provides an excellent analysis and evaluation of Hearn as a creative writer and emphasizes the importance of his studies of nineteenth-century French writers.

Lewis, Oscar. HEARN AND HIS BIOGRAPHERS. San Francisco: Westgate, 1930.

> This provides a much-needed perspective on the many, often biased, accounts of Hearn's unusual life.

McWilliams, Vera. LAFCADIO HEARN. Boston: Houghton Mifflin, 1946.

> In a reliable study, McWilliams draws upon Hearn's own writings and periodical accounts as well as the reminiscences by his son and wife, which had helped to revive interest in his work.

Miner, Earl. THE JAPANESE TRADITION IN BRITISH AND AMERICAN LITERA-TURE. Princeton: Princeton Univ. Press, 1958.

> This excellent general study points out the importance of Hearn's influence and reputation in Japan.

Mordell, Albert, ed. DISCOVERIES: ESSAYS ON LAFCADIO HEARN. Tokyo: Orient/West, 1964.

> A collection of scholarly essays by one of the leading Hearn schol-ars, this provides an overview of Hearn's reputation and accomplish-ments and includes information about some unpublished pieces.

Robert, Marcel. LAFCADIO HEARN. 2 vols. Tokyo: Hokuseido Press, 1950-51.

> Robert studies the relationship between Hearn's life and writings and analyzes the works written before 1897.

Stevenson, Elizabeth. LAFCADIO HEARN. New York: Macmillan, 1961.

> Stevenson's thoroughly documented biography is the best to date.

Temple, Jean. BLUE GHOST: A STUDY OF LAFCADIO HEARN. New York: J. Cape and H. Smith, 1931.

Thomas, Edward. LAFCADIO HEARN. Boston: Houghton Mifflin, 1912.

Tinker, Edward L. LAFCADIO HEARN'S AMERICAN DAYS. 1924; Rev. ed. New York: Dodd, Mead, 1925.

> Tinker provides important biographical information, gives entertain-ing anecdotal accounts, and includes some uncollected writings.

Yu, Beongcheon. AN APE OF GODS; THE ART AND THOUGHT OF LAFCA-DIO HEARN. Detroit: Wayne State Univ. Press, 1964.

> The first complete study of Hearn's philosophy and literary criticism, this approaches Hearn's writings as "philosophical voyages" of self-

discovery. The author argues eloquently and persuasively for Hearn's sensitivity and artistry and for his contribution not only to American but also to world literature.

RELATED GENERAL STUDIES

Hubbell, Jay B. THE SOUTH IN AMERICAN LITERATURE. (p. 24)
Pattee, Fred L. A HISTORY OF AMERICAN LITERATURE SINCE 1870. (p. 29)

OLIVER WENDELL HOLMES (1809-94)

Holmes's prose was marked by warm wit, perceptiveness, and wide reading; his style was based on the best talk to be heard. In his "Breakfast Table" series, he combined the techniques of prose fiction, drama, and essay, interspersed with poetry, becoming a master of a form well suited to his talents and ideas. Holmes created The Autocrat for the first number of the ATLANTIC MONTHLY in 1857, and these and others of his pieces helped set the tone for the magazine for many years. Holmes had a rare ability to systematize and articulate scientific knowledge; many of his medical essays remain classics in the literature. In his essays and lectures, he attacked bigotry in medicine, theology, and society with intelligent ferocity and determination. His lively discussions of human problems and explorations of ideas in his prose works remain relevant and readable today.

PRINCIPAL NONFICTION PROSE WORKS

BOYLSTON PRIZE DISSERTATIONS FOR THE YEARS 1836 AND 1837. 1838.
HOMEOPATHY AND ITS KINDRED DELUSIONS. 1842.
THE CONTAGIOUSNESS OF PUERPERAL FEVER. 1843.
THE AUTOCRAT OF THE BREAKFAST-TABLE. 1858. Rev. 1883.
THE PROFESSOR AT THE BREAKFAST-TABLE. 1860.
CURRENTS AND COUNTER-CURRENTS IN MEDICAL SCIENCE, WITH OTHER
     ADDRESSES AND ESSAYS. 1861.
BORDER LINES OF KNOWLEDGE IN SOME PROVINCES OF MEDICAL SCIENCE.
     1862.
SOUNDINGS FROM THE ATLANTIC. 1864.
MECHANISM IN THOUGHT AND MORALS . . . . 1871.
THE POET AT THE BREAKFAST-TABLE. 1872. Rev. 1883.
JOHN LOTHROP MOTLEY, A MEMOIR. 1879.
MEDICAL ESSAYS, 1842-1882. 1883.
PAGES FROM AN OLD VOLUME OF LIFE: A COLLECTION OF ESSAYS,
     1857-1881. 1883.
RALPH WALDO EMERSON. 1885.
OUR HUNDRED DAYS IN EUROPE. 1887.
MY HUNT AFTER THE CAPTAIN AND OTHER PAPERS. 1888.
HENRY JACOB BIGLOW. 1891.

OVER THE TEACUPS. 1891.
THE WRITINGS OF OLIVER WENDELL HOLMES. Riverside Ed. 13 vols.
   1891.

LETTERS AND JOURNALS

To date there is no separate collection of Holmes's letters. Letters are included
in John T. Morse, LIFE AND LETTERS, Mark A. De Wolfe Howe, HOLMES OF
THE BREAKFAST-TABLE, and Eleanor M. Tilton, AMIABLE AUTOCRAT, below.

LATER EDITIONS, SELECTIONS, AND REPRINTS

THE AUTOCRAT OF THE BREAKFAST-TABLE. Darby, Pa.: Arden, 1977.

THE AUTOCRAT'S MISCELLANIES. Ed. Albert Mordell. New York: Twayne,
1959.

DR. HOLMES' BOSTON. Ed. Caroline Ticknor. Boston: Houghton, Mifflin,
1915.

   This includes selected passages from the works fitted together in
   chronological order.

JOHN LOTHROP MOTLEY: A MEMOIR. Darby, Pa.: Arden, 1977.

MEDICAL ESSAYS. Darby, Pa.: Arden, 1977.

OLIVER WENDELL HOLMES: REPRESENTATIVE SELECTIONS. Ed. S.I. Haya-
kawa and Howard Mumford Jones. 1939; New York: AMS Press, 1976.

OUR HUNDRED DAYS IN EUROPE. New York: Arno, 1971.

OVER THE TEACUPS. 1970; Darby, Pa.: Arden, 1977.

THE POET AT THE BREAKFAST-TABLE. 1968; Norwood, Pa.: Norwood Editions,
1978.

THE PROFESSOR AT THE BREAKFAST TABLE. 1968; Darby, Pa.: Arden, 1977.

RALPH WALDO EMERSON. 1967; Philadelphia: R. West, 1973.

THE WRITINGS OF OLIVER WENDELL HOLMES. 15 vols. 1892; Grosse Pointe
Mich.: Scholarly Press, 1972.

This is a reprint of the Standard Library Edition of 1892, which includes Morse's LIFE AND LETTERS.

BIBLIOGRAPHY

Currier, Thomas F., and Eleanor M. Tilton. A BIBLIOGRAPHY OF OLIVER WENDELL HOLMES. New York: New York Univ. Press, 1953.

This is a definitive descriptive bibliography of editions, manuscripts, lectures, and other primary sources; it also includes selected secondary sources.

Ives, George B. A BIBLIOGRAPHY OF OLIVER WENDELL HOLMES. Boston: Houghton, Mifflin, 1907.

Ives includes a chronological checklist of Holmes's contributions to the ATLANTIC.

Menikoff, Barry. "Oliver Wendell Holmes." In FIFTEEN AMERICAN AUTHORS BEFORE 1900. Ed. Robert A. Rees and Earl N. Harbert. Madison: Univ. of Wisconsin Press, 1971, pp. 207-28.

This bibliographical essay presents an evaluation of biography and criticism.

Rutman, Anita, and Lucy Clark, eds. THE BARRETT LIBRARY: OLIVER WENDELL HOLMES: A CHECKLIST OF PRINTED AND MANUSCRIPT WORKS OF OLIVER WENDELL HOLMES IN THE LIBRARY OF THE UNIVERSITY OF VIRGINIA. Charlottesville: Univ. of Virginia Press, 1960.

A listing of Holmes's works is in Blanck's BIBLIOGRAPHY OF AMERICAN LITERATURE 4:233-340. Holmes is listed in the BIBLIOGRAPHY to the LITERARY HISTORY OF THE UNITED STATES, pp. 564, 933, 1225.

BIOGRAPHY AND CRITICISM

Crothers, Samuel. OLIVER WENDELL HOLMES: THE AUTOCRAT AND HIS FELLOW-BOARDERS. 1909; Freeport, N.Y.: Books for Libraries, 1970.

Highly favorable to Holmes, this is a readable account which points out Holmes's skill in analyzing human behavior.

Howe, Mark A. De Wolfe. HOLMES OF THE BREAKFAST-TABLE. 1939; Staten Island, N.Y.: Phaeton, 1972.

The author draws a pleasant picture of Holmes's professional and social relationships, using letters which Holmes wrote to James and Annie Fields.

Morse, John T., Jr. LIFE AND LETTERS OF OLIVER WENDELL HOLMES.
2 vols. Boston: Houghton Mifflin, 1896.

> Morse, who was Mrs. Holmes's nephew, had access to material
> which has since disappeared but was limited by a lack of knowl-
> edge of other material. A number of letters are reprinted with
> omissions and corrections not noted; however, the study provides
> a reliable chronology of Holmes's career.

Small, Miriam R. OLIVER WENDELL HOLMES. New York: Twayne, 1962.

> The author emphasizes Holmes's importance both as a physician and
> "medical scholar" and as a literary figure, pointing out ways in
> which Holmes was at odds with his own age.

Tilton, Eleanor M. AMIABLE AUTOCRAT: A BIOGRAPHY OF DR. OLIVER
WENDELL HOLMES. New York: Schuman, 1947.

> This definitive biography places Holmes in appropriate social and
> cultural perspective and perceptively examines his literary and
> scientific work. Holmes's subjects for his lecture tours are de-
> tailed in the study.

RELATED GENERAL STUDIES

Brooks, Van Wyck. THE FLOWERING OF NEW ENGLAND. (p. 17)
Curtis, George W. LITERARY AND SOCIAL ESSAYS. (p. 47)
Fields, Annie. AUTHORS AND FRIENDS. (p. 71)
Higginson, Thomas W. CONTEMPORARIES. (p. 82)
_____. OLD CAMBRIDGE. (p. 82)
Howells, William Dean. LITERARY FRIENDS AND ACQUAINTANCE. (pp. 350
    and 352, under Howells)
Jones, Howard M. HISTORY AND THE CONTEMPORARY. (p. 24)
Macy, John, ed. AMERICAN WRITERS ON AMERICAN LITERATURE. (p. 26)
Pritchard, John P. RETURN TO THE FOUNTAINS. (p. 66)
Rubin, Louis D. THE COMIC IMAGINATION IN AMERICAN LITERATURE.
    (p. 98)

WILLIAM DEAN HOWELLS (1837-1920)

In 1890, Howells was judged (above both Twain and Henry James) as America's foremost man of letters. As an influential critic and a nationally known editor, he encouraged and affected many writers whose reputation eventually exceeded his. The clarity and conviction of his critical position, expressed in such places as "The Editor's Study" in HARPER'S magazine, made it a rallying point for the new realism. Howells advocated a democratic realism in which ordinary people going about everyday tasks were the real heroes and heroines, a realism which, without being dogmatic, implied choice and a sense of values. Although Howells will probably remain best known as a novelist, his travel books are distinguished for their vivid impressions and full sense of time and place; his autobiographical volumes are still fresh and powerful; his reviews of continental writers considerably widened literary horizons in America; and his criticism stated significant principles for those writers who were active around the turn of the century.

PRINCIPAL PROSE WORKS

LIVES AND SPEECHES OF ABRAHAM LINCOLN AND HANNIBAL HAMLIN.
     1860.
VENETIAN LIFE. 1866.
ITALIAN JOURNEYS. 1867.
NIAGARA REVISITED. 1884.
THREE VILLAGES. 1884.
TUSCAN CITIES. 1886.
MODERN ITALIAN POETS: ESSAYS AND VERSIONS. 1887.
A BOY'S TOWN DESCRIBED FOR "HARPER'S" YOUNG PEOPLE. 1890.
CRITICISM AND FICTION. 1891.
A LITTLE SWISS SOJOURN. 1892.
MY YEAR IN A LOG CABIN. 1893.
MY LITERARY PASSIONS. 1895.
IMPRESSIONS AND EXPERIENCES. 1896.
LITERARY FRIENDS AND ACQUAINTANCE: A PERSONAL RETROSPECT OF
     AMERICAN AUTHORSHIP. 1900.
THE WRITINGS OF WILLIAM DEAN HOWELLS. Library Edition. 6 vols. 1910-11.
     This set includes: MY LITERARY PASSIONS, CRITICISM AND FICTION,

LITERATURE AND LIFE, LONDON FILMS with CERTAIN DELIGHTFUL
ENGLISH TOWNS, LITERARY FRIENDS AND ACQUAINTANCE, and MY
MARK TWAIN with A HAZARD OF NEW FORTUNES.
HEROINES OF FICTION. 2 vols. 1901.
LITERATURE AND LIFE: STUDIES. 1902.
LONDON FILMS. 1905.
CERTAIN DELIGHTFUL ENGLISH TOWNS WITH GLIMPSES OF THE PLEASANT
COUNTRY BETWEEN. 1906.
ROMAN HOLIDAYS AND OTHERS. 1908.
SEVEN ENGLISH CITIES. 1909.
IMAGINARY INTERVIEWS. 1910.
MY MARK TWAIN: REMINISCENCES AND CRITICISMS. 1910.
FAMILIAR SPANISH TRAVELS. 1913.
NEW LEAF MILLS, A CHRONICLE. 1913.
THE SEEN AND UNSEEN AT STRATFORD-ON-AVON: A FANTASY. 1914.
YEARS OF MY YOUTH. 1916.

LETTERS AND JOURNALS

JOHN HAY-HOWELLS LETTERS: THE CORRESPONDENCE OF JOHN HAY
AND WILLIAM DEAN HOWELLS, 1861-1905. Ed. George Monteiro and Brenda
Murphy. Boston: Twayne, 1980.

> This volume includes forty-two letters by Howells and seventy-one
> by Hay, with full annotations.

LIFE IN LETTERS OF WILLIAM DEAN HOWELLS. Ed. Mildred Howells. 2
vols. 1928; New York: Russell and Russell, 1968.

MARK TWAIN-HOWELLS LETTERS: THE CORRESPONDENCE OF SAMUEL LANG-
HORNE CLEMENS AND WILLIAM DEAN HOWELS, 1872-1910. 2 vols. Ed.
Henry Nash Smith and William M. Gibson, with Frederick Anderson. Cambridge,
Mass.: Harvard Univ. Press, 1960. Issued in one vol. as SELECTED MARK
TWAIN-HOWELLS LETTERS, 1872-1910. Ed. Frederick Anderson et al. Cam-
bridge, Mass.: Harvard Univ. Press, 1967.

SELECTED LETTERS OF WILLIAM DEAN HOWELLS. Ed. George Arms et al.
6 vols. projected. Boston: Twayne, 1979-- .

> Vol. 1, 1852-72, and vol. 2, 1873-81, were published in 1979;
> vol. 3, was published in 1980.

LATER EDITIONS, SELECTIONS, AND REPRINTS

A BOY'S TOWN. Folcroft, Pa.: Folcroft, 1973.

CRITICISM AND FICTION AND OTHER ESSAYS. Ed. with Introd. and Notes Clara M. Kirk and Rudolf Kirk. 1959; Westport, Conn.: Greenwood Press, 1977.

DISCOVERY OF A GENIUS: WILLIAM DEAN HOWELLS AND HENRY JAMES. Compiled and ed. by Albert Mordell. New York: Twayne, 1961.

> The introductory essay discusses the friendship of Howells and James; the volume reprints Howells' articles and reviews, in which he both defends and interprets James's work.

EUROPEAN AND AMERICAN MASTERS. Ed. with Introd. Clara M. Kirk and Rudolf Kirk. New York: Collier, 1963.

IMAGINARY INTERVIEWS. Folcroft, Pa.: Folcroft, 1973.

IMPRESSIONS AND EXPERIENCES. New York: Arno, 1972.

INTERVIEWS WITH WILLIAM DEAN HOWELLS. Ed. Ulrich Halfmann. Arlington, Tex.: American Literary Realism, 1973.

> A collection of all known interviews, this is a reprint of a special issue of the journal AMERICAN LITERARY REALISM, vol. 6, 1973.

LIFE OF ABRAHAM LINCOLN. Bloomington: Indiana Univ. Press, 1960.

> This reprint includes Abraham Lincoln's notes and corrections to the campaign biography.

LITERARY FRIENDS AND ACQUAINTANCE. Ed. David F. Hiatt and Edwin H. Cady. Bloomington: Indiana Univ. Press, 1968.

> This and the volume above are part of the CEAA[CSE]-approved SELECTED EDITION, below.

MODERN ITALIAN POETS. New York: Russell and Russell, 1973.

MY LITERARY PASSIONS. St. Clair Shores, Mich.: Scholarly Press, 1970.

MY MARK TWAIN. Ed. with Introd. Marilyn A. Baldwin. Baton Rouge: Louisiana State Univ. Press, 1967.

MY MARK TWAIN. 1910; New York: Haskell, 1977.

PREFACES TO CONTEMPORARIES. Ed. George Arms et al. 1957; Gainesville, Fla.: Scholar's Facsimiles and Reprints, 1978.

This collection of prefaces by Howells has an introduction and bibliographical notes by the editors.

A SELECTED EDITION OF WILLIAM DEAN HOWELLS. General ed. Edwin H. Cady. Bloomington: Indiana University Press, 1968-- . 41 vols. projected.

The volumes of this CEAA[CSE]-approved project will be the definitive texts.

SELECTED WRITINGS. Ed. and Introd. Henry Steele Commager. New York: Random House, 1950.

The selections include A BOY'S TOWN and MY MARK TWAIN.

WILLIAM DEAN HOWELLS AS CRITIC. Ed. Edwin H. Cady. London: Routledge and Kegan Paul, 1973.

This presents fifty-four of Howells' critical essays and has been a useful source of Howells' critical ideas, although it will probably be superseded by the volumes of criticism projected for the SELECTED EDITION, above.

WILLIAM DEAN HOWELLS: REPRESENTATIVE SELECTIONS. Rev. ed. Clara M. Kirk and Rudolf Kirk. 1950; New York: Hill and Wang, 1961.

The introduction to this volume is an excellent summary of Howells' achievements.

YEARS OF MY YOUTH AND THREE ESSAYS. Introd. and Notes David J. Nordloh. Bloomington: Indiana Univ. Press, 1976.

The text is established by David I. Nordloh.

BIBLIOGRAPHY

Beebe, Maurice. "Criticism of William Dean Howells: A Selected Checklist." MODERN FICTION STUDIES 16 (1970): 395-419.

This is a comprehensive but unannotated checklist.

Brenni, Vito J., ed. WILLIAM DEAN HOWELLS: A BIBLIOGRAPHY. Metuchen, N.J.: Scarecrow, 1973.

This is valuable for locating uncollected articles and reviews, although the entries are unannotated. A checklist includes columns written by Howells for HARPER'S MONTHLY, HARPER'S WEEKLY, and ATLANTIC MONTHLY.

Eichelberger, Clayton L. PUBLISHED COMMENT ON WILLIAM DEAN HOWELLS THROUGH 1920: A RESEARCH BIBLIOGRAPHY. Boston: G.K. Hall, 1976.

> This annotated listing demonstrates the kinds of critical commentary given to Howells during his lifetime.

Fortenberry, George. "William Dean Howells." In FIFTEEN AMERICAN AUTHORS BEFORE 1900. Ed. Robert A. Rees and Earl N. Harbert. Madison: Univ. of Wisconsin Press, 1971, pp. 229–44.

> This bibliographical essay discusses books and articles written about Howells' life and works.

Gibson, William M., and George Arms. A BIBLIOGRAPHY OF WILLIAM DEAN HOWELLS. 1948; Rev. ed., with Note by the Compiler, 1971. Darby, Pa.: Arden, 1980.

> This includes a checklist and collation of works by Howells, including periodical pieces, and of works by other writers for which Howells wrote introductions or prefaces. The bibliography in the revised edition of 1971 is not updated from 1948.

Woodress, James, and Stanley P. Anderson. A BIBLIOGRAPHY OF WRITINGS ABOUT WILLIAM DEAN HOWELLS. Arlington, Tex.: American Literary Realism, 1969.

> Published separately from a special issue of AMERICAN LITERARY REALISM, this covers the years 1860–1969.

An extensive listing of works by Howells is in Blanck's BIBLIOGRAPHY OF AMERICAN LITERATURE 4:384–448. George Arms is preparing a bibliography for the definitive SELECTED EDITION OF HOWELLS, above.

Howells is listed in the BIBLIOGRAPHY to the LITERARY HISTORY OF THE UNITED STATES, pp. 571, 934, 1225.

BIOGRAPHY AND CRITICISM

The works below deal primarily with Howells' criticism and travel literature or Howells in relationship to his contemporaries and society. Works dealing mainly with the fiction are excluded.

Brooks, Van Wyck. HOWELLS: HIS LIFE AND WORLD. New York: E.P. Dutton, 1959.

> The author briefly discusses the influence of Howells' criticism and essays, but focuses upon his relations with his contemporaries and his social and practical interests.

Cady, Edwin [H]. THE REALIST AT WAR: THE MATURE YEARS, 1885-1920. Syracuse, N.Y.: Syracuse Univ. Press, 1958.

> In this second of two biographical volumes, the author discusses Howells' "war" as a result of his advocacy of realism and his activities in defending realism as editor, critic, and author. This and the companion volume below are among the best biographies of Howells.

_____. THE ROAD TO REALISM: THE EARLY YEARS, 1837-1885. Syracuse, N.Y.: Syracuse Univ. Press, 1956.

> This includes Howells' years as a correspondent in Venice and as editor of the ATLANTIC MONTHLY.

Cady, Edwin H., and David Frazier, eds. THE WAR OF THE CRITICS OVER WILLIAM DEAN HOWELLS. Evanston, Ill.: Row, Peterson, 1962.

> This collection of essays illustrates the conflicting views of Howells as a realist and the rise and fall of Howells' reputation.

Carter, Everett. HOWELLS AND THE AGE OF REALISM. Philadelphia: Lippincott, 1954.

> The author uses Howells as a focus for the study of the development of American literary realism, including the attack on sentimental romanticism and the development of naturalism from realism.

Dean, James L. HOWELLS' TRAVELS TOWARD ART. Albuquerque: Univ. of New Mexico Press, 1970.

> This study explores Howells' development as a travel writer and analyzes his nine travel books. The author considers matters of style as well as Howells' views on European art, European-American relationships, and past cultures and traditions. Dean argues that Howells was a master of the genre of travel literature.

Eble, Kenneth, ed. HOWELLS: A CENTURY OF CRITICISM. Dallas, Tex.: Southern Methodist Univ. Press, 1962.

> The critical essays collected here document the course of Howells' growth as a writer and his place in American literature from 1890 to the 1950s.

Eschholz, Paul A., ed. CRITICS ON WILLIAM DEAN HOWELLS. Coral Gables, Fla.: Univ. of Miami Press, 1975.

> This collection of brief pieces and excerpts gives an excellent survey of Howells' reputation from 1860 to the 1970s and introduces Howells' major themes and artistic intentions.

William Dean Howells

Firkins, Oscar W. WILLIAM DEAN HOWELLS, A STUDY. Cambridge, Mass.: Harvard Univ. Press, 1924.

> This early biography considers Howells' contributions as travel writer and critic as well as novelist.

Gibson, William M. WILLIAM DEAN HOWELLS. Minneapolis: Univ. of Minnesota Press, 1967.

> In this brief study, Gibson argues that a new and more comprehensive view of Howells' critical theory is needed, particularly of some of the lectures and essays which are statements of Howells' critical theory, more important than CRITICISM AND FICTION.

Hough, Robert L. THE QUIET REBEL: WILLIAM DEAN HOWELLS AS SOCIAL COMMENTATOR. Lincoln: Univ. of Nebraska Press, 1959.

> Treating Howells less as a novelist than as a social reformer, the author shows Howells' impact on liberal thinking in this country.

Kirk, Clara M. WILLIAM DEAN HOWELLS AND ART IN HIS TIME. New Brunswick, N.J.: Rutgers Univ. Press, 1965.

> The study points out that Howells was part of the literary, artistic, and social movements of his time and shows the influence of painting and sculpture on Howells' theory of realism.

_____. WILLIAM DEAN HOWELLS, TRAVELER FROM ALTRURIA. New Brunswick, N.J.: Rutgers Univ. Press, 1962.

> Concerned with Howells' social thought, this discusses Howells' views and travels from 1889 to 1894, treating particularly the effect of Christian socialism on his thought and the experiences which affected TRAVELER FROM ALTRURIA.

Kirk, Clara M., and Rudolf Kirk. WILLIAM DEAN HOWELLS. New York: Twayne, 1962.

> This brief study discusses Howells as scholar, critic, and artist, dealing with his literary career and his life.

Lynn, Kenneth S. WILLIAM DEAN HOWELLS: AN AMERICAN LIFE. New York: Harcourt Brace Jovanovich, 1971.

> This is a thoroughly researched, sensitively written biography. Although the author's discussion focuses upon the fiction, he provides information on Howells' realism in relation to the midwestern culture in which Howells grew up and gives a good understanding of the influences upon Howells' early years.

McMahon, Helen. CRITICISM OF FICTION, A STUDY OF TRENDS IN THE ATLANTIC MONTHLY, 1857-1898. New York: Bookman, 1952.

This study of the journal includes reviews about and by Howells.

McMurray, William. THE LITERARY REALISM OF WILLIAM DEAN HOWELLS. Carbondale: Southern Illinois Univ. Press, 1967.

Although much of this work deals with Howells' fiction, it also shows the relationship between Howells' realism and the pragmatism of William James.

Wagenknecht, Edward. WILLIAM DEAN HOWELLS: THE FRIENDLY EYE. New York: Oxford Univ. Press, 1969.

In this sympathetic study which aims to get at Howells' "character and personality," the author describes Howells' reading interests and attempts to explicate his critical terminology.

Woodress, James. HOWELLS AND ITALY. Durham, N.C.: Duke Univ. Press, 1952.

The author discusses Howells' tastes in literature and his travels and shows the influence of Italy on his later career. The study provides a useful and perceptive approach to both the travel writing and the fiction.

RELATED GENERAL STUDIES

Cawelti, John. APOSTLES OF THE SELF-MADE MAN. (p. 19)
Clark, Harry H. TRANSITIONS IN AMERICAN LITERARY HISTORY. (p. 19)
Foerster, Norman, ed. THE REINTERPRETATION OF AMERICAN LITERATURE. (p. 21)
Macy, John, ed. AMERICAN WRITERS ON AMERICAN LITERATURE. (p. 26)
Mott, Frank L. A HISTORY OF AMERICAN MAGAZINES. (p. 61)
Paine, Albert B., ed. MARK TWAIN'S AUTOBIOGRAPHY. (p. 279, under Clemens)
Pizer, Donald. REALISM AND NATURALISM IN NINETEENTH CENTURY AMERICAN LITERATURE. (p. 30)
Pritchard, John P. CRITICISM IN AMERICA. (p. 65)
_____. RETURN TO THE FOUNTAINS. (p. 66)
Smith, Bernard. FORCES IN AMERICAN CRITICISM. (p. 66)
Stovall, Floyd. AMERICAN IDEALISM. (p. 32)
_____, ed. THE DEVELOPMENT OF AMERICAN LITERARY CRITICISM. (p. 68)

WASHINGTON IRVING (1783-1859)

Any listing of Irving's "nonfiction" prose is necessarily arbitrary because so many of his works do not fit into clear categories. A HISTORY OF NEW YORK, THE SKETCH BOOKS, and THE CONQUEST OF GRANADA all contain examples of pieces which could be called well-wrought essays; but these collections are generally categorized as fiction, while THE LIFE OF COLUMBUS, equally romantic in many passages, is considered history. Irving's best nonfiction prose is a skillful blending of history, authentic description, and romance. One of the first in America to write good history and biography as literary entertainment, Irving was also a pioneer in establishing a literary form for accounts of Western travel. Irving did not always acknowledge his sources; but he was a conscientious historian and biographer, his lucid, smoothly flowing style giving polish even to his late, more perfunctory, studies.

PRINCIPAL PROSE WORKS

LIFE OF THOMAS CAMPBELL. 1810.
BIOGRAPHY OF JAMES LAWRENCE. 1813.
A HISTORY OF THE LIFE AND VOYAGES OF CHRISTOPHER COLUMBUS. 1828.
VOYAGES AND DISCOVERIES OF THE COMPANIONS OF COLUMBUS. 1831.
THE CRAYON MISCELLANY. 3 vols. (A TOUR ON THE PRAIRIES, ABBOTS-FORD AND NEWSTEAD ABBEY and LEGENDS OF THE CONQUEST OF SPAIN.) 1835.
ASTORIA. 2 vols. 1836.
ADVENTURES OF CAPTAIN BONNEVILLE. 1837.
BIOGRAPHY AND POETICAL REMAINS OF THE LATE MARGARET M. DAVIDSON. 1841.
THE WORKS OF WASHINGTON IRVING. Author's rev. ed. 15 vols. 1848-51.
THE LIFE OF OLIVER GOLDSMITH. 1849.
A BOOK OF THE HUDSON. 1849.
MAHOMET AND HIS SUCCESSORS. 1850.
LIFE OF GEORGE WASHINGTON. 5 vols. 1855-59.

LETTERS AND JOURNALS

JOURNALS AND NOTEBOOKS. 5 vols. projected. Madison: University of Wisconsin Press; Boston: Twayne, 1969--.

> These volumes and the LETTERS, listed below, are being published as part of the definitive COMPLETE WORKS OF WASHINGTON IRVING, gen. ed. Henry Pochmann, sponsored by the CEAA (Center for Edition of American Authors, now Center for Scholarly Editions). The volumes which have appeared at the present time are: 1, ed. Nathalia Wright, 1969; 2, ed. Walter A. Reichart and Lillian Schlissel, 1980; and 3, ed. Walter A. Reichart, 1969.

JOURNAL, 1803. Ed. Stanley T. Williams. New York: Oxford Univ. Press, 1934.

JOURNAL OF WASHINGTON IRVING, 1823-1824. Ed. Stanley T. Williams. 1931; Hamden, Conn.: Shoe String, 1968.

THE JOURNALS OF WASHINGTON IRVING. 3 vols. Ed. W.P. Trent and G.S. Hellman. 1919; New York: Haskell, 1970.

LETTERS. 4 vols. projected. Boston: Twayne, 1978-- .

> The volumes of letters listed below will be largely superseded by this project, which is part of the definitive COMPLETE WORKS, below. Volumes 1 and 2, edited by Ralph M. Aderman et al., have appeared at the present time.

LETTERS FROM SUNNYSIDE AND SPAIN. New Haven, Conn.: Yale Univ. Press, 1928.

LETTERS OF WASHINGTON IRVING TO HENRY BREVOORT. Ed. G.S. Hellman. New York: G.P. Putnam's, 1918.

NOTES AND JOURNAL OF TRAVEL IN EUROPE 1804-1805. 3 vols. 1921; St. Clair Shores, Mich.: Scholarly Press, 1972.

NOTES WHILE PREPARING THE SKETCH BOOK . . . 1817. Ed. Stanley T. Williams. New Haven, Conn.: Yale Univ. Press, 1927.

TOUR IN SCOTLAND, 1817, AND OTHER MANUSCRIPT NOTES. Ed. Stanley T. Williams. New Haven, Conn.: Yale Univ. Press, 1927.

WASHINGTON IRVING AND THE STORROWS. Ed. Stanley T. Williams. Cambridge, Mass.: Harvard Univ. Press, 1933.

WASHINGTON IRVING'S DIARY: SPAIN, 1828-1829. Ed. Clara L. Penney. New York: Hispanic Society of America, 1926.

THE WESTERN JOURNALS OF WASHINGTON IRVING [1832-1833]. Ed. John F. McDermott. 1944; Philadelphia: American Philosophical Society, 1963.

LATER EDITIONS, SELECTIONS, AND REPRINTS

THE ADVENTURES OF CAPTAIN BONNEVILLE, U.S.A., IN THE ROCKY MOUNTAINS AND THE FAR WEST, DIGESTED FROM HIS JOURNAL BY WASHINGTON IRVING. Ed. with Introd. Edgeley W. Todd. Norman: Univ. of Oklahoma Press, 1961.

THE ADVENTURES OF CAPTAIN BONNEVILLE. Ed. Robert A. Rees and Alan Sandy. Boston: Twayne, 1977.

> This edition, vol. 6 of THE COMPLETE WORKS, below, contains new illustrations, maps, and explanatory notes.

ASTORIA: OR, ANECDOTES OF AN ENTERPRISE BEYOND THE ROCKY MOUN-TAINS. Ed. and Introd. Edgeley W. Todd. Norman: Univ. of Oklahoma Press, 1964.

ASTORIA; OR, ANECDOTES OF AN ENTERPRIZE BEYOND THE ROCKY MOUN-TAINS. Ed. Richard Dilworth Rust. Boston: Twayne, 1976.

> Vol. 15 of THE COMPLETE WORKS, below.

THE COMPLETE WORKS OF WASHINGTON IRVING. Gen. Ed. Henry A. Pochmann. 28 volumes projected. Boston: Twayne, 1969-- .

> This will be the definitive edition of Irving's works. Individual volumes which have appeared are cited by title, above and below.

THE LIFE AND VOYAGES OF CHRISTOPHER COLUMBUS. New York: AMS Press, 1973.

LIFE OF GEORGE WASHINGTON. Abridged Ed. by Jess Stein. Introd. Richard B. Morris. Tarrytown, N.Y.: Sleepy Hollow Restorations, 1975.

LIFE OF GEORGE WASHINGTON. 5 vols. Ed. Allen Guttman and James Sappenfield. Boston: Twayne, 1981.

MAHOMET AND HIS SUCCESSORS. Ed. Henry A. Pochmann and E.N. Felt-skog. Madison: Univ. of Wisconsin Press, 1970.

> Vol. 1 of THE COMPLETE WORKS, with historical note and textual commentary.

OLIVER GOLDSMITH: A BIOGRAPHY AND POETICAL REMAINS OF THE LATE MARGARET MILLER DAVIDSON. Ed. Elsie Lee West. Twayne, 1978.

SELECTED WRITINGS OF WASHINGTON IRVING. Ed. Saxe Commins. New York: Modern Library, 1945.

SPANISH PAPERS AND OTHER MISCELLANIES. 2 vols. Ed. Pierre M. Irving. New York: G.P. Putnam's, 1966.

A TOUR ON THE PRAIRIES. Ed. John F. McDermott. Norman: Univ. of Oklahoma Press, 1956.

VOYAGES AND DISCOVERIES OF THE COMPANIONS OF COLUMBUS. Ed. James Tuttleton. Boston: Twayne, forthcoming.

WASHINGTON IRVING: REPRESENTATIVE SELECTIONS. . . . Ed. with Introd. Henry A. Pochmann, 1934; St. Clair Shores, Mich.: Scholarly Press, 1971.

> Pochmann's introduction provides an excellent critical commentary on Irving's works.

WASHINGTON IRVING: THE WESTERN WORKS. Ed. Richard Cracroft. Boise, Idaho: Boise State Univ. Press, 1974.

WASHINGTON IRVING'S CONTRIBUTIONS TO "THE CORRECTOR." Ed. and Introd. Martin Roth. Minneapolis: Univ. of Minnesota Press, 1968.

THE WORKS OF WASHINGTON IRVING. Author's uniform rev. ed. 21 vols., 1860–61; New York: AMS Press, 1973.

> Long the standard edition, this is being superseded by THE COMPLETE WORKS, above.

BIBLIOGRAPHY

Langfield, William R., and Philip C. Blackburn, comps. WASHINGTON IRVING: A BIBLIOGRAPHY. New York: New York Public Library, 1933.

> This is an analytical and descriptive bibliography of first editions, intended primarily for the collector.

Pochmann, Henry A. "Washington Irving." In FIFTEEN AMERICAN AUTHORS BEFORE 1900. Ed. Robert A. Rees and Earl N. Harbert. Madison: Univ. of Wisconsin Press, 1971, pp. 245–62.

This fine bibliographical essay surveys and evaluates biography and criticism as well as editions, manuscripts, and other bibliographical items.

Springer, Haskell. WASHINGTON IRVING: A REFERENCE GUIDE. Boston: G.K. Hall, 1976.

This guide annotates scholarship, criticism, reviews, and miscellaneous commentary on Washington Irving and his works published between 1807 and 1974.

Williams, Stanley T., and Mary Allen Edge, comps. A BIBLIOGRAPHY OF THE WRITINGS OF WASHINGTON IRVING: A CHECK LIST. New York: Oxford Univ. Press, 1936.

This supplements the bibliography by Langfeld and Blackburn, listing all known printings of Irving's writings in all languages--appearing as complete individual titles, in collected editions, or as selections--as well as Irving's contributions to periodical and other publications, his letters, his journals, and secondary sources in Irving scholarship and criticism.

An extensive listing of Irving's writings is in Blanck's BIBLIOGRAPHY OF AMERICAN LITERATURE 5:1-96. A bibliographical volume edited by Edwin T. Bowden is planned for inclusion in THE COMPLETE WORKS, above.

Irving is listed in the BIBLIOGRAPHY to the LITERARY HISTORY OF THE UNITED STATES, pp. 578, 937, 1230.

BIOGRAPHY AND CRITICISM

Aderman, Ralph M. WASHINGTON IRVING RECONSIDERED. Hartford, Conn.: Transcendental Books, 1969.

This collects articles giving new viewpoints on Irving; nine are by editors of the volumes in THE COLLECTED WORKS, above.

Bowers, Claude G. THE SPANISH ADVENTURES OF WASHINGTON IRVING. Boston: Houghton Mifflin, 1940.

This is a popular but reliable biography about Irving's years in Spain.

Callow, James T. KINDRED SPIRITS: KNICKERBOCKER WRITERS AND AMERICAN ARTISTS, 1807-1855. Chapel Hill: Univ. of North Carolina Press, 1967.

Irving is an important figure in Callow's exhaustive discussion of the relationship between writers and painters in the nineteenth century.

Ellsworth, Henry Leavitt. WASHINGTON IRVING ON THE PRAIRIE: OR, A NARRATIVE OF A TOUR OF THE SOUTHWEST IN THE YEAR 1832. Ed. Stanley T. Williams and Barbara D. Simison. New York: American Book Co., 1937.

> This account by one of Irving's tour companions provides an interesting comparison to Irving's own TOUR ON THE PRAIRIES.

Hedges, William L. WASHINGTON IRVING: AN AMERICAN STUDY, 1802-1832. Baltimore, Md.: Johns Hopkins Press, 1965.

> Hedges reevaluates Irving's works by analyzing his use of various literary motifs; the study reveals Irving as a man of greater complexity of thought and response than most biographers and critics have indicated.

Irving, Pierre Munro. LIFE AND LETTERS OF WASHINGTON IRVING. 4 vols. New York: G.P. Putnam's, 1862-64.

> The authorized biography, this quotes liberally from Irving's letters and journals.

Kime, Wayne R. PIERRE M. IRVING AND WASHINGTON IRVING: A COLLABORATION IN LIFE AND LETTERS. Waterloo, Ont.: Wilfrid Laurier Univ. Press, 1977.

> Washington Irving's nephew played an important role in his life and in the establishment of his posthumous reputation. This study of the nephew and his biography of his uncle is well-researched and informative.

Leary, Lewis. WASHINGTON IRVING. Minneapolis: Univ. of Minnesota Press, 1963.

> This essay, first published in SIX CLASSIC AMERICAN WRITERS (1961), surveys Irving's career and praises his craftmanship and talent.

McClary, Ben H., ed. WASHINGTON IRVING AND THE HOUSE OF MURRAY. Knoxville: Univ. of Tennessee Press, 1969.

> McClary collects and comments upon letters between Irving and his principal English publisher.

Myers, Andrew B., ed. A CENTURY OF COMMENTARY ON THE WORKS OF WASHINGTON IRVING. Tarrytown, N.Y.: Sleepy Hollow Restorations, 1976.

> This collection of representative pieces, all postdating Irving's career and life, includes articles, reviews, speeches, and introductions to Irving's writings.

_____. WASHINGTON IRVING: A TRIBUTE. Tarrytown, N.Y.: Sleepy Hollow Restorations, 1972.

> Papers delivered at a symposium in 1970 are collected here.

Reichart, Walter A. WASHINGTON IRVING AND GERMANY. Ann Arbor: Univ. of Michigan Press, 1957.

> This discusses Irving's travels in Germany and German sources in his work as well as the influence of German romanticism on Irving's writings.

Spaulding, George E., ed. ON THE WESTERN TOUR WITH WASHINGTON IRVING: THE JOURNAL AND LETTERS OF COUNT DE POURTALES. Trans. by Seymour Feiler. Norman: Univ. of Oklahoma Press, 1968.

> De Pourtales' account provides an interesting contrast to Irving's TOUR and is a useful document of American travel.

Wagenknecht, Edward. WASHINGTON IRVING: MODERATION DISPLAYED. New York: Oxford Univ. Press, 1962.

> The author shows great sympathy for and understanding of Irving and his writings, painting a superb "portrait" of the man.

Williams, Stanley T. THE LIFE OF WASHINGTON IRVING. 2 vols. New York: Oxford Univ. Press, 1935.

> A thorough and definitive critical biography, this breaks new ground in the examination of origins and sources as well as evaluation of the works.

RELATED GENERAL STUDIES

Brooks, Van Wyck. THE WORLD OF WASHINGTON IRVING. (p. 17)
Herold, A.L. JAMES KIRK PAULDING, VERSATILE AMERICAN. (p. 432, under Paulding)
Macy, John, ed. AMERICAN WRITERS ON AMERICAN LITERATURE. (p. 26)
Rusk, Ralph L. THE LITERATURE OF THE MIDDLE WESTERN FRONTIER. (p. 130)
Spencer, Benjamin T. THE QUEST FOR NATIONALITY. (p. 67)

HENRY JAMES (1843-1916)

In addition to his fiction and plays, James published some 450 articles, principally literary criticism; travel pieces; introductions to various volumes by other authors; his own prefaces for the New York edition of his novels and tales; autobiographical writings; and letters. James's travel writings, especially THE AMERICAN SCENE, are among the best of the genre. Leon Edel credits James with giving to criticism "for the first time a valuable terminology for the discussion of the novel." Tightly written and clearly formulating James's principles of the novelist's art, the criticism emphasizes the importance of style and the integration of form and substance. James's notebooks also provide a rare glimpse of the creative process. The autobiographical volumes are considered by some critics to be among his best work. The style in James's nonfiction prose and criticism, despite its occasional mannerisms, holds up well. His contributions are both considerable and distinguished.

PRINCIPAL NONFICTION PROSE WORKS

TRANSATLANTIC SKETCHES. 1875.
FRENCH POETS AND NOVELISTS. 1878.
HAWTHORNE. 1879.
PORTRAITS OF PLACES. 1884.
A LITTLE TOUR IN FRANCE. 1885.
PARTIAL PORTRAITS. 1888.
ESSAYS IN LONDON AND ELSEWHERE. 1893.
PICTURE AND TEXT. 1893.
WILLIAM WETMORE STORY AND HIS FRIENDS. 2 vols. 1903.
ENGLISH HOURS. 1905.
THE QUESTION OF OUR SPEECH [AND] THE LESSON OF BALZAC. 1905.
THE AMERICAN SCENE. 1907.
VIEWS AND REVIEWS. 1908.
ITALIAN HOURS. 1909.
A SMALL BOY AND OTHERS. 1913.
NOTES OF A SON AND BROTHER. 1914.
NOTES ON NOVELISTS. 1914.

LETTERS AND JOURNALS

HENRY JAMES: AUTOBIOGRAPHY. Ed. F.W. Dupee. New York: Criterion, 1956.

> This includes James's three autobiographical books: A SMALL BOY AND OTHERS, NOTES OF A SON AND BROTHER, and the unfinished THE MIDDLE YEARS.

HENRY JAMES: LETTERS. Ed. with Introd. Leon Edel. Cambridge, Mass.: Belknap Press, Harvard Univ. Press, 1974-- .

> In addition to providing historical notes, Edel discusses the basis of his own selection of letters and the nature of the earlier selection by Percy Lubbock. Vol. 1, 1843-75, was published in 1974; vol. 2, 1875-83, in 1975, and vol. 3, 1883-95, in 1980.

HENRY JAMES AND H.G. WELLS: A RECORD OF THEIR FRIENDSHIP, THEIR DEBATE ON THE ART OF FICTION, AND THEIR QUARREL. Ed. with introd. Leon Edel and Gordon N. Ray. 1958; Westport, Conn.: Greenwood Press, 1979.

HENRY JAMES AND JOHN HAY: THE RECORD OF A FRIENDSHIP. Ed. George Monteiro. Providence, R.I.: Brown Univ. Press, 1965.

HENRY JAMES AND ROBERT LOUIS STEVENSON. Ed. Janet A. Smith. 1948; Westport, Conn.: Hyperion, 1979.

THE LETTERS OF HENRY JAMES. 2 vols. Ed. Percy Lubbock. 1920; New York: Octagon, 1970.

LETTERS OF HENRY JAMES TO A.C. BENSON AND AUGUSTE MONOD. 1930; New York: Haskell, 1969.

THE MIDDLE YEARS. London: Collins, 1917.

> This autobiographical volume was unfinished when James died.

THE NOTEBOOKS OF HENRY JAMES. Ed. and introd. F.O. Matthiessen and Kenneth B. Murdock. New York: Oxford Univ. Press, 1947.

THE SELECTED LETTERS OF HENRY JAMES. Ed. by Leon Edel. New York: Farrar, Straus, 1955.

THEATRE AND FRIENDSHIP. London: Cape, 1932.

> This collection consists of letters to Elizabeth Robins with a commentary by Robins.

LATER EDITIONS, SELECTIONS, AND REPRINTS

THE AMERICAN ESSAYS OF HENRY JAMES. Ed. Leon Edel. New York: Knopf, 1956.

THE AMERICAN SCENE. Introd. Irving Howe. New York: Horizon, 1967.

> This edition includes several photographs with captions taken from James's writing.

THE AMERICAN SCENE. Introd. and notes Leon Edel. Bloomington: Indiana Univ. Press, 1968.

> Edel's opinions about James's view of the American scene is in contrast to Howe's (see above). Edel sees the work as a protest, Howe as an attempt to get at "the essence of the American Experience."

THE ART OF FICTION, AND OTHER ESSAYS. Ed. with introd. Morris Roberts. New York: Oxford Univ. Press, 1948.

THE ART OF THE NOVEL, CRITICAL PREFACES BY HENRY JAMES. Ed. with introd. R.P. Blackmur. 1934; New York: Scirbner's, 1937.

> Blackmur's introduction to this collection is an excellent discussion of the prefaces.

THE ART OF TRAVEL: SCENES AND JOURNEYS IN AMERICA, ENGLAND, FRANCE AND ITALY FROM THE TRAVEL WRITINGS OF HENRY JAMES. Ed. Morton D. Zabel. 1958; Freeport, N.Y.: Books for Libraries, 1970.

FRENCH POETS AND NOVELISTS. Folcroft, Pa.: Folcroft, 1973.

FRENCH WRITERS AND AMERICAN WOMEN: ESSAYS. Ed. with introd. Peter Buitenhuis. Branford, Conn.: Compass, 1960.

THE FUTURE OF THE NOVEL. Ed. Leon Edel. New York: Knopf, 1956.

HAWTHORNE. Ithaca, N.Y.: Cornell Univ. Press, 1956.

THE HOUSE OF FICTION. Ed. Leon Edel. 1957; Westport, Conn.: Greenwood Press, 1973.

ITALIAN HOURS. Westport, Conn.: Greenwood Press, 1977.

LITERARY REVIEWS AND ESSAYS OF HENRY JAMES. Ed. Albert Mordell. 1957; New York: Grove, 1979.

> This collection includes more than sixty essays and reviews.

A LITTLE TOUR IN FRANCE. Folcroft, Pa.: Folcroft, 1973.

NOTES AND REVIEWS. Ed. Pierre La Rose. 1921; Freeport, N.Y.: Books for Libraries, 1968.

NOTES ON NOVELISTS. New York: Biblo and Tannen, 1969.

THE PAINTER'S EYE. Ed. John L. Sweeney. London: Hart-Davis, 1956.

PARISIAN SKETCHES: LETTERS TO THE NEW YORK TRIBUNE 1875-1876. Ed. by Leon Edel and Ilse Lind. 1957; Westport, Conn.: Greenwood Press, 1978.

PARTIAL PORTRAITS. Introd. Leon Edel. Ann Arbor: Univ. of Michigan Press, 1970.

PICTURES AND OTHER PASSAGES. Folcroft, Pa.: Folcroft, 1976.

PORTRAITS OF PLACES. 1883. New York: Lear, 1948.

> This reissue includes notes by George Alvin Finch on James as a traveler.

THE QUESTION OF SPEECH. New York: Haskell, 1972.

THE SCENIC ART, NOTES ON ACTING AND THE DRAMA, 1872-1901. Ed. and introd. and notes Allan Wade. New Brunswick, N.J.: Rutgers Univ. Press, 1948.

SELECTED LITERARY CRITICISM. Ed. Morris Shapira. 1964; Westport, Conn.: Greenwood Press, 1978.

> This collects twenty-three pieces written from 1865 to 1914.

THE SPEECH AND MANNERS OF AMERICAN WOMEN. Ed. E.S. Riggs. Lancaster, Pa.: Lancaster House, 1973.

> This collects two series of essays originally published in HARPER'S BAZAAR, 1906-07.

THEORY OF FICTION: HENRY JAMES. Ed. James E. Miller. Lincoln: Univ. of Nebraska Press, 1972.

> This is an excellent collection arranged from sources scattered throughout James's work, including essays, notebooks, prefaces, and letters. The editor also provides a bibliography of sources, an index to authors and works discussed, and a glossary of critical terms.

VIEWS AND REVIEWS. New York: AMS Press, 1969.

WILLIAM WETMORE STORY AND HIS FRIENDS. 1957; New York: Da Capo, 1969.

WITHIN THE RIM AND OTHER ESSAYS. 1919; Folcroft, Pa.: Folcroft, 1973.

BIBLIOGRAPHY

Babiiha, Thaddeo K. THE JAMES-HAWTHORNE RELATION: BIBLIOGRAPHICAL ESSAYS. Boston: G.K. Hall, 1980.

This gives a definitive description of what has been written about the relationship between Hawthorne and James, including an extensive analysis of the influence of Hawthorne upon James and James's criticism of Hawthorne's works.

Edel, Leon, and Dan H. Laurence. A BIBLIOGRAPHY OF HENRY JAMES. Rev. ed. London: Rupert Hart-Davis, 1961.

A thorough and meticulous bibliography, this includes books, letters, contributions to periodicals, and translations of James's writings.

Foley, Richard N. CRITICISM IN AMERICAN PERIODICALS OF THE WORKS OF HENRY JAMES FROM 1866 TO 1916. Washington, D.C.: Catholic Univ. of America, 1944.

Franklin, Rosemary F. AN INDEX TO HENRY JAMES'S PREFACES TO THE NEW YORK EDITION. Charlottesville: Bibliographical Society of the Univ. of Virginia, 1966.

This is keyed to Blackmur's 1934 edition of the prefaces (THE ART OF THE NOVEL, above).

Gale, Robert L. "Henry James." In EIGHT AMERICAN AUTHORS. Rev. Ed. James Woodress. New York: 1971, pp. 321-75.

McColgan, Kristin Pruitt. HENRY JAMES, 1917-1959: A REFERENCE GUIDE. Boston: G.K. Hall, 1979.

This lists major bibliographical sources, principal works by James, and writings about James, 1917-59, the latter with useful annotations, continued by Scura, below.

Phillips, Le Roy. A BIBLIOGRAPHY OF THE WRITINGS OF HENRY JAMES. New York: Coward-McCann, 1930.

Ricks, Beatrice. HENRY JAMES: A BIBLIOGRAPHY OF SECONDARY WORKS. Metuchen, N.J.: Scarecrow, 1975.

Scura, Dorothy McInnis. HENRY JAMES, 1960-1974: A REFERENCE GUIDE. Boston: G.K. Hall, 1979.

This is the companion volume to McColgan, above.

Stafford, William T. A NAME, TITLE, AND PLACE INDEX TO THE CRITICAL WRITINGS OF HENRY JAMES. Englewood, Colo.: Microcard Eds., 1975.

The author attempts "to list the name, title and those places that are described as places in all of James's published nonfictional work except his letters."

James is listed in the BIBLIOGRAPHY to the LITERARY HISTORY OF THE UNIT-ED STATES, pp. 584, 938, 1232 and Blanck's BIBLIOGRAPHY OF AMERICAN LITERATURE 5:1-96.

BIOGRAPHY AND CRITICISM

The listing below is limited to the important biographies and those works which discuss James in relationship to the rest of his family and to his times or those which deal to some extent with the nonfiction prose. The travel writings and the autobiographical and biographical writings have recently been treated in several articles. These are listed in the MLA INTERNATIONAL BIBLIOGRAPHY and AMERICAN LITERATURE and reviewed in AMERICAN LITERARY SCHOLAR-SHIP.

Anderson, Quentin. THE AMERICAN HENRY JAMES. New Brunswick, N.J.: Rutgers Univ. Press, 1957.

This study of the influence of the ideas of the elder Henry James upon the writings of his son deals primarily with the fiction, but it also illuminates ideas expressed in the essays and autobiographical writings. Edel's biography, however, refutes Anderson's theory that the younger James was seriously affected by his father's philosophical and psychological notions.

Banta, Martha. HENRY JAMES AND THE OCCULT: THE GREAT EXTENSION. Bloomington: Indiana Univ. Press, 1972.

In this study of the various spiritualistic movements of the nine-teenth century and James's relation to them, the author shows how James responded with both skepticism and creative imagination to these movements. In being affected by them, the author argues, James was very much a man of his time.

Beach, Joseph Warren. THE METHOD OF HENRY JAMES. 1918; Rev. ed. West Orange, N.J.: A. Saifer, 1954.

> Beach's analysis focuses upon the fiction, but, in this pioneering study, he sheds much light upon the literary and aesthetic principles which underlie James's fiction. Beach argues that James eliminated anything which obscured the ultimate design, or the "figure in the carpet," of his writings.

Brooks, Van Wyck. THE PILGRIMAGE OF HENRY JAMES. 1925; New York: Octagon, 1972.

> Brooks argues that James was alienated from the cultures of both Europe and America and shows little patience with James's later style. His treatment of James in NEW ENGLAND: INDIAN SUM-MER is more sympathetic.

Buitenhaus, Peter. THE GRASPING IMAGINATION: THE AMERICAN WRIT-INGS OF HENRY JAMES. Toronto, Ont.: Univ. of Toronto Press, 1970.

> This discussion of James's use of American materials has an excel-lent chapter on THE AMERICAN SCENE, showing James's use of imagery and careful structuring in this work.

Burr, Anna R., ed. ALICE JAMES: HER BROTHERS, HER JOURNAL. New York: Dodd, Mead, 1934.

> This is a good source of primary material.

Dupee, Frederick W. HENRY JAMES. 1951. Rev. 1956; New York: William Morrow, 1974.

> Dupee's biography is a straightforward record of the details of James's life and was the best study before Edel's volumes.

Edel, Leon. HENRY JAMES. Minneapolis: Univ. of Minnesota Press, 1960.

> This presents a good brief introduction to James.

_____. HENRY JAMES: THE UNTRIED YEARS, 1843-1870. Philadelphia: J.B. Lippincott, 1953.

> Edel's approach is psychoanalytic, relating James's inner life to his works. Edel uses vast amounts of unpublished family papers in this somewhat controversial but indispensable study. His entire five-volume biography (including this and the four listed below) is available in paperback (New York: Avon, 1978).

_____. HENRY JAMES: THE CONQUEST OF LONDON, 1870-1881. Phila-delphia: Lippincott, 1962.

_____. HENRY JAMES: THE MIDDLE YEARS, 1882-1895. Philadelphia: Lippincott, 1962.

_____. HENRY JAMES: THE TREACHEROUS YEARS, 1895-1901. Philadelphia: Lippincott, 1969.

_____. HENRY JAMES: THE MASTER, 1901-1916. Philadelphia: Lippincott, 1972.

_____. PREFACES OF HENRY JAMES. 1931; Folcroft, Pa.: Folcroft, 1970.

Edel explores the theories and method articulated in the prefaces to the New York edition.

Gill, Richard. HAPPY RURAL SEAT: THE ENGLISH COUNTRY HOUSE AND THE LITERARY IMAGINATION. New Haven: Yale Univ. Press, 1972.

In his long chapter on James, the author analyzes James's use of the country house in some of his nonfiction as well as his fiction.

Grattan, Hartley C. THE THREE JAMESES: A FAMILY OF MINDS: HENRY JAMES, SR., WILLIAM JAMES, HENRY JAMES. Introd. Oscar Cargill. New York: New York Univ. Press, 1962.

This study, which begins with the father of Henry James, Sr., (Henry and William's grandfather) points to some interesting psychological patterns which recur in family members.

Heimer, Jackson W. THE LESSON OF NEW ENGLAND: HENRY JAMES AND HIS NATIVE RELIGION. Muncie, Ind.: Ball State Univ., 1967.

This describes James's attitude toward New England; some of the material is derived from THE AMERICAN SCENE but few new insights are offered.

Hocks, Richard A. HENRY JAMES AND PRAGMATIC THOUGHT: A STUDY IN THE RELATIONSHIP BETWEEN THE PHILOSOPHY OF WILLIAM JAMES AND THE LITERARY ART OF HENRY JAMES. Chapel Hill: Univ. of North Carolina Press, 1974.

Hocks focuses upon Henry in this study, concluding that in his later works he "actualized" William's pragmatism.

Hyde, Henry. HENRY JAMES AT HOME. New York: Farrar, Straus and Giroux, 1969.

This describes James's English homes, includes long quotations from diaries, letters, and memoirs, and discusses James's visitors, friends, and activities during the early years of World War I.

Jefferson, Douglas W. HENRY JAMES. 1960; New York: Capricorn, 1971.

This is a brief study, but it deals at some length with James's autobiographical works.

Kelley, Cornelia P. THE EARLY DEVELOPMENT OF HENRY JAMES. 1930. Rev. ed., introd. L.N. Richardson. Urbana: Univ. of Illinois Press, 1965.

This remains an excellent study of James's early works and his attitudes toward his early achievements.

Long, Robert E. THE GREAT SUCCESSION: HENRY JAMES AND THE LEGACY OF HAWTHORNE. Pittsburgh, Pa.: Univ. of Pittsburgh, 1979.

The author compares themes and characters in the works of Hawthorne and James and points out that although much influenced by Hawthorne, James gives different values to experiences. James's interpretations of Hawthorne's themes indicate how he used the past, including Hawthorne's archetypal characters, to give depth to his own works.

McCarthy, Harold T. HENRY JAMES: THE CREATIVE PROCESS. New York: Thomas Yoseloff, 1958.

This is a brief study of James's aesthetic principles, his relating of theory and practice, and his concept of the responsibility of the writer to his work and society.

McElderry, Bruce R., Jr. HENRY JAMES. New York: Twayne, 1965.

This is a brief but solid critical and biographical introduction to James. Although he does not discuss the nonfiction in detail, McElderry states that "James's travel books, criticism, autobiography, and letters won for him a solid reputation in an age of great prose writers. These nonfictional works deserve to be read for their own merit, as well as for their illuminating commentary on his fiction."

Matthiessen, F.O. HENRY JAMES: THE MAJOR PHASE. New York: Oxford Univ. Press, 1944.

This excellent study focuses upon the fiction but provides an important basis for understanding some of James's critical theories and his techniques in his nonfiction.

_____. THE JAMES FAMILY: INCLUDING SELECTIONS FROM THE WRITINGS OF HENRY JAMES SENIOR, WILLIAM, HENRY, AND ALICE JAMES. 1947; New York: Vintage, 1980.

This studies the influence of the elder James on his children and gives a comprehensive picture of the latter half of the nineteenth century.

Maves, Carl. SENSUOUS PESSIMISM: ITALY IN THE WORKS OF HENRY JAMES. Bloomington: Indiana Univ. Press, 1973.

> The author traces James's visits to Italy and his attitudes toward the place, using for sources the travel writings as well as the fiction.

Nowell-Smith, Simon, comp. THE LEGEND OF THE MASTER. New York: Scribner's, 1948.

> This reprints anecdotes told about James by his friends and acquaintances and traces legends--some true, some inaccurate--about James.

Powers, Lyall H. HENRY JAMES: AN INTRODUCTION AND INTERPRETATION. New York: Holt, Rinehart and Winston, 1970.

> A good general introduction to James, this briefly discusses James's nonfiction, arguing a unity of attitude and consistency in all of James's work. The volume includes a useful bibliography.

Roberts, Morris. HENRY JAMES'S CRITICISM. 1929; New York: Haskell, 1969.

> Roberts demonstrates how James's critical theories are reflected in his fiction and discusses the criticism from the early reviews to the pieces collected in NOTES ON NOVELISTS.

Spender, Stephen. LOVE-HATE RELATIONS: ENGLISH AND AMERICAN SENSIBILITIES. New York: Random House, 1974.

> Spender discusses James's views of the French, English, and Americans and devotes some attention to THE AMERICAN SCENE.

Ward, Joseph A. THE SEARCH FOR FORM: STUDIES IN THE STRUCTURE OF JAMES'S FICTION. Chapel Hill: Univ. of North Carolina Press, 1967.

> In this thorough study, the author tells us much about James's aesthetic and critical principals and the structure of his fiction.

Wegelin, Christof. THE IMAGE OF EUROPE IN HENRY JAMES. Dallas, Tex.: Southern Methodist Univ. Press, 1958.

> The author studies the relationship of James's attitudes toward Europe and those previously held by Americans, tracing the development of James's treatment of the international theme in his writings.

Winner, Viola Hopkins. HENRY JAMES AND THE VISUAL ARTS. Charlottesville: Univ. Press of Virginia, 1970.

> The author convincingly argues that James often saw with a painter's eye and that the visual arts played an important part in his theory and practice of fiction.

Wright, Nathalia. AMERICAN NOVELISTS IN ITALY: THE DISCOVERERS:
ALLSTON TO JAMES. Philadelphia: Univ. of Pennsylvania Press, 1965.

> The author examines James's responses to Italy, especially Italian
> architecture, with some interesting comments on the importance of
> James's image of Italy as he was writing THE AMERICAN SCENE.

RELATED GENERAL STUDIES

Anderson, Quentin. THE IMPERIAL SELF. (p. 14)
Banta, Martha. FAILURE AND SUCCESS IN AMERICA. (p. 14)
Berthoff, Warner. THE FERMENT OF REALISM. (p. 15)
Blasing, Mutlu K. THE ART OF LIFE. (p. 77)
Brooks, Van Wyck. NEW ENGLAND: INDIAN SUMMER. (p. 17)
Brownell, William C. AMERICAN PROSE MASTERS. (p. 17)
Canby, Henry S. TURN WEST, TURN EAST. (p. 286, under Clemens)
Commager, Henry S., ed. BRITAIN THROUGH AMERICAN EYES. (p. 128)
Cooley, Thomas. EDUCATED LIVES. (p. 78)
Lewis, R.W.B. THE AMERICAN ADAM. (p. 25)
Matthiessen, F.O. AMERICAN RENAISSANCE. (p. 27)
Mordell, Albert, ed. THE DISCOVERY OF A GENIUS: WILLIAM DEAN
    HOWELLS AND HENRY JAMES (p. 352, under Howells)
Perry, Ralph B. THE THOUGHT AND CHARACTER OF WILLIAM JAMES.
    (p. 381, under W. James)
Rowe, John C. HENRY ADAMS AND HENRY JAMES. (p. 239, under Adams)
Smith, Bernard. FORCES IN AMERICAN CRITICISM. (p. 66)
Tanner, Tony. THE REIGN OF WONDER. (p. 32)
Vivas, Eliseo. CREATION AND DISCOVERY. (p. 33)

WILLIAM JAMES (1842-1910)

In his attempt to stretch language to capture a vision whole rather than to build a logical sequence of specific arguments, James has more affinity with someone like Emerson than with more conventional philosophers; however, as John Dewey noted, James's power of expression greatly enriched philosophical literature. During his career, James developed new concepts and shifted perceptions in his approach to philosophical problems, but the union of Christian mysticism with biological and psychological empiricism characterized his work from the very beginning. He found truth in the process of subjecting ideas to the test of practical consequences in action and emphasized the need to remain always open and imaginative in analyzing new experiences. He was a pioneer in applying the principles of evolutionary theory to the concept of mind and helped to shape the American belief in the value of individual effort and faith in the future. In clear, direct, and highly effective prose, William James presented an excellent synthesis of many of the important ideas of his time.

PRINCIPAL WORKS

THE PRINCIPLES OF PSYCHOLOGY. 2 vols. 1890.
PSYCHOLOGY: BRIEFER COURSE. 1892.
THE WILL TO BELIEVE, AND OTHER ESSAYS IN POPULAR PHILOSOPHY. 1897.
HUMAN IMMORTALITY: TWO SUPPOSED OBJECTIONS TO THE DOCTRINE. 1898.
TALKS TO TEACHERS, ON PSYCHOLOGY. 1899.
THE VARIETIES OF RELIGIOUS EXPERIENCE: A STUDY IN HUMAN NATURE. 1902.
THE SENTIMENT OF RATIONALITY. 1905.
PRAGMATISM: A NEW NAME FOR SOME OLD WAYS OF THINKING. 1907.
THE MEANING OF TRUTH: A SEQUEL TO PRAGMATISM. 1909.
A PLURALISTIC UNIVERSE: HIBBERT LECTURES ON THE PRESENT SITUATION IN PHILOSOPHY. 1909.

LETTERS AND JOURNALS

THE LETTERS OF WILLIAM JAMES. 2 vols. Ed. with a biographical introd. by his son, Henry James. Boston: Atlantic Monthly Press, 1920.

THE LETTERS OF WILLIAM JAMES AND THEODORE FLOURNOY. Ed. Robert C. LeClair. Madison: Univ. of Wisconsin Press, 1966.

THE SELECTED LETTERS OF WILLIAM JAMES. Ed. with Introd. Elizabeth Hardwick. New York: Farrar Straus, 1961.

Several letters are included in Perry's THE THOUGHT AND CHARACTER OF WILLIAM JAMES and Gay Wilson Allen's biography, below.

LATER EDITIONS, SELECTIONS, AND REPRINTS

AS WILLIAM JAMES SAID: EXTRACTS FROM THE PUBLISHED WRITINGS OF WILLIAM JAMES. New York: Vanguard, 1942.

COLLECTED ESSAYS AND REVIEWS. Ed. Ralph B. Perry. 1921; New York: Russell and Russell, 1969.

ESSAYS IN PRAGMATISM. Ed. and introd. Alburey Castell. New York: Hafner, 1948.

ESSAYS IN RADICAL EMPIRICISM. Ed. with Pref. by Ralph B. Perry. New York: Longmans, Green, 1912.

ESSAYS ON FAITH AND MORALS. Ed. Ralph B. Perry. New York: Longmans, Green, 1943.

INTRODUCTION TO WILLIAM JAMES: AN ESSAY AND SELECTED TEXTS. Ed. Andrew J. Reck. Bloomington: Indiana Univ. Press, 1967.

THE MEANING OF TRUTH. Ann Arbor: Univ. of Michigan Press, 1970.

MEMORIES AND STUDIES. Ed. Henry James, Jr., and Prepared by Horace M. Kallen. New York: Longmans, Green, 1911.

THE MORAL PHILOSOPHY OF WILLIAM JAMES. Ed. John K. Roth. New York: Crowell, 1969.

THE PHILOSOPHY OF WILLIAM JAMES. Selected with introd. Horace M. Kallen. New York: Modern Library, 1925.

PRAGMATISM AND OTHER ESSAYS. Ed. Joseph L. Blau. New York: Washington Square Press, 1963.

PRAGMATISM . . . TOGETHER WITH FOUR RELATED ESSAYS. Ed. Ralph B. Perry. New York: Longmans, Green, 1943.

SELECTED PAPERS ON PHILOSOPHY. Ed. and Introd. C.M. Bakewell. New York: E.P. Dutton, 1917.

SOME PROBLEMS OF PHILOSOPHY: A BEGINNING OF AN INTRODUCTION TO PHILOSOPHY. Prepared by Horace M. Kallen. New York: Longmans, Green, 1911.

THE VARIETIES OF RELIGIOUS EXPERIENCE. Ed. and Introd. Joseph Ratner. Hyde Park, N.Y.: University Books, 1963.

THE VARIETIES OF RELIGIOUS EXPERIENCE. New York: Doubleday, 1978.

WILLIAM JAMES--A SELECTION FROM HIS WRITING ON PSYCHOLOGY. Ed. and Introd. Margaret Knight. Baltimore: Penguin, 1950.

WILLIAM JAMES ON PSYCHICAL RESEARCH. Comp. and ed. Gardner Murphy and Robert O. Ballou. New York: Viking, 1960.

WILLIAM JAMES--PHILOSOPHER AND MAN. Comp. Charles H. Compton. New York: Scarecrow, 1957.

THE WRITINGS OF WILLIAM JAMES: A COMPREHENSIVE EDITION. Ed. with introd. John J. McDermott. New York: Random House, 1967.

THE WORKS OF WILLIAM JAMES. Ed. Frederick H. Burkhardt et al. 16 vols. projected. Cambridge, Mass.: Harvard Univ. Press, 1975-- .

> This is the MLA-sponsored, CEAA (now Center for Scholarly Editions) definitive edition of James's works. Vol. 6, THE WILL TO BELIEVE, was published in 1979.

BIBLIOGRAPHY

Compton, Charles H. WILLIAM JAMES: PHILOSOPHER AND MAN. New York: Scarecrow, 1957.

> Compton gives quotations from and references to William James in 652 books.

Perry, Ralph B. ANNOTATED BIBLIOGRAPHY OF THE WRITINGS OF WILLIAM JAMES. 1920; Dubuque, Iowa: W.C. Brown, 1964.

Skrupskelis, Ignas K. WILLIAM JAMES: A REFERENCE GUIDE. Boston: G.K. Hall, 1977.

> This lists writings about James, 1868-1974, including foreign works and dissertations.

John J. McDermott updates Perry with an annotated bibliography of James in THE WRITINGS, above.

William James is listed in the BIBLIOGRAPHY to the LITERARY HISTORY OF THE UNITED STATES, pp. 590, 942, 1237.

BIOGRAPHY AND CRITICISM

Allen, Gay Wilson. WILLIAM JAMES. Minneapolis: Univ. of Minnesota Press, 1974.

> Allen gives a good brief summary of James's career and an overview of the major works; this monograph is reprinted in Ralph Ross's collection, MAKERS OF AMERICAN THOUGHT (Minneapolis: Univ. of Minnesota Press, 1974).

_____. WILLIAM JAMES: A BIOGRAPHY. New York: Viking, 1967.

> The author had full access to the James family papers and, for the first time, to the letters and diaries of William James's wife, Alice. This is certainly among the best biographies of James to date, tracing, as Allen says, "the relationship between James's emotional and intellectual life--certainly important for a man who enthroned feeling with thought in philosophy."

Bixler, Julius Seelye. RELIGION IN THE PHILOSOPHY OF WILLIAM JAMES. Boston: Marshall Jones, 1926.

> This is a definitive study of the religious aspects of James's thought.

Blanshard, Brand, and Herbert W. Schneider, eds. IN COMMEMORATION OF WILLIAM JAMES, 1842-1942. New York: Columbia Univ. Press, 1942.

> This collects sixteen addresses by various scholars from a symposium on James.

Brennan, Bernard P. THE ETHICS OF WILLIAM JAMES. New York: Bookman, 1961.

> The author provides a systematic formulation of James's moral philosophy.

_____. WILLIAM JAMES. New York: Twayne, 1968.

This is an excellent introductory study which "aims to convey to a beginner the principal angles of James's philosophical vision." The author organizes James's published and some previously unpublished writings around the problems of "knowledge; truth and certitude; the philosophy of religion; the nature of the universe; the moral life of man."

Dooley, Patrick K. PRAGMATISM AS HUMANISM: THE PHILOSOPHY OF WILLIAM JAMES. Chicago: Nelson-Hall, 1978.

A good introductory study, this emphasizes the consistency rather than the tension in the humanistic philosophy of James, surveying James's views on the scientific study of man in psychology, his approach to man in ethics and religion, and his humanistic epistemology and metaphysics.

Knox, Howard V. THE PHILOSOPHY OF WILLIAM JAMES. New York: Dodge, 1941.

Knox gives an excellent brief exposition of James's thought.

Linschoten, Hans. ON THE WAY TOWARD A PHENOMENOLOGICAL PSYCHOLOGY: THE PSYCHOLOGY OF WILLIAM JAMES. Ed. Amedo Giorgi. Pittsburgh: Duquesne Univ. Press, 1968.

A pioneering account by a Dutch phenomenological psychologist, this study of James's psychology proposes he recognized that subjectivity determines appearance and makes it impossible to go "behind experience."

Moore, Edward C. WILLIAM JAMES. New York: Washington Square Press, 1965.

In this introductory study, the author attempts to give "appropriate emphasis to the various elements of James's thought so that the more notorious ones do not take an undue share of the spotlight."

Morris, Lloyd R. WILLIAM JAMES, THE MESSAGE OF A MODERN MIND. New York: Scribner's, 1950.

This general, popular survey of James's thought relates it to political issues of the twentieth century.

Otto, Max C. et al., eds. WILLIAM JAMES: THE MAN AND THE THINKER. Madison: Univ. of Wisconsin Press, 1942.

This volume collects centenary addresses and tributes to James.

Perry, Ralph B. IN THE SPIRIT OF WILLIAM JAMES. New Haven, Conn.: Yale Univ. Press, 1938.

The author contrasts James and Royce and discusses them in relation to American culture.

_____, ed. THE THOUGHT AND CHARACTER OF WILLIAM JAMES AS REVEALED IN UNPUBLISHED CORRESPONDENCE AND NOTES, TOGETHER WITH HIS PUBLISHED WRITINGS. 2 vols. 1935; abridged with additional material. Cambridge, Mass.: Harvard Univ. Press, 1948.

This excellent study by a distinguished philosopher and student of James includes some five hundred letters by James and provides other essential resource material.

Roth, John K. FREEDOM AND THE MORAL LIFE: THE ETHICS OF WILLIAM JAMES. Philadelphia: Westminster Press, 1969.

The author traces the development of James's conception of the self and of freedom and discusses his view that actions should maximize freedom and unity.

Sabin, Ethel E. WILLIAM JAMES AND PRAGMATISM. Lancaster, Pa.: New Era Printing Co., 1918.

The author compares James's and Dewey's concepts of pragmatism.

Seigfried, Charlene Haddock. CHAOS AND CONTEXT: A STUDY IN WILLIAM JAMES. Foreword by John J. McDermott. Athens: Ohio Univ. Press, 1978.

In this examination of James's theory of relations, the author focuses upon his radical empiricism, tracing the development of his position, presenting and evaluating the doctrine, and noting opposing points of view. The title refers to James's original interpretation of "pure experience," which, though chaotic, must be seen in the larger context imposed by past experience.

Turner, J.E. AN EXAMINATION OF WILLIAM JAMES'S PHILOSOPHY: A CRITICAL ESSAY FOR THE GENERAL READER. Oxford: B.H. Blackwell, 1919.

The author argues that James's genius was to stimulate thought and show that philosophy has relevance to everyday concerns.

Wild, John. THE RADICAL EMPIRICISM OF WILLIAM JAMES. Garden City, N.Y.: Doubleday, 1969.

This is a well-documented scholarly study which attempts to place James within the tradition of existential phenomenology. Emphasis is placed on THE PRINCIPLES OF PSYCHOLOGY.

Wilshire, Bruce. WILLIAM JAMES AND PHENOMENOLOGY: A STUDY OF THE PRINCIPLES OF PSYCHOLOGY. Bloomington: Indiana Univ. Press, 1968.

> The author compares James and Husserl and argues that James moved toward phenomenology when dualistic principles broke down.

RELATED GENERAL STUDIES

Ayer, A.J. THE ORIGINS OF PRAGMATISM: STUDIES IN THE PHILOSOPHY OF CHARLES SANDERS PEIRCE AND WILLIAM JAMES. (pp. 160-161)
Banta, Martha. FAILURE AND SUCCESS IN AMERICA. (p. 14)
Blau, Joseph. MEN AND MOVEMENTS IN AMERICAN PHILOSOPHY. (p. 161)
Cohen, Hennig, ed. LANDMARKS OF AMERICAN WRITING. (p. 19)
Conkin, Paul K. PURITANS AND PRAGMATISTS. (p. 165)
Edel, Leon. Biographies of Henry James (pp. 371-72, under H. James)
Hocks, Richard A. HENRY JAMES AND PRAGMATIC THOUGHT. (p. 372, under H. James)
Kuklick, Bruce. THE RISE OF AMERICAN PHILOSOPHY. (p. 169)
Matthiessen, F.O. THE JAMES FAMILY. (p. 373, under H. James)
Moore, Edward C. AMERICAN PRAGMATISTS. (p. 170)
Ross, Ralph, ed. MAKERS OF AMERICAN THOUGHT. (p. 239, under Adams)
Santayana, George. CHARACTER AND OPINION IN THE UNITED STATES. (p. 173)
Schneider, Herbert W. A HISTORY OF AMERICAN PHILOSOPHY. (p. 174)
Smith, John Edwin. THE SPIRIT OF AMERICAN PHILOSOPHY. (p. 174)
White, Morton. SCIENCE AND SENTIMENT IN AMERICA. (p. 177)
Wiener, Philip. EVOLUTION AND THE FOUNDERS OF PRAGMATISM. (p. 178)

JOHN PENDLETON KENNEDY (1795-1870)

Only secondarily regarded as a man of letters during his lifetime, Kennedy was known rather as a politician and man of public affairs. Today, only his fiction is regarded as lasting; however, his penetrating criticism of Jacksonian democracy in QUODLIBET, considered by Vernon L. Parrington to be one of the best of American political satires, remains very readable. His official biography of Wirt, though dull, was meticulously researched and reflected many of Kennedy's own ideas. His political documents are useful statements of principles upon which his other books were grounded. His pamphlet on THE BORDER STATES urged these states to attempt to effect a compromise; when war broke out between the states, Kennedy remained a Unionist. His essays, written for the NATIONAL INTELLIGENCER and collected as MR. AMBROSE'S LETTERS presented the conservative northern position in the conflict. As a source of information about the man and his ideas, Kennedy's nonfiction prose is, thus, a valuable resource.

PRINCIPAL PROSE WORKS

QUODLIBET. 1840.
DEFENSE OF THE WHIGS. 1844.
MEMOIRS OF THE LIFE OF WILLIAM WIRT. 1849.
THE BORDER STATES. 1861.
MR. AMBROSE'S LETTERS ON THE REBELLION. 1865.

LETTERS AND JOURNALS

Several of Kennedy's letters are included in Henry T. Tuckerman's biography, below. The John Pendleton Kennedy Papers in the Peabody Institute, Baltimore, totals 130 volumes, including a 33-volume set of manuscript journals, a brilliant autobiographical sketch to the author's nineteenth year, and 33 volumes of letters.

John Pendleton Kennedy

LATER EDITIONS, SELECTIONS, AND REPRINTS

THE COLLECTED WORKS OF JOHN PENDLETON KENNEDY. 10 vols. 1871-72; Hildesheim, W. Ger.: Olms, 1969.

> This edition includes the LIFE by Tuckerman and three volumes of miscellaneous writings edited by Tuckerman: AT HOME AND ABROAD, POLITICAL AND OFFICIAL PAPERS, and OCCASIONAL ADDRESSES.

QUODLIBET. Upper Saddle River, N.J.: Literature House, 1970.

SLAVERY, THE MERE PRETEXT FOR THE REBELLION. Pottstown, Pa.: Americanist, 1967.

BIBLIOGRAPHY

Griffin, Lloyd W. "The John Pendleton Kennedy Manuscripts." MARYLAND HISTORICAL MAGAZINE 48 (December 1953): 327-36.

> This gives a full listing of the extensive papers at the Peabody Institute Library.

A selected bibliography is included in Ridgely's study, below, and a detailed listing of Kennedy's works is in Blanck's BIBLIOGRAPHY OF AMERICAN LITERATURE 5:228-42. Kennedy is listed in the BIBLIOGRAPHY to the LITERARY HISTORY OF THE UNITED STATES, pp. 604, 947, 1243.

BIOGRAPHY AND CRITICISM

Bohner, Charles H. JOHN PENDLETON KENNEDY: GENTLEMAN FROM BALTIMORE. Baltimore, Md.: Johns Hopkins Press, 1961.

> This is a well-documented biography focusing upon Kennedy as a politician and political theorist. Kennedy is praised as one who "taught his countrymen that an American could mix politics and belles lettres and bring distinction to both."

Ridgely, Joseph V. JOHN PENDLETON KENNEDY. New York: Twayne, 1966.

> The author focuses upon Kennedy's fiction, giving a detailed analysis of the three novels and finding the nonfiction to be of little value. The study of the novels is detailed and informative; this brief consideration is one of the best critical comments upon Kennedy as a writer of fiction.

Tuckerman, Henry Theodore. THE LIFE OF JOHN PENDLETON KENNEDY.
New York: G.P. Putnam's, 1871.

> This is the "official" biography by Kennedy's literary executor. It
> is still a valuable source of primary material, although it has been
> superseded by Bohner's biography.

RELATED GENERAL STUDIES

Hubbell, Jay B. THE SOUTH IN AMERICAN LITERATURE, 1607-1900. (p. 24)
Parrington, Vernon L. MAIN CURRENTS IN AMERICAN THOUGHT. (p. 29)

SIDNEY LANIER (1842-81)

Although Lanier's place in American literature has been determined largely by his poetry, he was a highly capable critic. He was influenced by Poe in his criticism as well as in his poetry, but, unlike Poe, he held to a moral purpose for art. His critical estimates were colored by his belief that the great development of modern times was the emphasis on individuality and personality; this view led him into some rather erratic critical pronouncements as well as some original insights. Only a small part of his criticism was written for publication; most was derived from drafts for lectures and is somewhat rough and unbalanced. However, THE SCIENCE OF ENGLISH VERSE is a pioneering contribution to American criticism and is an excellent exposition of his notion of "temporal prosody" which helped to create the esthetic basis for later experimentation.

PRINCIPAL PROSE WORKS

FLORIDA: ITS SCENERY, CLIMATE, AND HISTORY. 1876.
THE SCIENCE OF ENGLISH VERSE. 1880.

LETTERS AND JOURNALS

LETTERS OF SIDNEY LANIER: SELECTIONS FROM HIS CORRESPONDENCE, 1866-1881. Ed. Henry W. Lanier. 1899; Freeport, N.Y.: Books for Libraries, 1972.

LETTERS: SIDNEY LANIER TO COL. JOHN G. JAMES. Austin: Univ. of Texas Press, 1942.

SIDNEY LANIER: POEMS AND LETTERS. Introd. Charles R. Anderson. Baltimore, Md.: Johns Hopkins Press, 1969.

Clarke's REMINISCENCES includes letters, and volumes 7 through 10 of the CENTENNIAL EDITION OF THE WORKS OF SIDNEY LANIER, below, include some one thousand letters edited by Charles Anderson and Aubrey Starke.

LATER EDITIONS, SELECTIONS, AND REPRINTS

THE CENTENNIAL EDITION OF THE WORKS OF SIDNEY LANIER. Ed. Charles
R. Anderson. 10 vols. Baltimore: Johns Hopkins Press, 1945.

> The introductions to these volumes include excellent commentaries
> and evaluations of Lanier's critical theories and writings.

THE ENGLISH NOVEL AND THE PRINCIPLE OF ITS DEVELOPMENT. Ed.
W.H. Browne. 1883. Ed. Clarence Gohdes and Kemp Malone as vol. 6 of
the centennial ed. 1945; Darby, Pa.: Arden, 1978.

FLORIDA: ITS SCENERY, CLIMATE, AND HISTORY. Gainesville: Univ.
Presses of Florida, 1973.

MUSIC AND POETRY: ESSAYS UPON SOME ASPECTS AND INTER-RELATIONS
OF THE TWO ARTS. Ed. Henry W. Lanier. 1898. Ed. Paull F. Baum and
included, with THE SCIENCE OF ENGLISH VERSE, as vol. 2 of the centennial
ed.; 1969; St. Clair Shores, Mich.: Scholarly Press, 1970.

RETROSPECTS AND PROSPECTS: DESCRIPTIVE AND HISTORICAL ESSAYS.
Ed. Henry W. Lanier. New York: Scribner's, 1899.

THE SCIENCE OF ENGLISH VERSE. Ed. Paull F. Baum as part of vol. 2 of
the centennial ed. Folcroft, Pa.: Folcroft Press, 1973.

SELECTIONS FROM SIDNEY LANIER: PROSE AND VERSE. Ed. Henry W.
Lanier. New York: Scribner's, 1916.

SHAKESPEARE AND HIS FORERUNNERS: STUDIES IN ELIZABETHAN POETRY
AND ITS DEVELOPMENT FROM EARLY ENGLISH. 2 vols. Ed. Henry W.
Lanier. Ed. Kemp Malone as vol. 3 of the centennial ed. 1902; New York:
AMS Press, 1966.

BIBLIOGRAPHY

DeBellis, Jack. SIDNEY LANIER, HENRY TIMROD, AND PAUL HAMILTON
HAYNE: A REFERENCE GUIDE. Boston: G.K. Hall, 1978.

> The guide includes an annotated checklist of writings about Lanier,
> 1868-1976.

Volume 6 of the CENTENNIAL EDITION, above, includes a listing compiled by
Philip Graham and Frieda C. Thies. A listing of Lanier's works is in Blanck's
BIBLIOGRAPHY OF AMERICAN LITERATURE 5:280-98. Lanier's manuscripts are
in the archives at Johns Hopkins. Lanier is listed in the BIBLIOGRAPHY to
the LITERARY HISTORY OF THE UNITED STATES, pp. 605, 947, 1243.

BIOGRAPHY AND CRITICISM

Clarke, George Herbert. SOME REMINISCENCES AND EARLY LETTERS OF SIDNEY LANIER. Macon, Ga.: J.W. Burke, 1907.

This is a good source of primary material.

DeBellis, Jack. SIDNEY LANIER. New York: Twayne, 1972.

This brief study focuses on Lanier's personal development as a poet and upon an analysis and evaluation of the poetry. It contains little reference to Lanier's criticism or prosody, although ideas presented in his letters, lectures, and essays are mentioned in passing and THE SCIENCE OF ENGLISH VERSE and the lectures on Shakespeare are briefly considered.

Jones, Mary C., comp. SIDNEY LANIER: A CHRONOLOGICAL RECORD OF AUTHENTICATED FACTS. Macon, Ga.: Privately printed, 1940.

A short monograph, this lists dates and activities, with notes and sources providing a useful reference.

Lorenz, Lincoln. THE LIFE OF SIDNEY LANIER. New York: Coward-McCann, 1935.

An anecdotal account, this is for the general reader rather than the scholar.

Mims, Edwin. SIDNEY LANIER. 1905; Port Washington, N.Y.: Kennikat, 1968.

The first full-length biography of Lanier, this relies heavily on his letters and stresses his lack of achievement as a result of his poor health and relatively short life.

Parks, Edd W. SIDNEY LANIER: THE MAN, THE POET, THE CRITIC. Athens: Univ. of Georgia, 1968.

An expansion of lectures given in 1968 at Wesleyan College, Macon, Georgia, this follows the three-part plan indicated by the title. After a brief biographical sketch, the author presents a summary and evaluation of Lanier's poetry and criticism and discusses his relationship with and judgment of other writers of his time. This is one of the best estimates of Lanier's contributions as poet and critic.

Spencer, Thomas E. SIDNEY LANIER: A STUDY IN PERSONALITY. St. Louis, Mo.: Hadley School, 1930.

The author examines Lanier's roles as a Southerner and a Nationalist.

Starke, Aubrey H. SIDNEY LANIER: A BIOGRAPHICAL STUDY. 1933; New York: Russell and Russell, 1964.

> This is the definitive biography, but the criticism, which offers a detailed interpretation of all of Lanier's works, is often unsatisfactory. The author presents Lanier as one who was highly sensitive to the development of the "New South."

Webb, Richard, and Edwin R. Coulson. SIDNEY LANIER: POET AND PROSODIST. Athens: Univ. of Georgia Press, 1941.

> Coulson adds his own analysis of the reputation and influence of Sidney Lanier to Webb's 1903 pioneering scholarly essay on Lanier's contributions as poet and prosodist. Webb praises Lanier's incisive prose style and his ability to assimilate and synthesize and gives a detailed summary of Lanier's theories of poetry. Coulson considers Lanier's position in American poetry and prosody as reflected in later critical appraisals.

RELATED GENERAL STUDIES

Abel, Darrel, ed. CRITICAL THEORY IN THE AMERICAN RENAISSANCE. (p. 62)
Baym, Max I. A HISTORY OF LITERARY AESTHETICS IN AMERICA. (p. 62)
Hubbell, Jay B. THE SOUTH IN AMERICAN LITERATURE. (p. 24)
Parks, Edd W. ANTE-BELLUM SOUTHERN LITERARY CRITICISM. (p. 65)

ABRAHAM LINCOLN (1809-65)

Critics and biographers have frequently acknowledged that Lincoln's leadership owed more to his powers of expression than to his policies or actions. One of the established masters of prose in the English language, Lincoln developed a style marked by lucidity, economy, honesty, and an unerring sense of pace and rhythm. He was not a conscious literary artist; his power and eloquence, unlike Webster's, did not lie in conventional rhetorical devices. He often used humor in story, anecdote, or quip to make a point or create an atmosphere, but the key to his use of language lies in its almost ideal adaptation of form to idea and emotion. He is one orator and statesman who unequivocally survives as a literary artist. His place in American literary history is secure.

COLLECTED WORKS

THE COLLECTED WORKS OF ABRAHAM LINCOLN. 9 vols. Ed. Roy P. Basler, with Marian Delores Pratt and Lloyd A. Dunlap. 1953-55; Westport, Conn.: Greenwood Press, 1974.

> This supersedes the collection below, although neither is complete.

THE COMPLETE WORKS OF ABRAHAM LINCOLN. 12 vols. Ed. John G. Nicolay and John Hay with general introd. Richard Watson Gilder. New York: F.D. Tandy, 1905.

> This collection, far from complete, was actually edited by Francis D. Tandy from the 1894 edition by Nicolay and Hay. It is still an important source for Lincoln's correspondence.

LETTERS AND JOURNALS

ABRAHAM LINCOLN: HIS AUTOBIOGRAPHICAL WRITINGS NOW BROUGHT TOGETHER FOR THE FIRST TIME. Ed. Paul M. Angle. Kingsport, Tenn.: Kingsport Press, 1947.

ABRAHAM LINCOLN'S SPEECHES AND LETTERS. Ed. Paul M. Angle. New York: Dutton, 1958.

AN AUTOBIOGRAPHY OF ABRAHAM LINCOLN. Ed. Nathaniel W. Stephenson. Indianapolis: Bobbs-Merrill, 1926.

> This collects and arranges speeches, letters, and conversations to cover Lincoln's life from 1809 to 1865.

THE LINCOLN PAPERS: THE STORY OF THE COLLECTION WITH SELECTIONS TO JULY 4, 1861. 2 vols. Ed. David C. Mearns. New York: Doubleday, 1948.

> In addition to a useful introduction, this extracts material from some five hundred documents and notes.

UNCOLLECTED LETTERS OF ABRAHAM LINCOLN. Ed. Gilbert A. Tracy. Introd. Ida M. Tarbell. Boston: Houghton Mifflin, 1917.

> This includes three hundred letters written for the most part between 1858 and 1861.

Several of the selections and biographical volumes listed below also include letters and autobiographical writings.

LATER EDITIONS, SELECTIONS, AND REPRINTS

ABRAHAM LINCOLN: A DOCUMENTARY PORTRAIT THROUGH HIS SPEECHES AND WRITINGS. Ed. with Introd. Don E. Fehrenbacher. New York: New American Library, 1964.

ABRAHAM LINCOLN: HIS SPEECHES AND WRITINGS. Ed. Roy P. Basler. 1946; New York: Kraus, 1968.

ABRAHAM LINCOLN: HIS STORY IN HIS OWN WORDS. Ed. with notes by Ralph Geoffrey Newman. New York: Doubleday, 1975.

ABRAHAM LINCOLN: SELECTED SPEECHES, MESSAGES, AND LETTERS. Ed. T. Harry Williams. New York: Holt, Rinehart and Winston, 1957.

ABRAHAM LINCOLN: SELECTIONS FROM HIS WRITINGS. Ed. Philip S. Foner. New York: International Publishers, 1944.

CREATED EQUAL? THE COMPLETE LINCOLN-DOUGLAS DEBATES OF 1858. Ed. with Introd. Paul M. Angle. Chicago: Univ. of Chicago Press, 1958.

THE ESSENTIAL LINCOLN. Ed. Gerald E. Stearns and Albert Fried. New York: Collier, 1962.

IN THE NAME OF THE PEOPLE: SPEECHES AND WRITINGS OF LINCOLN AND DOUGLAS IN THE OHIO CAMPAIGN OF 1859. Ed. with Introd. Harry V. Jaffa and Robert W. Johannsen. Columbus: Ohio State Univ. Press, 1959.

LIFE AND WRITINGS OF ABRAHAM LINCOLN. Ed. Philip Van Doren Stern. Introd. Allan Nevins. New York: Modern Library, 1942.

THE LINCOLN-DOUGLAS DEBATES OF 1858. Ed. Edwin E. Sparks. Springfield: Illinois State Historical Library, 1908.

THE LINCOLN-DOUGLAS DEBATES OF 1858. Ed. Robert W. Johannsen. New York: Oxford Univ. Press, 1965.

THE LINCOLN ENCYCLOPEDIA: THE SPOKEN AND WRITTEN WORDS OF ABRAHAM LINCOLN ARRANGED FOR READY REFERENCE. Comp. Archer H. Shaw. New York: Macmillan, 1950.

THE LITERARY WORKS OF ABRAHAM LINCOLN. Ed. Carl Van Doren. New York: Heritage Press, 1942.

THE LITERARY WORKS OF ABRAHAM LINCOLN. Ed. David D. Anderson. Columbus, Ohio: Charles E. Merrill, 1970.

THE LIVING LINCOLN. Ed. Paul M. Angle and Earl S. Miers. New Brunswick, N.J.: Rutgers Univ. Press, 1955.

THE POLITICAL THOUGHT OF ABRAHAM LINCOLN. Ed. Richard N. Current. Indianapolis: Bobbs-Merrill, 1967.

SELECTED WRITINGS AND SPEECHES. Ed. T. Harry Williams. Chicago: Hendricks House, 1943.

BIBLIOGRAPHY

Angle, Paul M. A SHELF OF LINCOLN BOOKS. New Brunswick, N.J.: Rutgers Univ. Press, 1946.

    The author gives a critical appraisal of eighty-one biographies, monographs, and collections of Lincoln's writings.

Monaghan, Jay. LINCOLN BIBLIOGRAPHY, 1839-1939. 2 vols. Springfield: Illinois State Historical Library, 1945.

Searcher, Victor. LINCOLN TODAY: AN INTRODUCTION TO MODERN LINCOLNIANA. New York: T. Yoseloff, 1969.

> A descriptive bibliography of "all books on Lincoln now in print; and all those published during and after 1955, even if not now in print."

There have been frequent bibliographical listings in the JOURNAL OF THE ILLINOIS STATE HISTORICAL SOCIETY (1908--), and the ABRAHAM LINCOLN QUARTERLY (1940-52). Lincoln is listed in the BIBLIOGRAPHY to the LITERARY HISTORY OF THE UNITED STATES, pp. 613, 950, 1246.

BIOGRAPHY AND CRITICISM

The listing below includes the standard biographies and the criticism discussing Lincoln as a literary man.

Anderson, David D. ABRAHAM LINCOLN. New York: Twayne, 1970.

> The author devotes this brief but enlightening study to a consideration of Lincoln's literary accomplishment and to the growth and development of his abilities of expression. He concludes that Lincoln's greatness was his ability to record "what he saw and understood for those whose eyes were not so keen, whose minds were less acute, and whose voices were mute. This is the ultimate test of great writing in any age, and it provides the proof of Lincoln's greatness as man and as writer."

Angle, Paul M., ed. THE LINCOLN READER. 1947; Chicago: Rand McNally, 1964.

> This includes 179 of the best of the biographical articles on Lincoln, some contemporary, others more recent.

Barzun, Jacques. LINCOLN, THE LITERARY GENIUS. Glenview, Ill.: Schori Press, 1960.

> Reprinted from a SATURDAY EVENING POST article that appeared in 1959, this praises Lincoln's ability to get at the heart of a problem and extract the central factor.

Basler, Roy P., ed. THE LINCOLN LEGEND: A STUDY IN CHANGING CONCEPTIONS. Boston: Houghton Mifflin, 1935.

> A collection of poetry, fiction, and drama dealing with Lincoln, this is a revealing study.

_____. LINCOLN, THE LITERARY GENIUS. New York: Grove Press, 1961.

> The author uses many quotations from Lincoln, incidents, and anec-

dotes to present a picture of Lincoln as a natural product of the spirit of the times.

_____. A TOUCHSTONE FOR GREATNESS: ESSAYS, ADDRESSES, AND OCCASIONAL PIECES ABOUT ABRAHAM LINCOLN. Westport, Conn.: Greenwood Press, 1973.

Two of the essays focus upon Lincoln as a literary man: one on his style, the other on his interest in Shakespeare.

Current, Richard N. THE LINCOLN NOBODY KNOWS. New York: McGraw-Hill, 1958.

This compiles and comments upon myths, legends, anecdotes, and contemporary accounts, emphasizing the ambiguous and debatable aspects of Lincoln's career.

Current, Richard N., and James G. Randall. LINCOLN THE PRESIDENT: LAST FULL MEASURE. New York: Dodd, Mead, 1955.

This is the concluding volume of Randall's biography, below.

Dodge, Daniel K. ABRAHAM LINCOLN: MASTER OF WORDS. New York: D. Appleton, 1924.

The author collects papers written by Lincoln, gives a critical analysis of the Gettysburg and inaugural addresses, and appraises Lincoln's messages to Congress and his presidential proclamations.

Edwards, Herbert J., and John E. Hankins. LINCOLN THE WRITER: THE DEVELOPMENT OF HIS STYLE. Orono: Univ. of Maine Studies, 1962.

The authors tend to become distracted from the works by the biography, but their discussion of literary aspects and poetic techniques is a good beginning, though brief.

Herndon, William H., and Jesse W. Weik. AMERICAN LINCOLN: THE TRUE STORY OF A GREAT LIFE. 3 vols. 1982; Ed. with Notes by Paul M. Angle as HERNDON'S LINCOLN. Cleveland: Fine Editions Press, 1949.

Written by Lincoln's former law partner, this biography contains much that has not withstood careful investigation, although the personal observations are revealing.

Howells, William Dean. LIVES AND SPEECHES OF ABRAHAM LINCOLN AND HANNIBAL HAMLIN. Reprinted as LIFE OF ABRAHAM LINCOLN. 1860; Bloomington: Indiana Univ. Press, 1960.

Although this campaign biography was hastily written, it shows Howells' literary skill. The 1960 edition gives the corrections in the 1860 text made by Lincoln in his handwriting.

Kempf, Edward J. ABRAHAM LINCOLN'S PHILOSOPHY OF COMMON SENSE. 3 vols. New York: Academy of Sciences, 1965.

> Although there are historical discrepancies which affect its scientific conclusions, this examination by a psychiatrist of the biographical evidence is interesting and occasionally insightful.

Kranz, Henry S., ed. ABRAHAM LINCOLN: A NEW PORTRAIT. New York: G.P. Putnam's, 1959.

> These twenty-two essays by experts include essays on Lincoln's literary skills and use of humor.

Mearns, David C. LARGELY LINCOLN. New York: St. Martin's, 1961.

> A collection of essays by the author on a variety of subjects, this is excellent reading and a reliable source for students of Lincoln.

Miers, Earl Schenck, editor-in-chief. LINCOLN DAY BY DAY: A CHRONOLOGY, 1809-1865. 3 vols. Washington, D.C.: Lincoln Sesquicentennial Commission, 1960.

> This detailed and well-researched account contains a remarkable wealth of information, not only about Lincoln but also about the times.

Nicolay, John G., and John Hay. ABRAHAM LINCOLN: A HISTORY. 10 vols. 1889; Abridged and Ed. by Paul M. Angle. Chicago: Univ. of Chicago Press, 1966.

> The one-volume condensation of the original excellent account focuses upon the war years, evaluating most of the important aspects of Lincoln's life and career.

Randall, James G. LINCOLN THE PRESIDENT: SPRINGFIELD TO GETTYSBURG. 2 vols. New York: Dodd, Mead, 1946.

> Randall's biographical volumes provide one of the best and most scholarly studies of Lincoln to date.

_____. LINCOLN THE PRESIDENT: MIDSTREAM. New York: Dodd, Mead, 1952.

> See Current and Randall, above, for the third, and concluding, volume of this biography.

Robinson, Luther E. ABRAHAM LINCOLN AS A MAN OF LETTERS. New York: G.P. Putnam's, 1923.

> This is a rather superficial account, less perceptive than Dodge's study, p. 394.

Sandburg, Carl. ABRAHAM LINCOLN: THE PRAIRIE YEARS. 2 vols. New York: Harcourt, Brace, 1926.

> Critics recognize Sandburg's volumes as being literature of the first rank as well as biography, but historians note that in his concern to paint a great epic, historicity suffers. Especially disturbing to the scholar is the lack of documentation.

_____. ABRAHAM LINCOLN: THE WAR YEARS. 4 vols. New York: Harcourt, Brace, 1936.

Thomas, Benjamin P. ABRAHAM LINCOLN. New York: Knopf, 1952.

> This is the best single-volume biography, covering a great deal of material simply and clearly.

RELATED GENERAL STUDIES

Brigance, William N., ed. A HISTORY AND CRITICISM OF AMERICAN PUBLIC ADDRESS. 2 vols. (p. 214)
Lewis, Edward R. A HISTORY OF AMERICAN POLITICAL THOUGHT FROM THE CIVIL WAR TO THE WORLD WAR. (p. 220)
Shaw, Warren C. HISTORY OF AMERICAN ORATORY. (p. 224)

HENRY WADSWORTH LONGFELLOW (1807-82)

Longfellow's contributions to the development of American prose were slight; but he wrote much prose which is of interest as the product of the poet. His scholarly essays and reviews, many of which were originally published in the NORTH AMERICAN REVIEW and were later included in the 1909 WORKS, are useful for the study of Longfellow's thinking about American literature and his place in it. Other essays show his wide acquaintance with various languages and literatures, including Old English. OUTRE-MER, his delightful travel book, combines descriptive sketches, observations on people and places, and local tales. The new edition of letters, below, shows Longfellow to be a lively and interesting correspondent; his meticulously kept journal is a potentially significant addition to his writings. Overall, his prose is clear and effective.

PRINCIPAL PROSE WORKS

OUTRE-MER. 2 vols. 1835.
PROSE WORKS. 1 vol. 1851. 2 vols. 1857. 3 vols. 1878-80.
FROM MY ARMCHAIR. 1879.
BAYARD TAYLOR. 1879.
Ed. POETS AND POETRY OF EUROPE. 1845. (Contains a long critical intro-
    duction)

LETTERS AND JOURNALS

THE LETTERS OF HENRY WADSWORTH LONGFELLOW. 6-7 vols. projected. Ed. with Introd. and Notes by Andrew Hilen. Cambridge, Mass.: Harvard Univ. Press, 1966-- .

Samuel Longfellow's LIFE, Kennedy's memoirs, and Thomas W. Higginson's biography include letters and excerpts from the journals. Robert S. Ward is working on a scholarly edition of the JOURNALS.

LATER EDITIONS, SELECTIONS, AND REPRINTS

COMPLETE WORKS. Standard Library Edition. 14 vols. 1891; New York: AMS Press, 1966.

> The SLE adds the three-volume LIFE by Samuel Longfellow to a reprint of the Riverside Edition of 1886.

HENRY WADSWORTH LONGFELLOW: REPRESENTATIVE SELECTIONS. Ed. with Introd., Notes by Odell Shepard. New York: American Book Co., 1934. Bibliog.

THE WORKS OF HENRY WADSWORTH LONGFELLOW. 10 vols. New York: Davos Press, 1909.

> This collects some of Longfellow's important prose material.

THE WRITINGS OF HENRY WADSWORTH LONGFELLOW. Riverside Ed. 11 vols. 1886; Philadelphia: R. West, 1973.

BIBLIOGRAPHY

Livingston, Luther S. A BIBLIOGRAPHY OF THE FIRST EDITIONS IN BOOK FORM OF THE WRITINGS OF HENRY WADSWORTH LONGFELLOW. 1908; New York: B. Franklin, 1968.

Rust, Richard Dilworth. "Henry Wadsworth Longfellow." In FIFTEEN AMERICAN AUTHORS BEFORE 1900. Ed. by Robert Rees and Earl Harbert. Madison: Univ. of Wisconsin Press, 1971, pp. 263-84.

An extensive listing of Longfellow's writings is in Blanck's BIBLIOGRAPHY OF AMERICAN LITERATURE 5:468-640. Selected bibliographies are included in the studies by Cecil B. Williams and Edward Wagenknecht and in the selections edited by Odell Shepard, above and below.

Longfellow is listed in the BIBLIOGRAPHY to the LITERARY HISTORY OF THE UNITED STATES, pp. 622, 954, 1251.

BIOGRAPHY AND CRITICISM

There are no full-length studies of Longfellow's prose works. The listing below excludes works devoted solely to the poetry.

Arvin, Newton. LONGFELLOW: HIS LIFE AND WORK. Boston: Little, Brown, 1962.

The author gives a well-balanced view of Longfellow as a humane, talented person who was a conscious craftsman.

Austin, George Lowell. HENRY WADSWORTH LONGFELLOW: HIS LIFE, HIS WORKS, HIS FRIENDSHIPS. Boston: Lea and Shepard, 1883.

This partially completed "authorized" biography collects vast amounts of memoranda and anecdotes.

Cameron, Kenneth W., ed. LONGFELLOW AMONG HIS CONTEMPORARIES. Hartford, Conn.: Transcendental Books, 1978.

This gives anecdotes and provides contemporary estimates of Longfellow's work.

Hatfield, James Taft. NEW LIGHT ON LONGFELLOW: WITH SPECIAL REFERENCE TO RELATIONS TO GERMANY. Boston: Houghton Mifflin, 1933.

This study focuses on Longfellow's Harvard professorship and his German friends and studies.

Higginson, Thomas W. HENRY WADSWORTH LONGFELLOW. Boston: Houghton Mifflin, 1902.

Higginson bases his study primarily on Samuel Longfellow's LIFE, below, but he introduces some new material in his well-written account. Higginson judges that Longfellow will be read not for insight but for comfort.

Hilen, Andrew R. LONGFELLOW AND SCANDINAVIA. New Haven, Conn.: Yale Univ. Press, 1947.

Hilen discusses Longfellow's philological studies and treats him more as a figure in literary history than as a poet.

Hirsh, Edward L. HENRY WADSWORTH LONGFELLOW. Minneapolis: Univ. of Minnesota Press, 1964.

The author praises Longfellow's use of language within the literary conventions of the time, although he notes that Longfellow has many limitations of insight and artistry.

Johnson, Carl L. PROFESSOR LONGFELLOW OF HARVARD. Eugene: Univ. of Oregon Press, 1944.

In this study, Longfellow, who devoted twenty-four years of his life to teaching languages and literature, is seen as a reluctant but conscientious teacher.

Kennedy, William Sloane. HENRY WADSWORTH LONGFELLOW: BIOGRAPHY, ANECDOTE, LETTERS, CRITICISM. Cambridge: Moses King, 1882.

Although the author's use of the material he collects is disjointed, this volume contains useful contemporary estimates and primary material.

Longfellow, Samuel. LIFE OF HENRY WADSWORTH LONGFELLOW. Vols. 1-2, 1886; vol. 3, 1887; 1968; Philadelphia: R. West, 1973.

The third volume, FINAL MEMORIALS OF HENRY WADSWORTH LONGFELLOW, completed this biography which was added to the COMPLETE WORKS (1891), above. The biography relies heavily upon selections from Longfellow's journals and letters. Compiled by Longfellow's younger brother, it presents a highly favorable portrait, yet remains an indispensable resource.

Thompson, Lawrance. YOUNG LONGFELLOW (1807-1843). New York: Macmillan, 1938.

This is a well-researched account of the early years and an attempt to modify Longfellow's image as a long-bearded old man.

Wagenknecht, Edward. HENRY WADSWORTH LONGFELLOW: PORTRAIT OF AN AMERICAN HUMANIST. New York: Oxford Univ. Press, 1966.

This is a revision, with some additions and a new organization, of the author's LONGFELLOW: A FULL-LENGTH PORTRAIT (New York: Longmans, Green, 1955). It is based upon careful study of manuscript and published sources and presents a finely balanced view of Longfellow, correcting many previous misconceptions.

_____, ed. MRS. LONGFELLOW: SELECTED LETTERS AND JOURNALS OF FANNY APPLETON LONGFELLOW (1817-1861). New York: Longmans, Green, 1956.

This collects the well-written and informative letters and journals of Longfellow's second wife.

Whitman, Iris Lilian. LONGFELLOW AND SPAIN. New York: Instituto de las Espanas en los Estados Unidos, 1927.

The author argues that Spain broadened Longfellow's appreciation of life and grasp of literary material.

Williams, Cecil B. HENRY WADSWORTH LONGFELLOW. New York: Twayne, 1964.

In this well-supported introductory study, the author calls for an objective reappraisal of Longfellow in terms of biography and literary history. He argues that Longfellow is important both for what he has contributed to American literary history and for what he continues to give in his works in terms of "quiet enjoyment" for each new generation of readers. One long chapter is devoted to Longfellow as a prose writer.

RELATED GENERAL STUDIES

Brooks, Van Wyck. THE FLOWERING OF NEW ENGLAND. (p. 17)

Emerson, Edward W. THE EARLY YEARS OF THE SATURDAY CLUB, 1855-1870. (p. 71)

Fields, Annie. AUTHORS AND FRIENDS. (p. 71)

Higginson, Thomas W. OLD CAMBRIDGE. (p. 82)

Howells, William D. LITERARY FRIENDS AND ACQUAINTANCE. (p. 350 and 352, under Howells)

Long, Orie W. LITERARY PIONEERS: EARLY AMERICAN EXPLORERS OF EUROPEAN CULTURE. (p. 130)

Macy, John, ed. AMERICAN WRITERS ON AMERICAN LITERATURE. (p. 26)

Pochmann, Henry A. GERMAN CULTURE IN AMERICA. (p. 172)

Pritchard, John. RETURN TO THE FOUNTAINS. (p. 66)

Woodberry, George E. LITERARY MEMOIRS OF THE NINETEENTH CENTURY. (p. 56)

JAMES RUSSELL LOWELL (1819-91)

Although his best-known criticism is in the form of verse (the political satire in the BIGLOW PAPERS and the literary commentary in THE FABLE FOR CRITICS), and his best prose can be found in his letters, Lowell's delightful familiar essays and his impressionistic but usually astute criticism make him a figure of some importance in American prose as well as poetry. As the first editor of the ATLANTIC MONTHLY and as professor of modern languages at Harvard, he influenced literary scholarship and criticism in America primarily through conveying to his readers and students his own enthusiasm for books. Lowell achieved wide recognition during his own lifetime as a man of letters and a critic. Later commentators have observed a lack of coherence and consistency in his writings; yet despite this lack of discipline, Lowell had a brilliant and sympathetic mind and made a significant contribution to American prose and criticism.

PRINCIPAL PROSE WORKS

CONVERSATIONS ON SOME OF THE OLD POETS. 1845.
FIRESIDE TRAVELS. 1864.
AMONG MY BOOKS. 1870.
MY STUDY WINDOWS. 1871.
AMONG MY BOOKS: SECOND SERIES. 1876.
DEMOCRACY AND OTHER ADDRESSES. 1887.
THE ENGLISH POETS, LESSING, ROUSSEAU. 1888.
POLITICAL ESSAYS. 1888.
THE WRITINGS OF JAMES RUSSELL LOWELL IN PROSE AND POETRY. 11
    vols. 1890.

LETTERS AND JOURNALS

BROWNING TO HIS AMERICAN FRIENDS: LETTERS BETWEEN THE BROWN-INGS, THE STORYS AND JAMES RUSSELL LOWELL. Ed. Gertrude Reese Hudson. London: Bowes and Bowes, 1965.

IMPRESSIONS OF SPAIN. Ed. J.B. Gilder. Boston: Houghton Mifflin, 1899.

> This consists of letters written to the secretary of state by Lowell as minister to Spain.

LETTERS OF JAMES RUSSELL LOWELL. 2 vols. Ed. Charles Eliot Norton. 1894; New York: AMS Press, 1973.

NEW LETTERS OF JAMES RUSSELL LOWELL. Ed. Mark A. DeWolfe Howe. New York: Harper, 1932.

THE SCHOLAR FRIENDS: LETTERS OF FRANCIS JAMES CHILD AND JAMES RUSSELL LOWELL. Ed. Mark A. DeWolfe Howe and G.W. Cotress, Jr. Cambridge, Mass.: Harvard Univ. Press, 1952.

Additional letters are in William Smith Clark's LOWELL: ESSAYS, POEMS, AND LETTERS and in Scudder's biography, below. Letters also appear in various periodicals from time to time (see AMERICAN LITERATURE or PMLA bibliographies).

LATER EDITIONS, SELECTIONS, AND REPRINTS

AMONG MY BOOKS. 1970; Philadelphia: R. West, 1973.

THE ANTI-SLAVERY PAPERS OF JAMES RUSSELL LOWELL. 2 vols. Ed. William Belmont Parker. 1902; New York: Negro Univ. Press, 1969.

> This collects papers published in the PENNSYLVANIA FREEMAN (1844) and the NATIONAL ANTI-SLAVERY STANDARD (1845-50).

THE COMPLETE WRITINGS OF JAMES RUSSELL LOWELL. Elmwood Ed. 16 vols. 1904; New York: AMS Press, 1966.

> This includes the Norton edition, above, of the letters and some posthumously collected writings.

CONVERSATIONS ON SOME OLD POETS. New York: Books for Libraries, 1973.

EARLY PROSE WRITINGS OF JAMES RUSSELL LOWELL. Ed. with pref. Note by Dr. Edward Everett Hall. Introd. Walter Littlefield. London: Lane, 1902.

THE ENGLISH POETS, LESSING, ROUSSEAU. Philadelphia: R. West, 1973.

ESSAYS ON THE ENGLISH POETS. Philadelphia: R. West, 1973.

THE FUNCTION OF THE POET AND OTHER ESSAYS. Ed. Albert Mordell. 1920; Port Washington, N.Y.: Kennikat, 1968.

JAMES RUSSELL LOWELL: REPRESENTATIVE SELECTIONS. Ed. with Introd. Harry Hayden Clark and Norman Foerster. 1947; Darby, Pa.: Arden, 1977.

> Several essays and letters as well as poetry are included in this collection. The annotated bibliography is a valuable guide to Lowell scholarship before 1946, and the introduction is excellent.

LATEST LITERARY ESSAYS AND ADDRESSES. Ed. Charles Eliot Norton. 1892; reprinted in THE COMPLETE WRITINGS, 1904; New York: Arno, 1972.

LECTURES ON THE ENGLISH POETS. 1897; Philadelphia: R. West, 1973.

LITERARY CRITICISM OF JAMES RUSSELL LOWELL. Ed. Herbert F. Smith. Lincoln: Univ. of Nebraska Press, 1969.

> The editor's introduction discusses Lowell's critical principles and finds them "remarkably contemporary." The selections include some of Lowell's best critical essays and illustrate his defense of poetry, his main critical principles, his assessment of the native and national in American literature, and his criticism of four contemporaries: Emerson, Thoreau, Howells, and Henry James.

LITERARY ESSAYS. 2 vols. New York: Arno, 1972.

LOWELL: ESSAYS, POEMS AND LETTERS. Ed. William Smith Clark, II. New York: Odyssey, 1948.

MY STUDY WINDOWS. New York: AMS Press, 1971.

THE OLD ENGLISH DRAMATISTS. 1892; Philadelphia: R. West, 1973.

THE ROUND TABLE. 1913; Norwood, Pa.: Norwood Editions, 1979.

BIBLIOGRAPHY

Cooke, George W. A BIBLIOGRAPHY OF JAMES RUSSELL LOWELL. Boston: Houghton Mifflin, 1906.

> This gives dates and places of first publication of all of Lowell's writings and lists notices and criticisms to 1906.

Livingston, Luther S., and J.C. Chamberlain. A BIBLIOGRAPHY OF FIRST EDITIONS IN BOOK FORM OF THE WRITINGS OF JAMES RUSSELL LOWELL.

1914; New York: Burt Franklin, 1968.

This lists items printed as individual volumes.

Rees, Robert A. "James Russell Lowell." FIFTEEN AMERICAN AUTHORS BE-FORE 1900. Ed. Robert A. Rees and Earl N. Harbert. Madison: Univ. of Wisconsin Press, 1971, pp. 285-306.

In this bibliographical survey of biography and criticism, the writer notes that the definitive study of Lowell is yet to be written.

A useful listing of Lowell's works is in Blanck's BIBLIOGRAPHY OF AMERICAN LITERATURE 6:21-105. Selected bibliographies are in the collection edited by Clark and Foerster, above, and in McGlinchee's brief study, below. Duberman's biography, below, includes an excellent listing of manuscript sources. Lowell is listed in the BIBLIOGRAPHY to the LITERARY HISTORY OF THE UNITED STATES, pp. 628, 955, 1252.

BIOGRAPHY AND CRITICISM

This listing does not include critical studies focused primarily on the poetry.

Beatty, Richmond Croom. JAMES RUSSELL LOWELL. Nashville: Univ. of Tennessee Press, 1942.

Admitting to a southern bias, Beatty finds fault with Lowell's political, critical, and literary judgments and does not add substantially to the knowledge of Lowell and his writings. However, the study is based upon thorough scholarship, and Beatty's insights are sometimes revealing.

Cameron, Kenneth W., ed. CONTEMPORARY DIMENSIONS: AN AMERICAN RENAISSANCE LITERARY NOTEBOOK OF NEWSPAPER CLIPPINGS. Hartford, Conn.: Transcendental Books, 1970.

Most of the entries in this collection have to do with James Russell Lowell.

Duberman, Martin B. JAMES RUSSELL LOWELL. Boston: Houghton Mifflin, 1966.

The author has made excellent use of manuscript sources to produce the best biography since Scudder's study. Factual materials not available to Scudder are used to give a detailed account of Lowell's life and personality.

Greenslet, Ferris. JAMES RUSSELL LOWELL: HIS LIFE AND WORKS. American Men of Letters Series. Boston: Houghton Mifflin, 1905.

This biography has some perceptive evaluations of Lowell as a writer.

Greenslet notes that Lowell's best prose is related to his conversational style.

Hale, Edward Everett, Jr. JAMES RUSSELL LOWELL AND HIS FRIENDS. Boston: Houghton Mifflin, 1899.

These reminiscences are superficial but present an entertaining account of Lowell and the members of his circle.

Howard, Leon. VICTORIAN KNIGHT-ERRANT: A STUDY OF THE EARLY LITERARY CAREER OF JAMES RUSSELL LOWELL. Berkeley: Univ. of California Press, 1952.

Viewing Lowell's life and times through his literature, Howard draws extensively upon Lowell's writings to provide many new biographical insights into the early years.

McGlinchee, Claire. JAMES RUSSELL LOWELL. New York: Twayne, 1967.

This is a superficial study, relying mainly upon the evaluations of other scholars to assess the works, but it provides an introductory survey of Lowell's life and writings.

Reilly, Joseph J. JAMES RUSSELL LOWELL AS A CRITIC. New York: G.P. Putnam's, 1915.

The author disparages Lowell's critical judgments, considering Lowell deficient in his knowledge of art and history, lacking in sympathy for science and classical art, and having little interest in drama and fiction.

Scudder, Horace. JAMES RUSSELL LOWELL: A BIOGRAPHY. 2 vols. Boston: Houghton Mifflin, 1901.

Although it was conceived primarily as a tribute, this was the standard biography for over sixty years, until Duberman's work, and is still useful as a source of basic data on Lowell.

Stewart, Charles Oran. LOWELL AND FRANCE. Nashville, Tenn.: Vanderbilt Univ. Press, 1951.

The author shows that French culture and literature influenced a number of Lowell's works.

Wagenknecht, Edward. JAMES RUSSELL LOWELL: PORTRAIT OF A MANY-SIDED MAN. New York: Oxford Univ. Press, 1971.

In this interpretive critical biography, the author focuses upon Lowell's temperament and personality. He finds Lowell to be a complex individual with great "unrealized potential." This is a sympathetic analysis of the characteristics which affected Lowell's achievements as a writer.

RELATED GENERAL STUDIES

Blair, Walter. HORSE SENSE IN AMERICAN HUMOR. (p. 97)
Brooks, Van Wyck. THE FLOWERING OF NEW ENGLAND. (p. 17)
Brownell, William C. AMERICAN PROSE MASTERS. (p. 17)
DeMille, George. LITERARY CRITICISM IN AMERICA. (p. 62)
Edel, Leon, ed. THE AMERICAN ESSAYS OF HENRY JAMES. (pp. 371-72, under H. James)
Foerster, Norman. AMERICAN CRITICISM. (p. 63)
Higginson, Thomas W. OLD CAMBRIDGE. (p. 82)
Howe, Mark A. De Wolfe, ed. MEMORIES OF A HOSTESS. (p. 73)
Howells, William Dean. LITERARY FRIENDS AND ACQUAINTANCE. (p. 350 and 352, under Howells)
James, Henry. ESSAYS IN LONDON AND ELSEWHERE. (p. 365, under H. James)
Pritchard, John P. CRITICISM IN AMERICA. (p. 65)
_____. RETURN TO THE FOUNTAINS. (p. 66)
Smith, Bernard. FORCES IN AMERICAN CRITICISM. (p. 66)
Tandy, Jennette R. CRACKERBOX PHILOSOPHERS IN AMERICAN HUMOR AND SATIRE. (p. 99)

HERMAN MELVILLE (1819-91)

Melville's reviews for LITERARY WORLD, particularly the well-known "Hawthorne and His Mosses," his impressionistic but magnificent description of the Galapagos Islands in "The Encantadas," and his journals of travel, edited and published after his death, deserve mention in a listing of nineteenth-century prose and criticism. Melville's reputation, like Hawthorne's, must rest upon his fiction; nevertheless, these relatively minor prose pieces bear the stamp of his greatness.

PRINCIPAL NONFICTION PROSE WORKS

PIAZZA TALES. 1856. (The only major collection containing nonfiction prose published during Melville's lifetime, this includes "The Encantadas.")

LETTERS AND JOURNALS

FAMILY CORRESPONDENCE OF HERMAN MELVILLE, 1830-1904. Ed. Victor H. Palsits. 1929; New York: Haskell House, 1976.

JOURNAL OF A VISIT TO LONDON AND THE CONTINENT. Ed. Eleanor M. Metcalf. Cambridge, Mass.: Harvard Univ. Press, 1948.

JOURNAL UP THE STRAITS. Ed. Raymond M. Weaver. New York: Colophon, 1935.

    See also MELVILLE'S JOURNAL, below.

THE LETTERS OF HERMAN MELVILLE. Ed. Merrell R. Davis and William H. Gilman. New Haven: Yale Univ. Press, 1960.

MELVILLE'S JOURNAL OF A VISIT TO EUROPE AND THE LEVANT, OCTOBER 11, 1856-MAY 6, 1857. Ed. Howard C. Horsford. 1955; Westport, Conn.: Greenwood Press, 1976.

    This is a critical reediting of the JOURNAL UP THE STRAITS, with explanatory and textual notes.

SOME PERSONAL LETTERS OF HERMAN MELVILLE. Ed. Meade Minnigerode. 1922; Freeport, N.Y.: Books for Libraries, 1969.

> This volume includes a bibliographical description of first editions of Melville's writings and most of Melville's contributions to periodicals and other publications.

LATER EDITIONS, SELECTIONS, AND REPRINTS

The list below represents the major sources for the nonfiction prose, although several other collections include sketches, reviews, letters, and excerpts from the journals.

THE APPLE TREE TABLE AND OTHER SKETCHES. Ed. Henry Chapin. 1922; Westport, Conn.: Greenwood Press, 1968.

> This collection includes "Hawthorne and His Mosses" as well as previously uncollected short fiction and nonfiction sketches.

COMPLETE WORKS OF HERMAN MELVILLE. Gen. Ed. Howard P. Vincent. Chicago: Hendricks House, 1947-- .

> Seven volumes in this edition have been published, including THE PIAZZA TALES (1948), but the project has not been completed.

THE ENCANTADAS: OR, ENCHANTED ISLES. Introd. and Notes by Victor Wolfgang Von Hagen. Burlingame, Calif.: W.P. Wreden, 1940.

GREAT SHORT WORKS OF HERMAN MELVILLE. Ed. with Introd. Warner Berthoff. New York: Harper and Row, 1970.

HERMAN MELVILLE: REPRESENTATIVE SELECTIONS. Introd. and Notes by Willard Thorp. New York: American Book Co., 1938. Bibliog.

> The selections include several book reviews and letters.

THE PORTABLE MELVILLE. Ed. Jay Leyda. 1952; New York: Macmillan, 1969.

> Several excerpts from the travel journals are included in this selection.

SELECTED WRITINGS OF HERMAN MELVILLE. New York: Random House, 1952.

THE WORKS OF HERMAN MELVILLE. Standard Ed. 16 vols. 1922-24; New York: Russell and Russell, 1963.

THE WRITINGS OF HERMAN MELVILLE. 25 vols. projected. Gen. Eds. Harrison Hayford et al. Evanston, Ill.: Northwestern Univ. Press, 1968-- . Bibliog.

The volumes published in this CEAA (Center for Editions of American Authors, now Center for Scholarly Editions) (CSE)-approved edition will provide the definitive texts, with historical and textual notes.

BIBLIOGRAPHY

Bowen, James K., and Richard Van Der Beets. A CRITICAL GUIDE TO HERMAN MELVILLE: ABSTRACTS OF FORTY YEARS OF CRITICISM. Glenview, Ill.: Scott, Foresman, 1971.

Most of these essays, published between 1950 and 1970, deal with the fiction.

Gross, Theodore L., and Stanley Wertheim. HAWTHORNE, MELVILLE, STEPHEN CRANE: A CRITICAL BIBLIOGRAPHY. New York: Free Press, 1971.

Annotations to the listings are thorough and informative.

Ricks, Beatrice, and Joseph Adams. HERMAN MELVILLE: A REFERENCE BIBLIOGRAPHY. Boston: G.K. Hall, 1973.

This listing is comprehensive, but there are no annotations.

Vincent, Howard P., ed. THE MERRILL CHECKLIST OF HERMAN MELVILLE. Columbus, Ohio: Charles E. Merrill, 1969.

Wright, Nathalia. "Herman Melville." In EIGHT AMERICAN AUTHORS. Rev. Ed. James Woodress. New York: Norton, 1971, pp. 173-224.

The Melville Society prints bibliographical listings of works about Melville from time to time. Useful listings are also in Minnegerode's SOME PERSONAL LETTERS and in HERMAN MELVILLE: REPRESENTATIVE SELECTIONS, ed. Willard Thorp, above. A substantial listing of Melville's writings is in Blanck's BIBLIOGRAPHY OF AMERICAN LITERATURE 6:152-81. Melville is listed in the BIBLIOGRAPHY to the LITERARY HISTORY OF THE UNITED STATES, pp. 647, 958, 1256.

BIOGRAPHY AND CRITICISM

There are no full-length studies of Melville's nonfiction prose; the listing below includes the standard biographies and general critical studies.

Anderson, Charles R. MELVILLE IN THE SOUTH SEAS. 1939; New York: Dover, 1966.

This details Melville's experiences from 1841 to 1845, drawing from journals, log books, crew lists, printed accounts in newspapers, and other material.

_____, ed. JOURNAL OF A CRUISE IN THE PACIFIC OCEAN, 1842-1844, IN THE FRIGATE UNITED STATES. Introd. and Notes by C.R. Anderson. Durham, N.C.: Duke Univ. Press, 1937.

This gives events, excerpts from the log, letters, and other documents from a ship on which Melville sailed; the notes review Melville's involvement in various events recorded.

Arvin, Newton. HERMAN MELVILLE. 1950; Westport, Conn.: Greenwood Press, 1973.

The author considers Melville's life and work from a Freudian point of view. This is a valuable study and a good introduction to Melville's work, but it is not always reliable in details.

Berthoff, Warner. THE EXAMPLE OF MELVILLE. 1962; New York: Norton, 1972.

This study, which outlines Melville's development as a literary craftsman, focuses upon the fiction; but Berthoff's analysis of the elements of Melville's style is relevant to the nonfiction prose as well.

Bowen, Merlin. THE LONG ENCOUNTER: SELF AND EXPERIENCE IN THE WRITINGS OF HERMAN MELVILLE. Chicago: Univ. of Chicago Press, 1960.

The author's examination of Melville's concept of self in relation to the universe gives insight into the imagery and tone which Melville uses effectively in his nonfiction prose sketches as well as in the fiction.

Bredahl, A. Carl, Jr. MELVILLE'S ANGLES OF VISION. Gainesville: Univ. of Florida Press, 1972.

Like the studies by Berthoff and Bowen, this one explores Melville's literary techniques, focusing on the function of perspective in Melville's style.

Chase, Richard. HERMAN MELVILLE: A CRITICAL STUDY. New York: Macmillan, 1949.

A controversial but penetrating study of Melville's use of myth and symbol, this establishes the relation of Melville's work to folk tradition in American literature.

Fogle, Richard H. MELVILLE'S SHORTER TALES. Norman: Univ. of Oklahoma Press, 1960.

The author examines several of the sketches, including "The Encantadas," as well as the short fiction.

Hetherington, Hugh W. MELVILLE'S REVIEWERS: BRITISH AND AMERICAN,
1846-1891. 1961; New York: Russell and Russell, 1975.

This provides a valuable overview of Melville's reputation during
his lifetime.

Hillway, Tyrus. HERMAN MELVILLE. Rev. ed. Boston: Twayne, 1979.

This is a brief but comprehensive and intelligent introduction to
Melville's thought and works.

Howard, Leon. HERMAN MELVILLE: A BIOGRAPHY. Berkeley: Univ. of
California Press, 1951.

An attempt to understand Melville "as a human being living in
nineteenth-century America," this remains one of the best biographies. Leyda's LOG, below, supplied the source material for this
work.

Leyda, Jay. THE MELVILLE LOG: A DOCUMENTARY LIFE OF HERMAN MEL-
VILLE, 1819-1891. 2 vols. 1951; New York: Gordian, 1969.

This is an indispensable sourcebook, documenting Melville's life
and activities in great detail.

Metcalf, Eleanor M. HERMAN MELVILLE: CYCLE AND EPICYCLE. 1953;
Westport, Conn.: Greenwood Press, 1953.

Written by Melville's granddaughter, this includes several letters
and makes use of family papers.

Miller, James E., Jr. A READER'S GUIDE TO HERMAN MELVILLE. 1962;
New York: Octagon, 1973.

Dealing with Melville's analysis of "man's response to evil," this
provides an interesting perspective on his works.

Mumford, Lewis. HERMAN MELVILLE. 1929; New York: Harcourt, Brace,
1962.

This is still an important biography, although factually unreliable,
because Mumford was the first to recognize the importance of the
relationship between Melville's life and his art.

Parker, Hershel, ed. THE RECOGNITION OF HERMAN MELVILLE. Ann Arbor: Univ. of Michigan Press, 1967.

These essays give important information about the development of
Melville's reputation since 1846.

Sealts, Merton M. MELVILLE AS LECTURER. Cambridge, Mass.: Harvard Univ. Press, 1957.

> This reconstructs lectures from newspaper accounts and details Melville's activities as a lecturer from 1857 to 1860.

_____, ed. MELVILLE'S READING: A CHECK LIST OF BOOKS OWNED AND BORROWED. Madison: Univ. of Wisconsin Press, 1966. Index.

> This provides, as well as an alphabetical listing of books, a chronological account of the reading and other source material.

Walker, Franklin. IRREVERENT PILGRIMS. Seattle: Univ. of Washington Press, 1974.

> Walker compares the accounts of journeys to the Holy Land by Melville, J. Ross Browne, and Mark Twain.

Weaver, Raymond M. HERMAN MELVILLE: MARINER AND MYSTIC. New York: George H. Doran, 1921.

> Though now outdated and superseded by other studies, this was the first important biography.

RELATED GENERAL STUDIES

Brooks, Van Wyck. THE TIMES OF MELVILLE AND WHITMAN. (p. 17)
Crawley, Thomas. FOUR MAKERS OF THE AMERICAN MIND. (p. 20)
Fussell, Edwin. FRONTIER: AMERICAN LITERATURE AND THE AMERICAN WEST. (p. 22)
Lewis, R.W.B. THE AMERICAN ADAM. (p. 25)
Matthiessen, F.O. AMERICAN RENAISSANCE. (p. 27)
Marx, Leo. THE MACHINE IN THE GARDEN. (p. 26)
Miller, Perry. THE RAVEN AND THE WHALE. (p. 27)
Munson, Gorham. STYLE AND FORM IN AMERICAN PROSE. (p. 29)
Richardson, Robert D., Jr. MYTH AND LITERATURE IN THE AMERICAN RENAISSANCE. (p. 30)
Rourke, Constance. AMERICAN HUMOR. (p. 98)

JOHN LOTHROP MOTLEY (1814-77)

After trying his hand at two novels which were unsuccessful, Motley decided that his forte was writing history; so he turned to the early history of the Dutch Republic. Influenced by Carlyle, Motley took a biographical approach to history, making heroes and villains of his historical characters. Motley also preached the virtues of Protestantism as opposed to the "ruthless decadence" and authoritarianism of Catholicism. Realizing the value of paintings in depicting historical events, Motley attempted to develop a unity of theme through what he called "startling and brilliant pictures." Motley also represented the ideas of his time in his histories, which, although largely superseded by later studies, remain documents of an age. He ranks below Prescott and Parkman as a scholar, but his works contain unexcelled examples of brilliant pictorial prose.

PRINCIPAL WORKS

MORTON'S HOPE; OR, THE MEMOIRS OF A PROVINCIAL. 2 vols. 1839.
    (Autobiographical novel)
MERRY-MOUNT: A ROMANCE OF THE MASSACHUSETTS COLONY. 2 vols.
    1849. (Historical novel)
THE RISE OF THE DUTCH REPUBLIC. 3 vols. 1856.
HISTORY OF THE UNITED NETHERLANDS, FROM THE DEATH OF WILLIAM
    THE SILENT, TO THE TWELVE YEARS' TRUCE--1609. 4 vols. 1860-67.
THE LIFE AND DEATH OF JOHN OF BARNEVELD. 2 vols. 1874.

LETTERS AND JOURNALS

THE CORRESPONDENCE OF JOHN LOTHROP MOTLEY. 2 vols. Ed. George
W. Curtis. New York: Harper, 1889.

JOHN LOTHROP MOTLEY AND HIS FAMILY: FURTHER LETTERS AND RECORDS.
Ed. Susan Mildmay and Herbert A. St. J. Mildmay. London: J. Lane, 1910.

    Motley's daughter and son-in-law edited these papers, which supplement the Curtis edition (above).

RECENT EDITIONS, SELECTIONS, AND REPRINTS

JOHN LOTHROP MOTLEY: REPRESENTATIVE SELECTIONS, WITH INTRODUC-
TION, BIBLIOGRAPHY, AND NOTES. Ed. Chester P. Higby and Bradford T.
Schantz. New York: American Book Co., 1939.

THE WRITINGS OF JOHN LOTHROP MOTLEY. 17 vols. Ed. George W.
Curtis. 1900; New York: AMS Press, 1973.

> This collection includes RISE OF THE DUTCH REPUBLIC, HISTORY
> OF THE UNITED NETHERLANDS, LIFE AND DEATH OF JOHN OF
> BARNEVELD, and the CORRESPONDENCE.

BIBLIOGRAPHY

A solid listing of Motley's writings is in Blanck's BIBLIOGRAPHY OF AMERICAN
LITERATURE 6:355-67. A selected bibliography is given in the SELECTIONS,
edited by Higby and Schantz, below, including several of Motley's periodical
pieces. Motley is listed in the BIBLIOGRAPHY to the LITERARY HISTORY OF
THE UNITED STATES, pp. 664, 1265.

BIOGRAPHY AND CRITICISM

Higby, Chester P., and Bradford T. Schantz. Introd. to JOHN LOTHROP
MOTLEY: REPRESENTATIVE SELECTIONS. New York: American Book Co.,
1939.

> The introduction contains excellent comments upon Motley's works
> by the two editors, one of whom is a literary critic, the other a
> historian.

Holmes, Oliver Wendell. JOHN LOTHROP MOTLEY: A MEMOIR. Boston:
Houghton Osgood, 1879.

> Holmes was a friend of Motley. His memoir remains the only full-
> length biography of the historian.

RELATED GENERAL STUDIES

Barnes, Harry E. A HISTORY OF HISTORICAL WRITING. (p. 213)
Bassett, J.S. THE MIDDLE GROUP OF AMERICAN HISTORIANS. (p. 213)
Bremner, Robert H., ed. ESSAYS ON HISTORY AND LITERATURE. (p. 16)
Gardiner, Harold C., ed. AMERICAN CLASSICS RECONSIDERED. (p. 22)
Henderson, Harry B. VERSIONS OF THE PAST. (p. 218)
Jameson, J. Franklin. THE HISTORY OF HISTORICAL WRITING IN AMERICA.
(p. 219)
Levin, David. HISTORY AS ROMANTIC ART. (p. 220)

Loewenberg, Bert James. AMERICAN HISTORY IN AMERICAN THOUGHT.
(p. 220)
Long, Orie W. LITERARY PIONEERS. (p. 130)
Macy, John. AMERICAN WRITERS ON AMERICAN LITERATURE. (p. 26)
Nye, Russel B. SOCIETY AND CULTURE IN AMERICA. (p. 29)
Whipple, E.P. RECOLLECTIONS OF EMINENT MEN. (p. 56)

JOHN MUIR (1838-1914)

Although Muir did not complete his first book until he was fifty-six and most of his works were published in the first years of the twentieth century, he had been writing for periodicals since he was thirty-three and, when he died, left sixty volumes of journals. Except for his autobiography, most of his books are derived from these journals and from notes which he took in the wilderness. Muir's wide travels and close observations gave him an expertise matched by few geologists and naturalists of his time; his writings and influence led to the establishment of a number of national parks and forests.

Muir must also be recognized as an outstanding nature writer. There is good evidence in both his journals and his published works that Muir worked hard to find the right words with which to transcribe his experiences. He was not always successful, but he succeeded well often enough to deserve a secure place in American literature.

PRINCIPAL WORKS

THE MOUNTAINS OF CALIFORNIA. 1894.
OUR NATIONAL PARKS. 1901.
MY FIRST SUMMER IN THE SIERRA. 1911.
EDWARD HENRY HARRIMAN. 1911.
THE YOSEMITE. 1912.
THE STORY OF MY BOYHOOD AND YOUTH. 1913.

LETTERS AND JOURNALS

JOHN OF THE MOUNTAINS: THE UNPUBLISHED JOURNALS OF JOHN MUIR. Ed. Linnie M. Wolfe. Boston: Houghton Mifflin, 1938.

LETTERS TO A FRIEND. Ed. Jeanne C. Carr. 1915; Marietta, Ga.: Larlin, 1976.

Letters as well as selections from the autobiographical writings are included in Bade's LIFE AND LETTERS, published as part of the WORKS (1923-24), below.

LATER EDITIONS, SELECTIONS, AND REPRINTS

In addition to the works listed below, several volumes have been reprinted recently by Larlin, Folcroft, AMS, and Scholarly Presses; selections have been reprinted as guidebooks by Outbooks (Reno, Nevada) and as the text for exhibit books by the Sierra Club.

THE MOUNTAINS OF CALIFORNIA. Garden City, N.Y.: Natural History Press, 1961.

MY FIRST SUMMER IN THE SIERRA. Boston: Houghton Mifflin, 1979.

RAMBLES OF A BOTANIST AMONG THE PLANTS AND CLIMATES OF CALIFORNIA. Introd. William F. Kines. Los Angeles, Calif.: Dawson's, 1974.

SOUTH OF YOSEMITE: SKETCHES BY JOHN MUIR. Ed. Frederic R. Gunsky. Garden City, N.Y.: Natural History Press, 1968.

THE STORY OF MY BOYHOOD AND YOUTH. Foreword by Vernon Carstensen. Madison: Univ. of Wisconsin Press, 1965.

STUDIES IN THE SIERRA. Ed. William E. Colby. San Francisco: Sierra Club, 1950.

> Seven previously uncollected articles by Muir from the OVERLAND MONTHLY (1874-75) are published here.

TRAVELS IN ALASKA. Boston: Houghton Mifflin, 1979.

THE WILDERNESS WORLD OF JOHN MUIR. Ed. Edwin Way Teale. Boston: Houghton Mifflin, 1954.

> This selection of Muir's works has been well edited with useful notes and commentary.

WORKS. Sierra Ed. 10 vols. Ed. William Frederick Bade. Boston: Houghton Mifflin, 1917-24.

> The WORKS include the following volumes: 1, THE STORY OF MY BOYHOOD AND YOUTH and A THOUSAND-MILE WALK TO CALIFORNIA; 2, MY FIRST SUMMER IN THE SIERRA; 3, TRAVELS IN ALASKA; 4, THE MOUNTAINS OF CALIFORNIA (Part Two); 6, OUR NATIONAL PARKS; 7, THE CRUISE OF THE

CORWIN; 8, STEEP TRAILS; and 9 and 10, THE LIFE AND LETTERS OF JOHN MUIR, ed. by William Frederick Bade.

BIBLIOGRAPHY

Bradley, Cornelius B., ed. REFERENCE LIST TO PUBLISHED WRITINGS OF JOHN MUIR. Berkeley: Univ. of California Press, 1897.

The most complete listing of Muir's works is in Blanck's BIBLIOGRAPHY OF AMERICAN LITERATURE 6:387-403. A listing of selected secondary sources before 1944, especially reminiscences and memoirs, can be found in Linnie M. Wolfe's SON OF THE WILDERNESS, below. Herbert F. Smith's study, below, contains a selected list of more recent secondary sources. Muir is listed in the BIBLIOGRAPHY to the LITERARY HISTORY OF THE UNITED STATES, pp. 666, 966, 1266.

BIOGRAPHY AND CRITICISM

Lyon, Thomas J. JOHN MUIR. Western Writers Series 3. Boise, Idaho: Boise State College, 1972.

> The author of this monograph takes Muir seriously as a writer and a thinker, although the study is too brief for extensive analysis of any of the writings. Lyon sketches an outline of Muir's life and compares Muir with Robinson Jeffers, Edward Abbey, and Gary Snyder in their views of the wilderness, nature, and society. Lyon concludes that Muir's greatness lay in "his ability to convey a whole, living sense of wilderness."

Smith, Herbert F. JOHN MUIR. New York: Twayne, 1965.

> This is a fine study, concentrating on the literary qualities of Muir's work. In his preface, Smith writes, "What I have tried to do in this study is to isolate the literary qualities of Muir's writing from the merely factual and informative, to deduce his metaphysics on the one hand and to examine and analyze the style of his writing on the other." Smith succeeds admirably, perceiving a depth and continuity in Muir's thought and a precision and method in his style that have not been pointed out in previous studies.

Wolfe, Linnie M. SON OF THE WILDERNESS: THE LIFE OF JOHN MUIR. 1945; Madison: Univ. of Wisconsin Press, 1978.

> This is a well-researched biography which contains accurate details about Muir's life but little commentary about the works.

Young, Samuel Hall. ALASKA DAYS WITH JOHN MUIR. 1915; New York: Arno, 1976.

> As a companion on Muir's trip to Alaska in 1879, Young learned to share Muir's enthusiasm for the wilderness. His account of their experiences gives a great deal of insight into Muir's character.

RELATED GENERAL STUDIES

Foerster, Norman. NATURE IN AMERICAN LITERATURE. (pp. 166–67)
Fox, Stephen. JOHN MUIR AND HIS LEGACY. (p. 167)
Osborne, Henry F. IMPRESSIONS OF GREAT NATURALISTS. (p. 172)

THEODORE PARKER (1810-60)

Preaching a modified Unitarianism which put theology into the realm of actions and attitudes, Parker sought to improve both church and state, attacking those who tacitly as well as openly supported slavery and war and condemning other abuses of power. Largely self-taught, he became an accomplished linguist and scholar. As editor of the MASSACHUSETTS QUARTERLY REVIEW for three years, he wrote essays and reviews on politics, history, religion, and literature. Although he was not a particularly original or brilliant writer, his sermons and lectures are structurally more logical and coherent than are most of Emerson's essays. By putting abstract ideas into understandable words, and by being a man of action as well as of words, Parker, perhaps even more than Emerson, helped to shape American transcendentalism. He was courageous in proposing political, religious, and social reforms, but he also had the ability to make his causes popular and has come to be seen as a representative thinker of the American renaissance.

PRINCIPAL WORKS

THE PREVIOUS QUESTION BETWEEN MR. ANDREWS NORTON AND HIS
    ALUMNI MOVED AND HANDLED IN A LETTER TO ALL THOSE GEN-
    TLEMEN. [by "Levi Blodgett."] 1840.
A DISCOURSE OF MATTERS PERTAINING TO RELIGION. 1842.
CRITICAL AND MISCELLANEOUS WRITINGS. 1842.
A CRITICAL AND HISTORICAL INTRODUCTION TO THE CANONICAL SCRIP-
    TURES OF THE OLD TESTAMENT. 2 vols. 1843.
A LETTER TO THE PEOPLE OF THE UNITED STATES TOUCHING THE MATTER
    OF SLAVERY. 1848.
A SERMON OF WAR. 1846.
SPEECHES, ADDRESSES, AND OCCASIONAL SERMONS. 2 vols. 1852.
TEN SERMONS OF RELIGION. 1853.
SERMONS OF THEISM, ATHEISM, AND THE POPULAR THEOLOGY. 1853.
ADDITIONAL SPEECHES, ADDRESSES, AND OCCASIONAL SERMONS. 2
    vols. 1855.
THE TRIAL OF THEODORE PARKER, FOR THE "MISDEMEANOR" OF A SPEECH
    IN FANEUIL HALL AGAINST KIDNAPPING: WITH THE DEFENCE. 1855.
THE BIBLICAL, ECCLESIASTICAL AND PHILOSOPHICAL NOTION OF GOD.
    1858.

THEODORE PARKER'S EXPERIENCE AS A MINISTER, WITH SOME ACCOUNT OF HIS EARLY LIFE AND EDUCATION FOR THE MINISTRY. 1859.

LETTERS AND JOURNALS

The LIFE AND CORRESPONDENCE OF THEODORE PARKER by John Weiss contains the most complete collection of letters to date. Frothingham's biography also includes some letters. See below for both.

LATER EDITIONS, SELECTIONS, AND REPRINTS

THE BOSTON KIDNAPPING. New York: Arno, 1969.

> This account of Parker's activities as an abolitionist includes Parker's speech at Faneuil Hall against the Fugitive Slave Law and tells of his role in the attempt to prevent the return of Anthony Burns, a fugitive, for which Parker was tried and indicted.

THE COLLECTED WORKS OF THEODORE PARKER. 14 vols. Ed. Frances P. Cobbe. London: Truebner, 1863-74.

> This edition is incomplete, with no footnotes, index, or bibliography; but it is occasionally more reliable textually than the centenary edition.

DISCOURSE OF MATTERS PERTAINING TO RELIGION. New York: Arno, 1972.

HISTORIC AMERICANS. Ed. with Introd. Octavius B. Frothingham. Boston: H.B. Fuller, 1870.

> This is a collection of essays based upon one of the last series of lectures by Parker. These essays show the care with which Parker researched and composed his biographical lectures.

LESSONS FROM THE WORLD OF MATTER AND THE WORLD OF MAN. Ed. with Pref. Rufus Leighton. Boston: American Unitarian Assn., 1865.

> This volume presents excerpts from Parker's writing about transcendentalism and his interpretations of Unitarian doctrine.

A LETTER TO THE PEOPLE OF THE UNITED STATES TOUCHING THE MATTER OF SLAVERY. St. Clair Shores, Mich.: Scholarly Press, 1972.

QUOTATIONS ON LIBERAL RELIGION. Ed. James H. Curtis. Boston: American Unitarian Assn., 1960.

THE RIGHTS OF MAN IN AMERICA. Ed. F.B. Sanborn. 1911; New York: Negro Univ. Press, 1969.

THE SLAVE POWER. Ed. James K. Hosmer. New York: Arno, 1969.

This includes a number of Parker's speeches and sermons against slavery and slave laws.

THEODORE PARKER: AMERICAN TRANSCENDENTALIST: A CRITICAL ESSAY AND A COLLECTION OF HIS WRITINGS. Ed. Robert E. Collins. Metuchen, N.J.: Scarecrow, 1973.

This reprints six significant discourses in full: "Transcendentalism," "A Discourse of the Transient and Permanent in Christianity," "The Political Destination of America and the Signs of the Times," "The Writings of Ralph Waldo Emerson," and "A Sermon of War."

THEODORE PARKER: AN ANTHOLOGY. Ed. Henry Steele Commager. Boston: Beacon, 1960.

This is an excellent collection, with a wider range of selections than those in Collins's edition, above.

THE TRIAL OF THEODORE PARKER. . . . Westport, Conn.: Negro Univ. Press, 1970.

WEST ROXBURY SERMONS, 1834-1844. Ed. S.J. Barrows. Boston: American Unitarian Assn., 1902.

This collects early sermons not reprinted elsewhere.

THE WORKS OF THEODORE PARKER. Centenary Ed. 15 vols. 1907-13; New York: AMS Press, 1976. Bibliog.

This edition is incomplete; but it is well edited, with introductions and notes.

BIBLIOGRAPHY

Volume 15 of the centenary edition, above, includes Charles W. Wendte's listing of primary and selected secondary sources up to about 1910. Selected bibliographies, including secondary sources, are in the studies by Albrecht and Chadwick, below. Commager's biography, below, includes a useful bibliographical essay for each chapter. Parker is listed in the BIBLIOGRAPHY to the LITERARY HISTORY OF THE UNITED STATES, pp. 678, 970, 1272.

Theodore Parker

BIOGRAPHY AND CRITICISM

Albrecht, Robert C. THEODORE PARKER. New York: Twayne, 1971.

> This is a good critical introduction to Parker's works and influence.
> The chronological discussion of the published speeches, sermons,
> and writings touches only briefly on Parker's life; but the evaluation
> of his ideas is objective and informative. In placing Parker in the
> context of his time, Albrecht argues that "to know Parker's work
> is to know the central political, social, and religious conflicts of
> the crucial period of his century."

Chadwick, John W. THEODORE PARKER, PREACHER AND REFORMER. Boston:
Houghton Mifflin, 1900.

> This is a sympathetic biography, showing Parker's influence in the
> theological developments of the time.

Collins, Robert E. THEODORE PARKER: AMERICAN TRANSCENDENTALIST:
A CRITICAL ESSAY AND A COLLECTION OF HIS WRITINGS. Metuchen,
N.J.: Scarecrow, 1973.

> In his critical essay in this collection, the author argues that Park-
> er deserves at least an equal rank with Emerson in the history of
> American literature. His praise of Parker's work as being a fine
> example of "a philosophic treatise," whereas Emerson's is "only a
> suggestive impressionistic literary essay," reveals the basis for his
> judgment.

Commager, Henry Steele. THEODORE PARKER. 1936; Boston: Beacon, 1960.

> This is an excellent evaluation of Parker's achievement and in-
> fluence.

Dirks, John Edward. THE CRITICAL THEOLOGY OF THEODORE PARKER.
1948; Westport, Conn.: Greenwood Press, 1970.

> Dirks provides a useful background for understanding the theologi-
> cal influences upon Parker and his impact in turn upon religion in
> New England. It includes the pseudonymous "Levi Blodgett Letter,"
> a reply to Andrews Norton's attacks on the transcendentalists.

Frothingham, Octavius Brooks. THEODORE PARKER: A BIOGRAPHY. Boston:
J.R. Osgood, 1874.

> This is still one of the best of the biographies of Parker, but
> Frothingham's biases clearly favor the kind of liberal intellectual
> transcendentalism for which Parker spoke.

Mead, Edwin D. EMERSON AND THEODORE PARKER. Boston: American Unitarian Assn., 1910.

This study focuses upon Emerson as a significant influence on Parker.

Weiss, John. LIFE AND CORRESPONDENCE OF THEODORE PARKER. 2 vols. 1864; New York: Arno, 1969.

Although valuable as a source of primary material, Weiss's LIFE is poorly organized and difficult to use.

RELATED GENERAL STUDIES

Aaron, Daniel. MEN OF GOOD HOPE. (p. 14)
Addison, Daniel D. THE CLERGY IN AMERICAN LIFE AND LETTERS. (p. 160)
Brigance, William N., ed. A HISTORY AND CRITICISM OF AMERICAN PUBLIC ADDRESS. (p. 214)
Cameron, Kenneth W. TRANSCENDENTAL READING PATTERNS. (p. 164)
Frothingham, Octavius B. RECOLLECTIONS AND IMPRESSIONS. (p. 72)
Gohdes, Clarence L. THE PERIODICALS OF AMERICAN TRANSCENDENTALISM. (p. 61)
Hutchison, William. THE TRANSCENDENTALIST MINISTERS. (p. 168)
Lader, Lawrence. THE BOLD BRAHMINS. (p. 219-20)
Lewis, R.W.B. THE AMERICAN ADAM. (p. 25)
Pochmann, Henry A. GERMAN CULTURE IN AMERICA. (p. 172)
Smithline, Arnold. NATURAL RELIGION IN AMERICAN LITERATURE. (p. 175)
Whittemore, Robert C. MAKERS OF THE AMERICAN MIND. (p. 177)

FRANCIS PARKMAN (1823-93)

Although it was THE OREGON TRAIL which made Francis Parkman famous, his greatest ambition was to write the history of the conflict between England and France for dominance in North America, and it was to this enormous project that Parkman, despite his illnesses, devoted much of his life. His powers of observation were excellent; he made himself familiar with the areas which he wrote about and was able to reconstruct scenes and events in great detail. Parkman combined conservative, even reactionary, social and political views with a forward-looking methodology and style. He questioned the benefits of democracy and showed evidence of racial bigotry, but he was painstaking in his research and precise in his choice of words. His ability to shape historical material into coherent narrative with concreteness, vividness, excitement and immediacy gives him a place in both history and literature.

PRINCIPAL WORKS

THE CALIFORNIA AND OREGON TRAIL. 1849.
    Issued with the better-known title of THE OREGON TRAIL, 1872.
HISTORY OF THE CONSPIRACY OF PONTIAC AND THE WAR OF THE NORTH
    AMERICAN TRIBES. 1851.
VASSAL MORTON: A NOVEL. 1856.
PIONEERS OF FRANCE IN THE NEW WORLD. 1865.
THE BOOK OF ROSES. 1866.
THE JESUITS IN NORTH AMERICA IN THE SEVENTEENTH CENTURY. 1867.
THE DISCOVERY OF THE GREAT WEST. 1869.
    Issued as LA SALLE AND THE DISCOVERY OF THE GREAT WEST, 1878.
THE OLD REGIME IN CANADA. 1874.
COUNT FRONTENAC AND NEW FRANCE UNDER LOUIS XIV. 1877.
MONTCALM AND WOLFE. 1884.
A HALF-CENTURY OF CONFLICT. 1892.

LETTERS AND JOURNALS

THE JOURNALS OF FRANCIS PARKMAN. 2 vols. Ed., Introd. and notes Mason Wade. 1947; Millwood, N.Y.: Kraus, 1969.

The JOURNALS contain material which contributed to THE ORE-
GON TRAIL and several of the other histories.

LETTERS OF FRANCIS PARKMAN. 2 vols. Ed. Wilbur R. Jacobs. Norman:
Univ. of Oklahoma Press, 1960.

These well-edited letters are an essential tool in the study of Parkman.

Twenty-three letters from Parkman to Henry Stevens are included in John
Buechler's "The Correspondence of Francis Parkman and Henry Stevens, 1845-1885,"
TRANSACTIONS OF THE AMERICAN PHILOSOPHICAL SOCIETY n.s. 57, pt.
6 (August 1967): 3-36. Additional letters and excerpts from letters and journals are included in the studies by Henry Dwight Sedgwick, Howard Doughty,
and Mason Wade, below.

RECENT EDITIONS, SELECTIONS, AND REPRINTS

THE CONSPIRACY OF PONTIAC. 2 vols. Ed. Joseph Schafer. New York:
Dutton, 1943-44.

THE DISCOVERY OF THE GREAT WEST. Toronto: Ryerson, 1962.

FRANCIS PARKMAN: REPRESENTATIVE SELECTIONS. Ed. Wilbur L. Schramm.
New York: American Book Co., 1938. Bibliog.

This collection includes notes, introduction, and a critical bibliography.

A HALF-CENTURY OF CONFLICT. Ed. with Introd. Samuel Eliot Morison.
New York: Collier, 1962.

THE JESUITS IN NORTH AMERICA. Williamstown, Mass.: Corner House,
1970.

LA SALLE AND THE DISCOVERY OF THE GREAT WEST. Williamstown, Mass.:
Corner House, 1968.

MONTCALM AND WOLFE. New York: Macmillan, 1962.

THE OREGON TRAIL. Ed. with Introd. Mason Wade. New York: Heritage
Press, 1943.

This edition contains an excellent critical introduction.

THE OREGON TRAIL. Ed. and introd. E.N. Feltskog. Madison: Univ. of Wisconsin Press, 1969.

> Feltskog's authoritative text, based upon a collation of all nine editions published in Parkman's lifetime, has excellent critical notes. It also includes Frederic Remington's illustrations and map.

THE PARKMAN READER. Ed. Samuel Eliot Morison. Boston: Little, Brown, 1955.

> This collection includes a listing of Parkman's works, letters, and journals and a valuable discussion of his revisions of his historical writings.

PIONEERS OF FRANCE IN THE NEW WORLD. Williamstown, Mass.: Corner House, 1970.

THE SEVEN YEARS WAR: A NARRATIVE TAKEN FROM MONTCALM AND WOLFE, THE CONSPIRACY OF PONTIAC, AND A HALF-CENTURY OF CONFLICT. Ed. John McCallum. New York: Harper and Row, 1968.

SOME OF THE REASONS AGAINST WOMAN SUFFRAGE. Ed. Norman E. Tanis. Northridge: California State Univ. Press, 1977.

> Tanis reprints, with notes and introduction, a pamphlet published "at the request of an association of women." The work had some popularity; the earliest edition to be dated (1884) was apparently the third printing of the pamphlet.

THE WORKS OF FRANCIS PARKMAN. Champlain Ed. 21 vols. Introd. John Fiske. Boston: Little, Brown, 1897-1901.

> The La Salle edition (20 vols., 1897-98), the New Library edition (13 vols., 1901-02), and the Frontenac edition (17 vols., 1923) were all printed from the same plates as the Champlain edition. The New Library and Frontenac editions include Farnham's LIFE OF PARKMAN. The La Salle edition has been reprinted (New York: AMS Press, 1969).

BIBLIOGRAPHY

A listing of Parkman's works is in Blanck's BIBLIOGRAPHY OF AMERICAN LITERATURE 6:541-56. Additional selective bibliographies of primary and secondary sources are in the studies by Charles H. Farnham, Robert L. Gale, and Mason Wade, below, and in Morison's THE PARKMAN READER and Schramm's FRANCIS PARKMAN: REPRESENTATIVE SELECTIONS. Parkman is listed in the BIBLIOGRAPHY to the LITERARY HISTORY OF THE UNITED STATES, pp. 680, 970, 1272.

BIOGRAPHY AND CRITICISM

Doughty, Howard. FRANCIS PARKMAN. New York: Macmillan, 1962.

> This is an excellent critical biography with a perceptive analysis of the major works and a fine examination of Parkman as a literary stylist.

Farnham, Charles H. A LIFE OF FRANCIS PARKMAN. 1900; 1969; New York: Scholarly Reprints, 1970.

> This is the best of the early critical accounts of Parkman's works and contains personal details available only to the author, who was Parkman's secretary. Farnham's tracing of the traits of Parkman's personality which carry over into the histories themselves is interesting; however, the interpretation of Parkman's later years has been disputed by subsequent biographers.

Gale, Robert L. FRANCIS PARKMAN. New York: Twayne, 1973.

> In this brief but perceptive study, the author provides a biographical sketch and considers Parkman's major works in chronological order. Gale concludes that Parkman "was a great historian, a fine nineteenth-century literary artist, and a brave man."

Pease, Otis A. PARKMAN'S HISTORY: THE HISTORIAN AS LITERARY ARTIST. New Haven, Conn.: Shoe String, 1968.

> This examination of Parkman's fusion of historical facts and literary artistry is detailed, well documented, and informative.

Sedgwick, Henry D. FRANCIS PARKMAN. Philadelphia: R. West, 1973.

> A sourcebook as well as a biography, this stresses Parkman's professional preparation and character and includes long excerpts from his diary.

Wade, Mason. FRANCIS PARKMAN, HEROIC HISTORIAN. 1942; Hamden, Conn.: Shoe String, 1972.

> In a reliable and readable biography, Wade makes extensive use of the letters and journals.

RELATED GENERAL STUDIES

Bremner, Robert H., ed. ESSAYS ON HISTORY AND LITERATURE. (p. 16)
Cohen, Hennig, ed. LANDMARKS OF AMERICAN WRITING. (p. 19)
Cunliffe, Marcus, and Robin W. Winks, eds. PASTMASTERS. (p. 215)
DeVoto, Bernard. THE YEAR OF DECISION, 1846. (p. 21)
Gardiner, Harold C., ed. AMERICAN CLASSICS RECONSIDERED. (p. 22)

JAMES KIRKE PAULDING (1778-1860)

Paulding's most important contributions to American literature were his works of fiction, but his literary and social criticism should not be ignored. His political satires were his good-humored contributions to the controversy between America and England about cultural development and social institutions. He also contributed literary criticism and travel commentary and was willing to experiment with a number of different forms covering a wide range of activities.

His LIFE OF WASHINGTON is a good early biography; his travel descriptions give realistic pictures of places, societies, and customs; his defense of slavery was based upon well-known arguments presented in a plausible way. His style, based upon that of the eighteenth-century essayists, has a more lasting quality than the romantic effusions of some of his contemporaries. His literary criticism and theories--presented in the introductions to his fiction, in his magazine articles, and in his essay, "National Literature," which appeared in the last part of SALMAGUNDI, SECOND SERIES--helped lay the foundation for the early development of American realism.

PRINCIPAL PROSE WORKS

THE DIVERTING HISTORY OF JOHN BULL AND BROTHER JONATHAN, BY
    HECTOR BULL-US. 1812.
THE UNITED STATES AND ENGLAND: BEING A REPLY TO THE CRITICISM
    ON INCHIQUIN'S LETTERS. 1815.
LETTERS FROM THE SOUTH. . . . 2 vols. 1817.
SALMAGUNDI, SECOND SERIES, BY LAUNCELOT LANGSTAFF, ESQ. 2 vols.
    1819-20.
A SKETCH OF OLD ENGLAND, BY A NEW-ENGLAND MAN. 2 vols. 1822.
JOHN BULL IN AMERICA; OR, THE NEW MUNCHAUSEN. 1825.
THE MERRY TALES OF THE THREE WISE MEN OF GOTHAM. 1826. (Narra-
    tive essays often classified as fiction)
THE NEW MIRROR FOR TRAVELLERS; AND GUIDE TO THE SPRINGS. 1828.
A LIFE OF WASHINGTON. 2 vols. 1835.
WORKS. 14 vols. 1834-37.
SLAVERY IN THE UNITED STATES. 1836.
With William and Washington Irving. SALMAGUNDI; OR, THE WHIM-WHAMS

AND OPINIONS OF LAUNCELOT LANGSTAFF, ESQ. AND OTHERS. 2 vols. 1807-08.

LETTERS AND JOURNALS

THE LETTERS OF JAMES KIRKE PAULDING. Ed. Ralph M. Aderman. Madison: Univ. of Wisconsin Press, 1962.

> The editor's introduction provides a useful brief summary and an evaluation of Paulding's life and career. The short introductions to each section and the critical notes give solid background information.

LATER EDITIONS, SELECTIONS, AND REPRINTS

JOHN BULL IN AMERICA. Upper Saddle River, N.J.: Literature House, 1970.
LETTERS FROM THE SOUTH. 2 vols. in 1. New York: AMS Press, 1973.
LIFE OF WASHINGTON. 2 vols. Port Washington, N.Y.: Kennikat, 1970.
SALMAGUNDI: SECOND SERIES. New York: AMS Press, 1974.
SLAVERY IN THE UNITED STATES. Westport, Conn.: Negro Univ. Press, 1968.

BIBLIOGRAPHY

Wegelin, Oscar. A BIBLIOGRAPHY OF THE SEPARATE PUBLICATIONS OF JAMES KIRKE PAULDING, POET, NOVELIST, HUMORIST, STATESMAN, 1779-1860. Printed in the PAPERS OF THE BIBLIOGRAPHICAL SOCIETY OF AMERICA, vol. 12, nos. 1-2, 1918.

> This listing is not always accurate and should be checked against others.

The checklist of Paulding's writings in Amos L. Herold's study, below, is reliable and includes contributions to periodicals. Paulding is listed in the BIBLIOGRAPHY to the LITERARY HISTORY OF THE UNITED STATES, pp. 684, 971, 1273.

BIOGRAPHY AND CRITICISM

Herold, Amos L. JAMES KIRKE PAULDING: VERSATILE AMERICAN. 1926; New York: AMS Press, 1966.

> This is a well-documented biography, giving a sympathetic view of Paulding as a talented writer and presenting a brief summary and an evaluation of his works.

Paulding, William I. LITERARY LIFE OF JAMES K. PAULDING. New York: Scribner's, 1867.

This portrait by the author's son provides valuable source material.

RELATED GENERAL STUDIES

Callow, James T. KINDRED SPIRITS: KNICKERBOCKER WRITERS AND AMERICAN ARTISTS. (p. 362, under Irving)
Irving, Washington. LIFE AND LETTERS. Ed. Pierre M. Irving. (p. 363, under Irving)
_____. JOURNALS AND NOTEBOOKS. Ed. Nathalia Wright. (p. 359, under Irving)
_____. LETTERS, Vol. 1, 1802-1823. Ed. Ralph M. Aderman et al. (p. 359, under Irving).
Pritchard, John P. CRITICISM IN AMERICA. (p. 65)
_____. LITERARY WISE MEN OF GOTHAM. (p. 65)
Wilson, James Grant. BRYANT AND HIS FRIENDS: SOME REMINISCENCES OF THE KNICKERBOCKER WRITERS. (p. 267, under Bryant)

EDGAR ALLAN POE (1809-49)

For most of his career, Poe was best known as a magazine critic. His essays and his brilliant reviews were frequently a vehicle for a statement of his literary principles. One of his important contributions as an editor and critic was to establish a method of judging works by a coherent set of aesthetic and technical standards. Unique among his contemporaries in America, he insisted upon the ultimate importance of aesthetic purpose in writing.

Poe, like Dryden, has often been accused of constructing his critical theories to conform with his own literary practices; however, he justifiably argued that a theory can be validated only by its practical application, and, like most writer-critics, his own works illustrate his aesthetic principles. In his study of Poe as a journalist and critic, Robert D. Jacobs suggests that "Poe is a crucial figure in the history of literary criticism, not because he oversimplified important issues," but because he raised the question of bringing art to the general public. Poe believed that a true artist can affect even the dullest sensibilities.

As a reviewer and critic, Poe avoided provincial nationalism although his tastes were contemporary and his critical temper sometimes unsteady. He remains, however, an important figure in American criticism and must be recognized for his development of a systematic critical theory and an original discipline of analytical criticism.

COLLECTED WORKS

COLLECTED WORKS OF EDGAR ALLAN POE. Ed. Thomas O. Mabbott, et al. Cambridge, Mass.: Harvard Univ. Press, 1969-- .

> Mabbott had completed the editing of volume 1, which contained the poems, and was working on the tales and critical writings at the time of his death in 1968. Volumes 2 and 3, containing the tales, were edited by Maureen C. Mabbott and Eleanor D. Kewer, and appeared in 1978.

THE COMPLETE WORKS OF EDGAR ALLAN POE. Virginia Ed. 17 vols. Ed. James A. Harrison. 1902; New York: AMS Press, 1965.

LETTERS AND JOURNALS

EDGAR ALLAN POE: LETTERS AND DOCUMENTS IN THE ENOCH PRATT FREE LIBRARY. Ed. Arthur H. Quinn and Richard H. Hart. New York: Scholar's Facsimiles and Reprints, 1941.

EDGAR ALLAN POE: LETTERS TILL NOW UNPUBLISHED IN THE VALENTINE MUSEUM. Ed. Mary N. Stanard. 1925; New York: Haskell, 1973.

THE LAST LETTERS OF EDGAR ALLAN POE TO SARAH HELEN WHITMAN. Ed. James A. Harrison. 1909; Folcroft, Pa.: Folcroft, 1974.

THE LETTERS OF EDGAR ALLAN POE. Ed. John W. Ostrom. 1948; with supplement, New York: Gordian, 1966.

SOME LETTERS OF EDGAR ALLAN POE TO E.H.N. PATTERSON. Ed. Eugene Field. Chicago: Caxton Club, 1898.

Supplements to Ostrom's collection have appeared in AMERICAN LITERATURE from time to time. Woodberry's LIFE, below, includes several letters.

LATER EDITIONS, SELECTIONS, AND REPRINTS

THE COMPLETE POEMS AND STORIES OF EDGAR ALLAN POE WITH SELEC-TIONS FROM HIS CRITICAL WRITINGS. 2 vols. Ed. Arthur H. Quinn. 1946; New York: Knopf, 1964.

CRITICAL EXCERPTS FROM POE. Ed. Isaac Goldberg. Girard, Kans.: Halde-man-Julius, 1925.

EDGAR ALLAN POE AND THE PHILADELPHIA SATURDAY COURIER. Ed. John G. Varner, Jr. Charlottesville: Univ. of Virginia Press, 1933.

EDGAR ALLAN POE: REPRESENTATIVE SELECTIONS. Ed. Margaret Alterton and Hardin Craig. 1935; Darby, Pa.: Arden, 1978.

AN INTRODUCTION TO POE: A THEMATIC READER. Ed. Eric W. Carlson. Glenview, Ill.: Scott, Foresman, 1966.

LITERARY CRITICISM OF EDGAR ALLAN POE. Ed. Robert L. Hough. Lincoln: Univ. of Nebraska Press, 1965.

> Hough's important introduction discusses Poe's significance as a critic, summing up his theories of poetry and short fiction.

THE LITERATI: SOME HONEST OPINIONS ABOUT AUTORIAL MERITS AND DEMERITS. New York: J.S. Redfield, 1850.

MARGINALIA. Ed. with Introd. Isaac Goldberg. 1924. Ed. with Introd. John Carl Miller. Charlottesville: Univ. Press of Virginia, 1981.

> This collects pieces published in the UNITED STATES MAGAZINE AND DEMOCRATIC REVIEW and in GRAHAM'S AMERICAN MONTHLY MAGAZINE. The 1981 edition reprints for the first time all seventeen installments of MARGINALIA exactly as Poe published them.

POE'S DOINGS OF GOTHAM: POE'S CONTRIBUTIONS TO THE "COLUMBIA SPY." Ed. by Thomas O. Mabbott and J.E. Spannuth. 1929; Folcroft, Pa.: Folcroft, 1974.

SELECTED POETRY AND PROSE. Ed. T.O. Mabbott. New York: Modern Library, 1931.

SELECTED WRITINGS OF EDGAR ALLAN POE. Ed. E.H. Davidson. Boston: Houghton Mifflin, 1956.

SELECTIONS FROM THE CRITICAL WRITINGS OF EDGAR ALLAN POE. Ed. Frederick C. Prescott. New York: H. Holt, 1909.

SELECTIONS FROM POE'S LITERARY CRITICISM. Ed. and Introd. John Brooks Moore. New York: F.S. Crofts, 1926.

BIBLIOGRAPHY

Dameron, J. Lasley, and Irby B. Cauthen, Jr. EDGAR ALLAN POE: A BIBLIOGRAPHY OF CRITICISM, 1827-1967. Charlottesville: Univ. of Virginia Press, 1974.

> This lists almost four thousand books and articles about Poe, including items in foreign languages.

Dameron, J. Lasley, and Louis Charles Stagg. AN INDEX TO POE'S CRITICAL VOCABULARY. Hartford, Conn.: Transcendental Books, 1966.

> The authors list terms and concepts (beauty, genius, style), give the phrase in which the terms occur, and cite the source.

Heartman, Charles F., and James R. Canny. A BIBLIOGRAPHY OF FIRST PRINTINGS OF THE WRITINGS OF EDGAR ALLAN POE. Rev. ed. Hattiesburg, Miss.: Book Farm, 1943.

> This is intended for collectors rather than scholars, but still retains considerable bibliographical interest.

Hyneman, Esther K. EDGAR ALLAN POE: ANNOTATED BIBLIOGRAPHY OF CRITICISM OF POE, 1827-1972, AND HIS CONTEMPORARY REPUTATION. Boston: G.K. Hall, 1974.

> This has more detailed annotations than Dameron and Cauthen, above, but also more errors.

Hubbell, Jay B. "Edgar Allan Poe." In EIGHT AMERICAN AUTHORS. Rev. ed. James Woodress. New York: Norton, 1971, pp. 3-36.

Moldenhauer, Joseph J. DESCRIPTIVE CATALOG OF EDGAR ALLAN POE: MANUSCRIPTS IN THE HUMANITIES RESEARCH CENTER LIBRARY. Hartford, Conn.: Transcendental Books, 1973.

> This publication details the manuscript holdings in the Humanities Research Center at the University of Texas, Austin; it includes letters, poems, tales, and essays.

Robbins, J. Albert. CHECKLIST OF EDGAR ALLAN POE. Columbus, Ohio: Charles E. Merrill, 1969.

> Included are books and major separate publications by Poe as well as biographies, checklists, scholarship, and Poe criticism.

Robertson, John W. BIBLIOGRAPHY OF THE WRITINGS OF EDGAR ALLAN POE. 2 vols. 1934; New York: Kraus, 1969.

POE STUDIES (1971--) continues the POE NEWSLETTER (1968-71) and includes essays, book reviews, and bibliographical items. Until 1968, the EMERSON SOCIETY QUARTERLY also included listings of items related to Poe. Poe is listed in the BIBLIOGRAPHY to the LITERARY HISTORY OF THE UNITED STATES, pp. 689, 972, 1275.

BIOGRAPHY AND CRITICISM

Allen, Michael. POE AND THE BRITISH MAGAZINE TRADITION. 1969; Darby, Pa.: Arden, 1978.

> The author shows the contemporary situation Poe confronted as a practicing journalist and his response to it and concludes that Poe's idealization of the artist as an elite member of society conflicted with the necessity for adjusting to popular demands and mass-producing techniques.

Alterton, Margaret. ORIGINS OF POE'S CRITICAL THEORY. Iowa City: Univ. of Iowa Press, 1925.

Alterton finds Poe's sources in Plato, BLACKWOOD'S, Schlegel, scientific journals, and the PHILOSOPHICAL TRANSACTIONS OF THE ROYAL SOCIETY OF LONDON.

Braddy, Haldeen. GLORIOUS INCENSE: THE FULFILLMENT OF EDGAR ALLAN POE. Metuchen, N.J.: Scarecrow, 1952.

The author considers, among other subjects, Poe's aesthetic models and his criticism.

Broussard, Louis. THE MEASURE OF POE. Norman: Univ. of Oklahoma Press, 1969. Bibliog.

The review of Poe's criticism in this study is somewhat sketchy.

Buranelli, Vincent. EDGAR ALLAN POE. Rev. ed. Boston: G.K. Hall, 1977.

This is a good introduction, emphasizing Poe's Romanticism and symbolism and adopting a balanced position between Freudian and anti-Freudian critical views.

Campbell, Killis. THE MIND OF POE AND OTHER STUDIES. 1933; New York: Russell and Russell, 1962.

The author's essays on Poe discuss his activities as a critic and journalist, as well as his poetry and fiction.

Carlson, E.W., ed. THE RECOGNITION OF EDGAR ALLAN POE: SELECTED CRITICISM SINCE 1829. Ann Arbor: Univ. of Michigan Press, 1966.

Most of the essays in this collection focus on the poetry and fiction, although Poe's criticism is mentioned.

Cooke, John Esten. POE AS LITERARY CRITIC. Ed. with Introd. and Notes by N. Bryllion Fagin. Baltimore, Md.: Johns Hopkins Press, 1946.

A contemporary of Poe, Cooke argued that Poe was an envious man who descended into "petty spites and rivalries" in his criticism.

Davidson, Edward H. POE: A CRITICAL STUDY. Cambridge, Mass.: Harvard Univ. Press, 1957.

This study focuses primarily upon symbolism in the poems and tales, but mentions Poe's criticism in the context of the Romantic tradition.

Goldberg, Isaac. POE AS A LITERARY CRITIC. Girard, Kans.: Haldeman-Julius, 1924.

The author discusses and attempts "to correlate in [Poe] the theorist, the pedant," and the practicing critic.

Ingram, John H. EDGAR ALLAN POE: HIS LIFE, LETTERS AND OPINIONS. 1880; New York: AMS Press, 1965.

This was the first good, corrective biography of Poe by an ardent defender.

Jackson, David K. POE AND THE SOUTHERN LITERARY MESSENGER. 1934; New York: Haskell, 1970.

This is a useful study of Poe's relations with and contributions to the MESSENGER.

Jacobs, Robert D. POE: JOURNALIST AND CRITIC. Baton Rouge: Louisiana State Univ. Press, 1969.

Giving a full account of Poe's career as a reviewer, editor, and literary theoretician, this is probably the definitive work on Poe's critical writings. The author discusses the influence of eighteenth-century aesthetic theories and nineteenth-century organic theories on Poe's development as a critic and examines "the operative regulations of Poe's practical criticism."

Moss, Sidney P. POE'S LITERARY BATTLES: THE CRITIC IN THE CONTEXT OF HIS LITERARY MILIEU. Durham, N.C.: Duke Univ. Press, 1963.

The author focuses upon Poe's literary criticism and the politics of the world of journalism, seeing Poe as a "champion of literary values" who was crushed by a third-rate opposition and contemporary publishing practices.

_____. POE'S MAJOR CRISIS: HIS LIBEL SUIT AND NEW YORK'S LITERARY WORLD. Durham, N.C.: Duke Univ. Press, 1970.

This documents the eclipse of Poe's reputation caused by the publication of the "Literati" series, the antagonism it aroused in his contemporaries, and his libel suit against the owners of the MIRROR.

Parks, Edd Winfield. EDGAR ALLAN POE AS LITERARY CRITIC. Athens: Univ. of Georgia Press, 1964.

The author describes Poe's sources, the shifts in his critical thinking, and his strengths and weaknesses as critic and craftsman. Parks argues that Poe's critical theories were mainly formed by his work as a magazine editor and critic.

Quinn, Arthur H. EDGAR ALLAN POE: A CRITICAL BIOGRAPHY, 1941; New York: Cooper Square, 1970.

One of the best factual biographies, this emphasizes Poe's role as an editor who excelled in criticism, fiction, and, chiefly, poetry.

Quinn, Patrick F. THE FRENCH FACE OF EDGAR POE. Carbondale: Southern Illinois Univ. Press, 1957.

The author focuses primarily on the fiction and poetry, but also discusses the influences upon the French of Poe's criticism and the conflict in Poe between the creative and the analytical faculties.

Rans, Geoffrey. EDGAR ALLAN POE. Edinburgh: Oliver and Boyd, 1965.

This evaluation of Poe's work begins with a discussion of EUREKA and Poe's criticism and examines these works against the background of Poe's literary theories and philosophy.

Regan, Robert, ed. POE: A COLLECTION OF CRITICAL ESSAYS. Englewood Cliffs, N.J.: Prentice-Hall, 1967.

Although this gives a good overview of critical attitudes, the focus is primarily on the fiction.

Richard, Claude. EDGAR ALLAN POE: JOURNALISTE ET CRITIQUE. Paris: Editions Klincksieck, 1978.

This is an excellent complement to Robert D. Jacobs' study (above) discussing Poe's literary theories, criticism, and journalism.

Woodberry, George Edward. THE LIFE OF EDGAR ALLAN POE, PERSONAL AND LITERARY. . . . 2 vols. 1885; 1909; New York: Biblo and Tannen, 1965.

This is still an excellent literary biography, although Woodberry was unaware of Rufus Griswold's forgeries of Poe's letters.

RELATED GENERAL STUDIES

Abel, Darrel, ed. CRITICAL THEORY IN THE AMERICAN RENAISSANCE. (p. 62)
Brooks, Van Wyck. THE FLOWERING OF NEW ENGLAND. (p. 17)
_____ . THE WORLD OF WASHINGTON IRVING. (p. 17)
Brownell, W.C. AMERICAN PROSE MASTERS. (p. 17)
Charvat, William. LITERARY PUBLISHING IN AMERICA. (p. 19)
_____ . THE PROFESSION OF AUTHORSHIP IN AMERICA, 1800-1890. (p. 19)
DeMille, George E. LITERARY CRITICISM IN AMERICA. (p. 62)
Duyckinck, Evert. A. CYCLOPAEDIA OF AMERICAN LITERATURE. (p. 47)
Foerster, Norman. AMERICAN CRITICISM. (p. 63)

Gardiner, Harold C. AMERICAN CLASSICS RECONSIDERED. (p. 22)
Howe, Mark A. De Wolfe. AMERICAN BOOKMEN. (p. 73)
Macy, John. THE SPIRIT OF AMERICAN LITERATURE. (p. 26)
Miller, Perry. THE RAVEN AND THE WHALE. (p. 27)
Minor, Benjamin B. THE SOUTHERN LITERARY MESSENGER, 1834-64. (p. 64)
Mott, Frank L. HISTORY OF AMERICAN MAGAZINES. (p. 61)
Munson, Gorham B. STYLE AND FORM IN AMERICAN PROSE. (p. 29)
Pochmann, Henry A. GERMAN CULTURE IN AMERICA. (p. 172)
Pritchard, John P. CRITICISM IN AMERICA. (p. 67)
_____. RETURN TO THE FOUNTAINS. (p. 66)
Smith, Bernard. FORCES IN AMERICAN CRITICISM. (p. 66)
Stafford, John. THE LITERARY CRITICISM OF "YOUNG AMERICA." (p. 67)
Stedman, E. Clarence. POETS OF AMERICA. (p. 52)
Stoddard, Richard H. RECOLLECTIONS PERSONAL AND LITERARY. (p. 76)
Stovall, Floyd. AMERICAN IDEALISM. (p. 32)
_____, ed. THE DEVELOPMENT OF AMERICAN LITERARY CRITICISM. (p. 68)
Wimsatt, W.K., and Cleanth Brooks. LITERARY CRITICISM: A SHORT HISTORY. (p. 31)

WILLIAM HICKLING PRESCOTT (1796-1859)

Influenced by Ticknor, Prescott became enthusiastic about the possibilities of Spanish history as a subject and dedicated himself to the studies which were to result in his four major works. Prescott was relatively free of nationalistic bias but was occasionally suspicious of Catholicism. He felt that good historical writing should have a dramatic form and purpose, unity through a central theme, and concrete details derived from primary sources. Prescott's scholarship was thorough and diligent, although his sources were sometimes questionable. His style, modeled after the eighteenth-century English essay, was admirably clear but has sometimes been judged as overly stiff and formal. His structure and dramatic sense were masterful. Despite some of the limitations of his use of language, Prescott was able to fit form to function in the best manner of the literary artist.

PRINCIPAL WORKS

HISTORY OF THE REIGN OF FERDINAND AND ISABELLA, THE CATHOLIC. 3 vols. 1838.
HISTORY OF THE CONQUEST OF MEXICO, WITH A PRELIMINARY VIEW OF THE ANCIENT MEXICAN CIVILIZATION AND THE LIFE OF HERNANDO CORTES. 3 vols. 1843.
BIOGRAPHICAL AND CRITICAL MISCELLANIES. 1845. Revised and enlarged, 1850. New ed., 1857.
HISTORY OF THE CONQUEST OF PERU, WITH A PRELIMINARY VIEW OF THE CIVILIZATION OF THE INCAS. 2 vols. 1847.
A HISTORY OF THE REIGN OF PHILIP THE SECOND. 3 vols. 1855-58.

This work had not been completed at the time of Prescott's death.

LETTERS AND JOURNALS

CORRESPONDENCE OF WILLIAM HICKLING PRESCOTT, 1833-1847. Ed. Roger Wolcott. Boston: Houghton Mifflin, 1925.

THE LITERARY MEMORANDA OF WILLIAM HICKLING PRESCOTT. 2 vols. Ed. with Introd. C. Harvey Gardiner. Norman: Univ. of Oklahoma Press, 1961.

> This includes Prescott's journals of literary work as well as his personal diary and gives insight into the labor and inspiration involved in his creative process.

PAPERS OF WILLIAM HICKLING PRESCOTT. Ed. C. Harvey Gardiner. Urbana: Univ. of Illinois Press, 1964.

> Consisting primarily of letters which document Prescott's life and career, these papers include correspondence with Bancroft, Motley, Irving, Holmes, Longfellow, Sparks, and Ticknor. Other materials are accounts, memoranda, publishing contracts, and miscellaneous papers.

UNPUBLISHED LETTERS TO GAYANGOS IN THE LIBRARY OF THE HISPANIC SOCIETY OF AMERICA. Ed. Clara L. Penney. New York: Hispanic Society of America, 1927.

RECENT EDITIONS, SELECTIONS, AND REPRINTS

BIOGRAPHICAL AND CRITICAL MISCELLANIES. Darby, Pa.: Arden, 1978.

HISTORY OF THE CONQUEST OF MEXICO. 2 vols. Abridged and Ed. by C. Harvey Gardiner in 1 vol. 1957; Chicago: Univ. of Chicago Press, 1966.

> Gardiner's introduction and notes to the 1966 edition are excellent.

"HISTORY OF THE CONQUEST OF MEXICO" AND "HISTORY OF THE CONQUEST OF PERU." New York: Modern Library, 1936.

HISTORY OF THE CONQUEST OF PERU. New York: Dutton, 1957.

HISTORY OF FERDINAND AND ISABELLA. Abridged and Ed. C. Harvey Gardiner. Carbondale: Southern Illinois Univ. Press, 1962.

PRESCOTT'S HISTORIES: THE RISE AND DECLINE OF THE SPANISH EMPIRE. Ed. with Introd. Irwin R. Blacker. 1963; reissued in paperback as THE PORTABLE PRESCOTT. New York: Viking, 1966.

> Blacker's introduction is an excellent critical commentary on the works included in this collection.

WILLIAM HICKLING PRESCOTT: REPRESENTATIVE SELECTIONS. Ed. William Charvat and Michael Kraus. 1943; Norwood, Pa.: Norwood Press, 1979.

The introduction to this collection presents an insightful discussion of Prescott as writer and historian.

THE WORKS OF WILLIAM HICKLING PRESCOTT. Montezuma ed. 22 vols. Ed. Wilfred H. Monroe. 1904; New York: AMS Press, 1968.

BIBLIOGRAPHY

Gardiner, C. Harvey. WILLIAM HICKLING PRESCOTT: AN ANNOTATED BIBLIOGRAPHY OF PUBLISHED WORKS. Washington, D.C.: Library of Congress, 1958.

Selected secondary sources are listed in the editions by Charvat and Kraus and by Blacker, above. A listing of manuscript sources is in Gardiner's biography and in Cline et al., eds., WILLIAM HICKLING PRESCOTT: A MEMORIAL, below. Prescott is listed in the BIBLIOGRAPHY to the LITERARY HISTORY OF THE UNITED STATES, pp. 700, 978, 1282.

BIOGRAPHY AND CRITICISM

Cline, Howard F., et al., eds. WILLIAM HICKLING PRESCOTT: A MEMORIAL. Durham, N.C.: Duke Univ. Press, 1959.

This includes modern critical articles, a checklist of manuscripts, and a collection of contemporary reviews.

Darnell, Donald G. WILLIAM HICKLING PRESCOTT. Boston: Twayne, 1975.

In this brief analysis of Prescott's career and works, the author finds much to admire in Prescott's treatment of history, seeing him as one "who, while writing a splendidly conceived and solidly based narrative history, had the imagination to perceive evil and also had the sense of moral responsibility to call it by its name."

Gardiner, C. Harvey. PRESCOTT AND HIS PUBLISHERS. Carbondale: Southern Illinois Univ. Press, 1959.

In addition to presenting Prescott's relationship with his publishers, this study discusses Prescott's character, his dedication to scholarly authorship, and his role in the publication of his books. It also contributes to an understanding of the publishing world, including the conflict over the international copyright.

_____. WILLIAM HICKLING PRESCOTT: A BIOGRAPHY. Introd. Allan Nevins. Austin: Univ. of Texas Press, 1969.

Based upon Gardiner's excellent knowledge of Prescott's memoranda and correspondence, this biography gives an accurate and well-detailed account of Prescott's life. As a factual and largely sympathetic source, this supersedes previous biographies, although it does not deal with the works.

Ogden, Rollo W. WILLIAM HICKLING PRESCOTT. Boston: Houghton Mifflin, 1904.

This short biography presents a good analysis of Prescott's political attitudes and his personality. Although not as thorough as Ticknor's biography, this served as a corrective to that work in its use of material which Ticknor ignored.

Peck, Harry Thurston. WILLIAM HICKLING PRESCOTT. 1905; New York: AMS Press, 1970.

Better in its criticism of the works than in its biographical details, this gives a useful evaluation and analysis of Prescott as a historian and a literary stylist.

Ticknor, George. LIFE OF WILLIAM HICKLING PRESCOTT. 1864; New York: AMS Press, 1968.

For many years the standard biography, this has now been superseded by Gardiner's work, above.

RELATED GENERAL STUDIES

Bassett, J.S. THE MIDDLE GROUP OF AMERICAN HISTORIANS. (p. 213)
Bremner, Robert H., ed. ESSAYS ON HISTORY AND LITERATURE. (p. 16)
Gardiner, Harold C., ed. AMERICAN CLASSICS RECONSIDERED. (p. 22)
Henderson, Harry P. VERSIONS OF THE PAST. (p. 218)
Jameson, J. Franklin. THE HISTORY OF HISTORICAL WRITING IN AMERICA. (p. 219)
Levin, David. HISTORY AS ROMANTIC ART. (p. 220)
Lewis, R.W.B. THE AMERICAN ADAM. (p. 25)
Loewenberg, Bert James. AMERICAN HISTORY IN AMERICAN THOUGHT. (p. 220)
Macy, John, ed. AMERICAN WRITERS ON AMERICAN LITERATURE. (p. 26)
Nye, Russel B. SOCIETY AND CULTURE IN AMERICA. (p. 29)

WILLIAM GILMORE SIMMS (1806-70)

Simms's current reputation rests largely on his fiction, and the recent proliferation of criticism has been focused principally on the novels; however, a good part of Simms's impressive output was in the form of critical essays. Some of his better criticism can be found in the SOUTHERN QUARTERLY REVIEW, which he edited, but much of it is unsigned and/or scattered in prefaces and in articles in other southern journals. In his criticism, Simms emphasized the importance of design in fiction--that is, an overall theme and plan of construction in narration and characterization. His theories of historical romance emphasize the importance of truth to the spirit of the past rather than accuracy of detail, and he makes a clear-cut distinction between the "romance" and the "novel." Simms's reviews and essays represent current opinion rather than original insights, but he was honest and fair in his judgments, and his nonfiction prose works are a solid contribution to American literature.

PRINCIPAL NONFICTION PROSE WORKS

SLAVERY IN AMERICA. 1838.
THE HISTORY OF SOUTH CAROLINA. 1840.
THE GEOGRAPHY OF SOUTH CAROLINA. 1843.
THE LIFE OF FRANCIS MARION. 1844.
VIEWS AND REVIEWS IN AMERICAN LITERATURE, HISTORY AND FICTION.
    1845.
THE LIFE OF CAPTAIN JOHN SMITH. 1846.
THE LIFE OF NATHANAEL GREENE. 1849.
SOUTH-CAROLINA IN THE REVOLUTIONARY WAR. 1853.
SACK AND DESTRUCTION OF THE CITY OF COLUMBIA, SOUTH CAROLINA.
    1865.

LETTERS AND JOURNALS

THE LETTERS OF WILLIAM GILMORE SIMMS. 5 vols. Ed. Mary C. Simms Oliphant et al. Introd. Donald Davidson. Columbia: Univ. of South Carolina Press, 1952-56.

The introduction and the brief biographical sketch, the latter written by A.S. Salley, are useful additions to these well-edited volumes.

LATER EDITIONS, SELECTIONS, AND REPRINTS

THE LIFE OF CAPTAIN JOHN SMITH. Freeport, N.Y.: Books for Libraries, 1970.

THE LIFE OF FRANCIS MARION. Freeport, N.Y.: Books for Libraries, 1970.

SACK AND DESTRUCTION OF THE CITY OF COLUMBIA, SOUTH CAROLINA. Ed. A.S. Salley. Freeport, N.Y.: Books for Libraries, 1970.

VIEWS AND REVIEWS IN AMERICAN LITERATURE, HISTORY AND FICTION. Ed. with Introd. C. Hugh Holman. Cambridge, Mass.: Belknap Press, Harvard Univ. Press, 1962.

> Holman's introduction is an excellent discussion of Simms's contributions as a critic and essayist. Holman notes that VIEWS AND REVIEWS was "a virtual manifesto in the young American literary world of the 1840s. Thus it was an important document in American literary and cultural history, whatever its weaknesses as criticism may be."

WORKS OF WILLIAM GILMORE SIMMS. 20 vols. 1853-56; St. Clair Shores, Mich.: Scholarly Press, 1973.

> Several of Simms's prefaces to these volumes, which include only the fiction and poetry, contain important critical statements.

THE WRITINGS OF WILLIAM GILMORE SIMMS: THE CENTENNIAL EDITION. 15 vols. projected. General Ed. John C. Guilds. Columbia: Univ. of South Carolina Press, 1969-- .

> Volume 4, edited by John R. Welsh, as SOCIAL AND POLITICAL ESSAYS, will include much of Simms's nonfiction prose.

BIBLIOGRAPHY

Kibler, James E. PSEUDONYMOUS PUBLICATIONS OF WILLIAM GILMORE SIMMS. Athens: Univ. of Georgia Press, 1976.

Salley, A.S. CATALOGUE OF THE SALLEY COLLECTION OF THE WORKS OF WILLIAM GILMORE SIMMS. Columbia, S.C.: Privately Printed, 1943.

Watson, Charles S. "William Gilmore Simms: An Essay in Bibliography." RESOURCES FOR AMERICAN LITERARY STUDY 3 (1973): 3-26.

Wegelin, Oscar. A BIBLIOGRAPHY OF THE SEPARATE WRITINGS OF WILLIAM GILMORE SIMMS OF SOUTH CAROLINA, 1806-1870. Hattiesburg, Miss.: Book Farm, 1941.

THE LETTERS OF WILLIAM GILMORE SIMMS, above, includes one of the fullest listings of Simms's periodical writings. Simms is listed in the BIBLIOGRAPHY to the LITERARY HISTORY OF THE UNITED STATES, pp. 720, 983, 1290.

BIOGRAPHY AND CRITICISM

Faust, Drew Gilpin. A SACRED CIRCLE: THE DILEMMA OF THE INTELLECTUAL IN THE OLD SOUTH, 1840-1860. Baltimore, Md.: Johns Hopkins Press, 1977.

> The author shows how Simms and his associates dealt with the social and cultural problems of the South just prior to the Civil War.

Holman, C. Hugh. THE IMMODERATE PAST: THE SOUTHERN WRITER AND HISTORY. Athens: Univ. of Georgia Press, 1977.

> The section on Simms in this study focuses upon his historical fiction, but it mentions his social and political views in its discussion of Simms's changing perceptions of revolutionary loyalists.

Parks, Edd Winfield. WILLIAM GILMORE SIMMS AS LITERARY CRITIC. Athens: Univ. of Georgia Press, 1961.

> This is the most complete summary and evaluation of Simms's critical essays. After surveying much of the criticism, Parks concludes that "he was a good but not a great critic."

Ridgely, J.V. WILLIAM GILMORE SIMMS. New York: Twayne, 1962.

> In this first full-length critical study of Simms's work, the author devotes one short chapter to Simms's literary theories. The discussion and evaluation of the fiction is well-considered and informative and includes, in passing, some mention of Simms's ideas about the qualities of good fiction and romance.

Trent, William P. WILLIAM GILMORE SIMMS. Boston: Houghton Mifflin, 1892.

> The only full-length biography to date, this contains valuable material unavailable elsewhere, but it is marred by Trent's hostility to the Old South, which Simms represented and defended.

Wakelyn, Jon L. THE POLITICS OF A LITERARY MAN: WILLIAM GILMORE SIMMS. Westport, Conn.: Greenwood Press, 1973.

> A study of the battles of party and personality in antebellum South Carolina, this analyzes private and public documents to support the conclusion that Simms sacrificed art and literary distinction to a defense of the South.

RELATED GENERAL STUDIES

Hubbell, Jay B. THE SOUTH IN AMERICAN LITERATURE, 1607-1900. (p. 24)
Miller, Perry. THE RAVEN AND THE WHALE. (p. 27)
Parks, Edd Winfield. ANTE-BELLUM SOUTHERN LITERARY CRITICISM. (p. 65)
Stovall, Floyd. THE DEVELOPMENT OF AMERICAN LITERARY CRITICISM.
   (p. 68)

HARRIET BEECHER STOWE (1811-96)

If Stowe had not written UNCLE TOM'S CABIN, her nonfiction prose would merit little more than a brief acknowledgment. On the other hand, UNCLE TOM'S CABIN is more prominent in the history of reform literature than as a contribution to American fiction. Stowe's nonfiction prose falls into the general categories of travel writings and regional sketches, religious essays, domestic advice, and biographical sketches. The descriptions of Florida in PALMETTO-LEAVES remain excellent documentary sources. Her biographical sketches are undistinguished; her study of Byron far more revealing of Stowe's personality than of Byron's life or relationships. However, her pieces on Christian womanhood reveal a strong streak of feminist independence.

Her best essays from the ATLANTIC were collected in THE WRITINGS, below. Other uncollected magazine pieces, primarily those from the Cincinnati JOURNAL, the WESTERN MONTHLY MAGAZINE, the CHRISTIAN UNION, GODEY'S LADY'S BOOK, and HEARTH AND HOME have gone largely unnoticed. Although carelessly and hastily written, and often sentimental or banal, these contain much of interest for a student of the period.

PRINCIPAL NONFICTION PROSE WORKS

SUNNY MEMORIES OF FOREIGN LANDS. 1854.
HOUSE AND HOME PAPERS. 1865. [by Christopher Crowfield]
LITTLE FOXES. 1866. [by Christopher Crowfield]
THE CHIMNEY-CORNER. 1868. [by Christopher Crowfield]
MEN OF OUR TIMES. 1868.
LADY BYRON VINDICATED. 1870.
PALMETTO-LEAVES. 1873.
WOMAN IN SACRED HISTORY. 1873.
    Reissued as BIBLE HEROINES, 1878.
FOOTSTEPS OF THE MASTER. 1876.
THE WRITINGS OF HARRIET BEECHER STOWE. 16 vols. 1896.

LETTERS AND JOURNALS

The biographical studies by Charles E. Stowe and by Annie Fields, below, include letters by Stowe. The papers in the Stowe-Day Memorial Library have been compiled and edited by Mair, French, and Royce, below.

LATER EDITIONS, SELECTIONS, AND REPRINTS

THE CHIMNEY CORNER. Plainview, N.Y.: Books for Libraries, 1972.

LADY BYRON VINDICATED. Philadelphia: R. West, 1973.

MEN OF OUR TIMES. Freeport, N.Y.: Books for Libraries, 1974.

PALMETTO-LEAVES. Gainesville: Univ. of Florida Press, 1968.

THE WRITINGS OF HARRIET BEECHER STOWE. 16 vols. New York: AMS Press, 1967.

BIBLIOGRAPHY

Ashton, Jean W. HARRIET BEECHER STOWE: A REFERENCE GUIDE. Boston: G.K. Hall, 1977.

> This lists, with annotations, writings about Stowe.

Hildreth, Margaret Holdbrook. HARRIET BEECHER STOWE: A BIBLIOGRAPHY. Hamden, Conn.: Shoe String, 1976.

> This contains an extensive listing of Stowe's writings; including periodical publications, pamphlets, and works in anthologies.

Mair, Margaret Granville, ed. THE PAPERS OF HARRIET BEECHER STOWE. A BIBLIOGRAPHY OF THE MANUSCRIPTS IN THE STOWE-DAY MEMORIAL LIBRARY. Ed. Earl A. French and Diana Royce. Hartford, Conn.: Stowe-Day Foundation, 1977.

Stowe is listed in the BIBLIOGRAPHY to the LITERARY HISTORY OF THE UNITED STATES, pp. 736, 989, 1298.

BIOGRAPHY AND CRITICISM

The works listed below exclude those devoted primarily to Stowe's fiction.

Adams, John R. HARRIET BEECHER STOWE. New York: Twayne, 1963.

This survey presents a critical estimate and summary of Stowe's principal works. It is fairly objective and informative, but Stowe's nonfiction prose deserves a more careful and sympathetic treatment.

Ammons, Elizabeth, ed. CRITICAL ESSAYS ON HARRIET BEECHER STOWE. Boston: G.K. Hall, 1980.

The collection contains commentary by such Stowe contemporaries as Charles Dudley Warner, William Dean Howells, and Henry James, by black writers Paul Laurence Dunbar, Langston Hughes, and James Baldwin, and by modern critics including Anthony Burgess, Leslie Fiedler, and Edmund Wilson.

Fields, Annie A. LIFE AND LETTERS OF HARRIET BEECHER STOWE. 1897; Detroit, Mich.: Gale Research Co., 1970.

Much of the material in this sympathetic biography was taken from Stowe's own MEMOIRS or from her letters.

Foster, Charles H. THE RUNGLESS LADDER: HARRIET BEECHER STOWE AND NEW ENGLAND PURITANISM. 1954; New York: Cooper Square, 1970.

The author characterizes Stowe as an "Edwardsean Calvinist" whose books are a symbolic representation of her theological struggles.

French, Earl A., and Diana Royce, eds. PORTRAITS OF A NINETEENTH CEN-TURY FAMILY: A SYMPOSIUM ON THE BEECHER FAMILY. Hartford, Conn.: Stowe-Day Foundation, 1976.

A collection of papers presented at a symposium honoring Lyman Beecher's two-hundredth birthday anniversary, this includes two essays dealing with Harriet.

Gilbertson, Catherine. HARRIET BEECHER STOWE. 1937; Port Washington, N.Y.: Kennikat, 1968.

A well-written biography, this places Stowe in the context of nine-teenth-century genteel aspirations and theological conflicts.

Johnston, Johanna. RUNAWAY TO HEAVEN: THE STORY OF HARRIET BEECHER STOWE. Garden City, N.Y.: Doubleday, 1963.

A popular biography, this attempts to explain Stowe in terms of her nineteenth-century backgrounds.

Moers, Ellen. HARRIET BEECHER STOWE AND AMERICAN LITERATURE. Hart-ford, Conn.: Stowe-Day Foundation, 1978.

This publishes a lecture delivered in November 1976 to the friends of the Harriet Beecher Stowe House and Research Library. An interesting "Note on Mark Twain and Harriet Beecher Stowe" is added.

Stowe, Charles E. LIFE OF HARRIET BEECHER STOWE: COMPILED FROM HER JOURNALS AND LETTERS. 1889; Detroit: Gale Library of Lives and Letters, 1967.

> The authorized family biography, this contains letters and other primary source materials. It was compiled and written by her youngest child while Stowe was alive and presents the image of herself that Stowe wished to present to posterity.

Stowe, Charles E., and Lyman Beecher Stowe. HARRIET BEECHER STOWE: THE STORY OF HER LIFE. Boston: Houghton Mifflin, 1911.

> This centennial biography contains new resource material but does not add to the biographical information of the earlier volume by Charles E. Stowe.

Wagenknecht, Edward. HARRIET BEECHER STOWE: THE KNOWN AND THE UNKNOWN. New York: Oxford Univ. Press, 1965.

> This sympathetic study, particularly of Stowe's inner life and family relationships, is based in part on unpublished letters. The author concludes that Stowe's literary affinities are more with Clemens and George Washington Cable than with the sentimental novelists.

Wilson, Forrest. CRUSADER IN CRINOLINE: THE LIFE OF HARRIET BEECHER STOWE. 1941; Westport, Conn.: Greenwood Press, 1972.

> An interesting and well-detailed biography with excellent documentation, this is a comprehensive and scholarly account of the life, although it does not say much about the writings of Stowe.

Wise, Winifred Esther. HARRIET BEECHER STOWE: WOMAN WITH A CAUSE. New York: G.P. Putnam's, 1965.

> This popular biography focuses on the years before the publication of UNCLE TOM'S CABIN.

RELATED GENERAL STUDIES

Beecher, Catharine. AN ESSAY ON SLAVERY AND ABOLITION. (p. 197)
_____. THE TRUE REMEDY FOR THE WRONGS OF WOMAN. (p. 192)
Beecher, Lyman. AUTOBIOGRAPHY. (p. 136-37)
Caskey, Marie. CHARIOT OF FIRE: RELIGION AND THE BEECHER FAMILY. (p. 256, under Henry Ward Beecher)
Merideth, Robert. THE POLITICS OF THE UNIVERSE: EDWARD BEECHER, ABOLITION, AND ORTHODOXY. (p. 221)

Rourke, Constance. TRUMPETS OF JUBILEE. (p. 223)

Rugoff, Milton. THE BEECHERS. (p. 257, under Henry Ward Beecher)

Sklar, Kathryn. CATHARINE BEECHER: A STUDY IN AMERICAN DOMESTI-
    CITY. (p. 224)

Stowe, Lyman Beecher. SAINTS, SINNERS AND BEECHERS. (p. 257, under
    Henry Ward Beecher)

BAYARD TAYLOR (1825-78)

Although Bayard Taylor was most ambitious to be a poet, his international fame and popularity during his lifetime came from his travel writings and journalism. His first trip to Europe was made with meager means, and his book about those travels was widely read. He covered the Gold Rush for Greeley's New York TRIBUNE; that experience was recounted in ELDORADO, which is probably his best travel piece. Most of his other travel books were also originally published as letters to the TRIBUNE. Taylor's travel writings were conventional, following the taste and style of the times, and they remain of interest as embodiments of a type rather than as unusual or original writing. The parodies of contemporary poets in THE ECHO CLUB remain mildly humorous. The lectures published as STUDIES IN GERMAN LITERATURE and the pieces collected in CRITICAL ESSAYS AND LITERARY NOTES, below, show Taylor to have been a lucid and perceptive critic.

PRINCIPAL PROSE WORKS

VIEWS A-FOOT; OR, EUROPE SEEN WITH KNAPSACK AND STAFF. 1846.
ELDORADO; OR, ADVENTURES IN THE PATH OF EMPIRE. 1850.
A JOURNEY TO CENTRAL AFRICA; OR, LIFE AND LANDSCAPES FROM
    EGYPT TO THE NEGRO KINGDOMS OF THE WHITE NILE. 1854.
THE LANDS OF THE SARACEN; OR, PICTURES OF PALESTINE, ASIA MINOR,
    SICILY AND SPAIN. 1854.
A VISIT TO INDIA, CHINA, AND JAPAN IN THE YEAR 1853. 1855.
NORTHERN TRAVEL. SUMMER AND WINTER PICTURES. SWEDEN, DENMARK
    AND LAPLAND. 1858.
TRAVELS IN GREECE AND RUSSIA, WITH AN EXCURSION TO CRETE. 1859.
AT HOME AND ABROAD: A SKETCH-BOOK OF LIFE, SCENERY AND MEN.
    1859.
AT HOME AND ABROAD. 2nd Series. 1862.
COLORADO: A SUMMER TRIP. 1867.
BY-WAYS OF EUROPE. 1869.
EGYPT AND ICELAND IN THE YEAR 1874. 1874.
A SCHOOL HISTORY OF GERMANY. 1874.
THE ECHO CLUB AND OTHER LITERARY DIVERSIONS. 1876.

LETTERS AND JOURNALS

THE CORRESPONDENCE OF BAYARD TAYLOR AND PAUL HAMILTON HAYNE. Ed. Charles Duffy. Baton Rouge: Louisiana State Univ. Press, 1945.

THE UNPUBLISHED LETTERS OF BAYARD TAYLOR IN THE HUNTINGTON LIBRARY. Ed. John R. Schultz. San Marino, Calif.: Huntington Library, 1937.

Additional letters are included in Hansen-Taylor and Scudder's LIFE AND LETTERS and in Richard Cary's THE GENTEEL CIRCLE, below.

LATER EDITIONS, SELECTIONS, AND REPRINTS

BAYARD TAYLOR'S TRAVELS. 11 vols. St. Clair Shores, Mich.: Scholarly Press, 1976.

BY-WAYS. Darby, Pa.: Darby, 1977.

CRITICAL ESSAYS AND LITERARY NOTES. New York: G.P. Putnam's, 1880.

ELDORADO; OR, ADVENTURES IN THE PATH OF EMPIRE. Facsimile rpt. with a Biographical Introd. by Richard H. Dillon. Glorieta, N.M.: Rio Grande Press, 1968.

A JOURNEY TO CENTRAL AFRICA. Westport, Conn.: Negro Univ. Press, 1970.

THE LAKE REGIONS OF CENTRAL AFRICA. Westport, Conn.: Negro Univ. Press, 1970.

THE LANDS OF THE SARACEN. New York: Arno, 1977.

STUDIES IN GERMAN LITERATURE. 1879; New York: G.P. Putnam's, 1974.

VIEWS A-FOOT. Darby, Pa.: Darby, 1977.

BIBLIOGRAPHY

Selected listings of Taylor's works and secondary sources are in the studies by Beatty, Smyth, and Wermuth, below. Taylor is listed in the BIBLIOGRAPHY to the LITERARY HISTORY OF THE UNITED STATES, pp. 738, 990, 1300.

BIOGRAPHY AND CRITICISM

Beatty, Richmond Croom. BAYARD TAYLOR: LAUREATE OF THE GILDED AGE. Norman: Univ. of Oklahoma Press, 1936.

This is a sympathetic biography presenting Taylor as a victim of American life. Although it contains some inaccuracies, it gives a clear picture of the literary and social standards and the tastes of Taylor's generation and provides a perceptive analysis of his character and career.

Cary, Richard. THE GENTEEL CIRCLE: BAYARD TAYLOR AND HIS NEW YORK FRIENDS. Ithaca, N.Y.: Cornell Univ. Press, 1952.

This brief work includes an account of the genteel tradition and letters from Taylor to Stoddard, Stedman, and Aldrich.

Conwell, Russell H. THE LIFE, TRAVELS, AND LITERARY CAREER OF BAYARD TAYLOR. Boston: B.B. Russell, 1879.

The author draws his information from the travel books, producing a timely (Taylor died in 1878) biography; but it is neither well written nor particularly informative.

Hansen-Taylor, Marie, and Horace E. Scudder, eds. LIFE AND LETTERS OF BAYARD TAYLOR. 2 vols. Boston: Houghton Mifflin, 1884.

This is eulogistic but is still useful as a source.

Hansen-Taylor, Marie, and Lilian Bayard Taylor Kiliani. ON TWO CONTI-NENTS: MEMORIES OF HALF A CENTURY. New York: Doubleday, Page, 1905.

An account of life with Taylor by his wife, this also includes some of Taylor's paintings.

Krumplemann, John T. BAYARD TAYLOR AND GERMAN LETTERS. Hamburg: Cram, de Gruyter, 1959.

The author treats Taylor as "the foremost literary intermediary be-tween America and Germany" in the second half of the nineteenth century.

Smyth, Albert H. BAYARD TAYLOR. Boston: Houghton Mifflin, 1896.

This biography in the American Men of Letters Series is still sound, although it is somewhat dated in its evaluations of Taylor's achieve-ments and stature.

Wermuth, Paul C. BAYARD TAYLOR. New York: Twayne, 1973.

This short study includes excellent summaries and evaluations of

Taylor's writings. The author examines Taylor in the context of the genteel tradition and explores the causes of his sudden and extreme loss of popularity. Wermuth concludes that "Taylor remains for us a figure of more historical than literary interest," but that he is interesting because he is so representative of his times.

RELATED GENERAL STUDIES

Allen, Walter, ed. TRANSATLANTIC CROSSING: AMERICAN VISITORS TO BRITAIN AND BRITISH VISITORS TO AMERICA IN THE NINETEENTH CENTURY. (p. 126)

Fields, James T. YESTERDAY WITH AUTHORS. (p. 71)

Howells, William D. LITERARY FRIENDS AND ACQUAINTANCE. (p. 350 and 352, under Howells)

Perry, Commodore Matthew C. THE JAPAN EXPEDITION. (p. 119)

Santayana, George. CHARACTER AND OPINION IN THE UNITED STATES. (p. 173)

Wilson, James G. BRYANT AND HIS FRIENDS: SOME REMINISCENCES OF THE KNICKERBOCKER WRITERS. (p. 267, under Bryant)

Woodberry, George E. LITERARY MEMOIRS OF THE NINETEENTH CENTURY. (p. 56)

HENRY DAVID THOREAU (1817-62)

Thoreau published only two books before his death; five volumes appeared shortly afterward, and, after his sister Sophia's death, excerpts from the journals began to appear. When the writings were collected in 1906, they amounted to twenty volumes. The editions being published by Princeton University Press using CEAA (CSE) guidelines will provide definitive texts of the literary works, journals, and correspondence.

Much of the biography and criticism of Thoreau has been written either to present a particular point of view or to counter another opinion. Early biographers were interested in overcoming Lowell's adverse commentary and the image of Thoreau as a solitary eccentric. Later biographies were often clouded by psychological interpretations based upon unreliable sources or unreasonable readings. No biography has yet appeared which can be called definitive.

Serious critical studies of Thoreau's literary art were also slow in coming. Matthiessen's study in AMERICAN RENAISSANCE (1941) was the first significant analysis of Thoreau's techniques and style. In recent years, however, several detailed treatments, most focusing on WALDEN, have appeared. Just as each generation seems to find its own image of Thoreau, each decade of scholars discovers new facets of both his art and his ideas.

PRINCIPAL WORKS

A WEEK ON THE CONCORD AND MERRIMACK RIVERS. 1849.
WALDEN. 1854.

LETTERS AND JOURNALS

THE BEST OF THOREAU'S JOURNALS. Ed. with Foreword by Carl Bode. Carbondale: Southern Illinois Univ. Press, 1971.

> This is a reissue of a volume first published in 1967 as THE SELECTED JOURNALS OF HENRY DAVID THOREAU.

COMPANION TO THOREAU'S CORRESPONDENCE. Ed. Kenneth W. Cameron. Hartford, Conn.: Transcendental Books, 1964. Index.

> This is a guide to the volume of correspondence edited by Bode and Harding, below. It provides annotations, key words and topics, and a few new letters.

CONSCIOUSNESS AT CONCORD. Ed. Perry Miller. Boston: Houghton Mifflin, 1958.

> Miller presents a "lost" volume of the journal, covering the period 1840-41, with a provocative introduction, notes, and commentary. The introduction points to evidence of Thoreau's sexual ambivalence in a discussion which contributes a great deal to an understanding of the man and some of his imagery. The comments on the journal are intelligent, stimulating, and often sympathetic.

THE CORRESPONDENCE OF HENRY DAVID THOREAU. Ed. Carl Bode and Walter Harding. 1958; Westport, Conn.: Greenwood Press, 1974.

EARLY SPRING IN MASSACHUSETTS. Ed. H.G.O. Blake. Boston: Houghton Mifflin, 1881.

> This is the first of the four seasonal excerpts from the journals edited by Blake. The other volumes are SUMMER (1888), WINTER (1888), and AUTUMN (1892), all published by Houghton Mifflin and included in their publication of the Riverside edition of the writings in 1893 and their later Walden ed., below.

FAMILIAR LETTERS OF HENRY DAVID THOREAU. Ed. with Introd. and Notes F.B. Sanborn. Boston: Houghton Mifflin, 1894.

THE HEART OF THOREAU'S JOURNALS. Ed. Odell Shepard. 1927; New York: Dover, 1961.

HENRY DAVID THOREAU: A WRITER'S JOURNAL. Ed. Laurence Stapleton. New York: Dover, 1960.

THE INDIANS OF THOREAU: SELECTIONS FROM THE INDIAN NOTEBOOKS. Albuquerque, N.M.: Hummingbird, 1974.

> This gives a sampling of the notebooks on Indians with transitional comments by the editor.

THE JOURNALS. Vols. 7-20 of the Walden ed. of THE WRITINGS. Ed. Bradford Torrey and Francis H. Allen. 1906; with Foreword by Henry S. Canby. 1949; two-volume edition prepared by Walter Harding. New York: Dover, 1962.

LETTERS TO VARIOUS PERSONS. Ed. Ralph W. Emerson. 1865; 1976; Darby, Pa.: Arden, 1979.

> Emerson selected and edited these letters to emphasize Thoreau's stoicism. Sophia Thoreau protested that they gave a distorted picture of her brother.

MEN OF CONCORD. Ed. Francis H. Allen. Boston: Houghton Mifflin, 1936.

> This compiles excerpts from the journals of Thoreau's comments on his fellow townsmen.

OVER THOREAU'S DESK: NEW CORRESPONDENCE, 1838-1861. Ed. Kenneth W. Cameron. Hartford, Conn.: Transcendental Books, 1965.

> The letters collected here deal mostly with business and legal matters.

THE RIVER: SELECTIONS FROM THE JOURNAL. Arranged with notes by Dudley C. Lunt. New York: Twayne, 1963.

> The collection presents seasonal comments excerpted from the journals, most of them on the rivers of Concord.

SOME UNPUBLISHED LETTERS OF HENRY D. AND SOPHIA E. THOREAU. Ed. S.A. Jones. Jamaica, N.Y.: Marion Press, 1899.

THOREAU'S CANADIAN NOTEBOOK. Ed. Kenneth W. Cameron. Hartford, Conn.: Transcendental Books, 1967.

THOREAU'S LITERARY NOTEBOOKS IN THE LIBRARY OF CONGRESS. Ed. Kenneth W. Cameron. Hartford, Conn.: Transcendental Books, 1964.

THOREAU'S WORLD: MINIATURES FROM HIS JOURNAL. Ed. Charles R. Anderson. Englewood Cliffs, N.J.: Prentice-Hall, 1971.

> These 250 paragraphs, or what Anderson views as short essays, from Thoreau's journals were selected for their "literary value" and their ability to stand alone as separate pieces.

THE WRITINGS OF HENRY DAVID THOREAU: JOURNALS. Ed. William L. Howarth. Gen. ed. John C. Broderick. Princeton: Princeton Univ. Press, 1979-- .

> Edited from manuscripts, indexed, annotated with appended material giving historical background and explaining editorial decisions, these volumes will provide the definitive edition of the journals. Vol. 1, 1837-44, published in 1979, contains some newly found unpublished material.

Letters and excerpts from the journals can also be found in many of the selections listed below: in Sanborn's THE FIRST AND LAST JOURNEYS OF THOREAU, in Cameron's collections, especially THE TRANSCENDENTALISTS AND MINERVA, and in Cook's THE CONCORD SAUNTERER. THOREAU SOCIETY BULLETIN and ESQ also publish such material from time to time. An important journal was published in 1962 as THOREAU'S MINNESOTA JOURNEY, edited by Walter Harding and issued as the THOREAU SOCIETY BOOKLET, no. 16.

LATER EDITIONS, SELECTIONS, AND REPRINTS

A good commentary on Thoreau's early editors is in Allen's THOREAU'S EDITORS, below.

THE ANNOTATED "WALDEN." Ed. Philip Van Doren Stern. New York: Clarkson N. Potter, 1970.

> This is a useful volume, including extensive notes, information about the publishing of the book, maps, and other material.

ANTI-SLAVERY AND REFORM PAPERS. Ed. with Introd. Walter Harding. Montreal: Harvest House, 1969.

CAPE COD. Ed. Sophia Thoreau and Ellery Channing. 1865; Ed. Dudley C. Lunt, 1951; New York: Crowell, 1961.

> A new edition of CAPE COD is scheduled to be one of the volumes in the definitive edition of THE WRITINGS.

COLLECTED POEMS. Ed. Carl Bode. 1943; Enlarged ed. Baltimore: Johns Hopkins Press, 1964.

COMPLETE ESSAYS. New York: Modern Library, 1940.

EARLY ESSAYS AND MISCELLANIES. Ed. Joseph J. Moldenhauer and Edwin Moser, with Alexander Kern. Princeton: Princeton Univ. Press, 1975.

> This is a volume in the CEAA(CSE)-approved definitive edition of THE WRITINGS being published by Princeton University Press.

EXCURSIONS IN FIELD AND FOREST. Ed. Sophia Thoreau and Ralph Waldo Emerson. 1863; Gloucester, Mass.: Peter Smith, 1973.

> Emerson's "Memoir," the widely read eulogy to Thoreau, was reprinted as the introduction to this volume.

THE FIRST AND LAST JOURNEYS OF THOREAU. Ed. F.B. Sanborn. Boston: Bibliophile Society, 1905.

> Sanborn's revisions and editing of Thoreau's manuscripts produce an

unreliable text which includes correspondence, excerpts from notebooks and journals, an early draft of A WEEK ON THE CONCORD
AND MERRIMACK RIVERS, and notes about a journey by Thoreau
to Minnesota.

HENRY DAVID THOREAU: THE NATURAL HISTORY ESSAYS. Salt Lake City,
Utah: Peregrine Smith, 1980.

THE ILLUSTRATED MAINE WOODS. Textual Ed. Joseph Moldenhauer. Princeton: Princeton Univ. Press, 1974.

> This and the volume below use texts from the CEAA(CSE)-approved
> edition of THE WRITINGS and include photographs taken early in the
> century by Herbert Gleason, who attempted to make a record on
> film of the places about which Thoreau wrote.

THE ILLUSTRATED WALDEN. Textual Ed. J. Lyndon Shanley. Princeton:
Princeton Univ. Press, 1974.

LIFE WITHOUT PRINCIPLE. Pref. by Henry Miller. 1946; Folcroft, Pa.:
Folcroft, 1977.

> This collects three essays by Thoreau with an interesting preface.

THE MAINE WOODS. Ed. Sophia Thoreau and Ellery Channing. 1864; New
York: Corwell, 1961.

THE MAINE WOODS. Ed. Joseph J. Moldenhauer. Princeton: Princeton
Univ. Press, 1972.

> Volume 3 of the definitive edition of THE WRITINGS.

MISCELLANIES BY HENRY DAVID THOREAU. Biographical sketch by Ralph
Waldo Emerson. 1893; New York: AMS Press, 1968.

THE MOON. Ed. Francis H. Allen. Boston: Houghton Mifflin, 1927.

THE PORTABLE THOREAU. Ed. Carl Bode. New York: Viking, 1947; New
York: Penguin, 1977.

REFORM PAPERS. Ed. Wendell Glick. Princeton: Princeton Univ. Press,
1973.

> About half of this volume consists of introduction, textual introduc-
> tion, and textual notes.

THE SELECTED WORKS OF HENRY DAVID THOREAU. Ed. with Introd. Walter
Harding. Boston: Houghton Mifflin, 1975.

SELECTED WRITINGS OF HENRY DAVID THOREAU. Ed. Lewis Leary. North-brook, Ill.: AHM, 1958.

THE SERVICE. Ed. F.B. Sanborn. Boston: Charles E. Goodspeed, 1902.

SIR WALTER RALEIGH. Ed. F.B. Sanborn. Boston: Bibliophile Society, 1905.

THOREAU ON THE ART OF WRITING. Ed. Franklin W. Hamilton. 1962; Flint, Mich.: Walden Press, 1968.

> This is a collection of Thoreau's comments on style, structure, and vocabulary with commentary and a summary by the editor.

THOREAU: THE MAJOR ESSAYS. Ed. with Introd. Jeffrey L. Duncan. New York: Dutton, 1972.

THOREAU: PEOPLE, PRINCIPLES, AND POLITICS. New York: Hill and Wang, 1963.

> This collects Thoreau's political essays and other political comments from the letters and journals.

THOREAU: PHILOSOPHER OF FREEDOM. Ed. James MacKaye. New York: Vanguard, 1930.

THOREAU: REPORTER OF THE UNIVERSE. Ed. Bertha Stevens. New York: John Day, 1939.

THOREAU: REPRESENTATIVE SELECTIONS. Ed. Bartholow V. Crawford. New York: American Book Co., 1934.

THOREAU TODAY. Ed. Helen Barber Morrison, with Introd. Odell Shepard. New York: Comet, 1957.

THOREAU'S FACT BOOK IN THE HARVEY ELKINS WIDENER COLLECTION IN THE HARVARD COLLEGE LIBRARY. Ed. Kenneth W. Cameron. Hartford, Conn.: Transcendental Books, 1966.

THOREAU'S VISION: THE MAJOR ESSAYS. Ed. with Introd. Charles R. Anderson. Englewood Cliffs, N.J.: Prentice-Hall, 1973.

THE THOUGHTS OF THOREAU. Ed. Edwin Way Teale. New York: Dodd Mead, 1962.

THE VARIORUM "CIVIL DISOBEDIENCE" BY HENRY DAVID THOREAU. Ed. with Introd. and Annotations Walter Harding. New York: Twayne, 1967.

THE VARIORUM WALDEN. Ed. with Introd. and Annotations Walter Harding. 1962; Reprinted with the entry above as THE VARIORUM WALDEN AND THE VARIORUM CIVIL DISOBEDIENCE. New York: Washington Square Press, 1967.

WALDEN. Ed. J. Lyndon Shanley. Princeton: Princeton Univ. Press, 1971.

Volume 2 in the definitive edition of THE WRITINGS.

WALDEN AND SELECTED ESSAYS. Ed. George F. Whicher. Chicago: Packard, 1947.

A WEEK ON THE CONCORD AND MERRIMACK RIVERS. Ed. Carl Hovde and the staff of the Thoreau Textual Center, William L. Howarth and Elizabeth Witherell. Historical Introd. Linck C. Johnson. Princeton: Princeton Univ. Press, 1978.

Volume 1 of the definitive edition of THE WRITINGS.

THE WORKS OF THOREAU. Selected and Ed. Henry S. Canby. 1937; Cambridge ed. Boston: Houghton Mifflin, 1948.

THE WRITINGS OF HENRY DAVID THOREAU. Walden ed. 20 vols. 1906; New York: AMS Press, 1968.

This long-standard set, also known as the Manuscript edition, will be superseded by the Princeton edition.

THE WRITINGS OF HENRY DAVID THOREAU. Gen. Ed. Walter Harding. Princeton: Princeton Univ. Press, 1971-- .

This will provide CEAA (Center for Editions of American Authors, now Center for Scholarly Editions)-approved, definitive texts of Thoreau's writings. Individual titles, which are out to this date, are listed separately, above.

A YANKEE IN CANADA, WITH ANTI-SLAVERY PAPERS. 1866; rpt. of 1892 library edition; New York: Haskell, 1969.

BIBLIOGRAPHY

Allen, Francis H. BIBLIOGRAPHY OF HENRY DAVID THOREAU. 1908; New York: B. Franklin, 1969.

Harding, Walter, ed. A BIBLIOGRAPHY OF THE THOREAU SOCIETY BULLETIN BIBLIOGRAPHIES, 1941-1969: A CUMULATION AND INDEX. Cumulated by Jean C. Advena. Troy, N.Y.: Whitston, 1971.

_____. CENTENNIAL CHECKLIST OF EDITIONS OF HENRY DAVID THOR-
EAU'S WALDEN. Charlottesville: Univ. of Virginia Press, 1954.

Harding, Walter, and Michael Meyer. THE NEW THOREAU HANDBOOK.
New York: New York Univ. Press, 1980.

> An updated revision of the 1959 edition, this survey is more selec-
> tive and has a long section on Thoreau as a literary artist. The
> HANDBOOK is an indispensable guide for both beginning student
> and scholar.

Hildenbrand, Christopher A. A BIBLIOGRAPHY OF SCHOLARSHIP ABOUT
HENRY DAVID THOREAU: 1940-1967. Hays: Fort Hays Kansas State College,
1967.

Howarth, William L. THE LITERARY MANUSCRIPTS OF HENRY DAVID THOR-
EAU. Columbus: Ohio State Univ. Press, 1974.

Jones, Joseph. INDEX TO WALDEN. Austin, Tex.: Hemphill's, 1955.

> This is a useful word and topic index.

Leary, Lewis. "Henry David Thoreau." In EIGHT AMERICAN AUTHORS. Rev.
ed. James Woodress. New York: Norton, 1971, pp. 129-72.

Sherwin, J.L., and R.C. Reynolds. A WORD INDEX TO WALDEN: WITH
TEXTUAL NOTES. Charlottesville: Univ. of Virginia Press, 1960.

> This is a useful concordance which gives insight into Thoreau's
> vocabulary.

Timpe, Eugene F., ed. THOREAU ABROAD: TWELVE BIBLIOGRAPHICAL ES-
SAYS. Hamden, Conn.: Shoe String, 1971.

> These bibliographical essays trace Thoreau's reputation in such coun-
> tries as France, Germany, Italy, India, and Japan.

White, William. A HENRY DAVID THOREAU BIBLIOGRAPHY, 1908-1937.
Boston: F.W. Faxon, 1939.

The THOREAU SOCIETY BULLETIN (1941--) regularly carries a bibliography of
Thoreau items. The Thoreau Society also regularly publishes booklets containing
material by and about Thoreau. THE THOREAU JOURNAL QUARTERLY, published by the Thoreau Fellowship; THE CONCORD SAUNTERER, published by
the Thoreau Lyceum; ESQ; and the AMERICAN TRANSCENDENTAL QUARTERLY
also carry bibliographical items. For a convenient listing of Cameron's collections of primary materials on Thoreau and transcendentalism, see his TRANS-
CENDENTAL AND AMERICAN RENAISSANCE BIBLIOGRAPHY (Hartford, Conn.:
Transcendental Books, 1977), which describes the sixty-six volumes of primary

materials issued by Transcendental Books. Thoreau is listed in the BIBLIOGRAPHY to the LITERARY HISTORY OF THE UNITED STATES, pp. 742, 991, 1302.

BIOGRAPHY AND CRITICISM

Allen, Francis H. THOREAU'S EDITORS: HISTORY AND REMINISCENCE. Monroe, N.C.: Nocalore Press, 1950.

> Originally issued as the THOREAU SOCIETY BULLETIN, no. 7, this describes and evaluates Thoreau's early editors.

Anderson, Charles R. THE MAGIC CIRCLE OF WALDEN. New York: Holt, Rinehart and Winston, 1968.

> In this thorough analysis of WALDEN, Anderson treats the work as a poem, revealing literary values which give impact and meaning to the work. This is an informative and often profound study, although the author's concentration on style leads him on occasion to underemphasize some major autobiographical elements.

Atkinson, Brooks. HENRY THOREAU, THE COSMIC YANKEE. 1927; Darby, Pa.: Arden, 1978.

> Good as a brief and very readable introduction to Thoreau, this is best in its discussion of Thoreau as a nature writer. An even better commentary by Atkinson, however, is his introduction to the Modern Library edition of Thoreau's writings.

Bhatia, Kamla. THE MYSTICISM OF THOREAU AND HIS AFFINITY WITH INDIAN THOUGHT. New Delhi: New India Press, 1966.

> This is an excellent brief summary of the relationship between Hindu thought and American transcendentalism.

Cameron, Kenneth W., ed. THOREAU'S HARVARD YEARS: MATERIALS INTRODUCTORY TO NEW EXPLORATIONS: RECORD OF FACT AND BACKGROUND. Hartford, Conn.: Transcendental Books, 1966.

> Like all of Cameron's volumes, this contains valuable primary material.

_____. THOREAU AND HIS HARVARD CLASSMATES: HENRY WILLIAMS' "MEMORIALS OF THE CLASS 'OF 1837" WITH A COMMENTARY AND INDEX BY K.W.C. Hartford, Conn.: Transcendental Books, 1965.

_____. TRANSCENDENTAL APPRENTICESHIP: NOTES ON YOUNG HENRY THOREAU'S READING: A CONTEXTURE WITH A RESEARCHER'S INDEX. Hartford, Conn.: Transcendental Books, 1976.

Canby, Henry S. THOREAU. Boston: Houghton Mifflin, 1939; Gloucester, Mass.: Peter Smith, 1968.

In some ways less useful than Canby's chapter on Thoreau in his CLASSIC AMERICANS, this has been criticized for Canby's Freudian analysis and his acceptance, without question, of the accounts of some of Thoreau's contemporaries as well as for errors of fact and detail. However, it remains one of the important biographical studies.

Cavell, Stanley. THE SENSES OF WALDEN. New York: Viking, 1972.

In this close analysis of the language and philosophical implications of WALDEN, the author presents some provocative insights into Thoreau's creative use of words and images.

Channing, William Ellery. THOREAU: THE POET NATURALIST. 1873; Ed. F.B. Sanborn. 1902; New York: Biblo and Tannen, 1965.

This is sketchy and is effusive in its admiration of Thoreau, but it is still a useful resource. Channing was one of the few among Thoreau's friends and admirers who recognized his literary skills. Channing utilized much material from Thoreau's journals and other published and unpublished writings, often without identifying the source.

Christie, John A. THOREAU AS WORLD TRAVELLER. New York: Columbia Univ. Press, 1965.

Showing how Thoreau used his voluminous reading in travel literature to give universal significance to some of his images and allusions, this study gives not only a good account of some of Thoreau's techniques but also a useful survey of nineteenth-century travel literature.

Condry, William. THOREAU. New York: Philosophical Library, 1954.

Written for the British Great Naturalists Series, this emphasizes Thoreau's nature writing and is one of the better short biographies.

Cook, Reginald L. THE CONCORD SAUNTERER: INCLUDING A DISCUSSION OF THE NATURE MYSTICISM OF THOREAU. Middlebury, Vt.: Middlebury College Press, 1940.

Cook focuses his discussion here more on Thoreau's interest in correspondences between man and nature than he does in the more important study below.

_____. PASSAGE TO WALDEN. 1949; New York: Russell and Russell, 1966.

The author praises Thoreau for his ability to embody in literature the relationship of man to nature and for the energy and "poetic imagination" of his prose. Cook concludes that "what Henry Thoreau assures the enlightened citizens of the Western world is the certainty that nature quickens and renews the human spirit through sympathetic relationship." The 1966 reprint identifies previously unacknowledged citations.

Derleth, August W. CONCORD REBEL: A LIFE OF HENRY DAVID THOREAU. Philadelphia: Chilton, 1962.

Written primarily for young people, this is clear and generally reliable.

Edel, Leon. HENRY DAVID THOREAU. Minneapolis: Univ. of Minnesota Press, 1970.

This is a good brief summary of Thoreau's life and writings.

Emerson, Edward W. HENRY THOREAU AS REMEMBERED BY A YOUNG FRIEND, EDWARD WALDO EMERSON. 1917; Concord, Mass.: Thoreau Foundation, 1968.

Edward Emerson's account helped to correct the notion that Thoreau was an unsociable eccentric and presented a superb portrait of Thoreau as a warm, friendly human being.

Foerster, Norman. THE INTELLECTUAL HERITAGE OF THOREAU. 1917; Folcroft, Pa.: Folcroft, 1974.

This analysis of Thoreau's literary background, originally published in the TEXAS REVIEW, emphasizes Thoreau's use of classical, Oriental, and seventeenth-century English sources.

Garber, Frederick. THOREAU'S REDEMPTIVE IMAGINATION. New York: New York Univ. Press, 1977.

An excellent study of Thoreau's attempts to understand and control the relationship of external nature and human consciousness, this focuses upon Thoreau's use of the phenomenal world in imaginative, symbolic structures and places Thoreau in the context of American and British romanticism.

Glick, Wendell, ed. THE RECOGNITION OF HENRY DAVID THOREAU: SELECTED CRITICISM SINCE 1848. Ann Arbor: Univ. of Michigan Press, 1969.

The collection consists of chronologically arranged essays, reviews, and excerpts from longer studies of Thoreau, beginning with Lowell's comments in A FABLE FOR CRITICS in 1848 and concluding with essays published in the 1960s. The steady increase of Thoreau's reputation and the increasing seriousness with which he has come to be regarded as a literary artist are well documented.

Greene, David Mason. THE FRAIL DURATION: A KEY TO SYMBOLIC STRUC-
TURE IN WALDEN. San Diego, Calif.: San Diego State College, 1966.

> Although the author carries symbolic interpretation to great lengths,
> his close analysis of sections of WALDEN is sometimes enlightening.

Harding, Walter. THE DAYS OF HENRY THOREAU: A BIOGRAPHY. New
York: Knopf, 1965.

> A sympathetic and thorough study, this will remain an indispensable
> source for future biographers. Harding attempts to present an ac-
> curate and objective chronicle of Thoreau's life and to portray
> "Thoreau the man."

_____, ed. HENRY DAVID THOREAU: A PROFILE. New York: Hill and
Wang, 1971.

> This reprints, among other studies, an influential dissertation writ-
> ten by Raymond Gozzi which presents a psychological study of
> Thoreau.

_____. THE THOREAU CENTENNIAL. Albany: State Univ. of New York
Press, 1964.

> This is a gathering of papers presented for the Thoreau centenary
> in 1962 by outstanding Thoreau scholars, including Joseph Molden-
> hauer, J. Lyndon Shanley, Carl Hovde, and Raymond Adams.

_____. THOREAU: A CENTURY OF CRITICISM. Dallas, Tex.: Southern
Methodist Univ. Press, 1954.

> Some of the best critical essays on Thoreau are collected here.

_____. THOREAU: MAN OF CONCORD. New York: Holt, Rinehart
and Winston, 1960.

> A selection of comments by Thoreau's contemporaries, this draws
> upon numerous sources and produces a vivid portrait of the man.

Harding, Walter, George Brenner, and Paul A. Doyle, eds. HENRY DAVID
THOREAU: STUDIES AND COMMENTARIES. Rutherford, N.J.: Farleigh
Dickinson Univ. Press, 1972.

> This is a collection of papers given at a Thoreau festival held at
> Nassau Community College, Long Island, in 1967. Among other
> studies, it includes a fine essay by Alfred Kazin and two essays
> on Thoreau's affinity with Indian thought.

Hendrick, George, ed. REMEMBRANCES OF CONCORD AND THE THOREAUS:
LETTERS OF HORACE HOSMER TO DR. S.A. JONES. Urbana: Univ. of
Illinois Press, 1977.

Hendrick collects letters written between 1891 and 1894 to a Thoreau scholar by a former student in the school conducted by Thoreau.

Hicks, John H., ed. THOREAU IN OUR SEASON. Amherst: Univ. of Massachusetts Press, 1966.

Many of these essays discussing Thoreau's relevance today were originally published in the MASSACHUSETTS REVIEW in 1962.

Hough, Henry B. THOREAU OF WALDEN: THE MAN AND HIS EVENTFUL LIFE. 1956; Hamden, Conn.: Shoe String, 1970.

A superficial and uncritical biography, this makes extensive use of quotation and anecdote. Thoreau's prose provides welcome relief from Hough's inflated rhetoric.

Hovey, Allen Beecher. THE HIDDEN THOREAU. Beirut: Catholic Press, 1966.

The author analyzes Thoreau's use of symbolism and mythology in his earlier writings.

Japp, Alexander H. THOREAU: HIS LIFE AND AIMS. 1901; Folcroft, Pa.: Folcroft, 1976.

First published under the pseudonym of "H.A. Page," this is an unreliable biography; but it attempts to correct the view of Thoreau as an egotistical recluse and demonstrates an enthusiastic appreciation of Thoreau's understanding of man and nature.

Jones, Samuel Arthur. THOREAU: A GLIMPSE. 1903; New York: Haskell, 1972.

Jones rejected the view that Thoreau was merely an imitator of Emerson and urged that Thoreau be read as one who made a "strenuous endeavor to apprehend . . . eternity." This is an important early study.

_____, ed. PERTAINING TO THOREAU. 1901; Folcroft, Pa.: Folcroft, 1976.

This collects early articles and reviews, including pieces by Lowell and Alcott.

Kleinfeld, Leonard F. HENRY DAVID THOREAU CHRONOLOGY. Forest Hills, N.Y.: Privately Printed, 1950.

Presented here are a detailed chronology of Thoreau's life with a useful parallel chronology of American literature and world history.

Krutch, Joseph W. HENRY DAVID THOREAU. 1948; New York: Morrow, 1974.

> Krutch gives an excellent discussion of Thoreau's ideas, showing that he went beyond Emerson in his own thinking and that he was clearly aware of the contradiction between his concern for individualism and his desire for social reform.

Lane, Lauriat, Jr., ed. APPROACHES TO WALDEN. San Francisco: Wadsworth, 1961.

> A useful introduction for students, this presents a brief analysis of WALDEN, excerpts from the work itself, and nineteenth and twentieth-century critical attitudes toward it.

Lebeaux, Richard. YOUNG MAN THOREAU. Amherst: Univ. of Massachusetts Press, 1977.

> Taking what he calls an "Eriksonian" approach to biography, the author focuses upon Thoreau's years from his graduation from Harvard in 1837 to his "declaration of independence" on July 4, 1845. Many of the author's insights, particularly the comments on the journals, are valuable; others seem implausible.

Lee, Harry. MORE DAY TO DAWN: THE STORY OF THOREAU OF CONCORD. Foreword by Brooks Atkinson. New York: Duell, Sloan, and Pearce, 1941.

> A biography in verse, this also presents several prose passages from WALDEN set up as free verse.

McIntosh, James. THOREAU AS ROMANTIC NATURALIST: HIS SHIFTING STANCE TOWARD NATURE. Ithaca, N.Y.: Cornell Univ. Press, 1974.

> The author presents a dialectic he sees as formed by Thoreau's desire for involvement in nature and his feeling of isolation from it. Thoreau's relationship to British and European romantic naturalists and the mind-nature dichotomy as it appears in Thoreau are also discussed.

Marble, Annie R. THOREAU: HIS HOME, FRIENDS AND BOOKS. 1902; New York: AMS Press, 1969.

> This is sentimentalized version of Thoreau's life, but the author had access to documents which have since disappeared and was able to speak with surviving friends of Henry and Sophia Thoreau.

Meltzer, Milton, and Walter Harding, eds. A THOREAU PROFILE. New York: Crowell, 1962.

> The text of this pictorial biography consists of quotations from Thoreau's autobiographical writings and comments and reminiscences by friends and contemporaries.

Metzger, Charles R. THOREAU AND WHITMAN: A STUDY OF THEIR ESTHE-
TICS. 1961; Hamden, Conn.: Shoe String, 1968.

>   Better on Thoreau than on Whitman, this study relates the theories
>   of both writers to transcendentalism and concludes that Thoreau
>   consistently followed an organic theory but was not much interested
>   in formal aesthetic principles.

Meyer, Michael. SEVERAL MORE LIVES TO LIVE: THOREAU'S POLITICAL
REPUTATION IN AMERICA. Westport, Conn.: Greenwood Press, 1977.

>   The author surveys American commentary on Thoreau's political
>   thought and writings from the 1920s to the early 1970s, noting
>   that "the explicit and implicit political assumptions of the critics
>   and their respective times have, in many instances, generated the
>   uses to which Thoreau has been put."

Moldenhauer, Joseph J., ed. THE MERRILL STUDIES IN WALDEN. Columbus, Ohio: Charles E. Merrill, 1971.

>   This is a solid and useful introductory guide to WALDEN.

Moller, Mary Elkins. THOREAU IN THE HUMAN COMMUNITY. Amherst:
Univ. of Massachusetts Press, 1980.

>   The author analyzes Thoreau's views on love, friendship, and com-
>   munity and concludes that he was more humane than misanthropic.

Murray, James G. HENRY DAVID THOREAU. New York: Washington Square
Press, 1968.

>   A good introduction to Thoreau's ideas, this uses some of the less
>   well-known essays in its summary of Thoreau's thought.

Oehlschlaeger, Fritz, and George Hendrick, eds. TOWARD THE MAKING OF
THOREAU'S MODERN REPUTATION: SELECTED CORRESPONDENCE OF S.A.
JONES, A.W. HOSMER, H.S. SALT, H.G.O. BLAKE, AND D. RICKETSON.
Urbana: Univ. of Illinois Press, 1980.

>   Letters by these five correspondents who were friends and acquain-
>   tances of Thoreau are edited here with accompanying biographical
>   sketches; the effect is to present a picture of Thoreau as social
>   critic rather than sentimental poet-naturalist.

Paul, Sherman. THE SHORES OF AMERICA: THOREAU'S INWARD EXPLORA-
TION. 1958; Urbana: Univ. of Illinois Press, 1980.

>   A study of Thoreau's essays, letters, and journals, this assesses the
>   growth of Thoreau's philosophy and inner life, emphasizing his
>   introspection, existential anxieties, and the therapeutic effect of
>   the stay at Walden.

_____, ed. THOREAU: A COLLECTION OF CRITICAL ESSAYS. Englewood Cliffs, N.J.: Prentice-Hall, 1962.

> This collects fourteen twentieth-century essays and two poems on Thoreau. Several of the essays are excellent, and the collection provides a good survey of Thoreau criticism.

Ricketson, Anna, and Walton Ricketson. DANIEL RICKETSON AND HIS FRIENDS. Boston: Hougthon Mifflin, 1902.

> A New Bedford Quaker, Ricketson read WALDEN when it was first published and began a correspondence and friendship with Thoreau that lasted until Thoreau's death. Their relationship is detailed in this biographical study.

Ruland, Richard, ed. TWENTIETH CENTURY INTERPRETATIONS OF WALDEN: A COLLECTION OF CRITICAL ESSAYS. Englewood Cliffs, N.J.: Prentice-Hall, 1968.

> The emphasis in these collected and excerpted essays is on myth and symbolism.

Salt, Henry S. THE LIFE OF HENRY DAVID THOREAU. 1890; 1896; Hamden, Conn.: Shoe String, 1968.

> A British biographer and critic, Salt was influential in introducing Thoreau to English readers. He systematically gathered material from friends, acquaintances, and published sources and produced what remains an excellent account of Thoreau's life and ideas.

Sanborn, F.B. HENRY D. THOREAU. 1882; Detroit: Gale Research Co., 1968.

> Expanded and rewritten as THE LIFE OF HENRY DAVID THOREAU (1917), this biography is discursive and sometimes inaccurate; but it brings together important details about Thoreau's life, prints much of Thoreau's correspondence with Horace Greeley, includes some college essays, and provides other valuable source material.

Sayre, Robert F. THOREAU AND THE AMERICAN INDIANS. Princeton: Princeton Univ. Press, 1977.

> This study demonstrates the contemporary stereotypical views of American Indians and shows how Thoreau, although he was affected by these views, managed to transcend them.

Scudder, Townsend. CONCORD, AMERICAN TOWN. Boston: Little, Brown, 1947.

> This gives a vivid picture of the social and intellectual activity of the town in Thoreau's day.

Seefurth, N.H. THOREAU: A VIEW FROM EMERITUS. Chicago: Seefurth Foundation, 1968.

> An appreciative sketch, this is intended to be inspirational in tone and substance, evaluating the significance of Thoreau in current times.

Seybold, Ethel. THOREAU: THE QUEST AND THE CLASSICS. 1951; Hamden, Conn.: Shoe String, 1969.

> The study focuses upon Thoreau's reading, especially of the classics, shows how he used quotations from the classics in his work, and discusses his career in light of his attempt "to discover the secret of the universe." The author tends to overemphasize the importance of the classics to Thoreau, overlooking the fact that he read in many other literatures as well.

Shanley, J. Lyndon. THE MAKING OF WALDEN. Chicago: Univ. of Chicago Press, 1957.

> An outstanding scholarly analysis, this examines several drafts of the work and shows how it was developed and polished.

Snyder, Helena A. THOREAU'S PHILOSOPHY OF LIFE, WITH SPECIAL CONSIDERATION OF THE INFLUENCES OF HINDOO PHILOSOPHY. Heidelberg: Univ. of Heidelberg, 1900.

> In one of the earliest dissertations on Thoreau, the author points out the parallels between passages from Thoreau and passages from the major Hindu scriptures.

Stein, William Bysshe, ed. NEW APPROACHES TO THOREAU. Hartford, Conn.: Transcendental Books, 1969.

> Most of the essays gathered here are close readings of various works, with an emphasis upon imagery, language, and structure.

Stoller, Leo. AFTER WALDEN: THOREAU'S CHANGING VIEWS ON ECONOMIC MAN. Palo Alto, Calif.: Stanford Univ. Press, 1957.

> Using a number of contemporary newspaper comments on Thoreau, Stoller argues that Thoreau increasingly recognized the dependence of the individual man upon the community and did not ignore the importance of social institutions. His thesis, eloquently but not entirely convincingly argued, is that when Thoreau climbed Mt. Katahdin in 1846, he lost his faith in natural goodness and turned "away from utopian social thought and toward a new synthesis" which involved an acceptance of industrial capitalism and commercial development of the land.

Stowell, Robert F. A THOREAU GAZETTEER. Ed. William L. Howarth. Princeton: Princeton Univ. Press, 1970.

> This collection of maps, photographs, and other material provides a visual representation of Thoreau's literal and metaphorical geography. It includes an index of place names from Thoreau's writings.

Taylor, J. Golden. NEIGHBOR THOREAU'S CRITICAL HUMOR. 1958; Folcroft, Pa.: Folcroft, 1974.

> This monograph is one of the best studies of Thoreau's use of humor as a technique of criticism.

_____, ed. THE WESTERN THOREAU CENTENARY. Logan: Utah State Univ. Press, 1963.

> The essays collected here are in honor of the Thoreau centenary in 1962.

Tuerk, Richard. CENTRAL STILL; CIRCLE AND SPHERE IN THOREAU'S PROSE. The Hague: Mouton, 1975.

> The author carefully analyzes Thoreau's use of the circle motif in various writings and presents some useful and original comments on several of the essays, although what he has to say about WALDEN has been said before.

Van Doren, Mark. HENRY DAVID THOREAU: A CRITICAL STUDY. 1916; New York: Russell and Russell, 1961.

> Van Doren's study, originally an undergraduate honors thesis at the University of Illinois, gives grudging praise of Thoreau's social criticism and use of concrete imagery, but objects to Thoreau's "intellectual and moral egotism" and concludes that Thoreau's "main product was nothing, and his main effort vain."

Whicher, George F. WALDEN REVISITED: A CENTENNIAL TRIBUTE TO HENRY DAVID THOREAU. Chicago: Packard, 1945.

> A brief introductory essay, this appreciation concentrates on Thoreau, the philosopher.

Wolf, William J. THOREAU: MYSTIC, PROPHET, ECOLOGIST. Philadelphia: Pilgrim, 1974.

> The author presents Thoreau as a "creative religious thinker," examining his works and ideas largely from a theological point of view.

RELATED GENERAL STUDIES

Alcott, Bronson. CONCORD DAYS. (p. 241, under Alcott)
Banta, Martha. FAILURE AND SUCCESS IN AMERICA. (p. 14)
Baritz, Loren. CITY ON A HILL. (p. 306, under Emerson)
Boller, Paul F. AMERICAN TRANSCENDENTALISM, 1830-1860. (p. 161)
Brooks, Van Wyck. THE FLOWERING OF NEW ENGLAND. (p. 17)
Bruel, Andre. EMERSON ET THOREAU. (p. 307, under Emerson)
Bruccoli, Matthew J., ed. THE CHIEF GLORY OF EVERY PEOPLE. (p. 17)
Buell, Lawrence. LITERARY TRANSCENDENTALISM. (p. 162)
Burroughs, John. INDOOR STUDIES. (p. 268, under Burroughs)
_____. THE LAST HARVEST. (p. 269, under Burroughs)
Cameron, Kenneth. CONCORD HARVEST. (p. 163)
_____. EMERSON AND THOREAU AS READERS. (p. 307, under Emerson)
_____. EMERSON, THOREAU, AND CONCORD IN EARLY NEWSPAPERS. (p. 163)
_____. THE MASSACHUSETTS LYCEUM. (p. 215)
_____. RESPONSE TO TRANSCENDENTAL CONCORD. (p. 163)
_____. TRANSCENDENTAL CLIMATE. (p. 163)
_____. TRANSCENDENTAL EPILOGUE. (p. 163)
_____. TRANSCENDENTAL READING PATTERNS. (p. 164)
_____. THE TRANSCENDENTALISTS AND MINERVA. (p. 164)
Carter, Everett. THE AMERICAN IDEA. (p. 18)
Christy, Arthur. THE ORIENT IN AMERICAN TRANSCENDENTALISM. (p. 164)
Crawley, Thomas E., ed. FOUR MAKERS OF THE AMERICAN MIND. (p. 20)
Ekirch, Arthur A. MAN AND NATURE IN AMERICA. (p. 166)
Falk, Robert, ed. LITERATURE AND IDEAS IN AMERICA. (p. 21)
Foerster, Norman. NATURE IN AMERICAN LITERATURE. (p. 166-67)
Foster, Edward H. THE CIVILIZED WILDERNESS. (p. 21)
Fussell, Edwin. FRONTIER: AMERICAN LITERATURE AND THE AMERICAN
     WEST. (p. 22)
Gohdes, Clarence. THE PERIODICALS OF AMERICAN TRANSCENDENTALISM.
     (p. 61)
Hicks, Philip M. THE DEVELOPMENT OF THE NATURAL HISTORY ESSAY IN
     AMERICAN LITERATURE. (p. 168)
Higginson, Thomas W. CARLYLE'S LAUGH. (p. 81)
_____. CHEERFUL YESTERDAYS. (p. 73)
Hoffman, Michael J. THE SUBVERSIVE VISION. (p. 23)
Huth, Hans. NATURE AND THE AMERICAN. (p. 168-69)
Jones, Howard M. HISTORY AND THE CONTEMPORARY. (p. 24)
Lewis, R.W.B. THE AMERICAN ADAM. (p. 25)
Lieber, Todd M. ENDLESS EXPERIMENTS. (p. 25)
Lynd, Staughton. INTELLECTUAL ORIGINS OF AMERICAN RADICALISM.
     (p. 221)
Macy, John. THE SPIRIT OF AMERICAN LITERATURE. (p. 26)
_____, ed. AMERICAN WRITERS ON AMERICAN LITERATURE. (p. 26)
Madden, Edward H. CIVIL DISOBEDIENCE AND MORAL LAW IN NINE-
     TEENTH CENTURY AMERICAN PHILOSOPHY. (p. 170)
Madison, Charles A. CRITICS AND CRUSADERS. (p. 221)
Matthiessen, F.O. AMERICAN RENAISSANCE. (p. 27)

GEORGE TICKNOR (1791-1871)

Ticknor is largely ignored by modern scholars; with the exception of David Tyack's fine study, little has been written about him in the twentieth century. Yet his HISTORY OF SPANISH LITERATURE is one of the first major works of American literary scholarship to receive recognition in Europe. It is a work which shows a relatively new approach in combining social and intellectual criticism--that is, viewing literature as an expression both of one mind and of the historical and social circumstances in which it was created. Ticknor preceded Longfellow and Lowell as the first professor of modern languages at Harvard and was a pioneer in introducing effective methods of teaching foreign languages. To Henry Adams, Ticknor became a symbol of a passing way of life, but Adams still felt that the LIFE, LETTERS, AND JOURNALS was a record of "permanent value as a vivid illustration of the conditions of the most cultivated society of New England."

PRINCIPAL WORKS

REMARKS ON CHANGES LATELY PROPOSED OR ADOPTED IN HARVARD UNIVERSITY. 1825.
THE REMAINS OF NATHANIEL APPLETON HAVEN. WITH A MEMOIR OF HIS LIFE. 1827.
LECTURE ON THE BEST METHODS OF TEACHING THE LIVING LANGUAGES. 1833.
HISTORY OF SPANISH LITERATURE. 3 vols. 1849.
PAPERS DISCUSSING THE COMPARATIVE MERITS OF PRESCOTT'S AND WILSON'S HISTORIES. PRO. AND CON., AS LAID BEFORE THE MASSACHUSETTS HISTORICAL SOCIETY, 1861.
LIFE OF WILLIAM HICKLING PRESCOTT. 1864.

LETTERS AND JOURNALS

GEORGE TICKNOR'S TRAVELS IN SPAIN. Ed. George T. Northrup. Toronto: Univ. of Toronto Studies, 1913.

Ticknor's journals, written while he was in Spain in 1818 and not included in LIFE, LETTERS, AND JOURNALS, are here edited with commentary and notes.

LETTERS TO PASCUAL DE GAYANGOS; FROM ORIGINALS IN THE COLLECTION OF THE HISPANIC SOCIETY OF AMERICA. Ed. Clara L. Penney. New York: Hispanic Society of America, 1927.

LIFE, LETTERS, AND JOURNALS OF GEORGE TICKNOR. 2 vols. Ed. George S. Hillard et al. 1876; New York: Johnson, 1968.

> This is composed of journals, a brief autobiography, and correspondence. Ticknor's daughter supplies a connecting narrative. It is the best primary source of material on Ticknor's life.

WEST POINT IN 1826. Ed. H. Pelham Curtis. [Boston]: n.p., [1886].

> These are letters to Mrs. George Ticknor.

LATER EDITIONS, SELECTIONS, AND REPRINTS

HISTORY OF SPANISH LITERATURE. 3 vols. New York: Gordian, 1965.

LIFE OF WILLIAM HICKLING PRESCOTT. New York: AMS Press, 1968.

BIBLIOGRAPHY

The best listing to date of materials by and about Ticknor is in Tyack's GEORGE TICKNOR AND THE BOSTON BRAHMINS, below.

BIOGRAPHY AND CRITICISM

Doyle, Henry G. GEORGE TICKNOR: TOGETHER WITH TICKNOR'S "LECTURE ON THE BEST METHODS OF TEACHING THE LIVING LANGUAGES." Washington, D.C.: n.p., 1937.

> This monograph, reprinted from the MODERN LANGUAGE JOURNAL (October, 1937), includes a brief bibliographical and critical introduction and notes on the lecture.

Hart, Charles H. MEMOIR OF GEORGE TICKNOR, HISTORIAN OF SPANISH LITERATURE. Philadelphia: Collins, 1871.

Rahv, Phillip, ed. DISCOVERY OF EUROPE: THE STORY OF AMERICAN EXPERIENCE IN THE OLD WORLD. Boston: Houghton Mifflin, 1947.

This includes a chapter on Ticknor's studies and travels in Europe from 1815 to 1819.

Ryder, Frank G. "Introduction." GEORGE TICKNOR'S THE SORROWS OF YOUNG WERTHER. Chapel Hill: Univ. of North Carolina Press, 1952, pp. ix-xxxiii.

In his introduction to Ticknor's translation of Goethe's novel, Ryder discusses Ticknor's years as a student in Germany.

Tyack, David B. GEORGE TICKNOR AND THE BOSTON BRAHMINS. Cambridge, Mass.: Harvard Univ. Press, 1967.

This is an excellent study of both Ticknor and the age and society in which he lived. The author uses Ticknor as an exemplar of New England nineteenth-century conservatism, documents his contributions to education, scholarship, and community, and notes the effect of the Civil War and its aftermath upon both Ticknor and the society which he represented.

RELATED GENERAL STUDIES

Brooks, Van Wyck. THE FLOWERING OF NEW ENGLAND. (p. 17)
Long, Orie W. LITERARY PIONEERS. (p. 130).
Whipple, E.P. RECOLLECTIONS OF EMINENT MEN. (p. 56)

BOOKER TALIAFERRO WASHINGTON (1856-1915)

Booker T. Washington's contributions to American prose are important not so much for their literary merit but for their value as documents of the way in which an intelligent man chose to deal with a profoundly difficult and often hostile situation. As an educator, speaker, national figure, and author (usually with the help of others) of numerous essays and an important autobiography, Washington deserves a place in American literature. His apparent simplicity was sometimes simple diplomacy, although some have seen it as subservience. The recent publication of his papers has revealed both his enormous power and his honest desire to work behind the scenes for first-class citizenship for blacks in America.

PRINCIPAL WORKS

BLACK BELT DIAMONDS: GEMS FROM THE SPEECHES, ADDRESSES, AND TALKS TO STUDENTS OF BOOKER T. WASHINGTON. 1898.
THE FUTURE OF THE AMERICAN NEGRO. 1899.
THE STORY OF MY LIFE AND WORK. 1900.
UP FROM SLAVERY. 1901.
CHARACTER BUILDING. 1902.
WORKING WITH THE HANDS. 1904.
FREDERICK DOUGLASS. 1907.
THE STORY OF THE NEGRO. 2 vols. 1909.
MY LARGER EDUCATION. 1911.
THE MAN FARTHEST DOWN: A RECORD OF OBSERVATION AND STUDY IN EUROPE. 1912.
With W.E.B. Du Bois. THE NEGRO IN THE SOUTH, HIS ECONOMIC PROGRESS IN RELATION TO HIS MORAL AND RELIGIOUS DEVELOPMENT. 1907.
THE NEGRO IN BUSINESS. 1907.

LETTERS AND JOURNALS

THE BOOKER T. WASHINGTON PAPERS. 11 vols. to date. Ed. Louis R. Harlan. Assistant Eds. Stuart B. Kaufman et al. Champaign and Urbana: Univ. of Illinois Press, 1971-- .

Volume 1 presents the autobiographical writings, including the original edition of UP FROM SLAVERY. Vol. II, published in 1981, covers the years 1911-12.

LATER EDITIONS, SELECTIONS, AND REPRINTS

BLACK BELT DIAMONDS. Introd. T. Thomas Fortane. New York: Negro Univ. Press, 1969.

BOOKER T. WASHINGTON. Ed., Introd., and Notes by Emma Lou Thornbrough. Englewood Cliffs, N.J.: Prentice-Hall, 1969.

> This collection includes excerpts from addresses and writings as well as comments by contemporaries.

BOOKER T. WASHINGTON AND HIS CRITICS: BLACK LEADERSHIP IN CRISIS. 2nd Ed. with Introd. Hugh Hawkins. Lexington, Mass.: D.C. Heath, 1974.

> Several excerpts from Washington's writings as well as criticism and commentary on his work and ideas are collected here.

CHARACTER BUILDING. New York: Haskell, 1972.

FREDERICK DOUGLASS. New York: Haskell, 1968.

THE FUTURE OF THE AMERICAN NEGRO. New York: Negro Univ. Press, 1969.

MY LARGER EDUCATION. Miami, Fla.: Mnemosyne, 1969.

THE NEGRO IN BUSINESS. New York: AMS Press, 1971.

THE NEGRO IN THE SOUTH. Foreword by Blyden Jackson. New York: AMS Press, 1973.

SELECTED SPEECHES OF BOOKER T. WASHINGTON. Ed. E. Davidson Washington. 1932; New York: Kraus, 1976.

THE STORY OF THE NEGRO. New York: Negro Univ. Press, 1969.

UP FROM SLAVERY. Introd. Booker T. Washington III and Denver Gillen. New York: Limited Editions, 1970.

WORKING WITH THE HANDS. New York: Negro Univ. Press, 1969.

BIBLIOGRAPHY

McPherson, James M., et al. BLACKS IN AMERICA: BIBLIOGRAPHICAL ES-
SAYS. Garden City, N.Y.: Doubleday, 1971.

Selected bibliographies are in the collections edited by Thornbrough and Hawkins, above.

BIOGRAPHY AND CRITICISM

Most of the early biographies are not listed below since they have been superseded by the studies listed here.

Bontemps, Arna. BOOKER T. WASHINGTON'S EARLY DAYS. New York:
Dodd Mead, 1972.

> Not intended for scholars, this is a well written lively account of
> Washington's activities from 1856 to 1895.

Du Bois, W.E.B. THE SOULS OF BLACK FOLK: ESSAYS AND SKETCHES.
1903; 1973; New York: Fawcett, 1977.

> Du Bois is highly critical of what he sees as Washington's compro-
> mises.

Harlan, Louis R. BOOKER T. WASHINGTON: THE MAKING OF A BLACK
LEADER. New York: Oxford Univ. Press, 1972-- .

> The first volume of this thorough biographical study comes up to the
> year 1901; it is clearly written and well documented and empha-
> sizes the complexity and contradictions in Washington's personality
> and character.

Mathews, Basil. BOOKER T. WASHINGTON, EDUCATOR AND INTERRACIAL
INTERPRETER. 1948; College Park, Md.: McGrath, 1969.

> This gives an account of Washington's life and achievements and
> an enthusiastic appreciation of the man.

Meier, August. NEGRO THOUGHT IN AMERICA, 1880-1915: RACIAL IDEO-
LOGIES IN THE AGE OF BOOKER T. WASHINGTON. Ann Arbor: Univ. of
Michigan Press, 1963.

> Meier focuses upon the development of educational and cultural in-
> stitutions in the black community and Washington's influence upon
> these institutions.

Scott, Emmett J., and Lyman Beecher Stowe. BOOKER T. WASHINGTON: BUILDER OF A CIVILIZATION. Garden City, N.Y.: Doubleday, Page, 1916.

> This is, perhaps, an overly laudatory account of the man and his doctrines, but it contains some useful primary material.

Spencer, Samuel R., Jr. BOOKER T. WASHINGTON AND THE NEGRO'S PLACE IN AMERICAN LIFE. Boston: Little, Brown, 1955.

> This is a well-balanced account, though less thoroughly researched and documented than Mathews' biography.

RELATED GENERAL STUDIES

Adler, Mortimer J., and Charles Van Doren, eds. THE NEGRO IN AMERICAN HISTORY. (p. 213)

Stepto, Robert B. FROM BEHIND THE VEIL: A STUDY OF AFRO-AMERICAN NARRATIVE. (p. 225)

DANIEL WEBSTER (1782-1852)

Webster's preeminence as an orator and his influence upon his own times cannot be questioned. However, few recognize how much his visibility and importance rests not only upon his rhetorical skills but also upon his literary abilities. He wrote little in a strictly literary sense except an incomplete autobiography and letters, but his speeches analyzed as literature reveal a considerable stylistic artistry. It is unfortunate that there have been no full-length studies of this art. In his excellent critical biography, below, Irving H. Bartlett points out that Webster revised his speeches carefully before their publication and that "he was looked upon as a literary giant as well as a great lawyer, orator, and statesman."

COLLECTED WORKS

THE SPEECHES AND ORATIONS OF DANIEL WEBSTER. Ed. with an Essay by Edwin P. Whipple. Boston: Little, Brown, 1879.

THE WORKS OF DANIEL WEBSTER . . . [Also called SPEECHES, FORENSIC ARGUMENTS AND DIPLOMATIC PAPERS OF DANIEL WEBSTER]. 6 vols. Ed. with Biographical Sketch by Edward Everett. Boston: Little, Brown, 1851.

THE WRITINGS AND SPEECHES OF DANIEL WEBSTER. National ed. 18 vols. Ed. J.W. McIntyre with a "Memoir" by Edward Everett. Boston: Little, Brown, 1903.

LETTERS AND JOURNALS

THE LETTERS OF DANIEL WEBSTER. . . . Ed. C.H. Van Tyne. 1902; New York: Haskell, 1969.

THE PAPERS OF DANIEL WEBSTER. Ed. Charles M. Wiltse. Assoc. Ed. Harold D. Moser. Hanover, N.H.: Published for Dartmouth College by the University Press of New England, 1974-- .

The first three volumes, published in 1974, 1976, and 1977, are correspondence.

THE PRIVATE CORRESPONDENCE OF DANIEL WEBSTER. 2 vols. Ed. Fletcher Webster. Boston: Little, Brown, 1857.

The collection includes Webster's brief autobiography written in 1829.

LATER EDITIONS, SELECTIONS, AND REPRINTS

DANIEL WEBSTER READER. Ed. Bertha M. Rothe. New York: Oceano, 1956.

This contains excerpts from the collected writings and speeches.

SPEAK FOR YOURSELF, DANIEL: A LIFE OF WEBSTER IN HIS OWN WORDS. Ed. Walker Lewis. Boston: Houghton Mifflin, 1969.

SPEECHES AND ORATIONS. Philadelphia: R. West, 1973.

WEBSTER AND HAYNE'S SPEECHES. . . . 1850; New York: Arno, 1979.

THE WORKS OF DANIEL WEBSTER. 11th ed. Boston: Little, Brown, 1959.

THE WRITINGS AND SPEECHES. 18 vols. New York: AMS Press, 1972.

BIBLIOGRAPHY

Clapp, Clifford B. "The Speeches of Daniel Webster: A Bibliographical Review." PAPERS OF THE BIBLIOGRAPHICAL SOCIETY OF AMERICA 13 (1919): 3-63.

Fletcher Webster compiled "A Chronological List of the Writings and Speeches of Daniel Webster" in volume 13 of the WRITINGS, above. A listing of secondary sources is in the study by Claude M. Fuess, below. Webster is listed in the BIBLIOGRAPHY to the LITERARY HISTORY OF THE UNITED STATES, pp. 755, 996, 1308.

BIOGRAPHY AND CRITICISM

Bartlett, Irving H. DANIEL WEBSTER. New York: Norton, 1978.

This is an excellent critical biography. The author notes that Webster became a symbolic charismatic leader by assuming the role of "guardian" or "defender" in the eyes of the people. Bartlett concludes that at his best Webster "represented the Establishment in America with an intelligence, dignity, and eloquence which have rarely been equaled in our history." At his worst, Webster's flaws were those of Americans in general--a fondness for money and power.

Baxter, Maurice G. DANIEL WEBSTER AND THE SUPREME COURT. Amherst: Univ. of Massachusetts Press, 1966.

This study focuses upon Webster's role as a constitutional lawyer, his influence in developing constitutional doctrines, and his effectiveness as an advocate. In this essentially legal biography, Baxter includes some discussion of Webster's rhetorical techniques.

Brown, Norman D. DANIEL WEBSTER AND THE POLITICS OF AVAILABILITY. Athens: Univ. of Georgia Press, 1969.

A study of Webster's presidential ambitions, this focuses upon political issues and party preferences, but also provides some insight into Webster's rhetorical responses to the issues and pressures of the times.

Carey, Robert L. DANIEL WEBSTER AS AN ECONOMIST. New York: Columbia Univ. Press, 1929.

The author draws extensively from Webster's speeches and letters in this analysis of his economic theory and philosophy of the tariff.

Current, Richard. DANIEL WEBSTER AND THE RISE OF NATIONAL CONSERVATISM. Boston: Little, Brown, 1955.

This is one of the first modern, book-length scholarly studies of Webster's influence in New England economic affairs.

Curtis, George T. LIFE OF DANIEL WEBSTER. 2 vols. New York: D. Appleton, 1870.

This authorized biography of Webster is unusually wise in its judgments and evaluations and remains an important source of primary information.

Dalzell, Robert. DANIEL WEBSTER AND THE TRIAL OF AMERICAN NATIONALISM, 1843-1852. Boston: Houghton Mifflin, 1973.

Based upon manuscript sources and Webster's own works, this scholarly study provides interpretation and analysis of key speeches but offers no significantly new information about Webster's nationalism.

Fuess, Claude M. DANIEL WEBSTER. 2 vols. Boston: Little, Brown, 1930.

A comprehensive and sympathetic biography, this presents Webster as a simple, unsubtle man of overwhelming personality and accomplishment.

Harvey, Peter. REMINISCENCES AND ANECDOTES OF DANIEL WEBSTER. Boston: Little, Brown, 1882.

Of the many memoirs, this is the most reliable.

Knapp, Samuel L. A MEMOIR OF THE LIFE OF DANIEL WEBSTER. Boston: Stimpson and Clapp, 1831.

Prepared with Webster's approval, this account by an associate is useful as a primary source.

Lanman, Charles. THE PRIVATE LIFE OF DANIEL WEBSTER. New York: Harper, 1852.

Webster's family attempted to suppress this reminiscence by his private secretary.

Lodge, Henry Cabot. DANIEL WEBSTER. Boston: Houghton Mifflin, 1883.

This is a reliable biography which depends much upon Curtis' earlier study. Lodge was disturbed by Webster's physical appetites and sexual promiscuity.

Lyman, S.P. THE PUBLIC AND PRIVATE LIFE OF /DANIEL WEBSTER. 2 vols. Philadelphia: J.E. Potter, 1852.

Much of this was published before Webster's death. It includes letters and several of the speeches.

Nathans, Sydney. DANIEL WEBSTER AND JACKSONIAN DEMOCRACY. Baltimore, Md.: Johns Hopkins Press, 1973.

Nathans examines Webster's career from the election of Andrew Jackson in 1828 to 1845. The author focuses upon the shift to voter-oriented partisan politics and analyzes Webster's efforts "to survive, comprehend, and manipulate the new politics." The study includes a comprehensive bibliographical essay on materials pertinent to the study of Daniel Webster during the Jackson years.

RELATED GENERAL STUDIES

WALT WHITMAN (1819-92)

During his lifetime, Whitman published only a small part of his prose works in book form. Since his death, a large number of selections from his newspaper articles, reviews, editorials, notebooks, and diaries have been edited and published. With the publication of such works listed below as the PROSE WORKS (ed. Floyd Stovall), the CORRESPONDENCE (ed. E.H. Miller), and the DAY-BOOKS AND NOTEBOOKS (ed. William White) and of other published and forthcoming volumes in the definitive edition of THE COLLECTED WRITINGS, reliable and systematic texts will be established for most of the important prose writings.

As a reporter and editor, Whitman was actively concerned with the problems of the nation and commented upon social and cultural issues, on moral and spiritual qualities, on literature and language, and on the place of the writer in society, as well as on the importance of personal identity, the theme of so much of his poetry. His prose writings, including those about the Civil War, deserve a secure place in our literature. As a critic, Whitman was subjective, and his taste, like Poe's, was sometimes defective. He was, nevertheless, a shrewd judge of his contemporaries; and his advocacy for a new literature springing from democracy, for an organic style, and for the predominance of power over form in literary expression were forceful and influential pronouncements.

PRINCIPAL PROSE WORKS

DEMOCRATIC VISTAS. 1871.
MEMORANDA DURING THE WAR. 1875.
SPECIMEN DAYS AND COLLECT. 1882.
SPECIMEN DAYS IN AMERICA. 1887.
NOVEMBER BOUGHS. 1888. (Includes "Slang in America" and "A Backward
    Glance O'er Traveled Roads" as well as poems)
COMPLETE POEMS AND PROSE OF WALT WHITMAN. 1888.
COMPLETE PROSE WORKS. 1892.

LETTERS AND JOURNALS

CALAMUS: A SERIES OF LETTERS WRITTEN DURING THE YEARS 1868-1880.
Ed. R.M. Bucke. 1897; Folcroft, Pa.: Folcroft, 1972.

LETTERS WRITTEN BY WALT WHITMAN TO HIS MOTHER FROM 1866 TO 1872.
Ed. Thomas B. Harned. New York: G.P. Putnam's, 1902.

WALT WHITMAN: THE CORRESPONDENCE. 6 vols. Ed. Edwin Haviland Miller. New York: New York Univ. Press, 1961-77.

> Volume 1 covers the years 1842-67; 2, 1868-75; 3, 1876-85; 4,
> 1886-89; 5, 1890-92. Volume 6 is a supplement with a composite
> index. This is part of the CEAA-approved definitive edition of
> THE COLLECTED WRITINGS under the general editorship of Gay
> Wilson Allen and Sculley Bradley, below.

WALT WHITMAN: DAYBOOKS AND NOTEBOOKS. 3 vols. Ed. William White. New York: New York Univ. Press, 1978.

> Part of the definitive COLLECTED WRITINGS, below, this publishes
> much material heretofore available only in manuscript.

WALT WHITMAN'S DIARY IN CANADA. Ed. William Sloane Kennedy. 1904; Folcroft, Pa.: Folcroft, 1970.

THE WOUND DRESSER: A SERIES OF LETTERS WRITTEN FROM THE HOSPITALS IN WASHINGTON DURING THE WAR OF THE REBELLION. Ed. Richard M. Bucke, 1898; with Introd. Oscar Cargill. New York: Bodley Press, 1949.

LATER EDITIONS, SELECTIONS, AND REPRINTS

AN AMERICAN PRIMER. Ed. Horace Traubel. 1904; Folcroft, Pa.: Folcroft, 1969.

AUTOBIOGRAPHIA; OR, THE STORY OF A LIFE, BY WALT WHITMAN. SELECTED FROM HIS PROSE WRITINGS. Ed. Arthur Stedman. 1892; Darby, Pa.: Arden, 1979.

THE BICENTENNIAL WALT WHITMAN: ESSAYS FROM THE LONG ISLANDER. Ed. William White. Detroit: Wayne State Univ. Press, 1976.

THE COLLECTED WRITINGS OF WALT WHITMAN. 19 vols. projected. Ed. Gay Wilson Allen and Sculley Bradley. New York: New York Univ. Press, 1961-- .

> Individual volumes of prose which have been published to date are

listed separately in this section. See also Miller's and White's editions of letters and journals, above.

COMPLETE POETRY AND SELECTED PROSE. Ed. James E. Miller, Jr. Boston: Houghton Mifflin, 1959.

COMPLETE POETRY AND SELECTED PROSE AND LETTERS. Ed. Emory Holloway. 1939; London: Nonesuch, 1964.

THE COMPLETE WRITINGS OF WALT WHITMAN. 10 vols. Ed. R.M. Bucke et al. With Bibliography and Notes by Oscar L. Triggs. 1902; Grosse Pointe, Mich.: Scholarly Press, 1968.

DEMOCRATIC VISTAS AND OTHER PAPERS. St. Clair Shores, Mich.: Scholarly Press, 1970.

FAINT CLEWS AND INDIRECTIONS. Ed. Clarence Gohdes and R.G. Silver. 1949; New York: AMS Press, 1971.

> This is a selection from the Whitman papers in the Trent Collection at Duke University.

THE GATHERING OF THE FORCES. Ed. Cleveland Rodgers and John Black. 1920; Philadelphia: R. West, 1977.

> This includes editorials, essays, and reviews written by Whitman for the Brooklyn DAILY EAGLE in 1846–47.

I SIT AND LOOK OUT. Ed. Emory Holloway and Vernolian Schwartz. 1932; New York: AMS Press, 1971.

> This is a collection of editorials from the Brooklyn DAILY TIMES.

MEMORANDA DURING THE WAR. Ed. R.P. Basler. 1962; Westport, Conn.: Greenwood Press, 1972.

NEW YORK DISSECTED. Ed. Emory Holloway and Ralph Adimari. 1936. Folcroft, Pa.: Folcroft, 1973.

> Some of these pieces written for LIFE ILLUSTRATED are of doubtful Whitman attribution.

NOTES AND FRAGMENTS. Ed. R.M. Bucke. 1899; rpt. in THE COMPLETE WRITINGS. 1902; Folcroft, Pa.: Folcroft, 1972.

THE POETRY AND PROSE OF WALT WHITMAN. Ed. Louis Untermeyer. New York: Simon and Schuster, 1949.

PROSE WORKS 1892. 2 vols. Ed. Floyd Stovall. New York: New York Univ. Press, 1964.

> Part of the definitive COLLECTED WRITINGS, this includes material published in the last edition of the COMPLETE PROSE WORKS and seven other pieces, including "A Backward Glance" and other prefaces.

RIVULETS OF PROSE: CRITICAL ESSAYS. Ed. Carolyn Wells and Alfred Goldsmith. 1928; Freeport, N.Y.: Books for Libraries, 1969.

SPECIMEN DAYS. Ed. Alfred Kazin. Boston: D.R. Godine, 1971.

SPECIMEN DAYS, DEMOCRATIC VISTAS, AND OTHER PROSE. Ed. Louise Pound. Garden City, N.Y.: Doubleday, Doran, 1935.

THE UNCOLLECTED PROSE AND POETRY OF WALT WHITMAN. 2 vols. Ed. Emory Holloway. Garden City, N.Y.: Doubleday, Page, 1920.

WALT WHITMAN AND THE CIVIL WAR: A COLLECTION OF ORIGINAL ARTICLES AND MANUSCRIPTS. Ed. C.I. Glicksburg. 1933; New York: A.S. Barnes, 1963.

WALT WHITMAN OF THE NEW YORK AURORA. Ed. Joseph H. Rubin and C.A. Brown. State College, Pa.: Bald Eagle Press, 1950.

> This collects pieces from the first New York daily, which Whitman edited for a time.

WALT WHITMAN: REPRESENTATIVE SELECTIONS. Ed. Floyd Stovall. 1939; Gloucester, Mass.: Peter Smith, 1962.

WALT WHITMAN'S BACKWARD GLANCES. Ed. Sculley Bradley and J.A. Stevenson. 1947; Freeport, N.Y.: Books for Libraries, 1968.

> This includes a facsimile reproduction of the manuscript of "A Backward Glance" and a discussion by the editors of the method of composition.

WALT WHITMAN'S CAMDEN CONVERSATIONS. Ed. Walter Teller. New Brunswick, N.J.: Rutgers Univ. Press, 1973.

> This consists of selections from Traubel's WITH WALT WHITMAN IN CAMDEN, below.

WALT WHITMAN'S CIVIL WAR. Ed. Nan Braymer. New York: Knopf, 1960.

> This has been compiled from notebooks, newspaper dispatches, letters, and other published and unpublished sources.

WALT WHITMAN'S NEW YORK: FROM MANHATTAN TO MONTAUK. Ed.
Henry M. Christman. New York: Macmillan, 1963.

> The volume collects articles published in the Brooklyn STANDARD,
> 1861-62.

WALT WHITMAN'S WORKSHOP. Ed. Clifford Furness. 1928; New York:
Russell and Russell, 1964.

> This contains speeches and prefaces, with a fine introduction
> and useful notes by the editor.

THE WORKS OF WALT WHITMAN: THE DEATHBED EDITION IN TWO VOL-
UMES. Prefatory note by Malcolm Cowley. New York: Funk and Wagnalls,
1969.

> The prose is collected in volume 2.

BIBLIOGRAPHY

Allen, Gay Wilson. THE NEW WALT WHITMAN HANDBOOK. New York:
New York Univ. Press, 1975.

> A comprehensive updated revision of the 1946 WALT WHITMAN
> HANDBOOK, this lists new editions, critical guides, criticism,
> and studies of reputation and influence.

_____. TWENTY-FIVE YEARS OF WALT WHITMAN BIBLIOGRAPHY, 1918-
1942. Boston: F.W. Faxon, 1943.

Asselineau, Roger. "Walt Whitman." In EIGHT AMERICAN AUTHORS. Rev.
Ed. James Woodress. New York: Norton, 1971, pp. 225-72.

Francis, Gloria A., and Artem Lozynsky. WHITMAN AT AUCTION, 1899-1972.
Detroit: Gale Research Co., 1978.

> This publishes photographic reproductions of pages from catalogs
> listing Whitman material.

Miller, Edwin Haviland, and Roselind S. Miller, eds. WALT WHITMAN'S
CORRESPONDENCE: A CHECKLIST. New York: New York Public Library,
1957.

Shay, Frank. THE BIBLIOGRAPHY OF WALT WHITMAN. New York: Fried-
man's, 1920.

Tanner, James T.F. WALT WHITMAN: A SUPPLEMENTARY BIBLIOGRAPHY,
1961-67. Kent, Ohio: Kent State Univ. Press, 1968.

Wells, Carolyn, and A.F. Goldsmith. A CONCISE BIBLIOGRAPHY OF WALT WHITMAN. 1922; 1930; New York: B. Franklin, 1968.

White, William. WALT WHITMAN'S JOURNALISM: A BIBLIOGRAPHY. Detroit: Wayne State Univ. Press, 1969.

> In addition to this volume, White is working on a full-scale bibliography of the writings of Whitman and an exhaustive checklist of recent books and articles about Whitman.

The WALT WHITMAN REVIEW, which succeeds the WALT WHITMAN NEWS-LETTER (1955-58), publishes a quarterly checklist of recent books, articles, and reviews about Whitman. Gay Wilson Allen's WALT WHITMAN AS MAN, POET, AND LEGEND, below, includes a bibliography compiled by E.A. Allen for the period 1945-60. Whitman is listed in the BIBLIOGRAPHY to the LITER-ARY HISTORY OF THE UNITED STATES, pp. 759, 997, 1310.

BIOGRAPHY AND CRITICISM

The listing below includes the standard biographies and those critical studies which deal with Whitman's prose.

Allen, Gay Wilson. THE SOLITARY SINGER: A CRITICAL BIOGRAPHY OF WALT WHITMAN. 1955; New York: New York Univ. Press, 1967.

> An indispensable source of biographical detail, this work attempts "to trace consecutively the physical life of the man, the growth of his mind, and the development of his art out of his physical and mental experience."

_____. WALT WHITMAN AS MAN, POET, AND LEGEND. Carbondale: Southern Illinois Univ. Press, 1961.

> A brief biography, this includes illustrations and a bibliography of writings about Whitman, 1945-60.

Arvin, Newton. WHITMAN. 1938; New York: Russell and Russell, 1969.

> This biographical study contains a good analysis of Whitman's political thought.

Brasher, Thomas L. WHITMAN AS EDITOR OF THE BROOKLYN DAILY EAGLE. Detroit: Wayne State Univ. Press, 1970.

> This is a thorough study examining Whitman's duties and contributions as editor of the most prominent Long Island journal of the time. The author argues that Whitman's ideas as expressed in the EAGLE reappear in LEAVES OF GRASS.

Canby, Henry Seidel. WALT WHITMAN, AN AMERICAN. Boston: Houghton Mifflin, 1943.

> The author makes a number of significant comments about Whitman's importance as a critic of democracy.

Holloway, Emory. WHITMAN: AN INTERPRETATION IN NARRATIVE. 1926; With a new Preface by the author. New York: Biblo and Tannen, 1969.

> This remains an important study which praises Whitman's enduring power, his flexibility, and his "stable center of gravity."

Johnson, Maurice O. WALT WHITMAN AS A CRITIC OF LITERATURE. 1938; New York: Haskell, 1970.

> This is one of the few studies of Whitman's critical writing.

Loving, Jerome M., ed. CIVIL WAR LETTERS OF GEORGE WASHINGTON WHITMAN. Foreword by Gay Wilson Allen. Durham, N.C.: Duke Univ. Press, 1975.

> These letters by Whitman's younger brother shed light upon the effect upon Whitman of his relationship with his brother. The introduction and notes provide an excellent source of information about the Whitman family.

Perry, Bliss. WALT WHITMAN: HIS LIFE AND WORK. 1906; 1908; New York: AMS Press, 1969.

> An early scholarly biography, this is still one of the clearest and most reliable accounts. Perry used material turned over to him by John Burroughs, but he did not have access to the important materials which were collected by Holloway, above.

Rubin, Joseph J. THE HISTORIC WHITMAN. University Park: Pennsylvania State Univ. Press, 1973.

> Through the use of newspaper accounts, Rubin recreates Whitman's early career before 1855. Included are articles on Long Island written by Whitman for the New York Sunday DISPATCH in 1849 and 1850.

Traubel, Horace. WITH WALT WHITMAN IN CAMDEN. 5 vols. 1906-1964.

> There are various publishers for this title: volume 1, Boston: Small, Maynard, 1906; volume 2, New York: D. Appleton, 1908; volume 3, New York: M. Kinnerley, 1914; volume 4, Philadelphia: Univ. of Pennsylvania Press, 1953; and volume 5, Carbondale: So. Illinois Univ. Press, 1964.

> These conversations remain valuable source material, although much of the bulk of it is tedious. Traubel records Whitman's judgments

about politics and literature, among other seemingly inexhaustible subjects. The last two volumes, 4 and 5, were edited from the notes which Traubel left unfinished at his death.

White, William, ed. WALT WHITMAN IN OUR TIME. Detroit: Wayne State Univ. Press, 1970.

Originally published as a special supplement to the WALT WHIT-MAN REVIEW, this includes essays on Whitman's ideas and influence as well as on his poetry.

RELATED GENERAL STUDIES

Brooks, Van Wyck. THE TIMES OF MELVILLE AND WHITMAN. (p. 17)
Crawley, Thomas E., ed. FOUR MAKERS OF THE AMERICAN MIND. (p. 20)
Foerster, Norman. AMERICAN CRITICISM. (p. 63)
Gardiner, Harold C. AMERICAN CLASSICS RECONSIDERED. (p. 22)
Jones, Howard M. BELIEF AND DISBELIEF IN AMERICAN LITERATURE. (p. 24)
Matthiessen, F.O. AMERICAN RENAISSANCE. (p. 27)
Metzger, Charles R. THOREAU AND WHITMAN: A STUDY OF THEIR ESTHE-TICS. (p. 473, under Thoreau)
Richardson, Robert D., Jr. MYTH AND LITERATURE IN THE AMERICAN RE-NAISSANCE. (p. 30)

JOHN GREENLEAF WHITTIER (1807-92)

Whittier will be remembered primarily as a writer of poetry, but he was also a reformer, philanthropist, and editor. His prose fills three of the seven volumes of his WRITINGS, but much of his journalistic work remains uncollected. Early biographers were interested in Whittier's activities as an abolitionist. Later studies have focused upon the paradoxes and contradictions in the man and the quality and context of the verse. Little has been written about his aesthetic ideas, his criticism, his interest in folk literature, or his correspondence. Although his prose will probably remain subsidiary to his verse, Whittier is, nevertheless, a prose writer of some importance.

PRINCIPAL NONFICTION PROSE WORKS

JUSTICE AND EXPEDIENCY. 1833.
THE STRANGER IN LOWELL. 1845.
THE SUPERNATURALISM OF NEW ENGLAND. 1847.
LEAVES FROM MARGARET SMITH'S JOURNAL. 1849. (Semifictional sketch
    of New England Colonial life)
OLD PORTRAITS AND MODERN SKETCHES. 1850.
LITERARY RECREATIONS AND MISCELLANIES. 1854.
THE WRITINGS OF JOHN GREENLEAF WHITTIER. 7 vols. Riverside Ed. Ed.
    Horace Scudder. 1888-89.

LETTERS AND JOURNALS

ELIZABETH LLOYD AND THE WHITTIERS: A BUDGET OF LETTERS. Ed. Thomas Currier. Cambridge, Mass.: Harvard Univ. Press, 1939.

THE LETTERS OF JOHN GREENLEAF WHITTIER. 3 vols. Ed. John B. Pickard. Cambridge, Mass.: Harvard Univ. Press, 1975.

    This is the definitive edition of Whittier's letters.

LIFE AND LETTERS OF JOHN GREENLEAF WHITTIER. 2 vols. Ed. Samuel T. Pickard. 1894; Boston: Houghton Mifflin, 1907.

> Most of the letters are selected to show Whittier's abolitionism or his problems with his publishers.

WHITTIER AND THE CARTLANDS, LETTERS AND COMMENTS. Ed. Martha Hale Shackford. Wakefield, Mass.: Montrose Press, 1950.

WHITTIER AS A POLITICIAN: ILLUSTRATED BY HIS LETTERS TO PROFESSOR ELIZUR WRIGHT, JR. Ed. Samuel T. Pickard. Boston: Charles E. Goodspeed, 1900.

> Elizur Wright was a prominent abolitionist.

WHITTIER CORRESPONDENCE FROM THE OAK KNOLL COLLECTIONS, 1830-1892. Ed. John Albree. Salem, Mass.: Essex Book and Print Club, 1911.

WHITTIER'S UNKNOWN ROMANCE: LETTERS TO ELIZABETH LLOYD. Ed. Marie V. Denervaud. 1923; New York: Haskell, 1973.

LATER EDITIONS, SELECTIONS, AND REPRINTS

THE COMPLETE WRITINGS OF JOHN GREENLEAF WHITTIER. 7 vols. 1894; New York: AMS Press, 1969.

THE CONFLICT WITH SLAVERY, REFORM, AND POLITICS. 1894; New York: AMS Press, 1969.

> This is volume 7 of the Houghton Mifflin COMPLETE WRITINGS, above, published in many editions. The title of this volume was originally THE CONFLICT WITH SLAVERY. POLITICS AND RE-FORM.

THE SUPERNATURALISM OF NEW ENGLAND. Ed. Edward Wagenknecht. Norman: Univ. of Oklahoma Press, 1969.

WHITTIER ON WRITERS AND WRITING. Ed. Harry H. Clark and Edwin H. Cady. 1950; Freeport, N.Y.: Books for Libraries, 1971.

> This collection of literary reviews and criticism from various periodicals shows that Whittier urged a stern independent criticism of American poetry.

BIBLIOGRAPHY

Currier, Thomas F. A BIBLIOGRAPHY OF JOHN GREENLEAF WHITTIER. Cambridge, Mass.: Harvard Univ. Press, 1937.

This is a valuable and comprehensive listing which identifies such primary sources as elusive poems, letters, essays, and tracts. Included is a bibliography by Pauline F. Pulsifer of secondary sources to 1936.

Keller, Karl. "John Greenleaf Whittier." In FIFTEEN AMERICAN AUTHORS BEFORE 1900. Ed. Robert A. Rees and Earl N. Harbert. Madison: Univ. of Wisconsin Press, 1971, pp. 357-86.

Keller gives excellent evaluations of biographical and critical studies.

Von Frank, Albert J. WHITTIER: A COMPREHENSIVE ANNOTATED BIBLIOGRAPHY. New York: Garland, 1976.

This lists standard editions, a guide to manuscript sources, biographies, journalism, and critical studies, all with extensive annotations.

Wagenknecht's study, below, includes a bibliographical essay on Whittier scholarship, 1936-66. The WHITTIER NEWSLETTER, published in Amesbury, Massachusetts, by John B. Pickard, provides additional bibliographical and review items. Whittier is listed in the BIBLIOGRAPHY to the LITERARY HISTORY OF THE UNITED STATES, pp. 769, 1001, 1313.

BIOGRAPHY AND CRITICISM

Bennett, Whitman. WHITTIER, BARD OF FREEDOM. Chapel Hill: Univ. of North Carolina Press, 1941.

A response to Mordell, below, this points out the positive, dynamic influence which Whittier exerted as poet, pamphleteer, and journalist. It is well written but is affected by its effort as a vindication of the poet.

Carpenter, George Rice. JOHN GREENLEAF WHITTIER. American Men of Letters Series. Boston: Houghton Mifflin, 1903.

This account is sympathetic but avoids the eulogistic extremes of some some of the other early accounts and is one of the best of these.

Eastburn, Iola K. WHITTIER'S RELATION TO GERMAN LIFE AND THOUGHT. Philadelphia: Univ. of Pennsylvania, 1915.

This is an interesting study of some of the influences on Whittier, but the author fails to show that the German influence was highly significant.

Hawkins, Chauncey J. THE MIND OF WHITTIER: A STUDY OF WHITTIER'S FUNDAMENTAL RELIGIOUS IDEAS. New York: Thomas Whittaker, 1904.

> The author defends the purity and strength of Whittier's convictions and principles of action, discussing his religious views in the context of Quakerism and Calvinism and contrasting them with the views of other poets, most notably Burns and Tennyson.

Higginson, Thomas W. JOHN GREENLEAF WHITTIER. English Men of Letters Series. New York: Macmillan, 1902.

> This biography is short but discerning. Higginson praises Whittier's ethical values and activism and argues that they improved rather than detracted from his creative abilities.

Kennedy, William Sloane. JOHN GREENLEAF WHITTIER: HIS LIFE, GENIUS, AND WRITINGS. Boston: S. Cassino, 1882.

> Kennedy did not approve of Whittier's Quakerism and in this early biography measured the writer's achievements from this viewpoint. He indicated that Whittier's life and religiosity dominated and sometimes degraded his art.

_____. JOHN GREENLEAF WHITTIER: THE POET OF FREEDOM. New York: Funk and Wagnalls, 1892.

> Better than the earlier work by Kennedy, this focuses upon Whittier's antislavery activities.

Perry, Bliss. JOHN GREENLEAF WHITTIER: A SKETCH OF HIS LIFE WITH SELECTED POEMS. Boston: Houghton Mifflin, 1907.

> Although this focuses upon Whittier's poetry, it does present Whittier as a poet who was primarily concerned with social and political issues and was profoundly influenced by his democratic idealism.

Pickard, John B. JOHN GREENLEAF WHITTIER: AN INTRODUCTION AND INTERPRETATION. New York: Barnes and Noble, 1961.

> This is an excellent critical guide, showing, among other things, how Whittier moved between various genres in his work.

Pickard, Samuel T. LIFE AND LETTERS OF JOHN GREENLEAF WHITTIER. 2 vols. 1894; Boston: Houghton Mifflin, 1907.

> Pickard argues that Whittier's political ambitions came to overshadow his literary ambitions. This is the authorized biography, giving an affectionate account of Whittier, the man, and investigating the relationship between Whittier's political life as a reformer and his life as a poet.

John Greenleaf Whittier

Pollard, John A. JOHN GREENLEAF WHITTIER, FRIEND OF MAN. Boston: Houghton Mifflin, 1949.

> This study focuses upon Whittier's public life, giving a good account of the man as poet, prophet, and politician. It is an accurate report of Whittier's reform and political activities but gives little interpretation or evaluation of his achievements.

Underwood, Francis H. JOHN GREENLEAF WHITTIER: A BIOGRAPHY. Boston: James R. Osgood, 1884.

> Underwood's biography formed the pattern for a school of later overblown discussions of Whittier as the representative of love, peace, and high ideals in both his life and art. However, the study is a good source of information for Whittier as an abolitionist and a contributor to the ATLANTIC.

Wagenknecht, Edward. JOHN GREENLEAF WHITTIER: A PORTRAIT IN PARADOX. New York: Oxford Univ. Press, 1967.

> This is one of the most interesting of the critical biographies to date, presenting Whittier as a complex man, destroying previous stereotypes, and placing Whittier's views in historical context.

RELATED GENERAL STUDIES

THOMAS WOODROW WILSON (1856-1924)

Although as a political leader Wilson is a twentieth-century figure, he is included here as a man of letters and an influential teacher who was a significant opinion maker of the last decade of the nineteenth century. Wilson thought of himself in his early years as a writer, as well as an historian, a teacher, and an academic leader; and his sympathy with the aims of literature can be seen in several of his essays. His style has been criticized, but he was always conscious of the importance of creating through skillful rhetoric what he called a "whole impression."

PRINCIPAL WORKS

CONGRESSIONAL GOVERNMENT: A STUDY IN AMERICAN POLITICS. 1885.
THE STATE: ELEMENTS OF HISTORICAL AND PRACTICAL POLITICS. 1889.
DIVISION AND REUNION, 1829-1889. 1893.
AN OLD MASTER AND OTHER POLITICAL ESSAYS. 1893.
MERE LITERATURE AND OTHER ESSAYS. 1896.
GEORGE WASHINGTON. 1897.
WHEN A MAN COMES TO HIMSELF. 1901.
A HISTORY OF THE AMERICAN PEOPLE. 5 vols. 1902.
CONSTITUTIONAL GOVERNMENT IN THE UNITED STATES. 1908.
THE NEW FREEDOM. 1913.

LETTERS AND PAPERS

THE PAPERS OF THOMAS WOODROW WILSON. 40 vols. projected. Ed. Arthur S. Link et al. Princeton: Princeton Univ. Press, 1966-- .

> Thirty-one volumes of this definitive edition of Wilson's letters and papers have been completed to date. The first twelve deal with his earlier years as a historian, author, and teacher.

LATER EDITIONS, SELECTIONS, AND REPRINTS

CONGRESSIONAL GOVERNMENT. Cleveland, Ohio: Meridian, 1965.

CONSTITUTIONAL GOVERNMENT IN THE UNITED STATES. New York: Columbia Univ. Press, 1965; 1979.

CROSSROADS OF FREEDOM: THE 1912 CAMPAIGN SPEECHES OF WOODROW WILSON. Ed. John Wells Davidson, with a Pref. by Charles Seymour. New Haven, Conn.: Yale Univ. Press, 1956.

A DAY OF DEDICATION: THE ESSENTIAL WRITINGS AND SPEECHES OF WOODROW WILSON. Ed. Albert Fried. New York: Macmillan, 1965.

DIVISION AND REUNION. New York: Peter Smith, 1962.

GEORGE WASHINGTON. New York: Frederick Ungar, 1975.

MERE LITERATURE AND OTHER ESSAYS. New York: Kennikat, 1965.

AN OLD MASTER AND OTHER POLITICAL ESSAYS. Freeport, N.Y.: Books for Libraries, 1971.

THE PUBLIC PAPERS OF WOODROW WILSON. 6 vols. Ed. Ray Stannard Baker and William E. Dodd. 1925-27; New York: Kraus, 1970.

SELECTED LITERARY AND POLITICAL PAPERS AND ADDRESSES OF WOODROW WILSON. 3 vols. New York: Grosset and Dunlap, 1925-27.

WILSON. Ed. John Braeman. Englewood Cliffs, N.J.: Prentice-Hall, 1972.

> Part 1 of this volume consists of excerpts from Wilson's writings with brief introductory notes.

BIBLIOGRAPHY

Turnbull, Laura S. WOODROW WILSON: A SELECTED BIBLIOGRAPHY OF HIS PUBLISHED WRITINGS, ADDRESSES, AND PUBLIC PAPERS. Princeton: Princeton Univ. Press, 1948.

Vexler, Robert I., ed. WOODROW WILSON, 1856-1924: CHRONOLOGY, DOCUMENTS, BIBLIOGRAPHICAL AIDS. Dobbs Ferry, N.Y.: Oceana, 1969.

Arthur S. Link's biographical volumes, below, include bibliographical essays. Wilson is listed in the BIBLIOGRAPHY to the LITERARY HISTORY OF THE UNITED STATES, pp. 779, 1004, 1318.

BIOGRAPHY AND CRITICISM

The listing below includes only those volumes which focus upon the earlier years of Wilson's career or upon Wilson as a writer.

Anderson, David D. WOODROW WILSON. Boston: Twayne, 1978.

> In this brief study, the author emphasizes the early years and assesses Wilson's writing and the development of his style and thinking.

Baker, Ray Stannard. WOODROW WILSON, LIFE AND LETTERS. 8 vols. Garden City, N.Y.: Doubleday, Page, 1927-38.

> This is the authorized biography and is a sympathetic study. Although it has been superseded by Link's study, below, and the PAPERS, above, this is still the best account of Wilson's early years.

Bragdon, Henry Wilkinson. WOODROW WILSON: THE ACADEMIC YEARS. Cambridge, Mass.: Belknap Press, Harvard Univ. Press, 1967.

> This is a study of Wilson's academic policies and techniques and his relationships with classmates, colleagues, and students. It also provides some useful insights into the development of Wilson's political views during the late nineteenth century.

Link, Arthur S. WOODROW WILSON: A BRIEF BIOGRAPHY. Cleveland, Ohio: World Publishing Co., 1963.

> This and the volumes below are solid studies, providing the best account of Wilson's life.

_____. WOODROW WILSON: A PROFILE. New York: Hill and Wang, 1968.

_____. WILSON: THE ROAD TO THE WHITE HOUSE. Princeton: Princeton Univ. Press, 1947.

> Other volumes in this definitive biographical study deal primarily with the presidential years.

Mulder, John M. WILSON: THE YEARS OF PREPARATION. Princeton: Princeton Univ. Press, 1978.

> The author treats Wilson's life prior to his entry into politics. An "intellectual history" as well as a biography, this points to the influences upon Wilson of his cultural backgrounds and the society around him.

Myers, William S., ed. WOODROW WILSON: SOME PRINCETON MEMORIES. Princeton: Princeton Univ. Press, 1946.

> A collection of recollections by Princeton contemporaries, this includes comments about Wilson as an educator and a thinker as well as some assessment of his political ideas.

Osborne, George Coleman. WOODROW WILSON: THE EARLY YEARS. Baton Rouge: Louisiana State Univ. Press, 1968.

> The author examines the years up to Wilson's becoming president of Princeton.

RELATED GENERAL STUDIES

Lewis, Edward R. A HISTORY OF AMERICAN POLITICAL THOUGHT FROM THE CIVIL WAR TO THE WORLD WAR. (p. 220)

INDEX

INDEX

The index includes authors, editors, and other contributors of primary and secondary works listed in this guide. Titles, some of which have been shortened, and section headings are also included. Numbers refer to page numbers; those numbers indicating main entries for individual authors are underlined. Duplicated titles for primary and secondary works are followed by the author's name (e.g. COMPLETE WORKS [Longfellow]). I would like to thank Lydia Sullivan, computer consultant at California State College, San Bernardino, for her assistance in preparing the index.

Index

Index

Index

Index

Camp, Charles L. 132
Campbell, Killis 438
Camp-Fire and Cotton Field 209
Camping and Tramping with Roosevelt 269
Camping with President Roosevelt 269
Camps and Prisons 207
Canary, Robert H. 252
Canby, Henry Seidel 18, 286, 375, 460, 465, 468, 496
Cannibals All! 201
Canny, James R. 437
Canoe and the Saddle, The 126
Cantor, Milton 235
Cantwell, Robert 335
Canyon Country 154
Cape Cod 462
Cardwell, Guy A. 280
Carey, Henry Charles 183
Carey, Mathew 60, 70
Carey, Robert L. 488
Cargill, Oscar 491
Carlson, Eric W. 302, 308, 435, 438
Carlyle and Emerson 311
Carlyle's Laugh and Other Surprises 81, 477
Carnegie, Andrew 183
Carpenter, Delores Bird 309
Carpenter, Frederic Ives 18, 303, 305, 308, 319
Carpenter, George Rice 36, 500
Carr, Jeanne C. 417
Carroll, Gordon 212
Carruth, Hayden 18
Carstensen, Vernon 418
Carter, Everett 18, 289, 319, 330, 477
Cartwright, Peter 70
Cary, Edward 457
Cary, Richard 457
Caskey, Marie 256, 453
Castell, Alburey 377
Catalogue of the Salley Collection of Simms 447
Cate, Wirt 206
Cater, Harold Dean 234
Catharine Beecher: A Study in American Domesticity 224, 454

Cathcart, Wallace H. 334
Cauthen, Irby B., Jr. 436
Cavell, Stanley 468
Cawelti, John G. 19, 319, 357
Célieres, Andre 308
Centenary Edition of the Works of Nathaniel Hawthorne, The 333
Centennial Check List of Editions of Walden 466
Centennial Edition of the Works of Sidney Lanier, The 387
Centennial Tributes 329
Central Still 476
Century 82, 87
Century of Commentary on the Works of Washington Irving 363
Century of Dishonor, A 195
Certain Delightful English Towns 351
Chadwick, John W. 275, 424
Chamberlain, J.C. 404
Channing, Edward T. 187
Channing, Ellery 462, 463
Channing, Grace Ellery 274
Channing, the Reluctant Radical 276
Channing, William Ellery 31, 58, 273-77, 468
Channing, William Henry 274, 275, 276
Channing Day by Day 274
Channing's Note-Books 274
Chaos and Context 381
Chapin, Henry 409
Chapiro, Jose 274
Chapman, John Jay 308
Chapters from a Life 76
Chapters of Erie and Other Essays 233, 234
Character and Characteristic Men 88, 338
Character and Opinion in the United States 173, 382, 458
Character and Writings of John Milton 274
Character Building 482, 483
Character of Napoleon and Other Essays 274
Characteristics of Emerson 316
Characteristics of Literature 53
Characters and Criticisms 49
Characters of Schiller 47

Index

Index

Index

Index

Index

Index

Index

Index

Index

Index

Index

Index

Index

Mathews, Cornelius 50, 57
Matthews, Brander 38, 50
Matthews, William 78, 79
Matthiessen, F.O. 27, 319, 338, 366, 373, 375, 382, 413, 477, 497
Mauve Decade, The 15
Maves, Carl 374
May, Samuel J. 209, 502
Mayberry, George 38
May-Day and Other Pieces 300
Maynard, Theodore 261
Mead, David C. 302
Mead, Edwin Doak 274, 313, 425
Meaning of Henry Ward Beecher, The 257
Meaning of the Times 186
Meaning of Truth, The 376, 377
Means and Ends of Education 135
Mearns, David C. 391, 395
Measure of Poe, The 438
Mechanism in Thought and Morals 346
Mediatorial Life of Jesus, The 258
Medical Essays 346, 347
Meek, Alexander B. 181
Meier, August 484
Meine, Franklin J. 93, 97
Meisel, Max 170
Meltzer, Milton 472
Melville, Herman 20, 334, 408-13
Melville as Lecturer 413
Melville in the South Seas 410
Melville Log, The 412
Melville's Angles of Vision 411
Melville's Journal of a Visit to Europe and the Levant 408
Melville's Reading 413
Melville's Reviewers 412
Melville's Shorter Tales 411
Memoir of George Ticknor 480
Memoir of Ralph Waldo Emerson, A 307
Memoir of the Life of Daniel Webster, A 489
Memoir of William Ellery Channing 275
Memoirs (of Charles Godfrey Leland) 74
Memoirs (of William T. Sherman) 75
Memoirs of Colonel John S. Mosby, The 210

Memoirs of Hawthorne 337
Memoirs of Henry Heth, The 210
Memoirs of John Quincy Adams 69
Memoirs of Marau Taaroa 233
Memoirs of Margaret Fuller Ossoli 322
Memoirs of the Life of William Wirt 383
Memoranda during the War 490, 492
Memorial of Horatio Greenough 53
Memorial of James Fenimore Cooper 294
Memorials of a Southern Planter 211
Memorials of Prison Life 194
Memorial to the Legislature of Massachusetts 193
Memories and Studies 377
Memories of a Hostess 73, 407
Men and Movements in American Philosophy 161, 318, 382
Mencken, H.L. 292
Mendelsohn, Jack 276
Menikoff, Barry 348
Men of Concord 461
Men of Good Hope 14, 318, 425
Men of Our Times 450, 451
Mental Development in Child and Race 142
Mere Literature and Other Essays 503, 504
Merideth, Robert 221, 257, 453
Meriwether, Robert L. 187
Merrill, Walter M. 202
Merrill Checklist of Herman Melville, The 410
Merrill Guide to Nathaniel Hawthorne, The 336
Merrill Studies in Walden, The 473
Merry-Mount 414
Merry Tales of the Three Wise Men of Gotham, The 431
Metcalf, Eleanor M. 408, 412
Method of Henry James, The 371
Method of Nature 300
Methods of Study in Natural History 152
Metzger, Charles R. 313, 473, 497
Meyer, Michael 466, 473

O

Index

Index

Index

Index

Index

Index

Index

Index

Index

Index

01

MAR 31 '83